| DATE DUE | | | |
|---|---|---|---|
| | | | |
| | | | |
| | | | |
| | | | |
| | | | |
| | | | |
| | | | |
| | | | |
| | | | |
| | | | |
| | | | |
| | | | |

# THE VALUE OF THE
# INDIVIDUAL

Karl Joachim Weintraub

# THE VALUE OF THE INDIVIDUAL

## Self and Circumstance in Autobiography

THE UNIVERSITY
OF CHICAGO PRESS
Chicago & London

KARL JOACHIM WEINTRAUB is the Thomas E. Donnelley Professor in the Department of History and the College, chairman of the Committee on the History of Culture, and dean of the Division of the Humanities at the University of Chicago. His *Visions of Culture: Voltaire, Guizot, Burckhardt, Lamprecht, Huizinga, Ortega y Gasset,* is also published by the University of Chicago Press.

The University of Chicago Press, Chicago 60637
The University of Chicago Press, Ltd., London

©1978 by The University of Chicago
All rights reserved. Published 1978
Printed in the United States of America

82 81 80 79 78    54321

The section on Franklin, in chapter 10, appeared in somewhat different form in the *Journal of Religion* for July 1976, © 1976 by The University of Chicago. The section on Gibbon, in chapter 11, also in somewhat different form, was given as a speech before the Stochastics in May 1976.

LIBRARY OF CONGRESS CATALOGING IN PUBLICATION DATA
Weintraub, Karl Joachim, 1924–
The value of the individual.

Bibliography: p.
Includes index.
1.  Autobiography.   I.   Title.
CT25.W37        128        77–9435
ISBN 0–226–88621–2

To Kathryn
*individuum ineffabile est*

# Contents

# Acknowledgments

Late in the 1960s, when I was busily engaged in research on the seventeenth-century Dutch figure Constantijn Huygens, I obtained the Danforth Foundation's E. Harris Harbison Award in Teaching. When I reflected on how I would use this most generous prize of nearly $11,000, I decided to fulfil two wishes: to visit some of the historical places known to me only from the study and teaching of Western civilization, and to take some time off to start on a reading program of autobiographies, books that rarely are short. The Danforth Foundation's generosity thus stands at the beginning of this project. I began to develop a course on the history of autobiography and found that the students in this course were, as students always are, a teacher's finest helpers; they helped shape my understanding of the subject. I have forgotten many of their names, though I remember their individual faces; I remain very grateful to them. The writing and rewriting of the book was, however, a very lonely task. That I might indeed have a book was not clear to me until three of my colleagues, and two students who had worked with me, agreed to read the second (in parts, the third and fourth) draft of the sizable manuscript. When I think of the colleagues and friends who were willing to submit themselves to the thankless task of reading and criticizing so many pages of text, I am helpless to find adequate expressions of gratitude. A church at least promises delayed rewards for such works of supererogation; without such rewards to give, I can only assure Robert E. Streeter, Donald Lach, Charles Wegener, Katy O'Brien, and Lynn Rivers Wilbanks of my deepest gratitude and admiration. For fine typing I owe thanks to Dorothy Kelty, Ann Johnson Silny, La Verna Moore, and Meredith Spencer. I am filled with admiration and gratitude for the good taste and tolerant thoughtfulness of Janet Feldstein, an editor par excellence, who gave final shape to the text. To the presidents, provosts, and faculty of the Humanities Division of the University of Chicago I am beholden for their gracious indulgence in permitting a dean some time away from his daily tasks to finish a book.

Finally, I feel a very special kind of gratitude for Katy O'Brien. With exemplary diligence, intelligence, and devotion, she has done the work for which one hires research assistants. Far more important is what she added to such labors in unbought grace by loyalty and love for the subject, and by a willingness to share problems and to attack difficulties with cheerfulness and Irish wit, at times when I most needed such support and such sharing of minds. Without the part of herself that she invested in the book, it would not have been the same.

# Introduction

This is an essay, an attempt, a trial. For anything more the author is neither learned nor wise enough. It is an essay despite its length and because of its length. It deals with a matter too massive to be mastered by a teacher and academic who must fulfill a multiplicity of obligations. The subject concerns a major component of modern man's self-conception: the belief that, whatever else he is, he is a unique individuality, whose life task is to be true to his very own personality. The essay rests on the conviction that this conception of personality, this idea of the individualized person, is a part of the modern form of historical consciousness. In attempting to trace the gradual emergence of some of the most important factors which helped to form this modern self-conception, I have not written a history of the period when the concern with individuality had become dominant; the essay ends at the threshold of that moment. The materials for this historical search are some of the autobiographic reflections of their self-searching which some men and women in our Western tradition have left to us. Although these do not allow us to reconstruct a full history, they can serve as signposts marking crucial moments of this complicated historical development. In this sense, then, the following is a historical essay of the gradual emergence of individuality in autobiographic writings from Augustine to Goethe. Those readers who need and wish to know no more about an author's conception of the problem and his working assumptions, may wish to turn immediately to chapter 1.

The problems dealt with in this essay came to me through a major professional interest in the history of history. The study of the different forms of historical conceptions and modes of historical consciousness held by Western man at different times led me, some twelve or fifteen years ago, to the conviction that there was a relation between the views men held of the past and their concepts of their own selves. A particular interest in that specifically modern historical outlook to which the ugly terms *historism* or *historicism* have been affixed brings one to views, assumptions, and attitudes, which, roughly speaking, have transformed the habits and perspectives of historians since 1800 A.D. This form of historical consciousness took root in a great fascination for the rich variety in human existence. Rather than considering variation a regrettable deviation from the perfect model of being human, this outlook places immense value on the specific goodness of each individually specified expression of the human experience. The variations in the different styles of life achieved by different peoples or "nations" are seen as a matter of great virtue and interest. Man, however limited he might be in each distinct formulation of his being, redeemed himself by the successive actualizations of his indefinitely variable potential. Each style of life has its own intrinsic justification; each has the right to be understood in its own terms; each deserves loving attention as another human search for humanity. History thus becomes the passing scene of possible human forms. And only history can make us understand our potential and our present.

The greatly enriched view of human reality which lies in this position has greatly attracted me. It proclaims a love for the individual moment and shrinks from judging it by norms other than those that apply to it. It plays down the historian's dominant moralistic and didactic intent and highlights his aesthetic pleasure in matters of nuances, modulations, and style. Such a contemplative viewing of humanity redeems itself by the cultivation of human wisdom rather than by the delivery of historical lessons. It takes utterly seriously the important juncture of time, and place, and cultural atmosphere, and men's own wills; it makes history a truly important form of knowledge. That it relativizes knowledge and judgment by its profound perspectivism has come to be its weakness; critics justly call for a countervailing stress on the common unities of human reality. But an awareness of its faults cannot gainsay the merit that lies in the historian's willingness to take seriously each form of being as a value in itself.

The historical thinkers formulating such views at the turn from the eighteenth to the nineteenth century dwelt on the individuality of great collective units such as peoples, "nations," national art styles, and poetry. It did not take long before this outlook could also be seen in the self-conception of individual human beings. Our modern forms of self-conception result from a very complex heritage. We are the heirs of the Greeks and of long experiments in rationality; we are bound by and wish to be bound to a common logos. We desire to be rational men. We are made to submit and ultimately learn to submit voluntarily to the common tasks of citizenship. We wish to deal responsibly with the commonly shared national and worldwide problems of man. We cultivate a common language and know it cannot be private; when the soul *speaks*, it cannot be simply the *soul* that speaks. We work in commonly binding disciplines, and in our professional life we aim at the fulfillment of professional ideals. And yet, while we have commitments to universal human objectives, modified as these may be by national differences, we also have come to place a very high value on our specific uniqueness as individuals. We are captivated by the spectacle of all the subtle differences between the I and the thou. We see genuine value in the belief that each person has a very special human form and something very much his own to give to the world. We feel a deep need to be true to the self. We feel frustrated when we think that our society does harm to the inviolable self, or that others prevent us from fulfilling our potential. We regret it when a specific human form does not obtain the opportunity to fulfill itself, to become what only it can be, and we are saddened when such a loss impoverishes the human cosmos. However much our processes of education must be directed toward the acculturation of the individual, so that he can function within prevailing culture patterns, we burden our educational systems with the additional charge that they be a means of personal self-cultivation. For we desire the formation of autonomous human beings, those who do set the law unto themselves, who follow their self-given norms with a sense of responsibility both to themselves and to humanity, who do build common knowledge, taste, insight into their own personalities and fulfill their specific potential to the fullest. We are deeply impressed by a genuine personality, one who has harmonized the varied givens and disparate demands of life into a personal style. We may recognize the dangers in this fascination with individuality, since it can be so easily bastardized into egocentric addiction to arbitrary whim, into a mindless glorification of doing "one's own thing," into the "idiocy" (in the sense by which the Greeks spoke of *idiotes*) of seeing in surrounding social patterns the enemy rather than the support of each self-search. Yet we are captivated by an uncanny sense that each one of us constitutes one irreplaceable human form, and we perceive a noble life task in the cultivation of our individuality, our ineffable self.

My aim, at best, can be to "suggest" that there may indeed be a discernible history of the gradual formation of this modern self-conception. For practical reasons I restrict myself to a few general reflections followed by a selective look at older modes of self-conception. Ideally the task requires a history of our Western culture; this is out of the question for this historian, although the reader may perhaps "sense," at times, that my effort here results from a lifelong labor to acquire a personal vision of our own tradition.

For the task at hand, some simple-minded limitations were set. The self-evident source materials for the story are the writings of men and women in which they undertook the difficult task of presenting their ideas about themselves. They have done this in many different forms: in prefaces to their works, poetry, letters, diaries, memoirs, and autobiographies. The differences between these types of writing are considerable. What I consider genuine autobiography turns out to be very much rarer prior to 1800 A.D. than might be expected. My underlying struggle with the genre and the reasons for the gradual formulation of the autobiographic task will, no doubt, be discernible in the reading of this book. I have attempted a more compressed and more systematic treatment of the problems in a separate article.[1] The choice of texts was thus dictated by their availability and their suitability for testing the growth and nature of self-conception. It should go without saying that a choice of other texts, analyzed by other minds, would result in a different history. To this historian the chosen texts seemed to function as the most revealing signposts along the long road, through a complex historical territory, that Western man has traveled in his effort to arrive at a sense of individuality.

I have not been able to find satisfying solutions for several structural problems of this history. Some of the difficulties proceed from the nature of the historical thesis that individuality is a specifically modern form of self-conception. Some of the features we are searching out come to the fore in the Renaissance; the notion comes fully into its own at the time of Goethe. In classical antiquity men were very little inclined to assign positive value to the ineffable self. In chapter 1, I therefore try to suggest, at least, some of the cultural features of antiquity that set limits to an overt concern with individuality. At the close of the ancient world, at its confluence with emerging Christianity, St. Augustine produced in the *Confessions* an autobiographical form and a view of the self (though not of individuality) of extraordinary power for the subsequent story; and it is treated in chapter 2. While medieval Christians—less imitative of the Augustinian model of self-analysis than might be expected— elaborated cultural forms and institutions that limited the view of their individuality, at the same time a social differentiation prepared the ground in which it later could flourish. Chapter 3, which owes a great debt to the pioneer work by Georg Misch,[2] attempts a compressed survey of medieval autobiographical forms and self-conceptions and suggests some of the reasons for the relative absence of individuality. Chapter 4, is meant to test these by focusing on the single figure of Abelard. There are no subsequent general chapters, since I believe that detailed analyses of modern autobiographical writings may cumulatively shed light on the general cultural conditions responsible for the emergence of individuality as a self-conscious concern. The full convergence of all the factors constituting this modern view of the self occurred only at the end of the eighteenth century. The book ends with a discussion of Goethe's *Dichtung und Wahrheit* and a very brief forward glance from there. But the insights grounded in Goethe's idea of individuality guided my search, and they are undeniably present in the earlier chapters. That the present superimposes itself on the past is an inevitable feature of the historical quest and of the autobiographical enterprise.

The analysis proper has been guided by the contrast between "model" conceptions of personality and individuality. This heuristic device posits, on the one hand, the adherence of men to great personality ideals in which their culture tends to embody its values and objectives—and, on the other hand, a commitment to a self for which there is no model. The ideal which most clearly expresses the view that the task of life and of self-formation rests on the imitation of a lofty model is the ideal contained in the *Imitatio Christi*. An ideal form of being beckons men and women to model their lives upon it. There existed, and continue to exist, many such model conceptions of the personality in our tradition: the ideal of the Homeric Hero, the Germanic hero, the truly "polis-minded" man, the Roman *pater familias*, of Aristotle's "great-minded man," of the unshakable Stoic, the ideal monk, the ideal knight, the ideal gentleman, the ideal teacher, and so on. All such ideals share certain formal characteristics. They prescribe for the individual certain substantive personality traits, certain values, virtues, and attitudes. They embody specific life-styles into which to fit the self. They offer man a script for his life, and only in the unprescribed interstitial spaces is there room for idiosyncrasy. To be sure, no two knights were ever the same, there are interesting differences between Achilles and Odysseus, and no "imitator" of Christ ever duplicated that life. But the all-important point is that, despite all variation, the men who sought to follow such models saw virtue in approaching and fulfilling an exemplary way of being human while placing very little value on idiosyncratic differences—if at all. The more the mind's eye is fascinated by the ideal model before it, the more a man will strive to attain *it*, and the less he will ask about the fit between the model and his own specific reality. He is unlikely to suffer from a sense of "falsifying himself" by fitting into the norms demanded by his model, to feel "hemmed in" if the ideal expresses the values of the society, or to lament the lost opportunities of his precious individuality. In youth the attractive and guiding powers of such ideals are powerful; they beckon one to be a good citizen, a good father, a good doctor, or teacher.

But the ideal of individuality is marked by the conviction that ultimately no general model can contain the specificity of the true self. The ineffable cannot be defined by the general—*individuum ineffabile est.* When the belief in individuality reaches its full force, this individual difference is seen to be a matter of great value in itself. The great fecundity of nature and of the human potential specifies each separate existence as a unique being of irreplaceable value. When this conception dominates man's awareness, it becomes his life's task to actualize the one mode of being which only he can be. There is both joy and terror in this task. It may fill a life with a sense of cosmic importance that can unhinge balanced sanity. The task of self-exploration and self-definition can consume life to the danger point of morbid self-inspection and egocentrism, where active life in the world ceases. It is exceedingly difficult to come to know one's individuality. But the mind fascinated by this vision of potential life finds no help in looking to models. By definition, they will not fit. Decisions must fit the inner law of one's being; there is very little room for role-playing. To fail one's individuality becomes in a sense a crime against the human cosmos. Models do have a function, even in this form of self-conception: they provide for those aspects of the personality where the self subjects itself to externally defined roles. But ultimately no model can set the terms for the precise and the unique manner in which a multitude of elements are coordinated by an individuality. A personality has its very own style.

Nothing in real life, or in its reflection in writing, ever fits the purity of conceptualizations. They are meant not to be substitutes for life but to serve in the discovery of complex interrelations in reality. No life can be purely a pursuit of a model or purely a concern with uniqueness. What counts is the respective weight of attention placed on either component, the question of the predominant theme. The same caveat must be heeded with regard to any of the other ideal-typical constructions employed in this search: historical-mindedness and an ahistorical stance, development and unfolding, memoir and autobiography. The conceptual distinction between a social situation in which the individual seems to be firmly embedded in the social mass (experiencing itself as an integral part of society, or as its mere prolongation) and a social situation where the individual thinks of itself as the constitutive element of society, is also too simple to fit a complex reality. But it can be used to help suggest that a very far-reaching differentiation of the social mass, in a variety of terms, seems to accompany the emerging fascination with personal individuality. At the one end of the spectrum one can posit a primitive tribal form of community with very little differentiation and near-complete identification of the individual with the socially given world; at the other pole stands a highly differentiated society in which each constitutive element is an individually different part of the whole. In between *may* lie the complex social reality.

It is wise to keep in mind two points in particular. Individuality and individualism, two terms forever being confused with each other, are seen here as having quite distinct meanings. *Individualism* has to do with the conception of the appropriate *relationship* between an individual and society. The *Oxford English Dictionary* defines it, in contrast to collectivism, as "the social theory which advocates the free and independent action of the individual." It is, therefore, a social theory which desires that form of society in which the degree of social control over the individual is kept to a minimum so that the individual can pursue his course with the highest degree of autonomy. Individualism leaves men as free as possible to define themselves. *Individuality*, however, had best be restricted to a personality conception, the form of self that an individual may seek. It is entirely thinkable that individualism does not lead to a preoccupation with individuality. If, in a society dedicated to individualism, everyone freely opts for the realization of a common model—that of a truly rational man, for example (as implied perhaps in Kant, Comte, Marx, or Freud)—a society of homogeneous personalities may be sought which denies the value of individuality. The complication lies in the fact that a society of individualities, however, seems to demand the freedoms of a society devoted to individualism.

The other point worth watching is that a study of the self-conception we call individuality deals with the desire or willingness of historical figures to perceive themselves as unique personalities. What is most important is that they place a value on being an individuality. From a modern point of view we may perceive them as individualities, but this is irrelevant to the purpose of this essay. The all-important historical question is whether or not an Augustine, an Abelard, a Petrarch did place a value on distinctiveness or whether each was more preoccupied with the pursuit of the typical and the model. And since this is a study of their professed self-conceptions, there is no need for psychohistory. The issue is Augustine's self-conception, to the extent that he reveals it, and not the question of whether he conceived of himself "correctly" or of how he related to his mother—the "correctness" of the view is not to be determined by this or that particular modern theory of the personality. The issue is the historical reconstruction of the view Augustine had of himself, not the reconstruction of "the" historical Augustine. If, to some readers, these are undesired restrictions, so be it. I do not deny the insights that psychoanalytical studies can bring to these same persons.

The search for these self-revelations in autobiographic writings can be an elusive one. One tracks them down wherever one can find them. I have tried to seek them in a very specific kind of writing, and some aspects of the "order" of the individual chapters depends on the character of this literature. A hallmark of autobiography is that it is written from a specific retrospective point of view, the place at which the author stands in relation to his cumulative experience when he puts interpretative meaning on his past. This moment, this point of view, needs to be recaptured for a proper understanding of the autobiographic effort; so must the motivation and intention of the author for writing autobiography at all. Thus the historical investigator can at times be led into complex analyses. The manner of the text, the very mode of writing, usually has to be seen as an important means whereby the author reveals his self-awareness. I have chosen to include a recapitulation of the life story as each writer saw it himself in each of the chapters of this essay, as further evidence of the understanding of the self and as a reminder of the bare bones of the story. Some readers will think it wrong to stay this close to textual analysis. I can only say that I have made a conscious choice of one of many ways of dealing with the problems.

This undertaking thus has significant limitations. They are not to be excused, but perhaps they may be understood. As soon as one begins to dig deeply into the vast problem of emerging individuation, one encounters a model piece of scholarship. The study of the history of autobiography owes an enormous debt to Georg Misch, the son-in-law of Wilhelm Dilthey who by his own methodological reflections pointed to the importance of autobiography for the historian. In 1904, the young Misch submitted a prizewinning essay to the Prussian Academy on the history of autobiography. The rest of his life was devoted to working out the details of his insights. He studied Arabic, Old Norse, and Byzantine writings to track down the autobiographic literature of our Western tradition. He wrote eight half-volumes with a total of 3,885 pages. By the time of his death in 1965, at eighty-seven years of age, Misch had reached the epoch of Dante—and the treatment of him was not quite completed. It was Misch's literary executors who rounded out the work by simply adding the 1904 version on the modern age. Since Misch barely reached the threshold of modernity—when the development of autobiography begins to come into its own—he only sparingly treated the problem of individuality. The problem of individuation, which was supposedly the theme of the whole enterprise, was again and again totally buried in Misch's detailed inquiry.

The debt I owe to such monumental scholarship is immense, even if, on reading the autobiographic texts on my own, I often come to quite different views of the subject. But a work such as Misch's haunts one's mind in another sense as well. I am reminded that life is too short for perfect scholarship; the promise of completion is always left *ad calendas Graecas*. None of the writers taken up can be mastered even by years of study; the truly great ones—Augustine, Montaigne, Rousseau, Goethe—are inexhaustible. Certainly no one who attempts them all can be expert on any one—and those who are experts will be critical of what I have done.

There is, then, no false modesty in calling this an essay. It is an essay—at best. All one can do when one is interested in a subject of this magnitude is to try to suggest an area of investigation in which there lies an interesting human topic. One takes a deep breath, takes his heart in hand, and works with as much care and intellectual responsibility as he can. Though the interest of one's students is encouraging, one wonders to the end whether he writes only for himself.

# 1

# The Problem of Individuality and Autobiography in Classical Antiquity

This essay will take St. Augustine's *Confessions* as its starting point. To begin here is not to say that "there was no autobiographic writing prior to the *Confessions*." There was such writing and it has received the attention of scholars.[1] But my interest is less in all the varied forms of autobiographic writing than in that proper form of autobiography wherein a self-reflective person asks "who am I?" and "how did I become what I am?" I search for conditions of self-conscious individuality. From this vantage point Augustine's great book has a certain claim for special consideration and the nature of classical autobiographic writing has a problematic character.

The justification for assigning a special position to Augustine lies also in a simple experience. In a systematic search in time through our Western heritage for the accounts in which men self-consciously sought to express the meaning of their personal experience, his book confronts us with striking prominence. All autobiographic writing prior to the *Confessions* retains a much lower profile. None has the scope, the fullness, the inner richness, and the intense personal focus of the *Confessions*. It makes no difference whether one's route is through Athens, Rome, or Jerusalem; at the end of the ancient world there suddenly looms that book whose sheer presence makes one feel like the traveler through the plains who suddenly comes upon the mountains. Everything that had seemed like an elevation before has been moved into a realm of different proportions.

It is not only that meeting up with one of mankind's great geniuses imposes a change in scale. Since Augustine, lesser minds have produced great autobiographies; and before him, men of comparable genius wrote of themselves in more restricted autobiographic forms.

Some ancients wrote of great deeds done (*res gestae*); some wrote on memorable events they had witnessed (*memoir*); some reported why and how they sought to become wise men (philosophers' Lives); but none opened up their souls in the inwardness of genuine autobiography. The essential cultural features and different human needs of the ancient world may help to account for the more stunted growth of an autobiographic activity which later gained so much greater prominence in the life of Western man. Though the effort to suggest these reasons can only produce plausibilities, it should be made, even tentatively. Anyone treading on ancient ground knows how easily clever arguments can be undone because the sands of Egypt may release an unexpected document or a new discovery may upset a previous textual reading.

Three dominant factors in the history of ancient Greece and Rome in particular suggest why the self-searching quest from which genuine autobiographic activity results—especially that from which individualistic traits of the personality conception emerge—had such limited results. One reason lies in the strong kinship ties marking the early phase of this civilization. Another rests in the intensely public character of *polis* life. The third factor is a reflection of the powerful hold that a rational model exercised over the later personality conceptions. Autobiographic memoirs, *res gestae,* and philosophers' Lives emerged much more readily in this cultural context than did autobiography with the inward orientation marking the *Confessions.* There was very little room for a personality conception to move in the direction of individuality.

The documents of early Hellenic life, as well as the later Roman reflections on the conditions of earliest Rome, suggest the long dominance of kinship ties. Ask a Homeric hero who he is, and most likely he will answer: I am Telemachus, the son of Odysseus, the son of Laertes, the son of Autolykus. Ask a Roman, and he may enumerate the names of the *maiores,* his "better ones" who went before. Individuals were embedded in the social mass of given blood relations. In fundamental ways, often so hard for us who live in a highly differentiated society of individualists and individualities to understand, these earlier lives are enmeshed in and derive their meaning from basic social and kinship relations. In the sixth century a Solon, in his "Fragment on Justice," considers it perfectly just that the yet unborn children will pay for the *hubris* of their fathers. The more strongly one knows oneself as a prolongation of a family, fully as a part of a tightly linked kinship group, the less offensive such a view of justice is. Until we reach reflections of a different world at the end of Aeschylus's *Oresteia,* the sons of the family know that it falls upon them to secure justice by revenging the unjust acts committed by others. *Phylae* and *gentes* are the real bases of power in a society where public power is undeveloped.

In these societies, the pervasive kinship structure joins hands with an intensely aristocratic view of life which left a lasting mark on all ancient culture. For the "good life" one depends entirely on the welfare of the *oikos* or the *patrimonium*, the family estate. What one has seems more important than what one is. In a society with such a narrow economic base of well-being, only the great families have power; only they can afford chariot warfare and cavalry service. Only they "stand out" or are eminent; only they are *nobiles;* only they have names. "Good" sons have "good" fathers. Virtue is a matter of breeding. In the *Iliad* there is but one name without a genealogy: Thersites, the bold-spoken one, whose fate was not promising. When Romans thought of proletarians, they thought of that vast mass of "nameless" ones who could serve the public good only with their children (*proles*). Even after the middle of the fifth century B.C., an Athenian writer, the so-called Old Oligarch, assumes it as axiomatic that nothing good can come from the have-nots without family names. In Greece, only the belief in *Themis,* a sense for some basic order among men, protected the lowly against the arbitrary willfulness of his prominent neighbor. The Roman client system gave protection to the weak through a religiously formalized association with the patricians and gave the patricians a base for formidable power. What, as Walpole said, was the greatness of Rome but the history of a thousand great families?

As polis life gradually emerged in both Hellenic and Roman society, the tough strength of the kinship hold over men was still reflected in the prolonged struggle of transforming blood loyalties into polis loyalty. Over centuries, the constitutional developments, insofar as they are known, suggest the tenacity of this conflict. Almost any of the struggles between senate and plebs in fifth- and fourth-century Rome has the marks of this transformation. Perhaps in this particular *res publica* the basic power of kinship prevailed longer than in any other polis; the greatness of the republic rested very much in the fact that here the powerful clans had learned at an early time to merge their interests to an extraordinary degree with the public ones. The Lycurgan constitution in Sparta was, in many respects, the imposition of an intense commitment to public affairs upon a clannish community. In Athens the Solonic constitution had aimed at intersecting the tribal order by property classifications; at best it was a halfway house. Cleisthenes' grandiose gerrymander (of either 510 or 508 B.C.), by enforcing identification with a *deme,* a residence, sought to secure polis loyalty over the clannish interests of the great families. All in all, it took protracted developments to bring men to a greater readiness to identify with the city more than with the family. The gradual shift from subsistence farming to a somewhat greater reliance on a money economy, and the severe social crises accompanying such a shift, helped to loosen the social weave. And the broader social base of power which lay in the change to the superior military effectiveness of heavy infantry was perhaps the prime factor in the growth of polis power. The hoplite phalanx and the Roman legion were extraordinary teachers of polis-mindedness.

What kind of self-conception might a man hold in this older world? For early Rome we have no evidence to answer this question. For the early Greek world we do have one great source: Homeric poetry. The epic, at least, permits a reconstruction of "Homeric man," albeit not a self-awareness of anyone but the poet, or poets.

Homer's man, like Homer's audience, is the aristocratic hero. Blood ties are of extraordinary importance to him. The poet pays a striking attention to genealogies: heroes meet for combat before Troy and recount their noble lineage, often even in direct speech; horses are shown to be noble by being given their line of descent, and so are fine weapons. The audience is clearly given to understand that, although a servant woman, Odysseus' housekeeper Eurycleia is "noteworthy": as daughter of Ops, she is a name-descendant. The worth of each is very much a matter of the worth of a family. Sons are prolongations of the life of the fathers. The setting within a given social mass is imprinted on each life.

Most men "disappear" in the relatively undifferentiated mass; the heroes stand out as separate individuals. Their strength of will, at first sight, seems to belie the domination of society. Who, in our literary heritage, is a more strong-willed egotist than Achilles? The Myrmidons, his people, entirely depend for their safety on this man whose chariot-fighting protects the poor on foot, much as tanks protect infantry. By his stature he seems to dominate society. What is left, then, at first sight, of the argument that man is prevented from self-definition as a separate individual by the realities of a tightly knit kinship society?

The hero stands out, but only as the representative of his society's values. He cannot function in contradistinction to his group. He certainly would not have understood anything about an inner law of life by which an individuality seeks to direct its course. Homeric man does not seem to have a character-organizing center such as our modern conception of an ego. The hero is governed by the strong flow of instinct and passion. His great actions result from a special form of energy (*menos*) which frequently comes from the outside: the God "put *menos* into the hero's nostrils." *Psyche* seems to refer to the breath that leaves the corpse and goes as a shade to Hades; it does not seem to function as a coordinating force for the whole being. It is altogether striking how "open" Homeric man is to the forces of the surrounding world and how they direct his life. Emotions such as love, anger, fear, and courage "jump at him"; thoughts come to him. When Helen, on the battlements, sees Menelaus, on the battlefield, and wonders how all these terrible events came about, she does not hold herself responsible—a god had seized her. Agamemnon attributes the fatal quarrel with Achilles to Zeus's sending *Até*; the man struck by endangering blindness does not function as a self-directed being.

The hero has his fate, but hardly as the consequence of a self-formulated plan for fulfilling the chosen personality. His moral compass is set entirely by the forces within a typical shame-oriented society. Fear of shame (*aidos*) is the prime motive for action, for the men on the battlefield as well as for a young noble girl like Nausicaa, who refuses to walk the streets with the stranger Odysseus. Fear of publicly incurred shame functions in the place of an inner-directed conscience. With all their love of life, fear of shame is stronger for Achilles and Hector than any well-reasoned argument for self-preservation. Their self-esteem, their sense of honor, their glory are publicly given and recognized attributes. Glory, a good name, is the chief objective of the struggle of life. There is no comfort for men such as these in what was for them the strange thought that virtue, unacknowledged by others, might receive a reward in a hereafter. A person's "name" depends on the belief of others that it is worthy of respect and remembrance. Glory is a gift bestowed by admirers. Personal excellence (*arête*) is publicly proven "virtue" in the contest, the *agon* with equals worthy of competition. There is little comfort in "having meant well" but not having done well. Always try to be the best and take the risk of the uncertain outcome. Excellence, personal distinction, and eminence come to the competitor who is proven best. The hero is the supreme accomplishment of a style of life and the ideal of personality held in common. The intensely agonistic spirit that dominated Hellenic and Hellenistic life for so long afterward is the spawning ground for a model conception of the aristocratic personality: the ideal of the *aner kalokagathos*, the man harmonizing the ideal aristocratic values, in the last analysis the product of good breeding. From this ideal one does not move easily in the direction of individuality. The stimulant for self-accounting lies in the telling of great deeds and accomplishments. From it result *res gestae*, perhaps memoirs, but hardly autobiographic self-reflection of the more contemplative inward kind.

Something resembling individualism, a certain manner of self-assertion against society, could, however, result from such a personality ideal. Later in the fifth and fourth centuries, some of the strong personalities almost seem to act as if the quality of polis life were the gift of its great personages rather than the product of any common struggle for excellence. Something about Alcibiades, Pausanias, Lysander, and Alexander suggests individualistic traits, but in a sense they are throwbacks to the older Homeric hero and not newly emerging personality types. At an earlier time, when much of the older kinship world was weakening and the polis world was only beginning to assert its hold, aspects of individualism also came to the fore in such poets as Hesiod, Archilochus, Alkaios, and even Solon.[2] But this individualistic tone becomes more muted as the polis imposed an intense public-mindedness on hoplite and citizen. The polis proved to be the strongest force throughout the fifth century at least.

The polis represented that great social effort whereby men around the Mediterranean overcame their tribal limitations and lifted themselves to a higher level and a greater potential for a decent life. In its Hellenic forms especially it was a most formidable achievement, and it affected Western civilization forever. As Aristotle still saw it in the fourth century: the polis came into existence for the protection of life; later on it existed for the sake of the good life. This enormous collective effort demanded the whole man. The polis developed by forcing the individual into submission to its claims; it imposed, in Jacob Burckhardt's apt phrase, a state servitude on the individual (*Staatsknechtschaft des Individuums*). A hoplite phalanx, rows of heavily armed infantry (where the shield of one's neighbor could provide protection for one's right side), could move effectively only when the next man could be trusted, when each man had the same objectives and was willing to submit his self-will to the will of the whole. The phalanx must have been an extraordinary molder of a common spirit. In the ideal which the Spartan polis represented for so many Greeks, the life order of the Lycurgan *cosmos*, and the order of training (*agŏgé*) that set the mold, claimed the entire man, leaving no room for private life. In Athens, which so often appears to us moderns through facile misreadings as the more "liberal" society, the same state servitude prevailed, even if, toward the end of the fifth century, the individual also begins to procure a greater measure of private existence for himself.

Man was taught by his polis to perceive his very essence in being a *zoon politikon*, a polis creature, a public man. He had no freedom to choose between a life committed to the public good and a decent private life. The good private life was derived from the good life obtained as citizen only. And those who thought it possible to live without the polis were *idiōtes*; only gods or beasts had this option, as Aristotle suggests even at a time when the polis ideal had already passed its highest point. In a world where the polis aimed at near self-sufficiency (*autarky*), where citizenship was jealously guarded (at one point an Athenian citizen was defined as one with an Athenian father and mother—in other words: the polis was a closed "corporation"), the fate of the exile seemed worse to many than death. The *metic*, willing to live on "foreign" soil in order to exploit opportunities in trade, can hardly have served as a model for a father to hold up to his growing son. How utterly contemptuous still is the remark of a first-century-B.C. Roman on this point: in a famous letter to his brother Quintus, Marcus Cicero sneers at that miserable type of citizen who prefers making money in the provinces to full participation in public life at Rome—a decaying republic which Cicero himself, at times, compared to a stinking garbage mound.

Active public life, in which a good man could test his mettle, was the model of existence. It retained its hold on the minds of men even though models of private existence developed throughout the Hellenistic age and during the period of the Roman empire. As long as this model prevailed, a premium lay on the individual's public role. Perhaps the finest expression of this ideal was Pericles' Funeral Oration, as Thucydides immortalized it. When Pericles gave that speech, commemorating the first to fall in the Peloponnesian War, he undertook to hold up to the Athenians the mirror of their polis ideal, and he obviously contrasted it with the ideal of the Spartan enemy. The whole argument is drawn up to suggest that the Athenian citizen, even without the strict Spartan training order, is by his nature and his heritage as fully committed a public man as his foe. The history of Athens, its laws and its *mores*, make him so. So does his fear of incurring public shame. Only *because* he is so firmly a public-minded citizen can the Athenian afford what the Spartan fear of endangering the Lycurgan *cosmos* cannot permit: a measure of private life, cultural refinement, and the alleged luxury of a democracy's deliberations and discussions. The order of priorities is perfectly clear: the mark of personal well-being depends on the well-being of the polis. Personal excellence is a derivative of the excellence of the community. The praiseworthy exertions of the public man will cover, like a cloak, his private shortcomings. The polis, the concerted effort and common achievement, is the "collective" hero, and Pericles speaks of Athens as if she were a Homeric hero. The individual derives value and gratification from fully participating in something greater than himself, some work of excellence and splendor which no single individual could equal. Excellence flows from the collective hero, the polis, to the individual, always the lesser hero.

A startling reversal of this position occurs when Alcibiades, only a few decades later, claims a special position for himself by virtue of the glory that flows from his achievements for the polis, and when Socrates seems to suggest in the *Apology* that good individuals will make a good polis. If the ideal expressed in this Periclean speech had a pervasive hold—and Thucydides strongly suggests that Pericles' leadership ultimately rested in his ability to tell men what they knew to be true—then it is hardly likely that a father in such a society brought up his sons to seek self-fulfillment in the private cultivation of individuality. What could individuality mean to Pericles' listeners when he tells the women not to lament the lost son, but to go home and replace him by another one? Contrast that attitude with the sentiments of a Wilhelm von Humboldt writing to his wife that despite all the fine children still living none can ever replace the lost individuality of a long deceased boy. How much more telling of that Greek age of "public man" is Aeschylus's desire to have his life summed up on his tombstone, not as the immortal poet, but as the valiant fighter at Marathon. *Se non e vero, e ben trovato.*

The disappointments men experienced with the polis—of which the internecine Peloponnesian War was so symptomatic—loosened the grip of the ideal of polis-mindedness on some men, and these were often the best. The older ideal of the "gentleman," harmonizing the desirable virtues unreflectingly in a unified personality, the *aner kalokagathos,* was gradually being displaced by a greater differentiation of social functions characteristic of a more sophisticated society requiring trained specialists. Now some men might find a form of self-fulfillment in performing a specialty at which they were particularly good. The mercenary hoplite, the medic, the trained orator, the sophist, and even the philosopher-king and the expert grammarian, botanist, and mathematician are expressions of this phenomenon. So is Socrates with his insistence that he has a special mission that takes all of his time. To some men at least, the alternative option of finding meaning in a private existence now offered itself. A Xenophon might either seek the attainment of brave deeds in adventure—but no longer in the service of his own polis—or simply transfer his abilities of public leadership to the running of a private household: the pots and pans on his shelves are marshaled like the phalanx he might wish to command if the times still valued such talent.

Various processes contributed to this diversification of life-styles through which, in Hellenistic times, the more intense cultivation of individual personality could develop alongside the survival of the public ideal: a general sophistication of techniques in economic, military, and legal affairs; the infiltration of "foreign" ways and religions, especially in such "open" societies as Athens and the Ionian poleis; and above all the sophists' abrasive effect on an unquestioned polis consensus. The intellectual reorientation accompanying (or underlying?) such developments had two aspects. On the one hand, it sought to keep alive the ideal of the public man; on the other hand, it took a turn (according to Nietzsche, the fatal turn) toward independence, placing life at the disposal of thought. But when the real polis presented men with such extraordinary problems as the events of the Peloponnesian War or the inability of the jealous poleis to unite against the threat from outside, the polis ideal continued strong. The great political philosophies now tried to provide the intellectual blueprints for building the perfect polis with which to overcome the imperfect but inescapable public life. Political utopia is less a looking forward to new institutions than an attempt to reendow with life the old models from which men have not been able to free themselves. Educational schemes often aimed at the cultivation of civic virtue more than private virtue. A sophist like Isocrates wanted individuals to be trained in intellectual and cultural skills so that they could function all the better as polis creatures. The grandiose model personality which Aristotle presented in the ideal of the "great-minded man," the *aner megalopsychos*, retains the qualities of the eminently public man and man of affairs, despite the intrusion of a new fascination with the "theoretical life." For the locally prominent in the many poleis dotting the Mediterranean world, the aristocratic ideal of public service to their community long remained the natural outlet for their talents and the most readily available road for satisfying the craving for public honor.

To some extent, intellectual trends adapted themselves to changing reality. There were men who understood that the autarkic polis, the "exclusive" polis, had no future and had to be overcome. Early Panhellenic ideas may have been reactions to the suffering of internecine warfare or a warning against the encroaching threat of the larger territorial state. From this halfway station, philosophical thought and taste eventually moved to the rationalization that the whole cosmos in which men moved (especially when conceived as a rational order of things) constituted the true polis. Why should it matter to the true cosmopolitan whether home was Athens, Rome, or Alexandria? These men could be reconciled to the new order in which overarching territorial states, usually governed by princes, absorbed the independent poleis, leaving them as important centers still of administration and cultural life, but no longer as the crucial unit of life on which fate depended. In some important ways the large state and ultimately the universal empire were conducive to promoting private life. As Seneca asked in the first century A.D.: who stands to benefit more from the good universal ruler than the lover of wisdom? for if the ruler be good, the wise man, without a bad conscience, can devote himself to the pursuit of wisdom.

The life of Socrates—whether historical truth or poetic transformation—suggests the turn toward a personality conception that offers a genuine alternative to the ideal of the public man. Here the danger of misrepresentation or misunderstanding is great. The following argument is concerned more with discerning certain possibilities in the Socratic position than with ascribing this new focus to Socrates personally. What was fresh and important for the future should be stressed more than the balance of old and new. For from several important perspectives Socrates was a polis creature, whose life-style was unthinkable without the polis, and who worked actively for the best of all poleis. So was his pupil Plato; but less so his pupil Antisthenes who stressed the importance of individual development. Our concern must be with the tensions created for Socrates' public commitment when other interests began to impinge. These may not have been unreconcilable tensions for Socrates himself, but out of them grew the viable alternatives of a fully private life.

When Pericles spoke of the measure of private life which Athens could grant its citizens—exactly because their public commitment could be taken for granted—it is easy to visualize Socrates as a prime beneficiary. Indeed, it was he who most conscientiously heeded the call to public duty and the superior claims of the laws to which the individual should submit himself. But he did not seek personal fulfillment in the public role, except as he may have defined such a role for his own purpose. For him, fulfillment came instead in the pursuit of the philosopher's mission. And from that shift in emphasis emerged new possibilities.

One Socratic line of argument inverts the process of personality formation suggested, however vaguely, in the Funeral Oration. As Pericles would have it: the children of Athens have the excellence of Athens. The fear of public shame makes them behave. The philosopher says instead that all good comes from a virtuous soul. The norm of behavior is not the opinion of the market place but the inner dictate of reason. The very "discovery" of the soul, as the governing form within man, sets a different task of self-formation than prevailed in the older ideal of the *Kalokagatheia*. And the shift from a shame-oriented morality to an internalized rational ethic imposes on the individual who follows it (perhaps only a few did) a never-ending rational investigation into the grounds of its action. Social control gives way to autonomy, even if the real lawgiver is not the idiosyncratic self but a universal conception of reason. Intensive work on the human personality, bringing a unified being to the harmonious expression of its inner governor, gives to life a different tone than that set by letting inherited nature unfold itself. The cultivation of personality becomes a consuming task, even if it may be placed in relation to a still wider social one. For Socrates the process is shared in common with other men; he sees the task in reaso*ning*, which occurs in dialogue, not monologue. But already, not far in the future, looms that human type for whom the imparted truth—and no longer the truth actively being uncovered—sets the simpler life task: fit the self into the given rational model.

While this Socratic turn, and its spiritualizing of individual life, was a highly significant step in the individuation of our Western personality, it impeded rather than promoted the growth of a sense of individuality. The premium lay on following reason, and the objective of all effort was to become the wise man. But "in the realm of reason individuality is a stranger."[3] The more universal that reason is thought to be, the more each life, in accord with reason, shares its form with every other one. I go where the logos leads me, you go where the logos leads you; if we truly followed the logos, we ought to come out at the same point. Only much later, with the coming of a strong historicism giving each life the conditions to which to apply reason, was this conception of universal reason countermanded; only then did man seem to rest willingly with the proposition that a universally valid reason, supplementing inexplicably different but valid life premises, does not lead to uniform positions.

But in the ancient world the trust in a unifying logos was too strong for this. The more this trust went with a belief in a firm order of the world, the cosmos itself as an expression of a rational order, the more the personality conceptions adhered to the demands of a universalized and universalizing rationality. The transition to the larger Hellenistic states, and ultimately the incorporation of the entire polis world into the Roman Empire—which until the second century A.D. was a federation of poleis under the hegemony of the strongest one—strengthened a cosmopolitanism in which the rational cosmos had become one's true polis. Fitting the self into this rational order of the world became for many the task of life. The ideal of the wise man who had learned to live in harmony with nature (i.e., reason) was, despite variations in detail, the model existence preached by the great philosophical systems which were the Hellenistic heirs of that Socratic turn. This ideal could be reconciled with the other model of the public man, most eminently in Roman forms of Stoicism which, in their tie to natural law, had a long career in the Western tradition. The frequently voiced dilemma of having to make the personal choice between the *vita activa* and the *vita contemplativa* clearly suggests the side-by-side existence of alternative modes of personal life.[4]

The extant autobiographic writings of the ancients mirror such a choice of personality conceptions. "Lives of philosophers," emanating from the various schools, join memoir and *res gestae*, the record of great deeds done, as the other autobiographic genre of antiquity. However sketchy these philosophers' Lives are, they sufficiently suggest the dilemma of presenting a self under classical conditions. One simple inhibition lies in the belief that a wise man really should not talk about himself; when he does, he does so only for didactic purposes. Another handicap lies in the pervasive distrust of idiosyncrasy. The whole undertaking thus tends to be dominated by the need to show the degree to which the personal life was true to the admired typical model. This could almost be done by formula: What was the author's descent? What were his relations to teachers and later to disciples? His relations to women, family, and friends? How exemplary was he in controlling his passions? What was his external appearance, his moral behavior, his style of life? What were his writings, teachings, and wise sayings? The interest in individuality is minimal at best; the genetic understanding of the personal development pales, by comparison, before the interest in the didactic value of the personality. Much of this value is drawn from the presentation of the exemplary struggle with fate, a force so often seen chiefly as the obstacle standing in the way of living as a genuinely wise man, whose wisdom is continually tested through his encounter with destiny.

Here the conditions for successful biography are the same as for auto-biography; rarely does the autobiographer reveal insights unavailable to the biographer. The art of literary portraiture, however, was highly de-veloped within this schematic view of the personality. The true incentive for writing autobiographic literature may have been weak, but such a statement does not call into question the artistry of ancient historians and biographers. Quite the contrary: the literary forms and devices were available, and the formal power of ancient writers was great. Though they had the literary tools and talent to write exemplary autobiographies, they had little incentive for doing so. Thus the suggestion is reinforced that the relative absence of autobiography is indeed an index of the restrictions on the dominant personality ideals and the cultural condi-tions on which they rested.

During the millennium from 800 B.C. until 200 A.D., the conditions of ancient life neither stimulated nor promoted the growth of autobiog-raphy. The ancients did not put a premium on the life devoted to settling the quandary: who am I? how did I become what I am? in what sense am I a distinctive personality? and what complex interplay of external forces and internal characteristics accounts for my specific configuration? There was no need to use autobiography as a basic quest for the self, or as a tool for self-clarification. But there did exist, in that aristocratic, agonis-tic, and public-minded civilization, a need for self-glorification and self-justification. Now the representation of great deeds done, the public role of personality and its effects on the world, is given a straightforward presentation. In Plato's "Seventh Letter," for example, the heavy stress on the value of a truly rational existence leaves very little room for the wonder of an individualistic personality development. The term *de-velopment* is actually a key to the limitations of all these genres that have their real strength in the art of static portraiture. The representation of developmental possibilities seems to be exhausted in a technique show-ing the gradual attainment of a given nature, or of a model of existence. Only in the heroic struggle against fate can one occasionally discern a weak development of the person. Not yet do we find that element which later on becomes so essential for the full potential of autobiography—the conception of a genetic personality development founded in the aware-ness of a complex interplay between I-and-my-world.[5] Compared to Judeo-Christian conceptions, and certainly compared to later historicist ones, the ancient personality conception has a more static mark. Portraiture and moralistic exemplification are more germane to it. From many perspectives, then, there are reasons for the limited growth of autobiography in antiquity. What growth there was, however, provided the later Western developments with basic literary forms and devices which became integral parts of the autobiographic tradition.

Prior to 400 B.C., at least some poetry has an autobiographic quality; rarely is this genre devoid of autobiographic moment.[6] Most noteworthy are the personal references in the work of Hesiod, Archilochus, and Solon. But anyone desiring to reconstruct a life from these autobiographic details is stumped by their paucity. Such prose writers as Herodotus and Thucydides only give us the barest hints about their own person. Only in Xenophon's *Anabasis*, written in the third person, do we find a memoir with autobiographic content; it has a strong tone of political apology and dwells on deeds done.[7]

From the fourth century we possess three extant documents with a decidedly autobiographic content. Two of these are in the form of legal speeches, and one is a famous letter. Isocrates, very late in life, around 354 B.C., wrote a defense speech for an Antidosis trial, which he probably never gave. The occasion is imagined to be a public one; the presentation of the personality is held entirely to a schema of the public man, living by the ethos of a virtuous citizen, albeit, in Isocrates' version, he is less of a hero than an average, slightly philistine, Athenian burgher. Sophistic education goes hand in hand with the cultivation of civic virtue, not private virtue; the cultivation of personal qualities still stands strongly in the service of the public function. This is even more true for Demosthenes' oration "On the Crown" (330 B.C.), an autobiographic justification for his opposition to Philip II of Macedon. The account of his life and character is meant to provide the context for understanding his political advocacy. As for Plato's famous autobiographic "Seventh Letter," scholars do not even agree as to whether it was written by Plato or by one of his pupils.[8] In any case, it is of particular interest for what it reveals about the author's dilemma: to opt for a life of political action or one of undisturbed withdrawal into philosophy? That account is centered on Plato's Sicilian experiences at the court of Syracuse where the old philosopher, having abstained from political life in his own Athens, thought he had a chance for translating philosophy into action. It is an honest assessment of his failure to do so. It also, however, is an account that mixes factual reporting of events with high philosophic thought; it gives us less of an insight into the person than into a philosopher with a practical problem concerning the remainder of his life. The dilemma of the choice between the *vita activa* or *vita contemplativa* had henceforth a model representation.

While Hellenistic writers extended the scope of biographic literature, we only have references to nonextant autobiographic works, all of which seem to have been memoirs or accounts of great deeds. Polybius tells us that Hannibal is alleged to have written a monumental record of his deeds and that Aratus of Sicyon wrote memoirs on military and political affairs. We find scattered references to autobiographic inscriptions and memoirs by Hellenistic rulers. The political convulsions of the Post-Gracchan age in Republican Rome stirred a number of Romans to write political "apologies" and accounts of their own activity. Through Cicero, Tacitus, and Plutarch we know of the political autobiographic writings of Aemilius Scaurus, Rutilius Rufus, Q. Lutatius Catulus, and above all of a great memoir by the dictator Sulla. Caesar's commentaries on the Gallic and the civil wars can hardly qualify as autobiography, even if the third-person accounts give occasional insights into his personality. There is no self-contained autobiography of Marcus Cicero, who otherwise is the ancient man we know best. His remarkable corpus of letters, especially those to Atticus and other close friends, have many self-revealing, self-reflective, and self-assessing moments. He frequently inserted personal data in his other writings; and in the *Brutus* he sketched his own development as orator in the framework of a history of oratory. Again we find the deep conflict over choosing between the *vita activa* or *contemplativa*; there is in Cicero a real awareness of the different roles a man can and must play (the term *persona*, meaning originally "mask" or "role," now figures more prominently), and Cicero occasionally possesses the ability, until then rarely encountered, to step outside of himself to measure his actual performance against the model of the statesman's life at which he had aimed (a rare quality in a man who would, most of the time, delude himself about his actual power). Had he written an autobiography, he might have given us the richest one a classical man could produce; but there is nothing in the available material to suggest that it would have transcended the limitations ascribed to the classical autobiographic effort.

The remains from the period of the principate do not alter the picture substantially. Symbolically, at the beginning of the age stands *the* monumental *res gestae*, par excellence, the "Queen of the documents" as Mommsen called it, the account of Augustus's deeds. This man, who changed the course of history so fundamentally, had the most grandiose material for his *Res Gestae*, the inscription found on the temple to the

Goddess Roma at Ancyranum. "At the age of nineteen, I acquired on my own decision and my own account an army and restored liberty to the state which had fallen under the tyranny of a faction"—how many lives can start their account thus? The first sentence lifts the life onto a plane where nothing could rival it. At the same time, no other document can show as well as this the world of difference between the *res gestae* of a public man and real self-reflecting autobiography. One of mankind's most extraordinary personalities records his deeds and the intent of his policies—but reveals absolutely nothing of his inner life. We know that he also wrote an earlier autobiography, but would its content, if extant, reveal any more? As for later imperial *vitae*, the only reliable references we have are to those by Hadrian and Septimius Severus—reserving that of Marcus Aurelius as a special case.

Among the less politically colored autobiographic writings under the principate we have the self-revealing portions of the poetry of Horace, Ovid (especially *Tristia* 4.10), and Propertius. There similarly are autobiographic reflections strewn through the writing of philosophers such as Seneca and Epictetus. A larger work, the "writer's autobiography" (*Schriftstellerautobiographie*) of Nicholas of Damascus, the counselor of King Herod, is largely an apologetic self-portrait and mostly a self-encomium, written in the "modest" third person. Its fragments have not made a great impression on its few readers[9]—the personality loses itself in memoir or in schematic self-praise. The *Life* of the Jewish historian Josephus again is basically an account of his military and political conduct during the period of the great rebellion. The Pauline letters reveal a good deal about the writer, but their very specific didactic purposes undercut their value as autobiography.

From the second century A.D. there are autobiographic references in Lucian's satirical poetry and even more in "the strangest of all autobiographic products in Greek literature,"[10] the sacred orations of the rhetor Aelius Aristides who talks about himself by recording the dreams and visions he experienced as a practitioner in the Asclepius cult. Then there is the book *To Myself* by the Emperor Marcus Aurelius, which publishers have so frequently marketed as one of the world's great autobiographies. But is this remarkable book an autobiography at all? Book One, with its carefully drawn list of what "I owe to others who formed me," might still sustain the impression that it is. But all subsequent eleven books have the quality of momentary jottings that warrant instead the characterization of "an active diary."[11] They represent the attempts of a man, for whom the world is on the verge of seeming meaningless, to recall to his mind each morning the few insights he values, the few certainties by which he can hold his personality together for the job he must perform. They are a collection of basically Stoic teachings, repeated almost as incantations so that they may stay alive, and amplified by personal reflections on daily occurrences. There is no active self-exploration in this, no self-revelation for the profit of others, no real self-portraiture. The whole is dominated by the man's need to hold madness at bay. Marcus succeeded, by the use of this daily recall, in containing his life within a horizon of Stoic rationality—however cheerless and joyless that life was. As one reads his jottings, one senses that the more refined world of the universal principate could not be preserved much beyond his time.

In the rapidly changing world of the third and fourth centuries some autobiographic writing was produced. The rhetor Libanius wrote a self-revealing declamation. But mostly the Christian apologists claim the attention of the searcher into the remains of the genre; in the second century Justin Martyr was such an apologist, and later on one may look at the writings of Priscillian, and Nestorius. From a literary point of view the most accomplished work prior to Augustine may have been the "Song of Himself" written by the Eastern churchman Gregory Nazianzen. Deeply felt Christian needs now merge with the literary forms prepared by classical antiquity. The high profile of Augustine's *Confessions* finally appears on the scene. It stands out with such a prominence in proportion to everything preceding it that it is difficult to resist the assertion it is here that the true autobiographic tradition of the Western world took off.

# 2
## St. Augustine's *Confessions:* The Search for a Christian Self

The historian of autobiography often finds a rich harvest in the great periods of crisis when the lives of Western men take decisive turns. In the "classical" ages, possessing the more coherently elaborated cultural configurations (which says no more than that they have a less contested repertory of answers and techniques for the perplexing questions of life), individuals less urgently face the need to account for the meaning of their existence. The ages of crisis, in which the firm assumptions about man and his world are being called into question, force upon the individual the task of doubting and reinvestigating the very foundations on which his self-conception traditionally rested. Even the meager harvest of ancient autobiographic writing supports this impression in part: there was the brief flowering of autobiographic poetry in the period of transition from the old aristocratic tribal society to the early polis; there was the crisis of personal reorientation thrust upon man by the crisis of which the Peloponnesian War was symptomatic; and the crisis of the dying Republic and the Roman civil wars brought autobiographic efforts to the fore. The cultural configuration of the High Middle Ages presents a more stable and uniform, a less problematic autobiographic type than the much more labile cultural context of the Renaissance and Reformation. Without wishing to turn such loose reflections into anything like a historical law—a law we moderns could not test since we can hardly perceive the configuration of our own culture, and a law presumably contradicted directly by the consideration that any intense personal crisis in a stable age can release all the motivations necessary for producing autobiography—it is still noteworthy that the great early "autobiography" under discussion here belongs to an age of the most profound cultural changes Western man experienced.

Augustine lived from 354 to 430 A.D. The century between 350 and 450 was, in terms of its external events, no more momentous than any other such stretch of classical history. With the exception of the period from 50 to 200—the largest segment of which Gibbon, no less, considered one of man's happiest ages—the ancient world had fairly consistently experienced great political upheavals. The half century from 250 to 300 may well have been more tumultuous than that from 400 to 450; and the years from 300 to 400 may, on the whole, have appeared fairly secure to most citizens of the empire. Thus it made a great difference for any subjective sense of well-being *where*, in such an extensive empire, and in just what period a man experienced the times. The extant books of the last great Roman historian, Ammianus Marcellinus, cover the quarter century in which Augustine grew up to be a man. They in no way convey the sense that this intelligent historical observer thought his world to be one in decline. Nor did Augustine, despite the shock of the disastrous battle at Adrianople or the sack of Rome by the Visigoths or the Vandal invasions of his own North African lands, ever view the history of his day with the kind of gloom that pervades the mind of Gregory the Great, one hundred and fifty years later. Repeated struggles occurred between the holders of imperial power and rival claimants; sometimes imperial rule was unified (for instance between 353–75, and 379–95), sometimes it was not. There were barbarian raids on Roman territory, but somehow the empire had always seemed capable of absorbing the invaders. No one at the time had the advantage of hindsight by which the modern historian knows that the division of the rule became definite in 395, and that, in the weaker and more exposed western half, the barbarians would rapidly become permanent masters. It is hard to perceive anything in the political events alone that would have produced a radical change in a man's self-conception (as the events around 400 B.C. and 49 B.C. could have done).

Perhaps the social and the economic changes of this period were of greater consequence. Ancient life, having been centered so intensively upon the urban complex of the polis in its varied forms, became less and less urban. Especially in the western part of the empire, the flight of the urban elite into the countryside had been going on for at least a century prior to 350 A.D.; the development of the villa and its supporting colonate system was a significant first step in the direction of a manorial form of organization. The urban-based money-and-exchange economy was fairly steadily giving way to the growth of a more self-sufficient subsistence economy. But in ages that move more slowly than ours, such changes rarely have a dramatic impact on the self-consciousness of men.

But there was one kind of change in that century that was bound to have a fundamental effect on the mind of man. In quantitative demographic terms the world was Christianized in the century between 300 and 400 A.D. When Constantine opted for Christianity in the early third of the fourth century, Christians were a small minority, perhaps 10–20 percent of the total population, though they were more concentrated in certain areas. Their mentality bore the marks of a tightly compressed community of saints beleaguered by a pagan state, populace, and culture. After their acceptance into the basic order of things, the scene changed. By 450 A.D. a person was altogether more likely to be formally a Christian than a pagan. The relation of Christians to the political order had changed. The Edict of Milan in either 312 or 313 merely declared toleration for Christians and an end to persecutions, though the emperor "favored" the Church; Julian the Apostate, in his short reign from 361–63, failed in his counterthrust of organizing a pagan church; by 382 Bishop Ambrose of Milan had forced the Emperor Valentinian II to remove the altar of Victory from the Roman senate chamber; under the Emperor Theodosius Christianity had, practically speaking, become the "official" religion of the state. The struggle for the external acceptance of the Church having been won, the great conflicts were now internal ones: the great controversy over Arianism which preoccupied so much of Christian life in the fourth century, the Donatist schism still so important to Augustine's African Christianity, the doctrinal issues that would gradually emerge in the Pelagianism against which he fought so long, and, if one may put it thus, the implicit attack of monasticism on a Church endangered by the secularizing trends to which her victory in the world had exposed her.

Augustine's life must be seen against the background of these changes through which a classical style of life was being transformed into a Christian one; in essential ways it was a process of amalgamating opposites. He was born into a family in which the mother Monica was a devout Christian, the father, apparently quite self-consciously, a pagan; only shortly before his death did Patricius make his peace with the Church— Augustine was then eighteen years old. Both parents ambitiously pushed the son's chances for worldly success, at considerable financial sacrifice to themselves, by providing him with the typical classical education. The education to which he was submitted had not really changed in centuries; it was still designed to form a learned man of eloquence, the orator, serving society in a wide variety of public functions. For a young man of very modest circumstances, as was Augustine, this training was his only chance of "becoming someone." He made good use of the opportunity and was eminently successful: at the age of thirty, as public orator of

Milan, then the capital of the western half of the empire, a great marriage and high public career were his for the taking. The pattern of his education had thus enabled him to develop his personality according to the model through which a very ripe civilization had for a long time sought to express one of its dominant ideals of the good man. That Augustine's own spiritual development brought him into conflict with this classical ideal became, of course, the dramatic theme of his life. And the world-historical significance of his life derives from the transformation he wrought in this ideal by means of his extraordinary spiritual powers. Augustine struggled toward the formulation of an ideal of personality and of culture which profoundly affected the course of our civilization. Thus he bridges the ancient and the medieval worlds; he should be seen as a man representing an age in between these two huge blocks of time, an age in its own right, of which he was the most representative man.

What kind of book is the *Confessions*? Augustine wrote it in the years between 397 and 401 A.D., shortly after he had succeeded Valerius as bishop of Hippo in 395. By then, a decade had intervened between his conversion experience in August 386, his resignation from his "professorship" at Milan, his philosophical activity at the retreat at Cassiciacum, his baptism by Ambrose in 387, the death of Monica at Ostia in 388 and that of his son Adeodatus and his friend Nebridius in 390, the attempts to set up scholarly monastic retreats at Thagaste and at Hippo, and his ordination to the priesthood there in 391. He was already the author of several writings and was becoming a prominent spokesman for orthodoxy, especially in its struggle with the still troublesome Donatist heresy and with Manichaeanism.

As is typical of most autobiographic efforts, there may have been external stimuli for writing this book: friends requesting a fuller account of what had happened to him, the need to put to rest still resurgent suspicions that he was either a Manichaean or a Platonist, the priest's loss of contact with the friends who had joined him earlier in trying to build a common life of Christian contemplation as a devoted band of *servi Dei*, the fact of his sudden entrance into the Church, actually without much prior notice.[1] While some friends were possibly most interested in a narrative of his life, others may have desired to learn from his theological reflections or to receive samples of his extraordinary exegetical artistry. The text bears enough traces to show that Augustine is incidentally also concerned with the demands of a human audience.

Was this multiplicity of demands also responsible for the alleged disparity between Books 1–9 and 10–13 which readers who have not stopped reading at the end of Book 9 discern? The first nine books contain a fairly chronological account of Augustine's life down to his impending return to Africa before 389. Book 10, in sharp contrast, is essentially a series of reflections on memory as a human power, Book 11 a set of reflections on the nature of time, and, on the surface at least, Books 12–13 are exegetical exercises on the beginning phrases of the first Book of Moses. A continuous reading is, at first, somewhat perplexing. Have incompatible parts been forced together here? Or should one resort to the simpler explanation that in these books Augustine, as in a later work like *De trinitate,* did not compose his writing well?[2] The answers to such questions depend on a much more basic question: what kind of book is this? and in what sense is it an autobiography at all?

Most obviously: Augustine called this a book of confessions. So many writers have used this title subsequently for autobiographic writings, that the word has become bland, especially in the mouths of those who no longer had a God to whom to confess. For Augustine's enterprise all the shades of meaning of "confessing" were central, and without a God as the all important recipient the book would be senseless. On one level, there is public acknowledgement of transgressions here, made directly to God, *confessio peccati,* fully in keeping with the custom of the times in which public confession in church was the rule. This was a matter between the sinner and his God, but it was laid out in the presence of the community, although the details were secret even then. For Augustine, confession was also an act of total surrender to God, a handing over of oneself, entirely and with utter confidence, into the hands of the only power which could help. It was both public acknowledgement of the central creed and the beginning knowledge of truth. But what was, for Augustine, most important was the *confessio laudis,* the praising of the Lord in the old biblical sense. Now he had begun to understand the mysterious ways of the Lord and had felt the power of His hand in his own life. Emanating from this vital experience, every one of his utterances became a stuttering and stammering confession of praise and of neverending wonder. All the other modes of "confessing" remain present: *confessio peccati,* for only the soul that perceives its vagrancy gives thanks for guidance; confession of belief in gratitude for everything that the soul is now permitted to understand more clearly; the complete surrender that derives from the utter sense of wonder that, paradoxically, man can stand only when he no longer stands on his own. All confession rests in the imparted sense of grace, and the heart filled with this flows over in *confessio laudis.*

The very first lines set the tone completely:

> Great art Thou, O Lord, and greatly to be praised [*laudabilis valde*]: great is Thy power, and Thy wisdom is infinite. And man, who being part of what Thou hast created, is desirous to praise Thee [*laudare te vult homo*] this man, bearing about his own mortality with him, carrying about him a testimony of his own sin [*testimonium peccati*], even this testimony that God resists the proud; yet this man, this part of what Thou hast created, is desirous to praise Thee; Thou so provokest him, that he even delights to praise Thee. For Thou hast created us for Thyself and our heart cannot be quieted till it may find repose in Thee. . . .for they shall praise the Lord that seek after Him; for they who shall seek shall find; and finding they shall praise Him.

This opening note of praise is repeated at the end of the whole work. In Book 13 Augustine has wrestled with the Mosaic text for an understanding of creation. His grappling can only lead him to conclude as he began: in a prayer of praise and a prayer requesting peace. Having studied the account of creation, he, like God on the Sabbath, came to understand that it is good. "When a man sees anything that is good it is God that sees in him that it is good; and that to this end plainly, that He himself might be loved in that which He made" (13.31). "Thy works praise Thee, that we may love Thee, that Thy works may praise Thee" (13.33). "Grant, O Lord, Thy peace unto us: for Thou hast given us all things. Give us the peace of Quietness, the peace of the Sabbath, peace without any evening" (13.35). "But Thou being the good, needing no good, art at rest always because Thy rest Thou art Thyself. And what man is he that can teach another man to understand this? Or what angel another angel? Or what angel, man? Let it be begged of Thee, be sought in Thee, knocked for at Thee; so, so shall it be received, so shall it be found, and so shall it be opened" (13.38).

The book ends as it begins—as confession in a manifold sense. And the few hundred pages in between are writing of the same kind. But in reading it, it is necessary to perceive the activity that each book expresses and not simply its subject matter.

The truly remarkable unity of the *Confessions* seems ultimately to rest in three closely related aspects. Firstly, the act in which Augustine is engaged, the actual activity represented in the writing, is the same from start to finish. He is confess*ing*. He is not, like some later autobiographers, narrating a lived life in terms of what it now can be seen to have been. He does, in part, surely give such a view to his life, but not as an end in itself. What really matters to him are the consequences of confessing. In any case, the narration of that past life fills only one half of the entire book. The present and the future—and above all, eternity, incomparable to time in any sense—are as much on his mind as is the past. The life described is being viewed entirely within the perspective of the present as it now is and as it is affected by past and future and eternity. Augustine knows himself to be on an incompleted journey; he speaks of himself as a man on the road, *in viam*, concerned, to be sure, about the whence and the whither also. But the *Confessions* are not the log of the distance already covered.

Secondly, this book derives its unity from its "presentness." Unlike the genuine memoirist, Augustine is not simply moved to record an eventful life, even if he also has a sense that his life's story is worthy of being known by others. In the true autobiographic mode, he is instead moved by a deeply felt need to understand the meaning of his being and his life. The sheer act of writing is thus an act of self-orientation. For this it is of equal importance to understand present life, to understand the way in which this life has come to be, and to understand the pull exerted by the vision of life to be. By thus interlacing all the segments of time the book reaches into that realm in which genuine autobiography lives. From that point of view, Books 10–13 are as central to the "autobiography" as the alleged autobiographic Books 1–9. But the weight of the present presses down on the assessment of the whole existence. The past is ordered entirely in the terms that have come to give meaning to life by 397 A.D. As a consequence, the historically necessary telescoping of the past does not result in evenly balanced segments. Book 1 treats the problems of infancy and early boyhood; Book 2, on early adolescence, gives more than half of its span to the analysis of robbing a pear tree; Books 3–4 and half of 5 depict life at Carthage between 371 and 383 (there was an interlude of one year's return to Thagaste, 375–76) and dwell on the problems of friendship, love, death, literature, the theater, philosophy, and, most intensely, on Augustine's association with the Manichaeans. When he reaches Milan at the end of Book 5, he is thirty years old. The next four books, 6–9, cover a span of only four years in which we see the gradual turn to Catholicism, the encounter with Ambrose, Simplicianus, Neoplatonism, the conversion, the stay at Cassiciacum, baptism, the Ostia vision, and Monica's death. And then the years from 388 to 397 are a blank—except insofar as they are Augustine's "present life" and are thus outlined by the content of Books 10–13.

Much that was formatively interesting in that life was not presented at all, or was revealed in only brief glimpses. But throughout the book Augustine adheres to a rigorously maintained sense of relevance. Like any good autobiographer, he sacrifices a precise chronological progression, occasionally introducing specific events where they fit in terms of meaning rather than being tyrannized by their accidental placement in time. Augustine's entire assessment of life is dominated by the consciousness of his conversion experience in 386. Thus the *Confessions* belong to that type of autobiography in which one datable moment in life enables a human being to order all his experience retrospectively by the insight of one momentous turn.[3] The book, however, was actually written ten years after that turning point, at a time when the meaning of that central experience had been able to mature into insight. That it would have been a different "Confession" had it been written in 386, can still be sensed by reading the earlier *Soliloquies*.

In the third place, the unity of this work is derived from the view of the world and life to which Augustine has struggled through by 397 A.D. He is now forty-three years old. He is a clearly defined personality beginning to have a great impact on the world. He visibly moves according to a hierarchy of values; he knows his priorities and his horizons. The many tumultuous events and intense relationships of the past can be assigned to the appropriate layers of his being. The personality has succeeded in building the precious and the painful experiences into its very essence. And out of such diverse intellectual and spiritual stimuli and strains a coherent, life-directing rational order has been born. Most men never succeed in unifying the disparate elements of human existence, but by 397 Augustine's spirit has managed to fuse them into that kind of inner and outer order that gives the personality its recognizable traits. Everything he touches bears the touch of that personality. And the order that prevails in him imparts itself also to his "confessions."

Thus, while the work remains technically a confession, Augustine works out the presentation of a life course as no one prior to him had done. With a unified view of his experience Augustine can confess his life to the God who gave him the vision of a new life within the order of creation. In a true sense Augustine is returning the gift to God. His devoted life is all that he can give and his consuming concern is to return it in the best condition. For all of this he needs the act of orientation and the self-assessment allowed by the act of confessing. The compelling ground rules here do not permit willful self-deception. The recipient of the gift cannot be deceived. And the powerful demands of the Christian's internalized ethics make utter honesty and careful scrutiny of motives an absolute command. There is no prize for a self-formulation based on any one of the older models of existence, no reward for denying given realities in the pursuit of an ideal not suited to this specific person. Augustine must lay bare the real self in all its complexity rather than focusing on its model-fitting traits. This confession would in every respect be negated by willful deception.

Under these conditions Augustine's act of confessing becomes largely identical with self-searching, self-questioning, self-discovery, self-description, and self-assessment. The act of writing is itself a process of bringing to self-consciousness again the nature of this personality and its implications for the course of life. A self-formulation built from a keen awareness of internal as well as external surrounding conditions occurs within the compactness of a book. But it is the self-awareness of neither a fully formed personality nor a completed life. As long as man is on earth he continues to seek such self-clarification and will try to fashion his life by the insight thus gained. The self-clarification is steady, but gradual. Seeking-Finding-Praising, these are the never-ending activities of man on earth. The all important moment of conversion was not a resting place in the ardent search for peace, but a narrow portal beyond which lay the real struggles of life; only now the seeker is more fully aware of God's help. Augustine both fears and rejoices at what he still may discover in himself. The searching goes on in the present, as in the past, as it will in the future, until the soul, lifted into eternity, will no longer face the problems of knowledge which exist merely in the passing of time.

Whether this is indeed an autobiography will always be a matter of legitimate debate. But though the word autobiography itself is not older than the eighteenth century, the *Confessions* were built out of elements that have remained at the very heart of autobiographic writing: self-questioning, by asking the context of one's life to surrender the secrets about the self; self-discovery, by perceiving the order in the disparate elements of life; self-evaluation, by tracing the meaning as a continuous pattern. The *Confessions* artfully present self-conscious interpretation of a life and a being from the vantage point of a meaningful center. At the end the reader knows that he has met a personality in the concreteness that gave its life a near palpable texture and a meaningful pattern. No self-written life before Augustine had this scope, fullness, intensity, and life-like quality. But while the following discussion will attempt to discuss the Augustinian conception of the personality from which the autobiographic reach of the *Confessions* derives, it will also point to the factors that delimit the work as an autobiographic act.

What is Augustine's conception of the self? how did it develop? and what possibilities and problems resulted from his notion of the personality?

When Augustine began to write the *Confessions* he was still struggling with the problems of human life. He had by no means reached the secure resting place from which many a later autobiographer surveyed his past in calm retrospection. He could not review his life with that wondrous detachment at which Goethe aimed, that "irony in a higher sense." Augustine knew himself to be ever steeped in the travail of continuous self-clarification. He was still a problem to himself. He very much "needed" the activity of writing out the confessions as an instrument of self-clarification, especially, perhaps, Books 10–13.

Yet he had gained by then a position which enabled him to find his way. He was now a more surefooted traveler, with a firm sense of direction. He knew the location of the land of peace that held the source of wisdom from which the true answers came. He more clearly discerned what questions to ask, where and how the answers might be found. Above all he had gained the precious inner certainty that derives from an assurance of not having been abandoned helplessly to a search that has no answers. His quest for understanding and meaning was securely grounded in a basic trust that life had been endowed with fundamental meaning and that man had been so created that his search for meaning could be crowned with success. He felt tranquil in trusting a growing religious tradition and ecclesiastical authority which permitted reason the advantage of a secure starting point and then provided continuing support in the intellectual's unavoidable quest for full understanding. The flood of insights released by an all-consuming experience had had ten years to be channeled into a deepened view of the human problem. For Augustine, this decade had been filled, on the one hand, with contemplation in which the philosophical formulations of Neoplatonism could serve to generalize experience beyond the merely personal, and, on the other hand, with the involvement of the presbyter and bishop in the affairs of human beings entrusted to his care. A much more generalized view of the human condition could thus merge with the individual experience. The elements for a coherent conception of man had coalesced. The exercise of the *Confessions* was its test and its acknowledgment.

The writer of the *Confessions*, of course, had the full benefit of hindsight for reinterpreting his very first actions by the light of later knowledge. Yet, his reflective account of the later vision can be stripped to show how he came to his subsequent understanding.

Augustine never questioned the assumption that the object of man's striving is happiness, neither before nor after the conversion. Though as he himself grew as a person he assigned to happiness an increasingly more elevated value; the very idea of happiness remained, for him, the driving impulse of life. Happiness is the fulfillment of desires—but if lasting happiness *is* to result, the desires must become good ones. The worthier the object of our love is, the greater is our happiness. Certainly, happiness must mean absence of pain, simple pains of the body, but as Augustine grew more and more into the intellectual that he was, he hoped above all for the absence of that gnawing pain of doubt and uncertainty that can turn a mind into a hell. Happiness has to be the full possession of the desired object; as long as this does not obtain, man is in the clutch of intense longing. To be loved, to be accepted, to be harbored is but happiness's complement. Augustine thus always expressed his intense longing for happiness in his consuming wish for peace: peaceful satiation of desires and longing, peace with oneself, peace with others, peace with the world around one, and peace of mind.

The quest for peace was the driving force of this life. At different stages of existence it expressed itself in different forms; but it was always driving him onward. Augustine's description of infancy already shows the strength of such longing. He acknowledges honestly: I do not remember, I cannot remember, but I am sure from what others told me about myself, and from what I myself later could observe in babies, that I was like this: happy when I could suck mother's milk, smiling when satisfied, crying and kicking when my needs went unanswered, and jealous when love was being diverted from me. Man may be helplessly dependent in that state, and yet he is strongly self-willed and by no means simply an innocent body.

Augustine's recollections of early boyhood relate closely to the memory of his schooling. "So many before us had trampled out that road that we were forced to take, multiplying [our] toil and sorrow" (1.9). The boy did not choose this work; he wanted to play and to gain the respect of others by winning. He liked to watch games and shows. But others had placed their ambitions in him and sent him on that road "one had to take" in order to become someone in this world. For Augustine this was humiliating suffering. The fear of being beaten made him behave, and that same fear was the cause for his first prayers. The demands of culture and the will were bound to clash. And yet his memories also betray the delight he began to take in the instruments of culture. The description (1.8) still carries the touch of wonder in the discovery that words could serve to communicate wishes and in the later fascination with the power of poetry when words and imagination were joined.

Though others had set Augustine on this road, he soon discovered that one could gratify ambition and gain respect by being good at the games of a verbal culture. And he did become very good at it, far better in Latin than in Greek, but increasingly expert in what this literary culture demanded. When the simple school at Thagaste no longer served him well, his father, Patricius, borrowed money and sent the growing boy first to Madaura and finally to the metropolis of Carthage. He thus escaped the pressures of a home very much dominated by a possessive mother and beset by the tensions between parents. While he continued as a good student, his growing virility (in which the father took great delight) and his insatiable longing for love and companionship led him into the liaisons that his culture permitted but his Christian mother lamented. He found himself in an adolescent group life in which the shame over being thought different was stronger than the aversion to such senseless mischief as robbing a pear tree of its fruit—and not even for the taste of the pears. The enjoyment of sight and touch and the gratification of respect and the longing for love seemed all important.

The later Augustine did not express it thus, but his characterization of the early self-formation very strongly brings to the fore the formative power of the social and cultural world around him. On the one hand, he was a being with a fine intellectual capacity, strongly developed senses, a great need for love, friendship, and respect, and a strong will for self-assertion; on the other hand, there were the limited resources of the family, its inner tensions, the sense-gratifying accommodations of late classical society with its decided aesthetic bent, and above all, the literary culture that offered a chance for advancement. Many of these external conditions helped to shape Augustine permanently, and for a long time his richly unfolding inner life sought its expression in the model of existence offered by an old and tested culture. In many regards Augustine became a strikingly representative man of the age that came to bear his name.[4]

Especially significant is the formation Augustine underwent in his "professional" training. Its aim was to produce an orator, a representative of a profession long cherished by the classical world. This ideal, going back at least as far as Isocrates in the fourth century B.C., and adopted later by the Romans of Cicero's day and adapted to typically Roman ideals, sought to express a human type capable of serving society by commanding the total culture. He could do so either by public service before "the bar" (although the rhetor's training in the law had become minimal by the fourth century A.D.), or in the important area of public address, or as the trainer of future public leaders. Although continuous tensions existed between this ideal of the cultured man and that of the philosopher, the truly wise man—Plato's quarrel with Isocrates was already an early indication of such stresses—it was possible to combine both. Cicero had done so, and his example was of particular significance for Augustine. The training of the truly erudite man had been formalized and routinized centuries earlier and, in most essential features, it had not changed much by Augustine's time. In schooling the emphasis was placed heavily on the cultivation of the verbal and literary arts and on the fairly passive absorption of "book learning" typical of any age of erudition.

Almost as by a process of natural selection Augustine was gradually fitted into the eventual role of *"vir eloquentissimus ac doctissimus."* His sharp intellect, his prodigious memory, his verbal facility, and (albeit that he denied it later on) his apparent self-discipline predestined him to great success along the hewn path of this cultural ideal. Even Monica's Christian bias and hopes for her son were no obstacle; there is nothing to suggest that she ever considered the road of erudition incompatible with being a good Christian. She spent her criticism on her son's nonascetic, to her immoral, life. Augustine underwent a training in the customary disciplines and acquired intellectual and verbal-literary habits which he never shook off as a bishop, though he would try later to give them new functional justifications. And his success was astounding: hardly twenty years old, he has made himself independent as a teacher; hardly thirty years old, he has become the public "professor" for the capital and court city of Milan. He is now a man filled with erudition and devoted to the cultivation of *scientia.*

But for Augustine the self-cultivation of the man of culture became wedded at an early point of his intellectual career to the philosopher's pursuit of wisdom. A chance reading of Cicero's *Hortensius* redirected the intellectual search. It "altered his affections," he found in it a new object of love, the love of wisdom, *philosophia* (3.4). He now began to see a meaningful distinction between lasting wisdom, *sapientia,* and expert knowledge, *scientia.* This newly found road of endeavor was as much an expression of an old classical ideal as the role of the most learned and most eloquent man. It promised the happiness of inner peace by means of full understanding. While Augustine as the man of passions and ambitions does not disappear from the pages of Books 3 through 7, these books dwell heavily on the development of his intellectual and spiritual life.

Wisdom was meant to lead to true happiness. But which wisdom would serve? The form that would have presented itself most readily must have been the eclecticism of Cicero and Seneca which was handed on in the literary traditions. Was it ever a source of comfort for Augustine? Did he as a young thinker already rebel against the inherent contradiction of a philosophy promising happiness by means of such Stoic values as *fortitudo,* resignation to the evils of life, which he voiced much later on in Book 19 of the *City of God* when he lunged out at such a philosophy? In the description of his development in the *Confessions* he deals at greater length with his experimentation with the wisdom of the gnostic sect of the Manichaeans. Urged on by his need for absolutely certain knowledge, especially on the troublesome question of the origin of evil acts, Augustine drew very close to this group of ascetically inclined intellectuals desiring to reform Christianity, in part, by detaching it from the Jehovah of the Old Testament.[5] This Manichaean movement carried to Augustine the appealing promise, typical of all gnostic sects, that a very specific esoteric knowledge about the true nature of good and evil could free a man from the powers of evil. A special appeal of the doctrine lay in the promise of alleviating the inner sense of guilt by relieving the individual of responsibility. The dualism of this world view, with its plausible intellectual answers to the question of good and evil, preoccupied Augustine intensely. For nine years he sought in this sect the answers to the questions troubling him; gradually intellectual doubts grew. When the answers of the greatly acclaimed wandering magister of the Manichaeans, Faustus of Milevis, seemed unable to satisfy Augustine, he gradually turned away from the movement which later on, as priest and bishop, he had to combat as heretical. The predictable reaction to disappointing promises of certain knowledge came: he fell into skeptical despair. To be sure, he did not doubt that three and seven make ten, but could one be certain at all about any of the answers to life's great questions? Was there any answer to the question of the origin of good and evil? and, above all, was there wisdom anywhere that could grant peace?

In this skeptical state of suspension, Augustine's development came under the influence of seemingly chance encounters. In 383 A.D. he decided to leave Carthage for Italy; by a deception he freed himself from his now widowed mother, and with his common-law wife and son he set sail for Rome. As it turned out, the students at Rome did not pay their tuition, but friends secured for him the more promising position as professor of rhetoric at Milan. Monica joined him there in 385. One of the key encounters came with the great Catholic bishop of Milan, St. Ambrose, whom he heard preach repeatedly. Here at last was a Christian whom the intellectual in Augustine could truly respect. Ambrose's art of exegesis showed to the doubter that the Bible when interpreted symbolically attained a coherent and an unexpected depth of meaning far more significant than Augustine obtained with his accustomed literal interpretation. One of the great obstacles standing between the intellectual and the all-important Scripture gave way before this newly discovered power of a symbolical interpretation. The pressure of this new insight, supplemented by Monica's continuous urging that he throw in his lot with Catholicism, was great; but so were the doubts that kept Augustine in suspense. As yet he had no answer to the problem of good and evil, and, above all, there was no access to the Christian God as long as he could not conceive of him in other than material form.

This intellectual and spiritual crisis took a new turn when Augustine became acquainted with the most profound revitalization any form of classical philosophy had experienced in late antiquity: the Neoplatonism of Plotinus (who had died ca. 270 A.D.) and his disciple and editor Porphyry. Augustine had access to this thought in the Latin translations made by the rhetor Victorinus, who, some decades earlier, had also experienced a noted conversion. This intensely spiritualized philosophy provided Augustine, at a time when he most needed it, with satisfying epistemological answers based in a monistic metaphysical system. In its ethical teachings he found an insistence upon the good as an active power; Manichaeanism had in the long run disturbed Augustine with its teaching of passive suffering as the best means to assure the dominance of the good. Augustine may well have found an immediate point of contact with Neoplatonism in the realm of aesthetic issues which he had recently sought to work out in his now lost work *De pulchro et apto*.

Augustine found in Neoplatonism positions that were to remain a part of his world view. That he thought of it as a most important encounter, even later on when he saw the points at which his Christian convictions could not be reconciled with this philosophy, is supported by the fact that he devoted almost all of Book 7 to his initial struggle with Neoplatonic thought. Perhaps Chapter 17 of that book stated in most succinct summary form what he found so persuasive:

> I was most certain, too, that "from the foundations of the world men have caught sight of Your invisible nature, Your

eternal power, and Your divineness, as they are known through Your creatures" (Romans 1:20). For I wondered how it was that I could appreciate beauty in material things on earth or in the heavens, and what it was that enabled me to make correct decisions about things that are subject to change and to rule that one thing ought to be like this, another like that. I wondered how it was that I was able to judge them in this way, and I realized that above my own mind, which was liable to change, there was the never changing true eternity of truth. So, step by step, my thoughts moved on from the consideration of material things to the soul, which perceives things through the senses of the body, and then to the soul's inner power, to which the bodily senses communicate external facts. Beyond this dumb animals cannot go. The next stage is the power of reason, to which the facts communicated by the bodily senses are submitted for judgment. This power of reason, realizing that in me it too was liable to change, led me on to consider the source of its own understanding. It withdrew my thoughts from their normal course and drew back from the confusion of images which pressed upon it, so that it might discover what light it was that had been shed upon it when it proclaimed for certain that what was immutable was better than that which was not, and how it had come to know the immutable itself. For unless, by some means, it had known the immutable, it could not possibly have been certain that it was preferable to the mutable. And so, in an instant of awe, my mind attained the sight of the God who Is. Then at last, "I caught sight of Your invisible nature, as it is known through Your creature."

This, as Augustine said to a friend in 387 (Epistle 4:2), had to be a key argument in his quest for certain knowledge. Such reasoning freed him gradually from his skeptical materialism and opened the road to a spiritual view of the world.

This encounter with Neoplatonism occurred at a time when a turn to Catholicism had become a real possibility for Augustine for other reasons as well. Catholicism at Milan was, at this time, strongly influenced by Neoplatonism, and the men with whom Augustine associated thought of it as a complementary philosophy to their Christian convictions. While Augustine always thought such a confluence possible and desirable, up to a point, he must even then have been perturbed by certain implications of this philosophy, especially those troublesome for the notion of the Incarnation and the God-Man Jesus. When he now turned to a more intensive reading of Saint Paul's letters, the pull toward Catholic Christianity must have become the stronger force in his life. His own account makes clear that, at the time he reached the end of Book 7, he was *intellectually* prepared to cast his lot with the Catholic church.[6]

The most dramatic sequence of experiences now hit him with tremendous force, a force that was to alter his life. Augustine had come to the point where he somehow understood that there, there on that other side of this threshold, lay the promise of the very life he sought: the peace of trusting belief, loving acceptance, a lifelong supportive institution, genuine reconciliation with Monica, and now the suddenly opened horizons of the vision of a spiritual world in which satisfying truth could be found to rest securely. There it lay: "I had now found that Pearl of price, which I ought to have bought . . ."—and then it turned out to be unattainable! Stripped of its later meaning-giving theological language, Augustine's report on his condition prior to the conversion portrays that deeply perverse human situation of knowing what one desires, reaching for it, straining and straining—and not being able to reach it. Even the language of his later rethinking still conveys the extraordinary sense of panic in this shaking experience: "my inner self was a house divided against itself," "my voice sounded strange," "driven by the tumult in my breast," "I was beside myself with madness," "I was frantic, overcome by violent anger with myself," "I tore my hair and hammered my forehead with my fists," "all my bones cried out" (8.8). In this utterly frantic state came the experience in the garden, the uncontrolled weeping under the fig tree, and the child's guiding voice: *tolle, lege*—take up and read.

What, in Augustine's opinion, had happened? and in what sense was this point at which he found himself the turning point that could give meaning to all the life before and the life to come?[7]

Augustine's self-presentation attacks the central issue: at the very moment when a man concentrates all his effort on leading the life he sees as the desired one, he is confronted most forcefully by his inability to do so. He becomes utterly frantic over his helplessness in accomplishing an ardently desired life task. Exactly at the moment of greatest despair comes the reversal—the experience of the comfort lent by a secretly guiding hand. Then the scales fall off the eyes—and whether they do so at once or only gradually is much less important for the effectiveness of the experience than the realization that this is the turning point. At the time of the writing of the *Confessions*, an entire vision of the human condition rested on the fulcrum of that great personal moment.

Just as Augustine despaired of ever attaining the good life by his most strenuous exertion, the overpowering experience of helplessness turned into the consoling trust of dependence. The creature came to understand its own dependency: that it could not be the creator of its own life. The issue nestled in that little question which was posed by the apparition of Continence: Why stand on yourself and thus not stand at all? *Quid in te stas et non in te stas?* (8.11). The moment of acknowledging human inadequacy and acknowledging divine power is one and the same moment, if only in the poetic condensation of retrospection. Throwing away one conception of self and finding the true self resting in another, a higher one, were complementary acts. The low point of self-despair and the rising ascent in trust were intimately linked. Only the ultimate disillusionment with self-will, self-reliance, self-love could lead to the giving up on oneself which, in turn, could result in living from within the full trust in a completely life-sustaining power.

This sense of growing trust that his life was indeed in the hands of God allowed Augustine a unified conception of his existence. Throughout the book he confesses this trust as God's gift to him. The confident acceptance of the ultimate power of the Good as the sole creator of the world and as the prime mover of history—a changed view whereby evil is seen not as the power contrary to the good but as a degree of privation of the good—leads to the equally confident belief that creation is a good order, that there is meaning in life long before you can see it, and that the individual has not been abandoned to a senseless struggle. Now, as Augustine looks back on his confused past, every detail evokes in him the constantly repeated confession: You, my God, did this . . .!

At this point Augustine discerned a basic direction and directedness in his past life that he knew must have come from another source. The example of Monica, her exhortations as well as the dreams and visions that foresaw his final conversion to her faith, stood out above all else; but equally direct guidance had come from reading the *Hortensius,* from the encounter with Ambrose, the Neoplatonic books, Simplicianus's account of Victorinus's conversion, and Ponticianus's report on the monks of the desert. For a very clear reason these directing forces appeared in enormous concentration the closer Augustine had come to the conversion point. But even the moments when he had strayed furthest from the (now seen) central line of his life had had their mysterious efficacy. The suffering schoolboy had his meaning, as did the rage of the infant; all the vagaries of friendships, the seductions of bad company, and the erroneous wanderings of the intellectual search—they all had had to be as they had been. Now, of course, they seemed so lamentably wasteful. They surely had been not God's dictated course but the errors of a misguided self. But the confessing Augustine was forever awed to discover how God had returned a perversely willful, meandering creature to His road. Everything had gradually been channeled toward that great moment of surrender that accompanied the totally disillusioned view of his true condition. "Oh Lord, You were turning me around to look at myself. For I had placed myself behind my own back, refusing to see myself. You were setting me before my own eyes so that I could see how sordid I was, how deformed and squalid, how tainted with ulcers and sores. I saw it all and stood aghast, but there was no place where I could escape from myself" (8.7). It seemed that everything within him and everything surrounding him had forced the one issue: surrender of the self, radical acknowledgment of the complete dependence on God. Even for that you could only declare yourself to be ready; the act of lifting you across the threshold was an act reserved to God. On the other side of it, then, lay this never to be wiped out sense of wonder at the truth: only he who loses his soul can gain it.

One part of the *Confessions* had to express a renewed concern with the past, though the gaining of that vision of true coherence had only a limited utility. The motives are all fused. Grateful love for the gratuitous gift of a meaningful life is the dominant note. It is most strongly amplified by the sense of awe at the discovery of meaning in what had seemed meaningless; all the pain, the suffering, the errant wanderings had not been in vain. But there is more: the intellectual need to understand the unity of the person amid such seeming confusion of will, of love, of affects, and of errant thought. The grateful acknowledgment for the measure of understanding already granted is accompanied by humble but persistent pleas for enlightenment of the darkness still spread over so much. The aesthetic pleasure in retracing the artistry of God's work is joined by the didactic purpose of presenting, for the profit of others, the view of a life so mysteriously regained.

But it is this very question (what function will these confessions have for my fellowmen?) that serves to bring out in Augustine an impatience to be done with this personal past (10.3). The reconstruction of that past can have no purpose in itself. It does not even have any great significance for Augustine in his effort to relieve himself of his sense of guilt over past sins. The *confessio peccati* is much less important as an unburdening than as a starting point for gaining greater insight. The deeper one penetrates into this many-layered book, the clearer it becomes that Augustine has no interest in the past except as it lies in the present and the future. It is his intention neither to present a character formed in the course of a noteworthy life nor to suggest in any way that he has, after such a sequence of startling events, come home safe. Even the account of a life is only an exercise; it is to be used, not to be enjoyed or possessed as an end in itself. His important distinction between *uti* and *frui* is part of the new sense of the purpose of things and of human activities.

The entire rethinking of the personal past had utility only as one step in the life-consuming process of self-clarification. The conversion experience had not brought the restless wanderer to the peaceful resting place that must be the objective of all seeking after happiness. In one sense, quite the contrary had occurred. The bitter confrontation with the self that was so severely limited led to the knowledge that the haven of happiness was out of reach during the voyage of this life. The classical ideal of the wise man with his blueprint for happiness, the *artifex vitae* as the proudly independent builder of his own life, was an utter illusion. The peace of full understanding, of true lasting *sapientia*, kept beckoning, much more irresistibly than ever before. But it was now seen to lie in the beyond where it dwelled with its creator. A terrestrial life consumed in the pursuit of *sapientia* could only be a continual exercise toward eternal truth, a preparing of the entire being for the possibility of such a possession. For Augustine it was the real promise of the *vita beata* to live forever in the presence of real truth.

Man was *at best* a pilgrim and thus in need of understanding his wandering nature and the conditions of his pilgrimage. The conversion signified the very moment of enlightenment whereby a blind stumbling and a vagrant wandering about could be converted into a fully purposeful pilgrimage, a *peregrinatio* homeward. Out of the basic Christian teachings and the spiritual metaphysics of the Neoplatonists Augustine formulated a vision of the pilgrim on such a pilgrimage.

The conversion experience—in its unfolding of meaning within meanings, one after another—surely contained the lesson of man's inadequacy. His power of knowledge was defective, his power of love was inadequate, his power of control over his complexities was limited. All of Book 8 is an analysis of the perversity of the will, which rested in its defectiveness. The issue of a will striving for good *and* for evil had to come to the ex-Manichaean. But for Augustine the evil in these human conflicts was not the reverse of good, as the Manichaean dualism had implied. Rather, human defects were damaged parts of a good creation, damaged by the false use of man's free will. In his Fall man had lost control of himself as a unified being and had become prey to the mul-

titude of perverted forces within which pulled him in so many conflicting directions that he lost himself and his way. Blinded by his self-love,
and its concomitant pride, he could neither understand that it was his
dominant need to become whole again nor perceive the means to do so.

The healing process had to start with a chance to see the defective
state of the self. Only then could the trust in the healer do its work.
There was no sudden cure; all of life had to be given to it. The miracle lay
in the promise of healing. Man had to learn to trust creation, for there
was nothing wrong in it except his own self-inflicted disorientation. In
his sense of feeling lost he had to search the purpose in the creator who
had left the decipherable signature of His will on the creation and had
also revealed knowledge which man could not attain on his own. Finding the way back home meant finding one's place in creation, finding
where one rested in the presence of God, fully living out of the strength
flowing from Him and His work.

Augustine always associated this pilgrimage home with an upward
motion. Man had fallen out of place, away from the light into darker
regions; his weight always endangering him to fall back even further.[8]
Conversion was thus *metanoia* in the truest sense of turning around
toward the task of the upward motion. Certainly, man needed God's
help for this. But the possibility of an upward return was no idle promise.
Man was an in-between-creature, above the animals, below the angels
and God; a composite creature of body and soul. He was capable of
knowing, of loving, and of willing. But his senses and his body could
force such actions into their own service and thus deprive the soul of its
potential power. The promise of health was given in the ability of the
soul to bring order to this whole being by turning all its actions toward
that upward movement: to assign to things and to the senses their
controlled usefulness instead of permitting them to function as ends in
themselves. A man thus engaged in seeking his health would abhor all
waste of time, of talent, of idle curiosity, of mere sense gratification, of
senseless and aimless activity. The full horror with which Augustine now
regarded his youthful "crime" in robbing the pear tree with his band of
youthful companions came with his newly gained understanding that it
symbolized the utter depravity of a totally senseless act.[9] Distraction had
to give way to attraction (11.29); all the power of love had to be turned to
the love of the one being most worth loving. "Too little does he love
Thee who loves anything together with Thee which he loves not for
Thee" (10.29). The will had to will toward the will of that loved being
only. And all knowledge must have such concentrated purpose. What

do I want to know? God and my soul. Nothing else? Nothing else whatsoever.

Augustine was far too much the intellectual to accept a lesser task for his life than the continuous striving for fuller and fuller understanding of God and His relation to Augustine's soul. But loving, willing, and understanding would all function in harmony the more the whole being regained its wholesomeness. All three modes of activity reinforced one another: concentration of will made understanding possible; but only the attractive power of love and of understanding enabled the will to concentrate; growing understanding and growing love and growing attention were all part of the same process. The act of understanding starts for Augustine with the loving trust of belief. The given propositions of faith are the ground and the objective of understanding. I believe, so that I may understand—*credo, ut intelligam,* as Anselm of Canterbury phrased it later. "Faith seeks, but it is understanding that finds. Understanding is the reward of faith ... Eternal life is not belief in Him, it is knowing Him."[10] The pilgrim striving toward that high end spends his life in refining, softening, honing, improving his whole being so that it may steadily become more capable of that final reward of understanding. In that sense, pilgrimage is testing and exercise, *exercitatio animi.*

This, perhaps more than anything else, Augustine sought to express in the *Confessions.* The analysis of the past is never simple remembrance. Each component that he lifts back into consciousness becomes an appropriate occasion for such an *exercitatio animi.* Each part will ultimately interweave with all the others to form one continuous process of seeking and understanding. The early account of birth (1.6) gives rise to a process of speculation and questioning which is still going on at the end (13.24), where the concern has been raised from a matter of curiosity about the creation of a personal life to a deeply moral concern for the creation of all mankind. All the questioning begun in connection with the young boy's discovery of the mysterious working of words (1.8) leads, over so many recurring exercises of the mind on the wonder of signs and symbols, to the attempt to understand the function or nature of revelation for Moses and ultimately to the Word of the Trinity. The analyses of learning processes move from the considerations about grammar school to the highest reaches of the mind in the grasping for God's intention as revealed in creation and Scripture. All the early books are an exercise in which the mind strives for a finer understanding of the entrapment which the things of this world prepare for the soul. And the account of the vision at Ostia becomes a compressed presentation of all the steps whereby the soul is freed from such entrapment in order to reach the infinite. The book which will show in detail how thoroughly Augustine has executed these exercises is still to be written.[11]

Books 10 to 13 each seem to be such an *exercitatio animi* in its purest form. They are the most forceful evidence that for Augustine life itself is such a never-ending process of conditioning the soul and the mind and the whole being for the ultimate contemplation of truth in the *vita beata*. The exercises in these books are more concentrated, less disjointed than those in the earlier Sections (except perhaps in Book 13, which has a tendency to become a catalogue of beliefs). The reason surely is that Augustine is now "within himself" in a different way; the continuity of Books 1 to 9 is broken because the world's effects at that earlier time still impinge so strongly on the shape of his personal life. In these later books he can follow the logos where it leads. This does not mean, however, that these books are appendixes to the life story, or simple samples of Augustinian thought. They remain truly autobiographic. And in a very real sense the earlier books rest in these later ones.[12]

In Book 10 Augustine comes quite naturally to the question: what do I love when I love God? who am I as I love God? where is the locus of my activity? (10.6). After a consideration of the limited understanding allowed to all the external parts of the creation, Augustine leads us through these queries to the mystery of memory. In this "stomach of the mind" (10.14) all his life is stored. "Without it I could not even speak of myself" (10.16). And Augustine becomes a problem to himself as soon as he recognizes how much there may be hidden of him in this cavern of memory, how much he may have forgotten, what horrors he may still have to discover. He knows, however, that the real contact with the divine can be made only in these inner recesses of himself. For here the Ideas and the Forms have their life by which we know and judge. From this inwardness our search is guided. "The woman who had lost a coin searched for it by the light of a lantern, but she would never have found it unless she had remembered it" (10.18). The power of remembering a lost happiness pulls us back onto our pilgrimage (10.20, which has images both of Plato's cave and Adam in Paradise). On this pilgrimage we seek to rise by the power of reflection that Truth has let penetrate into our innermost being. In this inwardness our life is truly lived. On this inwardness depends the unification of the personality. This is a most essential part of the discovery of the inner unity of man. Life from moment to moment is an extension of the self forward and backward. A man carries the coherent form of a self, made by the constant formation of what is not yet, in his own consciousness.

The exercise on Time, in Book 11, is equally wonderful. By adding the notion of expectation to that of memory, Augustine arrives at that internalized sense of time which may be crucial for the living person. "There are three times, a present of past things, a present of present things, and a present of future things. Some such different times do exist in the mind, but nowhere else that I can see. The present of past things is the memory; the present of present things is direct perception; and the present of future things is expectation" (11.20). Augustine touches in his search for meaning on a vast set of subjects. They are all indicative of the degree to which all the different parts of his being begin to function in unison. In this inner life that he has discovered, the mediation occurs between the physical man, the spiritual being, and the realities impinging upon him from the Beyond. Nothing is more expressive of this than his imagery: the heart has its ears, its mouth, and its eyes; the mind has its ears, its mouth, and its eyes.

The being thus being unified addresses itself to the task of learning more—and now directly from God. On one level, the last two books become simply reflections on the first few lines of the first book of Moses. In Book 12 Augustine struggles heroically with the phrase "the Heaven of Heaven." After many pages of exercising his mind on this mystery, he catches himself: "O Lord, my God, how much have I written on so few words!" (12.32). He then makes the transition to Book 13: "Let me then continue to lay before You my thoughts on the Scriptures, but more briefly." Later this becomes: "Beyond this let my faith speak for me" (13.12). In consequence, the text then swells with biblical quotations. But all these pages are not separate sets of pure theological speculations in which Augustine exhibits his exegetical skill. Nor is the choice of texts on which this skill is being exercised indifferent or arbitrary. To be sure, an Augustinian *exercitatio* always amounts to more than the subject matter warrants since so much of its value lies in its very activity. But the struggle with Genesis has its precise meaning in relation to the entire *Confessions*. On the crudest level, it serves an apologetic function: here Augustine can show whether he is cured of his earlier Manichaean leanings and also that he is aware of where love for Platonic thought must give way to biblical fact. On another level, the *exercitatio* on these very matters offers Augustine a superb chance to let his priestly and his episcopal role mingle with his personal life. Reflections on the general nature of man and especially his concern with the foundations of the sacraments break out into the open. And yet the ultimate function is still the one related to Augustine's inner search. For the *exercitatio* leads to the jubilant acknowledgment of the goodness of all creation. The entire *exercitatio* of the *Confessions*, especially as *confessio laudis*, rests in this sense that basically all is right in the relations between creator, creation, and the creature struggling back toward its creator—the returning Prodigal.

A finely tuned harmony prevails in this book between the autobiographic form and the confessing personality. It is not the harmony of a carefully thought out, systematized work; it rests in a life unified by a central shaping experience. It permits Augustine to balance a tightly disciplined form, which he can make to look so artless, with a spontaneity that expresses itself in poetic bursts of writing.

In this autobiographic effort the form was created by the personality's need to explain the meaning of life, a need which again and again was to account for the impulse toward autobiography. And the assigning of meaning is itself dominated by a gradually expanding consciousness of the powerful experience that shook the entire personality. This experience was, in a way, historically conditioned, even necessitated. To be sure, the ancient style of life and the style of Christian life gradually forming itself—these two incompatibles—had coexisted for some time prior to Augustine. But only in Augustine do we get the full account and the intensely vivid description of the tensions, the clash, and the fusion which two contemporary life-styles like these could produce in an individual. Many others must have felt it; some even left us their reflections. But Augustine presented the encounter in the model form of a dramatically compressed life story that is unequaled. Perhaps presentation in that form had to await a man capable of experiencing problems with his intensity, his inner need to live life to the fullest, the ineradicable bent of mind that impelled him to understand the forces of his life and to lead a life consciously shaped by such understanding. By training and early intention his life was meant to follow to self-fulfillment the course that the ancient world had summed up in the ideal of the rhetor, the man of eloquence, of culture. But that ideal of the self-sufficient shaper, of man in his pride assigning the creation of the good life to his talents and the forms given by his culture, was perhaps already too severely undermined for a questioning intellectual like Augustine. Such an ideal was not meant to function for such an intensely "religious" nature as Augustine's—or for one who was fated to have a mother like Monica. Indeed one needs a term like religion in order to suggest that Augustine belonged with those who could not rest easily with a matter-of-fact sense of the world, demanding instead the absolute answers which religion could furnish. He needed an outlet for the sense of awe and

mystery which the world evoked in him despite all his hard-headed intel-
lectuality. For a while his Manichaean interests were perhaps a most
suitable middle ground.

At any rate, the crisis came in the form of a radical reversal. The sense
of self that a man can derive from strong self-reliance and pride in the
human accomplishment—and on this much in the ancient world
rested—had to give way to self-negating humility befitting an overwhelming sense of dependence upon a transcendent power. Now *res
gestae* could only be seen as *opera dei*. The ambition to count for something in this world by measuring up to its esteemed models collapsed.
The objective of earthly happiness was transferred to a hope for a reward in a life beyond. The various mystery religions had used this
promise for a long time to console those who could not give meaning to
their life by participating in the highly aristocratic intellectual and public
culture of antiquity. But the case of Augustine is symptomatic of the
cultural problem that occurs when the culture bearers themselves lose
trust in the efficacy of their culture. Then the valuation of cultural institutions and techniques becomes a different one. The thoughtful individual experiencing this shock, no longer able to find the answers for his
life in the given ones of his culture, suddenly faces immense tasks in
reorienting himself—including, perhaps, the task of helping to transform his culture.

It was a remarkable aspect of Augustine's self-conception that he did
not let the radical conversion experience cut his life into radically separate halves. If he had done this, he would not have become involved in
the immense process of giving meaning to the "worthless" portion.
Instead he used the turn in his life to reintegrate his former existence, as
a revalued part, into the vision of his new self, and through his own
efforts he served the culture as a whole as well.

The conceptual device he used in sorting out the details of his own
life, the highly significant distinction between the *uti* (that which had
value only as something to be used) and the *frui* (that which alone had a
right to be enjoyed as a value in and for its own sake), proved itself to be
a powerful device in probing all elements of culture. Was I wrong in
striving for eloquence? Yes, as long as I pursued it for the wrong motive
and assigned a use and a value to it which it should not have. No, if I
used it in the search for the only truth and beauty that deserved enjoyment. There is, therefore, a proper place and a function for Christian
eloquence. And the same is true for erudition, music, dialectic, logic,
law, and all institutions; they can have instrumental value only when

they are pursued for the right ends. The basic elements for this kind of reevaluation are appropriately present in the *Confessions*; later on the bishop worked them out in a more systematic fashion in *De doctrina Christiana*, the *City of God*, and other works. In one sense, he perpetrated an enormous act of barbarism on the rich inheritance of a thousand-year-old culture by thus sorting it out: saying Yes to this because it may be useful to me as a Christian, and No to that because it is wasteful. But in another sense, he performed a culture-creating act as well as saving a "decadent" culture. He preserved what could survive in another life-style and infused it with a new vitality streaming forth from a source that the older cultural context lacked. He also endows the cultural functions with an active sense: where before there was a premium on passive *possession* of knowledge, now the virtue comes to lie in its active pursuit. The personal culture which Augustine fashioned for himself out of the Christian rededication of his old training and interest also served, in generalized form, for the culture of an age which was neither purely classical nor yet medieval, but which deserves its own nomenclature as Christian Antiquity or, as Marrou says, Theopolis, or the Age of Saint Augustine.

Augustine had a profound dedication to his fellow men. It is tempting to see autobiography as a prime illustration of human egotism. Indeed, there is one center to the *Confessions*: the relationship Augustine saw between God and his soul. Other human beings, even Monica, remain on the periphery. But the personality of the Christian pilgrim which he created for himself readmits the deepest possible concern for his fellow creatures. For the pilgrimage is one made in communion, and to make possible the pilgrimage of others is a prime law. But though this element is present in the *Confessions*, it is subordinate. Yet the man who had found his own way to the pilgrimage had, by the time he wrote the *Confessions*, sacrificed his most cherished plan for contemplating God with a few like-minded *servi Dei* and had surrendered to the never-ending tasks of the bishop in the out-of-the-way little town of Hippo.[13] "And do not place your own ease before the needs of the Church, for if no good men were willing to minister to her in her travail, you would find no means of being born yourselves" (Epistle 48:2).

The self-presentation in the *Confessions* is that of a human being in motion. Christian man is a pilgrim. Behind him lies darkness, before him the light. "Let him walk on for fear that darkness may engulf him" (10.23). He should do so by discarding unnecessary baggage and concentrating upon a lifelong job of helping the soul pull the whole being upward. It might seem that this ruthless simplification of the personality discards a good deal of human reality; but this is not so. The Gnostic, the Manichaean solution of sloughing off the responsibility for the evil within, for the material body (that cage of the soul) and its needs, was not an acceptable one. For the difference between Manichaean and Christian was that, while the one saw the life task in learning to separate what had unjustly been condemned to coexist, the soul with the body, the other saw the salvation in reuniting in one healthy whole what man by his own fault had permitted to be torn asunder. It was the pilgrim's task to let the power of the soul reconstitute the whole being in a new-found wholesomeness. The starting point must be in accepting all the givens, accepting the creature as a dilemma unto itself, and ultimately accepting creation as truly good. Implicit was the never-ending concern that the whole being—will, reason, affection, emotions—be aimed toward the one thing worth loving and pursuing. No single human factor in its perverted isolation should ever be permitted to lead the whole being astray again. Thus the ideal involved a personality unified in self-awareness. Inward and outward harmony was the ultimate objective, but the self-presentation could depict only the process of personality formation, the step-by-step growth in gaining more and more understanding, in training the will, in learning to love, in struggling for the inward order, in trying to let the soul take over. That is why the nature of the *exercitatio* and the form of the confession were so eminently fitting for each other.

This Augustinian self-conception and self-presentation have a complicated bearing upon the notion of individuality. The text in no way suggests that Augustine self-consciously thought of himself as a unique individual with the life task of translating his uniqueness from mere potentiality into actuality. Although he certainly was conscious of personal idiosyncrasy, he did not see it as anything of value in itself or deserving of cultivation. Quite to the contrary, the indications are that he saw in the story of *one* Christian soul, the one he could know best, the *typical* story of all Christians. In one life he sought to understand the drama of all. In a way, he reconstructed his life with the help of a "theory of Man" which gradually was taking shape. And it could be shown that, by analogy, Augustine saw in the course of his lifeline the lifeline for the whole history of mankind. In making the *Confessions* public, unique events were not merely being presented for their intrinsic value—the offering of a *typical* life had a didactic purpose. The conversion account could thus become a model of conversion as such, and so it functioned for centuries to come.

The transcendental relatedness of the Augustinian conception of the personality constitutes another barrier for freely admitting the notion of individuality. At the heart of Augustine's experience lay the insight that the self was not sufficient unto itself. Man was neither wise nor strong enough to set himself the law. He was not good enough for the dimly perceived but so strongly felt vision of perfection. A stronger power than he pulled him beyond himself, instilling a transcendent yearning he could not satisfy on his own. As an autonomous being man was impoverished. The soul can function as a healing and unifying force only when it has divine assistance. The self gains strength in dependence upon God, in an unbreakable relatedness to the creator of man's purpose. In that conception the self desiring to be its true self is a being living in and out of another being (*ein Auf-Gott-Bezogensein*), and becoming a full self is a growing surrender of the self to God. Such a God-related self does not aim at dissolving itself in the Godhead; Augustine never lets man's yearning for God end in a desire for a merger with the totally different Deity. Man retains his specified nature as a creature. But Augustine's formulations do not lend themselves to a conception of an autonomous self facing the task of bringing into actuality a self-determined self. Perhaps Christians will always have to acknowledge this barrier to individuality.

And yet within this Augustinian self-conception lie important elements which could eventually contribute to the emergence of individuality. The God who counts every hair is the God to whom every single soul is important. All of creation exists for the striving homeward of each errant soul. God's care in the running of the world extends to the providential usefulness of the smallest personal minutia. He is also the master who knows everything and who cannot be deceived. The impetus given by all of this to the most intense and careful self-analysis and self-cultivation was of great importance. Even the humblest striving could be seen to have cosmic value. A Christian need for the most careful self-testing and self-understanding gave rise to habits of self-inspection on which the later emergence of individuality depended. All the aspects contributing to the unification of the personality in terms of its inward coherence and consciousness were of similar importance. And despite Augustine's dominant concern with the typical Christian experience, there is enough room in the model for a differentiation among souls.

There is, of course, a world of difference between those who are given grace and those who are not, although man is not permitted a judgment on the latter (13.23). But those who receive grace can also differ strongly. The bishop knew it and, clearly, the intellectual son of Monica knew it.

However essential the restless search for rational understanding was to him personally, he never denied the full Christianity of the mother who could not follow him at all in his philosophical thirsting. There was enough in such a view of a differentiated Christianity from which men eventually could move toward a world filled with individuality. Here was a step toward a view of creation filled with uniquely different souls, each of which serves the purposes of the creator by its uniquely individual lifeline. However profound the differences between an Augustine and, say, a Leibniz, there are internal lines within the culture which connect them as well.

Since the notion of a specific historicity is essential for the conception of individuality, it remains to assess Augustine's thought on that point briefly. Compared to the more static classical views which undervalued development, there is a marked shift in Augustine, who perceives a matter of value in the notion of process. In one way, he therewith expresses a basic difference between the Hellenic and the Judeo-Christian views of the world. Athens gave birth to the philosophical and natural-scientific conception of the world as a rationally understandable cosmos. Jerusalem gave rise to historical-mindedness; the essence of its world view lay in the belief that the universe was a willed creation of a God standing outside it and using it for his inscrutable purpose—though He had not written His message into the structure of nature, to be read off there by a human reason proportioned to do so, His will might be fathomed from an attentive reading of history. Thus the Christian felt a prime need to understand what had happened to him. He could not afford the anachronism of acting as if the Crucifixion had not occurred. Despite some countercurrents in Augustine, such historical-mindedness was so strongly developed in him that, in the *City of God*, he could formulate the basic framework for viewing history by which the Western world oriented itself for nearly one and a half millennia. And in the *Confessions* he took his life as a biographic datum and told its story.

While much of this constitutes a historicizing of human realities which the classical mentality, without being crossfertilized by influences coming from the Jewish tradition, could not have achieved, it is still only a step toward that historicist view of the self-concept on which the notion of individuality depends. The difference between the Augustinian belief in a basic human nature and the historicist exaggeration that man has no nature, only a history, is still a wide one. Since Augustine sought to present his own life story as the typical model for any Christian life, he thereby diminished the value of historic specificity. He carefully reported the concrete historical details of his personal life; but do they have historical meaning or only symptomatic value? To be born into that particular family, for instance, was important; but was it important for his self-conception that his birth occurred in that specific historical constellation of the year 354 A.D.? Is it an essential mark of Augustine's self-conception that a truly different life would have resulted from a fate of having been born instead ten years to either side of 354? The concrete conditions and events against which the course of his life rubbed were significant as occasions for releasing or stimulating the inner processes whereby the soul could become its true self. They were not significant to Augustine as building blocks out of which a self builds a larger self through conscious integration. For Augustine, becoming a true self meant being able in many ways to shed the influence of "external accident or coincident." Passage through time pales in significance before the desire to be released from its bounds.

It all but follows from this low appreciation of historical concreteness that Augustine's self-presentation lacks any self-conscious trace of the powerful effect his own personality had upon the world around him. Such an omission does not stem from a fear of pride since he could have presented his achievements as the works of a chosen instrument of God. The reason must lie in the fact that he placed little importance on a conception of the interplay of a self and the historical world of which it is a part, that interplay in which a self, having formed itself in a specific world, works back upon the world by partially making it its own, changing it in terms of what it has become by having interacted with it. But Augustine is the man who most profoundly affected the world around him through his own central experience. He effectively shaped the life of the Catholic church, its dogma, its theology. He formulated Christian conceptions of society and of history which deeply entered into the life stream of this whole civilization. He was so centrally responsible for the then viable fusion of the two traditions entwined in Western civilization that it is perfectly proper to give his name to his age.

# 3

# The Problem of Autobiography and Individuality in the Middle Ages

In the *Confessions* St. Augustine had given an exemplary presentation of a Christian life. But that very Christian phase of our civilization, the Middle Ages, did not make much use of the great Augustinian model of autobiography. The conditions in which Augustine came to an understanding of his own experience were radically different from those faced by medieval autobiographers. Brought up as a classical man, he underwent a profound and conscious reorientation of his life when he fully came to accept Catholicism. But medieval men were born as Christians, brought up as Christians, and moved in an increasingly Christian world. Thus their autobiographic efforts would not simply continue to use the model of the *Confessions*.

When we see that the greatest history of autobiography we possess, that by Georg Misch, ranging in eight half-volumes from Egyptian tomb inscriptions to the nineteenth-century writer Theodor Fontane, devotes 2,724 pages of its total of 3,881 pages to the story of autobiography during the Middle Ages, the assumption that this form of self-presentation flourished in that age seems justified.[1] Yet while the harvest of medieval autobiographies is indeed larger than that of antiquity, it is still very small when compared to the thousands of modern bibliographic entries. Very rare still were "self-contained" autobiographies, those that attempted to give a coherent view of a life in one single writing. During the period from 500 to 1400, not more than eight to ten such works were produced[2] (leaving aside the Arabic and Byzantine texts which Misch also studied). But a number of medieval authors wove segments of autobiographic content into writings devoted to wider objectives. And several of them did this in more than one work, thus producing a characteristic cumulative genre that can be called "additive autobiography."

This chapter is meant to suggest, at least, certain general aspects of medieval autobiography by means of brief looks at *some* representative samples.[3] It also seeks to suggest, by means of broad generalizations, something about the nature of the cultural conditions affecting the character of medieval autobiography. The subsequent chapter on Abelard's *History of My Calamities* may then serve as the test case for the argument that self-conscious concern with individuality was not a mark of this central millennium of our civilization.

Historians of the Middle Ages have increasingly come to insist on the complexity of the period; sometimes it appears to them so intractably complex that their nominalist aversion to generalizations takes the upper hand. In part it is precisely this many-layered quality of medieval civilization which contributed to basic processes of social differentiation and thus ultimately to the emergence of individuality as a consciously cultivated value.

A simple reason for the perplexing patterns of this civilization was that at least three different cultural components had "fused": (1) the inheritance of antiquity, more of which was being revived as the age advanced, (2) a tradition of religious thought which was already, at the end of the Patristic age, a complicated amalgam of Judaic, Christian, and Oriental elements, and (3) a Germanic barbarism. To this one must add, at different places and at different times, influences coming from Celtic and Slavic groups and from the impact of fluctuating relations with the high civilizations of Byzantium and Islam. Since parts of Europe had been Romanized and others had not, these latter parts received the influence of classical elements in a somewhat different manner. The phenomenon of a "renaissance" is in itself witness to the complexity of a civilization; the successive waves of a Carolingian Renaissance, an Ottonian Renaissance, and a twelfth-century Renaissance vividly suggest a complicated pattern of classical influences feeding into a developing culture.

Since the decline of the Roman Empire, life had taken on a more exclusively agrarian-rural character in most parts of Europe, though Italy and Spain had preserved more active urban centers. When northern towns grew fairly rapidly after 1000 A.D. as somewhat alien bodies amid a basically rural order, they created a new element of tension in society, affecting the development of different areas of Europe in quite different ways. Local differences were marked; moving a distance of fifty miles might bring one to quite a different "world." Often not even consisting of one homogeneous ethnic stock, society was in fundamental ways differentiated into estates, status groups, and all sorts of functional layers with distinctive privileges and life-styles. Particular social groups might show internally an "egalitarianism" uncharacteristic of society as a whole. Despite the presence of certain universalizing fictions, political power was in reality only a limited control over relatively small areas, bridged by networks of authorities intersecting one another in a most complicated fashion. Even the degree of unity gradually being established in some areas left Europe divided into a community of "nations," with different tongues, traditions, and life-styles, a division that was to be its lasting fate.

But running through this undeniable diversity and the many layers of intricate social arrangements were also unifying features that provided a distinctive character to the total configuration. Many events and developments affected Europe as a whole. Certain needs were commonly felt needs; and some of the responses toward meeting them functioned as models far beyond their point of origin. Conquering Germanic war bands left to those in their wake the subsequent tasks of absorbing Germanic law and Germanic languages. Domestication of an aristocracy of barbaric origins resulted ultimately in a pervasive chivalric life-style having extraordinary consequences for the formation of European ideals of the personality. Shared conditions of soil, climate, rural labor, and techniques, especially in the grain-producing northwestern sector that was in many ways so dominant, accounted for the prevalence of a form of rural organization for which the "textbook manor" is not an overly false generalization. The political, military, and legal institutions of feudalism, merging with this rural order, aimed, despite all variations, at a model widely held. Not all Europeans were ruled by kings, but the ideal of kingship had some meaning for most. The gradual growth of monarchical power, with its own developing "administrative" and legal apparatus, later could make use of such unifying features as rested in the revival of Roman legal traditions. Almost all of European life was affected by the population boom that followed 1050 A.D. and similarly by the retrenchment that set in around 1350. The growth of towns, as one expression of this demographic trend, gave rise to a style of life with certain unifying features: the guilds, a growing lay literacy, newly felt religious needs, problems of defense, class divisions between patricians and the poor, and even the common tensions between country life and urban life.

That this European world was a Christian one was, of course, the most unifying factor of all. Europeans shared a Book, dogma, ritual, and an ethic; the dominant pattern of daily life resting in a common religion marked everyone in that world even if there was room for interesting variation. A basic view of world and life, on some points sufficiently diverse to allow lively discussion, was so coherent and dominant that no one could question it effectively in its fundamentals. In "the" Church Europe had a culture-creating and a unifying force that has rarely been equaled. An extraordinary display of intelligent energy went into the effort to form a unified Church out of a considerable variety of churches and practices. It was thus a more unified sacramental institution that then took seriously the objective of sanctifying as much of life as possible, undertaking thus the paradoxical task of creating a coherent Christian civilization (paradoxical, at least, in the sense that the antithetical gap could never be bridged between the other-worldly aspirations of Christianity and the tasks of civilization that are always secular in intention). That there was an implicit thrust toward this goal for a long time before it was purposefully undertaken after the middle of the eleventh century, and that it was tenuously "achieved" in the thirteenth, remains, despite all conflicting trends, the hallmark of Europe's Middle Ages.

It is this Christian framework that is the dominant and pervasive fact in the personality conceptions of which Europeans left traces in their autobiographic accounts. Except for James I of Aragon, all autobiographers were clerics. All their lives were confined within realities that they, as self-conscious Christians, could not and would not break through. The instrumentalities of the literary culture on which their self-orientation and self-expression depended were in the control of the Church; lay literacy opened new possibilities only gradually. Until the thirteenth century, Latin remained the unifying tongue for autobiography. Education was in the hands of the Church and the transmission even of classical models was, for the most part, affected by the Christianity of the transmitters. To be sure, the Church was the great *complexio oppositorum,* and there was room within its all-embracing arms for fascinating variation. But arms are confining. The more the Church strove to make real that Christian civilization of which the "medieval synthesis" is an expression, by bringing king, knight, burgher, peasant, monk, and priest within a common framework of life, a life dominated by sacraments for every important moment of existence, the more it also maintained the barriers that stood in the way of self-conscious individuality.

Not long after Augustine's death, the Western world became culturally so impoverished that men showed no capacity to imitate the model of the Christian personality he had presented in the *Confessions*. The history of autobiography, admittedly a barometer of limited registry, certainly attests to the existence of a "Dark Age" between 450 A.D. and the Carolingian world of the eighth and ninth century. Men of this age left us but the sparsest evidence of their selves, even if one resorts to such different literary forms as Anglo-Saxon poetry or the letters of that great man, Pope Gregory I. Such an exceptional man as Boethius (ca. 480–524) permits us a glimpse of his vital relation to philosophy; it is at best an autobiographic trait. Around 459, Paulinus of Pella wrote a *carmen*, the "Eucharisticos," in which he links his Christian confession of sins with the misfortunes of his wanderings in a world made insecure by barbarians on the move—but without telling us much about himself as a person. Occasionally an author will reveal something of himself in that peculiar autobiographic form of autobibliography; Gregory of Tours, Bede, King Alfred in his translation of Boethius, impart a little bit about themselves in discussing, or in simply listing, their literary activities.

Certain aspects of two early writings coming from the more peripheral areas of Europe, Ireland and Spain, may serve to suggest what form the autobiographic enterprise took then. One of these may have been written by St. Patrick.[4] While the *Vita* received the title *Confessio*, evoking expectations of Augustinian influences (although it was really too early for them), the form much more readily fits the frame of the developing hagiographic legend literature. In general, the form in which Athanasius had presented the life of St. Anthony remained for a long time a much more persuasive model than Augustine's *Confessions*. It was a much simpler form, eminently suited to frame the typical Christian experience, and it was free of the metaphysical underpinnings of Augustine's endeavor. A frequently found motif of the period, St. Patrick's lament over his lack of schooling, attests to the need for a form that was simple enough to accommodate a quite uncoordinated reporting of events experienced, deeds done, visions granted, and the confession of sin. Despite the inadequacy of his Latin, Patrick knew how to fill this form with the details of his monastic, missionary, and episcopal existence that he thought most important.

The hagiographic form was especially suitable to a presentation of the monk's life; the *Lamentatio* of the Spanish hermit St. Valerius (ca. 630–95) illustrates this. The ideal of the monk was to dominate much of early medieval autobiography and much of the literature was written by monks. More than anyone else they became the custodians of writing; their libraries could also furnish them with models of ancient portraiture—those derived from Suetonius and Sallust eventually became important influences. But the monk is handicapped as an auto-biographer. He can indulge in self-interest only to a point; he represents the ideal personality in whom self-will has given way to divine will. The ever-repeated motive for writing such accounts at all is an intensely didactic one, the wish to furnish others with exempla of the struggle between God and Devil for a soul. An often recurring theme is the turn from a sinful *vita activa* in the world to the *vita contemplativa*, which by this time always means acceptance of the monastic ideal of seclusion, a theme of major importance for monks of aristocratic origins, like Valerius. The presence of this theme, the conflict that was so often described between these two ways of life, is in itself an indicator of the dominance of the monastic ideal.

Misch undertook to trace the forms of self-conception expressed by the secular aristocracy in the heroic literature and sagas celebrating its style of life; as a parallel he even studied the old heroic poetry of the Arabs prior to Mohammed as well.[5] He was especially interested in the Icelandic sagas which, though written down only late in the Middle Ages, had preserved in their island isolation many of the older social realities. His analysis of this autobiographically important literature evokes impressions of a barbaric warrior world in which powerful personalities expressed themselves, particularly when struggling to preserve their traditional ways against the introduction of Christianity. But such expression stylized itself by the traditional heroic norms of an undifferentiated sib society. The individual bard expresses something "General" and "Typical"; he sees a common ideal in individual terms. "The We precedes the I."[6] The limits set for distinctive individuation within the Germanic sib society must have been similar, in most regards, to those already suggested for the very early Greek world. When finer forms of individuation ultimately came to this Germanic warrior aristocracy, they were molded by the forces of Christianity. The indomitable warrior berserk was over centuries domesticated into a Roland and was finally turned into a Parsifal searching for the Holy Grail.

Even with the onslaughts of Moors, Vikings, and Magyars on Charlemagne's realm, and despite the growing internal disorders of life, there seems to be a bit more light and sophistication in the late and post-Carolingian autobiographic writings. Up to approximately 1070 A.D., the actual number of autobiographic accounts is not larger than in the earlier darker ages, but they have grown in inner complexity and richness. Two of the three we shall discuss here are examples of the "additive autobiographies" we have mentioned, in which the author does not write one self-contained life of himself but reveals himself in various writings. In itself this practice need not be astounding, but if it can be shown to be expressive of more fundamental aspects of the medieval mentality, it becomes a weightier matter. The reactions of modern editors to these dispersed autobiographic data suggest something of the difference in outlook. There are some who, in reading a medieval writer's works, cannot resist the temptation to peel out the precious autobiographic matter, shucking the other contextual matters in which the writer embedded them, and then stringing up, like pearls, the author's personal revelations for the reader, as if to say: *voilà un homme!*[7] By turning what was written in additive form into a picture of a coherently presented personality, they seem to give expression to the modern conviction that the real value lies in the self-aware unified personality. But in meeting this phenomenon of the additive autobiographical account one surely must assume that, for the medieval writer, there was something right and fitting in placing his self-presentation in the contextual matter in which he perceives it to have significance. If, in other words, it was "natural" and proper for a medieval writer to view his self in relation to its context, to view the self as a prolongation of itself within its surroundings, as an integral part of its enveloping world, then the phenomenon of additive autobiography may indeed say something of importance about that specific form of self-conception. There were other forms of personal accounts, but it is noteworthy that both the self-contained and the additive autobiographies, each in its own way, express the strong support medieval men found in the cultural forms in which they found it easiest to express themselves.

One such additive autobiographer, who interested Misch very much, was Bishop Ratherius of Verona (ca. 890–974). As a descendant of an impoverished aristocratic family, Ratherius entered monastic life in Lorraine and was affected by the currents of the Cluniac reform movement. The family pulled him out of the monastery again and involved him in feudal intrigues over ecclesiastical property, quarrels typical of this age. Later on he became bishop of Verona, lost his see, regained it, and lost it again. When he went north again, he was made bishop of Liège, but he lost this see as well after two years. The struggles he undertook to recover his bishoprics, extending over decades, turned him into a writer. In four different kinds of writings he spoke of himself and his troubles. The earliest was a moral portrait of his times in which he satirized the immorality of the clergy who dislodged him from his bishopric. He thus uses the discussion of a general issue to insert the personal history which in part he hides behind the phrase "a certain bishop." In a sense he speaks less about the person Ratherius by concentrating instead on his conception of the episcopal role; the largest part of the self-definition is in the identification with the priestly office. He sees a conflict between an immoral clergy and laity and a man holding reform ideas of ecclesiastical office. He does submit himself to the criticism that he should have stayed in the monastery. This theme he repeats in all the writings—but he stayed in the world. The fiasco at Liège led him to send explanatory and fighting epistles in all directions. These he subsequently pulled together and furnished with a self-revealing preface. Again he spoke in the third person, and further complicated the self-presentation by describing a man with crazy ideas of "the right" to which he felt entitled, thus satirizing the perverted justice to which his political and ecclesiastical enemies adhered. When, in his sorrow, he briefly stayed in a friendly monastery, he wrote there a confession in dialogue form, confessing to a priest instead of God, and confining his confessions to a confession of sins only. He accused himself of every imaginable sin, and grossly exaggerated them. By generalizing through repeated statements of the sins of which "he and such as he" are guilty, he used his confession for satirizing the mores of his age. Still later in life he drew a literary portrait "On the character of a certain someone," presenting himself obliquely through the accusations others might or did voice against him instead of offering direct self-criticism.

Behind all the jocose hide-and-seek of these writings a pattern emerges. Ratherius deals with himself by dealing with the traits of the cultural context in which his life moves. He fights for himself by setting his case in the wider framework of a satire on the prevailing immorality. He makes his legal case by satirizing the legality of others. He hides the personal confession in a tract on the need of Christian confession in general. He indirectly tries to defend his reputation with a catalogue of what others say about him. He laments that he left the comfort and peace of the monastery where he might have been able to be true to himself; amid the dreadful inconstancy of the world he finds it more difficult to understand himself. He is always interested in the general. The ups-and-downs of secular life become *exempla* of the human condition. Perhaps God meant it to be so insecure; he gave Saul a kingdom and took it away, he gave Judas an apostleship and took it away, he gave Satan heaven and then hell.

Thus Ratherius does not present a view of his own self as a writer would do who is conscious of an inner organizing center in the personality. He instead describes himself as a person whose inner order is dependent on the fact that there is an order in the surrounding world in which he exists.[8] He knows himself neither as a person who projects the order of his own experience on a surrounding world (as some modern men conceive of this) nor as a self-regulating organism coexisting with a surrounding world having its independent order. From among the many different conceptions men can formulate of their relation to the surrounding world in which they live, Ratherius chooses one in which the self and the cultural world of which it is a part are in closest harmony. He can present something about himself by presenting those aspects of his world and those cultural forms which give meaning to his actions, intentions, and experience. He apparently saw no need to compose a unified vision of his person and felt comfortable with revealing one aspect of himself in one specific context of his life, another in another situation, leaving a total impression of the person to the effect of reading about it in many different writings. In this way, "additive autobiography" may be suitable to a person who has no need to perceive himself as an individuum unified in its own consciousness (what Jacob Burckhardt called *ein geistiges Individuum*). The propensity to understand one's own life in terms of the verities offered by the prevailing culture (or those verities accepted by the individual as valid ones for itself) also suggests the power of models for the personality given in the culture.

When the conditions of life were less complicated than they were in Ratherius's case, it was easier for an author to present a view of his personality. This was true of Othloh of Emmeram (ca. 1010–70), a plain man of peasant extraction who spent his life almost entirely as a monk in the rich Benedictine cloister of Emmeram outside Ratisbon. He became a schoolmaster and deacon but could not advance further in that very aristocratic establishment. In his writings he tried to hide his authorship and even asked his fellow monks: "Since you know who I am, please do not give away my name. My work might seem despicable because of my lowly person."[9] He was in some ways a simple scribe who copied the Psalter nineteen times and the Gospels five. But he also wrote some devotional literature himself and into these works he wove short self-presentations, which, taken together, form another additive autobiography. Unlike Ratherius, Othloh had only one role to play, being a good monk. Thus he could concentrate his autobiographic tasks on a straightforward portrayal of his monastic conception and its development. Like Ratherius, he had been affected by the reform spirit which expressed itself most strongly in his repeated insistence that a good monk should shun secular literature.

The scene in which he reports how he was saved, by being turned away from his earlier love for Vergil and Lucan, is typical of his manner of self-presentation. He gives an account of a dream vision in which he was visited by a man who beat him mercilessly until he seemed to be floating in his own blood. When he awoke he puzzled out what this could mean. He then remembered that in a dream St. Jerome had similarly been beaten for his love of Cicero. Not daring at first to compare himself with St. Jerome, Othloh hesitated over the interpretation. He went on to recount all sorts of other divine chastisements and only gradually became persuaded that his own dream must have the same meaning as St. Jerome's. The model is there, and he adapts the personal experience to it. Cured of his love for Vergil, he soon is worried, however, about a monk writing books, but eventually he finds the justification: I do this not for my own sake, but so that the wonderful visions and personal experiences can serve as fruitful *exempla* for my fellow monks. "I thought it useful to acquaint many with these as I believed that it concerns all human beings when one of them, be it for chastisement or for comfort, is visited by God, for as he said in the Gospel 'What I say to one, I say to all.' "[10] The personal element had to serve the typical and the general, from which it in turn drew its meaning. The potential distinctiveness of individual experience is minimized.

The same features can be illustrated from the *Lamentatio* of the abbot Jean de Fécamp (ca. 990–1078), a man who saw the whole purpose of his life in being a good monk and who writes as if he had been born a monk rather than having to be converted to that status, lamenting that his high office involves him too much in worldly affairs. The extreme self-abasement of his confession of sins and his confession of faith go hand in hand. A good monk should live only for the *vita contemplativa*. He should govern his entire life by St. Jerome's advice to follow closely in the footsteps of the monastic fathers. Clear models direct the person, and it is Jerome who is the exemplar. The ideal of the great athlete of God, modeled upon St. Anthony and the early fathers, still gives meaning and direction to individual life.

To men whose self-orientation depended so much on the uncontested validity of their norms and models, a world growing more complex was bound to present difficulties. By the eleventh century Western civilization had begun its geographic expansion from a narrowly confined area to eventual world dominance. European consciousness of the world expanded correspondingly. The reaches of the civilization were extended considerably by the Reconquista in the Iberian peninsula and the islands of the western Mediterranean, the Christianization of Scandinavia, Bohemia, and Hungary, and by the steady push of Latin Christians into the areas east of the Elbe River. The northwestern pockets of remaining Celtic elements were brought more fully into the context of European civilization. The crusades to the eastern Mediterranean opened the West more effectively for the cultural influences of Islam, Byzantium, and eventually of even the Mongol and Chinese world beyond. At the same time the ties to the classical inheritance were retied much more tightly. The revival of the study of Roman law and Greek-Arabic science and medicine opened up the possibility of more secular intellectual careers. The new poetic forms of the troubadors and goliards permitted new expressions of personal experience. New forms of intellectual training and the cultivation of new forms of knowledge, at the cathedral schools and later the universities, gave new vigor to men's rational pursuits. Processes of self-orientation became more complex. New monastic orders, designed to meet different needs from those answered by the older Benedictines, enriched religious life. Augustinian canons and later Dominicans and Franciscans, moved self-consciously out into the world, and eventually such lay movements as the Béguines and the *Devotio moderna,* no longer living by a common rule, went even further in disregarding the lines which once had separated monks from those living in the world. The distinction between orthodoxy and heretical idiosyncrasy was tested more forcefully. Finally, the complications created by the rapid rise of town life, its economic activities, its social and cultural innovations, produced tensions in the fabric of medieval culture from which a more differentiated world would eventually result.

Yet the very same centuries of growing complexity were also marked by remarkable efforts to unify and order the Latin Christian world. The political history of the period is bewildering in its details, but underneath the confusion new forces were clearly laying the foundations for the future political order of Europe. Feudalism itself became a more recognizable order, and within its framework, though contending against it, princely power grew. In Western Europe the confines of the future nation-states, most of them the creation of dynasties, were being marked off more distinctly. Men's loyalties to certain political entities grew. More systematic forms of administration would serve to give greater coherence at least to smaller princely realms or to practically independent city-states. While Europe as a whole may not have been more unified than before, most individuals lived in an increasingly more coherent political order.

The unity Christianity imposed on Europe during the High Middle Ages strengthened the whole cultural configuration. The great Gregorian reform movement not only created greater ecclesiastic unity by the extension of papal power and the systematic elaboration and application of canon law, but it also led to a more thoroughly Christianized civilization. The priests' control of the now more fully elaborated sacramental system, enveloping the life of each European from birth to death, gave the Church an effective tool for assuring greater cultural coherence. All the factors driving toward a more explicit Christian life proved stronger, for a while at least, than the centrifugal tendencies of other complex cultural forces. By the thirteenth century, popes could function as the arbiters of Europe. A future saint rules France, a Christian knight rules Aragon; Germany no longer is a threat, and the Hohenstaufen "devil's brood" in Sicily is to be wiped out by papal "mercenaries." The Albigensian crusade was a warning to heretics. The potential dangers of the new urban style of life seemed to be contained through the Christianization of guilds and by the work of canons and friars. A crude warrior aristocracy had been partially transformed by Christian values, whose most effective image was perhaps the papally sponsored ideal of the Crusader, who, now becoming enamored with the etiquette of *courtoisie* and prepared to perceive an ideal in Parsival, was a far cry from the uncouth and uncontrollable barbarians with whom Bishop Gregory of Tours had had to contend. Scholasticism had turned the skittish forces of reason into handmaidens of the faith. A pervasive mode of symbolic thinking sustained adherence to a basic Christian view of the world. That the unity of the medieval synthesis was a tenuous one is only of subsequent interest. Before the fourteenth century the autobiographic efforts of men stayed entirely within the confines of this fundamentally Christian mode of human self-conception.

Between 1100 and 1300 A.D. self-conception in autobiography adhered to the basic models, though now in greater variation and with greater inner richness. Self-aware individuality is not yet to be found. Some traditional autobiographic habits—of the historians who speak occasionally of themselves or the authors who provide an autobibliography—are from now on a customary and expected part of the scene. Some of the larger fragments of autobiography—here discussed from a topical rather than strictly chronological viewpoint—hardly depart from the older models. In the first half of the twelfth century, for instance, Petrus Diaconus, the "archivist" of Europe's most famous Benedictine monastery on Monte Cassino, glorifies his institution in a way that lets glory fall upon himself, whom he no doubt considered one of the "great men of Monte Cassino." At times the language seems hard to reconcile with Benedictine humility. "This deacon"—the humble third person still being employed—"grew into a monk already as a child and while maturing in the monastery, acquired such a mind that he totally understands the Sacred Scriptures, which others hardly learn to do even with the help of teachers."[11] The form of reporting, the hiding in semi-anonymity, is old-fashioned; the heightened degree of writer's pride is new. An even more old-fashioned version of the typical conversion to a monastic existence comes late in the thirteenth century from Pietro of Murrone, the short-lived Pope Coelestinus V (1294), the *Papa angelicus* of the Spiritual Franciscans, whom Dante, however, consigned to hell for cowardly resigning the papacy. In a *confessio laudis* Pietro celebrates God's providential help in permitting him, in early life (to which the autobiography is restricted), to become a rigorous ascetic by guiding him with dreams, visions, signs, and miracles and giving him the strength to fend off the Devil, who was bent on defeating his *askesis*, his ascetic training.

Other autobiographic writings of the age contain a variety of details that suggest new trends. In a typical story of conversion to the *vita contemplativa* of monastic life, the Cistercian Ailred of Rievaulx (1110–67) gives an account of the role of human friendship. Here *Laelius*, Cicero's dialogue on friendship, is given a function equal to the *Hortensius*, that was so significant for Augustine, and the Augustinian conversion account is, with some self-consciousness, employed as a model. In a separate dialogue Ailred investigates the problem of friendship and persuades himself that it can be a step on the road to monastic perfection: friendship with men may teach true friendship with God, and the monastery may become the haven for those seeking the ideal union. Thus the personal experience of a strong human affection, easily a disturbing element in a monk's life, is integrated into the monastic ideal of a new order priding itself on a harsher ascetic commitment.

A number of autobiographic accounts from the twelfth century reveal how significant the revival of older knowledge and fresh philosophical activity was in the lives of men. The most dramatic of these is Abelard's *History of My Calamities*, to be discussed in the next chapter. Some self-portraits of a more fragmentary nature than Abelard's show how fresh intellectual pursuits affected various thinkers in various ways. The

*Meditations* of the Carthusian Guigo of Chastel (fl. 1110) have the same formless quality as the reflections of Marcus Aurelius. The book is auto-biographic insofar as the author tells us of his immense effort to achieve his spiritual progress even if to others he had always seemed so firm in his faith. Guigo combines his Christian outlook with "Platonism in Augustinian form," but he does so without recognizing the potential tension. Philosophical meditation is seen as a useful instrument for free-ing oneself from the claims of the world in order to achieve a full dedication to God. Aesthetic and moral reflections are made to serve Guigo's religious quest. Without doubting the inherent compatibility of all the elements, he blends rational reflection (used to persuade himself of the uselessness of worldly desires) with full devotion to the monas-tic ideal, and with the prior's concern for the moral welfare of his institu-tion. A similar trust in the ultimate consonance of divine and philosophic truth is present in Adelard of Bath's *De eodem et diverso* (ca. 1108). The weighty autobiographic moment comes when man is con-fronted with choosing between the road that leads to love of wisdom (*philosophia*) or the one that leads to the love of the world (*philocosmia*), a choice reminiscent of Origen's writings. Adelard chiefly concerns him-self with defending that kind of philosophy and science which allows a man to penetrate the world of ultimate reality hidden behind the sense experiences. To this belief in a discernible rational world order is joined a lifelong interest in Arabic and Greek science and mathematics as well as an insistence on active reasoning as a way of overcoming the limitations of human authorities, though not the limits set by revelation.

John of Salisbury (ca. 1118–80), a representative of the more literary than philosophical school of Chartres, shows another side of medieval intellectual life in the self-reflections strewn throughout his two major works, the *Metalogicon* and the *Policraticus*. As a student of such very different masters as Abelard, Gilbert de la Porrée, William of Conches, and Bernard of Chartres, he was highly qualified by his experience to weigh the appeal of the main intellectual tendencies of the age and their effect on his own formation. Though for him philosophy answered an important human need, he turned against the overemphasis on logic and dialectic, seeing virtue in combining them with literary studies. The cultivation of refined literary style and a rational-moralistic humanism seemed to him perfectly compatible with his Christian faith. He kept his distance from the controversies between the fideists and mystics like St. Bernard of Clairvaux, and the rational theologians like Abelard or Gil-bert de la Porrée. He became neither a philosopher in the technical sense, nor a theologian. He preferred the *vita contemplativa* but did not choose to find it in monastic life. He served the Roman curia and two archbishops of Canterbury, always prepared and willing to defend his master Thomas à Becket. Late in life John was bishop of Chartres. He witnessed much, he experienced much, he had sophisticated ways, but he felt neither the need nor the inclination to write his life as a coherent whole. The awareness of a complex self was not pulled together in a unified vision.

In the conversion account of one of his contemporaries, the Premonstratensian abbot Hermann of Scheda, the intellectual currents of the time are reflected in yet another fashion. This onetime Jew from Cologne, shaken in the faith of his fathers at an early age by contact with Catholics, recounts his intensive rational search for the resolution of a conflict posed by the two religious traditions in his life. These debates and internal disputations show something of the contemporary attempts to obtain a rational understanding of dogma. But his conversion was not accomplished by rational persuasion. Instead he attributed his acceptance of the Christian faith on trust to a suprarational act of divine grace by which God sent him dream visions and divine signs that helped him to combat the Devil's temptations. He joined a new order in which commitment to asceticism and fideism far outweighed impulses toward a rational ordering of religious experience.

None of these self-revelations permits a conclusion that involvement in the intense intellectual currents of the times occasioned the kind of inner crisis in self-definition which leads to new personality conceptions. Quite the contrary, the accounts again and again point to the vital strength of the models of personality even when individuals had more complex experiences. The more intensive preoccupation with rational thought did not lead these men outside their firm Christian confines; though it might, as with Abelard, cause conflict with certain representative sectors of society, it did not necessitate a search for a personality model that was not already sketched out in the Christian tradition.[12] It is striking with what ease a slightly transformed conception of the *vita contemplativa* could be fitted into the life of a monk as well as into that of a bishop or clerk. The same men, moving freely from England, to France, to Italy, or to Spain, could assume the same roles anywhere, a fact that suggests how universally binding the cultural strictures were by which this revival of learning and thought was kept within Christian boundaries.

All of these writings, with the exception of Abelard's *vita*, were only partial autobiographies, and at that largely additive ones. Perhaps clerics could with relative ease integrate the diverse intellectual strains to fit the different aspects of their devoted religious lives, especially when they were content to speak only of partial aspects. It remains to be seen what happened to fuller self-presentations and also to those with a more decidedly secular content.

How difficult it was for some of these men to present their lives as coherently conceived wholes is shown by the *Monodiae* (songs for one voice) written by Guibert of Nogent around 1115 A.D. The younger son of a not very prominent aristocratic family, his father died early, leaving him to the care of a widowed mother and rough-mannered relatives. At a young age he entered a monastery, studying briefly with Anselm of Bec, who helped him develop skill in biblical interpretation. Guibert wrote moral-theological tracts and a history of the first crusade based on the report of a participant. At the age of fifty he was elected abbot of the small abbey of Nogent and, with his learning, he played a role in the church life of the important area north of Paris. When he decided to write his own life he at first sought to model it after Augustine's *Confessions*. Beginning, like Augustine, with the word *confiteor*, he then offers a confession of sins, in typical self-deprecatory fashion, following it up with a *confessio laudis*, which does not sound very Augustinian. He thanks God for his noble birth, his wealth, and his good looks. He assigns a large place in his early account to his mother whose beauty he greatly admired and whom he considered instrumental in turning him to the religious life. The important junctures in his life are all caused by supranatural intervention in the form of dreams, terrifying nightmares, voices, and visions. Although he accepted the monastic life eagerly, he was not entirely free from later regrets about having sacrificed the possibility of fame and fortune in the world. His mother's dream visions persuaded him to settle in his monastic choice and to hope for ecclesiastical preferment. He records the customary monastic struggles against the temptations of secular literature and his failure to be sufficiently humble toward his monastic brethren. He eventually became a devoted monk and fought with zeal for the moral reform of the world.

When Guibert had reached this point early in writing his life, the Augustinian model used at the very beginning has already begun to crumble in his hands. His story becomes loaded with examples of aristocrats who, like him, had become monks. Guibert shows no understanding for the drama of Augustine's conversion or the metaphysics supporting Augustine's account. Guibert's life had no clear turning point.

When he reaches his account of the abbot of Nogent, he can no longer use the model at all. Instead he talks about himself by talking about his abbey; local ecclesiastical history and autobiography melt into one.[13] Book 2 describes the abbey, its history, its claims to precedence, its struggles with rapacious nobles, the local stories that had come to Guibert's attention. Into these accounts he weaves excerpts from the sermon he gave on his accession and the story of his "saintly" mother's death. Book 3 contributes even less to any view of Guibert as a person. For historians, it is fascinating in its presentation of the early accounts of a revolt of burghers against the local lord, the bishop of the city of Laon, in an effort to bring a town under their own control, a struggle typical of the urban developments of the twelfth century.[14] But for the historian of autobiography it is a perplexing matter: the autobiographer, not even an active participant, has simply become the chronicler and the moral judge of events.

The *Monodiae*, as a whole, are thus a composite of quite diverse but traditional genres: the Augustinian model, which is not really held to; standard accounts of conversion to the monastic *vita contemplativa* which change abruptly into the history of an institution; and a conclusion which becomes pure *memoir*, things-I-have-witnessed. Each of these segments is internally broken by Guibert's narrative lust for exemplary stories of hagiography, miracles, and visions. Here a life with diverse segments instinctively employs equally diverse forms that express each segment without any concern for internal coherence. Here there is no unified personality imposing the order of its own unity on the whole.[15] Guibert as interested observer offers a mirror of that world of which he is a part. It is fortunate he had a gift as a raconteur.

A truly magnificent storyteller, Giraldus Cambrensis (ca.1146–1223), grants a somewhat modified view of this discrepancy between the life experience itself and the ability to give a coherent account of it. Once more the autobiographic segments are spread throughout diverse writings, although one of these, his *De rebus a se gestis*, describes a central thread: the frustration of his nearly lifelong efforts to become bishop of St. David's in southern Wales. There was much diversity in this life: family ties to the conquering Normans and to the Celtic world of Wales and Ireland, studies in Paris where he later taught, participation in the conquest of Ireland, close relations to the court of Henry II, witness to the tragic end of the Angevin realm, a gradual retreat from the court under Richard and John, and several visits to Rome in behalf of his episcopal aspirations. But we see the repeated threads of his lifelong association with St. David, the persistent struggle for the bishop's see and his advocacy of a consistent ecclesiastical policy, an apparently steady sense of humor, and a lasting aversion to monks—all of which tempered any other-wordly devotion to asceticism. In his later life he gradually turned from vigorous involvement in the affairs of the world to a more contemplative existence—but never in the cloister. He admired Thomas à Becket and always fought for the canonical rights of the Church. His letter to Archbishop Langton in 1215 shows his distaste for monkish withdrawal: "For your wise and pious discretion knows right well which are dearer to Christ, most excellent prelates or hermits wandering alone and anchorites shut up within their cells? The former rule, the latter are ruled; the former feed their flock, the latter are fed.... Prelates restore to God with great increase the talents committed to their charge and cease not to win souls, for which Christ laid down his life; but the recluse, intent only on their salvation, hide the talent committed to them."[16] By valuing Christian work in the world so positively, he seems a fitting contemporary to St. Francis, and by his interest in canon law and good administration a fitting contemporary of Innocent III. His interest in learning drove him not so much into the arms of philosophy as to literature. He presents the world of his experience with literary charm and ease. But he presents himself only in and through the world that harbors his experience. Where the affairs in which he is involved take him, there he presents himself. Like other medieval autobiographers, he mirrors his personality in the presentation of his world.

Somewhat later in the thirteenth century, the king of Aragon, James I (1208 or 1213–76), wrote a book *On the Deeds of James*. Even more than the work of Giraldus Cambrensis, this autobiography tends toward the genre of *res gestae* and memoir, though its impact is enhanced by the identity of its author. The story was written in Catalan instead of Latin, it moves chronologically, and seems to be based on an earlier daily record. The world of action that is recorded has a clear and ever-present center in the king who describes it. The psychic or mental distance between actor and recorder cannot have been a great one; the accounts have that "naïve" quality in which the recollection of the act has not been greatly transformed by conscious reflection on it. The story is largely made up of the king's struggle with the nobility, and of the three great campaigns by which he wrested the Balearic Islands, Valencia, and Murcia from the Moors; a plan for a crusade late in life is added. Since James was famous for constantly pursuing long-range plans and policies, it is remarkable that the record of his deeds does not present them in orderly detail. There is little of broadly conceived policy here—James I reflects on the bare outlines of his days, rather than the pattern of deeds and events. Much for which he was famous he does not recount at all; he cheerfully records incidents that are not particularly flattering to him. His conception of the role of king gives unity to the revelations of his person: he must conquer and he must serve God; he must rule effectively what has been entrusted to him, protect those who need his protection, and break those who try to break the power of kingship. He is the model of the royal crusader, the Iberian who sees life as a lasting struggle against the Moor. He is the model of the Christian king, touched by chivalric convention, with a clear sense of his power and his task. His efforts to record the deeds of a man fulfilling his royal role did not seem to occasion a need to reflect on his personal individuality.

Finally, we touch with hesitation the medieval autobiography possessing the greatest artistic unity, Dante's *Vita Nuova* (1294?), which has been the subject of so much learned interpretation and controversy. From certain points of view it may not be an autobiography at all. Perhaps it is simply "a treatise by a poet, written for poets, on the art of poetry."[17] The book benefits from the great artistic unity that can be derived from placing one vital experience, a great love, in a center from which it never veers. Thirty-one poems, arranged with an extraordinary concern for symmetry, are accompanied by the poet's prose account of the occasion for each poem and by his extended commentary on their basic structural forms. The whole has a coherently executed biographic lifeline, but whether it is almost entirely a fictionalized one, an intensely stylized version of real experience, a conventional invention, or chiefly an example of metaphysical-theological symbolism; whether, as has been suggested, it is an *apologia* whereby Dante meant to prepare his entry into the political life of his city, or indeed the poetic compression of a genuine experience—all this has been and will continue to be inconclusively debated. A fuller discussion of the autobiographic question in Dante would have to consider the *Convivio* and the *Divine Comedy* as well. Some fanciful modern editor could even compose Dante's autobiography by stringing together these dispersed self-revealing nuggets. A fuller analysis of Dante might show evidences of the medieval rather than the modern autobiographic stance—the conventions of high medieval poetic art, the intensive use of symbolism, the scholastic mentality, and the fundamental realities of an unquestioned metaphysical-religious ethos: the same characteristics that can be seen in self-revelations of such troubadours as Wolfram von Eschenbach and Ulrich von Lichtenstein.

At the end of such a sketchy survey, let us take one last view of a typical self-representation in medieval garb, one that may help to sum up the basic argument. Suger (1081–1151), the greatest abbot of St. Denis, was a near contemporary of Abelard (1079–1142). Unlike the "persecuted" philosopher, Suger felt at home in his world. He entirely merged with it. True, he participated less than Abelard in the excitement and fresh intellectual activity that affected so many autobiographic accounts of the times, yet his presence touched the diverse threads of contemporary French life. St. Denis was of central importance to the French crown; it was the "national" monastery of France. Its patron saint was, next to God, the mightiest protector of the realm. Suger and the future king Louis VI (Louis the Fat) met there as young pupils, and continued a relation of trust by which Suger was carried deep into the affairs of the kingdom. Later, the succeeding Louis VII retained Suger as a fatherly adviser who ruled the kingdom in the absence of the royal crusader and proudly returned it to him in an improved state. This statesman-abbot, earning the title *pater patriae*, had a developed sense of the need for a strong monarchy; he even had a primitive sense of "national consciousness." He consecrated on his altar, with fervor, the oriflamme, the "national" flag under which the country prepared its war against a threatening emperor from east of the Rhine. Suger, as Ranke said, had "a vital awareness of right and justice, their connection with might and the duty of the monarchy to maintain right."[18] Where he thought right to be on his side, he did not hesitate to enforce it by arms. But loving orderly peace even more, he was known for his never-ending work as mediator and link of peace—*mediator et pacis vinculum*. As one of the most eminent churchmen of the realm, he was as instrumental as his contemporary, St. Bernard of Clairvaux, in bringing about that close relation between the growing power of France and the even more significantly growing power of the twelfth-century papacy.

But he tells us very little of his great work in building a stronger France. In writing a life of his royal friend, Louis the Fat, he keeps himself modestly in the background, though the book records policies he probably initiated and events in which he participated. He loved to talk about such things, however, keeping his monastic brothers awake till late in the night; one of them, Guillaume the monk of St. Denis, thought it fit to record the abbot's life.

Suger wrote more freely about himself and his own actions in a number of writings related to his abbey and the great church he built there. Again we have additive autobiography in which the author merges his own story with the history of his institution. One of these records is entitled "What was done under his administration"; the other chief example is the "Little Book on the Consecration of the Church of St. Denis." In these Suger reveals himself as an eminently practical man whose managerial ability, energy, and initiative rebuilt a monastic establishment that had fallen into bad disrepair since the days when he had lived there as a very young peasant boy and had grown into a young monk. He reestablished the abbey's control over its vast land holdings, preferably by peaceful means and by buying out rival claimants, though he willingly resorted to legal force when necessary. He saw to it that the personal lot of the monastic tenants was improved, and by thus providing order, clear lines of command, and a legitimate outlet for the self-interest of all concerned, he tripled and quadrupled the abbey's income. Land and dwellings that had not been efficiently used were turned to productive use. He went everywhere, inspected everything personally, gave directions for the regulation of minutiae, and bestowed his personal care on each detail. At the same time he reformed the life-style of his Benedictines, not in the fashionable excessively ascetic style dear to St. Bernard (who had felt called upon to criticize the morals of St. Denis monks under the previous abbot!), but very much more in the humane and practical fashion of St. Benedict of Nursia himself.

At the center of all his activity stood his work for the fulfillment of a lifelong wish: to rebuild the basilica so it would be large enough to accommodate the crowds seeking the presence of the greatest relics in France and to house these in a splendor befitting their power. This church, meant to outshine Hagia Sophia in Constantinople, was to be consecrated as a shrine to St. Denis in the presence of kings, nobles, churchmen, and peasants! His whole being, his very personality merged with this first Gothic "cathedral." His initiative launched the project. His planning and administrative reforms procured the money for making the building possible. He selected the builders. He was involved in the planning of every detail: the basic structure, the windows, the altar, the altar vessels, the selection of every gem and stone. He drove the project forward with his boundless energy and his practical talent for innovation. Every part of his religiosity entered into the undertaking: his love for the saints and the Virgin, his love for the sacraments, his love for the monastery to which he had been brought by his poor parents when he was but nine years old, his love for God for whom only the very best would serve. He felt the hand of Providence in this work done by sinners, for Providence had shown them an abandoned quarry when no marble seemed available, Providence had guided the search for the exact number of huge trees for the roof beams—not one more, not one less!— in a forest where everyone had said that no such trees grew. And in the writings of Dionysius the Areopagite, whom he, in the tradition of his monastery, identified with the abbey's patron saint, he found the Christianized Neoplatonic philosophy about the *anagogicus mos*, the "upward leading" method providing him with the spiritual justification for all this material splendor: by the right means man can learn to move from the contemplation of worldly beauty to the great beauty beyond.

Here builder and building are one—the inscriptions of his name and his verses on light metaphysics that grace the "cathedral" walls tell only part of the story. The great art historian Panofsky characterized Suger as a "centrifugal personality,"[19] one who projected himself onto the world around him and whose self-affirmation is only self-effacement. He is indeed the archetypical medieval man who presents his own self in his work and reveals his character in his action. He shows himself fully as a part of his surroundings and in the forms that his culture permits. In the work that consumed him, every part of his being rightfully expressed itself; he was fitted for it by all that he was, all that he wanted, all that he believed and prayed for. He did not have to struggle to find appropriate forms of self-justification. Those forms were at hand, and he could simply fill them with his activity. And the same virtues, talents, capacities, beliefs, and habits that made him a success in building his church, also made him a success as an abbot, made him a success as churchman working in the secular world outside the cloister wall, and made him a success as a regent of a realm. It was as if his world had fitten him for self-fulfilling action.

As Misch says (though not in these precise words[20]), it is not necessary for a powerful personality, strong in deeds and in words, to have its form-giving center within itself if it can instead derive its coherence from a firmly formed world in which the collective mentality and spirit of a culture are expressed. If these cultural forms are firm, they can offer sustenance and shelter. The world of the Middle Ages had a coherence that enabled an extraordinarily talented man like Suger to combine many diverse elements: Platonism *and* catholic orthodoxy, an almost unbounded soaring of the senses and emotions into the timeless Infinite *and* a tangible cult of relics, childlike confiding piety *and* pleasure in economic well-being, self-conscious trust in his own election *and* deprecating judgment of his worldly success, as well as exceeding humility in turning to his monastic brethren, who are meant to pray for him. Thus he could engage in his energetic activity without being hindered by the intellectual incompatibility of such heterogeneous matter. His medieval world provided habits of mind, ritual, symbolic forms, traditions, and patterns for doing things that permitted him to fuse such diverse activities into a productive whole.

When such men, in such a world, in which the contents of self-consciousness and the consciousness of a whole society were practically the same, wrote autobiography at all they had no need for complex processes of self-exploration or self-orientation. For them, the notion of individuality might even have been an embarrassment.

# 4

# Peter Abelard:
# The Power of the Models

The famous *Story of My Misfortunes* was actually written between 1132 and 1136, most probably 1134, in the form of a letter to an unnamed friend. It may well be the most readable of all medieval autobiographies. But when modern readers, with modern habits of romanticizing a love relation, read the *Story* together with the exchange of letters between Abelard and Heloïse, they frequently also color the autobiographic account wrongly with their reading of the drama of the two lovers. In a "book" of barely eighty pages,[1] Abelard tells a dramatic story about a truly memorable life. A lively style permits the author's personality to come through with immediacy. A life so coherent and compact in its presentation is rare in the history of medieval autobiography.

Though Abelard's life fully deserves attention in its own right, his manner of presentation has also a particular relevance to an essay that asks when Western man came self-consciously to conceive of himself as an individuality. Older historians such as Jacob Burckhardt and Karl Lamprecht suggested that medieval men did not hold this modern form of self-conception. More recently Georg Misch devoted most of a lifetime to discovering the typical modes of self-characterization that medieval men did employ. The survey in the preceding chapter was meant to suggest some of the cultural conditions under which medieval autobiographers presented a view of their selves without resort to the conception of individuality. Abelard's *Story of My Misfortunes* is ideally suited to test these contentions. It is the one medieval autobiography in which a breakthrough to a conscious recognition of individuality might have occurred most readily. The tensions between Abelard and his society often seemed unbearable to him. His character was such that he might have dared to assert his individuality self-consciously had he wanted to do so.

Some modern authors will argue that this breakthrough did occur. A recent study of this autobiography maintains: "But it was Abelard, always fighting to defend and to extend the frontiers between the self and the world, who most fully experienced and most clearly articulated a new sense of personality. At the center of his *Story of Calamities*, at once its author and its subject, stands the autonomous individual who carries his world within, who faces constantly the private decisions and dilemmas, as well as the struggles with his environment, that force him repeatedly to define himself anew, the individual who by choice and action shapes itself."[2] At least two of the justly revered scholars on matters medieval use Abelard in order to attack claims made in behalf of the Renaissance. Abelard was one of the "esprits prégothiques" to whom Johan Huizinga devoted lectures at the Sorbonne in 1930. While Huizinga clearly treats him as a representative of the twelfth century, he obscures this by anachronistically treating him as a parallel to Erasmus. In an earlier long article on "The Problem of the Renaissance," Huizinga lists Abelard first among those medieval figures who make it impossible to claim individualism for the Renaissance, thus arguing explicitly against Lamprecht and Burckhardt.[3] And the doyen among the historians of medieval philosophy, Etienne Gilson, uses both Heloïse and Abelard even more vigorously in his effort to do away with the periodization scheme prevalent in post-Burckhardt scholarship. "Abelard is a fatal obstacle to Burckhardt's thesis, Heloïse ... a far more dangerous one.... their story ... is a kind of touchstone serving to test and evaluate the various definitions of the Middle Ages and the Renaissance which turn up from time to time."[4]

A number of dry arguments about method intersect in these efforts to use Abelard as the cutting edge between two distinct conceptions of periodization. One question is whether periodization is a wise historical procedure at all: Gilson thinks not; Huizinga, though he disliked the artificiality of period concepts, saw no way to avoid them.[5] Yet, periodizing history has a general usefulness; if used in the sense of Max Weber's "ideal types," these dangerous generalizations "Renaissance" and "medieval" can be fruitful heuristic devices that help to bring order to the chaos of historical data. The second question is whether the Renaissance is an invention of professors: Gilson likes to think it is, especially of secularistic-modernistic ones with a grudge against the Middle Ages; Huizinga mainly warns against attributing so much modernity to the Renaissance. These arguments between modernists and medievalists are not going to be settled soon. As an unabashed admirer of

Burckhardt, and one working on the specific issue of individuality, I am inclined to see significance in the change in life-style occurring in fourteenth and fifteenth-century Italy; it warrants a belief that, in many regards, that age is closer to modernity than the medievalists wish to acknowledge. The third question is whether the criteria employed in differentiating two ages are sensible ones. Both Gilson and Huizinga reject the idea that individuality and/or individualism are useful criteria; I contend that changing forms of self-conception are a useful indicator of changing cultural configurations, and that the lack of individuality is a mark of medieval culture and the emergence of self-conscious concerns with individuality suggests the rise of the modern world. We must remember that individuality and individualism should not be equated; saying that someone is recognizable as an individuality is not the same as saying that this person thought of himself as an individuality, or behaved as if he were one, or consciously cultivated individuality as a value to be sought.

The point at question in this chapter is whether Abelard, when trying to justify his life, reflects in his own self-presentation that mode of self-consciousness, that ideal of being a self which is involved in the notion of individuality. Understood in this sense, the analysis of Abelard's autobiography can still be, as Gilson intended it, a "touchstone."

When Abelard wrote the account of his life he was in his middle fifties. By then he had suffered for at least seven years as an abbot over the unruly monks of Saint Gildas de Rhuys in Brittany. Conditions in this monastery seem to have been impossible—at least they seemed so to Abelard, who wished to take the ascetic life seriously. Monks lived with their concubines and children; some apparently had their own property; the surrounding "nobility" viewed the establishment as a perfect hunting ground for their own rapaciousness. Although Abelard had been elected unanimously, several of the monks soon sought to get rid of the troublesome abbot, and Abelard accused them openly of having mixed poison with the wine of his chalice and of seeking any opportunity to kill him. At a meeting of French churchmen at Morigny in 1131 he obtained help from the pope; a papal legate visited St. Gildas and removed some of the ringleaders, but the situation did not improve. Abelard's feelings of insecurity were intensified by his failure to understand the Celtic tongue of the region: "I . . . as it were, see a sword dangling above my head so that I can scarcely be at ease at meals" (p. 77). With the help of a friendly noble he fled.

He must have felt a need to justify his action; it was not the first time
that he had left a monastic establishment. Later utterances of contemporaries make the point. In the eyes of someone like Saint Bernard he
seemed completely unreliable, the "monk without calling," "the abbot
without an office," and Otto of Freising accused him openly of a breach of
monastic discipline.[6] The scandal with Heloïse lay back in the past,
fifteen years or so; but when the nuns over whom she ruled as abbess
had been deprived of their monastery at Argenteuil, Abelard had offered to her community his abandoned abode near Troyes and had
begun to function as spiritual adviser to a nunnery. He might have felt
that such a role needed explanation as well. In 1136 Abelard is known to
have been established once again as a teacher in Paris where such later
luminaries as Alexander III, John of Salisbury, and Peter Lombard were
among his students, and where he continued to elaborate his main
work, the *Theologia Scholarium*, which had brought him the censure of
the Council of Soissons in 1121. That he may have been planning such a
return to teaching when writing his autobiography seems at least plausible.

There were thus enough reasons for writing an *apologia pro vita sua*.
The document bears such marks. Abelard's professed reason for writing, however, is to bring comfort to a friend in distress by permitting
him to compare his affliction with a story of real calamities! Except for
the references to this friend at the beginning and near the end, we hear
next to nothing of him, and the story deals entirely with Abelard's
troubles. That he may have been in the mood to get the past off his
chest, prior to entering a more public life again, and that he may indeed
have been the prime beneficiary of the catharsis that can lie in writing, is
very possible as well. As often happens in autobiography, all these
motives may have been present—they may have interpenetrated and
complemented one another.

The story Abelard told, at any rate, is fairly straightforward and is
largely arranged in chronological sequence. The oldest son of a lesser
aristocratic family in the French-speaking part of Brittany, he was born
not far from the city of Nantes. His father had a great love of learning
and cared diligently for the education of his eldest boy. When the growing Abelard faced a choice of career, he decided not to take on the
customary military role of the oldest heir and went to France instead for
further intellectual training. For a while he attached himself to William
of Champeaux at Paris, receiving training primarily in dialectic, or logic,
from a master in the "Platonic" tradition who had a good reputation
(which even Abelard acknowledged). Pretty soon he created animosities

by constantly engaging the master in arguments. Presuming upon talents beyond the capacity of his years, Abelard set himself up as a master of a school in the vicinity of Paris; he must have been twenty-one or twenty-two years old. His success was great, and he soon made a name for himself as a dialectician. Apparently having overworked himself in the process, he went home to recover—where some of his more eager students followed him. Upon his recovery he returned to Paris and started fresh debates with William, attacking the radical realism to which William held in the discussion of universals. Again Abelard set up a rival school, and the fight over students was on. But just as he seemed to be achieving success over his rival, he returned on family business to Brittany, where both his parents had entered monastic life. A little later, he went to Laon to "learn divinity" from Anselm. He found him to be "devoid of reason," and although he had not yet studied theology, Abelard dared Anselm's students to select any scriptural text so that he, Abelard, might show them what real intelligence could accomplish. They assigned him an obscure prophecy of Ezekiel's and came to his announced lecture hoping to make him look ridiculous. "But those who did attend thought my lecture so good that they praised it highly and constrained me to comment on the text in the same vein as that in which I had lectured" (p. 23). As an archdeacon of the church at Laon, Anselm had a stop put to this effrontery, and Abelard went to the Paris school to assume the mastership William of Champeaux had vacated after being made bishop of Châlons. At Paris Abelard, now in his thirties, built a strong school pursuing the interests he had begun at Laon, applying his great dialectical skill to questions of theology. He became both rich and famous.

In that splendid position, approaching the age of forty, Abelard met the eighteen-year-old Heloïse, the niece of canon Fulbert. "She was a lady of no mean appearance while in literary excellence she was the first" (p. 26). Living as a tutor in Fulbert's house, Abelard carried on his secret love affair with Heloïse until she came to be with child. By stealth he took her to Brittany where she gave birth to a boy, named Astrolabe. Abelard, trying to conciliate the offended uncle, offered to marry Heloïse provided that this were done in secret to prevent damage to his reputation. Heloïse opposed this marriage strenuously, but obeyed her lover. When Fulbert began to divulge the secret of the marriage, Abelard placed Heloïse in the monastery of Argenteuil where she had spent her early childhood. Fulbert thought himself tricked again. Some nights thereafter, Abelard was surprised in his sleep and castrated. Deeply enraged, he sought revenge through the ecclesiastical courts (a fact he does not mention in his story, but which we know through a letter by Fulco of Deuil). Racked with shame, Abelard decided to enter monastic life. "Filled as I was with such remorse, it was, I confess, confusion springing from shame rather than devotion the result of conversion, which drove me to the refuge of monastic cloister" (p. 40). And very much against her own will, he forced Heloïse to take the veil. They did not see each other again for about a decade.

In the abbey of St. Denis, during the years just prior to Suger's election as its abbot, Abelard took up his teaching again, apparently attracting monks as well as laymen and secular clergy. The competition aroused the hostility of masters of other schools, and before long Abelard saw himself charged with holding unorthodox positions on crucial matters of faith. At the Council of Soissons in 1121 he hoped to be able to defend his book on the Trinity, but his opponents succeeded in having the text condemned in advance. He was forced to throw it into the flames with his own hand, and then, instead of being given a chance to explain his orthodoxy, he was simply compelled to recite the Athanasian creed as proof of his conformity. He was returned to the custody of St. Denis, where he had already made himself unpopular by criticizing the lax manners of the monks. That this was not unjustified criticism, we know from a letter in which St. Bernard somewhat later congratulated the new abbot Suger on cleaning up the establishment. Abelard created even more offense by the pursuits of his inquisitive mind: in a passage of the Venerable Bede he detected evidence against the cherished tradition that the patron saint of the abbey was the Denis the Areopagite whom Paul had made bishop of Athens. Abelard might as well have expected the bestowal of a cardinal's hat in gratitude for proving to the Roman curia that St. Peter never came to Rome. Unable to weather the storm he had unleashed, he thought it the wiser course to steal out of St. Denis at night, entrusting himself to the protection of a prominent nobleman, the count of Blois. He was now a renegade monk; but through powerful friends at the royal court and with the conditional consent of Suger, who had just been made abbot, Abelard was eventually freed of his obligations to St. Denis.

In an isolated area near Troyes, Abelard now created a hermitlike retreat for himself around an oratory he named the Paraclete. It did not remain an isolated retreat for long: "When my former students discovered my whereabouts, they began to leave the cities and towns and to flock there to dwell with me in my solitude" (p. 57). A small academic community grew up that Abelard sought to hold to his ascetic life-style. But in fairly short time he began to feel insecure again. "I was dwelling in this place in bodily retirement though my fame was spreading throughout the whole world.... Since my former adversaries could avail nothing by themselves, they stirred up against me certain ... new Apostles in whom the world had great confidence" (p. 63). One of these "new Apostles" certainly was Norbert of Xanten, the founder of the Premonstratensian order; it is not clear whether the other was his companion Hugh of Fosse or the great Bernard himself.[7] For Abelard, these clerics indeed represented new and different forces to deal with; they were spiritual enthusiasts capable of intimidating the secular authorities on whom he had relied. He now felt helpless and despondent. "God is my witness that whenever I learned of a meeting of ecclesiastics, I supposed it was to condemn me. Like one who expected to be struck by lightning, I was straightway overcome with fear that like a heretic or one irreligious I would be dragged before a council ..." (p. 64). In fright, he fled and became abbot of St. Gildas de Rhuys. While there, he learned that Suger had successfully reclaimed Argenteuil for St. Denis and that Heloïse and her nuns were homeless. He offered them the forsaken establishment of the Paraclete, a deed which Pope Innocent II approved in 1131. Abelard took on certain functions as a spiritual adviser to the nuns, but as calumnies began to spread about his activities, he discontinued his visits and continued the struggle with his unruly brethren at St. Gildas.

At this point the autobiography ends. We know of the remaining eight years of Abelard's life that after 1136 he was established at Paris as a teacher once more; as was his steady custom, he revised his former books and also wrote new ones. With Heloïse, who had learned of his self-revealing letter, *The Story of My Calamities*, he exchanged those astounding letters on which their immortality has rested. By 1139–40, the alarm felt by some of the clergy over certain of Abelard's theological formulations had brought St. Bernard into the field against him. Once again Abelard hoped that a formal debate of the issue might prove his orthodoxy; once again, the condemnation of his positions occurred prior to the formal proceedings of the Council of Sens in 1141.[8] As soon as Abelard learned what was going on, he denied the jurisdiction of the council, withdrew, and appealed to the papacy. There Bernard had secured his condemnation before the somewhat sickly Abelard had even reached Cluny on his way to Rome. Innocent II "condemned ... the perverse teachings of Peter ... together with their author, and ... imposed perpetual silence upon him as a heretic."[9] Abelard received the hospitality of the great abbot of Cluny, Peter the Venerable, who also arranged for the final reconciliation with Bernard as well as with the papacy. In one of the priories of Cluny, Abelard died in 1142 at the age of sixty-three.

Most readers of this dramatic document will carry away the impression of having met a conceited genius who brought on himself many of the calamities he bemoans. And our great modern art of dissecting and classifying human psyches will readily deliver such terms as "masochist" and "paranoid." That Abelard may be an appropriate case for an intelligent psychiatric study is not to be denied here. But if one stays with a common-sense analysis of his life, there seem to be reasons enough for a man to exclaim that he feels persecuted. Abelard found his teaching career repeatedly obstructed by people whom he considered inferior and who, in open competition, could not hold on to their students. His marvelous intellect, able to apply a sharply honed logic to any question, was found to lead him into conflict not only with more naïve minds but also with those profound ones who were assuming the defense of a Christian fideism against potentially irresponsible intellectual games. One council forced him to burn his own book without giving him a chance to defend his orthodoxy. When he wrote his autobiography, the condemnation by another manipulated council lay in the future, but did it not justify his fear of being treated as a heretic? Repeatedly he was accused of still adhering to older formulations he had long ago corrected in the light of persuasive criticism; at the Council of Sens, St. Bernard argued with seeming unawareness that Abelard had been rethinking and refining his ideas for the past twenty years.

Though students sought him out wherever he went, even in the monastery and the hermit's isolation, the masters grumbled over this seducer of youth. He undoubtedly considered it an honorable action to offer Fulbert the satisfaction of marrying his niece, though it is hard to see what profit the canon could derive from a marriage kept secret. But Fulbert agreed to the "deal," and Abelard felt betrayed by the steady leaking of the secret and, of course, he was justifiably enraged by the castration. When, as a monk and abbot, he insists upon monastic discipline, he makes himself unpopular, and eventually his life is threatened. When one surveys his life with a modern sense of the inviolable right of any individual to choose the life he deems fitting to himself, one is tempted to say: if a human being was ever justified in complaining that his society did not permit him "to be himself," Abelard had that right. In one passage of his autobiography Abelard comes very close to that sentiment himself. "God knows, I fell into such despair that I was ready to depart from the Christian world and to go to the Saracens, there, by paying whatever tribute was demanded, to live a Christian life among the enemies of Christ" (p. 64).

But—and this is a most weighty but—Abelard did no such thing. He went to Brittany to become an abbot: "as it turned out I fell in with Christians and monks by far more savage, and worse than Saracens" (p. 64). And what may look at first sight like an individual's revolt against a society in the defense of his individuality turns out to be no such thing. It is possible to argue that Abelard did not really reveal what he thought of himself. His personality seemed inscrutable enough to some of his contemporaries. St. Bernard called him *ambiguus*, "appearing in many forms"; someone wrote an epitaph saying "Here lies Petrus Abelard. He alone was able to know who he was [*cui soli patuit scibile quidquid erat*]." He not only went to his grave with much of his self unrevealed, but the self he did reveal does not have traces of self-conscious individuality. Those who would want to assume the burden of proving that apologetic needs falsified the representation of his self would still have to reflect on why he felt it necessary to hide behind the culturally given forms.

As one turns to an analysis, then, of the manner in which Abelard saw fit to present his life, there are three major considerations that forbid an attribution of self-aware individuality to this man and also to his wife: (1) the form he chose for presenting his story; (2) his intensely agonistic character; and (3) the conception of his appropriate role.

The frame in which Abelard chose to present his life bears great similarity to the traditional hagiographic genre. The basic structure of the life is the typical one expected of a good Christian. It fits the standard conversion account. The man to whom God gives a great talent misuses it in search of his own self-glorification. Pride, the greatest of Christian sins, is his sin. Twice God has to "turn him around" and teach him humility. Worldly fame and worldly gain, "the success that always puffs up fools" (p. 25), lead him into the snares of carnal allurements and lechery just at the point when he esteems himself as the sole reigning philosopher. "And while I was labouring under my pride and lechery, God's grace provided a cure for each, though I willed it not" (p. 25).

However outraged his human sense of dignity was by castration, however strongly he may have sought revenge for such an outrage, he ultimately came to accept his punishment as divine and just. "I fell to thinking ... how by a just judgment of God I had been afflicted in that part of my body by which I had sinned; how just was the betrayal by which he whom I had first betrayed paid me back" (p. 39). The letters to Heloïse, written after the autobiographic one, heavily underscore the sentiments of such passages. Abelard does not describe this as a sudden conversion, immediately effective. He admits that he initially joined a monastery because it seemed the best refuge for hiding his shame; the real commitment to monastic life grew only subsequently. The first attempt by God to turn him around was to be followed by a second divine blow "for my pride which my scholarship especially nursed in me in accordance with the saying of St. Paul 'Knowledge puffs up.' This was accomplished by humiliating me through the burning of the book which was my special glory" (p. 25). Again the lesson may have sunk in only gradually; Abelard's account of the proceedings at Soissons, thirteen years after the events, still bristles with indignation. He admits that at the time he quarreled with his divine judge. "Oh God, who judges equity, with what bitterness of soul and anguish of mind I, in my madness, I reproached you and in anger accused You ... Good Jesus, where were you?" (p. 52). But the basic lesson Abelard drew from the double experience was that he should not be a philosopher of the world so much as of God. He died in the firm belief that he had placed the talent God had given him in the gift of his mind at the service of God's teaching. He would not have wished to become a philosopher if that had meant contradicting Paul; he would not have wished to be another Aristotle if that meant parting from Christ.

The very mode of existence to which Abelard turned after these "conversions" was one that expressed for his world the desire to lead the truly Christian life. The figure of the monk was still the model of the devoted Christian. In that world conversion meant, for the most part, conversion from a secular to a monastic life. Abelard the rich teacher of the *jeunesse dorée* was to become the teacher of the poor, the strict ascetic inveighing against the loose morality of St. Denis, the hermit of the Paraclete, the spiritual adviser of a nunnery, and the reform-minded abbot of a reform-defying semibarbaric monastery. True, there was the very serious matter of having fled from St. Denis without permission, but Abelard himself presents this (in words attributed to the royal seneschal Stephen, who was seeking the release from Suger) as the consequence of the impossibility of reconciliation between a true ascetic and monks refusing to be monks.[10]

The flight from St. Gildas later on is justified by the repeated attempts

on his life; unwillingness to incur martyrdom does not imply unwillingness to be a strict monk. Nor does Abelard present himself as a monk
without sin, though he tried to remain virtuous. "Once a monk, Abelard
went the whole way. He was more a monk than any other monk. He
was a monk in the only manner he could do anything—without compromise, without measure, with the fierce energy of a will struggling
against despair."[11] Perhaps Gilson is too laudatory in view of Abelard's
lapses, but his description fits the character of the man. The letters to
Heloïse do sound like those of someone who has been "converted."
And the autobiography has a form to suit that image. A Benedictine will
have to come to the point where God's will has replaced self-will.
Abelard concludes his account with just such a reflection.

> in all things we are right in saying to Him: "Thy will be
> done." What great consolation those who love God
> have ... "We know that for those who love God all things
> work together unto good." The wisest of men carefully noted
> that ... "Whatsoever shall befall the just man, it shall not
> make him sad." From this he shows that they clearly depart
> from righteousness who are wroth at some hardship which
> they have to bear, knowing full well that it comes upon them
> by divine dispensation. These follow their own will, not that
> of God, and through their secret desires they range them-
> selves against the import of the words: "Thy will be done,"
> putting their own before the will of God. [Pp. 79–80]

In the spirit of these words which he wrote some eight years
before his death, his conduct upon learning of the papal condemnation, following the Council of Sens, was one of abject obedience;
even his great antagonist St. Bernard was reconciled with him. More
telling still is the testimony of Peter the Venerable in a letter to
Heloïse announcing Abelard's death to her.[12] He praises Abelard
as the good monk, humble in attitude and bearing, not unworthy
to be compared to saints like Germain, Martin, and Gregory the
Great. There was nothing obligatory about making such comparisons. They may suggest, at least, that some of the best among Abelard's
contemporaries accepted him as a devoted monk and that the frame of
the *typical* devoted Christian life into which he fitted the account of
himself was indeed fitting.

A second line of argument showing that Abelard had no sense of
individuality concerns his prevailing sense of honor. Perhaps the argument cannot furnish a decisive proof of the contention that he was

devoid of a sense of individuality, but it, at least, makes it implausible that he possessed it. On whatever page one may open Abelard's account, it will be clear that humble acceptance of God's will is not necessarily accompanied by humility toward his fellow men. He remained a proud man with a great sensitivity to questions of reputation and disgrace, which he reconciled in his own mind with his humility before God.

Abelard lived in a nonegalitarian world even if its basic Christianity had egalitarian elements. His society was governed by concern for rank, class, status, at times even caste, and the corollary facts of privilege, status consciousness, loyalty to family, and loyal adherence to the style of life befitting one's class or rank. The degree to which the emblems of status adhered to a man, and the extent to which they were formative agencies in his personal life, also suggest their strength as obstacles to the formation of individuality.

Abelard's own words intimate the power of his social background in shaping his person and personal life-style. He was the oldest son of a Breton nobleman who was himself imbued with a love of letters before he girded the soldier's belt, and who imparted this love to his favorite son. When Abelard had to make a choice between learning and his hereditary status and obligation, he relinquished to his brother the inheritance and the privileges of a first-born son. "I renounced the field of Mars to be brought up at the knee of Minerva" (p. 12). But he carried many traits peculiar to the court of Mars into the realm of Minerva. Around 1100 A.D. there did not yet exist the more firmly fixed forms in which the scholar and intellectual later could pursue an academic lifestyle. Before the universities had become established, scholarly work was carried on in monasteries or at the cathedral schools. The phenomenon of numbers of students in search of learning, who were not closely tied to monastery and cathedral school, the movement out of which the universities developed, was more the *result* of the activities of such men as Abelard than a factor in forming his behavior. His new "profession" thus did not furnish him with prepressed forms of conduct and self-conception into which he could simply fit himself.

The change from Mars to Minerva meant for Abelard an exchange of weapons: "the equipment of dialectic," the armor of logic, replaced the lance and sword. One form of contest gave way to another: "and [I] chose the contests of disputation above the trophies of warfare" (p. 12). The transformed knight sets out in search of adventure: "practising logic I wandered about the various provinces ... like the peripatetics" in quest of intellectual tournaments. The first lance was broken with William of Champeaux at Paris; when Abelard thought himself the victor, he set up his own school to compete, and he applied the rules of warfare: maneuver for positions of strength, then seek the contest and best the opponent, preferably to chase him out of the field; see that you do not get vanquished yourself, and then reap the applause of the students. Realizing that the first school at Melun lay too far out of town, at the first chance, he transferred it to the town of Corbeil, nearer to the city of Paris, so as to have more occasions for frequent disputation. Abelard describes his second campaign against William, which he began after his return from Brittany:

> But because he [i. e., William of Champeaux] . . . had put a rival in my former chair, I pitched camp for my school outside the city on Mount St. Geneviève, that I might, so to speak, lay siege to him who held my place. When my master heard of this, immediately and with no sense of propriety, he returned to the city and brought what students he had and his community back to his former monastery as if to raise the siege of his soldier whom he had abandoned. . . . The disputes which followed the return of my master to the city between my students and him and his students and the outcome which fortune gave to my students and to me among them, facts have long since told you. But to speak with due moderation, let me boldly repeat those words of Ajax: "If you ask the result of this contest, I was not worsted by it." [Pp. 19–20]

Abelard seeks out masters less to learn from them than to tilt dialectical lances with them. He appears in the school of Anselm of Laon, where he might have learned something he knew nothing about: explication of the Scriptures. Abelard looks the scene over, decides that the old man is a mere babbler; then he issues a challenge: assign me any text, I'll cope with it. To the warning that he may be untrained for this, he answers "indignantly . . . that it was not my custom to advance through practice but rather through intelligence" (*ingenium*= innate nature) (p. 23). His intelligence was an exceedingly sharp weapon, and he used it as one. Abelard approached the two Councils of Soissons and of Sens[13] as intellectual tournaments; the Council at Sens he consciously seems to have designed as a disputation with Bernard. Each time Abelard hoped that he could show in open contest that his attackers were wrong. Each time the rules were changed; no opponent entered the arena, and the tournament was simply turned into an occasion for orthodoxy to declare him out of bounds.

Abelard had the mentality of the aristocratic fighter. Despite depressions of shame and impotence, he always rallied and fought his battles again. He never surrendered, and fully accepted that intellectual struggle for a fuller understanding of the secrets of faith, even if only by the analogies of human reason, the task for which God had equipped him so well. All his life Abelard remained sensitive to attacks on his honor and eager to preserve a good name. He could see nothing un-Christian in that transference of an arch-aristocratic habit. Quite the contrary: he defended it with theological arguments. When he decided to serve as spiritual adviser to Heloïse's nuns, who had moved to the Paraclete, he felt deeply offended by suspicions that sexual desire drew him to that position: "and I . . . am tortured more by the loss of my reputation than I was from the mutilation of my body" (p. 71). He then draws a justification for such concern from an Augustinian text: "As it is written: 'Better is a good name than great riches.' And St. Augustine reminds us in a sermon on the Life and Morals of Clerics: 'The man who, relying on his own conscience, neglects his reputation is cruel.' And just above he says: 'We take forethought . . . for what is honorable, not only before God, but also in the sight of men. For ourselves our conscience suffices, for your sake our reputation should not be sullied but should exercise an influence among you. . . . There are two things, conscience and reputation; conscience for yourself, reputation for your neighbor'" (p. 71). That argument could have served him all his life, affording a unification of potentially discordant attitudes.

Whatever personal factors may have accounted for his deep-seated concern with honor, such a concern was also an expression of a life-style built upon the central importance of the *agon*, the contest with others— the ultimate measure of the quality of a person and his work. It is somehow very difficult to envisage Abelard, like Thomas Aquinas or Bonaventura later, quietly sitting in a cell, reasoning out his argument. He needed the give and take of discussion; and his intellectual work profited because he kept refining his arguments as he had to contend with objections. He always stated that he would be willing to discard any of his opinions that failed to stand the test of an opponent's objections. Although dialectics then so often meant only logic, it must have had a more profound meaning for Abelard.

For such an eminently agonistic creature as Abelard, individuality would have been a dilemma. It was important to him to prove himself "the better and the best"; *that* he could only do in a contest with peers. Any claim of incomparable uniqueness would have placed him *hors de combat*. Abelard's constant claim in the autobiography is that he bested others at the same task, that he was better as a dialectician, better as a monk. He steadily attributed the opposition he aroused to envy of his superiority and not to a willful departure from established norms, or innovating practices whereby he would have placed himself outside of his culture. It is one thing to see that Abelard made it difficult for others with his aggressiveness, and that they in turn made it often painfully difficult for him to live; it is quite another thing to turn Abelard into one of those unique men who by his very being and work could not fit into the society in which he lived.

It is tempting to see Abelard's problems as the result of his love affair, involving indecorous behavior not acceptable to his contemporaries. But *that* was never the experience to which Abelard himself attributed his calamities! From his perspective, the misfortunes were clearly tied to his excellence as a thinker and teacher, which aroused the persecuting envy of those whom he bested. His troubles, with the councils that condemned him and with the "new apostles," were, in his view, due to the machinations of envious rivals. He saw nothing extraordinary in his intellectual activity. Nowhere does he create the self-conscious impression of having engaged in an activity that was bound to create a conflict with the established order. The image of the near-Enlightenment rationalist who could not but clash with the narrow fideism of St. Bernard is a creation of modern historians; it was not a part of his self-image.[14] To be sure, Abelard (mostly in his ethics, perhaps) and Gilbert de la Porrée, for instance, went further in their rationalism than St. Bernard thought healthy for the faith, and it would not be surprising had Abelard thought of Bernard as one of the blind-leading-the-blind who was unwilling to see the benefits of that wondrous divine gift, human reason. But the application of reasoning to matters of faith was not a unique, extraordinary activity whereby Abelard placed himself inevitably in contradiction to his culture and time.[15] Abelard may have been conscious and proud of innovation in philosophic argument. But he did not derive from his philosophic activity a sense of uniqueness, of being exceptional, of being especially daring—or a sense of the potential collision course with a world of faith. Nothing contradicts the conclusion that he thought of himself increasingly as a Christian Philosopher.

The term Christian Philospher leads to the third and the weightiest of the arguments as to the unlikelihood that either Abelard or Heloïse had any sense of individuality. Abelard and Heloïse lived their lives by the guidance of models. They did not write a script to fit their own lives and personalities; they strove hard to fit their lives and personalities into scripts already written. As might be expected: this trait comes to the fore most strongly in times of crisis, when they were faced by the choice of vital alternatives. One may then speak of their "role-playing," provided that this implies neither a self-conscious pretense nor a desire to hide a reality from a hostile world.[16]

One such crisis was the decision to marry. A complicated set of reasons went into this decision; whether or not the deepest human level of this love story will ever be clearly intelligible may well be doubtful. Abelard was almost forty years old when, according to his account, he decided to seduce the eighteen-year-old Heloïse—and then fell in love with her. After the boy Astrolabe was born, and when it became obvious that Abelard needed a reconciliation with his conscience ("After a while I ... blamed myself for the deceit which love had wrought" [p. 31]) and a reconciliation with the furious uncle, Abelard made the offer of a secret marriage to Fulbert. He must have understood that by keeping it a secret Fulbert's concern for his own reputation as guardian of a ward could not be satisfied for long. Heloïse later warned Abelard on the same point. But Abelard's overriding objective was that his own reputation should suffer no injury. When he returned to Heloïse with the decision to marry her, it was she who argued the issue of the reputation even more forcefully: it would be impossible to be a great philosopher and a married man. The fact that he was a clerk and a canon of the Church only made her surer.[17] She put the issue to Abelard very clearly: the question was one of self-conception, not of legality in any sense, or of appearance in the eyes of the world. A philosopher can be great only if nothing else in the world can claim him. Abelard was born to be a great philosopher, created for all mankind, not for a single woman. Keeping the marriage a secret would not help; the real problem was that as a married man she could claim him and involve him in all the distractions of a household. How could one combine philosophy and the noise of servants or squealing babies? Abelard had already neglected his teaching when he fell in love with her, as he himself makes very clear.

Heloïse makes a few statements in her own language but then she buttresses these with a long list of authorities. The Apostle, that is, St. Paul, had declared it the higher glory not to marry; so had St. Augustine, St. Jerome, Elias, and Josephus. More extensive still is Heloïse's list of the great models. Socrates, haunted by his Xantippe, is the great warning to all subsequent philosophers. Cicero and Seneca taught the virtue of independence. The monks and St. Jerome are the models who turned love of wisdom into devoted lives. The truly great philosopher lives the life he teaches. The immense dignity of the figure of the true philosopher, the only role appropriate for Abelard, was for Heloïse the insurmountable obstacle to the marriage. For herself she preferred the role of the great *amica*, the true friend, to that of the wife. With a knowledge of the classics, so exceedingly rare in a twelfth-century woman, Heloïse drew her model of the disinterested love of friendship from Cicero's *De amicitia*. Pure love was for her the disinterested love of the *amica* who thus could in no way diminish the glory of the loved man. That was still the position she held when she later resumed her exchange of letters with him.

The fact that Abelard insisted on the secrecy of the marriage for the protection of his reputation shows that he basically shared Heloïse's opinion. But he had given his word to Fulbert and, above all, he wanted Heloïse for himself. As he told her later (*Epistle* 5), without the marriage tie she would have been free to give her heart to another. Thus, wanting the best of both worlds, he trusted in the possibility of secrecy and forced Heloïse to marry him. The secret, of course, became known and the tragedy took its course. He fled into the monastic world and he forced Heloïse to take the veil, the step to which she never became reconciled, as her subsequent letters show.

It is striking that Abelard does not report the taking of this step—for Heloïse the most fateful step—by giving us her own words or her own reasoning. In answer to some who were present at the consecration scene, wanting to dissuade the young woman from changing her life so radically, Heloïse broke into tears and sobs and then quoted the speech from Lucan's *Pharsalia* in which Cornelia, Pompey's wife, imposes a punishment on herself for having ruined the great man's career by her marriage. " 'Great husband, undeserving of my bed! What right had I to bow so lofty a head? Why, impious female, did I marry thee to cause thy hurt? Accept the penalty that of my own free will I'll undergo . . .' And while uttering these words she hastened to the alter and straightway took from it the veil blessed by the bishop and bound herself in the presence of all to the religious life" (p. 40). Her own familiarity with another literary model provided the appropriate script and the very words for the most crucial moment of her life.

This habit of identifying the personal experience with that of great precursors appears at numerous places in the autobiography. After his castration it was to be expected that Abelard would at times look at the parallel case of Origen, the great intellectual who sought to fuse philosophy and theology, and in the service of such an ideal had mutilated himself (p. 71). When Abelard needed models of persecution, he readily resorted to comparisons with St. Anthony (p. 52), with Athanasius ("and to compare a flea to a lion and an ant to an elephant, my rivals persecuted me with no less venom than did the heretics hound Athanasius" [p. 64]), with St. Benedict struggling against his recalcitrant monks ("How often they tried to poison me as happened in the case of St. Benedict. The same reason which led so great a Father to leave his perverse sons openly encouraged me after his example to do the same" [p. 76])—even with the Apostle and Jesus himself (pp. 78–79). For his dominant model, Abelard fixed his sight on St. Jerome, the intellectual church father with whom he shared so much more than with St. Augustine. Jerome, supplemented in this case by Plato, the Pythagoreans, and Elisha, gave Abelard the inner justification for his teaching activities in the wilderness of the Paraclete. Jerome provided the parallel for his flight to St. Gildas: "And so the envy of the French drove me to the West as that of the Romans drove Jerome to the East" (p. 65). Especially during the crisis created by his wish to serve as spiritual adviser to Heloïse's monastic establishment at the Paraclete, Abelard sought comfort in the very same relation that Jerome had cultivated with St. Paula and other noble Roman ladies devoted to the ascetic life (pp. 70 ff.).

A detailed analysis of the correspondence between Heloïse and Abelard tends to corroborate their strong dependence on such models. Such dependence should not be written off as a literary convention; if it were, its prevalence would still have to be explained. Such dependence on role models is not found in the autobiographies of authors who seek to understand themselves as an individuality. The more a human being possesses a sense of ineffable individuality, the more he will, in moments of critical decision, ask himself: what decision would be truly an expression of my special nature? and the less will he find comfort in models. The objective to be yourself, in your own peculiar terms, demands that critical decisions be made in terms of inner needs and inner "laws." Such a self-consciousness seems to be missing both in Abelard and in Heloïse, his pupil.

For the modern reader, with his much more developed sense of individuality, a large part of the great drama of these two lovers lies in the fact that neither of these seemingly self-willed and striking human beings could find forms truly expressive of their experience but instead had to bend this experience to fit the prevailing forms of their day. Neither he nor she could perceive how to unite in one life the great model conception of the Christian philosopher and their deeply felt love. What was to be the place of the erotic experience in his life? Two centuries later, Dante had his own wife *and* described the ideal of love in Beatrice; Petrarch sang of the idealized eros in his love for the Laura he never touched *and* had two children by a peasant woman to whom he simply turned with his sexual need. Abelard may have wished to combine it all in his relation with Heloïse *and* remain in some way faithful to the ideal of the devoted philosopher. Heloïse may have seen the ideal for herself in the figure of the "disinterested *amica.*" It did not work. Like all of us, Abelard also strove for a unified interpretation of himself. This meant that he had to reinterpret the love affair to make it fit his self-image. Though at the time of the love affair, he had written love poetry for which he was famous, in retrospect, as autobiographer, he has come to perceive the early phase of his love as a simple expression of lust. In his prideful conceit he had set out to seduce Heloïse to probe all the delights of lust. Now he censures himself for having forced her into sexual relations by the threat of beatings—and once even in the refectory of the monastery where he had hidden her. From the later vantage point he now sees that he received a fitting punishment for the sin of lust. God thus rescued him for his true work. When, upon resuming contact in the correspondence, Heloïse reveals that she has not followed him in this interpretation of the love affair, Abelard is profoundly shocked and then uses all his powers of persuasion to have her acquiesce in the view of the providential order of their lives which he had gained by then. She makes it plain that her role as abbess has not displaced her old love for him; but rather than argue she lapses into silence on the matter, and the subsequent letters turn into a discussion of monastic history. In the attempt to integrate his love experience into the course of a life now seen as a whole, Abelard assigns to love in its early phase the role of lust so that it can function properly as a factor in the divinely imposed conversion; he wishes to see the marriage as a spiritually transformed union in which two struggling human souls support each other in their devout attempts to find the way to God by serving as abbess and abbot. For Abelard the role as Christian Philosopher has won out.

When one thus views the form of the autobiography, the prevalence of status features clinging to the knight as well as the monk, and finally the need to lean on models in critical issues of self-perception, it is difficult to think of Abelard either as an example of the autonomous, self-defining personality, or as an individuality, or as an earlier version of the "Renaissance man." In almost all model conceptions of life there is always room within the basic frame and matrix for strongly idiosyncratic elements. And so with Abelard. He had a remarkable love affair, he had an arresting fate, and he stands in his age as a striking figure. He was an extraordinary thinker: he reconstructed much of Aristotelian logic before most of the *Organon* was recovered; he worked out a daring ethical theory about the primacy of intention; and he very directly pointed the way to the scholasticism that within one century became one of the great glories of medieval Catholicism. But he stood in his age and not outside it. Despite all the tensions with his society, in the essential features of his self-conception and self-portrayal he remained within the forms his culture provided. Despite his pained outcry that he might remove himself from that world, he did not break through its confines. One of the magnificent aspects of medieval Catholicism was the very coexistence of Abelard and Bernard, Francis and Thomas Aquinas, Heloïse and Mechthild of Magdeburg. But such diversity was held together by a very strong matrix outside of which medieval man neither would nor could live his life.

If one looks at the Middle Ages in terms of the self-conceptions men revealed in their autobiographic accounts, several unifying features stand out. In Saint Augustine's *Confessions* this age received a grand model for conceiving of the typical Christian experience. But it is—at first glance—a startling fact that as a model this book served that age so little. There were a few attempts to imitate it, but they were not especially successful. None achieved the inner unity of the conception which Augustine imposed on his work. But then none of them rested on Augustine's experience of a conversion from a highly developed intellectual pagan world to a Christian life, since almost all medieval men writing autobiography were born into a firmly established Christian world. For their "conversion" experience the hagiographic form, especially of monk's lives, was the more fitting model. Then too, they were born into a social world differing fundamentally from Augustine's. It was a multilayered society that ultimately was to express itself in the notion of a more corporatively construed whole. It possessed many diverse lifestyles, appropriate to status and social function, which might touch and influence one another but were not easy to merge. In that context someone who was and remained a monk could write a more unified life than one who changed from one status group to another or sought to combine them. In essence these life-styles had their model conception, and men lived lives appropriate to the status to which they belonged. Or, as the Germans can say this: *es wurde standesgemäss gelebt.* On the one hand, it seems altogether plausible that the differentiation of society expressed in this multilayeredness and corporative structure, especially when put in conjunction with other differentiating forces such as growing language and "national" patterns, was a factor in preparing that ever greater differentiation in which each individual existence distinguishes itself from the whole. On the other hand, it is striking how much power such model conceptions as the ideal monk, the true knight, etc., held over the self-consciousness of men within each status group. The basic view of the world and of life demanded by the Christian conception of the human drama seemed impenetrable.

In that world, though there were conditions that later might feed a sense of individuality, no man who sought to express his self did so self-consciously as an individuality. Only an ahistoricist point of view can criticize that world for such a "failure." Each age carries the standards for its own happiness and greatness within itself. And it is memorable, of course, that around 1800, at the very time when the ideal of individuality asserted itself strongly, there were many sensitive Europeans who looked back longingly to an age when men rested more securely within the confines of their cultural context and did not have to assume the awesome task of having to define their own individuality.

# 5
# Petrarch:
# The Introspective Turn

There came a time when man's self-conception rested less securely on a dominant view of the world and of life than it had, on the whole, during the Middle Ages. The experiences which Petrarch (1304–74) turned into a vision of his personality announced changing conditions and changing self-definitions. Despite vital continuities between the medieval and early modern world, the accents on important aspects of life were beginning to fall differently. Subtle changes in men's attitudes and in the conditions of their existence become noticeable. When such changes appear to be related to a later culture pattern, the temptation is strong to see evidences of modernism in a changing context that, as a whole, cannot be given such a label. A tug-of-war over Petrarch's "modernity" is bound to look silly; but the fascinating complexity of his life, his work, and his personality is likely to categorize him thus— especially in an essay tracing the emergence of a modern phenomenon.

As an Italian, writing both in Ciceronian Latin and in the Tuscan vernacular that Dante had raised to the status of a high literary language, Petrarch was affected by cultural changes peculiar to his "country." The phase of the development for which Petrarch is here being claimed is only later part of a general European development. Initially the Renaissance is an Italian phenomenon. Jacob Burckhardt expressed that very clearly when he entitled his book *The Civilization of the Renaissance in Italy.*[1] By calling this Italian Renaissance "our nearest mother," he suggested that our lineage as moderns was formed in other historical phases as well. He also knew that he was trying to characterize a culture pattern peculiar to a cultural elite. On a larger scale, the formative forces released by that development became "sociologically productive" only later on, fully so only during the Enlightenment.[2] Despite the limitations Burckhardt placed on his argument, his famous thesis has particular value for the present investigation because his view of the Renaissance is predicated on an idea of the emergence of a specific personality type. Roughly schematized, the underlying idea is that the insecurities and the instability peculiar to many lives in northern and central Italy during the fourteenth and fifteenth centuries necessitated a stronger reliance on one's own resources. Many a human being thus had to become what Burckhardt calls *"eine auf sich selbstgestellte Persönlichkeit,"* a personality that had to stand on its own and rely on its own inner and outer resources.[3] An "objective" view of the surrounding realities becomes forced upon the personality; a sober statistical inventory of controllable resources helps one to cope more than the best formula for what "should" be or how a man "ought" to act. In this sense there occurs a "discovery of the world and of man" leading to insights and attitudes that differ substantially from the medieval human cosmos. For some, the great repertory of answers to human problems which had worked for men of the older culture *may* now no longer be functional. The less the old institutions and customs sustain life, the less the old morality and convictions about the world contain answers and guidelines, the less the old models are applicable—the more these men are thrown upon their own devices for understanding and maintaining themselves.

In such circumstances personality development can move in several quite diverse directions. A man may adhere, as much as he can without difficulty, to the traditional life-style; most Italians, and in most essential respects, presumably did just that. Or it may happen that a man "discovers" himself in his peculiarity: as the "expert," perhaps, whose whole being only "lives" in politics, as was the case with a Machiavelli. Or a man may come to define himself by the ideal that is the very opposite to that of the expert: as *l'uomo universale*, the type of man captivated by the vision of the full human potential compressed into one lifetime (Alberti, Leonardo de Vinci).[4] Still another man may seek to coordinate the diversity of human realities and thus, in contrast to subordinating all in a hierarchical order of priorities, he will develop himself as a "harmonious personality" (for Burckhardt, Lorenzo de Medici, Pico della Mirandola, and Aeneas Sylvius Piccolomini, the later Pope Pius II were examples). Other aspects of self-definition cut into and/or across such categories. A man may give himself to an objective task that imposes limits upon his willfulness, or, by his own choice, he may impose objective norms upon himself and thus become an "autonomous" individual. Or again, he may instead surrender himself to his whims and willfulness (what Burckhardt calls *Willkür*) and thus "capsize" in pure "subjectivism," as did several of the humanists and tyrants of the age.

The reviving interest in classical antiquity can assist as well as thwart such personality developments. The alternative models antiquity provides may serve as support to men who need to lean on something until they can stand on their own; insofar as there is a consonance of some sort between the genuine needs of Renaissance men and the ancient models, these can be beneficial supports. Where the reliance on the ancient model thwarts a self-development which ought to occur according to the inner demands of the personality, the ancients lead men astray. Burckhardt thus assigns to the "Renaissance" as such only a supplementary role in the total process which slowly gave rise to the characteristically "modern" European personality.

Burckhardt expressed the most crucial mark of this personality in a difficult notion: *der Mensch wird geistiges Individuum und erkennt sich als solches;* that is to say, man recognizes himself as an individual being whose coherence lies in the dimensions of his mind or spirit. With growing self-consciousness man is aware that his distinctive quality as an individual personality rests on the unified conception he has of himself. He is not a coherence simply because the world around makes him so; he is a unity only insofar as he himself makes a coherent personality out of his individual experience of an objective world. It thus is important for a man to understand that his knowledge of himself is conditioned by his very own circumstances, that he himself creates a mental coherence of his experience of the world, and that in thought and action he gives expression to his unified view of experience.

As a result, man may more self-consciously pursue a life-style to suit the personality he cultivates. Such a self-conscious person will not find the self, the state, or the society, as finished givens of nature; he will perceive these as human creations, as works of art, or as artifices (this is what Burckhardt means by speaking of the state as *Kunstwerk,* an artifice like a clock). Society conceived as an artifice (*Gesellschaft*) replaces the notion of society as an organically grown community (*Gemeinschaft*). The notion of a society composed of willful individuals responds better to the new individual consciousness than the notion of a traditional community in which the individual finds, ready-made, his organic function. A more widespread fascination with things in their individual specificity rather than in their broad generality becomes the by-product. Burckhardt juxtaposes this concern with individual quality (by using the neuter form of *das Individuelle,* a much more comprehensive term than the individual human being) to a concern with generality (*das Allgemeine, irgendeine Form des Allgemeinen*). But men's pursuit of the distinctive marks of all individual existence does not necessarily lead to a full preoccupation with man as an individuality. And yet, the growth of the notion of individuality is predicated on man's self-conscious awareness as a "mental or spiritual" individuum (*geistiges Individuum*). In that notion lies the fundamental significance of Burckhardt's "theory" for the story traced here.

In Petrarch's life and personality some of the strains emerge that are dominant in the web of the Renaissance a century later. Yet there are features of his personality that make him much less the herald of a coming age. The cultural mutations begin, and the shifting tensions fashion him into an interesting figure in the study of changing self-perceptions. Though Petrarch left us no genuine autobiography, a fuller study than can be undertaken here might show how all his writings taken together are autobiographic in a much more profound sense than the work of Dante and others before him. His writings tend to be "emanations of personality."[5] Petrarch cultivated literary forms, above all the personal letter, which are especially suitable to self-revelation. He most self-consciously rewrote, amended, and edited his letters with a remarkable concern for the manner in which he might represent himself.[6] He could select a momentary experience such as the ascent of Mt. Ventoux and gradually turn it into a piece of writing elegantly mixing the immediate experience with the reading of a meaningful Augustinian passage, and with symbolic interpretations of the diverse observations of the man while climbing that become as a whole a miniature portrayal of life. Such habits do not make it easy to build a historical reconstruction of his life. In his hands the literary form of the dialogue became once again a skillfully employed medium for self-revelation. And the special kind of relationship existing between a poet's experience and his lyrical poetry is particularly evident in Petrarch's Italian verse.

The Petrarchan document most immediately interesting to this study of autobiography is the *Secretum*. It is neither a life story nor an explicit interpretation of life's course. But it is extraordinarily interesting in revealing the processes whereby a man, at a crucial moment in his life, tries to catch hold of himself as he seeks to determine his future path. Petrarch wrote most of it between October 1342 and March 1343, and, if modern scholarship is correct, he inserted some passages as late as the early fifties.[7] In 1342 Petrarch was not yet forty years old, but his lyric poetry had made him a figure of great renown. Born in exile, a sign of insecurity so typical of many Renaissance lives affected by the unstable politics of their city-states, he had studied law at Montpellier and

Bologna and then had entered the services of Cardinal Giovanni Co-
lonna as a minor cleric. When not on one of his frequent travels, Petrarch
lived in Avignon, then the seat of the papacy and the domicile of the
Laura he immortalized after having fallen in love with her on April 6,
1327, when he first saw her in the church of St. Clare. Disliking the
hectic life of Avignon, he acquired in the late thirties a modest country
house in Vaucluse where he hoped to find the peace and freedom for
thinking, studying, and writing. His immediate family consisted only of
brother Gherardo, to whom he was particularly close, and whose wish
to enter a strict Carthusian monastery was to play an important role in
the "crisis" out of which the Secretum grew. Around 1337, an illegitimate
son had been born to Petrarch by an unknown mother; later in 1343, i.e.,
shortly after writing the bulk of the Secretum, his long-beloved daughter
Francesca was born to him under similar circumstances. Throughout his
twenties and thirties Petrarch had begun to cultivate the friendships,
often bearing the mark of Cicero's amicitia, which continued to be so
important to him until the end.

The most grandiose experience of Petrarch's life occurred on April 8,
1341, in the Senatorial Palace on Rome's Capitoline Hill. There, decked
out in the fine robe of his sponsor, King Roberto of Naples, Petrarch was
crowned poet laureate in the name of that anachronism, the Senate and
the Roman People, which had last bestowed such favors on the poet
Statius in the first century A.D. In a splendid ceremony the laurel crown
was given to him with seven other awards that might turn anybody's
head: he was declared to be magnum poetam et historicum, designated a
magister, accredited as professor of poetic art and history; he had won
the right to crown other poets, obtained Roman citizenship, and received formal approval of his writings, present and future![8] A formal
procession then wound its way to the still modest St. Peter's where
Petrarch deposited his crown on the altar. On the return home to the
Vaucluse, this "most famous private citizen then living" stayed for a
while near Parma (where he thought he had a chance for an important
benefice) and wrote major sections of his great epic, Africa.

When Petrarch found himself again in his old surroundings in the
Provence in the summer of 1342, all these diverse experiences conspired
to produce an intense personal crisis. His soul was sick; his many cares
were in deep conflict with one another, and the turmoil left him restless.
So he sought a cure by confiding his troubled state to the pages of De
secreto conflictu curarum mearum, the Secret Conflict of My Cares. "That
this discourse, so intimate and deep, might not be lost, I have set it

down in writing and made this book; not that I wish to class it with my other works, or desire from it any credit. My thoughts aim higher. What I desire is that I may be able by reading to renew as often as I wish the pleasure I felt from the discourse itself. So, little Book, I bid you flee the haunts of men and be content to stay with me, true to the title I have given you of 'My Secret': and when I would think upon deep matters, all that you keep in remembrance that was spoken in secret you in secret will tell to me over again."[9]

This extraordinarily personal document consists of three dialogues between "St. Augustine" and Petrarch while the allegorical figure of Truth rests in the corner of the room as the guarantor of an unrelenting dedication to veracity. As "Augustine" is more a Petrarcan transformation of the historical Augustine than the words of an unretouched saint speaking in his own terms, Petrarch created a scene in which Petrarch talks to Petrarch about Petrarch with the announced intention to be as honest with himself as possible. The choice of the dialogue form is of intrinsic significance in itself. Petrarch claims to model it upon Cicero's *De amicitia*: "my dear Master learned this mode himself from Plato" (p. 6). Actually Petrarch does not follow the Aristotelian-Ciceronian type of dialogue in which the use of interlocutors often serves only as a device for presenting positions already worked out. Instead he adopts the spirit of the Platonic dialogue in which the give and take of question and answer follows the *logos* in an unfolding process of thinking aloud. Petrarch uses this dialogue for self-discovery, self-testing, and self-clarification. The form is thus ingeniously adapted to a perspectivistic procedure of introspection in which a man tries to step outside of himself, hoping that contrasting viewpoints may illuminate what, without a change of position, remains unclear.[10] The perspectivism goes further than the presence of merely two speakers might suggest, for neither one hesitates to evoke images of the Petrarch that was, the Petrarch that might have been, and the Petrarch that might be. Despite contradictions that will emerge sufficiently during the course of analysis, the choice of such a perspectivistic procedure suggests something most interesting: the diminishing importance of guiding models. Petrarch's problem is to understand Petrarch; he may subsequently judge himself by comparison to models (as he does, for instance, by holding up to himself the example of brother Gherardo who had meanwhile become a monk); but there seems to be an implicit understanding among the interlocutors that the task is not simply to assess the "actual" Petrarch against the "ideal" Petrarch. The matter of conscience, especially of the "neglected" Christian conscience, is a very important matter indeed; but in its deepest sense the entire search proceeds from the troubled awareness that conflicting "Petrarchs" seem to constitute one personality. What he needs is a cure for what he is and not another model to displace the present complexity.

Selecting Augustine as the other interlocutor *seems* to suggest, however, that a guilty Petrarch wishes to listen to his conscience. This suggestion would be stronger if Petrarch's portrait of Augustine were more a true reflection of the actual bishop of Hippo and less a reflection of what of Christianity is still alive within the author. This figure of Augustine functions *less* (it does do so in part) as an objective model Christian conscience than as a very self-critical part of Petrarch himself. While it is, of course, important that the figure is a Christian one, it is also important to recognize that other models could have functioned as a Christian conscience, such as Petrarch's own brother, any number of good friends, or even the great saint whose name he shared. The Augustine who earned the title "Doctor of Grace" actually would have presented an embarrassing dilemma to Petrarch; the Christian position of the real Augustine is as noticeably absent as his role as bishop is. The parallels in the lifeline of the historical Augustine attracted Petrarch. There is the parallel of the subtle author of the *Confessions*, also engaged in an intensely honest search of himself. Particularly important for this dialogue is the man seeking understanding of himself so that he might *act* the right way. Petrarch saw in Augustine another man struggling for possession of his soul who, like himself, had an urgent desire to do something with his life; a man who had hated dissipating both himself and the precious drops of time allotted to him. In him Petrarch felt the affinity of a kindred soul in search of peace of mind, a lover of books, and a friend of friends.

Like Petrarch, Augustine had experienced the pull of two distinct and conflicting ideals, though they came into his life from opposite directions and found different solutions. The classical man went over to Christianity, the Christian became enchanted with visions of classical antiquity. And ultimately the access to the realities of antiquity was easier for Petrarch when it came through that Christian intermediary who had been educated as an ancient, who had also loved Cicero, and who could link Petrarch with that world of classical humanity through the more comforting form of a Christianized humanism. Thus though in one sense the figure of Augustine was "modellike," it was not his function to serve as an objective counterweight to Petrarch. Here, after all, was a figure whom Petrarch had made a part of Petrarch and who could talk to other parts of Petrarch. And yet—there is something about this "Augustine" which stands apart from Petrarch, which can serve as mentor and model, and which resembles the saint of old. The very ambiguity remains a part of the life of the dialogue.

As soon as Augustine appears on the scene in the little artful prologue, Truth announces to him that Petrarch is sick with cares and is in need of hearing the very human voice of such an excellent physician. No specific diagnosis of Petrarch's sickness is made at first; the problematic details only emerge in the course of the conversations, which stretch over three days. Instead Augustine uses the first dialogue to drive home a general lesson: if you are sick, you must cure yourself! Petrarch declares himself helpless to do so, and indirectly he raises the question as to whether man can save himself. Can he master his own life? Is he really responsible for his own failure? Can he be happy through his own effort? Augustine, however, thinks that dear Petrarch simply does not try hard enough, that Petrarch does not want to try hard enough, that he does not concentrate hard enough on the problem, and that he is dissipating his energy. According to this Petrarchan Augustine, a man can help himself once he understands the seriousness of his situation and then bends all his energy and will to the task of extricating himself. In order to throw Petrarch full face into the problem, Augustine reminds him of his mortality. His patient, somewhat astonished at receiving such a reminder even though he had written poetry showing his awareness of death's imminence, assures the physician that he is haunted by the mark of mortality on himself—so much so that he is actually shivering. But Augustine unrelentingly presents one image of death after another to Petrarch. If Petrarch would only once truly feel the touch of mortality, then he might find comfort in the other half of the definition of man as a mortal but rational animal. Reason will give Petrarch the means for bringing his passions under control and for curbing the motions of his spirit. With the view fixed on what truly avails, and with unified will and energy pursuing the objective, man ascends out of his misery along the road of high meditation.

*Meditatio alta*, the gradual raising of man by contemplation of the highest things, begun and fed by constantly reflecting on death—that is the essence of Augustine's cure as suggested in Book 1. The emphasis is on man's mastery of his body and his passions so that he may *will* more perfectly. It sounds like pagan Stoic doctrine but most likely it is not. Certainly, Augustine here places so much stress on man's free will that one forcefully has to remind oneself that the speaker is supposedly the doctor of grace. Ironically even, Augustine sums up for Petrarch, in ambiguous terms underscoring this self-reliance on will, the personal experience described in the *Confessions* (8.8): "I wonder how many times I must reply that it is want of will not want of power, which is the trouble ... I too was tossed about, when I was beginning to contemplate entering upon a new way of life. I tore my hair; I beat my brow, my fingers I twisted nervously; I bent double and held my knees; ... yet nevertheless I remained what I was and no other, until a deep meditation at last showed me the root of all misery and made it plain before my eyes. And then my will after that became fully changed" (pp. 19–20). Petrarch answers that he indeed remembers "the story of that health-bringing fig tree, beneath whose shade the miracle took place." So it is Petrarch who, curiously enough, by introducing the crucial term *miraculum*, hints at the role of grace in this process. The theme is buried immediately in an Augustinian literary discourse on the virtue of fig trees; but Petrarch's question whether man can indeed save himself suggests that the issue is still being dealt with in Christian and not in pagan terms. Thus even the un-Augustinian Augustine expresses a Christian position: the popularized, nontheological, late medieval belief that God will help if man truly wills, a position that in its essentials can coincide with Stoicism. Such a position could well have been taken by most good Catholics of the time; even Erasmus did so later, though Luther protested against such a belief in the efficacy of human will. To be sure: even if this part of the dialogue still does move ultimately in a Christian frame, it remains highly significant that there is no strong reference to fundamental Christian terms. Though at one point Petrarch briefly suggests that his inability is a punishment (p. 17), no word otherwise reveals a concern with original sin and the need of priest and sacrament. The stress remains on the human will toward the *meditatio alta*. Petrarch is rationally persuaded and grants Augustine's argument. Still, his soul is sick. At the end of the first dialogue Augustine suggests that the real trouble lies in being overwhelmed by too many diverse impressions, sowing too many seeds in one small space of ground, and in being tossed around by a constant discord of desires. "But as we have now prolonged our discussion enough for today ... let us take a breathing space in silence" (p. 46).

When they meet again to take a closer look at this inner conflict (*intestina discordia*), Augustine hurls at Petrarch a whole catalogue of faults, all of which are meant to show that he is too deeply absorbed in worldly cares. Petrarch is taken aback: "Stop a little, I beg you, lest, over-whelmed by the weight of so many reproaches, I have no strength or spirit to reply" (p. 55). For the entire second dialogue the writer, without explicitly stating it, employs an interesting device: Petrarch's detailed problems are brought into discussion by reflecting them one by one in a typically Christian mirror of behavior. Each of the seven deadly sins passes in review, and Petrarch's conduct and desires are measured off against these norms.[11] Petrarch has no difficulty in gaining Augustine's agreement that there is not really much of a personal problem with three of these—*invidia, gula, ira*. Petrarch is relatively free of envy. Augustine himself makes short shrift of gluttony: "We will say nothing of gour-mandising, for which you have no more inclination than a harmless pleasure in an occasional meeting with a few friends at the hospitable board" (p. 75). And he is equally prepared to "leave on one side anger also, though you often get carried away by it more than is reasonable, yet at the same time, thanks to your sweet natural temperament, you commonly control the motions of your spirit" (p. 75). Petrarch agrees: "but hitherto I have not been able quite to arm myself at all points from some little gusts of irritation" (p. 76).

The problems are weightier with the four remaining sins: pride (*superbia*), lust (*luxuria* or *cupiditas*), "sloth" (*accidia* or *aegritudo*), and covet-ousness (which appears here as *rerum temporalium appetitus*). Lust of the flesh is the least enigmatic matter. Petrarch simply admits that he is no stone and is at times severely tormented by lust; he would like to be able to resist, "but of what avail is any human succour?" (p. 79). Augustine recollects his own experience and agrees: "None can be chaste except God give him the grace of chastity." Still, in praying for it you must truly desire it and you must watch that the passion does not secretly creep into hidden corners. The patient answers that he knows this and tries to prove it by a long quotation from the *Aeneid* (which will be dealt with later on).

Augustine attacks the sin of pride by accusing Petrarch of being much too concerned about worldly vanity. Petrarch is too proud of his intellect (*ingenium*), his literary knowledge (*librorum actio*), his eloquence, and his physical beauty. But Petrarch brushes these accusations aside by assert-ing that if these were faults of his youth, he now thinks very lowly of himself and of his fellow men, and that his intention, at least, is to be humble. Augustine is not persuaded: "It would be an easy task to refute all you have advanced, but I prefer that your own conscience should send the shaft of shame to your heart rather than words of mine" (p. 57).

The very weighty matter is dropped here; despite all statements to the contrary, any reader of Petrarch will find it difficult to believe that even the old Petrarch was not proud of his mind, his knowledge, his eloquence, and his beauty. Indeed it is striking that this whole discussion of the most crucial Christian sin moves on such a relatively superficial level.

Under the rubric of "desire for things temporal" Augustine brings up two points: *avaritia* and *ambitio*. The full treatment of the latter is reserved for Book 3, which deals with the problem of Petrarch's concern with fame. But there is a lengthier discussion of Petrarch's concern with worldly possession.[12] While he is at first inclined to assert that there is not a man in the world more free of this fault than he himself, Augustine soon forces Petrarch to acknowledge that he is no longer satisfied with his humble rural existence, that he has moved into the distracting life of the cities again, and troubles himself about provisions. Petrarch laments having succumbed to the claims of a noisy world and anxiety about an approaching destitute old age. He does not desire wealth, but he cannot face a life of real poverty. "Neither to want nor to abound," not to have to depend on others, "there you have my heart's wish" (p. 69). What can be so bad in wishing for the security of the half ducat more than you need? "Then you must drop your humanity and become God, if you would want nothing" is Augustine's reply. It is interesting that Augustine does not quarrel with Petrarch's pursuit of a Horacelike *mediocritas* and that Augustine warns instead against letting such antlike activities distract Petrarch from fulfilling the life nature prescribed for him: When you still gave promise of becoming a great man, your satisfaction never lay in such pursuits!

The discussion in the last one-third of the second dialogue dwells on the fascinating sin of *accidia*, Petrarch's famous melancholia (a term he does not employ himself). "You are the victim of a terrible plague of the soul—melancholy, which the moderns call *accidie*, but which in old days used to be called *aegritudo*." "The very name of this complaint makes me shudder." For whole days and nights Petrarch is tortured by a deep despair producing a bitter disdain of life in him. "In such times I take no pleasure in the light of day, I see nothing, I am as one plunged in the darkness of hell itself, and seem to endure death in its most cruel form. But what one may call the climax of the misery is that I so feed upon my tears and sufferings with a morbid attraction that I can only be rescued from it by main force and in spite of myself" (pp. 84–85). Augustine does not quite know what to make of this illness but pushes Petrarch's hint that there is a connection between fortune and *acidia*. True, fate has dealt Petrarch hard knocks—the exile, the loss of an inheritance—but can he claim that he had to suffer more than others? Will it not help to compare his good fortune with the lesser fortune of others? But Petrarch sees no comfort in this. He remains troubled that Fortune has made him dependent on others and that she keeps from him the peace of mind and the serenity of soul that will allow him to be the full master of his life. In one sense the discussion is really about Petrarch's melancholic temperament, about a writer who characterized so much in life as "bitter sweetness" and "sweet bitterness." *Acidia*, the word employed, fits the medieval theological meaning only insofar as it suggests incapacitating despair. The symptoms described still bear some relation to the monastic illness of the black hour when nothing makes sense, as described by Cassian of Marseilles around 400 A.D. Any suggestion of the later Renaissance theory of temperament consciously connecting melancholy and creative effort can at the most be sensed here—nothing of the sort is stated. [13] Petrarch can nicely describe the mood that grips him; he does not really know how to overcome it. Augustine tries to give all sorts of "reasonable" advice, but frankly sounds a bit helpless—if not actually a bit silly. Twice he returns to a suggestion of "positive thinking": make use of wholesome maxims! "Take notice in your reading if you find anything dealing with anger or other passions of the soul, and especially with this plague of melancholy . . . put marks against them, which may serve as hooks to hold them fast in your remembrance. . . . By this contrivance you will be able to stand firm against all the passions" (pp. 99, 102).

Thus passing muster before the seven deadly sins, Petrarch reveals a good deal of the tensions within himself. He does not deny that he has a good mind, that he knows much, that he writes well, and that he is good-looking—but he intends to be humble about it. He is a good-natured, not an envious, person and he likes the simple life. He acknowledges his sexual weaknesses but laments them openly. He is indeed concerned with the things of this world, fears poverty, and is not inclined to resist the lure of fame. And he is often in the grip of his melancholic temperament without knowing how to extricate himself. While his assent to Augustine's criticism implies a self-critique of what he is and has been, it seems almost of equal importance that the conflicting tendencies within Petrarch are thus straightforwardly recorded. At the end both men agree that it has been a long day, and, as Petrarch insists that the number three is particularly dear to him, they postpone further discussion to a third day.

On their last meeting, Augustine returns to the theme of concentrating upon the upward ascent by meditating on the highest things. He singles out as the worst obstacles in the way two vices that Petrarch himself considers as noble virtues, alas: his love for Laura and his love of fame. At first it seems altogether unbelievable to Petrarch that his great love for Laura could be seen as detrimental. Why, everything good in him was brought out in the cultivation of that love! This was not an ignoble passion but an ever-growing love for honor, virtue, sublime truth, devotion to a beautiful soul rather than a body. "To her I owe whatever I am, and I should never have attained such little renown and glory as I have unless she by the power of this love had quickened into life the feeble germ of virtue that Nature had sown in my heart. It was she who turned my youthful soul away from all that was base, who drew me as it were by a grappling chain, and forced me to look upwards" (p. 121). Augustine counters all this with assertions that even noble things may be loved the wrong way, that this earthly love for a mortal has detached the mind from the love of heavenly things. "Every creature should be dear to us because of our love for the Creator. But in your case ... held captive by the charm of the creature, you have not loved the Creator as you ought. You have admired the Divine Artificer as though in all His works He had made nothing fairer than the object of your love" (p. 125). Augustine relentlessly pushes Petrarch to admit that he actually departed from the right road at just the time when he first met Laura. In order to cure himself of this love, let him remember that he is getting old, that death is ever waiting, and let him move from these surroundings in which everything reminds him of his love. Whereto? to Italy, of course! Such physical removal is no ultimate cure, but as Petrarch cannot bring himself to love another, let him at least gradually cut the ties with the past and thus prepare himself for the ultimate cure that lies in the ascent to heavenly things. Petrarch still believes in the nobility of his love; but he grants Augustine's argument that such love for a mortal has become an obstacle in the way of his devotion to the highest life.

The conversation then turns to Augustine's last admonition: give up your ambition for literary fame! do not waste any more time on your *Africa* ("Get out of Africa and leave it to its possessors" [p. 184]); turn to yourself, take possession of yourself and use the little time left to prepare yourself for heaven. Petrarch will gladly admit that time triumphs over fame and that public renown may well be a fickle thing. Nor will he deny that there are higher things than his poetry. But no Augustinian argument makes him willing to set his work aside. The bitterest thought of all is that time may not allow him to finish his epic. He will always value the heavenly things above all else; he will certainly not relinquish them—but: "I may be postponing those riches" (p. 173). While he is mortal, he will pursue mortal blessings; it is right to seek them while we are here below. "What must I do then? Abandon my unfinished works? Or would it be better to hasten them on, and, if God gives me grace, put the finishing touch to them? If I were once rid of these cares I would go forward, with a mind more free, to greater things; for hardly could I bear the thought of leaving half completed a work so fine and rich in promise of success" (p. 184). To which Augustine replies: "Which foot you mean to hobble on, I do not know. You seem inclined to leave yourself derelict, rather than your books." Petrarch promises to be true to himself. "I will pull myself together and collect my scattered wits, and make a great endeavor to possess my soul in patience. But even while we speak, a crowd of important affairs, though only of the world, is waiting my attention" (p. 191). He will try to follow the path to salvation more than he has done. "But I have not strength to resist that old bent for study altogether" (p. 192). Augustine sees that they have come full circle. "We are falling into our old controversy. Want of will you call want of power. Well, so it must be, if it cannot be otherwise." For three days Augustine's arguments have been the stronger ones; but the dialogue ends with a Petrarchan self-assertion against an argument he accepts as the correct one; and the interlocutors part by agreeing to differ.

Strictly speaking, the *Secretum* is no autobiography. Dialogue has only a limited capability for fulfilling central autobiographic demands. But this particular dialogue became in Petrarch's hands an eminently suitable instrument for self-investigation, self-clarification, and ultimately for self-orientation. The whole book is one intensive search for the individual reality Francesco Petrarca. What am I really? Have I become what I thought I would become? What is happening to me? Am I really right in living as I do? For the introspective process that must generate the answer to such questions the perspectivism of the dialogue is excellently suited. The activity of writing, which concretely places one position over against another instead of letting the sense of juxtaposition pass in an "unobjectivized" thought, gives greater weight to the introspection. The authoritativeness of Augustine gives that interlocutor the power of the whip hand; Petrarch's inner doubts about his recent life necessitate the strength of that Augustinian conscience. While the dominance of the

Augustinian position in part imbalances the perspectivism (it does so, of course, only insofar as this Augustine is not identifiable by what is genuinely alive within Petrarch), it furthers the truthful self-questioning. Often Petrarch will assert something about himself; again and again, Augustine will counter with such stings as : you are great at self-justification—you always find pretexts for your errors—you have a bad conceit of yourself—come on, stop trying to hide behind your finger! Always there is the question: is it really so? Increasingly, Petrarch feels driven into corners, fearful of what Augustine may still bring up. Truth, the silent interlocutor, makes her presence felt.

The search for the true motive behind the apparent motive must help guard against the greatest danger: deceiving oneself about oneself. There is movement and sequence in this self-discovery; it appears as a genuine process of clarification. The whole expanded range of Petrarch's sensitivities is brought into play: his observational skill, his great concern with whether his language adequately expresses what he wants to say, his careful analysis of direct experience which he joins with the suggestive formulations of the classics he has come to know so well. And the pressure is heightened, in good Christian tradition, by the mental experiment: Death may be very imminent! therefore, take your accounting seriously! Employ any tricks that can force the self upon the self; its truths lie wholly within itself, and only introspection can uncover them.

There is need of such careful scrutiny since the fundamental experience is one of complexity. Petrarch "feels" and knows himself to be a battleground of quite diverse longings, hopes, values, and beliefs. His dilemma can be seen as the conflicting experience and claims of the two inheritances composing the complex amalgam of Western civilization. But while much value and plausibility remains in that view of a clash within Petrarch between traditional Christianity and the fascination with reviving antiquity, his own view of Christianity is already well "secularized" and his view of antiquity is still "Christianized."

Petrarch is a Christian, feels himself to be a Christian, and desires to be a truer Christian. The crisis from which the *Secretum* results stems from his very uneasiness that the world has been too much with him during the past ten to fifteen years. The reminders of a perilous life are coming forcefully now: some of the good friends have died, another illegitimate child is on the way; Gherardo is about to enter the monastery. And where should a man go who, not yet forty, has reached the pinnacle of the coronation at Rome? During the 1340s the world was getting darker: Laura dies in 1348, more friends precede and follow her, the chance for the benefice near Parma comes to nothing, and Italy is being ravaged by the plague. All of Petrarch's writings show that his Christian consciousness had begun to reassert itself strongly, a trend to last until his death. Here is no sudden "reversal," no "conversion," worked in a soul that has lost its religion. A sonnet from the year 1338 shows that the mood growing stronger in 1342–43, and thereafter, had precursors. "Father in Heaven, after my wasted days, after my nights spent in vain dreaming, because of the full desire kindled in my heart by the beholding of one who, to my sorrow was so lovely, may it please Thee now that by Thy light I may turn to a better life, and to fairer tasks, so that my cruel adversary shall have spread his nets in vain. 'Tis now, my Lord, the eleventh year since I took upon me the pitiless yoke that presses most fiercely on those who are most submissive. Have pity on my sinful suffering! Recall my straying thoughts to a better theme: remind them that Thou wast on the Cross today."[14]

The *Secretum* was not occasioned by a special holy day; it is not the reverse pendulum swing; its mood is that of a thoughtful reassessment not resulting in a sudden switch of the rudder but leading to a gradual resetting of compass bearings. Petrarch deeply respected his brother's decision to enter the monastery, and he had a feeling for the beauty of monastic life; yet he knew himself well enough to admit immediately that such a radical turn was impossible for himself even if it might be the better course. "And I see the better course and I cling to the worse."[15] The turn for himself was a shift a few degrees away from certain worldly involvements; creating some more room within him for "his" Christianity. His conscience, guided by Christian norms, is more troubled; he is more willing to see that what seemed to be virtues were perhaps vices; he is willing to subject even the dearest things in his life to the scrutiny of a Christian conscience; and above all he prepares himself to face, in the most serious vein, the Augustinian teaching that life must be a more demanding search after the divine. From all of this could eventually come the older Petrarch of the "penitential Psalms," the pilgrim to Rome in the mid-century Year of Jubilee, the writer *On His Own Ignorance*, the old man getting up in the middle of the night for services, the Petrarch who wished to build a chapel for the Virgin. A good son of the Church, who followed her customs and did not question her dogma consciously—that he had always been.

But the limitations are here as well. The name of Christ appears frequently in a later writing like *On His Own Ignorance*; it plays no role in the

*Secretum.* There is a remarkable silence about such central Christian verities as original sin, incarnation, redemption, grace, the sacraments, or
the helping priest. There is no real confession though much is being
"confessed." Petrarch is very apprehensive that death may come before
life's tasks are accomplished; he shows no fear of damnation. He has a
gnawing concern for his soul; but he expresses no real concern for the
brotherly care of other souls. In a perverse way, the arguments for a
more Christian life are often drawn from the pagan philosophers; the
Petrarch who discovered the beauty of the Bible still lies in the future.
And on crucial issues the power of the Christian commitment simply
fails. Petrarch remains suspended on the tensions of his conflicting
cares.

The power of attraction that the ancients exercised over him did not
wane—but it found a powerful countervalence in the strengthened assertion of Christian persuasions. The text of the *Secretum* is filled with
classical quotations, most frequently coming from Cicero, Vergil,
Horace, Seneca, and Juvenal. They are neither literary ballast nor
erudite exhibition. They function in the argument even where it is an intensely "Christian" one. They certainly are for Petrarch the finest formulations of human insights, "classical" formulations. The ancient authors
are authoritative in all *formal* matters; and as Petrarch is deeply concerned with the problem of expression, it is not surprising that, in
the middle of deadly serious moral issues, he engages Augustine in
philological discussions. The classical authors also function as catalysts:
their formulations of their experiences permit Petrarch to analyze and
formulate his own. The "world" he had found in ancient writers was
sufficiently incorporated: the resonance of kindred experiences was
working. But this does not say that Petrarch either was a "classical man"
or "had a Roman soul."

He often saw these ancients only in the refracting lens of his Christian
disposition, and sometimes he deformed them by his "medieval" habits.
One passage in the second dialogue should be made a textbook case for
"how not to read the ancients." Augustine, who has just urged Petrarch
to consider that the sin of lust is a severe obstacle in the way to the
divine, finally quotes Plato: "Nothing so much hinders the knowledge of
the Divine as lust and the burning desire of carnal passion." Petrarch is
most eager now to persuade Augustine that he, Petrarch, has learned
this lesson well. "To let you see how much I welcome this teaching, I
have treasured it with earnest care ... also where it lurks hidden in the
forests of other writers, and I have kept note in my memory of the very

place where it was first perceived by my mind." He then quotes a long passage from the second book of Vergil's *Aeneid* describing the night when Aeneas desperately tries to put up a final resistance to the Achaeans who have entered Troy. At the crucial moment Aphrodite appears, to lead him away. And Petrarch goes on in his own words: "Now wherever he wandered accompanied by the goddess of love, through crowding foes, through burning fire, he could not discern, though his eyes were open, the wrath of the angered gods, and so long as Venus was speaking to him he only had understanding for things of earth. But as soon as she left him you remember what happened; he immediately beheld the frowning faces of the deities, and recognized what dangers beset him round about . . . . From which my conclusion is that commerce with Venus takes away the vision of the Divine." And Augustine pats him on the back: "you have discerned the light of truth. It is in this way that truth abides in the fictions of the poets, and one perceives it shining out through the crevices of their thought." Vergil, of course, wrote not allegory but a simple epic narrative. Aeneas must be rescued from the senseless slaughter to fulfill his later historical role—so Aphrodite comes to lead him away. When he balks she convinces him that the cause of Troy is lost by permitting him to be witness to the deliberation of the gods, and thus it is finally revealed to him that the fate of the city is sealed. And there is excellent reason why Aphrodite, in particular, should extricate Aeneas from this dilemma—after all, she was his mother![16] Petrarch had not shed the medieval habit of looking for symbolic meaning where none was intended, and instinctively to pursue it was bound to lead to a strangely anachronistic reading of the ancients.

But if he "Christianizes" the ancients, he "paganizes" the Christian Augustine as well, making him, for instance, a man always aiming at Aristotle's "golden mean," or one who insists upon leading a life according to nature (for instance, pp. 63, 67). Petrarch's philological or historicist defects are not the present issue, of course; he shared these defects with most Renaissance humanists. The refracted images of the ancients (like those of apostolic Christianity for the later Christian humanists) are themselves an interesting index of the age. However much Petrarch may have misunderstood or misused the ancients, by his intensive fascination with them he had absorbed attitudes and ideas profoundly affecting his view of life and the world. He had absorbed a strain of secularism and humanism that had interposed itself permanently between himself and his longing for heavenly things. Natural man, with his human capacities and his worldly objectives, had become a focus of Petrarch's outlook. He could try to accommodate this view to his Christian sentiments but could not displace it effectively. The dream of nobleness and the self-esteem resting in a sense of personal ability left an unconquerable pride in human accomplishment and an everlasting concern with fame. Trust in the powers of intellect and of the eloquent word never left him completely. The skeptical strain, becoming stronger in later years, is not yet important to the *Secretum*. Even his "Augustine" argues in the terms of Seneca's *artifex vitae*, the man of reason who learns to master his passions and puts himself in control of his life. Several times he urges Petrarch to live according to his nature, to fulfill his natural potential. Is this a Christian concern with nature? What counts is less the wonder of creation than the extension of human experience in the natural surroundings, the moods that nature releases in man. Beauty is important as a concrete experience first, and only subsequently does it serve as a reminder of the beauty of the Creator. Life in this world is not simply a pilgrimage to the beyond; it also has value in itself.

The issue for Petrarch, therefore, is often how to be happy in *this* life. In the *Secretum*, Fortune figures as a much more prominent reality than Providence. She stands in the way of human accomplishment; she interferes with a man's effort to lead the life he truly desires. Man must learn to resign himself to an everlasting struggle with Fortune. Again and again these secular-humanistic strains have to capitulate to the Christian verities alive in Petrarch, but they remain strong enough to prevent a thorough Christianization of his personality. And it was his special fate to live with these conflicts more self-consciously perhaps than anyone since St. Augustine.

The very act of writing the *Secretum* is an expression of Petrarch's deep desire for the unification of his personality. In nothing are you whole, are you truly one (*nusquam integer, nusquam totus*), complains Augustine about him at the end of the first day's discussion.[17] How can Petrarch form himself into one, into a unified person? A man should come to the tranquility of mind which reflects his inner harmony. The life one leads ought to be a life of one's own, in the forms fitting the personality. One should *be* and *act* as one. A great part of the discussion between the two interlocutors revolves around this: What are the fitting surroundings for Petrarch? What is the appropriate life-style? The deep concern for bringing form and substance into harmonious relation was not only the preoccupation of the writer but one of the key problems that pervaded his life. In certain clearly compressed experiences Petrarch succeeded in pulling all the strands together; the famous letter on the ascent of Mt. Ventoux (Epistle Fam. 4) presents a wide range of his manifold diversity in its final form, an extraordinary example of Petrarch's power to unify it in one artistic whole. To do this with all of life was immensely more problematic. How could one simultaneously give form to the world as an artist *and* overcome the world as ethical philosopher? But the *Secretum*—and Petrarch's later life—give witness to his strong desire for a unified personality.

But is there any evidence in all this activity that Petrarch thought of himself as an individuality, as has been maintained?[18] There is much talk between Augustine and Petrarch about the need to be oneself, to avoid the example of the masses, to lead the life appropriate to one's nature. Isolation from a world that might "falsify" him is almost the methodical principle of Petrarch's self-formation.[19] Intensely desiring to know what he is, he must rely on introspection; the answer is only within himself. And the suspicion that Petrarch was inclined to think of himself as a singular man rises at times. All this, to be sure, may suggest the self-conscious presence of individuality, but it can also be explained without it. There is really no evidence of a belief that among the innumerable ways of being human, Petrarch expresses a unique mode of existence.

The continuing reliance on authority, and the Augustinian insistence on *the* correct Christian life, intimate that Petrarch is striving for a single universal ideal of human perfection. But if the sense of *individuality* remains unspoken, there is much that suggests the force of *individualism*. Petrarch knows that he must rely on himself. He must determine the form of his own life although the constitutive elements are the established molds of the ancient and Christian writers. What he will be in life will depend on what he makes of himself, and this self-forming process is for Petrarch less one of collaboration with the world than a struggle against its interference. And individual personal glory will be the reward for this struggle. Very little social consciousness impinges upon this self-cultivation. It would thus seem that Petrarch reveals in the *Secretum* the marks of Burckhardt's "*auf sich selbstgestellte Persönlichkeit*"—he has to stand on his own. Among the categories of personality development he would seem to resemble most closely the man who seeks somehow to unify a diversity of human realities into a "harmonious personality," an objective that can be pursued without hitching oneself to the star of individuality.

Even if the self-conscious cultivation of individuality is, at best, a minimal objective for Petrarch, he is aware of his own complexity. The *Secretum* is alive with a never-quieted apprehension about the difficulties of self-knowledge. How often does one deceive oneself? What hidden matters will this probing Augustine still lay bare? Self-discovery goes hand in hand with self-acceptance. Petrarch's submission to Augustine's Christian admonitions may seem contradictory. But such acquiescence in the correctness of Augustine's line of argument does not prevent Petrarch from reasserting his heart's inclinations for Laura and his mind's preoccupation with his studies. He is willing to acknowledge that, in terms of such Christian standards as the Seven Deadly Sins, some of his qualities appear to be vices, but he will not deny that it is part of the "real" Petrarch to be proud of his abilities, to be worried about a decent living, to have illegitimate children, and to long for fame and recognition and being loved for what he is. If Augustine is to argue himself into weariness by inveighing against *acidia*, Petrarch can only counter: but I am melancholic, and I do not know what to do about it! Nor does Augustine. The unification of personality would be a less problematic matter if indeed he could follow the Christian advice of *exire a saeculo*: extricate yourself from the world, and concentrate fully on the ascent to God. It is instead a difficult process to become one whole (*totus, integer*) because to achieve unification by discarding Petrarch's ill-fitting traits is possibly to destroy him. When he sees that simple models do not fit him, he ultimately declines to allow himself to be fitted onto any Procrustean bed. In such an attitude lies the future promise of individuality.

Petrarch is thus faced by a lifelong effort to contain somehow the tensions of his complex and often contradictory personality, the diverse longings of his much-demanding heart (*multivolum pectis*). This self-centered (not God-centered) striving to become the man he gave promise to become consumes him—and it is held up by Augustine as the ultimate task. Therein lies Petrarch's melancholia: he quarrels with Fortune because she deprives him of the chance to master his life. The mental experiment with imminent death is focused on this issue. If death comes now, can I account for what I have done? Can I say: I have reached the end, that I am myself? The anxiety arises in the awareness that death may intervene before the task of life is completed and not in the fear of what comes hereafter. If Petrarch had known Marcus Aurelius, he might have found the same concern. As to the life beyond he simply trusts in God's mercy, even though Augustine warns him about such easy confidence. When Augustine poses the question: What would you do if you had only one more year?, Petrarch assures him that he would "be extremely careful to employ it on serious things" (p. 173). From there the discussion turns to the incomplete *Africa*, and the need of completing the work.

Self-fulfillment comes with creative activity. The sentiment still resonates in one of Petrarch's last letters. In 1373 Boccaccio wrote to Petrarch urging him to conserve his strength and to let his pen finally rest. Petrarch was irritated by this letter; in the end he answered it by giving what has been called his "valedictory."

> Constant toil and application are the food of my spirit. When I begin to seek rest and to work but slowly I shall soon cease to live. I know my own strength.... Not content with the long works that I have begun, and for the completion of which neither my life nor twice the span of my life would suffice, I am looking every day for new and different tasks.... To me, indeed, it seems that I have just begun: however it may seem to you or to others, that is my judgment of myself. If in the midst of all this the end of my life should come—and it cannot now be far away—I could wish, I confess, that it might find me, as they say, *vita per acta iuvenem* [i.e., at the conclusion of life with the strength of my youth]. But since, things being as they are, I cannot hope for that, I do hope that death may find me reading or writing, or, if it should so please Christ, in tearful prayer.[20]

At the end life is still either praying or studying. There are no regrets in having given life to the double task of doing one's Christian duty *and* of pursuing creative productivity in the hope of secular fame.

# 6
## Benvenuto Cellini:
## The Naïve Individuality

Burckhardt's double-pronged formula for the Italian Renaissance as a period of "discovery of world and of man" can be verified more fully in biographic writings than in the autobiographic genre. A wealth of material shows the double fascination with describing the appearance of men and the appearance of the earth on which they moved; the representation of striking personalities and eventful lives was handled with increasing skill. Memoirs of men with interesting experiences were not infrequent; one thinks especially of Aeneas Sylvius Piccolomini and, in a somewhat different sense, of the historian Guicciardini. Family histories have some prominence (as they do at the same time in northern Europe). Most humanistic writings had room for the autobiographic comments eagerly inserted by such an agonistic race of men. But genuine autobiography was not written frequently. The two full autobiographies discussed hereafter belong to the world of sixteenth-century Italy and were written when the Renaissance began to be affected by Counter Reformation trends. On the whole, however, they remain Renaissance expressions.

The autobiography of the Florentine artist Benvenuto Cellini (1500–1571) will always be an unforgettable human document for its readers. It led Burckhardt to comment: "Whether we like to hear it or not, there lives in this figure a wholly recognizable prototype of modern man."[1] Goethe, who translated Cellini while working on *Wilhelm Meister*, remarked on his universal significance: "there appears a man who should be recognized as a representative of his century and perhaps even as a representative of all humanity [*sämtlicher Menschheit*]. Such natures can be viewed as spiritual fuglemen[2] [*geistige Flügelmänner*] who suggest to us with strong expressions what has indeed been written into every human breast albeit often only in weak and unrecognizable markings."[3]

The historian of autobiography is plainly thankful for finding in this document the rare self-revelation of an artist from a great artistic age; and the historian of individuality will treasure Cellini for his naïvely unreflective self-consciousness. Whether or not the claims of publisher's blurbs are correct that this is "one of the world's three or four best" autobiographies[4] may be a matter of either taste or opinion. When judged by the full panoply of technical demands that a "perfect" auto-biography would need to satisfy, the *Life of Benvenuto Cellini* is marked by numerous flaws. When you ask for more than formal excellence, or when you hope that the human greatness of the life behind the book will lift you to a high plane of experience, then Cellini keeps you earth-bound. Still, the book fully deserves its reputation as a spellbinder. That reputation is touched by irony: written, so to say, with the left hand, it circulated only in manuscript and was not printed until 1728; since that time it has gained Cellini a fame that he expected would flow instead from his works of art. Would he have put into the world such a rival to his art if he could have foreseen this?

When Cellini was fifty-eight years of age, he felt, by his own account, in better health, in a more contented state of mind, and less harassed by misfortune than at any time in the past. The time of his great travels was over. He had settled down as a respected citizen of his native Florence. It was a most auspicious time for taking his own advice: "All men, what-ever be their condition, who have done anything of merit, or which verily has a semblance of merit, if so be they are men of truth and good repute, should write the tale of their life with their own hand. Yet it were best they should not set out on so fine an enterprise till they have passed their fortieth year."[5] By his own criteria he was qualified as autobiog-rapher: he was past forty and had no doubt whatever of his deeds of merit; surely by the standards of his age a man, whatever his condition, was qualified "to write the tale" by virtue of his talent rather than by mere birth. A "man of truth"? Perhaps! The world does not always permit a man to be simply what he is. "We must live as we find others do; and so it is but natural some little vainglory should creep into a thing of this kind" (p. 2 [1:2]). So, since the foolish world insists, let us reveal the family tree: it all began with Fiorino de Cellino, a valorous man, and one of Julius Caesar's chief captains. With some grandiose reasoning the founding of Florence and the naming of the city are all tied to the Cellini ancestry. "I glory in my descent from men of valour. . . . But much prouder am I of having been born in a humble station, and of having laid an honourable foundation for my house, than if I had been of great lineage and by my vices had blackened and defaced it" (p. 5 [1:2]). I, for one, do not mind declaring, by this excursus at the outset, that I intend to relish Cellini's "cheeky" sense of truth rather than to join the chorus of critics who accuse him of lying and who even spend their time in proving that he does! Interest in his own self-conception is by no means diminished by this fabulist's skills.

Cellini's prime motive for writing was the drive for aggrandizement which had filled his whole life. He intends to give only the story of his adventures; repeatedly he warns that he is not writing the history of his time (cf. pp. 62, 139, 257 [1:38; 1:90; 2:43]). In contrast to so many other autobiographers, he expresses no concern with a didactic purpose. The first line of his prefatory sonnet, in which he offers his "life's struggling story" to the God of Nature, with many thanks, has, at best, perfunctory charm. "I know all the waste and sorely blame the precious time I have in trifles spent. Yet, since remorse is vain, I'll be content." He knows he has a good story to tell and, having tried his powers at everything else, he might as well try this. The enterprise obviously gave him great pleasure. Untrained in literary skills, but supported by his dramatic sense and depictive power, he simply told his story in the Florentine dialect. He enjoyed letting his memory flow freely. "I have taken great care to say nothing of things for which I should have had to fumble in my memory."[6] The narrative skill is "natural" and seems to be inborn. The book is narration in essence. The very beginning sections of the manuscript were done in his own beautiful calligraphy, then the patience obviously ran out—"patience than which nothing is harder to me" (p. 232 [2:73]). After all, he had his other work to do! So: "I reflected that I was losing too much time, and that this was but excessive vanity." He found himself a fourteen-year-old boy, who was not too strong, but who could write at least. "Thus while I worked I dictated to him my Life. And as I took no little pleasure in the thing, I worked all the more diligently and was the more productive." Three-fourths of the book (to his return from France) were completed in this manner in five months during 1558; he completed the remainder by 1566, working on it intermittently. Rarely can the historian "see" the creation of his documents. But this scene obtrudes itself on the mind's eyes: Cellini chiseling away at some marble or fixing jewels onto a silver box, pouring out his adventures, while the poor boy, with a hasty script (which most of the manuscript is said to have) tries to keep pace with the excited narrator. The very mode of recounting this life is a signal mark of the personality that here reveals itself.

As any reader of the book knows, Cellini tells a fairly straightforward story of his varied adventures. The early family history dwells on the father's attempt to turn the boy into a musician. Benvenuto hated the accursed fifing and, against parental wish, he became a goldsmith's apprentice at the age of fifteen. "He could not force us from our natural bents, which bound me to the art of design" (p. 14 [1:10]). The great world of designs around him obviously inspired him; he reports that he studied in the Campo Santo in Pisa and was especially attracted by the great designs of Michelangelo and Leonardo da Vinci in the Signoria in Florence. At the age of sixteen he left Florence and found his way to Rome, which remained the center of his activities and adventures until 1537. With good patronage, and with his skill and energy, he soon was independent, and his work was in great demand. In the Medici pope Clement VII he had a particularly lavish patron, and for a while Cellini was even in charge of the papal mint. In detailed accounts he reports his working habits and speaks of his intricate designs, mentioning the many works in gold and silver by which he proved his mastery during the first half of his life. Just as important to his story, however, are the ever eventful relations with patrons and competitors—intense and often quarrelsome competitiveness being his lifeblood. Interwoven in the artist's life are fascinating sketches: the constant matters of honor that mostly end in bloodshed and scrapes with the law, the Bohemian idylls of artists' "balls," feats of hunting and skillful handling of handguns, innumerable love affairs, one of which led to involvement with a necromancer in the famous night scene in the ruins of the Colisseum, frequent short travels, and equally frequent fevers ending in a miraculous continuation of life. Two large sections of Book 1 are given to his fabulous deeds in defending the Castello di San Angelo against the imperial troops during the 1527 siege of Rome, and finally to his imprisonment there after being accused of absconding with some papal jewelry entrusted to him, his relations with his fantastically weird jailor, and his adventurous escape and "mystical" visions in prison. A lot to pack into a lifetime; and this was only the first half!

The first half of the second Book deals with his French sojourn as a gold- and silversmith (or should one say gold and silver sculptor?) for Francis I. Set up like a grand seigneur, and conducting himself like one, lavishly supplied with working materials and opportunities for wild love affairs, Cellini was for some time in his element, until the hostility of the king's mistress, Madame d'Étampes, the wartime pinch on resources, and the court's eagnerness to protect French men and women against this highhanded Italian artist, persuaded Cellini to return to Italy in 1545. Here ends the story as he told it in the five months in 1558; the last fourth of the book was added gradually. It tells of his settling down in Florence, the strained patronage relations with those "merchant" dukes there, his rivalry with the sculptor Bartolommeno Bandinelli, and a risky adventure in land speculation. The tone is calmer now, the weapons stay sheathed; Cellini has settled down. The core of this Florentine period is the dramatic account of his life as a sculptor: the pouring in bronze of the Perseus statue, the work on the Escorial Crucifix, and the disappointed hope of laying his hands on a perfect piece of marble. The text ends abruptly in 1566, carrying the story no further than 1562. Of the remaining decade of his life we know from other sources that he took his first tonsure, but instead of going to the monastery married his housekeeper in 1565 and acquired a family. He suffered much from the gout; though chosen to represent "sculpture" at Michelangelo's funeral in 1564, he regretfully had to stay home. After his death of pleurisy in February 1571, he was buried in a fine public ceremony.

From his own account he thus appears as a man of enormous diversity. He was the master goldsmith, silversmith, and jeweler who bedazzled all his patrons with his virtuosity. He easily made the transition to sculpture in bronze and marble. The intricacies of design and the painstakingly precise working procedure of goldsmith and "fine mechanic" must have demanded intense concentration and a largely sedentary life. Yet the account leaves the impression of constant activity and movement, somewhat diminished only in the last fourth of the book. His fascination with weapons, his apparent skill in handling them, his ingenuity, self-reliance, and reckless sense of bravery might as well have made a great soldier of him. He could have been an inventor and engineer with his practical sense, his love for intricate works, his urge to try what had not yet been tried, and the facile inventiveness of his extremely agile mind. The show he put on (probably only in his mind) to reveal to Francis I and his court some of the completed life-size silver figures at Fontainebleau intimates a love for the theatrical and a talent for baroque stage management that could have made him famous—if fame could have been had by such activity in his time. He had a marvelous sense of the dramatic, of skillful timing, of quick and easy characterization, and an obvious power of invention; with a bit more early education he could have become a first-rate dramatic writer. He is, of course, a marvelous storyteller.

As a human being he moves with the same self-understood ease among the workmen in his shops, his fellow craftsmen, the great artists of the day, popes, cardinals, the emperor, kings, and dukes, as well as the demimondaines of Rome or Paris or the worst band of cutthroats. With the same ease he could shift from one mood and activity to the next. One moment he is chuckling away over the deceitful play of an artist's fancy-dress party; the next minute he may turn to the stealthy pursuit, through the dark streets, of an enemy into whose throat he drives his dagger. He will cheerfully tell of his pleasing ride through the countryside on a Good Friday, during which he suddenly gets involved in killing a man in a senselessly provoked fight, and then he will continue with ribald humor to tell about a poor fellow wounded in the fight needing now to be stitched up by a doctor who puts a spoon in his mouth to measure an opening for food! (pp. 204–8 [2:3–5]). Oh, we had a marvelous trip, thank you. He will leave everything behind to travel to Naples to find his Angelica again—as the daemons in the Colisseum had prophesied he would; and he will leave her just as abruptly when her old mother makes a nuisance of herself, and on the return trip will have the next amorous adventure. He can gratefully pray to God for providential help and turn from prayer to a killing. From the most vindictive verbal attacks on a rival sculptor he can turn to sincerest admiration of Michelangelo's greatness. In the enforced inactivity of prison he can make of himself an ascetic and mystic who talks directly to God and receives signs from Christ, and in his own blood he writes a long poem of his visions. And the same man who takes such delight in his feats of arms, who always tells of all his haggling about payment, can with rapture talk about the luminous halo "granted" to him after the "martyrdom" of "false" imprisonment.

If he was not quite *l'uomo universale* of the Renaissance, he was a man of enormous diversity and versatility. "He is a man who can do all and dares do all, and who carries his measure in himself."[7] The striking thing is the unity of the personality. An effortless ease holds the diversity together. In all his variety there is uncannily the same Cellini. The bravura in telling his life as a piece of one pouring goes hand in hand with the completely unproblematic view of himself and of the world in which he moves. As no thought-out scheme of interpretation underlies this rapidly moving account, as there is no given script for this life, no model personality simply to fill with the details, the peculiar unity comes unreflectingly from within his person, and it imparts a "Celliniesque" quality to everything he touches.

He "carries his measure in himself." This key phrase of Burckhardt contains a problem worthy of somewhat more detailed investigation. The statement might be taken to say that Cellini is the "autonomous personality," the person who gives himself the law by which he acts and lives. Such a person chooses from among a variety of norms and submits his life to the freely accepted standard. Something of the sort lay in the Socratic turn, in the Augustinian desire to learn to fuse with the divinely willed, and later in Petrarch's struggle to sort out the valid norms for his life. The less such a choice of norms is a selection of given alternatives, the more it is a self-conscious choosing of what fits the demands of one's own personality, the more we approach the phenomenon of individuality. Do we encounter this in Cellini? It may be hard to answer this affirmatively since the reader will have the impression that Cellini does not submit to "law" at all and that he is, therefore, one of those Renaissance figures exemplifying "arbitrary subjectivism." If that view were correct, then the Burckhardt phrase about a "measure" would be altogether incorrect, since rule by a measure is the opposite of *Willkür*, arbitrary willfulness. Another difficulty with the phrase may derive from the fact that a reading of the Cellini text simply does not leave one with the impression that this man ever consciously engaged in reflective choice about the course of his conduct. The conception of a man "giving" himself the law seems thus eminently unsuitable to such an unreflective nature. Burckhardt knew this, and his formulation says that Cellini carries such norms within him, leaving unexplained the way in which they came to be put there.

Cellini's self-representation is surely that of a freely standing, independent personality (*"auf sich selbst gestellte Persönlichkeit"*). He has a sovereign self. He has no master outside of himself. He expressed this in a variety of ways. He left home because he wanted to be his own man and no one else's, and in that he succeeded (p. 20 [1:14]). This strong sense of independence rested to a large degree in his own sense of the complete mastery of his craft. His ingenuity, skill, and virtuosity were his own to command, and they always put him in demand. Once, in a youthful political argument, in which he was accused of "serving" Florentine tyrants, he said: "I am a poor goldsmith, and serve him who pays me" (p. 137–38 [1:89])—but this shows, more than anything else, his totally apolitical outlook. Certainly, as a worker in jewels and gold and marble he was dependent on patrons. The king of France told him so bluntly: "With all your great abilities you can do nothing by yourself. You can only show your greatness through the opportunities we put in your way. I counsel you therefore to appear more docile—less proud, less headstrong" (p. 258 [2:44]). Cellini was quite prepared to acknowledge that Francis I gave him "such a chance of making wonderful masterpieces as had never fallen to the lot of any of my artist peers" (p. 268 [2:53]), but he made that argument to the face of the Florentine "merchant duke" from whom he wanted to elicit greater liberality. In this late phase of his life he was to suffer from such dependence for the first time; how he itched to get his hands on that block of perfect marble, and what a bitter blow it was to see it awarded to a rival, who—of course—ruined it! Whenever he had to deal with his niggardly Florentine patron, he knew he had blundered in leaving France. Francis wanted him back. "The king found it impossible to swallow his great vexation at my departure; yet would he gladly have had me back, if it could have been contrived with due regard to his dignity. But, feeling myself altogether in the right, I would not bend the knee. . . . I stood upon my dignity, and wrote in haughty terms, like a man with right upon his side" (p. 274 [2:59]). Throughout his life that was his typical attitude: "I would not bend the knee." The need to scrounge material to work on was real, but there was lively competition for his skills. As long as he could move, he knew: "I shall never lack bread wherever I go" (p. 276 [2:59]).

Cellini moved with his patrons on a footing of easy equality and behaved toward the great of this world as though he were their peer. In initial encounters he is, obsequiously, on his best behavior. As soon as he feels secure ground under his feet, his natural self-confidence overcomes all barriers of etiquette or respect for social distinctions. Friars, priests, and cardinals are always willingly abused when they touch his anticlerical nerve with haughty dealings. When cardinals bother him in his defense of the papal fortress he gets them forcefully out of the way ("at last I had them locked up and gained only their ill-will thereby"), and after nearly having dropped a cannon barrel on Cardinal Farnese ("how much better it would have been for me had I killed him"—Farnese being the future pope who later incarcerated Cellini), he pointed two of his falconets down the stairs, stepping with a lighted fuse between them, and vowed to shoot any high and mighty lord who troubled him (pp. 57–58 [1:36]). Popes were somewhat more sacred to him; but in his close relation to Clement VII, which resembled that of great artist and great patron more than that of vicar of God and mere lay sinner, he so unabashedly pushes his interests that the pope bursts out: "That devil of a Benvenuto will not brook being spoken to. I was disposed to give it to him, but he shouldn't be so haughty with a Pope" (p. 87 [1:45]). When Cellini feels unjustly treated, he frankly tells the pope's messengers to inform their master that such injustice could not be condoned in a pope and that he, Cellini, would not be intimidated (pp. 93–95 [1:61]). Nor did he hesitate to berate the Holy Father to his face in front of "many lords of high degree": "he reddened somewhat, and looked as if he were ashamed ... and then, afraid I might read him another lecture worse than the last" he praised my medals and promised me a good reward! (pp. 108–9 [1:71]).

He who treated popes this way certainly had no fears in dealing with a mere emperor. "I answered that I should have far greater courage in speaking to the Emperor, seeing that he was clad like me, and that it would seem as if I were addressing a man made like myself; which was not the case when I spoke to his Holiness, in whom I saw a far greater divinity, partially because of his ecclesiastical trappings, which were as a kind of halo about him" (p. 140 [1:91]). What, then, could a mere merchant duke of Florence or the court of a French king expect? When the cardinal of Ferrara, acting as the agent of Francis I, sends a messenger telling Cellini to get ready at once and come by post, Cellini's answer is simply that his art is not carried on in the post and that he will go at his leisure. When told in reply that "just in the manner I had described, the sons of the Duke were wont to travel," Cellini bursts forth "that the sons of my craft were used to go as I had said; that not being the son of a duke, I did not know the customs of such; also that if he used such language in my hearing, I would not go at all" (pp. 210–11 [2:7]). Madame d'Étampes, the powerful mistress of Francis I, sought to put Cellini in his place. He is ordered to appear for an audience but then told to wait. "I clothed myself with patience, than which nothing is harder to me. However, I kept calm till after her dinner-time. Then, seeing it was getting late, hunger roused such a fury in me that, unable any longer to bear it, I consigned her devoutly to the devil, and took myself off" (pp. 232–33 [2:23]). In Francis I he had at first found a patron after his own heart; aside from the royal liberality with materials, Cellini appreciated the fact that this king paid him the respect a great artist is entitled to expect. The king visited his studio, and, in the beginning, at least, Francis seemed to realize that an exceptional man deserves exceptional treatment.

Undoubtedly, a good part of Cellini's ease in dealing with the high and mighty must be assigned to a streak of incredible brashness and ill-mannered conceit. The tone in which he reports his conduct—evident in the preceding pastiche of citations—often becomes the rodomontade of the gamin who rose too quickly in the world and never acquired manners. Surely his patrons, offering him a finger, must frequently have been infuriated by the impertinence with which Cellini grabbed the whole hand. Even if another part is the braggadoccio of an old man now securely lodged before his fireplace, there is something genuine about the self-conception needing this unintimidated ease before the great of the world. This genuine sense of worth, on which the treatment of others rested, was rooted in the trust in his own skill and in his high conception of the artist as a superior human type.

Cellini could afford that absolute and wonderful self-confidence which derives from full mastery of his work. He had learned to master every facet of his goldsmith's craft and he never stopped growing. He could have made a comfortable living simply by his stunning expertise in setting jewels. But he was ever drawn to untried tasks and the kind of experimentation from which new skills developed. All that could be learned as a trick of the trade was eagerly assimilated. And as soon as an established rival was heard to say that this or that could not be done, Cellini would try to think of a new technique for accomplishing the allegedly impossible. Such challenges made him tingle with life down into his fingertips. He possessed a genuine fascination with the technical matters of his craft and found obvious relish in describing techniques. Technical ingenuity and skill counted for very much with him, perhaps to the danger point of esteeming virtuosity in execution at the cost of greater aesthetic values.

With this striving for highest technical skill went a willingness for work. Even in the retelling of later years one can sense the frenzy of activity in which he found himself. He frequently worked on several projects at the same time, never more frenetically perhaps than in France where Francis heaped so many artistic jobs one on another that many were never completed. Surround Cellini with the requisite materials, pose a challenging task for him, give the promise of appreciation and reward, and he begins to live at his highest energy and power. He forgets his love affairs, sometimes even his illness, over his work; it is remarkable how often he thought that he worked himself into a feverish state. He hated the pressures that patrons, overly eager to see the work in progress, exerted upon him. He wished to work as he saw fit. But he also hated to have his time wasted by others, and proudly reports the remark of the cardinal of Ferrara to Francis I: "Sacred Majesty, Benvenuto here is most anxious to work. Indeed it may be almost called a sin to waste the time of an artist like him" (p. 215 [2:10]). This attitude toward the full exploitation of time remains a Renaissance phenomenon of the highest interest; Cellini shares it with such as Alberti, who most carefully allocated the minutes of his day, and with Leonardo, who did not even wish to waste the minutes between lying down and passing over into the realm of sleep. Cellini's very positive attitude toward work and the use of time is intimately connected with the urge to express his creative power. There is no classical banausic aversion to working with one's hands; there is no monastic acceptance of work as an ascetic discipline and a remedy for *accidia* and the sins that come with leisure. This is certainly not yet the disciplined, methodical, steady labor of the Puritan personality rooted in essentially different grounds. But as a moment in that centrally important transition whereby work, at first negatively valued, gradually evolves into a most positive aspect of life, the very element by which the personality so often seeks self-fulfillment in our modern world—as such a moment this Celliniesque frenzy with work remains important.

Work had to be the full involvement of the whole man. Cellini shows no tendency whatever to avoid any step or to leave the manual labor to underlings. When Francis I tries to turn him into a studio entrepreneur who is unwilling to waste his strength on manual labor, Cellini rejects the notion immediately: "I should fall ill at once if I did not work; nor would the work, under these circumstances, be of that quality which I should desire" (p. 222 [2:15]). The work had to be his, and the satisfaction lay in the full power of creation. One of the most important aspects of his self-conception is, therefore, the frequency in remarking, *en passant*, that he does not copy but always makes his own designs.[8] Thus the work is his from conception to completion. It involves the most genuine sense of creation: unworked raw material meets with artistic conception and is executed with skillful fingers; at the end there is something of ingenuity and beauty where there was nothing before. One can still taste in Cellini's text his pleasure in preserving the secrecy of the work until it was ready to be carried proudly to a patron and suddenly unveiled. There was magic in this translation of an inner vision into the palpable beauty of gold, silver, bronze, and marble. There was intense frustration when anything or anyone blocked such creation. To be alive when an almost perfect piece of marble is found and to lose the chance of creating perfect beauty from it because silly political intrigues award it to a blockhead of a rival were supreme frustrations to the old Cellini. Interestingly, though, he is less sorry for himself than for the marble: "the great wrong which the marble suffered" (p. 327 [2:99]), "Oh unhappy marble!" (p. 330 [2:101]). Hope against hope, he worked on a design and a model—but the marble eluded him. So he took his own funds and set to work on "one of the most difficult things in the world": the man-sized white marble Christ on the cross of black marble for the church in which he wished to be buried.

This sense of the creative power within him must have grown throughout his lifetime. He had started as a jeweler-goldsmith, moved on to platework in silver and evermore toward sculpture in gold and silver, finally advancing to the bronze work of the Cosimo bust and the Perseus, and the complex marble crucifix. In connection with an early piece of work he made some significant remarks: "all those diverse crafts I set myself to learn with the greatest eagerness ... though I found it no easy matter, yet such pleasure did I take in it that its great difficulties were a rest to me. And this sprang from a special gift lent me by the God of Nature, a temperament so healthy and well-proportioned that I could confidently carry out whatever I had made up my mind to do. These arts ... are entirely different from one another, so that a man skilled in one of them rarely attains to equal success in any other, whereas I strove with my whole strength after them equally; and in its own place I shall show that I succeeded" (pp. 37–38 [1:26]). It was of the utmost significance for his personality that he experienced this "plastic power" of his own creativeness.

Cellini found this awareness of his powers in constant contests with rivals. He continued to test his excellence in competition to the end. He needed the rivalry and the sense of superiority gained in constantly besting others. He was not the kind of artist who could quietly perfect his works and find satisfaction in the thought that upon his death the world might discover a studio full of unexpected masterpieces. Surely, he wanted the fame, the honor, and the rewards now. But more important was the opportunity for personal *virtù* (the sense of excellence produced by the full exercise of one's powers) to "prove" itself before the eyes of the world. The challenge summons forth the fullest exertion of the faculties, and only this full flow of the expanding powers fills the agonistic creature with the sense of personal value. That Cellini was such an agonistic being, through and through, is reflected in the interesting turns of his self-account.

In the early period we find such statements as: "It was a great pleasure ... to engage in such a contest with so able a man" (p. 27 [1:20]), "I felt spurred to an honorable rivalry with this man also" (p. 37 [1:26]), "The best reward of my labors ... was to have equalled the work of so accomplished a man" (p. 48 [1:31]), "I answered that it would be all the more honor to compete with so first-rate a master" (p. 141 [1:92]). And later, in fighting for the marble he wanted so intensely, he offers a general insight into the positive power of competition: "I went on to tell how their fathers had bred great talents in the noble school of Florentine art only by pitting the best artists against each other in honorable rivalry. So was the wonderful cupola, and so were the exquisite doors of San Giovanni made ... now a crown of genius on their city's head, the like of which had never been seen since ancient days" (p. 326 [2:99]). But when he "fights" for his marble by pleading for open competition rather than an "administrative" decision, he no longer believes in the competitive urge, since he is now convinced that there is no one left worth competing with.

For, after all his victories, Cellini knew himself to be absolute master among the living. He proudly asserts his unchallengeable excellence. Now the rivalry is with himself and with the greatest art against which one may test oneself. As a young man, full of admiration for the divine Michelangelo, he had received the visiting master's praise: "and this was such an incitement to me to do well as I cannot describe" (pp. 65–66 [1:41]). The young man was equally filled with admiration for the works of the ancients, looking for them wherever he could see them. With growing mastery in his craft they became, like Michelangelo and Donatello, objects of rivalry. After besting the best among the living masters in tinting diamantés, he concludes: "Since I have beaten Miliano, let us now see if I can beat myself" (p. 142 [1:92]). He now carries out what the masters think impossible and takes delight when others say "that of surety I was a great demon, for I had done what by mere art could not be achieved" (pp. 293–94 [2:73] and 299 [2:77]). Remarks about having outdone the ancients occur more frequently (p. 108 [1:71], p. 214 [2:9], p. 255 [2:41], p. 260 [2:45], p. 284 [2:65])—"I would compete with the ancients, with hope to surpass them" (p. 288 [2:69]). Particularly suggestive is the occasion when the painter Francesco Primaticcio tried to blacken Cellini's name before Francis I by suggesting to the king that he should try to get copies of classical sculpture to get a taste of real art. "The beast ... had not had the pluck to try and rival me with the work of his own hands; but played me the very Lombard trick of depreciating my work by copying antiques. Now although he had these casts excellently made, the effect he produced was just the opposite to what he had intended" (p. 249 [2:37]). In the late Florentine period Cellini will proudly report that even Michelangelo places a Cellini bust above the work of the ancients. And now the contest with that much admired contemporary is on as well (p. 301 [2:79]). "How could my work possibly be valued at its true worth, since there is not a single man in Florence today fit to do it? . . . my master, Michel Agnolo Buonarroti could have done it when he was younger . . . but now that he is a very old man, assuredly the task would be beyond him" (p. 322 [2:97]). And when Cellini works on the crucifix he tells the duchess: "But I am so confident in the result of the hard, disciplined study I have devoted to my art, that I think to gain the palm, even were the great Michel Agnolo Buonarroti in the running, from whom alone in all the world I have learnt what I know. And I would much rather have him as rival, with all his skill, than those others with their little; for I should reap great honors in contest with the great master; but there is little credit to be had in surpassing the rest" (p. 328 [2:100]). Whether he is right or wrong in his judgment of his art is much less relevant a matter than to note how much the sense of accomplishment and of his own personal worth flows for Cellini from the conviction that he has run the race by full exertion of his powers and now stands unequaled in the world. Though he had never run away from the *agon*, he had expanded to his full potential in rivalry with the best. Personal *virtù* thus tested, let him face the world with unequaled self-assurance.

Cellini's "sovereign self" was the mark not only of Cellini-the-artist but of Cellini-the-man as well. He was a man of great self-reliance and independence from his early youth on. He was not only fearless in the defense of his own interests but often forbiddingly reckless. Not infrequently he acted both immorally and illegally in his own interest— though that he would not have thought. The term *immoral* is actually of great problematic interest. It never occurred to Cellini to rely on the processes of the law for obtaining what he thought to be his right; he will take care of such matters himself, often highly enraged—"by nature I am somewhat [!] choleric" (p. 23 [1:17])—and with mail on his chest, and dagger in hand. Thus he will get "his" justice for himself as well as for his workmen or for his murdered brother. When others have him hauled into court, the legal proceedings settle nothing as far as he and his sense of justice are concerned. In his youth he takes offense at the judgment of a Florentine court, and immediately takes up a stiletto, rushes alone into the house of his enemies, and deals out his blows. He flees from the courts, disguised as a monk; as soon as he is safely outside the city, "Off, I threw my frock, and was a man again" (p. 25 [1:18])—the fifty-eight-year-old narrator, recalling events some forty years past, still relishes the moment of recovering his freedom.

Thirty years after the Florentine escapade, he faces a French court of

law for his highhanded evictions of several parties from quarters he
desired. One man he simply turned out: "in a short time I dismantled
his whole house, and turned all his property outside my castle. The
treatment was somewhat severe; but I had recourse to it because he had
said to me that he knew not a single Italian strong enough or daring
enough to move even a nail from his wall" (p. 235 [2:25]). When he does
the same to the other man, he is hailed before the law. "In France they
are wont to make no end of capital out of a suit against a foreigner" (pp.
236–37 [2:27]). The court scene is to him an absolutely unrealistic affair;
"a place of justice is indeed an Inferno." He describes it as though he
were a nonparticipant in a peculiar show, full of admiration for the act
put on by the judge: "I stood there marvelling at that astonishing man,
with the Pluto-like face, in his watchful attitude, now lending ear to one,
now to the other, and answering each with ability. Now it has always
delighted me to see and savour every kind of skill; and this struck me as
so wonderful that I would not have missed it for anything." It is an
unreal world for the man used to solve his own affairs. After describing
this show, how does he go on?

> Now to return to my own business. When I learned what was
> the kind of judgment I had to expect from these men of law,
> and saw no other way of helping myself, I had recourse for
> my defense to a great dagger which I possessed—for I have
> ever delighted in having fine weapons [!]. The first I assaulted
> was the man who had brought the unjust law-suit against
> me; and one evening I wounded him so seriously as to de-
> prive him of the use of his legs, as well as injuring his arms.
> But I took care not to kill him. Then I found the other man
> who had brought the suit and gave him what made him glad
> enough to stop his litigation. Thanking God for this and all
> His other mercies and hoping I might now be left unmolested
> for a time ... [I returned] ... so that I might complete the
> works I had begun [pp. 237–38 (2:28)].

The elements coming together in this startling account—which did not
startle Cellini at all!—are revealing. A mere quarrel with someone in his
way, to which a dare is added by slurring his "nation," results in treatment he considers severe but fully justified. The relevance of the law to
his doings is quite unintelligible to him; taking justice into his own
hands is his preferred way. Reaching for the beautiful dagger rouses his
aesthetic delight about weapons but no trace of a moral concern. The
questionable justice in depriving someone of his legs is apparently

ennobled by not killing him. What he did to the second man he does not even find worth mentioning. And then he thanks God and goes back to his work. The trust in his sovereign self, as though there were nothing problematic about it, is extraordinary. Responsibility for your life is yours. He treats the human world in all this as an indifferent matter and assumes that the divine order is there for support. The same could be shown in hundreds of other episodes Cellini recounts. When he is ill, he is inclined to be his own doctor. When he faces danger, he tells his companions "that I was man enough to fight my own battles, that I needed no greater champion than myself" (p. 110 [1:72]). The wisdom in which he repeatedly sums up his attitude is simply: God helps those who help themselves.[9]

The extraordinary self-confidence in which Cellini creates his art and acts as a man of the world rests on a knowledge of his *virtù*. But this self-confidence is amplified by a fitting view of the world. He takes the world around him simply as a given. Men should accept it as it is; those who do not wish to live by its customs are told by him, with a disdain which makes it clear that he does not believe in such a possibility, "those who wanted things done in their own way should make a world for themselves" (p. 119 [1:79]). Cellini shows no intention whatsoever of reforming the human world, and he seems unconcerned about a titanic struggle with the cosmic order which a Nietzschean glorification sought to attribute to the Renaissance. He certainly does not feel responsible for the human order of things; he is only responsible for Cellini living in what might as well be a natural order. He cannot be found worrying about social questions. It is not particularly illuminating to call him the supreme egotist (which he may have been, though he was capable of considerable kindness) and to maintain that he treated the world as his oyster. The point is, rather, that he does not worry because the world is no problem to him. It is there as the stage (but even this word is misleading as there is no scene behind the scene) on which men act and create. How they live and whether they succeed depends first of all on their strength, on their *virtù*, and secondly on a blending of forces beyond their control. The world is what it is, but men are what they make of themselves. If they do not take care of themselves, they have only themselves to blame. To be sure: the universe is governed by forces not under man's control, but even these only amplify Cellini's urge for exercising his *virtù*.

Cellini rather consistently distinguishes between the power of two "agents" in his life: Fortune and Providence. Such dualism is in no way a "theoretical" problem for him. As is so characteristic of his entire attitude to life, he does not puzzle about it, he does not worry about it, he does not thoughtfully reflect about it—he takes it as a simple given with which to live. He makes a frequent association of Fortune and the Stars. He proposes no "theory" on the matter, but it is noteworthy that he speaks of Fortune and the Stars rather consistently when he requires an agency for explaining adversity and evil experiences that cannot be attributed to intelligible motivations of his human enemies.[10] He does not seem to think of Fortune or the Stars when things go well, because he holds Providence responsible for all good turns. The one experience leading him to reflect on the "problem" shows this in an interesting fashion. Cellini felt innocent when he was put in the papal prison; he had helped himself by his astounding escape from San Angelo; but was caught and incarcerated again. Being thus "inactivated," for the second time, and obviously troubled by this turn of events, he reflects: "It seemed to me that I was in the position of unlucky persons walking in the streets, when a stone falls from some great height on their head and kills them, which may be clearly assigned to the influence of the Stars. Not that the Stars in any way plot against us, to do us good or ill; but these accidents come to pass through their conjunction, to which we are subject. Yet I reflected, I know I have free will; and if my faith were active and devout, I am very certain that the angels of heaven would bear me out of prison. . . . But since God thinks me unworthy of such a favor, it is clear that celestial influences work out their malignity on me" (p. 181 [1:115]). In this deliciously confused argument it is at least clear that Cellini thinks of God as the real power to countermand the power of the Stars (cf. also 108 [1:71] and 304 [2:82]). When He does not, man can either employ magic or he can continue the battle against Fortune; the latter is Cellini's usual response. In typical Renaissance fashion, a man shows his *virtù* in his struggle with adversity, and at the end he may say proudly: "My cruel fate hath warr'd with me in vain" (p. 2).

Fortune and the Stars were inscrutable abstractions, but Cellini felt securely harbored in a belief in personal providence. He is a lively witness to the untroubled continuation of a popular Catholicism among those in Italian society who either were never seriously touched by Renaissance humanism or secularism or who found no conscious difficulty in reconciling such attitudes with the simpler faith in the miraculous. His attitude and belief often point to that great reservoir of popular faith on which the Counter Reformation, as real a part of his life as any part of the Renaissance, could draw. His belief in Providence is simple.

He is never concerned with general providence or the course of world history; he is ever convinced of personal providence as it affects his own life. All the traditional elements of a belief in such personal providence are there: God combats the power of the stars when He sees fit to do so; He who punishes the unjust will help Cellini in his right; He employs the king of France as his instrument for rescuing Cellini; He used Cellini's imprisonment to check his vainglory; He sends ills so that good may come from them; God blinds Cellini's enemy at the appropriate moment so that he may pass safely; but He will just as readily stop Cellini from a rash attack on Bandinello and give him instead the grace for excellent works of art, "to kill off all my rascally enemies" by that form of revenge (p. 286 [2:66]). God helps Cellini in general to be a good artist, but he charmingly enough grants him little artistic triumphs as well. Before the Perseus was poured, Duke Cosimo is firmly convinced that all the bronze will settle in the lower part of the figure. Cellini assures him that, quite to the contrary, the danger is that not enough bronze will settle in the foot. The master predicted: the toe will not be complete. Then we are told of the fantastic scene in which the metal is melted and poured; suddenly it is all gone; Cellini rushes in a fever into his house and takes all the tin tableware and throws it into the furnace for his statue. "I cried 'O God, who in Thy limitless strength didst rise from the dead, and glorious didst ascend to Heaven ... !' In an instant my mould filled up and I knelt down and thanked God with all my heart" (pp. 298–300 [2:77]). Repeatedly he will acknowledge that it all was "nothing short of a miracle ... the whole operation seemed as if it had been guided and brought to a happy end by Almighty God." The statue seemed to be perfect. "On the one hand I rejoiced; on the other I was half annoyed, but only because I had said to the Duke that it could not happen so. However, when all was disclosed, I found the toes ... wanting.... Though this would give me a little extra work, I was glad, nevertheless; for I could show the Duke that I understood my own business." Thus God helps the artist he favors; but a rascal like Bandinello, who will not even receive the grace for completing his pietà, dies (p. 329 [2:101]).

With comforting trust in a particularized providence goes an unproblematic acceptance of the various means by which such a popular Catholicism supports its believers. Cellini had as cynical an anticlerical streak as had other Renaissance Italians, but that, of course, did not diminish his need for certain priestly functions. He has special use for confession, and with good common sense he fully exploits his relation with Clement VII to receive absolution from the highest earthly agent. And when a pope "sins" against Cellini by having him incarcerated, Cellini formally forgives the Church and appeals directly to the pontiff's superior, St. Peter (pp. 181–82 [1:116]). He is eager to participate in processions, he promises to go on a pilgrimage, and he quite frequently reports his prayers, psalm singing, and in prison even his Bible reading. Now, in view of Cellini's own account of repeated killings and violent deeds—about which he himself at times gets worried (p. 240 [2:29])—it may be difficult to think of him traveling on a horse and to accept his own account that "I never ceased singing psalms and saying prayers to the honor and Glory of God all that journey" (p. 318 [2:94]).

But it seems desirable to admit, first of all, that for such a man it may indeed be possible to unite such diverse strains in one person. Secondly—and most important for the present argument—the function of these devout activities, as of the instinctive trust in Providence, has a significant bearing upon the very unification of such a personality, even if the activities are not as such necessarily a sign of "true" Christian devotion. Once the impetuous deed has been done, the internal pressures of conscience find a release by means of these religious practices. As soon as Cellini has the sense of pardon and continued providential support, he is free to let his nature lead him to the next deed. Precisely because he has such an unproblematic belief in the efficacy of such practices, the psychic accounting is a simple matter. The enormous energies, instead of dispersing themselves in moralistic worrying, can express themselves almost instinctively and naturally, in renewed activity.

During the siege of San Angelo, the pope witnesses, "greatly pleased and astonished," how Cellini with one of his shots cuts a man in half. "I told him what ingenuity I had used . . . . Then kneeling down, I begged him to remove from me the curse of this homicide and of others I had committed in that castle in the service of the Church. Whereupon the Pope, raising his hands made the sign of the cross broadly over my face, gave me his blessing and his pardon for all the homicides I had committed, or ever should commit, in the service of the Church Apostolic." So I went back to the "infernally cruel business," "hardly ever was shot of mine in vain, . . . killed more than thirty men in that blast" (p. 59 [1:37]). It could be said that there were special dispensations here; but there always were "special" reasons for Cellini's violent actions. When he takes bloody revenge for his brother's death, the pope admits him in audience again, and tells him simply: "Now that you have recovered,

Benvenuto, give heed to your way of life. And I, catching his meaning said I would do so. Without delay I opened a handsome shop ..." (p. 81 [1:51]). After sexually abusing one of his French models, he is for a while uncertain what course to take: "Whether to make off without a word to anyone, and let France go to the devil, or to fight this thing out and see for what end God had created me ... when just as I rose for my departure, some invisible one took me by the shoulder and turned me about. Then a rousing voice said in my ear 'Benvenuto, do as you are wont, and fear not.' On the spot I changed my mind ... and said to my Italian friends 'Arm yourselves well, and come out with me'" (p. 240 [2:29–30]). A touch of Providence, and he is himself again.

Although the greatest disaster that hit him was certainly his imprisonment, it also became the occasion for his most treasured religious experiences. Initially in despair, he tries suicide. But, "I was seized by some invisible thing and thrown four cubits' length from the place.... I felt I had been visited by some power divine, my guardian angel" (p. 184 [1:118]). More and more he sees the hand of God in the entire experience. God speaks directly to him ("Go now and rest and have no fears"). And ultimately Cellini has a mystical experience: "I was taken up and carried away by that invisible power, and brought into a place where the unknown being manifested himself visibly in human form" (p. 189 [1:122]). He sees the Christ on the Cross and he sees the Virgin; he wakes up with his forehead marked, and has several meetings with his guardian angel. His "miraculous" release occurs, and from then on, at sunrise, he may wear a halolike shadow around his head. For Cellini all of this could only serve to enhance and to exalt his sense of life being securely anchored in providential care. As he said in the "capitolo," written in prison in his own blood: "I raised my thoughts to God on high, Asking his pardon for my every sin.... I saw an angel coming down from heaven ... 'Thou shalt bear thy body's burden yet a while ... for God shall scatter every foe of thine, waging with them a bitter war, but thou, happy and free, art blessed by Him'" (p. 200 [1:128]).

Cellini thus found support for his actions in an unproblematic view of the world and in a simple trust in personal providence. One matter, in addition, deserves attention if we are to understand his uncomplicated conscience and his singularly striking way of acting without troubling reflection on the action. Although a sovereign self, Cellini was not the sort of man to invest much mental and psychic energy in considerate moral self-legislation. He is neither a Petrarch, weighing with great care conflicting standards of life, nor a Pico della Mirandola, struggling for a syncretistic unity of values, nor a Machiavelli, breaking consciously with one moral code for the overriding sake of a fitting political morality, nor a Castiglione, intent upon equipping an ideal courtier with norms of behavior and etiquette. Conventional morality would have been a disabling impediment to Cellini.

But neither was he a totally amoral creature simply pursuing its whims. He needed a regulative agency within him that could function with immediacy, without requiring thoughtful weighing of alternatives. For many of his actions Cellini could very simply rely on an instinct for self-preservation and self-assertion in harmony with his view of the world in which men had to take care of themselves and prove their *virtù*. In the self-assertion and the need for "virtuous" self-aggrandizement lay a tie to the other powerful regulative mechanism within him: his sense of honor. His own sense of worthiness was completely linked to his belief in being an honorable man. He will repeatedly insist that his word is sufficient guaranty; he is utterly disdainful, even of a pope, when he is convinced that a man went back on his word. That he may have been guilty of the same failing is not the issue; one attempts no claim of consistency for Cellini. Only once does he directly admit a mistake, and then not too impressively: "If I did not own that in some of these incidents I did wrong, my account of the others, in which I know I did well, would be suspect. So I own I made a mistake in revenging myself so violently on Pagolo Micceri" (p. 246 [2:34]). Long-range bookkeeping that totals up virtues and faults does not interest Cellini at all; what counts for him is the conduct in its immediacy.

In the immediate action Cellini is guided by his sense of honor. He turns to defensive action at the slightest suggestion of a personal offense. Often the issue must be fought out then and there. But at other times, when he either has his choler under control or sees no immediate chance for action, he will pursue the matter stealthily, like a cat, until he has his satisfaction. One of the most symptomatic scenes of this sort occurs on his return from a trip to Venice with some less "manly" companions. At Chioggia the innkeeper insists on being paid in advance. Cellini takes this as a direct slur on his honor. But he and his fellow travelers pay and stay the night. "We had indeed excellent beds.... Yet all the same I never closed an eye all night for thinking how I could have my revenge." When the party steps on the boat to leave the next morning, Cellini excuses himself, allegedly to pick up a pair of slippers he had forgotten. Returning unnoticed to the rooms, he "took a little razor-edged knife, and cut the four beds . . . into shreds . . . damage to the tune of more than fifty crowns." Then he returns to the boat with bits of the bed hangings wafting from his pockets and reports to his companions. One of them is aghast: "Let us bind up our swords, for God's sake! And no more pranks, for I have felt all the time I have been with you as if the knife were at my throat." But to Cellini this was no prank and his companion no man. He concludes the episode: "To my comrade I had seemed a bad companion for having resented insults, and defended us both against those who would have harmed us. But I thought his conduct much worse. . . . Let him be the judge who looks on dispassionately" (pp. 119–21 [1:79]). And thus ended the matter for him, as it always did, when he had achieved his sense of satisfaction and the balance of honor was restored. One can sympathize with his companions's constant feeling of having a knife at his throat. It is indeed as if Cellini carried a penumbra around himself; it was dangerous to enter the domain of such a sovereign personality with the slightest hostility. He could be effectively disarmed by a simple refusal to play his game of honor. In a quarrel with the Micceri, Cellini pulls his sword, points it at the man's throat: " 'Base coward . . . Recommend yourself to God, for you are a dead man!' Too terrified to move, he called out thrice 'O mother mine, help me!' I had meant to kill him on the spot; but hearing him utter these foolish words, half my anger passed away. . . . So I kept the point of my sword at his throat, now and then giving him a little prick. . . . But when I saw that he did nothing to defend himself, I did not know what more to do" (p. 245 [2:33]). You do not fight with a coward; you trick him instead into a marriage with a loose woman!

Numerous other incidents of the sort show how this sense of honor functions automatically among equally sovereign peers and automatically stops him from impetuous action where no matter of honor is to be pursued. It is a sense of honor that functions in a simple nonreflective manner. While it does not presuppose thoughtful moral reflection, it does function as a genuine moral substitute and as a regulative agent that prevents, within its own standards, absolutely criminal and arbitrary willfulness. Cellini seems unintelligible without it—but so perhaps is modern man. Jacob Burckhardt, more than a century ago, and very much with an eye on his own contemporaries, put it thus:

> Let us begin by saying a few words about that moral force which was then the strongest bulwark against evil [*die dem Bösen aufs stärkste entgegenwirkende sittliche Kraft*]. Those highly

gifted men thought they would find it in the form of a sense of honor. That is that enigmatic mixture of conscience and egotism [*Selbstsucht*], which often survives in the modern man after he has lost, whether by his own fault or not, faith, love, and hope. This sense of honor is compatible with much selfishness and great vices and is capable of astonishing illusions; yet, all the noble elements that are left in a character [*Persönlichkeit*] may gather around it, and from this source may draw new strength. It has become, in a far wider sense than is commonly believed, a decisive rule of conduct for the cultivated Europeans of our day [*die heutigen individuel entwickelten Europäer*], and many who still hold faithfully to religion and morality [*Sitte*] are unconsciously guided by this feeling in the gravest decisions.[11]

It may always be tempting to classify Cellini's personality with those boundlessly willful Renaissance creatures who accepted no limitation of any sort, until, driven only by their momentary whims and unbridled arbitrary self-will, they capsize in sheer "subjectivism." But he was too "autonomous" for that. There were laws and objective limitations by which he willingly let himself be bound. He accepts the world as it is and accommodates himself within the framework that it offers. He feels securely anchored in his experience of providential support; he needs and eagerly accepts the comfort of his Church—one may indeed wonder how he would have fared with the self-reforming Church of a few decades later. And he is guided by his sense of honor, his need to prove his *virtù*, and the binding framework of the *agon*.

Most important of all: he submits to the canons of his art. He does so ultimately; for there was a crisis point where he strove to go beyond it. Advancing ever further in skill and technique, intensely filled with a growing trust in his creative power, he faces the moment of temptation to ask from matter what matter cannot give. The danger point comes in France. Here he finds in Francis I a royal patron with a sense for the grandiose and a willingness, for a while at least, to support Cellini lavishly with materials and projects. Some of his work then moves in the direction of gigantesque, elaborate, virtuose intricacy and theatrical illusionism. He promises a fountain "the richest and most ingenious I could think of" (p. 229 [2:20]). He starts a head of Mars, so huge that his assistant Ascanio can place a bed for his paramour in a corner of the hollow head; the good Parisians looking at the monstrosity from their roofs see a figure moving through its eyes and promptly think of it being haunted (p. 256 [2:42]). Cellini is told to make twelve silver candlesticks, six gods, six goddesses, each the same size as Francis I. When one of these, the Jupiter, is finished, Cellini decides to present it late at night in the long gallery of Fontainebleau. He acts more in the spirit of a theatrical producer than a sculptor willing to let the forms of his statue speak for themselves. A thin veil is hung over the Greek god "to enhance its majesty," a lighted torch is put in his hand, and "when I saw his Majesty come in, I made my lad Ascanio push the statue gently forward; and as my contrivance [!] was arranged with some skill, this movement gave to the striking figure an additional appearance of life" (pp. 254–55 [2:41]). It is as if Cellini fears that a plain style will offer no occasion for showing off his virtuosity of skill. Ordinary size may not impress. A statue does not suffice as a statue: it should be dressed up, move, be alive, roll its eyes, and perhaps even utter some divine wisdom.

Cellini, even in his best work, ran the danger of succumbing to his fascination with sheer technical virtuosity and a nascent baroque tendency toward theatricality. The subtle balance between clean, beautiful lines, and that overornateness in which technical skill can assert itself, is often in danger of tilting. The great virtuoso easily stands in the way of the potentially great artist. But fortunately for his well-being as an artist and as a man, he lost the French paradise. In the more limited conditions of his native Florence, Cellini's artwork regained a more classical formal restraint. The attempt to capture spurting blood in bronze may still jar the aesthetic experience of the Perseus-Medusa statue; a decidedly theatrical effect was obviously sought; but the whole is still in formal balance. It is as if a very fundamental sense for plastic beauty and enough of a sense for the limitations of the artistic medium ultimately brought Cellini to submit to the canons of his art, just as the more settled existence in his native city, and the freely given admiration of its citizens let Cellini be a more securely contained self.

This same fundamental "plastic power" of the sculptor also enabled him to present his life as a whole and to leave the ineradicable impression of a formed person. When Cellini tells his life, he has no thought-out underlying interpretative scheme. He does not attempt to illustrate an underlying "philosophy of life" or "philosophy of personality." It seems altogether implausible that the very act of telling his life revealed to the narrator himself what he really was or anything he had not known already. The autobiographic effort here is not undertaken for the sake of self-clarification or self-interpretation. Cellini does not see himself as a historically, slowly developing self; except for the matter of the growth of his artistic skill—important as it is—and the gradual "settling" in Florence later, there is not much development to be noted. Cellini seems to remain recognizably the same. Thus the need to reach understanding by tracing the gradual growth of the self does not function as an autobiographic key either. By telling his life Cellini uses an alternative way for asserting his very being once again; perhaps it is even another form for immortalizing his fame. He does not write memoirs: things I have witnessed. There is not a scene in which Cellini is not the central actor. The sack of Rome seems to be "put on" as a scene in the world-historical drama so that we may learn of Cellini, the virtuoso cannoneer. But he does not write *res gestae*, things done for the public, and he does not even dwell much on the way in which he affected the world around him. His real theme is: How Cellini asserted himself—and his life was crowded with opportunities for doing just that. The question remains, how could he give unity to such a presentation, in the absence of an underlying interpretative scheme. The answer lies, of course, in his complex, though unified personality, and in his artistic power.

Aside from the discernible thread of his developing technical skill and the advancing artistic *agon* in which he proves his growing artistic capacity, the book consists of, say, a hundred episodic scenes dealing with most diverse matters. These are in essence narrative and are linked by the continued presence of the same central character. This blatant egocentrism has the great advantage of providing a focus; the horizon is always drawn by his own ken, and everything within view has a relation only to him and his present objective. Cellini prehended the world around him by what Goethe calls *Anschauung*, that capacity for absorbing the surrounding reality in its immediate impact and for perceiving somehow, without analytical reflection, its constitutive configuration. For Cellini the essential feature of the surrounding circumstances is always the way in which they offer themselves as scenes for personal action, scenes on which he can project his personality. The episodes thus become moments in which a life presents itself in great condensation, showing the whole man in pursuit of an immediate objective. Cellini's dramatic sense stands him in excellent stead; he can quickly sketch the setting and focus on the central action, and he relies much on direct speech. The man who takes in the world through the eye presents it in words with pictorial descriptiveness. The scenes have a visual immediacy and dramatic compactness. In an age that perhaps can be said to have had less a philosophy of life than a style of life, one is tempted to see something fitting in such reliance on *Anschauung* and in the ability of presenting experiences in such graphic descriptiveness, or *Anschaulichkeit*. It is as if Cellini's memory is stocked with the imprints of visible scenes; in retelling his life, *stante pede* without carefully planned analysis and reflection, while working on something else at the same time, the images and scenes roll out in rounded words preserving all the life of immediate experience. Pouring the Perseus in bronze—altogether an unforgettable scene: "I raised the mould with the utmost care by means of windlasses and strong ropes to an upright position; and suspended it a cubit above the level of the furnace, paying attention that it hung exactly over the middle of the pit. Then gently, gently I let it down to the bottom of the furnace, sparing no pains to settle it securely there" (p. 295 [2:74]). He can still "feel' the very strain in his hands while lowering something gently and can still follow his eye movements in centering the contraption. The same form-giving power that makes a whole scene also succeeds, somehow, in unifying all the episodes into a panoramic view of a whole life in which an instantly recognizable rounded figure moves.

The artist who could thus tender his life as a work of art presents as a personality an interesting problem in the history of individuality. The self-conception with which Cellini represents himself hardly seems "conceived"; he is, in the true meaning of the word, naïve. There is something utterly "artless," nonreflective, intentless about his self-conception. Cellini seems to have no intention of sitting down and figuring out what he is or how he wishes to present himself. He is not in search of himself. He would have no understanding of Petrarch's problem as to how one can become a whole, an integral person. He would get irritated with the minute self-investigation which Cardano imposes on himself. How can one imagine Cellini on an analyst's couch? He is what he is and he has no intention of making anything else of himself. He does not hold before his view models of action or models of being. Certainly, he compares himself to others; and in pursuing the artistic *agon*, and in following a code of honor shared with honorable peers, he belies a self-conscious pursuit of individuality. But he knows nothing about such a self-conscious pursuit except the instinctive feeling that "a man must do what he must" (p. 50 [1:33]). Cellini cannot be anything other than his own individuality even if he does not know what that means. He cannot present himself according to any schema other than that dictated by his individuality. But in a perfectly naïve way he can present Cellini by the depiction of his words. He can present himself as an individuality. That such individuality could unreflectingly come into its own, could assert itself, and could thus naïvely render itself in its retold life, in an age in which the freestanding person has come to the fore, is a vital step in the movement toward the conscious cultivation of individuality.

# 7

# Jerome Cardano:
# A Scientist Views the Complex Self

Cellini (1500–71) and Cardano (1501–76) were contemporaries but meant nothing to each other. Neither of these important Renaissance writers of autobiography could have taken his own measure by comparing himself with the other. Both men stood in the world the Renaissance had brought about; Cellini simply profited from that fact, Cardano began to weigh its historical meaning. The waves of the beginning Counter Reformation wash up against both lives: Cellini the artist proudly exhibits his emotional brand of religion; Cardano the scientist, speculating daringly about religious matters in his middle years, is in his old age imprisoned briefly under the strict regime of Pope Pius V, from whom, at the very end of life, he nonetheless obtains a pension. Though the age of exploration does not touch Cellini at all, it moves Cardano deeply. Cellini simply takes the world as it is and lives his life as artist and man of *virtù;* for the questioning Cardano the nature of the world and man's role within it have become challenging problems. Both Cellini and Cardano stand in their world as free, independent personalities driven by an irresistible desire for glory and fame. The artist surrenders to this desire with an ebullient assertiveness; the scientist soberly resigns himself to an indomitable passion for fame which his mind refuses to take seriously. Both believe that man immortalizes himself through creativity; but while the artist thrives on a sense of power to create what was not there before, the scientist finds fulfillment in the discovery of reality—as a doctor resigning himself to do hazardous battle with nature, and as a thinker searching for the clues to knowledge which will enable man to maintain himself somehow amid the forces of nature. The artist's unquestioned trust in the unity of closed form permits him to shape his art and his life. But under the pressure of the scientist's analysis the coherent forms of daily experience begin to disintegrate; when the thoughts about various infinities and relativities disturb the mind, the certainty of a world of closed forms gives way to a much more desperate search for some kind of causal nexus in a troublesome complex world. Both men provide important evidence for the gradual emergence of individuality; but while Cellini lived out and unreflectingly presented his individuality in an unproblematic manner, Cardano, pondered his own existence in a somber mood of sober querying and established his singularity piece by piece. His autobiography has been celebrated as the first "scientific" effort to get hold of the elusive human self.

Cardano was a prolific writer; his Latin is difficult, and his ideas are tied to a sixteenth-century world of science that a nonexpert finds difficult to penetrate and even the experts have been hard put to elucidate.

Cardano's book *De vita propria* is an autobiography written by an old man in the last year of his life. At seventy-four years old, fairly comfortably settled in Rome, the author could rely on several earlier writings in which he had looked at his life in the form of either horoscopes or discussions of his own books. He was an inveterate notetaker—the last volume of the *Opera omnia* he calls *Paralimpomena*, "things left out" of other books, a cleaning up of "all the chips that remained in the workshop." In writing his autobiography he was presumably surrounded by hundreds of note cards recording the minute and innumerable details with which he filled his story. He outlined the main events of his life in one of the early chapters; as we shall see, he thought it the least interesting aspect of his story. It was to be sure essentially a scholar's life, but it was not uneventful.

Cardano was a native of the duchy of Milan, a place about which Cellini would speak with utter disdain whenever he met a Milanese. His father, a jurisconsult, had a large number of relatives with whom Jerome Cardano later fought an endless number of lawsuits over property. The senior Cardano was a good mathematician, who had several times been consulted by Leonardo da Vinci. His wife seems to have come from very humble circumstances, and father and mother may have had the sort of arrangement which makes it likely that Jerome was technically born an illegitimate child. For this reason, the medical board of Milan later refused repeatedly to have him accredited. He was a nervous and sickly boy who suffered from nightmares and visions. When he was nineteen he began his academic training at Pavia, and, although his father wept when Jerome decided on a medical rather than a legal career, the young man obtained his doctor's degree in 1525 at Padua. For years thereafter, he lived in small country towns such as Sacco, outside Padua, or Gallarate, outside Milan, in very poor circumstances. "I ceased to be poor because I had nothing left" (p. 15 [4].)[1] He married at Sacco and had three children—a girl, and two boys who later were to break his heart. Between 1529 and 1539, he made several unsuccessful attempts at medical accreditation in Milan, but was admitted, "contrary to every expectation," only in 1539. Meanwhile he lectured in mathematics, made a very modest living by his medical practice, gambled, played chess, and observed the wondrous world around him. After 1536, his books began to appear, and he gradually acquired a reputation in medicine, mathematics, and astrology. Fame and wealth came to him during the forties. He turned down an appointment as physician to the Farnese pope Paul III because of the pope's age: "Why should I leave certainties for uncertainties?" He rejected a munificent offer from the Danish king for reasons of climate and "because the Danes are given to another way of worship" (p. 16 [4]). In 1552, however, he accepted an invitation to cure the archbishop John Hamilton of Scotland of asthma (by recommending that he sleep on a pillow covered with leather) and had a profitable and triumphant tour of northern Europe.

By 1546, his wife had died and Jerome was in charge of bringing up the children. In 1559, the oldest boy Giambatista, a doctor like his father, killed his unfaithful wife and, despite Cardano's desperate attempts to save him, he was executed in April 1560. It was the darkest hour in Cardano's life; after successfully soliciting an invitation to a professorship at Bologna in 1562, he "fled" there. By this time the youngest son Aldo had become a good-for-nothing, gambling away his father's money, stealing from his locked money boxes, and perhaps even provoking the Inquisitors to proceed against his father. After the boy had gotten into constant difficulties with the law, Cardano finally disinherited him. On October 6, 1570, Cardano was imprisoned, for alleged impieties and erroneous theological statements in his books, at the order of the Holy Office at Rome; his name was erased from Bologna's faculty rolls. He was permitted to abjure in private; further lecturing was not forbidden, but he was advised to abstain. He himself appointed four cardinals "to look after the revision of De rerum varietate," the book considered the most offensive.[2] After seventy-seven days in prison, and another eighty-six days of house arrest, Cardano was free once more. His student and friend Rodolfo Silvestri now took him to Rome where the old man lived as a private scholar. "At the present, to be exact, four years have passed since I entered the city, and five since my incarceration. I have passed my days as a private citizen, except for my reception by the College [of Physicians] of Rome, on the 13th of September. The Pope is my patron in the matter of a pension." On September 20, 1576, Cardano died peacefully, leaving behind him 131 printed works and 111 books in unpublished form (he had burned 170 manuscripts).[3] The *De vita propria* was the last book on which he worked.

In its formal structure this book is unlike any prior autobiography. Although Cardano declares in the first sentence of his Prologue: "This Book of My Life I am undertaking to write after the example of Antoninus the Philosopher, acclaimed the wisest and best of men," the comparison with Marcus Aurelius's *To Himself* does not fit Cardano's intent and structure. The other models he occasionally mentions— Galen, Josephus, Sulla, Caesar, and Augustus—do not fit either, but the brief references may mean no more than that Cardano intends to write about himself like others before him. His characterization that this is "merely a story" seems as useless as his use of the term *narrative*. Except for chapter 4 ("A brief narrative of my life ... "), the fifty-four chapters of this book are each given to topical discussions or enumerations hardly deserving of the title. Personal matters are arranged quite unlike the diarylike entries of Marcus Aurelius. Some of the parts reflect the usage of Suetonius's biographic art which had become standard humanist fare: native lands and forebears (1), my nativity (2), certain traits of my parents (3), stature and appearance (5), manner of life (8), my friends (15), my enemies (16), religion and piety (22), rules of conduct (23), marriage and children (26), journeys (29), honors (32), my teachers (34), my students (35), books I have written (45), testimony of illustrious men concerning me (48), familiar sayings of mind (50). But these parts are interspersed with quite unusual topics, to say nothing of their often singular content. A relatively large set of chapters are set aside for a discussion of external issues and habits such as Cardano's health (6), his exercises and sports (7), his gambling and dicing (19), dress (20), manner of walking and thinking (21), dwelling places (24), and the quality of his conversation (53). The content of his last will and testament comes in a middle chapter (36), and a systematic attempt to review his changes from youth to old age comes toward the end (52), but before a chapter on conversation. And chapters with "strange" titles are spread throughout: a meditation on the perpetuation of my name (9), those things in which I take pleasure (18), happiness (31), certain natural eccentricities (37), five unique characteristics by which I am helped (38), things absolutely supernatural (43), concerning my own existence (46), and guardian angels (47). To use one of his favorite terms: the whole has the appearance of a "farrago." There is an underlying order, however: the first eight chapters deal with man in his natural condition; the chapter on the pursuit of fame (9) then initiates the discussion of training, habits, intellect, and spirit by which a man makes more of his life than nature and circumstance alone can do. Even if this order is not rigorously maintained, it is still remarkable that such a "farrago" enabled Cardano to develop a "portrait" of himself at all.

The chosen form of presentation is, of course, related to the book's intention; but as the author's goals are not stated very explicitly, they emerge only gradually and, in part, have to be guessed. In the Prologue Cardano dwells on the lack of originality in his undertaking. He has not been witness to really great events, though he had "many noteworthy experiences." He emphatically rejects the idea that he intends to instruct anyone by the book. The strongest hint of purpose is his assertion that recognition of truth is always a worthy objective. He intends to collect "experiences"; the "story," presented "without any artifice," is meant to recount his life, not events. When in a later chapter he discusses the books written by himself, he simply states: "The Book of My Life I was moved to write, because this seemed meet, necessary, and in accord with the circumstances. And it is not unpleasant for me so to review my days, if I may put any faith in the sentiments of Epicurus" (p. 234 [45]). The first sentence of this statement may well relate to an introductory one he places at the beginning of this discussion of all his books: "The reason I was induced to take up writing I think you have already learned. I was, in fact, urged by a dream, and thereafter twice, thrice, and four and indeed many times the suggestion was thus presented.... But I was also urged by a great longing to have my name live" (p. 224 [45]).

Cardano addresses the general reader:[4] the book is not simply an instrument for self-discovery, or self-possession as in the case of Marcus Aurelius. In one pasage only (p. 13 [4]), when he lists all the details of an election to the doctor's degree, he becomes self-conscious about these and quickly suggests that he writes down insignificant facts only for his own satisfaction. "I do not record such personal items for others' eyes." But in the very next sentence, speculating again that he will have readers, he hints at the real reason for the details: the readers should "note that the beginning and outcome of important events are not always evident." The minutiae are significant in the story of his life; and he goes on to record much more "shocking" personal items. The intention for writing, then, is first of all his powerful desire to achieve fame through his books. But this reason hardly helps to account for the form he has chosen. The other stated reasons are the inner force that has "moved" him to undertake this task and his pleasure and benefit in viewing and revealing truth. That these reasons are indeed intrinsically related to the form will have to be shown by further analysis.

Cardano does not present his life as a consecutively told story, as Abelard, for instance, did by tracing his life through an account of its most critical moments. Unlike Augustine, Cardano does not present his past through the "meaning-giving" terms of a central experience, integrating the concrete events in an over-all view of a unified life. Nor does the book, written at the very end of life, display the process of self-recovery and orientation that marked Petrarch's *Secretum*. The contrast to the contemporary Cellini is particularly interesting. The artist presents his whole life by narrating, in historical sequence, condensed scenes in which the whole man shows himself; he permits a unified view of his self by portraying his full being in different situations and actions. There is a narrative sequence in this, albeit little evolution of personality can be discerned. In Cardano's autobiography the procedure is reversed. The outline of his life is given in one short early chapter; the general changes that mark the transition from infancy to old age are set forth in an even shorter late chapter. And in the chapters in between he draws on any phase of his life for illustrating the topical issue under discussion. Thus the emphasis is not on showing how he came to be what he now is; nor is it on a simple understanding of what he now is, as is the case in the late books of Augustine's *Confessions*. Indeed, the question of development is neglected, as it is so frequently prior to the eighteenth century. As the personality stands before the reader's eyes, it is a composite of separate parts that have been subjected to a laborious analytic process.

Cardano drew some of his analytical categories from model character studies such as Theophrastus, whom he generally admired, and from such classical historians as Plutarch, Suetonius, and Sallust, thus staying within a humanistic mold. Others, however, were derived from the peculiar structure of his own life and from his world view. He was fascinated by factual correctness, but was little given to idealizing: "the well known *gnothi seauton* (Know Thyself) seemed the best guide" (p. 49 [13]). He would be neither a Marcus Aurelius, "writing as they think they ought to be," nor a Josephus, giving "true accounts, but with all their shortcomings carefully suppressed." He understood that his many unorthodox views might lead to trouble (p. 57 [14]). He foresaw that the act of recording his praises and his vices might be misunderstood. "Any who cast aspersions upon the praises I have enjoyed by intimating that I

am boastful and extravagant, accuse me of faults of others, for those sins
are not mine, I resent such, and defend myself; I attack no one. Why
then do I trouble to make this examination of myself when I have given
testimony so many times of the emptiness of life? My excuse is the praise
spoken by some, who think that a man who has attained so much
distinction does not have his shortcomings" (pp. 50–51 [13]). He desired
fame, yet he realized that fame might be withheld from a man like the
one he might reveal himself to be. The fame he hoped for was to come
from his scholarly books, from his mathematical writings, and especially
from his commentaries on the Hippocratic corpus on which he had
lectured and worked most of his life—not from the autobiography. Yet
even the account of his life in all its stark factual nakedness might ultimately bring fame to someone who, like him, counted his perpetual
search for truth his finest quality! "Even if any hope I have for fame
should fail me, my ambition is worthy of praise" (p. 35 [9]). At the very
end of the book he worries briefly that some might think he listed his
medical achievements in an earlier chapter as a form of advertising to
gain more patients. He quickly brushes this aside. "I did it that men, in
so far as they can seek out the truth, may know me for such as I am—in a
word, a teller of truth, an upright man" (p. 291 [54]).

Cardano's stated intention is to let the facts speak. He himself is
willing to face his reality as it is, without being distracted by any precon-
ceived theory. What reality he sees, he intends to relay to his reader—no
matter how peculiar or unbelievable it is. Facts are determined by the
same standards used to construct and record his "scientific" views of the
world. Cardano's scientific activity exhibits a tension (different from our
modern one) between a restless curiosity that aims for erudite information about the world, on the one hand, and a concern for a critical testing
of the evidence, on the other. His desire to possess all available knowledge, and his wish to test that knowledge are not always compatible. In
his mathematical work, probably the arena of his most lasting renown,
this tension played no role. But it quickly comes into play with questions
of physical fact. Cardano's deep-seated desire for knowledge and his
eagerness to show off his erudition are so strong that he will not sus-
pend judgment until the knowledge is thoroughly tested. The phenom-
enal public success of his "encyclopedic" works, such as the *De subtilitate
rerum* (which saw five editions alone between 1550–54) and the *De
rerum varietate* (three editions between 1557–58), shows that he was in
tune with his age.

But while he was not engaged in the careful testing of every building stone that went into his scientific edifice, he was not uncritical in sorting out the material. He is generally inclined to record knowledge already shared by others, but he most certainly will weigh one source against the other. He does so without a marked prejudice against any group of men: he is not prepared to place any statement of an ancient author above that of a medieval one, or to prefer Christian to Arabic, a modern to ancient, although he is generally persuaded that he lives in an advanced and advancing age. He will attack Aristotle, Galen, or Ptolemy as well as defend tham against men too eager to found new sects. He challenges the continuing prestige of Aristotle with a common-sense proposition: if, for the sake of truth, Aristotle was free to depart from his teacher Plato, then we surely have the same right of review.[5] When he trusts a source, he will accept its less than certain data: Theodore Gaza and George of Trebizond would not have lied about the existence of mermaids, ergo Cardano reports the existence of the lovely creatures.

Cardano has two main means for testing information: for one, do the data fit or not fit within his general view of things? and, for another, do the data agree with his personal experience and observation? Convinced that the order of nature is no accident, he concludes that the influence of the stars must certainly be responsible for departures from natural regularity.[6] Convinced that something with an imperfect internal structure cannot be turned into something with a perfect internal structure, and that gold has such a perfect structure, he rejects the very possibility of alchemy.[7] Since he is in general inclined to think in terms of polarities, and since he is convinced that all matter has psychic life, he will unquestioningly make use of data suggesting that vines hate cabbage, that the olive tree loves the myrtle, and that pumpkins dry up when approached by a menstruating woman.[8] Where theory runs counter to his ordinary experience, he will not take the theory seriously. Though he knows of Copernicus, he rejects his theory on the ground that it implies that the earth would have to move so fast that he himself would have to be able to notice it.[9] Reports about long-living animals are many; Albertus Magnus asserts a goose may live to be sixty years; Cardano himself had seen a finch as old as thirteen in a cage; ergo, Albertus may be trusted. In the most professional aspect of Cardano's life, his medical practice, this reliance on personal observation and repeated experience expressed itself most strongly. This is not to say that he built his medical practice on observed data alone; his medical opinions are full of the current theories of the day. But he modified such theories freely on the basis of his own experience, and he undertook his general attack on the prevalent authority of Galen by confronting Galen with the insights of Hippocrates exactly because Hippocrates taught us to rely on experience and direct observation. Cardano considered his commentary on the Hippocratic corpus his best ground for future fame.

The all-important method for correcting or testing any transmitted knowledge through critical experiments based on hypothesis is in general missing from Cardano's scholarship. It is occasionally present in his medical practice, but even there experimentation seems to consist merely in repeated observation. In his own life his intuition served as his most important agent for discovery. He records "an intuitive flash of direct knowledge. This I employed with increasing advantage. It originated about the year 1529; its effectiveness was increased but it could never be rendered infallible except toward the close of 1573 . . . a gift which has not deserted me . . . . Its component parts are an ingeniously exercised employment of the intuitive faculty, and an accompanying lucidity of understanding. An altogether pleasing faculty . . . profitable for my influence, my training, for gain, and for confirming the results of my studies . . . it is certainly the most highly perfected faculty which man may cultivate" (p. 165 [38]).

In his attitude toward fact and its discovery, then, Cardano by no means stands outside his age. Like others, he is still the captive of authority. He gives no evidence of the radical distrust of tradition that Descartes would show in insisting on building a system only on reliably tested knowledge. Cardano can thus mingle reliance on critical observation with all the fantasy of tradition. To gain fame by erudition is as strong a desire as the wish to be celebrated for fresh discovery. But even if, in the light of a different scientific attitude, his factual foundation may be shaky, Cardano's fascination with fact is all-consuming and genuine. For him, every fact has a cause, and his drive to find it is unrelenting, though his method for establishing it is often uncritical.

Cardano held firmly to the idea that any matter in the universe is endowed with life to the degree that the world soul penetrates it; conversely the existence of the soul is affected by the nature of the matter it enters. When he wrote his *Vita*, he therefore placed the material and physiological conditions of his existence at the beginning. He saw life as, to a considerable extent, a set of givens. A man is born in certain geographic surroundings which, though arbitrary, are hardly inconsequential in accounting for fundamental differences.[10] To the discussion of the geographic setting of his birth, Cardano adds the customary humanistic genealogy. Noteworthy from the outset is his concern with numerical precision: the place of origin for the Cardani is twenty-four miles from Milan; of a far-off relative, Milano Cardano, we learn that in 1189 he had been "prefect of Milan for seven years and eight months by the ecclesiastical as well as the civil calendar"; we are given a long list of the different ages reached by relatives; he lists the exact number of relatives alive, etc. Similarly, precision about the time of birth is of vital importance: his birth occurred at 6:40 o'clock, September 24, 1501[11]—although, ironically there has been subsequent debate whether this is actually correct!

The all-important matter, of course, is how the stars stood: "Although the malefics were not within the angles, nevertheless Mars was casting an evil influence on each luminary ... *therefore* I could easily have been a monster, except for the fact that the place of the preceding conjunction had been 29° in Virgo, over which Mercury is the ruler." Cardano reports that he had to be torn from his mother's womb, was almost dead at birth, then revived in a bath of warm wine "which might have been fatal to any other child." Thus he is marked by special features from the outset. "To return to the horoscope, since the sun, both malefics, and Venus and Mercury were in the human signs, I did not deviate from the human form. Since Jupiter was in the ascendant and Venus ruled the horoscope, I was not maimed, save in the genitals, so that from my twenty-first to my thirty-first year I was unable to lie with women." All in all, the constellations were not promising for a noteworthy life; yet he will mention at the end of the chapter that the Emperor Augustus was born on the same day, and that the date also coincided with Columbus's first sailing (which involved one of the frequent errors in arithmetic of which Cardano is "guilty"). Thus, the givens were generally unfavorable—but then, givens are not the only forces in life.

In two early chapters (3 and 5), Cardano describes the physical appearance of his parents as well as himself. He dwells on telling characteristics: his father was never without a black skullcap; his whitish eyes enabled him to see at night; from his fifty-fifth year he lacked all his teeth. In describing himself, Cardano overwhelms us with details: my feet are wide near the toes, too high at the heels, "so that I can scarcely find shoes"; the thickly fashioned right hand has dangling fingers ... my left hand ... is truly beautiful with long, tapering, well-formed fingers and shining nails"; he has a cleft chin, and very small, half-closed eyes; "over the eyebrow of my left eye is a blotch or wart, like a small lentil, which can scarcely be noticed"; he has rather too shrill a voice, with a tone too harsh and high; "I am not inclined to speak in the least suavely, and I speak too often." But after all these characteristic details, Cardano paradoxically concludes that he presents "a picture so truly commonplace that several painters who have come from afar to make my portrait have found no feature by which they could so characterize me, that I might be distinguished."

A chapter "concerning my health" follows, and again the detail is perplexing. "Now I have fourteen good teeth and one which is rather weak"; "I had hemorrhoids"; "I ignored a rupture ... from my sixty-second year on I greatly regretted [this]"; "in 1536 I was overtaken with ... an extraordinary discharge of urine ... from sixty to one hundred ounces in a single day"; "[I had insomnia] lasting about eight days a year, never missed a year"; "when I was 55 I was troubled with daily fevers for forty days, at the crisis of which I was relieved of one hundred and twenty ounces of urine on October 13, 1555"; during his youth, his heart often throbbed violently, though it could be quieted by pressing the hand on it; from the hour of retirement until midnight Cardano was never warm from his knees down (later we learn how he learned to cure this affliction by warm bathing); he is afraid of high places and shuns those where mad dogs had been sighted. And so on, and so on. Since he is so very conscious of frequent attacks of pain, he is overcome by unbearable mental anguish when he is temporarily painless. "Accordingly I have hit upon a plan of biting my lips, of twisting my fingers, of pinching the skin of the tender muscles of my left arm until the tears come. Under the protection of this self-chastisement I live without disgracing myself" (p. 25 [6]). We are given similar details of his sports and exercises. The long list of personal idiosyncrasies becomes almost unbearable in a chapter on "Manner of Life." He stays in bed ten hours, eight of which he sleeps; when he cannot sleep, he walks around the bed and counts to a thousand several times. He puts ointment made of poplar sap, bear grease, and oil of water lilies on seventeen spots of his body (he forgot to list the spots). For breakfast he likes a bit of bread steeped in broth, and "those large Cretan grapes called Zibbibos or red raisins"; for the midday meal he takes "simply an egg yolk with two ounces of bread or a little more"; on Fridays and Saturdays he varies his diet. For supper he orders "a dish of beets, a little rice, a salad of endive; but I like even better the wide-leafed spiny sow thistle, or the root of the white endive." He gives details about meats with directions for preferred methods of preparation. But he prefers fish to meat and provides a guide to his tastes in a carefully categorized list of sea and fresh-water fish. "Fresh water crabs ... please me; sea crabs are too tough, and eels and frogs I find too disgusting, as is the case with fungi." Carp ought to be three to seven pounds. White meats are better than dark meat; bluish parts are less easily digested; "garlic does me good," and so on.

It is evidently important to Cardano to provide such detail. Usually the physical observations are given without comment. He has no inhibition about discussing hemorrhoids or urine. While writing the *Vita*, Cardano remembers an uncompleted book: "The Treatise on Urinary Diseases.... These demonstrate the wonders of nature, since in a subject so lightly esteemed, so many remarkable features are embraced, and so to the universe we must concede the wonders of its parts" (p. 228 [45]). What at first may seem to be an almost indifferent listing of weighty and insignificant matters may indeed rest on thoughtful reflection. There is not only hypochondria here but a genuine fascination with physical detail. He hints that there is a relation between physical attributes and spiritual existence.

But though he no doubt takes all this very seriously, his sense of fun and his mischievous streak suddenly take over. He concocts fanciful categories and plays with numerical relations. He lists one category of fifteen items, another one containing only eleven; yet he exclaims: "fifteen!" as though there were significance in mere numerical parallels. "I have reduced the whole to a system as is the fashion in matters of theology, with much profound meditation and brilliant reasoning. For without this illuminating logic, certain things, which are actually most clear, would seem not quite so evident to you!" (p. 31 [8]). But what is fun on one level may have a profounder implication after all. It is the concrete fact that is truly important to Cardano. The system for system's sake, the symbolism and fascination with numerical parallels that preoccupied the scholastics—such is not Cardano's game.

In Chapter 9, "A meditation on the perpetuation of my name," Cardano turns from the observations of his "physiology" to the intellectual and spiritual categories through which he analyzed his life. "Life is twofold: the material existence common to the beasts and the plants"—but of which man partakes insofar as he is matter—"and that existence which is peculiar to a man eager for glory and high endeavor" (p. 32 [9]). Nature and the conditions of birth necessary for high endeavors did not favor him. A cool calculation of his resources should have dissuaded him from even trying to reach for fame. But "something" within Cardano—he simply says a dream—spurs him on. His critical reason immediately forecloses any ambitious hopes: "How will you write what will be read? ... what remarkable facts do you know that readers care for?" (p. 32 [9]). And how long do books last? Even the exceptional one that may outlast ten thousand years, will eventually disappear. The hope for fame in the tomorrow will ruin your today. Hannibal, Alexander, Caesar, they sacrificed their lives, and yet their works perished. Where now is the Roman Empire? "Absurdly and strangely enough—in Germany" (p. 34 [9]).

But whatever reasons reason may marshal, whatever persuades the rational part of Cardano, does not silence the simple ambition to count for something. "Be that as it may, an unshakable ambition remains . . . my desire is for renown, so many things to the contrary, so many obstacles in my way" (p. 35 [9]). In this argument Cardano presents a very telling aspect of his approach to the world, to life, and to himself. His ambition for fame is a stubbornly fixed fact; it may be irrational, it may be unreasonable, but it is an undeniable reality within himself. After an early unplanned, opportunistic existence in which he simply follows his whims, the ambition for fame dominates his life. As he makes clear in the chapter (10) immediately following, his ambition was in important respects a ruinous force: for, by concentrating on his work and his books, he neglected his sons, [12] and set the stage for bitter disappointment. [13] But as soon as Cardano admits the validity of all the "shoulds" and "oughts," he knows how ineffective they are against what is and what happened. The very chapter in which he lists "Things in which I feel I have failed" (51) ends with a reassertion of the very achievements of his ambition: "I have the knowledge of many sciences. . . . I have books published, and many ready to be published; I have reputation, position, and substance honestly acquired; . . . [I have] an understanding of many mysteries" (pp. 278–79 [51]).

These contradictions are real for Cardano; ultimately he desires to understand them, but first of all they have to be admitted as facts. Fact does not cease to be fact simply because the reasons for it cannot be seen. "The proposition that the exterior angle is equal to the sum of the two opposite interior angles—there is no reason why this should be so, but that it is so, is simply a fact." Cardano does not know why he is so taciturn, but he knows he is; he knows he has a quick temper, often says things in an unpleasant manner, gives in to immoderate whims; he knows he has only flimsy excuses for his gambling; he knows all the arguments why he should not gamble; he knows he hurt his family and wasted his time (which he abhors) and yet he admits the shortcomings—and, once at least (p. 277 [51]) he wonders out loud: was it really such a vice? Such admissions do not seem to be simple Christian confessions of human inadequacy. Every admission of error, vice, and failing has its full equivalent in a proud assertion of his knowledge, virtue, and success. Nor can this process of balancing be explained by the plain suspicion that Cardano takes perverse delight in showing himself as either a disgusting old man or an interesting eccentric; he has an even stronger urge to reveal his true greatness. He steadily returns to the argument that there is no excuse for an illusive complacency ignoring "conditions, a pretense of not being aware of what we know exists, or a will to set aside a fact by force" (pp. 54–55 [13]).

The irrationality of the basic fact—of ambition, of error, of vice—does not prevent Cardano from seeking his fame and his human fulfillment in the pursuit of knowledge, in understanding, and in reasonable conduct. Quite the contrary: the deep-seated urge to understand the puzzles of nature and of his private life asserts itself in the face of stubborn fact, and in part because of it. He seeks his very fame in the ability to understand and to explain. And he believes that this urge is in full accord with the very purpose of man. Man has been created so that he may (a) perceive the divine; (b) as a creature of the middle, link the divine with the mortal; (c) come to dominate the mortal; and (d) devise all that can be devised by the mind.[14] Medicine was in all these regards a fitting professional choice. As a doctor he could fulfill his "duty to care for human life." Contrary to the legal career his father urged on him, medicine was for Jerome "a pursuit relying rather upon reason and nature's everlasting law, than upon the opinions of men" (pp. 39–40 [10]). The driving force in his life was the desire to know and understand nature and man—who despite his "physiological" foundation within nature had a spirit for controlling her—to help himself and others by such understanding, and to be remembered for his effort.

But if this desire for understanding and its concomitant fame was the dominant drive—even the unifying factor in Cardano's life—there were also competing desires in the complexities of the personality and frequently obstacles in the complexities of events. Cardano found it impossible to lead a life fully consistent with his professed aim. In a very brief aside he suggests how perverse life could be: the very knowledge in which he took such pride might come to stand in the way of his pursuit. Consulting the stars about his own course, he was told that he would hardly reach the age of forty, certainly not more than forty-five! But as it turned out, the "very year in which it was believed the end of my life was at hand, brought with it the beginning of living" (p. 37 [10]). Thinking himself unfit to lead a purposeful life and lacking in the kind of human prudence that helps others to do so, Cardano decided to pursue his aims as "an opportunist." He would combine, as best he could, governance by wisdom and his own unreasoned preferences. He would act "as seemed advantageous when each occasion arose" (p. 36 [10]). He determined upon a course of life "not such as I would have, but such as I could." "I have lived my life as best I might . . . I continue to exist as well as I can" (p. 36 [10] and p. 35 [9]).

A profound sense of the complexities of life made it very difficult for Cardano to perceive any coherent structure. He saw the separate analytical parts of himself but had only a blurred view of the whole of existence. He was preoccupied by his fascination with the potential significance of each detail. Thus he approached the study of his own realities in the complex analytical manner that gives the book its peculiar structure and its inherent difficulty for the reader. The same sense of complexity accounts for the manner in which Cardano contradicts himself again and again. He was full of contradictions, and the very mode of presentation enables him to maintain one thing in one context and almost deny it in the next. But the analytical separation of materials also allows the conflicting aspects of the personality to stand distinct from one another without being subjected to reconciliation, coordination, or subordination. Thus the sense of life's complexity is heightened.

After the short block of chapters (9–11) in which Cardano systematically speculates about the desire for fame, its consistent (or inconsistently consistent) pursuit, and the lack of prudence in this pursuit, some forty chapters of highly diversified subject matter follow. In contrast to the very early chapters, they seem to be related somehow to aspects of Cardano's intellectual, scholarly, professional, and spiritual existence. To be sure, we hear again about breakfast made up of fifteen Cretan grapes (p. 282 [52]), the palpitating heart, weak teeth, and copious discharge of urine (p. 196 [41]), the sulphurous odor of his flesh, and the itching skin, etc. (p. 155 [37]); but now such items do not form a massive block of mere physiological detail; instead they are integrated into discussions of knowledge, medical practice, or striking circumstances.

Readers may have differing views of the meaning and function of these chapters, but it is possible to bring a few concrete issues to the fore by imposing a rough scheme of categorization. Cardano lists in a sober, matter-of-fact manner how such things as the places in which he dwelled (24), his marriage (26), law suits (28), journeys (29), teachers (34), and students (35) were related to his professional life. The listings are often extraordinarily dry: houses he has lived in (though always with the precise address!), names of students, or what subject was learned from which teacher. Brute facts leave the reader guessing at their significance. At other times, Cardano is aware of the reader's bewilderment. "But you will ask to what purpose is this account of all these cities?" (p. 100 [29]). He proceeds to make clear that, just as he has learned from Hippocrates how a doctor must learn to watch the physical setting of his patients, he must insist on similar relations between such subjects as geography and mathematics, history, botany, etc. Though the nature of these relations is not worked out here—they were in part in other books—the reader is left with the growing sense that Cardano suspects that such relations do exist and do matter. In other chapters he dwells on such relations. A chapter on dress (20) moves from considerations of health, economy, remissness of servants, indifference to personal matters in order to have more time for study, to the teachings of Galen, and finally to a calculation of how many combinations are possible with four basic garments! This chapter is followed by one on "Religion and Piety" (22). Sandwiched in between lies a perplexing, one-page chapter on "My manner of walking and of thinking." At first one supposes that it belongs with the earlier physiological discussions. But the coupling of walking and thinking suggests that Cardano is concerned with the manner in which external appearance is conditioned by internal life. "Because I think as I walk my gait is uneven." How I walk depends on how I feel. In part my walk depends on the manner acquired in youth; in part it depends on the subject matter on which I think. Since I think about many topics that are very alien to the men around me, my walk must appear to be startling ("my gait" may be "a subject for comment . . . a by-word!"). Thus the whole matter leads to philosophical speculation: all things controlled by hard necessity are variable; only the mind can govern with constancy and thus adhere to the good even when the influence of external factors is hostile. "Sustained thought takes such complete possession of me that I may neither eat, nor enjoy myself, nor even succumb to grief or sleep . . . a great good which may ward off evil and offer relaxation, . . . yet should it cease, I know not whether the result would be a help or a hindrance" (p. 77 [21]).

Thus Cardano compacts in one short chapter observations about external characteristics and the internal condition which they express, a reflection on how this appearance may strike others, all sorts of speculations about diverse topics, and ultimately the stated ambivalence: did this habit help me or not? In similar fashion, Cardano treats his habit of assuming "an expression quite contrary to my feelings" (p. 51 [13]), from which all sorts of difficulties arose. Sometimes he is incredibly rude. When the German humanist Pirckheimer pays him a courtesy call, Cardano receives him with the abrupt query: Do you have money? If not, I do not intend to have any concern for these Transalpines.[15] He acknowledges the lack of charm in conversation which has made his life difficult, although at the end he counts the blessings such a defect brings him (53).

While other chapters are straightforward accounts of what he owes to friends and patrons (15), to his enemies and rivals (16), to his customs and vices (13) as well as of his virtues and constancy (14), it is striking that the deeper he penetrates his accomplishments the more the writing leads to a discussion of extraordinary gifts and circumstances. Again, there is no strict order but nonetheless a discernible pattern. In Chapters 22 and 23 he simply announces that God, the Virgin, and St. Martin helped him to bear the hardships of life and that, with such help, he has learned to turn adversities to some advantage. In the long chapter 30 he begins to list perils, accidents, and diverse treacheries against him: his sudden decision to cross the street just before a cornice falls, a near drowning, a fall from a carriage, near misses in attacks from dogs, poison, irate gamblers, beams designed to be dropped on him, etc. He supplies every instance with dates and select details. From all this he concludes : "when I observed how I was protected more by Divine Providence than by any wit of my own, I ceased to exercise any further anxiety for my safety in dangers" (p. 117 [30]).

A little further on, in the long chapter 37, Cardano becomes concerned with "natural" eccentricities, marvels, and dreams. He discusses his visions, the fact that no blood was ever spilled when he was present, not even on a hunt, unusual sequences he incurred in throwing dice, the way in which his whole house burned down leaving only the beds with their unharmed occupants, the premonitions concerning his elder son's misfortunes, and the numerous dreams with their steadily prophetic content. All are "gifts of a bountiful God, who is in debt to no one, much less to me" (p. 161 [37]). The emphasis on special gifts, special circumstances, extraordinary powers, becomes ever stronger. Later chapters have headings such as "Things absolutely supernatural" and "Guardian angels." Chapter 38 on "Five unique characteristics by which I am helped" begins: "Up to this point I have discussed myself as an ordinary human being, so to speak; and as a man even somewhat lacking, in comparison to other men, in natural endowment and education" (p. 163 [38]). But Cardano has the gift of hearing from afar whether men speak well or evil of him: if he hears a hum in his right ear they speak well, a hum in the left betokens the speaking of evil. As the greatest of all gifts, he has been given intuitive powers making possible the real achievements of his mind and profession. He receives omens, physical objects behave in unnatural fashion in his presence, he is saved from illnesses, he learns to read a language from one day to the next, and he considers it a very special favor to have lived in an age when the whole world was discovered, when the compass was first used, and when printing was invented (sic). "O what arrogant poverty of intellectual humility not to be moved to wonder!"[16] Finally, as one of but a handful of men in all recorded history, he was given a personal spiritus or daimon. Only in his seventy-fourth year, "in the act of writing this autobiography" (p. 240 [47]), did he fully grasp the way in which this spirit, this guardian spirit, had assisted him. The spirit never speaks to him directly, "but he points the way to one thing through others of another nature" (p. 243 [47]). As a spirit, it had to mingle with Cardano's "matter"; when it errs, "it therefore errs through the fault of the medium" (p. 244 [47]). Why he has been granted such assistance, he cannot tell; but again and again he concludes that he owes all his accomplishments to the special talents granted to him.

Intermingled with these chapters analyzing the power of his faculties are evidences of Cardano's attempt to draw up the balance sheet of his accomplishments and failures. Many of these chapters present simple lists: "Honors conferred" (32), "Dishonors" (33), the "Successes in my [Medical] practice" (40), "Books I have written" (45), and "Testimony of illustrious men concerning me" (48). The latter, for instance, contains a numbered list of authors who had mentioned him in their printed works: e.g., no. 8, "Amato the Portuguese in his *Commentatio in Dioscoridem*"; or no. 19, "Konrad Gesner mentions me in various places"; or no. 28, "François de Foix ... whose censure I took for praise: in his *Geometria*"; or no. 35, "Gabrielle Fallopio: in his *Liber de Metallis et Fossilibus* in which he freely contradicts me." Such meticulous tracking down of his name—and without the help of a clipping service!—surely suggests an enormous labor and ego, although it is surprising that only the shortest possible mention (see nos. 51 and 66) is given to Scaliger and Tartaglia, men of great fame with whom Cardano had engaged in controversies of great furor, from which in both cases he emerged "victorious."[17] In other evaluative chapters, Cardano aims at a more general assessment. "The purpose of this chapter is to discover whether I actually know anything, or whether I only seem to know" (p. 168 [39]). Systematically he goes through the disciplines and comes to the sober conclusion that he had mastered only ten of the thirty-six important branches of learning. He is proudest of work in arithmetic, which "I have advanced ... as a science, tenfold, and medicine not a little" (p. 171 [39]). In a later chapter (44)—and in chapter 45 where he comments on his own books—he cuts through this subject matter differently, asking himself: what are the main points of my teachings that are worth something? He takes pride in having left (and apparently having counted!) "about five-thousand suggestions for treatment, all told. Of problems solved or investigated I shall leave something like forty-thousand and of minutiae two hundred thousand, and for this that great light of our country [Andrea Alciate] used to call me 'The Man of Discoveries' " (p. 219 [44]). Cardano also has chapters on "things in which I failed"—there are fewer of these—in which lamentations about the disastrous stories of the two sons, especially the older one, are dispersed.

In four compact chapters (31, 46, 49, 53), Cardano is willing to draw a summary evaluation: was my life worth living? Life was in many important respects unbearably cruel; much of it is affliction, waste and vanity, and plain meanness. No animal is viler or more treacherous than man. He is polluted with the burden of his own filth and water; his belly is full of worms, he scratches his lice, he stinks from his armpits, his feet, and his foul mouth. There is more unhappiness than happiness—and man's condition is equally shared by all.

But Cardano obviously said "yes" to life. Happiness is a matter of degree: "it makes for happiness to be what you can, when you cannot become what you would." We "should recognize what we have at our command" (p. 120 [31]). The orderliness of his life and his achievements in skill and in knowledge gave him a sense of affirmation. "There is ... good in the exercise of some art in which one is skilled," with which one may "alleviate misfortune" (p. 275 [50]); there is good in "meditating upon the manifold transmutation of all nature and upon the magnitude of Earth" (p. 123 [31]). The love of knowledge resonates all through Cardano's book: it is a wondrous privilege to be able to know, to understand, to come to see the interrelation of things. "One thing alone is sufficient for me: to understand and grasp the meaning of all these wonders would be more precious to me than the everlasting dominion of all the universe; and this I swear by all that is holy" (p. 213 [43]).

In reading this perhaps most puzzling of all autobiographies, one desperately latches on to some unifying principle in hopes of catching some glimpse of the personality that seems to be forever fleeting away in analytic dissection. Cellini's grandiose talent for imposing a unifying form on disparate detail is displaced in Cardano by an insistent drive to reduce the form to its immensely variegated components. This does not deny the considerable talent for presenting vast bodies of material in systematic order that Cardano showed in many of his "scientific works."[18] He had an intense urge to grasp things in their vast inter-relatedness. But when he wrote the autobiography, the analytical men-tality (and it was "still an undisciplined analytical mentality"[19]) proved to be the much stronger motivation. The scientific framework for view-ing the world as it was given to him in his cultural heritage was fleshed out with his own ideas and "discoveries." When he turned to the details of his own personality, no preconceptions would fit: The need to take careful stock swamped the power to present a recognizable portrait to the reader. The personality remains an enigma; perhaps it even eluded Cardano himself. Thus the true value of the autobiography may well rest in his attitude and the manner in which he studied personality.

More than any previous autobiographer, Cardano reveals a growing awareness of individuality. He is certainly conscious of his own unique-ness. He delights in revealing oddities that differentiate him from others. But quite often he insists that the others have similar traits; they simply may not be as willing to admit them (pp. 54–55 [13 and 14]). While he may thus be pursuing two objectives simultaneously—(1) the discovery of self; and (2) the use of such self-analysis in the interest of constructing a general anthropology—he asserts in the process some general conditions which eventually become important for recognizing individuality.

Cardano begins to have a sense for the "relative" aspects of things in general and for the human condition in particular. With this sense of the relative goes a growing interest in speculating about infinity. He shares these concerns with others of his century. The impact of the voyages of discovery forces such insights on men; the rediscovery of antiquity works in the same direction. Montaigne was to be confronted most forcefully by such implications of relativity. The problems of infinity come to appear more frequently in mathematics and in the line of cosmic speculations that runs from Cusanus to Bruno. Cardano only shares such attitudes and experiences in part. He retains a model of a closed geocentric world; he does not conceive of an infinite acentric universe; but he becomes obsessed with the vastness and infinity within this shell. "O reader ... do not set up for yourself as a standard human intellec-tual pride, but rather the great size and vastness of earth and sky; and [compare] with that Infinity these slender shadows in which miserably and anxiously we are enveloped" (p. 214 [43]). Cardano is not as aware of the non-European world as are some of his contemporaries, but he considers it of great significance that he lives in an age when the whole world has become known. Despite all respect for the ancients, he has a sovereign sense of assurance that his own age has its own value and that what was fitting for the Greeks is not fitting for the Italians (p. 234 [45]). He frequently ponders how different circumstances, character, law, and custom effectuate differences in a human condition that, on principle, is equal for all (see especially pp. 217–19 [44]).

He is increasingly concerned with speculation about the differentia whereby the specific emerges from the general. The geographic setting and the precise constellation of time are of particular interest. The book starts with a mention of his native land and goes on to give a horoscope. It may be remembered that in the interesting chapter on Happiness, he expressed his gratefulness that "all events of my life have come and passed in an orderly fashion, as if by rule" (p. 119 [31]). He adds to this the insight that his life could only be what it was because every moment came in the precise sequence required. "Had this not been the case and had the numerous commencements of the succession of events begun a little too late, or a little too soon, or had the conclusion been delayed, my whole career would have been subverted." For a human being to have such a perception of the unique relation between his moment of time and his personal constitution, a consciousness that every specific point in a spatial-temporal coordinate system can only be filled by one unique existence, is an inescapable milestone in man's journey toward a sense of individuality.

What is noteworthy about Cardano, however, is the weight that he places on the "stellar" configuration of the moment rather than on the historical. In other words, he is inclined to relate his personal existence to a firm order in nature more than to a historical order. He can thus have an extraordinarily strong assurance that his life fits in the general, natural order of things—and all his striving goes into the effort to discover the cosmic details. While he has a measure of awareness that his life has the distinctive marks of being born after the Renaissance, after the discoveries, during a period of immense political turmoil for Milan especially, and especially after the invention of printing, he is generally not inclined to search the explanation for the peculiarity of his personality in the formative interplay of the I and the specific historical world.

He has a "negative" stance toward his social world as well. He will do his social duty, and he desires the support and acclaim of the world; but most frequently he wishes to be left alone. He is not a social creature and, despite all his talk, he is not a good family man. To have children and grandchildren is to perpetuate one's biological substance; Cardano has an almost primitive need to cling to that form of immortality. The real objectives of his life "are the product of solitude and not of the society of men . . . . What, therefore, have I to do with men?" (pp. 386–87 [53]). He pursues his individuality by separating it out of the social world; the perception of bizarre detail aids in the process. He is aware of being distinct, of being different, of being uniquely favored by a Providence that has even granted him a special spirit and so many special gifts. It might even be said that he perceives his real self in his "genius," as that word was used by Romans. But he has no clear concept or term for such an idea as individuality. What is crucial here is the attitude he brings to the process of self-discovery rather than the deciphering of his own personal enigma.

Cardano was a fascinating fact to Cardano, and no one could record his life as well as he himself. The purely factual is approached as if it were a sacred matter; the acceptance of the real is a sacred obligation. The old Stoic doctrine that the nature of each part is determined by the character of the whole is as valid for him as it was for so many others of his day. A world-soul penetrates every existence in a panpsychic cosmos. For Cardano, there is therefore no such thing as accident in a world order where every fact is causally related to another.

Even the greatest help toward knowledge that a man may get, a guardian spirit, does not reveal reality directly, but "he points the way to one thing through others of another nature" (p. 243 [47]). The deeper the conviction that all facts are interlinked, the more a discovery of the vast causal complexities reinforces Cardano's trust that there is a causal explanation. His profound sense of extreme intricacy and complexity never leads him to deny the still more pervasive trust that all such complexity is a manifestation of an underlying order. Because he combines such convictions, his pursuit of fact and cause is unrelenting.

> It is ever legitimate to draw inferences from even the most insignificant events, when they are uncommonly persistent, since . . . even as a net consists of meshes, all things in the life of man consist in trifles repeated and massed together now in one figure now in another like cloud formations. Not only through the very smallest circumstances are our affairs increased, but these small circumstances ought gradually to

be analyzed into their infinitely minute components. And
that man alone will be a figure in the arts, in display of judgment, or in civil life, and will rise to the top, who understands
the significance of all these influences, and knows how to
heed them in his business. Wherefore in any events whatsoever things are of apparently no significance ought to be
duly observed [p. 195 (41)].

Thus, for Cardano, the constant and careful pursuit of facts and their
causal interrelation is a necessity of life. The world has no teleological
order in which man can trustingly relax.[20] Enmeshed in a vast web of
interacting facts, man can only maintain himself through his understanding of the complex causal nexus. Cardano the healer was deeply
persuaded of this. A doctor should know all the theories, of course, and
all the learnable facts, but, in addition, he must learn as much as possible about the patient, preferably through observing him for a while
before acting, keeping careful records of peculiarities. "He must have a
care for heat, water, the bedroom, sanitation, silence and the patient's
friends. Fear, depression, or a fit of anger may bring on a patient's death
even though the disease of which the patient is suffering is curable" (p.
182 [40]). Medicine is a many-sided art, "many agencies working together" (p. 200 [42]), and the doctor must draw on all his faculties. Again
and again Cardano will explain his success as a consequence of intuition,
the divinely granted gift. What else is this faculty for him but the
privilege of arriving at the fact and cause he needs to know by a short-
cut across the vast complexity of causal interrelations? Despite all the
genuine love Cardano had for knowledge as a prize in itself, he finds
greater satisfaction in equating knowledge with divination. A man must be
able to understand the signs around him and within him if he somehow
wishes to maintain himself in this intricate web of causes. He cannot afford to neglect any form of knowledge, any divinatory art. Astrology, metoposcopy (the art of reading a man's character and fate from his
face), prognostic arts of all sorts have to be taken seriously—although
they may be swindler's tools in some hands and must thus be treated
with care.

Most important for Cardano is the realization that all knowledge has
its value in supporting life. He knew many dark moments of despair,
and to the very end he preserved a basic skepticism about the extent and
reliability of human knowledge. But his determination to do battle with
life, to overcome adversity by wisdom, and to maintain himself by
understanding the network of causes won out. There is something very

telling in the fact that he was the gambler who gambled away his wife's jewelry but tried to win some insight into the workings of chance by calculations of permutations and combinations of large numbers.[21] One is tempted to see in his insatiable pursuit of knowledge the secret hope of arriving at a "calculus of life," a tool for mastering one's existence. A science of life, an art of calculation, here holds the place occupied for others by the less systematic "art of life," the art of being a gentleman, an *honnête homme.* Cardano, beset by his somber moods and the often unbearable problems life posed for him, grasped for such a calculus of life as the only hope. He found comfort in his belief that Providence granted him special insights into mysteries other men could not fathom. And in his conviction of the pursuit of knowledge as a key to the mastery of life may well lie the unity of this enigmatic personality and this difficult autobiography.

# 8
# Montaigne's *Essais:*
# The Models Fail

When Voltaire in the eighteenth century surveyed human history, it seemed to him that the medieval world had been the most chaotic in which men had ever been condemned to live. From his enlightened vantage point, the centuries following this Gothic barbarism were marked by a gradual turn to greater order through rational progress and simplification. When one surveys the modes of human self-conception, however, a striking reversal of this Voltairean view takes place. On the whole, when the men of the Middle Ages reflected on the nature of their selves, they found a support for their self-conception in the order of their cultural world; the autobiographers of the Italian Renaissance world had to call upon untested inner resources to unify their personal image in the face of the many instabilities surrounding their lives. Men now undertook the processes of self-assessment and self-orientation in a world where the previously undoubted propositions were being called into doubt—a doubt evoked, in part, by a weakening hold of an older, established world view and, in part, by the strengthened appeal of an alternative life-style. The manner in which Petrarch had to find his bearings between conflicting values never faced Abelard. Cardano's whole life, his confrontation with overwhelmingly complex facts and causal relationships, was so pervaded by a sense of insecurity that he was virtually driven to a pursuit of knowledge in order to keep the personality somewhat afloat. The expansion of man's mental horizon, the need to accommodate increasingly more intricate data—and often with a mind ill-prepared to fit together the elements of strongly divergent world views, made the act of self-orientation more difficult. The vast increase in book learning that accompanied the ready availability of print, and the compartmentalization of knowledge added even further complexities. The changing social, political, and economic conditions of life must have aggravated the problems of self-clarification for all those who took up the task.

The northwestern European who began to feel the influences of the Italian Renaissance faced even greater problems. A mentally alive Frenchman in the middle years of the sixteenth century was likely to confront complexities even more formidable than those of his Italian counterpart. The revival of classical thought, values, and life-style was bound to take a different form in a northern setting that lacked even the superficial parallels between the ancient polis and the Italian city-states, the kindred ethnic relation which made it so natural for a Cellini to trace his own stock to Caesar's captain, the linguistic affinities, the very landscape with its archaeological remains. At the same time, the vitality of feudal traditions was even stronger in that northern sphere; and so was the scholastic manner of viewing the world and dealing with its questions. For Frenchmen born thirty years later than Cellini and Cardano, the impact of the overseas discoveries was to be even more profound, though not different in kind from their effects on southern contemporaries. And in the depths of their being they might be disturbed by the revolutions in religious outlook which, in their northern form, never convulsed Italy.

The full impact of such a growing complexity in man's outlook on the world showed itself in the self-reflections of two of the greatest French minds. Only Michel de Montaigne (1533–92) will be treated here. His famous *Essais*, though hardly a genuine autobiography, constitute a pivotal document in the gradually growing consciousness of man's individuality. The other man, René Descartes (1596–1650), will appear off and on as a symbolic reference point in the history of the personal quest reaching from Petrarch beyond Montaigne. Ironically, Descartes wrote the "truer" autobiography in his *Discours de la méthode*, which by title hardly qualifies as a vehicle for an autobiographic account. He chose to respond to the complexity of the tradition which had formed itself during the Renaissance with a radical solution: he left it behind and started from a clean slate. Montaigne, much more embedded in this tradition, struggled with it, albeit in a seemingly playful fashion. Descartes, sixty years younger, already belongs essentially to a different world. Two men of different styles, with different solutions to the problems of life—yet for both the act of self-orientation began in the same troubled confrontation with the inherited intricacy of opinions and ideas.

The *Essais* are the product of a life in retirement. At least Montaigne thought he had retired when in 1571, "since a long time tired of the servitude of *parlement* and public office," he withdrew to the quiet tower library on his family estate. Without benefit of our modern expectations of longevity, he thought at the age of thirty-eight of the years that "might remain." He dedicated his leisure to the memory of La Boétie, a cherished friend until his death in 1563. Perhaps he would do some writing. He ratified his decision and sealed the reasons for his retirement by having them inscribed on his library wall, along with the famous florilegium of maxims.[1]

In general, life had been good to him. He was born in 1533 into a family which, only within the previous century, had made the transition from solid bourgeois merchants in wines and salted fish to the noble estate of Montaigne, not far from Bordeaux. His father, Pierre, had been in the Italian wars with Francis I and had subsequently held important positions in the city of Bordeaux, finally becoming its mayor. His mother came from a family of baptized Portuguese Jews and was to outlive her son by a decade. As the two-year-old Michel was entrusted to a German tutor who knew no French, he learned Latin before he learned his mother tongue. For subsequent schooling he attended the excellent Collège de Guyenne and the University of Bordeaux and went on to Toulouse after the revolt of Bordeaux in 1548 was followed by terrible repression. At the age of twenty-one, he was appointed by Henry II as counsel to the Cour des Aides at Périgueux, and from there he advanced to the *parlement* of Bordeaux. Here he met La Boétie, his literary and intellectual friend. In 1565, Montaigne married the daughter of one of his legal colleagues, and upon the death of his father in 1568 he became the seigneur of Montaigne. As unrest over religious issues began to cut deeply into the life of Bordeaux, (as well as that of other regions of France), the *parlement* sent him on frequent emergency missions to the royal court.

When the civil wars broke out in 1572, Montaigne was at work on the *Essais*; most of Book 1 (excluding such "personal" essays as nos. 26 and 31) was written during the tumultuous years 1572–73, reflecting in its subject matter the many political and military issues of the day. Montaigne, a Knight of the Order of Saint Michel and a chamberlain to Charles IX, joined the royal army in Poitou but was not involved in battle. Throughout the many years of civil war he remained loyal to the king's cause and to his own personal style of Catholicism. A brother and a sister, however, had thrown in their lot with the Huguenots. Montaigne repeatedly sought to mediate between Henri de Guise and Henry of Navarre (who, in 1577, also made Montaigne his chamberlain), but in general he tried to live quietly on his estate and in his chosen retirement. Most of Book 2 was written in 1577–78; one or two years later he inserted the most personal essays—Book 1: 26 and 31; Book 2: 10, 17, and 37—and in March 1580 the first edition of the *Essais* was published at Bordeaux. By then Montaigne had begun to suffer from a kidney stone, a family ailment his grandfather and father had also known, and he sought relief in a long journey, visiting spas in Germany and Italy.

The *Journal de voyage en Italie* is, aside from a few letters, the other major source of information about him. While taking the waters at Lucca, he learned that he had been elected mayor of Bordeaux. He conscientiously filled the position until June 1585, trying his best to hold the surrounding territory for the crown. His relations with Henry of Navarre (who had become heir apparent upon the death of the duke of Anjou in 1584) continued to be cordial. But on the whole the eighties were hard years: a frightful pestilence ravaged the Bordeaux region, Montaigne's house was pillaged, he himself was held up by bandits while traveling to Paris, and in Paris he was put into the Bastille to be freed only by the direct intervention of Catherine de Medici. Yet he had continued to expand the published essays of Books 1 and 2 and added the grand third Book, publishing the whole at Paris in 1588. After the murder of Henry III in 1589, Montaigne supported Henry IV, but he stayed even more aloof from political involvement than before. By about one-fourth, he expanded the *Essais* into what has now become known as the Bordeaux edition. On September 13, 1592, he died peacefully on his estate at the age of fifty-nine.

The retirement Montaigne had sought in 1571 had thus been inter-sected repeatedly by official business and by the affairs of a most trouble-some age. Yet the tasks that fell on him interrupted but did not alter the mode of retirement he had chosen as his own. The *Essais* are the result of a long process of self-discovery; undertaken without any clear idea about what they might become, the volumes turned more and more into a book about Montaigne. The book has no order other than the order that was Montaigne. It is not a book of memoirs, though Montaigne filled it with observations about the world around him. It is not an active diary, like the one Marcus Aurelius used to remind himself of the wise maxims that alone could make life bearable—though it swarms with wise maxims. It is not an *apologia pro vita sua* of a man having to justify his life's course to others, even if the author did see his own self fully justified in what he found. It is not a confession motivated by the need to unburden a burdened soul or to praise the Lord for a life that suddenly seemed meaningful, although Montaigne does confess what others usually like to hide and although he did write in a spirit of profound gratitude for all that sustained his life. It is not an autobiography released by a sudden insight into the structure and meaning of a unique life. Nor is it, like Petrarch's *Secretum*, the product of a specific crisis that has brought a need for an act of orientation; or the result of sudden enlightenment, as is Descartes's *Discourse on Method*. Surely, Montaigne is fascinated by his own discoveries, and he does display some of the voluble chattiness of old men, but he does not portray his life as a Celliniesque adventure of creative daring.

Though Cardano and Montaigne were entirely different sorts of men, the largely contemporary works of the *Vita* and *Essais* show in some respects an amazing affinity. Neither of the two authors could fulfill his self-defining task by relying on the customary literary forms; writing itself thus became an experiment. Both books are the works of old men. Both are deeply marked by the analytical approaches of their authors. Montaigne, with a much sunnier temperament, shares neither Cardano's tormented hunting for explanatory causes nor his seemingly unshakable trust in knowledge. Nor does he share the Italian's hunger for fame and self-perpetuation. But Montaigne and Cardano do share a problem and an approach. The age-old quest for understanding the human condition became for both a fresh endeavor because they were bewildered by the vast variety of traditional answers. Where the tradition of the authorities failed, especially when it presented a normative ideality of which both men were suspicious, and where there was no firmly established view of the world to offer existential answers, sober self-analysis was the only alternative. Thus Cardano and Montaigne turned to careful observation of themselves, creating in the process a form for their search that led each in his own way to the brink of discovering individuality as something of great value.

In the essay that he ultimately placed first (though it was not the first one written),[2] Montaigne inducts his reader into the problem of choice and the perplexing variety of opinions. The title itself suggests the problem: "By Diverse Means We Arrive at the Same End." The troubling days of the civil war assigned the specific topic for speculation: is it better to avert the victor's revenge by appealing to his sense of pity or to his respect? In his exposed castle Montaigne faced the problem concretely enough. The first sentence states in general terms that "the commonest way" in dealing with offended victors is to submit and to appeal to their sense of commiseration and mercy. The next sentence starts with a "however": it is also true that audacity and steadfast resistance, "entirely contrary means," may be effective in gaining forgiveness. This short two-sentence introduction of a dilemma then gives way to an analysis of concrete historical examples.

A story about Edward the Black Prince illustrates that he, as a victor, was totally unmoved by the weeping women and children imploring his mercy, though he was stirred by the sight of three brave Frenchmen trying to hold out against his army. A second example, involving the Albanian hero Scanderbeg, adds a variation: Scanderbeg pursues a fleeing soldier who had been unable to move him by humble submission but who, in his extremity, awaits him sword in hand. "This resoluteness ... put a sudden stop to the fury of his master." As Montaigne realizes that those who might not know of Scanderbeg's valor and strength could interpret this reaction as prudence or cowardice, he immediately adds all the necessary elements for the correct understanding of the story. In another example Montaigne tells the story of the Emperor Conrad III and the courageous women of Winesberg, carrying their husbands on their backs out of the defeated city. In a B insertion,[3] Montaigne later added that he himself would lean toward mercy by compassion. But yet ... Montaigne stops himself: the Stoics despise pity as a vicious passion; we should aid the afflicted but without giving in to sentiment. Again, he voices a "But": is it really a sign of strength to be unmoved by pity and to be moved by valor? It could be argued that pity is a softer human reaction while respect for valor derives from strength. "But" some examples prove that the weak and humble are as much moved by the sight of proud valor—witness the Theban people trying Pelopidas and Epaminondas or the reaction of the army of Dionysius the Elder toward the steadfast courage of the persecuted Phyto. "Truly man is a marvelously vain, diverse, and undulating [*ondoyant*] object. It is hard to found any constant and uniform judgment on him." To prove the point once more, Montaigne offers a story about Pompey being moved by the valor of a lone brave man holding out for his city, and another story about Sulla remaining totally unmoved in a very similar situation. Then, in a longer B insertion, Montaigne analyzes two stories about Alexander the Great, "the bravest of men and one very gracious to the vanquished."

Such examples complicate the lessons of the earlier ones by questions about motivation. After the difficult siege of Gaza, Alexander is outraged rather than pacified by Betis's lack of submission and has him

dragged to pieces behind a chariot. Montaigne then poses three questions about the story: was bravery so common to Alexander that he
could not marvel at it any longer? or did he consider it his own
monopoly, thus being envious when meeting it in others? or was his
rage so uncontrollable that he could not be moved by other passions
until it abated? Montaigne does not answer his questions directly but
instead tells the story of Alexander's capture of Thebes, in which many
brave men lost their lives, and Alexander was neither moved to pity by
their valor nor able to satisfy his thirst for revenge at the long day's
butchery. And on this inconclusive note the essay ends.

Thus, in barely three and a half pages of text, Montaigne provides a
marvelous insight into his own perplexity about a matter which to many
might seem to be resolvable by a simple rule of conduct. The commonest
way is . . ., but there are striking examples to the contrary. A concrete
analysis of the contradictory examples shows how complicated everything becomes when one considers the precise nature of the situation
and of the characters involved. Seemingly stable characters suddenly
change their moods. Montaigne's brief look into himself reveals more
complications: though by nature he is inclined one way, the philosophy
to which he gives most credence at the time teaches the contrary conduct. And what may look like the same actions in the various examples
actually seem very different when the possible motives are taken into
account. Motives that are seemingly the same may in actuality be different. Sometimes motives clash with other motives: the analyses of the
Alexander stories, dwelling on the theme of his rage, are introduced by
the general statement that Alexander was the bravest of men and *si
gratieux* to the vanquished. The unavoidable conclusion must be that
general maxims and norms do not hold true for actions of a specific type
when all the complications of circumstance, character, and motivation
are taken into account. "L'homme . . . un subject merveilleusement . . .
divers et ondoyant."

Hundreds of pages from the other essays could be adduced to deepen,
expand, substantiate, elaborate, heighten, and aggravate this sense of
wonderment over the complexity of man and his situation. Since man is
born for action,[4] since he is an active creature fulfilling himself through
action, we thus have a most serious dilemma: By what norms can man
guide himself?

It might seem reasonable to assume that such norms can somehow be
extracted from that grand storehouse of human wisdom in the steadily
expanding library built around the core of classics inherited from the

dead friend La Boétie. Page upon page of these books deliver moral and practical recommendations by which a man may set his course. But every fresh recommendation clashes with a preceding one. How is one to choose between them? Man acts, or tries to act, with his sights trained on an ultimate good. Philosophers, however, have quarreled over nothing so intensely as this question of the *summum bonum;* by Varro's count, attempts to answer this most weighty question in antiquity had already brought forth 288 philosophical sects. The experts apparently cannot decide, and the poor layman is left at a loss. The careful consideration of every nicely told story brings Montaigne to matters of motive, or the nature of the specific setting making it difficult to apply the exemplary lesson to his own situation. Under close inspection "every example limps, and the connection drawn from experience is always faulty and imperfect" (p. 1046). To be sure, wherever you look you will find that men can act with firmness and decisiveness, that they are guided simply by unexamined prejudice, by instinct, or by the custom and habit that is second nature. Quite possibly, custom and habit are fully justified grounds for action. But the mind asking the question about the right or the correct action is as much baffled by the wide variety of custom and dogmatic beliefs as by "the racket from so many philosophical brains" (p. 496). "There is nothing in which the world varies so much as in customs and laws" (p. 564). What seems a barbaric aberration to the Frenchman may be a life-sustaining practice to someone else. A thoughtful man, more and more inclined to acknowledge that values and behavior are relative to changing settings, may still be sufficiently haunted by the age-old persuasion that "the bean in the cake" (p. 496) can be found, to look under these shells of appearances for the absolute truth. At least Montaigne does not avoid the inquest into the supposed grounds of action, be these instinct, reason, dogma, passion, or custom.

The strongest among the old traditions suggested that man, as a rational creature, could find the truth by following reason. One of the chief activities in that great age of erudition was to reason away the apparent incompatibilities of the diverse philosophical dogmas and produce a clarified elixir of truth. Descartes, the most heroic mental Hercules, looked upon all this array of traditional opinion as if it were an Augean stable not even worth clearing; it was better to let it decompose under its own weight so a free man might see where he could get by rigorously following the logos from a clean start. Neither of these two roads appealed to Montaigne. "There is, they say, a true and a false, and we have in us the means of seeking it, but we have no touchstone by which to test it" (p. 486). Early in life he must have already had a plain measure of practical sense and that protective wit by which one who is skeptically inclined eschews the temptation of reaching for absolute certainties; not even the enthusiastic adoration of La Boétie and his rigorous Stoicism, which still pervades many of the early essays, had been capable of displacing the habit of soberly questioning all presumptions. A reading of the classical skeptics, especially of Sextus Empiricus, reinforced this tendency so strongly that it gained the upper hand over any inclination to rest securely in absolutes.

In the longest of Montaigne's probings, the "Apology for Raymond Sebond"—an essay with many functions written between 1575 and 1580—he settled accounts with the presumptions of reason. How much could man really come to know by the exercise of his reason? Much of our reasoning is but the art of syllogism for which we require true premises. "Now there can be no first principles for men, unless the deity has revealed them to us; of all the rest, the beginning, middle, and end are but dreams and smoke" (p. 522). "True and essential Reason, whose name we steal by false pretences, dwells in the bosom of God" (p. 523). However much we may want to stretch our reason, we will find it restricted to a world of appearances. The thing itself is not accessible to us. All we can know is a world of phenomena. But this also means that our senses inevitably obtrude themselves on our operations of knowing. How easily these senses can deceive us! One sense affects another and modifies it. We have been limited to five such organs for coming to know phenomena; how many senses that we do not possess, and cannot even think of, are really needed to fathom the nature of phenomena more concisely? In the use of any one sense we are often inferior to the animals. Like the senses, all our other mental attributes color our rational judgments; our imagination wields its particular distortions. Pain and pleasure affect our mental capacities, and so do our varied and everchanging moods. The personal peculiarities of the knower are inextricably intertwined with his knowledge.

Montaigne drew no lessons of despair from such reflections. His famous motto "What do I know?—Que scay-je?" did not have the answer: Nothing! Its purpose was to stir man to activity, not to let him subside in self-satisfied ignorant sloth. It was a constant invitation to double-check what was really known, and it was a permanent call to stand guard against presumptuous nonsense. Montaigne had not the slightest intention of clouding the functions of his mind by an extravagant sort of skepticism. His skeptical stance kept close to the original meaning of the word: to look out, to espy, to look out so as to discover. Such skepticism was meant to open up the right kind of relation to the knowable world, not to foreclose it. It was neither the radical skepticism that hangs itself on hyperbole nor the initial skepticism through which a Descartes fashioned for himself a refounded rationalism.[5]

It cannot be said that Montaigne's epistemological reasoning rested in profound philosophical thinking. He argued neither rigorously nor systematically. He proceeded here as he always did by picking up the various propositions he encountered, holding them up to the light for his personal inspection, and then stating with much perspicacity the doubts and thoughts they evoked in him. He was neither logician, nor philosopher, nor scientist. At most, he admitted to being an "unpremeditate and accidental philosopher" (p. 528) who could not avoid discussing all sorts of issues. To be a school philosopher meant to be an expert; and no such truly aristocratic mind as his would tie itself down to such a professional stance. "Philosophy," he thought most fittlingly, "is but sophisticated Poetry" (p. 518). He felt more comfortable with the modest proposition. As a free man Montaigne considered it his birthright to take up any question that interested him, and he would always do so thoughtfully. He was most interested in contemplating the practical life of man, the world of action, especially the world of ethics which told a man how to deal with the never-ending problems life presented. So if his skepticism was not profound philosophy, it was an eminently practical position, entirely in keeping with his personality and interests. His perspectivist outlook upon a world of phenomena, a world without openings toward transcendent metaphysical certainties, secured him in his realm of interest. The scientific study of physical phenomena did not attract him, not even as a physiological study of man as a sensate being in a sensible external world.

Montaigne's doubts about reason as a sure road to absolute verities profited him well in the religious controversies threatening to tear his country apart during most of his later life. If there was ever a practical danger in man's presumptuous reasoning, its effects were surely to be seen in the murderous quarrels resulting from "our overweening conceit that would make the Deity pass through our sieve" (p. 509). Through this defective strainer of our mind we try to sift questions so difficult that upon cool reflection it would seem that it would have been better to abstain from the effort. "How many quarrels, and how momentous, have not been caused in this world by doubt as to the meaning of that syllable *Hoc*" (p. 508) in Jesus' statement *Hoc est corpus meum*, This is my body. In our reasoning about the nature of the will and the intentions of God we show an unbelievable presumptuousness and end up with hundreds of conceptions, each claiming to be the truth. "Man is indeed out of his wits! He cannot create a mite and he creates Gods by the dozen!" (p. 511). In such matters it seemed well to ask: what do I know? Montaigne considered it a "probable and defensible idea" that God was "an incomprehensible power, the origin and preserver of all things, all goodness, all perfection, graciously accepting the honor and reverence rendered him by human beings, under whatever aspect, whatever name, and in what manner soever" (p. 493). When necessary, this deity will reveal to us what we need to know about absolutes. But such revealed knowledge is of a special quality, coming to our assistance from beyond our mental horizon. Since we cannot very well reason about it, we should accept it on faith.

Without much reasoning or theological finesse Montaigne ensconced himself behind this form of fideism. It was for him a personal protective cover. It was also a public necessity to adopt an unquestioning attitude toward his Catholic faith, especially in an age when inveterate theological innovators and fantasts felt entitled to overthrow all authority simply because they thought they had the freedom of interpreting anything by their own dim lights. Perhaps Montaigne doubted that he could know better than centuries of thoughtful churchmen and simply accepted the teachings of an old institution which had sufficiently proven its viability. His skepticism and his conservatism were ever easy allies. For a century his Church may not have been quite certain how to judge such fideism. When Montaigne was in Rome, in November 1580, he received the personal imprimatur of the censor; in 1676, after men had had a chance to read the book with more care, the *Essais* were put on the *Index*. By 1713, the papal bull *Unigenitus* finally rejected all such forms of unquestioning fideism. But by having placed theology so entirely beyond the ken of his unending inquiry, Montaigne had gained for his lifetime the freedom to follow the bent of his mind and personality.[6]

The lovers of wisdom, the philosophers who, according to Montaigne, should have taught us the right use of reason, left us instead with its exaggerated claims: "That the human Reason is controller-general of all that is outside of us and within the heavenly arch; that she embraces everything, that she can do everything; that by her means everything is known and understood" (p. 523). He had come to think of such claims as total fantasy. Reason is indeed an important, even a noble tool of man. It is an indispensable aid to life as long as it helps us to understand ourselves and our surroundings. Montaigne had come to disavow it as soon as it began to dictate terms to life and to substitute its fancies for a sober view of reality. As but one part of the human reality, it could not be permitted to assert itself at the cost of everything else. Thus Montaigne was persuaded that logic was insufficient for cutting through all the conflicting opinions to some promised quintessence of truth. He did not see how reason might be helpful in regulating behavior by universal rules of conduct in a world of habit-forming customs at least as diverse as opinions. And if, under changing conditions and fluctuating motivations, there is as much variation between myself and myself as there is between you and myself (p. 321), then a general anthropology has at best a very limited usefulness for the delicate questions of life and death facing me from minute to minute.

The wisest course was to use reason in close conjunction with all the other faculties for assessing reality around us and taking stock of our very own situation. Instead of chasing after elusive general verities, let us come to know what we are closest to.

The more decided turn toward the study of the self came as a very gradual groping of which Montaigne left us the record on the pages of the *Essais*. He did not have the benefit of a sudden illumination. His life had no such sudden turning point as there was in that of Descartes, who lived under the clear impression that on the night of November 10–11, 1619, he had suddenly come to understand where he had earlier gone wrong and how his life might henceforth proceed directly toward its desired goal. From the World of the Books, a welter of confusing and contradictory opinions, Descartes had turned to the study of the Book of the World, in which the actions with far-reaching consequences seemed to be based on just as much ignorance; only by freeing himself in a radical fashion from the errors of books and of the world, could Descartes hope to find within himself the grounds for the absolute certainty of knowing that he craved. Here again the inability to cut through the inherited wisdom led back to the self, but in his case the self had regained through its doubts a firm trust in rationality. Montaigne had had to face the same welter of opinion and custom, but his limited respect for the powers of pure reason had never brought him to the radical thought experiments of Descartes. Rather than rejecting opinion and custom, Montaigne continued to use them, but now less as potential authorities and guides than as mirrors. He reflected upon them, as upon anything that would stimulate his reflections, until in these very reflections he noted the reflected self. Different turns in the face of very similar experiences led to different personality conceptions. *Esprit de géometrie et esprit de finesse* . . . .

When Montaigne had started to write, he had no clear conception of what he wanted to do. The untroubled manner with which he included among his own writing twenty-nine sonnets of his friend La Boétie[7] suggests the lack of a clear program. But the longer he kept writing down his loose reflections, the more he came to a clear objective: I myself, Michel de Montaigne. The very act of writing had become a process of discovery. Any lead brings author and reader to an interesting quotation here, an observation about a current event there; he had always to come back to the same observer, the same judge, the same doubter, the ever-questioning self. Had he had a live friend like La Boétie, all these subjects might have been matters of private correspondence or conversations. But to whom was he talking now? Who was meant to read this? If anyone did, what was he to gain from the fact that these random remarks all started with personal interests and always came back to the same observer? Throughout, Montaigne continued to wonder about this issue of an audience. But the eminent success which met the publication of the first two books in 1580 greatly strengthened his determination to make this ever more a book of self-exploration.

What were these jottings anyway but a constant exploring of the intricate questions faced by every man who had to act in given circumstances? and was it indeed *every* man or only *this* man? What were these but probings of a complex human reality? a weighing of judgments? The verb *essayer* in all its shades of meaning gives the title to a literary form in the process of being created: the word strongly emphasizes an activity. It was the activity in which he was so deeply engaged that was important, not the final result. "All this fricassee that I am scribbling here is nothing but a record of the essays of my life—toute cette fricassée que je barbouille icy n'est qu'un régistre des essais de ma vie" (p. 1056). Montaigne's objective lay indeed in this constant process of "registration." "It is in the last analysis a method of auscultation, of the observations of one's own inner movements . . . . a ceaseless listening to the changing voices which sound within him."[8] It rests on the profound insight that a man does not discover his self by brooding over his nature, by simply staring within himself, or by deciding what he is in the light of the latest mood and impression. The worst mistake was to identify oneself with the fanciful self-images that had taken possession of the mind either by wishful thinking or by the falsifying power that the great models of man exerted. But Montaigne was less concerned with forming himself than with discovering his self, and so there was no use in ticking off attributes of character like items on a checklist: do I have this trait or that one in sufficient strength? "Others form man; I describe him, and portray a particular, very ill-made one, who, if I had to fashion him anew, should indeed be very different from what he is. But now it is done" (p. 782). The only method was to listen constantly and carefully to what was stirring inside, and to follow with an honest self-registration.

Montaigne found no ready guidelines for such a procedure. He knew that he was probing for something new; he was a conscious pioneer. In a way he had stumbled upon a method and a subject by having employed the hours of his voluntary retirement in random scribblings on whatever struck his fancy. Some essays had turned into fairly consistently executed arguments; much more typical, however, were the freely roaming ones. Later on he saw no need to change the format, although the now more clearly understood objective gave to the writing a more centered focus on his own self-consciousness. The later essays, especially those of Book 3, became longer and unabashedly self-centered; but by repeated insertions the ones already written were padded so that they also came to highlight the author more directly. Chapter headings became only slightly more meaningful.[9] The form remained essentially the freely talking discourse of an old man ("I speak to my paper as I speak to the first person I meet" [p. 767]), with time on his hands, writing when he liked and as the inspiration of the moment guided him, unconcerned over problems of composition or exposition (p. 105), expressing himself in the inimitable images that seemed to come to him naturally. He had no need to invent topics. A phrase from a recently read book, an experience of the moment, any chance encounter, could serve as a springboard. Jump into the matter and see where your thoughts carry your pen! And what does it matter if an observation leads to a totally different topic? That a phrase of Seneca or Plutarch "has carried me away from my theme ... there is profit in change" (p. 670). At the end of an essay Montaigne sometimes did not remember what he had wanted to say at the beginning (p. 549). The chosen subject need not be a lofty one; it need not have a universal appeal. Quite the contrary. Trifles leave very telling marks; the seemingly insignificant detail of the humblest daily action may reveal more about a man than his loftiest professions. "Every theme is equally pregnant for me. A fly will serve my purpose.... I need only begin with a subject that I fancy, for all subjects are linked to one another" (p. 854).[10]

Most important, all the subjects would show him the reflections of an observing self that had penetrated them. Each subject taken up had started from a personal interest; every freely floating thought was still held on a string anchored at the vital center of the self. Thoughts were not thought for their independent beauty but were self-communings by which a self tested itself; as if on tenterhooks they were painlessly being pulled into the light of self-observation. In thousands of little mirrors Montaigne saw the vast and fascinating variety of Montaigne reflected.

Thus watching himself for years in his writings, he saw himself "in passage," adding new variants here and there, hardly ever erasing or correcting. The contradictions were part of the reality. Such writing had a remarkable effect: with every added page the book and the author became more consubstantial. "I have no more made my book than my book has made me" (p. 648). "All the world will recognize me in my book, and my book in me" (p. 853). The author had not foreseen that such a fusion would occur; but the more he understood it to be the right result of all this weighing of opinions, this testing of judgments, this probing of unexpected findings, the freer he felt in pursuing his course. Self-discovery and writing were the same. The more value he saw in this form of unveiling the self, the less apologetic he became about drawing the little warts and scars of this fine self-portraiture. "But whatever I make myself known to be, provided I make myself known such as I am, I am carrying out my plan. And so I make no excuse for daring to put into writing such mean and trivial remarks . . . . The meanness of my subject forces me to do so. Blame my project if you will, but not my procedure" (p. 636).

In Montaigne's conception of himself as "a mean subject" lay hidden a vast program. Evidently self-auscultation demanded a radical commitment to honesty. He thought he was honest with himself, and, despite the sneers of Pascal and Rousseau,[11] there is no reason to doubt his commitment to truth. It was a commitment not to "ideal" man but to "factual" man, to a mean subject. The real problem with honesty was less in seeing honestly what was to be seen than in accepting what one saw.

Much of the work was a sober leveling of presumptuous edifices. Man had to be taken down from the lofty heights where fanciful ideals had sought to place him. Since "we love to embroil ourselves in unreality, as being conformable to our being" (p. 1004), we first have to get rid of masks and role-playing. Our worst forms of self-deception forever derive from pretentious self-glory. "Presumption is our natural and original infirmity. The frailest and most vulnerable of all creatures is man, and at the same time the most arrogant. He sees and feels himself lodged here in the mud and filth of the world, nailed and riveted to the worst, the deadest and most stagnant part of the universe ... and he goes and sets himself in imagination above the circle of the moon, and brings heaven under his feet" (p. 429).

We had best purge the mind of such arrogant nonsense by means of a sober comparison with the animals who share our earth. Of course, we think we are their masters, but "when I play with my cat, who knows but that she regards me more as a plaything than I do her?" (p. 430). While we may think that they are stupid, they seem eminently capable of dealing with the needs of existence. We may think that we are guided by lofty philosophical principle, but how much do we instead follow appetites, whim, instinct, or passion? And our various capacities do not necessarily strengthen one another. Cruelty we share with animals as a natural instinct, but our imagination can turn a regrettable but life-supporting instinct into a horror unknown to the beasts. What other animal need suffer fear amplified by a lively imagination? Though we have willpower and may think of ourselves as self-directed beings, fateful accident is usually more responsible for our specific condition than is intelligent and consistent planning.

The great teachers have told us again and again that our superiority lies in our rationality. But were philosophers happier and better men? Does a professor at the University of Paris cope more effectively with life's exigencies? Reason is such a brittle tool, and madness lies so close to genius; having seen the mad Tasso in his cell at Ferrara (p. 472), Montaigne was reminded of the delicate balance of sanity—if indeed a reminder was needed. Who knows whether animals have reason? Or whether reason does us any good if we cannot control it. Even the skeptic in Montaigne concluded sadly: "My sexual appetites are less dissolute than my reason" (p. 407). Even in its presumption of controlling the will, the passions, and the instincts, this restlessly meddlesome rationality can only fail.

Our much-praised conscience is frequently the result only of custom, a second nature functioning much like instinct. Despite all good intentions we are even driven to use bad means for good ends. Neither can we brag about our physique. We are luckiest when the body functions without causing us pain. We are born between urine and feces. Our beauty is blemished, and "we have more reasons than any other animal to cover ourselves" (p. 463). Love and sex are pleasurable sensations, but, surely, a sober mind will have to smile at the ludicrous positions of making love. Not reason, nor any other talent can help us master the ever-moving flux that carries our existence. Impermanence besets us, and our very special problem is that we are the animal that knows of its own mortality.

Montaigne's manner of hauling down man from the lofty pedestals where his desire for self-glorification had placed him may in part resemble the typical Christian techniques of self-abasement. But it led to something quite different. Montaigne had no more intention of engaging in public self-flagellation or shouting *mea culpa* than Rabelais did in evoking the creatural view of man. Montaigne does not use the baroque images of a Pascal speaking of Man, the fallen Monarch, condemned by his own guilt to remember the lost glory while facing the Nothingness of his existence. Man's confrontation with his inadequacy is not intended as a way to bring him from disgust with himself to the complete religious surrender described by countless Christians as the salvation through a divine power willing to help whenever man would understand that he could not save himself. Montaigne was concerned not with heaven but with man's natural life. He fought no religious struggle; he fought the claims that ideality made on man. For ages man had been misled by teachings insisting that he follow this or that ideal. Imitate Christ! Learn to die with the wise dignity of the Stoic! Idealize your love life! Be a spiritual athlete who learns to deny the demands of the body! Man lived like a prisoner in the well of a panopticon where each beautiful model surrounding him promised him freedom and greatness if he would only follow it. He was intoxicated with ideas of greatness and needed nothing so much as sobering up. "What end is served by these lofty heights ... on which no human can sit and those rules which exceed our strength and our use. I often hear people propose to us ideal patterns of life [*images de vie*] which neither they nor their listeners have any hope of following" (p. 967).

The skeptic had developed an aversion toward the very thought of forming man by any formal rhetorical ideal, especially a humanistic one. Much subsequent labor was devoted to taking apart all formalistic culture, brick by brick. Montaigne had come to suspect all teachings that pointed us toward the superhuman. He was looking at himself honestly, comparing himself with the other creatures, and he found himself to be a creature among creatures, all of whom were the children of nature. This naturalistic, creatural view of man was not his invention. It was a Christian notion, but Christians had seen in it the human curse that could be lifted only by the saving hand of God. However, by the sixteenth century this creatural view of man had begun to take on a more positive coloration; Rabelais glorified it. "His creatural treatment of mankind no longer has for its keynote, as does the corresponding realism of the declining Middle Ages, the wretchedness and perishableness of the body and of earthly things in general; in Rabelais, creatural realism has acquired a new meaning, diametrically opposed to medieval creatural realism—that of the vitalistic-dynamic triumph of the physical body and its functions."[12] The development had its peculiar paradox. During the ages when man had most self-consciously related himself as creature to the Creator, his creaturalness seemed to him most seriously flawed, albeit self-inflicted. As he came to value himself as a creature, he more and more lost sight of the Creator. Montaigne saw Nature as the mother of all creatures, although she functioned as God's vice-regent. In an early essay, discussing the origin of things, he first spoke of the "reverence for the infinite power of God," then later crossed it out and substituted Nature for God (p. 179; fn. p. 1477). The paradox suggests the deep change in man's view of himself and of the world in which he moved. Arthur O. Lovejoy drew attention to the precise parallel in his discussion of the change that occurred at the same time from an earth-centered view of the world to an acentric view.

> The habit of mind naturally appropriate to a finite and geocentric universe did not much manifest itself in the age when the universe was actually so conceived, but appeared at its maximum long after such a conception had become, for science and philosophy, obsolete.... a metaphysical and practical otherworldliness coexisted for centuries with a cosmological finitism; ... when the latter began to be theoretically abandoned, the preoccupation of men's minds with supersensible and supratemporal realities also steadily diminished.... It is *after* the earth had lost its monopoly that its inhabitants began to find their greatest interest in the general movement of terrestrial events ... [and] *homo sapiens* bustled about most self-importantly and self-complacently in his infinitesimal corner of the cosmic stage.[13]

Montaigne was preoccupied with man and only noted the cosmological revolution incidentally. He found both peace of mind and intellectual fascination in the creatural condition of man, a "mean" subject. Once man was cured of his ideal striving, he could learn to accept what he really was. Freed from the tyranny of false rational claims, he could find room for the complex composition of his polymorphic being. Instead of following this "should" and trying to obey that "ought," he could simply be, and be himself.

Self-knowledge was the only road to this acceptance of our natural condition. Without an incontrovertible science of man that could teach the self about itself, the knowledge of man could come only through understanding the self. When the individual was unable to carry a firmly established view of the meaning of life into his own life, the meaning of life had to be derived from the individual experience. Indeed, "each man is a good education to himself, provided he has the capacity to spy on himself from close by" (p. 357). In one way, Montaigne would take an interest in Michel before taking an interest in Man. But within Michel he also discovered more: for "everyman carries within him the entire form of the human condition" (p. 782). Montaigne refrained from speaking presumptuously in behalf of Man in general. He retreated instead into the security of speaking only of himself. But ultimately the image of the self and the image of Man were to supplement each other.

The manner Montaigne had chosen for self-discovery would by necessity involve him in the more general condition of Man. He might seem secluded in his retirement, but he neither could nor would study himself as an object placed in atmospheric isolation. He could not analytically dissect a life taken out of the total encumbering human context. He only becomes aware of himself by watching his reactions to the world, by viewing himself in the mirrors of his fellow men, by testing his own judgments against the propositions advanced by others. Protected by nature, the creature is also embedded in nature. And as a social being man is entwined in the social weave. Abstracting a man from the full situation of his life would simply bring back the false constructs of idealized man. This determination to apprehend the subject within the complex network of its living situation, rather than to obtain the theoretical purity which knowledge can have when abstracted from the experimentally isolated object, separates Montaigne from the coming scientific revolution. He remains a perspectivist and a moralistic phenomenologist. The generalized abstract formulation of his understanding is much less his forte than his graphical, picturesque, metaphorical style.

His inveterate habit of leaving most of the self buried in the stuff surrounding it has often puzzled the reader. It has often tempted men to impose a "better order" on the *Essais*. Montaigne's wisdom is so appealing that it is hard to resist marketing anthologies with such titles as "Montaigne on Love," "Montaigne on Death," "Montaigne on the

State." Such ordering was already begun very early in the seventeenth century by his "pupil" Pierre Charron, who thought he could make the *Essais* of more value to scholars by giving them greater logical and topical coherence. Fine and good, if one wants nuts of wisdom cracked loose from the individual shells that hold them. Others find it irresistible to follow the opposite course: shuck the rambling ideas, and peel out the human being! And then we get such products as *"The Autobiography of Michel de Montaigne; comprising the life of the wisest man of his times: his childhood, youth, and prime; his adventures in love and marriage, at court and in office, war, revolution, and plague; his travels at home and abroad; his habits, tastes, whims, and opinions,* selected, arranged, edited by . . ." with such chapter headings as "A Jumble of Habits," or "My Philosophy of Life" thrown in for free. And the editor assures us: "Since the autobiography comprises hundreds of passages brought, some of them into a single sentence, from widely separated sources, I should warn anyone who wishes to turn to the French that he will often be baffled by my juxtapositions. . . . Yet it is my belief that I have nowhere betrayed Montaigne's thought or intention."[14] But either of the two "enlightening" approaches subverts the purpose which the *Essais* had for Montaigne. He may mislead us when he says that he is drawing his portrait, but he does not deceive if one is willing to watch the activity instead of looking for the finished picture. "I cannot keep my subject still. It goes along befuddled and staggering with natural drunkenness. I take it in this condition, just as it is at the moment I give my attention to it. I do not portray being: I portray passing. Not the passing from one age to another, or, as the people say, from seven years to seven years, but from day to day, from minute to minute. My history needs to be adapted to the moment. . . . If my mind could gain a firm footing, I would not make essays, I would make decisions; but it is always in apprenticeship and on trial" (p. 782).

Less concerned with imposing an order on experience than with finding the self in the midst of a profusely intricate living context, Montaigne took note of the way in which the many layers of reality surrounding us and within us interact. So many different parts of his own self seem to come into play and to impinge upon one another in this act of registering his own reactions to the world. His prejudices guided him to reading matter different from the choice his reason wanted to make. The impact of an immediate experience made him see but one meaning in an issue with many meanings which, taken up at another time, seemed to say something very different. His momentary whims and moods detoured thoughts and steered him in directions he had never wanted to travel. His uncontrollable imagination, leading the logic of his argument astray, involved him in thought experiments taking him back to the inner experience with vastly expanded understanding. He watched how the state of his body affected the course of his thought, and he became more willing to let the body have its rights. There was no use and really no justification, even if the Stoics demanded ever so insistently, to tell a troublesome kidney stone not to interfere with a fine train of thought. That stone with all its painfulness was a real part of Montaigne, and he was determined to grant it its right of occupancy within his personality. The creatural view of man readmitted the claims of the physical functions and stipulated that a sensible balance be kept between spirit and physique. One of the first lessons to acknowledge was that our knowledge is by no means a rational product but one that fully reflects the involutions of our whole composite self.

Yet, discovering the variegated richness of our living context by perceiving the endlessly varied interplay of mind, soul, and body was only the first step. Whatever Montaigne observed in himself or in others, he was always aware of the weighty presence of that second nature, habit or custom. "The young of bears and dogs show their natural disposition, but men, being very soon influenced by customs, opinions, and laws, easily change or disguise their nature" (p. 148). The inveterate traveler, always more at ease in the saddle than in a chair, studied the customs of the world with never satiated curiosity. He was proud of every Gascon oddity that stuck to him; yet he was more prepared than any other man of his age to understand with sympathy the life-style of the Brazilian aborigines to be seen at Rouen. When he was shown samples of Chinese writing at the Vatican Library, he was more grateful than disturbed at the thought of living in such a varied world.

Assuredly, the variety of custom left a man with puzzling questions. What in this multilayered being, "man," was the effect of nature? What of general custom? And what of local or even personal idiosyncrasy? And just as the different layers seemed distinguishable, the next situation presented them in different combinations and with different effects. Montaigne had no inclination to shed the weight of custom in order to find the natural being underneath; he hardly even aimed at finding one common human denominator, a quintessence of human behavior and institutions which would play down the interesting variety. Occasionally he might talk as if he thought that customs and habits were but masks. The weight of most of his observations suggests his conviction that there was no "pure" man to be extricated from this second nature. Habit was as integral and as life-sustaining a reality of the individual human being as was his creatural nature. And if man was this intricately composite product of nature and nurture, if there was no rational test for custom other than its life-supporting usefulness, surely it would be a bit foolish to reform man in terms of either some "ideal" nature or some untestable intellectual substitute for decently functioning habits.

The more Montaigne probed and judged himself as a member of the human community, the more he was persuaded of the meanness of his subject. He derived value and comfort from the discovery that he was of the common sort. The study of the fundamental human condition revealed more reliable verities than all the high-flown ideals and pretentious promises of philosophy. It was better to accept the common "vulgar" humanness than to be rich in borrowed excellence. "A little man is an entire man just as well as a big one" (p. 93). "The surname the *Great* we give to princes in whom there is nothing transcending the greatness of the common people" (p. 295). Every test showed that we falsify our lives when we strive to get beyond our "vulgar," common humanity.[15] Montaigne learned to accept it and from it draw ever more strength.

But if the study of himself in the full setting of his existence allowed him to perceive the common human condition, it also forcefully made him recognize the specific man he was. True, he could not fix the subject, it would not stand still. The perspectivist manner of viewing the subject always returned slightly altered views. And our own complexity stands in the way of drawing a portrait with heavy contours. "We are made up of bits, and so shapelessly and diversely put together, that every piece, at every moment, plays its own game. And there is as much difference between us and ourselves, as between us and others" (p. 321). Still, there is nothing we can know better than ourselves. Even if the disjointedness in the portrait was necessitated by the very mode chosen for tracing the subject ever anew, the accumulation of all the many brushstrokes revealed discernible patterns.

Whom, before Montaigne, can we know more intimately through the details he revealed of himself? He did not, like Cardano, pack chapters full of individual peculiarities, but left the tracers of his thoughts, his feelings, his wisdom, his quirks, his habits, his physique, and all his oddities spread throughout the *Essais*. They appear "naturally" where the living context had evoked them for the writer. He was so right in saying that he had become consubstantial with his book, and that the reader would encounter him there. There indeed he is with his rolling painful stone, his habits in the saddle, pacing his library, sitting with his feet higher up than his posterior, receiving his guests, observing his peasants at work, or dying from the plague, remembering his fine father and not saying anything about his mother, forgetting about his own children, or confessing his own inadequacy as a landlord and a builder. The myriad of little oddities giving depth to the portrait and flavor to the personality enliven the broader lines of the personality: his torment at the buzzing of a fly, his love of good smells, his hatred of chess and of beer, his preference for a hard mattress, his indifference to salad and all fruit except melons, his prodigality at bonnetings, the fast eating habits that made him bite his tongue, or his blushing embarrassment when his eyes accidentally would fall on a part of a letter someone else was read-ing. All in all, the evidence of his experience was that "there is no one who, if he listens to himself, does not discover in himself a pattern all his own—*une forme sienne, une forme maistresse*" (p. 789).

By learning to view himself in the full setting of his life, Montaigne came to see the general elements of the human condition in an indi-vidual experience. But he also noted how the strength of his individual peculiarity left its marks on a wider vision. The full test lay in the relation he gradually developed toward death. As a work of retirement, the *Essais* were in no small measure meant to be an exercise in self-preparation for the death that loomed at the end of the years still left. He had begun to write these pieces at a time of many compelling reminders: within the course of only a few years, Montaigne lost La Boétie, his father, and his first-born child, and the horrors of the civil war and of Saint Bartholomew's Massacre were even further food for reflec-tion. A decade later the plague ravaged the countryside.

Montaigne had an insatiable curiosity about death. Very early in his writing he concluded: "There is nothing about which I am so desirous of gathering information, as the death of men. . . . If I were a maker of books I should compile a register, with comments, of different deaths" (p. 88). There is no question that, even then, the possibility of *his* own death stimulated his curiosity and that many of the hallmarks of his later position are adumbrated here. Yet it is striking that his earlier reflections dwell on death as a general phenomenon; he speaks of *la mort*. He compiles registers of diverse manners of dying and weighs the philosophers' opinions on how a man *should* meet death. For a while the Stoic teachings of his dead friend direct Montaigne's thought to a fitting heroic stance in facing death, and Cato the Younger serves then as the model. Let a man try to disarm death so that death is not the master; let him die as a free being and not as the heedless victim. "They go, they come, they trot, they dance, but of death never a word.... Let us disarm him of his strangeness, let us become familiar and conversant with him ... bring him before our imagination in his every shape" (pp. 84–85). Many of the most familiar shapes of death do not occupy Montaigne at all. He offers no images reminiscent of the Dance of Death; the typical Christian thoughts about death and an afterlife are missing.

Becoming conversant with this mysterious end of life increasingly came to mean for Montaigne acquiring familiarity with his own impending death. The heroic stance gradually disappears. The model of Socrates replaces the model of Cato. Nature, benignly leading us all to our end, is more and more seen to be the guide. A bridge built of observations on personal illness and the process of aging gradually leads from here to there. In the reflections on the deaths of many around him, Montaigne less and less inspects various models for dying and more and more delivers the lesson that each man dies in his own way. Mere reasoning about death gives way to experiential testing and probing. In essay 2:6, "On Preparation," Montaigne dissects the recollection of the experience of lying in a two-hour swoon after having been thrown from a horse. He remembers the hazy but not frightening feeling of lying there half-conscious between life and death; he recalls the pleasurable feeling of growing languid and simply letting himself go. "It would, in truth, have been a very happy death.... I was letting myself slip away so gently, so gradually and easily" (p. 357). By more such probings he steadily found revealing ties between life and death. The erstwhile enemy of life becomes its more familiar companion, adding to its value and meaning. A life and a death should correspond to one another. Above all, every death should be such that no life is falsified in its conclusion. As landlord of his own estate, Montaigne thought it most fitting that death find him among his cabbages, quite unconcerned either about having to go or leaving his gardening undone. At other times Montaigne wished for the chance to die in the saddle, somewhere away from home so that he might be buried without the tears and lamentations of the relatives. By now he is on familiar terms with death. Very fittingly, the language shows that the earlier generalized concern with death, *la mort*, had turned to the use of the phrase *ma mort*. "Je me contente d'une mort ... toute mienne" (p. 956). The individual had made the inevitable end of his life a familiar part of existence; no single part of life would falsify the whole. The art of living seemed to be consubstantial with the art of dying. And the ultimate value seemed to lie in being true to oneself.

The *Essais* contributed to the self-consciousness of individuality (a word Montaigne never used) in part by describing these forms of self-awareness. But it is of equal importance that Montaigne placed a positive value on his very own specificity. He saw more significance in his writing than the simple discovery of his peculiarities and the perverse satisfaction of being distinguished by and remembered for his oddity. He felt a need to orient himself among an immensely rich but bewildering inheritance of models and ideals. His growing skepticism about the value of any ideal had led him gradually to a reasoned and constantly tested perception that truth, for him, could lie only in what he was. Truth lay in the individual existence when it took care not to falsify itself. The judgment of any action required consideration of the precise circumstances in which it occurred; morality had to fit the case. "Men are diverse in inclination and strength; they must be led to their own good according to their nature and by diverse routes" (p. 1029). That this problem was perceived by many in his age is perhaps best exemplified by the casuistic ethics that developed through the efforts of so many contemporary Spanish and Jesuit theologians. It was altogether fitting that Montaigne would write at such length against any form of pretence, presumptuousness, and remorse. He had learned to accept himself, and he would "not meddle with telling people what they are to do in the world" (p. 191).

The full acceptance of the self in all its peculiarity was accompanied by the positive valuation of all diversity. "No quality is so universal, in the appearance of things, as diversity and variety" (p. 1041); "I find in myself such infinite variety and depth" (p. 1052); "variety alone satisfies me, and the enjoyment of diversity" (p. 966). The acceptance of individual distinctiveness thus seemed secured in an immensely rich perspectivist view of the world. Man was not an impoverished creature thrown out of paradise but a protégé of nature functioning within an entirely fitting order in which not even uselessness itself was useless (p. 767).

This sense of trusting acceptance of the natural world and of man's creaturalness had its counterpart in the acceptance of the historically given social world of custom and institutions. The convulsions of his own time, especially as they were rooted in the presumptuousness of

religious innovators, left Montaigne deeply suspicious of any revolutionary activity. He saw no virtue in deliberate change, because he did
not think that man was intelligent enough to know how and what to
change. All the talk about ideal constitutions was as much presumptuous nonsense as the grandiose-sounding recipes for making better men.
In the light of reason, custom and habit might indeed look arbitrary and
deficient, but reason was once again overreaching itself when it deemed
itself capable of construing ideal solutions to complicated matters. Customs might be arbitrary, and the world of custom Montaigne inspected
seemed overly rich in alternatives, but the real justification of customs
lay in their ability to stand the test of men's complicated lives. Rules of
life should enable us to play the game of life; that is all we can and
should expect of them. The art of education, therefore, should aim at
making the custom of its particular world acceptable to the child; as for
the rest, it should enable the child to develop according to its nature and
to be true to itself. It was hard, often heartbreakingly hard, to live in
sixteenth-century France. Montaigne, as much as others, hoped for a
better life. He tried to live up to his social duty, and actually he had a
much fuller public life than he was ever willing to reveal in the *Essais*, [16]
where the role of mayor and public man was not meant to obtrude on
the tasks of the retired experimenter. But his hopes and labors for a decent
life never left the solid ground of the humanly possible. The Church, the
state, the customs of his land were a given order, which, like the order of
nature, enabled the individual to exist. Montaigne preferred such
functional orders to the phantoms of reason.

This preference for the firm ground of a given world order did not,
however, give Montaigne a historically oriented view of existence. There
are elements of his mental make-up which became an important part of
the late-eighteenth-century historicist position. The parallels are in the
sense of elation over the manifold diversity of life, the respect for the
uniqueness of each situation, and the fascination with the variations
brought out with a shifting perspective. Montaigne's view of the world
was an enormously expanded one; it was practically worldwide. His
loving acceptance of multiform appearances was stronger than his desire
for rational uniformity. He could understand himself as a part of his
surrounding world. But would he have thought it a meaningful question
to ask whether he would have been something distinctively different
had he been born in 1523 or in 1543 instead of 1533? He hardly conceived
of the personality as a historically grown reality. However much we
credit him with a sense of change, it is not possible to equate that sense

of change with a historicizing penchant. Nature for him is in constant flux, but she is not evolving. His view of social reality bears the same statical marks. He looked upon the troubles of his time as a vast disturbance of the order that ought to prevail; he hoped to see this order restored. He neither saw nor wanted to see in these troubles a historical transformation of his society. Montaigne thought that his own life and being could not be fixed, and he found himself to be recording "passage." He obtained this sense of passage in part from observing how differently he now thought about certain matters as he took them up again. Indeed, by separating out the different chronological layers in his writing, Montaigne scholarship of the twentieth century has made it possible to discern something of the evolution of his thought.[17] But Montaigne's very habits of working (which indeed make this scholarship possible) clearly suggest that he himself did not intend to write a history either of his thought or of his person. He simply interlaced his later reflections with the views already recorded as if to stress his fascination with the perpetually enriching process of moving around the same object once again. Flux and impermanence were part of reality, but it had no direction—surely not a historical one.

His life was filled with the wonder of discovering—perhaps even better, uncovering—the richness of the world as he could constantly experience it anew. In the process he found what was truest in him, that which one might call his individuality, but he uncovered it only in its specificity and not yet in its historical dimension. He came to value this personal distinctiveness. Most of his energy as a writer was spent on uncovering it, laying it open for inspection, accepting it, securing it against falsification, and simply "letting it be." For this task life still had room. Except in some of his thoughts on education, he did not consider the question of how an individuality comes to be. There was no more time and ultimately no need to face the lifelong task of personality formation. The *Essais*, after all, were the writing of an "old" man who had retired with a desire to learn how to die. In this they were wonderfully successful in bringing him to an acceptance of the fact that his very own death was meant to be an unfalsified part of the whole.

One matter remains slightly paradoxical in considering the relation of the *Essais* to the issue of individuality. Montaigne had found his way to his own self by turning against the world of models. But while the objective of the *Essais* was so personal, they yet left to the world, especially the world of Frenchmen, an ideal personality conception of a grand career. Essential traits of the *honnête homme*, that great ideal of the seventeenth century, were contained in Montaigne's conception of the *homme suffisant*. They point beyond—to the ideal of "education," of *Bildung* and *gebildetes Menschentum*, to which the generation of Goethe, and especially Goethe himself, felt drawn. Montaigne's own search thus left behind the vision of a model; but it was a model that had much room for the growth of individuality.

Montaigne had fused diverse elements of a rich inheritance in his conception. On the one hand, the old Ciceronian ideal held up the model of a man of *urbanitas* enjoying *otium cum dignitate*. It entailed the cultivation of a life-style, with material sufficiency to free it from *banausia* or the need for gainful employment (*negotium*), a life with the freedom for the activities that make man truly human and civilized, a life fit for a man who derives his dignity from placing his talent in the service of *humanitas*. On the other hand, many men in the sixteenth century, partially those under the influence of the Ciceronian ideal, had begun to turn the old chivalric model into the idea of the perfect courtier, or the perfect gentleman. Though neither of the two ideals could serve Montaigne as a simple model, there was much in his situation to which they appealed. Consciously or unconsciously, his life was affected by the fact that his aristocratic class had lost or was losing its older functional justification. He derived no sense of fulfillment from the role of the warrior, the official, or the seigneur building and improving his estate in the way in which his father was still able to do. The ancient aristocratic devotion to the role of the public man did not leave him enough room for his private self; he found the role of the courtier totally false. No conception of *persona*, in the old sense of role or masque, could serve him. He evinces a typically aristocratic disdain for any form of "profession." The first great lay writer of French prose sought to avoid any semblance of the professional writer possessing expertise or being marked by professional pedantry. He would have been offended had anyone looked at him as an author "by profession."

The only real function left for this aristocrat was the living of a full life. "My trade and my art is living" (p. 359). The individual, sufficient unto his world and to himself, faces the task of living his life. He has no rules for this, no prescriptive philosophy. Instead of the calculus of life for which Cardano hoped, Montaigne's man needs training in the art of life. The great diversity of his existence can be mastered only by an art that balances and harmonizes. "Our life is composed, like the harmony of the world, of contrary things, also of different tones, sweet and harsh, sharp and flat, soft and loud. If a musician liked only one kind, what would he have to say? He must know how to use them together and blend them. Our existence is impossible without this mixture, and one element is no less necessary for it than the other" (p. 1068). Nature and artfulness blend in the grace with which a man masters the situations into which life throws him. Here is a personality ideal which prescribes very few concrete virtues, but insists instead on the elegant blending of diverse human elements. It does not prescribe so much that a man be this or that, that he do this or that; it suggests only that a man had better have a style all his own! Here is an "open" conception of a human model in which many an individual could cultivate his individuality.

Different men responded differently to the complex choices which life posed for many Europeans of the early modern centuries. Some of these responses furthered the slow growth of a sense of individuality; others represented ideals of life less consonant with that notion.

In the face of a complex world, Montaigne found refuge in the undeniable concreteness of his personal existence. In the process he uncovered a specific self that was hardly less complicated and intricate than the world of nature, custom, and opinion in which it had to live. At least, a man could rest with a sense of security in that reality which was truly his own. But this ideal of an individual art of mastering the multiform existence in a harmoniously balanced personality was by no means the only ideal for Europeans.

Descartes, sixty years younger, reacted in much more radical terms to the complex tradition. His autobiographic account in the *Discours de la méthode* is symptomatic of the radical break with many traditional elements, a break beyond which looms the more ordered world of intelligible causality on which Voltaire looked and for which Cardano already had had a deep longing. Growing distrustful that he would ever find certainty of knowledge in the vast accumulation of ancient and scholastic tradition, Descartes radically cleaned the slate and on that *tabula rasa* sought to draw the full outlines of a knowledge erected entirely on rational certainty. At least he thought he was doing this, and he may never have been aware of how much he was "the last of the Greeks" and the heir of the scholastics. This abrupt jump from a radical doubt about man's inherited thought into an untrammeled trust in pure rationality, this respectless housecleaning on the grand scale, helped to simplify life. In that sense this Cartesian revolution in thought—in part supporting the simultaneous rationalization of the natural science, and in part supported by it—made a rationalistic outlook on reality once again an obstacle to the growth of the sense of individuality to which Montaigne had contributed so fundamentally. It took another two centuries for Europeans to find the appropriate balance between the claims of their rational culture and their recognition of the factors difficult to accommodate within it.

But there also lay in this Cartesian turn to rationalism the very opposite tendency toward the ultimate individualization of thought. It was clearly perceived by the great seventeenth-century Bishop Bossuet. In a letter to the Marquis d'Allemans, a disciple of the Cartesian philosopher Father Malebranche, Bossuet, in defense of his Church, voiced a warning. From Descartes's declaration of the autonomy of the human mind would follow an uncontrollable diversity of opinion.

> For under the pretext that one only must admit that which one understands clearly—which, when brought within certain limits, is very true—everyone grants to himself the liberty of saying: I understand this, and I do not understand that. On this basis alone, men approve and reject whatever they wish, without considering that besides our clear and distinct ideas there are confused and general ones which nonetheless embrace such essential truths that one would overthrow everything by denying them. There is introduced under this pretext a freedom of judgment which has as its result that men boldly put forward whatever they think without regard to Tradition. [18]

# 9

# Seuse, St. Teresa, and Madame Guyon: The Mystic's Inward Search and the Authoritative Model

 The Christian model of man was dominant long into modernity. If it were my task to trace domin-ant personality conceptions rather than to probe for the gradual emergence of that later conception of self we call individuality, then surely the weight of this essay would lie on the subtle variations of a basic Christian personality type. Most of the key characteristics of the basic Christian personality could already be found in the Augustinian model: the sense of man's inadequacy, his dependence upon grace, the submission of human rationality to a higher form of truth, a fundamental transcendent longing, an acceptance of the world as a crea-tion and of the self as a creature, a gradated reality in which spirit is of more value than matter, the conception of life as a pilgrimage deriving its value from a value beyond life, and the commitment to an absolute ethic of brotherly love. With varying stresses on any one of these com-ponent elements, the total configuration shifts substantially. Thus the variations on such a basic type can be bewilderingly complex. Think of the differences, indeed, that distinguish an Augustine from a Thomas Aquinas, a Gregory VII from a Francis of Assisi, or an Abelard from a Bernard of Clairvaux. And yet there remains a basic Christian experi-ence, creating conditions which were partially conducive to the quest for a self that later eventuated in a perception of individuality. The way in which this same experience also placed obstacles in the way of such a self-conception, should be evident from the analyses of Augustine and of medieval personalities such as Abelard.

The return to the Christian personality at this point does not signify any intention of dealing in a systematic manner with the late medieval and post-medieval variations of this type. I only consider here a few autobiographic writings and in no way aim to recapture the fuller range of the Christian experience in a slightly more modern setting. The treatment in this chapter of a few mystics—Heinrich Seuse, Teresa of Avila, and Madame Guyon—and in the next chapter of a few Puritans—John Bunyan, Richard Baxter, and the "secularized Puritan" Benjamin Franklin—aims at a broader understanding of neither the mystical experience nor the Puritan one. Every text in this essay is used for quarrying a few specific stones to construct a very limited argument. The mystics' texts are meant to suggest, at least, the debt our modern personalities owe to the sensitive reaching for the limits of inner consciousness to which the mystic is driven by his quest and by his desire to present this inner world to others. The Puritan's systematic self-testing may then be compared with this. And the weighty matter of how each strives differently for a unification of the personality, a process proceeding under different aegises in the Catholic and the Calvinist Protestant, should at least be looked at briefly. Neither the human type coming out of the mystical experience, nor that coming out of the Puritan experience, need to eventuate in what we call individuality. And yet their contribution to this ideal is not altogether negligible.

## HEINRICH SEUSE (SUSO)
### (CA. 1295–1366)

The mystical strain in medieval Christianity had appeared in such early masters as Augustine and Gregory the Great, and had subsequently been strengthened by St. Bernard, the Victorines, and St. Francis in the twelfth and early thirteenth centuries. It flourished in the Rhenish region in the fourteenth century in four great exemplars: Master Eckehart, Johannes Tauler, Heinrich Seuse (all three members of the Dominican Order), and Jan van Ruysbroeck (an Augustinian canon). Eckehart, the oldest, was the intellectual fountainhead for this group; Tauler and Seuse were his students at the Dominican training center at Cologne; Ruysbroeck, as the youngest of the group, may still have heard Eckehart. Tauler, one of the most powerful Christian preachers of all time, was instrumental in spreading the mystic element. Ruysbroeck, "the Admirable," the most poetically eloquent of this group, was to have particular importance for Geert Groot and the "Modern Devotion." Seuse, by virtue of an autobiographic writing named "The Book That Is the Seuse," is the one great mystic, prior to Teresa of Avila and Francis de Sales, who remains most accessible as a person.[1] He does not figure as an intellectual innovator like Eckehart, nor as a popular preacher like Tauler, nor as a reformer of monastic life like Teresa, nor as a great mystic poet like St. John of the Cross. His pastoral care made him important for and beloved by some around him; through his writings he influenced such later figures as Thomas à Kempis, Canisius, Spee, Angelus Silesius, and, stretching the ages, Görres. He is particularly interesting for the manner in which practical mysticism, visionary mysticism, and speculative mysticism were unified in a single life.

Almost all that we know about him we know from himself, although ironically, the early form of the *Life* owes much to the hand of Elsbeth Stagelin, a nun from Töss, outside Winterthur, to whom Seuse had a close pastoral-confessional relation.[2] He related few external facts of his life. He considered himself a Swabian. His father, of noble descent, was active as a businessman at Konstanz. Seuse so abhorred these worldly interests that he later took the family name Seuse from his mother, whom he adored for her godly life. As a thirteen-year-old boy he was placed in a Dominican monastery on an island in Lake Konstanz, where he lived until about 1348. Since he was too young to enter the monastery legally, his father gave a considerable sum to the Dominicans. Seuse subsequently suffered greatly whenever he thought that his monastic position had been bought by committing the ecclesiastical sin of simony. When he was roughly eighteen, he suddenly (*mit einem geswinden kere* [8:14]) "converted" to a rigorous monastic life.[3]

As an intellectually gifted young man, he was sent by his order to Cologne for advanced studies, and there he met Eckehart and probably also Tauler. But afterward he did not follow the customary course for a Dominican—further training in theology at the University of Paris. Either he had turned away from purely intellectual pursuits or he had become suspect by his association with Eckehart, who was tried in the last year of his life (1327), seventeen of his propositions being subsequently condemned by the papacy. Seuse remained faithful to his master, but avoided discussion of the controversial theses. In one of his recorded visions he had a conversation with Eckehart, now speaking to him from the Beyond. On his return, Seuse must have served as a lector to his monastic community, which was exiled for a while by the imperial city Konstanz when it became involved in the intense struggles between Louis the Bavarian and the papal curia. Between 1326 and 1334, Seuse wrote three of his books: *The Little Book of Truth, The Little Book of Eternal Wisdom,* and its Latin version, the *Horologium Sapientiae.* Eventually Seuse must have been involved in many pastoral duties of his order, traveling far and wide, and advancing to the position of prior. Sometime around 1348, he was transferred to Ulm, where he redacted his works into the definitive *Exemplar,* adding now the *vita* which Elsbeth Stagelin had started to compile from his letters and her records of conversations. He died in Ulm in 1366.

The *vita* is less a strictly chronological account than a topically ordered depiction of a life advancing in religious perfection. The book is meant to teach by the example of a lived life. Experiences and occurrences are thus taken out of chronological context and are freely transposed to an appropriate place in the lesson. Seuse perceived the meaningful pattern of his life in the conception of a gradual advance along the *via purgativa* to the *via illuminativa* to a final destination on the *via unitiva.* He only touches lightly on the first five years of his young monastic existence: an easygoing, unfocused living unto the day (*sin gemüte ungesamnet* [8:6]), in which, from a retrospective view, God protected him from real harm. The turn to a serious devotion came at eighteen. Everyone was surprised at the change: "the one said this, the other that, but how it was, nobody found out." And Seuse does not tell. He stresses instead the "advance battles" (*vorstriten* [8:20]) that a "beginning man" must fight, especially in resisting the tempting voices trying to distract. He could not tell how long this battle lasted, but he knew he had learned to turn away from material things and tempting company. Wanting at least to suggest what it was that made him bear up under the next phase of the struggle, he inserted some early chapters on ecstasies and visions. Especially memorable was his experience of a sudden "displacement" of his soul—whether inside his body or outside of him he could not say. He heard and saw what cannot be put in words, something formless, without a specific way of being (*wiselos*), and yet having all the forms and manners of pleasure. Was it day? Was it night? He could not say. Eternal life's very own sweetness broke into his presence: "if this is not heaven then I do not know what heaven is" (10:26). Perhaps it lasted an hour, perhaps but half an hour. He came to himself with a pang of pain such as the dying must experience. The memory of this hour was to stay with him; no outsider could notice any change, but on his inside "the powers of his soul were filled ... with a fragrancy, just as if one empties a good-smelling ointment from a box and the box retains the good fragrance" (11:15 ff.). An intense experience, vaguely describable as to its precise nature but described poetically in its effect on a man's soul, filled him with a heavenly longing by which it could at least orient itself. To this Seuse adds an account of his "spiritual wedding to the eternal wisdom," referring the reader to his *Little Book of Eternal Wisdom* for a fuller understanding. In many respects the *vita* is the account of a spiritual troubador and knight declaring his devotion to serve a divine spiritual Queen of Love.

The servant of eternal wisdom, now knowing whom he wants to serve and what he hopes to gain at the end of the road, enters then as a "beginning man" upon an upward climb. An established tradition had sufficiently defined the means and the objective of the way. As Augustine had put it (in *Sermo*, 261:7), *"per hominem Christum tendis ad Deum Christum,"* through Christ the man upward to Christ the God. The generalized form for this spiritual quest having long been given, Seuse filled in the details of the prescribed forms with vivid pictorial concreteness. He identified in minute detail with the suffering Christ, in a manner fully befitting a representative of that late medieval symbolic-allegorical mentality which Huizinga has analyzed in such detail in his *Waning of the Middle Ages*. So that Seuse may be constantly reminded of his devotion to the suffering Christ, he stabs the initials IHS on his chest with an iron ink stylus, right over the heart. "As often as the heart beat, the name was moving" (16:27 ff.). Every action of the day was turned into a symbolic service, expressed in graphic form: Seuse would only drink by parsing his draft into five swallows in memory of Christ's five wounds, and as both water and blood flowed from the wound in the side, Seuse doubled his last swallow. Every apple was cut in four—three parts eaten in the name of the Trinity, the fourth eaten unpeeled in memory of the young Jesus, because children eat apples unpeeled. Every daily action became more and more his very own specific act of identification with the suffering Christ. He especially cultivated the virtue of silence and thus seems to have become a lonely monk in his community.

While a number of the chapters in part 1 dwell on these more charming aspects of the *Imitatio Christi*, the stress lies on an intense identification with Christ's suffering. By extreme acts of ascesis Seuse concentrates on breaking the body's powers to distract from religious devotion. The core of these exercises was Seuse's personalized version of the Stations of the Cross. His walk across the monastery became an extended journey on which, at appropriate locations, he sought to recapture Christ's last suffering walk on earth. The cloister door became the town gate through which Mary comes helplessly with the hot blood of her son's wounds splattered on her, and the servant "in the innermost of his heart falls down before her ... greeting her with the words: *Eya, ergo advocata nostra*" (37:3 ff.)—falling into the Latin formula, but inserting the children's talelike German exclamation "Eya," giving it thus his spontaneous personal mark even in the retelling. The chancel steps lead to Golgotha; the crucifix comes alive while the Savior is being undressed and nailed to the Cross in dreadful pain so that the servant takes his own scourge and "nails himself with heartfelt yearning to his Lord on his cross" (*und negelt sich mit herzklicher begierde zu sinem herren an sin Kruzz* [36:16 ff.]).

Seuse uses everything around him for completing the inner imaginative identification. But in order to accomplish it the will must be made less dependent on the body. And whenever the *Anfechtung* comes, when the inner doubts assault him as to whether he has a right to be with his Christ, he intensifies the ascesis. For more than twenty years Seuse, day in, day out, submits himself to painful tasks of suffering. He sleeps on a hard wooden door, and finally restricts himself to the use of a narrow wooden chair. He dresses his hands in spiked gloves so that he will learn not to strip off the hairshirt in his sleep without scratching himself bloody. He wears a wooden cross on his back, the size of a palm, with thirty iron nails sticking into his skin ("in memory of all the savior's wounds and the five wound marks of his love" [41:8 ff.]), driving the nailed cross into himself by batting his back against a wall whenever he feels a special need to revive the power of his memory or wishes to punish himself. For eight years the sores never healed. By innumerable other ascetic devices, and by fasting and thirsting, he often came close to death. When he was forty years old, "having chilled his blood and destroyed his nature" (40:26 ff.), he received a signal from God that such exercises were no longer wanted. He then threw his torture tools into the river.

The extraordinary aspect of these chapters, in which the reader seems to be looking into a torture chamber, is that they conjure up the presence of a man whom many justly came to call the Sweet One, a man who was known in his monastery as Brother Amandus. When, at the beginning of part 2, he draws the lessons from his own experience, he advises others to be more moderate and sensible in their own ascesis.

The purgation of the body now left room for that inner kind of suffering through which an "advancing man" may come to acquire the art of true tranquility (*rechter gelassenheit*).[4] With this inner art of total acceptance a man can bear the problem of being undone himself (*sölicher entwordenheit* [54:4]), taking everything God and men may deal out, seeking only God's honor and love—even when love does not seem to be given. Rather than imposing suffering on himself, a man is now tested by how well he can bear the suffering thrown upon him. The little fearful rabbit under the bush, trembling at every leaf that falls, must come out from under the bush and live fearlessly in a world in which suffering is the rule (54:23 ff.). The page must become a knight. The lamb must live among wolfish men (134:10). You do not suffer to become inured to more suffering by more suffering; you bear suffering not to look forward to the end of suffering, but to look forward to more. A man who advances in *Gelassenheit* yearns to suffer all the "painful heart pains" (*wetundes herzleid* [91:1 ff.]) of humanity, the pains of all wounds, the groans of all the ill, the sighs of all the sad, the tears of all the weeping, the insults of all the oppressed, and the needs of all widows and orphans. For in this lay the humanity of Christ. Looking outside his cell one day, Seuse saw a wild dog tearing a cloth; he rescued that torn cloth for himself as the reminder of what he had to expect as his own worldly fate.

Further chapters are filled with accounts of assaults on his honor and on his self-esteem. He depicts the courage needed for remaining a Christian. In marvelously vivid fashion he thus describes concrete occurrences that express his inner growth in dramatic pictorial form. He tells of the rescue of his sister who had dishonored herself by leaving the nunnery for a sexual escapade. He describes the suspicion he had to endure when he was accused of having poisoned the drinking water of a town ravaged by pestilence. And he recounts the story of the help he gave to some fallen women, one of whom turned on him, accusing him of being the father of her bastard child, thus bringing upon him a long period of suffering in which he was left without any human support in his innocent loneliness. When those who should have known and trusted him turn against him, he recalls that the Lord also had to have his Judas: why, then, should the friend of the Christ not suffer from his Judas too? (pp. 125–26)

But this was only half a turn. An inner voice finally points to true *Gelassenheit:* "To a man with whom all is right, a Judas no Judas in that sense shall be, but a helper of God leading him to what is best" (126:4–6). Only when pride is driven out to make room for God's will, only when a love (*eros*), striving upward toward the highest perfection, can express itself also as love (*caritas*) for the lowest creature, only then can the soul come to touch the ground of all grounds. He who finds innerness also in the outward, finds innerness in a richer measure than he who receives innerness only in the inward region (*Svem inrkait wirt in usserkait, dem wirt inrkait inrlicher, denn dem inrkait wirt in inrkeit* [167:15 ff.]).

The differentiation among degrees of *Gelassenheit* becomes ever finer toward the end of the book, the distinctions among experiences ever subtler, as the soul becomes ever more illuminated for its meeting with that realm where God dwells in his Godhead.[5] Nothing borrowed from nature can help to describe the ultimate mystical experience; no symbolic language, no pictorial usage, can serve in speaking of Pure Being, of the Pure Oneness that is all. Only a language of negation, negating all we know, can be used to hint at a Nothing that is not nothing but Being totally different from what we know as being. "This Oneness is called a Nothing because the human spirit finds no expression to say what it is. The Spirit [*geist*] only knows that it will receive [*enthaltet*] from one which is other than itself. That is why that which it will have is in a certain way a something as a nothing, but it is for man's spirit a nothing after its own way of Being" (187:12–16).

The life of a man advancing in *Gelassenheit* is thus seen by Seuse as a continuous process of forming: man must be unformed from his creatureliness, then formed in Christ, transformed in God (*ein gelassener mensch müss entbildet werden von der creatur, gebildet werden mit Christo, und überbildet in der Gotheit* [168:9 ff.]). The problem for Seuse, as for every Christian mystic (in distinction, for instance, to the mystic of Neoplatonist persuasion) is the difficulty of unifying a practical-emotional mystical strain and a purely speculative-contemplative one. The intense domination of the will in ever-tighter ascetic exercises must be reconciled with the surrender of the will in opening the self to the penetration of visions. A cultivation of passive *Gelassenheit* and a mysticism of suffering must go together with active service of love for others. The strongest yearning for a flight from all existence toward unification with the ultimate ground of all existence goes with the most intensive, imaginative identification with the lowest beings in a suffering creation. A quiet intellectual speculation, aimed at a knowledge denying all conceptualization and words, is to be joined to a highly elaborate symbolical mentality and an emotional poetic urge. The *Imitatio Christi* of the Stations of the Cross and the speculative mysticism of Eckehart were to be held together somehow.

In essence there was nothing new in this dilemma; every intensely experiencing Christian knew of the paradox of his Christianity. Augustine and Gregory the Great struggled with the need to reconcile a contemplative and an active mysticism, and so did every Christian mystic after them.[6]

The Church, this enormous institutionalized *complexio oppositorum*, sought to reconcile irreconcilables. But in Seuse's time some of these separate elements presented themselves in strikingly formulated examples. The mystical speculation in a theologically trained scholastic like Eckehart, in an age when the logical limits of understanding had been explored, had a profound appeal for some of the best minds of the fourteenth century; it was pushing the limit of what could be contained within Catholic doctrine, and it is noteworthy how carefully Seuse seeks to restrain the speculation as it moves too precariously toward pantheism. A late medieval figure like Seuse could find a more emotional-imaginative-visionary-poetic strain of mysticism in the impressive formulations of St. Bernard of Clairvaux and, in part, in those of St. Bonaventura. Seuse's emotional lyricism shows, in addition, the strong influences of the flourishing *Minnesang*. The ideal of the *Imitatio Christi* was powerfully expressed in the example of St. Francis, with whom Seuse also shares the loving intimacy with flowers and animals. In Seuse this was wedded to an infatuation with the chivalric ideal (cf. especially chapters 43 and 20), combining an erotic lyricism and the notion of testing oneself through struggle and service. This later medieval phase saw an extraordinary advance in a highly symbolic mode of thinking about the world and of self-expression.

The problem surely was how all these elements could be experienced and presented in a unified form. Seuse, like all medieval Christians, found the major containing frame in the doctrinal and institutional framework of his Church. He took care, pride, and comfort in staying within this frame by seeking to avoid the extremes of speculation, adhering to the sacramental system, preserving the rigors of monastic commitment, stressing the key virtues of charity, humility, and hope, and insisting on works and moral conduct as the absolute prerequisites to mystical experience. He submitted his works for approval to superiors.

But even within this frame Seuse had to deal with serious tensions. As a devoted monastic he valued the seclusion of his cell, but in much of his life he was deeply engaged in the outside world. His pastoral cares, especially those related to his order's supervision of nunneries, took him outside the monastery walls for long periods. As a highly intelligent and well-trained member of a teaching and preaching order, he nonetheless turned against the academic task. As a knight of the spirit he had to deny to himself any concern with personal honor. As a speculative mystic he had to deny himself the symbolic-pictorial habit of mind. As a devotee of the active *Imitatio Christi* he had to find room in his life for extended contemplation *and* long periods in which to perform the harshest ascetic acts. In his day-to-day life the most diverse elements could stand together in an unproblematical fashion so long as he made no conscious attempt at intellectual systematization.[7] The striking concreteness of his imagery, which seems to refer directly to things he has seen himself, the personal tone in all accounts of emotional experiences, the manner in which personal elements always creep into prescribed formulas that might simply have been taken over, all of this attests to a highly personalized experience. The astonishing richness of his language seems to derive directly from the fact that he tries to express common cultural matters in the intense and oversubtle amplification of an internalized experience. His writing has the poetic quality which never results from repeating given formulas but only from the felt need to externalize an inner experience. There are thus no grounds for doubting that his life somehow contained the most diverse elements. How he could present his life as a whole with a meaningful pattern when he sought to set it on parchment is another question, however.

The structure of the life as written departs in certain fundamental ways from the life as lived. It does so for very revealing reasons. Seuse had reported personal experiences and reflections to his spiritual daughter Elsbeth Stagelin, orally and in writing. She had begun to compose those into a larger whole. When Seuse took over, the dominant motive for writing was didactic; he meant to offer his own experience for the teaching and edification of others. He speaks not in the first voice but always as "he," or "the servant of eternal wisdom." By this didactic intention he placed a higher premium on presenting an orderly view of the *typical* phases of a mystic's way upward than on a faithful rendition of the factual sequential order of the personal life. The elements are called forth by the needs of the teaching design. The basic structure is dictated by the desire to show the rising order in the three stages of the *via purgativa–via illuminativa–via unitiva*. The life roughly corresponds to this scheme insofar as it was taken up by ascetic devotion during early manhood and abandoned after the age of forty for an intense concentration on the attitude of *Gelassenheit*, a passive surrender ultimately leading to mystical union. Similarly, the enthusiastic emotional pursuits of the *Imitatio* in imaginative acts of identification, and the chivalric service of the servant of the Heavenly Queen and the bridegroom of Christ later give way to the more speculative wisdom of the internal sufferer gaining his heavenly peace. Seuse placed the movement toward mystical union at the end of the book, as the end of life, although he described the attractive power of this element at the very beginning. Undoubtedly

Seuse believed, and must have experienced, and certainly intended to teach, that the true ascent to God depended on the gradual ordering of the inner man by means of the earlier steps on the road. But what thus appears as the final objective obviously reflects the author's early experiences: his sudden turn at eighteen was related to a vision of Eternal wisdom, and the encounter with Eckehart occurred in his formative years. His own *Little Book on Truth*, a dialogue on the deepest questions of speculative mysticism, was written before the *Little Book on Eternal Wisdom*, which deals more explicitly with the practical side of mysticism and asceticism. But when he put together all writings in the *Exemplar*, he reversed the order by placing the speculative *Book on Truth* after the *Book on Eternal Wisdom* in order to complete the parallelism of the steps of the way preached in the *vita*. The teaching function demands its own order.

And yet, the more confused pattern of the personal experience interferes continuously with the clear didactic purpose, though it does provide the complex richness that makes it more than a typical guide to the mystic life. For instance, in submitting to a set of extreme ascetic exercises, Seuse had placed before his eyes the lives of the desert fathers as reported in the *Apophthegmata*, one of his favorite books. Though he factually reports these acts, they occasionally seem colored by the outlook of an older man who now places less importance on them. When he feels he has to advise others, he warns against ascetic excesses, telling the nuns especially to seek only those suitable for the weaker sex. The different elements of the mystical way, though basically subordinated to the typical pattern, repeatedly enter into his discussions where the experience of life had inserted them, even though the pure order of thought may not require them. Thus he fuses the concerns with the typical and the general and with the individual and the personal in a lively fashion.

As an autobiographer, Seuse ultimately faced an exceedingly difficult problem: how to present his speculative mysticism in a didactic account of his life? Judged as an integrated autobiography, Seuse's work cannot be regarded as a success. A series of chapters in which he states speculative mystical teachings without making any attempt to have these reflect the life context in which they came to him are simply affixed at the end. The long chapter 49, for instance, is simply a list of proverbs "on the truly inward man." Thus the account of his life is totally driven by the desire for union between his own truth and the ultimate ground of all truth, and the personal experience that provided the ultimate meaning is never described.

The mystic's inherent dilemma is, of course, that he cannot truly speak of his greatest experience. At best he can suggestively hint at the realm where he finds his ultimate solace. Even when he claims the privilege of having directly experienced a reality totally beyond the one in which we are bound, he can speak of this only through the mediation of the indirect language formed by the experience of this world. Christian teachings also offered built-in barriers to a continuous speculative contemplation of that other reality beyond. In the early patristic age, pure Gnosis had been abandoned as a false road, incompatible with the idea of a transcendent Creator and the unity of creation. Matter and spirit were not to be separated as antithetical deities, but corrupted matter was meant to be refitted by the power of the spirit for wholesome existence. Earthly life retained an intrinsic value not to be denied by complete abandonment. Firmly within his tradition, Seuse knew this. As a Dominican he had absorbed a rationalistic scholastic outlook; it is not clear how much he was aware of the doubts being raised about man's rational powers within the scholasticism of his own day. But the example of Eckehart was always a live warning to him concerning limitations of the mind's ability to face the ultimate questions. He warned his spiritual daughter not to push rational investigation too far. And although Thomas Aquinas remained Seuse's rational authority, he felt a particular affinity for Thomas's exact contemporary Bonaventura, the more mystically inclined Franciscan scholastic.

One likes to think that Seuse would have liked the Zurbaran painting of the two Parisian doctors: Thomas surrounded by all the accouterments of learning while Bonaventura is unveiling a crucifix in a totally bare cell—as if to say "And that is the only book and all the learning I need." True blessedness lay less in words than in works. The mystic would use the strength gained by having been permitted to sense the power of the Beyond, for work in this world. Lift your heart, and the *Sursum Corda* leads upward so that the refreshed heart may then live here among the lowly again. However powerful the attraction of pure contemplation, it was no more complete in itself than rigorous ascesis. When God is being born in the soul, true innerness finds its external expression as well. The tradition that insisted on contemplation *and* charity, on grace *and* works, protected the mystic from dissolving active life in the vast reaches of eternity.

Despite the inherent yearning of all mystics for overcoming the separated self in union with the ultimate, the mystic in the Western tradition was left with the task of forming a self for serving his God and his fellow men. The fascination of *The Book that Is the Seuse* emanates from the undetachable presence of a distinctive person among all the didactic material. The autobiographic section does not simply resemble the older autobibliographies in which the writer explains the background of his books. The living person presented by Seuse is instead the "existential" ground in which the written works rest. What is given in the generalized conceptualizations, the typical forms of the teachings, is inextricably tied to the experience of a person living the teaching and doctrine. Within the didactic form and content, provided mostly by the culture of the day, there was thus room for an individualized presence. The universal Christian message was being experienced in a personalized way. Seuse heard his Christ say that He had died for him as well as all others. "The dear Christ did not say 'Take my cross on yourselves, but each man take *his* cross on himself'" (107:11 ff.). The heavenly Queen had a very personal relation to Seuse; he adorned his cell with his own picture of her and had his very own way of serving her. Though as a *gelassener* man he dissolved his own suffering in the universal suffering, his experience remained personalized and individualized. In Seuse, the concrete individualization of every experience is always part of a symbol pointing to a universal fact.

And the language in which all of this is presented is a very personal language, despite the self-negating habits of talking in the third person—"There was a servant of Eternal Wisdom who . . . ." The writing has a lyrical quality, even when it tells of self-torture. It employs simile derived from direct experience; it has an emotional sweetness entirely in keeping with the harmony of the person. It seeks to express sensations and emotions and insights of an inward experience, and it approaches the limits of what can be said. The Augustinian habit of speaking of the inward organs of inward senses such as the heart of hearts, the eye and ear of the heart, the fragrance of the soul, is continued here. "I placed myself before my inward eyes" (18:1). Seuse makes heavy use of the adjectival reinforcement of the noun and loves to talk of silent silence, painful heart pain (*wetündes herzleid*), *gelassene Gelassenheit*, innerly innerness; he uses such contrasting terms as imageless imagery. Though at times he plays with words, the language never loses its meaning. *Alle di wile liep bi liebe ist, so enweis liep nit, wie liep liep ist; swenn aber liep von liep gescheidet so emphindet erst liep, wie lieb lieb waz.* All the while that love is near love, it does not know how lovely love is; but when love parts from love, then only love senses how lovely love was (234:13 ff.). The very intensity of experience, and the utterly serious motive in speaking of it, drive the reaches of language into further recesses. Freeing himself (probably not by a conscious choice) from Latin, with its more firmly established formulas for expressing the religious life, Seuse used a special talent for phrasing in concrete lifelike language what easily could have turned into a learned abstraction. His significance as a prose writer and his contributing influence on German prose have long been recognized.[8]

Every bird will sing according to the way its beak is grown, so a very personal expression of the most inward life of a human being is thus a cultural good as well. Unlike Augustine, Seuse did not have to form for himself the very elements of a *Weltanschauung* in which to find a place for his Christian self. The rich developments of a thousand years gave him a firmly established Christian framework and the basic forms in which to fit the individual Christian experience. Seuse is the interesting example of the way in which the most common ideal can be experienced in an intensely personal way. The Christian insistence on the distinct value of each soul, the inward seriousness of the devoted Christian life, and the very personal relation of the soul and its God—such strong elements in the mystic—were feeding grounds for the continued exploration and reexploration of the inner richness of the human personality. Which personality conception ties the individual more to a model of being than the *Imitatio Christi*? And yet—in Seuse—even this ideal of forming the self in the image of another, becomes in its own paradoxical way, a part of the story of individuality.

## St. Teresa of Avila
### (1515–82)

In the Escorial, the national monument of sixteenth-century Spain, the manuscript of St. Teresa's *Life* lies next to a page from Augustine. The life of the saint, so indifferent to worldly glory except when it was a matter of God's glory, coincided with the Spanish century. The role of Spain in world history was inextricably bound to the vitality of its religious life. While the dominant forms of Spanish religiosity had only tangential relations to mysticism, Spain in the sixteenth century was the scene of the greatest mystical movement of all times. St. Teresa, St. John of the Cross (1542–91), Luis de Leon (1527–91) are great names in modern mysticism; the Spain of their times is said to have produced more than 3,000 mystical writings, of which many are still in manuscript only. As religious writers, employing the Spanish vernacular, the great mystics helped form language as well as literature at a time when many of the great Spanish theological works were still being written in Latin. This great flowering of mysticism occurred, moreover, at a time when some mystical tendencies had resulted in movements that were suspect to Church authorities fearsome of heresy and divisive particularism. But the mysticism of the reformed Carmelites St. Teresa and St. John of the Cross remained eminently within orthodoxy, unlike the dangerous, more troublesome strains of the Dejamiento (Abandonment) and Molinist Quietism of the late sixteenth and early seventeenth centuries. In St. Teresa especially, this mysticism led to extraordinary practical activity. As the key figure in the reform of the Carmelite Order, both female and male, she played a national role, even though it is clear that she would never have conceived of it thus. In a land where up to one-fourth of the adult population may have been clerical, lay and monastic, where the Cortes of 1626 claimed to find 9,088 monasteries, she herself founded some 17 monastic establishments. The woman who wrote in the simple direct manner of the people about her practical work as well as her subtlest mystical experience was indeed a national figure and one of the most popular of all modern saints. That she, disclaiming any learning, should have her work placed next to the work of the greatest Christian mind, is an apt tribute to the broad reach of mysticism within Christianity.

The *Life of Teresa* does not equal the maturer expression of the mystical life given in her later book *The Interior Castle*. But my interest is in the autobiography. And this interest is limited to those few orthodox elements which can, in part, be contrasted with the later Quietism and with certain elements in Puritan contributions to the genre.

The *Life* was Teresa's first book; she most likely began to write it in 1561 when she was over forty-five years of age. She did so at the request of her confessor. The first draft was completed by the middle of 1562. She was then commanded to amplify it, and she completed it toward the end of 1565. The writing of the book thus followed within four to five years the point that she considered the beginning of a new phase of her religious life (1556–57). By then she had experienced her first visions and raptures; the transverberation of her heart belonged probably to the year 1559. Having made a vow of greater perfection, she had taken steps, after 1560, for the first foundation of a reformed convent at Avila. Thus the writer was filled, on the one hand, with the experience of extraordinary signs of divine grace in the heart of a great sinner, and, on the other hand, with the firm conviction that she had been commanded to reform her order in the face of all the expected opposition. The power of the book thus lies in the joining of an intense longing for mystical union and devotion to a practical task.

The autobiography basically follows the chronological lifeline of experience. Teresa arranged the presentation in five blocklike segments. The first nine chapters deal with her early life to the point when she found the appropriate manner of praying. Chapters 10 through 22 are a more systematic discussion of the basic forms of prayer. They reflect the basic phases of Teresa's experience but are not held to a strict chronological scheme. In Chapters 23 through 31 she resumes her personal story, now dwelling heavily on her visions and raptures. Chapters 32 through 36 relate the founding of the convent of St. Joseph at Avila. In the concluding chapters, 37–40, she reports more of the effects that visions and revelations had on her life. The first sentence of the short prologue, and many passages throughout, stress that her confessor had commanded her to write the book in order to explain her ways of prayer. The theme of the "unwilling author" is deliberate: I have "to steal the time" for writing, "My writing hinders me from spinning. I am living in a house that is poor, and have many things to do."[9] She consistently insists that as an unlearned woman she ought not to be writing. Yet, in her last seventeen years after completing the *Life*, she wrote many works and very many letters. What had started as an aid in the relation between confessor and the confessing sinner—and many passages suggest that Teresa's words were not meant for anyone else—became in the reworked second version a book with a clearly didactic purpose, most likely to teach the nuns of her new foundations. It is very much a "talking" book; the writer speaks what she writes. And, depending upon the issue, she addresses whoever seems to be the most appropriate recipient at the moment: at times she talks to God the Father; at times the father addressed may be the confessor; and at other times the intended recipients are the novices of her convents. At first the account of the founding of St. Joseph was not included in the *Life*; the decision to include it meant giving more than a confessional content to the book. But the confessional part was not quite to the liking of the author either: "I could wish that I had been allowed at the same time to speak distinctly and in detail of my grievous sins and wicked life. But it has not been so willed; on the contrary, I am laid herein under great restraint; and, therefore, for the love of our Lord, I beg of everyone who shall read this story of my life to keep in mind how wicked it has been."[10] Much of this suggests that the autobiography is not quite what the author would have written had she voluntarily undertaken to present her life. And yet the book she wrote expresses much of what she was and what she experienced. It has long been valued as one of the great autobiographies in the Western tradition.

The lives of all saints fit a basic Christian pattern; the hagiographic form was one of the earliest and most dominant biographic models in Christian literature. The sinful life of the creature is bisected by the experience of conversion and subsequently becomes a life devoted to doing God's will. This basic pattern is also present in Teresa's autobiography. But, on the whole, it is remarkable how little her self-presentation is dictated by the imperative of literary models. The life she presents runs its course very much within the containing forms of a firmly established cultural matrix, reported simply as the expression of her direct experience. Or perhaps one should only say that Teresa seems plainly unconcerned with fitting her life to any consistent pattern; she is recounting what she knew to have been her experience. But since it was an intensely Christian quest, fitting many of the characteristic elements of sixteenth-century Spanish spirituality, the life has model-like features. Teresa had a great love for Augustine's *Confessions,* but aside from sprinkling the expected praise of the Lord for his merciful acts through her pages, there was little that she borrowed directly from that model. Though Teresa often speaks of her habit of envisaging phases in the life of Christ, there is very little stress on the *Imitatio Christi,* even though she insists on having the Christ near her so that she may talk with him. Her life as a mystic fits into the basic pattern of the successive phases of the *via purgativa—via illuminativa—via unitiva.* However, it is very characteristic that, when she comes to talk of the *via illuminativa,* she complains that she herself does not really know what "they" mean by using the language of mystical theology. She makes no pretense at theological learning, and she expects her confessors to "edit out" what should not be in the text. She does not write for literary laurels, and if she were not filled to the bursting point with the exaltation of her experience, she would not be writing at all. The value of the book for mystical theology, or for understanding the person, lies in the directness of the style whereby she transmits to the reader her observations of herself and of the phenomena in which she was interested.

For the first fifty years of the life—and the autobiography is limited to those—the external events form but a meager story, though the details of her life after 1565 would indeed have made for a stirring story of "adventure." The founding of her convents, and the stormy history of the first few decades of the reformed Discalced Carmelite order, offer a story of extraordinary events which she herself later told in her *Book of the Foundations*. [11] Until the founding activity went beyond St. Joseph's, Teresa spent most of her life in Avila. She was born there in 1515 in a fairly well-to-do family that had eleven other children. She felt particularly close to one brother, nearly her own age; they read saints' Lives together and dreamed their children's dreams of becoming martyrs. "We settled to go together to the country of the Moors, begging our way for love of God that we might be there beheaded" (1:4). They built little hermitages for themselves. "I used to delight exceedingly, when playing with other children, in the building of monasteries, as if we were nuns; and I think I wished to be a nun, though not so much as I did to be a martyr or a hermit" (1:6). When Teresa was thirteen, she lost her mother, from whom she had acquired a great enthusiasm for books of chivalry, that fashionable distraction signifying for the truly religious person an undue attachment to worldly things. The distractions of company and servants ("whom I found ready enough for all evil" [2:7]) are singled out as the dangers of her life at that time.

Three years later, around 1531, Teresa is on her way toward the life of a nun. She enters the Augustinian convent at Avila as a boarder. Her thoughts are brought back to eternal things, but her heart is still hard: "I could not shed a tear even if I read the Passion through" (3:1). In retrospect it seemed to her that servile fears of hell, rather than love, drove her to the religious life. But at least she developed the habits of vocal prayer and of reading good books. After a period of growing inner conflict, in which she acquired the gift of tears, and a spell of ill health, she took the Carmelite habit at the Convent of the Incarnation at Avila in November 1536. While by external standards she was a good nun (at one point even converting a lax priest), she often suffered from an internal restlessness, found it difficult to concentrate, and lamented the fact that no confessor could adequately guide her in her desire for meditation. Between 1538 and 1540, she had to leave the convent because of serious illness in which she suffered attacks of catalepsy that left her paralyzed for months. She then chose her patron saint, St. Joseph. From the time of her return to the monastery until the 1550s, she mentions no external event other than her father's death in 1543. Her descriptions of this long period are devoted entirely to an account of her inner struggle to find her way to the right kind of prayer. The laxness of her order disturbed her, but the true problem was her difficulty with mental prayer and meditation, which she suspended for a while when she became persuaded that she had no right to seek the comfort of God's presence before she had truly cleansed herself of sin. She gradually returned to forms of mental prayer, helping herself by reflecting upon Christ's Passion, identifying especially with the mystery of the prayer in the Garden. Simply habituating herself to the practice was helpful: "My soul gained very much in this way, because I began to practise prayer without knowing what it was; and now that it had become my constant habit, I was saved from omitting it, as I was from omitting to bless myself with the sign of the cross before I slept."[12]

The great aridities of the inner life are gradually turned into a watered garden, as the soul, through the various habits of self-willed prayer, is being prepared for a kind of infusion in which God himself comes to be seen as the active force. At this point in her account, Teresa inserts the long section of Chapters 10–22 in which she tries to give her statement of the various stages of prayer. It seemed that life was different now. "Hitherto, my life was my own; my life, since I began to explain these methods of prayer, is the life which God lived in me—so it seems to me" (23:1). Sometime around 1555–56, when Teresa was about forty years old, she apparently made very rapid advances in the quiet prayer of contemplation and experienced numerous visions and raptures. Prayer, as she said in her finest definition of it, "is nothing else, in my opinion, but being on terms of friendship with God, frequently conversing in secret with Him who, we know, loves us" (8:7).

She had ever more strongly gained the conviction that a sinner who is truly intent upon conversing with God and taking His signs of loving acceptance will more and more pass into His power. God creates the conditions for truly communing with Him, and she felt increasingly enabled to partake of such communion and to receive the divinely infused power. Visions and raptures were increasingly reported during this period, but they were mainly intellectual and imaginary visions, never corporeal ones. One of the most interesting of Teresa's descriptions of an intellectual vision is in her *Relations* no. 7, given to the Jesuit Rodrigo Alvarez.

> As for the vision about which you, my father, wish to know something, it is of this kind: she sees nothing either outwardly or inwardly, for the vision is not imaginary; but, without seeing anything, she understands what it is, and where it is, more clearly than if she saw it, only nothing in particular presents itself to her. She is like a person who feels that another is close beside her; but because she is in the dark she sees him not, yet is certain that he is there present. Still, this comparison is not exact; for he who is in the dark, in

some way or other, through hearing a noise or having seen that person before, knows he is there, or knew it before; but here there is nothing of the kind, for without a word, inward or outward, the soul clearly perceives who it is, where he is, and occasionally what he means. Why, or how, she perceives it, she knoweth not; but so it is; and while it lasts, she cannot help much to retain the image thereof—she cannot do it, for it is then clear to her that it would be, in that case, an act of the imagination, not the vision itself—that is not in her power; and so it is with the supernatural things. [13]

At first Teresa was very fearful at such experiences, and for a time she intensely struggled with doubts as to whether they might be all delusions. So many in that age saw things and heard things and were proven to be charlatans or fools. At first she was even fearful of reporting the experiences to her confessors; but she scrupulously gave an account of them. Her confessors submitted her to tests; whereupon the power of the visions grew stronger. Some demanded ascetic exercises from her which she found very difficult to perform in her fragile state of health. Some even commanded her to resist the experiences; she dutifully sought to obey. Even when she thought that God himself declared to her that the priest was mistaken in imposing his tyranny on her, she obeyed God's minister, trusting that God himself would change the priest's mind. [14] By and by she found growing understanding from her confessors, especially from the Jesuit Baltasar Alvarez and the famous Franciscan Peter of Alcántara. As every test to which she submitted herself strengthened her belief that these were indeed divinely infused graces, and as she relied on the test of assessing the genuineness of the experience itself by the effect it had on her soul and on her entire conduct, she grew ever stronger in her inner trust. By 1560, she was able to translate this gain in her rich inner experience, in strength, and in devotion to sanctity, into the immense practical work of reforming her order and, thereby, much of the religious life of Spain. In the autobiography she reports only the labors in setting up her first foundation, St. Joseph at Avila. All the devotion, humility, and patience she had acquired were now called into play as she struggled to meet the opposition of the diocesan authorities, jealous monasteries, and the town of Avila, which was violently opposed to having an unendowed monastic establishment, devoted to abject poverty, within its walls.

On reading and rereading this book, one is left with an impression that a life filled with extraordinary content has been presented in a remarkably direct fashion. Unlike Seuse, Teresa only occasionally hides behind the use of the third person or such locutions as "the servant of Eternal Wisdom then learned . . ." The scene is always the one Teresa herself can survey; the attention is fixed on what goes on within her. The reader is tied to her extraordinary inner life by the nexus of her continuous reports on her feelings. So much of this book consists of the descriptions of her joys about special experiences, her expressions of sadness over her lack of humility, her statements of her fears in encountering new forms of grace she had never thought of or heard of and had never expected, her feelings of being torn between what she felt to be true and her desire to be obedient to unsympathetic advisers, her sense of shame in not being worthy of all this attention, and above all, of course, her never-ceasing wonderment and astonishment that all of this was happening to her, that God "on a dunghill so foul and rank has made a garden of flowers so sweet" (10:15). The test for the quality of prayer was always the quality of the emotional state in which it left her. She "classified" the different types of prayer and the different stages in the upward movement by their effects on her spirit, soul, and body. Her certainty about the nature of her visions and raptures is measured by the degree to which she recognizes their recurring effects on her.

What she gives in writing results from the power and the delicacy of her observation. She expresses an awareness of her experience and her spiritual state without much dissecting analysis, "philosophizing," or theologizing. Only very rarely does she couch these observations in the ready-made formulations that her religion, after all, had formed over centuries. She rarely uses the Bible for adorning her personal experience. She simply reports what she knows about herself. She is certain about what she reports when she says, as she often does, "I know this by experience." She will, at times, try to explain what she has experienced, and then will temper it by a "thus it seems to me." And every so often she recounts an experience and states that she has no idea what it was or what it meant; only after repeated occurrence may she acquire the insight. She will occasionally make subtle distinctions between types of visions, between visions and raptures, and many of these have remained persuasively valid to the experts; but her real interest seems to be in telling what happened to her and what the effects on her were.

Chapters 10–22 are, of course, a grand attempt at a systematic discussion of prayer in its various stages; since prayer stood at the center of Teresa's spiritual life, the summation of this, her experience, was bound to be the element that most directly lent itself to teaching others, especially the nuns of her reformed order. On most of the essential points there seems to be extraordinary agreement between her analysis and that of a much "more theoretical mind," such as St. John of the Cross (who, of course, was influenced by her). When she is less clear, as she is for instance on the difficult point of transition from the "prayer of active recollection" to the "prayer of passive recollection" and the underlying problem of the "ligature of the senses," such a "lapse" seems to be the result of her own confused experience early in life in trying to free herself from the limitations of discursive prayer.

As an autobiographer of a life of mysticism, Teresa was at her best when she could simply recount her experience and directly describe the state of her consciousness. In the later book, *The Interior Castle*— considered by many her greatest work—her chosen symbol obliged her to spin out the implications of the symbolism, either that of the crystal-clear diamond with its many passages and chambers, or that of the Mystical Betrothal. In the *Life* very little use is made of such symbolic transformation of the experience—the systematic discussion of prayer in Chapters 10–22 uses the rather simple image of the four ways of watering a garden, a symbol so fitting for a Castilian experience (11:11). But even here the bulk of the discussion is effectively guided by her predisposition to describe the various states of the soul as she has come to understand them through her long experience. The emphasis is always more on a direct description than on an attempt to systematize the experience by fitting it into a theological scheme.

The most basic frame of the mystical experience—the three-stage ascent over the purgative, the illuminative, and the unitive way— underlies her experience as well, but she leaves her individual imprint and now the accents are placed differently. The elements of the illuminative and unitive way are much more mingled than in Seuse, for instance, and it is in the unitive phenomena that her interest lies. The purgative way is handled in a much more subdued fashion than in Seuse, for whom the disciplining of the flesh was such a dominant matter at first. The struggle with the distractions of the world, the difficulties arising out of the laxity of the unreformed convent in which she had to fight such struggles, was a big topic for Teresa. And she is, of course, famous for turning her order into a much more ascetically disciplined one. But with her fragile health in early life, ascetic exercise had to be less extreme physically. She believed in discretion in those matters in which each one had to find his own appropriate means. There is a time for partridges and a time for hard fasting. "Take care, then, of the body, for the love of

God, because at many other times the body must serve the soul; and let recourse be had to some recreations—holy ones—such as conversation, or going out into the fields, as the confessor shall advise. Altogether, experience is a great matter, and it makes us understand what is convenient for us. Let God be served in all things—His yoke is sweet; and it is of great importance that the soul should not be dragged, as they say, but carried gently, that it may make greater progress."[15] Purgation is an important matter, but it has a sweeter quality for her. When she notices her distraction, the hourglass she watches while praying, she tries to help herself by "picturing" the Christ in the Garden within her and intensifying her inner love. In contrast to later Quietist "perversion" of Catholic doctrine, Teresa insisted very much on what the Christian could and must do himself before he can experience the true inner arrival of God. Go to the well to haul up the water, again and again, and do the necessary weeding. But since one of her initial stumbling blocks had been to think wrongly that she should not commune with God as long as she was not purer, she later knew how to live with a sense of the extraordinary mercy of divine communion while remaining conscious of the shame of her own littleness. "The soul seems to me like a little ass, which feeds and thrives because it accepts the food which is given it, and eats it without reflection" (30:22). "The inward stirring of my love urges me to do something for the service of God; and I am not able to do more than adorn images with boughs and flowers, clean or arrange an oratory, or some such trifling acts, so that I am ashamed of myself. If I undertook any penitential practice, the whole was so slight, and was done in such a way, that if our Lord did not accept my goodwill, I saw it was all worthless, and so I laughed at myself" (30:25). The central experience of her life was that God does commune with such a soul. Seuse, at the end of his book, spoke of this union only in a series of intellectual propositions; Teresa presented it not in dogmatized summation but as a day-by-day part of the lived experience with its effect on her personality.

The great power for careful and delicately probing observation may well have been one of Teresa's natural gifts. When one considers that it is also found in her contemporaries Cellini, Cardano, and Montaigne, one is tempted to think of it as an emergent "modern" trait. In her case, however, the needs arising from her relations with confessors provided an enormous impetus for cultivating the powers of observation as well as the powers of simple, clear description. Volumes can be written on this topic of Teresa and her advisers. Suffice it now to point to some essentials.

The core of the mystic's existence is the absorption in the all-claiming, all-consuming personal relation of the soul and God. In this lies the force for the intense discovery of the inward life of man—and also the threat of uncontrolled subjectivism. For Teresa, the barrier against such subjectivism lay in her absolutely unquestioning faithfulness to her Church. When she heard of a threat of inquisitional procedure, she exclaimed: "I heard this with pleasure, and it made me laugh, because I was never afraid of them; for I knew well enough that in matters of faith I would not break the least ceremony of the Church, that I would expose myself to die a thousand times rather than that anyone should see me go against it or against any truth of Holy Writ" (33:6).

Her advisers and confessors were her links to religious orthodoxy. Early in her career she suffered because she could not find advisers truly responsive to her needs for understanding guidance.[16] She found none who could help her in her early struggles with mental prayer. But she gradually learned to seek out experienced and learned men, especially among the Jesuits who became established at Avila in the early 1550s. When Teresa's visions and locutions came, she was very much in need of guidance. She was fearful about her experience; she was afraid of being laughed at. Above all, she was at first suspicious that she might be deluded, that she might imagine her experiences, that they were indeed Satan's work. Some advisers told her that they were most likely the devil's work, signs of her lack of humility which had better be corrected by more strenuous ascetic exercises; and one of them thought she would do better by not talking about her experience. On several occasions a situation thus arose in which her inclination, her own sense of the right course, and her steadily stronger experience of divine realities stood in conflict with the position taken by her confessor.[17] Each time, Teresa consciously placed her obedience to the confessor ahead of what she believed to have been God's directive to her, always seeing in priest and confessor the minister placed there by God. When her visions and raptures recurred ever more strongly, and as experienced and learned men now patiently listened to her and searched the texts, the point of full concurrence between Teresa's irresistible experience and the Church tradition within which it had a place finally came. The book she had started as an exercise in testing her faith could thus become its testimonial: "So, then everything here beyond the simple story of my life your reverence must take upon yourself—since you have so pressed me to give some account of the graces which our Lord bestowed upon me in prayer—if it be consistent with the truths of our holy Catholic faith; if it be not, your reverence must burn it at once—for I give my consent. I will recount my experience, in order that, if it be consistent with those truths, your reverence may make some use of it; if not, you will deliver my soul from delusion, so that Satan may gain nothing there where I seemed to be gaining myself" (10:13).

Books like Teresa's became schools where men learned ever better to observe themselves and to speak of their inner life. The mystical, Quietistic and Pietistic literature of the coming centuries shows that men were trying to register ever subtler stirrings of their soul—perhaps at times to the point of oversickly self-indulgence in which every little twitter seemed important. Against this danger Teresa was protected by a need to test her experience against the established norms of an old tradition. She preserved a sane balance between contemplation and action by converting so much of her energy, released by mystical pursuits, into the practical work of a reformer who had to struggle very hard for her reforms. Her conception of life admitted human variation: each one needs his own pace, and the fitting surroundings "where they may save their souls in the way of their own spirit" (36:31); there are many rooms in my Father's Mansion. Yet those were but variants of the Christian way, and, in essence, her self-conception stayed within the tradition of the model life.

## Madame Guyon
### (1648–1717)

Thoughtful churchmen had always known that the noblest of Christian desires for closer union with the divine could, by the slightest misstep, endanger the Christian faith. A very subtle line separates the potential saint from the potential heretic. All of Christian orthodoxy has been a delicate balancing of fundamental paradoxes. The problems of observing subtle distinctions and the quality of nuances were especially pronounced in mysticism, which contains so many untestable and indescribable experiences, and is so closely associated with the most intricate issues of grace. The Catholic church of the seventeenth century, already steeped in the problematics of grace presented by Jansenism, also had to face the dilemma of mysticism in the form of Quietism. Much of the early activity of this "movement" had been centered at Rome around the Spanish priest Miguel de Molinos (1640–97?) whom the Holy Office there had tried and condemned between 1685 and 1687 for the principles of his *Guida spirituale* (published in 1675) and the alleged crimes of his personal life. Teachings of a very similar type, though not necessarily influenced directly by Molinos, emerged in French aristocratic circles in the 1680s, bringing into prominence one Jeanne Marie Bouvier de la Motte, better known as Madame Guyon.[18] Though she fully deserves attention in her own right, historians have chiefly remembered her as the cause that pitted Bossuet against Fénelon in an intense fight over the orthodoxy of certain mystical teachings, especially the possibility of totally pure, totally disinterested love.

A pupil of Madame Guyon published her collected works in thirty-nine volumes. Some of her poetry has survived in the translations of Cowper. The works most influential in her lifetime were a treatise on quiet prayer (*Moyen court et très facile de faire oraison* [1685]). However, her subsequent fame as a writer, especially among Protestants, has rested on her long autobiography, which she completed in 1709 during her house arrest at Blois. The book had been begun at the behest of a confessor when she returned to Paris in 1686.[19]

The life is told in a straightforward chronological fashion. The events are meant to have significance only as occasions for her religious life. Clearly an *apologia*, the book has a missionary, didactic intent. Madame Guyon held, by descent and by her later marriage, a socially prominent position, though she was not a member of the highest nobility among which she later often moved. Early in the book she takes up her theme of being the maltreated martyr for God—"Having sacrificed myself in the strength of pure love to thee" (p. 11). Neglected by an unloving mother, Jeanne Marie spent much of her youth in a cloister, where she nourished an early desire to be a nun. As she tells it, quiet prayer was already her solace in the early years. In obedience to her father she married a much older man whose mother and servants came to tyrannize her. Rather than fight against this, she made an elaborate cult out of suffering every conceivable indignity. She attributed the loss of a child and her own beauty to her mother-in-law's stubborn refusal to let her see a doctor during the plague. But, as she says repeatedly, her enemies were not really enemies, only the servants of God's Will. Her central tenet was to ask nothing for herself but to turn to God with selfless love. She thus presents her married life as a grand schooling for learning that all-important lesson. Encounters with the Benedictine Mère Granger and several other spiritual figures of the time, and the reading of mystical literature, especially the writings of François de Sales and his pupil Madame Chantal, convinced Madame Guyon ever more firmly that the right way to find God was to find him within herself. Asceticism took the form of an extreme willingness to suffer.

To this period of her married life also belongs the first encounter with the young Barnabite Father La Combe, to whom her later life was tied in an exceptional fashion. "He told me he had remarked in my countenance, a deep inwardness and presence of God, which had given him a strong desire of seeing me again: and God then assisted me to open to him the interior path of the soul, and conveyed so much grace to him through this poor channel, that he has owned to me since, that he went away, changed into quite another man" (p. 104). After her husband's death, Madame Guyon felt called upon by God to leave her children behind (with the exception of one girl whom she took along) and settle in the regions around Geneva to regain heretic souls for God. The bishop of Geneva at Annecy wanted her to direct a foundation for "nouvelles catholiques" at Gex but cooled in his enthusiasm when he found she had not brought her wealth along. Father La Combe, meanwhile, had come to the area to head the Barnabite institution at Thonon. He became her spiritual director—while she converted him to the right way of prayer. "God showed me, that he had given him to me, to draw him into one more pure and perfect . . . the Lord made known to me, as I was at prayer in the night, that I was his mother, and he my son" (pp. 203–4). To some this visionary priest and this prophetess of prayer were near saints, to others they seemed a suspect couple.

Madame Guyon had the great power of attracting other people; her general goodness and willing suffering made her many friends, though no one ever lived near her for very long. Her spiritual activity repeatedly occasioned conflicts with the ecclesiastical authorities which eventually resulted in their request that she leave. She never understood how much an enthusiastic interloper, albeit a prophetess, might threaten established parish routines. The entire objective of the mission to the "Calvinist Rome" of Geneva seems to have been forgotten fairly soon. For some five years she, and often Father La Combe as well, moved from diocese to diocese in the general area bounded by Grenoble, Marseilles, Genoa, Turin, and Geneva. The lady gained more and more sureness in her mystic ways, her sense of having been selected by God for a "new building" of his faithful growing apace.

In 1686, La Combe was recalled by his superiors to Paris. She followed him. A year later he was arrested, suffering a miserable and long incarceration until he finally passed away in a state of insanity. For a while Madame Guyon enjoyed the protection of Madame de Maintenon, the morganatic wife of Louis XIV, and taught in her establishment for young ladies at Saint-Cyr. She became deeply involved in the confrontation slowly brewing between Bossuet and Fénelon, her newly won protector, over the orthodoxy of quietistic forms of mysticism. High-level conferences were arranged for testing her writings; she submitted in part, but refused the far-reaching kind of recantation that Bossuet demanded. Finally, she endured a lengthy imprisonment in the Bastille, from which she was "released" only in 1702. She quietly lived out the rest of her life in family circles near Blois, where she died in 1717, attesting in her last will that she had always been a faithful daughter of the Church. Although her orthodoxy had been the initial occasion for the momentous confrontation of France's two great churchmen, their attention ultimately shifted away from her to the battle over mysticism in the French church, a struggle in which the Papal Curia also became involved. In 1699, a papal judgment, having to do as much with political as theological issues, condemned Fénelon and the woman he had protected.[20]

By the very nature of the problem, the controversies that arose in the late seventeenth century over the nature of the newer forms of mysticism could produce only partial answers. The key issues of Pure Love for God, unmarred by the pursuit of personal interests, and mental prayer in which human will gives way to Divine Will were embedded in the mystical tradition. Effective theological barriers could be set up only where these teachings led to the total condemnation of all human effort, the stress on near-permanent passivity and annihilation of human will, the real denigration of outward acts of mortification and of good works, and the claim for a sin-free state of the inspired person. But it was always extremely difficult to determine in any one specific case whether these crucial limits were being transgressed. Cardinals, inquisitors, bishops, and even a pope at first approved of Molinos's teachings. His condemnation was hastened by sudden accusations against his private morality. Any number of bishops and persons of saintly reputations gave testimonials for Madame Guyon; the bishop of Vercelli had his happiest moments "when he could spend half an hour chatting with her about God."[21] A pious, immensely learned, and theologically subtle man like Fénelon defended her basic position to the end. It proved most difficult for a theologian like Bossuet, hampered by his lack of a sympathetic understanding of mysticism, to pinpoint any single statement by her as clearly heretical.

Yet, if one takes the lady's *Life* as an expression of her religious state, its very tones and nuances leave the uneasy feeling that mysticism is here tipping toward its most dangerous side. In part this is caused by the exuberance of her expressions. Her style is not unrelated to a deeper-lying dilemma. Even her great defender Fénelon recoiled at times from her way of expressing herself, though he believed in the basic goodness of the life behind it.[22] She draws sympathy when in straightforward fashion she speaks of her servants' and mother–in-law's conduct to her; she is winning in her gesture when she simply tells how she gave a beggar the buttons of her dress when she had nothing else to give (p. 174). But the continuous reports of her willing suffering are meant to justify everything she does—though she says: "Whatever they said against me, love would not allow me to justify myself" (pp. 96, 396). Her assertion of utter humility is somehow marred by the frequency of statements such as these: "I was a victim incessantly offered upon the altar to Him who first sacrificed himself for love" (p. 91); "God ... has given me a very great facility to bear the faults of my neighbor"; "Oh, my Love, if there is a heart in the world of which thou art the sole and absolute master, mine seems to be one of that sort" (p. 285); "Oh my God, methinks, thou has made of me a prodigy, a monument of thy goodness and wonderful works" (p. 341); "The more any soul is favored with eminent grace the more nearly is it united with me" (p. 216); "I had nothing for myself; all was for others; yet I wanted nothing. I was like those nurses who are full of milk, though they are not themselves fed thereby" (p. 283).

She always wished to convince others of the utter importance of an inner freedom from the troubles of this world. "Christ showed me that my soul was above the vicissitudes and inconstance of events" (p. 241). Her lessons never have the sobriety and humanness of Seuse's *Gelassenheit*. When her children, her father, her husband, and her mentor die, she reports each time with pride that she did not weep. "I believe had everyone perished, I should not have been moved, my peace was so profound" (p. 120). What should be made of the utter selflessness of a person—"letting [herself] be consumed by love all the day long" (p. 222)—who repeatedly will state that those dear to her had to die so that she might come to be firmer in her God? There is a difference between a Seuse wanting to be permitted to identify with the suffering of all humans so that he might learn from it and this woman exclaiming: "Let me, oh my God, be the scapegoat, charged with the iniquities of thy people. Spare them all, but spare not me" (p. 367). Teresa was filled with the wonder of her betrothal to Christ, but she spoke of it in awe and with restrained taste. Each year Madame Guyon celebrated her wedding to the Lord while being married to a man whose jealousy she could not understand. But when Father La Combe became interested in anyone else, she would immediately accuse him of falling victim to a counter-

saint (p. 311). In one of her famous dreams (pp. 256 ff.), she was taken to
a lodge on Mount Lebanon where her divine spouse showed her a room
with two beds in it. "For whom are these? He answered: One for my
mother, and the other for thee, my spouse." Surely God deserves the
right to a more tasteful reporting of his inspirations.

Madame Guyon's inner life filled her with absolute certainty about her
own acts and her apostolic mission: "I could do nothing but what the
Lord made me do" (p. 280). She had curative powers. She was given
great power over souls. The Devil feared her excessively: "I was to him
like a thunderbolt" (p. 234)—Teresa merely fended him off by throwing
holy water at him. While Teresa viewed her trances and visions as highly
awesome moments during which the daily immersion in ordinary life
was temporarily suspended or transcended, Madame Guyon more permanently feels herself in divine states. "I found myself every day more
transformed into him [the Lord], and had continually more knowledge
of the state of souls without ever being mistaken or deceived therein,
though some were willing to persuade me to think the contrary" (p.
251). She thought that her books were written in total inspiration. When
she becomes suddenly inspired to read Holy Scripture, she produces in
several months twelve octavo volumes of commentary on the Old Testament and eight on the New Testament! "Thus the Lord made me go on
with an explanation of the holy internal sense of the Scriptures" (p. 278),
leaving only occasional passages unclear when her own reflection interfered with the divine guidance of the transcribing hand. Only later on,
when Bossuet began his intensive questioning of her writings, does she
sigh about errors of scribes and admit: "I doubt not but my own weakness may [!] have been too much mixed with the sacred intelligences of
his pure light. But can the dirt of the ground tarnish or injure the sun?"
(p. 357). Anyway, as she insisted, Bossuet should have judged her by
his feelings and not by his head, and Jesus himself should have presided
over a hearing on her writings (p. 374).

The more the world persecuted her, the surer she, of course, became of
her apostolic mission. God has used her to accomplish conversions and
to destroy the temple built by mere human endeavor. God commands her
to go to Geneva, but there is no report of her having converted any Calvinist there. Her successor in those regions, and for that same sort of
work, Madame de Warens, at least captured Rousseau—for a while.
Madame Guyon saw herself as a stone God had designed for a new building (p. 178); Christ showed her to herself as the Woman in Revelations
(p. 241); she is the chosen spouse to lead others; she is to be a

spectacle to God, to the angels, and to man (p. 262); there was nothing in her that was not also in Christ and in Holy Scripture (p. 284); she is to be crucified with Christ, and she hears him say "I became a man to save men. If thou are willing to finish what is behind of my suffering, and that I form in thee an extension of my quality of Redeemer, thou must consent to lose the happiness thou enjoyest" (p. 346). No spiritual director, no confessor could cope with such certainty; and indeed Madame Guyon's relations with confessors were either nonexistent or ineffective.[23] She nowhere denies the sacraments, but there is no mention of them either. The institutionalized Church and the hundreds of traditional means by which it sought to assist weak human creatures, disappear into the background; the certainty of the inner life, almost in a self-corroborating fashion, dominates her existence.

The test for any certainty lies in the subjective strength of her feeling. Reason, the rules of logic, play no role. She takes pride in the destruction—actually the word used is "annihilation" (as it was for Pascal)—of ordinary human powers. She had no need to study a theological tradition. "I study nothing; but there are given me immediately, as occasion requires, expressions and words very forcible" (p. 395). The whole tradition of Augustine—in its insistence on the painful continuous intellectual struggle to understand God's mysteries by approximation only, the stress on the pilgrimage as the only earthly life possible for inadequate human beings, his hard-headed sense that the touching of the divine, dwelling in eternity, was not even describable for men caught in the web of time, the sense of the basic precariousness of human life—most of this is lost, or very much in danger of being lost, in this orgy of selfless love and near-continuous permanence of a divinely infused state of perfection.

It is difficult to see what might function now as a check, a bridle, a limit to the expansion of the purest subjectivism. And it really is no wonder that the same Bossuet who fought the dangers of an authority-free subjective element in the Cartesian notion of the innate "clear and distinct idea," also emerged as the fighter against this unchecked and uncheckable form of mysticism: by adding his active concern to that of other churchmen, he aroused his Church against its dangers. Madame Guyon did not become a saint; her popularity proved to be greater among Protestants. However, by the vigorous defense of the whole mystical tradition, Fénelon not only fought for the possibility of its survival but also put the mantle of his great personality protectively over one who died firmly in the belief that she was a good daughter of her church.

The intense pursuits of mystics helped to uncover and to unlock the vast inward richness of man. Both the subtlety of human observation and man's ability to speak of the riches he found benefited from their inner search. Many of the mystics played a powerful part in enriching the language of their communities. They stressed a primacy of feeling and of spontaneous inner knowledge, which no subsequent view of the human personality could neglect. By their practice they also furthered man's imaginative powers of expression. Others besides mystics and pietists were making their contribution to the refined observation and rendering of human realities. By the beginning of the eighteenth century the art of literary portraiture—as it could be found in Saint-Simon's memoirs, for instance—had learned to combine the subtlety of analyzing internal conditions with detailed descriptions of the externally visible. Description can move from a remark about a wart to description of a character trait, and from an internal sensation to its palpable expression on a face or in a gesture. Deeper into the century, a pietist like Lavater began to preach the "science" of physiognomy.

While the mystic drew attention to sensibilities and inner urgings that mere rationality might not have cultivated, his most basic personality conception could move only in a limited degree toward that of individuality. The ideal of the *Imitatio Christi* is the most complete fixation on a model way of being. In the yearning for mystical union lies a powerful urge to cancel out the importance of the independent personality. The mystics who correctly understood the dangers of denying creatural realities knew, with the help of their Church tradition, where they had to guard a line and how to take their own extraordinary experience as part of a more general conception of the Christian person to which ordinary humans could adhere. Where mystic leanings overstepped the normative lines drawn to guard the existence of sinful mortals, a dangerous, uncontrolled and uncontrollable subjectivism opened up which should not be confused with the ideal of individuality, but which later on was mistaken as such by all sorts of romantics.

# 10

## Bunyan, Baxter, and Franklin: The Puritan Unification of the Personality

 The European developments occasioned by the Protestant Reformation, or, if one prefers, the Protestant Revolt, influenced personality conceptions in various ways. The Reformation was a factor in breaking up long-lived European unities. The break it caused in Latin Christendom was irreparable for centuries. The inevitable interpenetration of politics and religion accompanying this break further divided Europe into a community of nation-states with different languages and lifestyles. In nineteenth-century historiography, Luther was seen as a champion of individualistic liberty and free thought. This view is now as untenable as the occasional twentieth-century views that make him responsible for typically German quiescent submissiveness to amoral political authoritarianism. There is truth, of course, to the simple proposition that his revolt against the authority of the Catholic church altered established patterns of authority and established new ones. In Luther's view the individual Christian was still tied to the absolute authority of the gospel, with a rigor no less than the one by which the practicing Catholic was bound to the authority of a sacramental sacerdotic institution. Luther had an invincible trust that the sacred word communicates its unmistakable meaning with immediate clarity to each attentive reader; but as the text proved itself resistant to such a simple flow of uniform, self-evident meaning, it became clear over time that one central interpretative authority had now given way to ever-multiplying centers of authority. For even if, within a century, Lutheran orthodoxy and a biblical form of scholasticism had come to rival Catholic orthodoxy, the step once taken led inevitably to splitting up the Christian community into more and more self-assured sects and subsects, until the individual finally claimed a right to his own personal variant.

Protestantism thus stimulated a process of differentiation in the direction of individual autonomy; the same stimulus also worked to break down established status groups. As was the case with the political and cultural differentiation of Europe, Protestantism was less the prime cause than simply one additional powerful factor affecting historical processes already at work. The once sharp distinction between monastic and secular life had already been blurred by the growth of mendicant orders and such movements as the Beguines and the *Devotio moderna*. In Protestant thought the distinction was totally eliminated, and every believer was ideally expected to live by an innerworldly asceticism. As the theoretical distinction between clergy and laity disappeared, status distinctions in the religious world were leveled. Lutheranism, especially, left the secular differentiation into social status groups still untouched. But radical sects also transferred the ideals of religious egalitarianism to the social and political order and stimulated notions of a more egalitarian democracy. The powerful Protestant insistence that each man fulfill his calling forcefully drove society in the direction of individualistic differentiation.

While all of these factors may have helped to prepare the soil in which individuality might grow, there is no reason to assume that Protestantism, any more than Catholicism, had a "natural" or inevitable leaning toward that specific mode of self-conception. Essential elements within Protestantism were as inhospitable to that ideal of selfhood as was Catholicism. In some ways Protestantism may have contributed more to the eventual growth of individualism, which expressed a conception of the ideal relation between individual and society, than to the personality conception of individuality. This is a matter of importance for our story, since it seems altogether likely that the ideal of individuality needs the social conception of individualism—while it is certainly not true that individualism is dependent upon the ideal of individuality.

Luther himself wrote no autobiography, though he told us a good deal about his personal experience. Calvin told us very little about himself. During the first century only minor autobiographic accounts were written by Protestants; the history of autobiographic literature at the time is much more dominated by the autobiographies of Catholic mystics. But around the middle of the seventeenth century there occurs a striking reversal in this pattern: writings that are clearly autobiographic in intent and form appear in great numbers among English Puritans and sectarians and, a while later, among German pietists as well. The convulsion of the Puritan Revolution occasioned many extraordinary life experiences and provided opportunities for much personal religious experimentation. But the more important stimulus lay probably in certain theological innovations in the doctrine of grace. Precise causes are, as always, difficult to determine for such a phenomenon, but it is possible to restate some plausibilities that have been advanced over the years.[1]

Greatly compressed, the key elements of the argument are these. In certain segments of Post-Calvin Calvinism the insistence on the central doctrine of predestinarian grace and damnation occasioned intensely felt psychological needs for a sense of the certainty of personal salvation. Calvin himself had strongly warned against a persistent inquiry into one's personal state of salvation. To him such an unprofitable activity distracts man from fulfilling the one task for which he is here: to work everlastingly for the greater glorification of the Creator who, as an expression of his freely given love and inscrutable wisdom, predestined some to salvation among a totally sinful humanity deserving eternal damnation for its perverted will. To be preoccupied with the well-being of the self was thus a bit like idolizing the creature (or what Weber calls *Kreaturvergötterung*). "For men to search their own glory is not glory."[2] Even when a man is not certain of his salvation, his sense of gratitude and love should make him work actively to glorify God and enable his fellow men to do the same. We must adhere to God's commandments for the society in which He meant us to work for Him. A hero of faith, such as Calvin, could perhaps live with unconcern for his personal fate; but a large number of the ordinary men who followed him could not resist the immense psychological pressure of asking: Am I one of the elect? And how can I be certain of being in a state of grace? The pastoral response to this irresistible quest for the *certitudo salutis* was that it was a duty to regard doubts as Satanic temptations, that a man ought to consider himself chosen, and should find the certainty in the signs of his daily struggle to live for God.

This slight shift to a greater emphasis on the elements of Effectual Calling had tremendous effects on the formation of a certain personality type.[3] The individual himself, in his "unprecedented inner loneliness,"[4] sought the signs of election, of certainty of faith since faith alone would save; in other words, he looked for a sign of the works of God within him. He could not rely on sacraments as a means of access to grace; he had no priest to whom he could confess and who could alleviate the sense of sinfulness for a while by means of penitential acts, and thus he was denied that great spiritual comfort available to the Catholic for whom works counted as well as faith. "The means to a periodical discharge of the emotional sense of sin was done away with."[5] Misplacing trust in false men, frittering away one's concentrated energy on the emotional and sensual gratifications of a culture, employing superstitious magic for forcing God's unforceable hand, abusing time and natural functions, became sinful distractions for a soul carrying on its intercourse with God in deep spiritual isolation. The *fascinans* with the awesome Majesty of God, His total otherness and transcendental character, no longer permitted such urges toward mystical union as were partially still alive within Lutheranism. At best, God works in man, and man can be His instrument.

Thus enormous weight was thrown upon disciplined ascetic action. Only the elect will do the good works which can truly glorify God, and which are never undertaken as means for "purchasing" grace. Active work in one's calling is the "technical means . . . of getting rid of the fear of damnation."[6] What was demanded was not a series of good works but "a life of good works combined into a system."[7] A man engaged in such a quest could not afford a situation where the right hand knows not what the left hand does, or where the irrational disorders of a surrounding society might interfere with his constant quest. A high premium was thus placed on the inner unification of the personality, on bringing a methodical order into conduct, and on a rational (i.e., "purpose-rational") control of the surrounding world in which man might lead an acutely alert, intelligent existence.

Max Weber was interested in this religious personality as the prototype of the highly disciplined modern working man and entrepreneur. His search for a personality type motivated by a strong religious urge to work in such a disciplined manner while refraining from consuming the fruits of his labor was an attempt to explain how nascent capitalism could have developed into the coherent purpose-rational system of industrial capitalism. It was thus important for Weber to assume that such a personality, once it had been fashioned by intensely religious forces, could become secularized and could work without the initial religious motivation.

The Protestant's need for open access to the saving Word, and the corresponding devaluation of sense-gratifying aesthetic ritual other than hymn singing, made for an intensely literate subculture. By the seventeenth century it was also easier to publish, especially in brief pamphlet form. Inspired laymen, men and women of the humblest station, frequently appear among the writers of the day. No excessive learning was required; a man was qualified by the quality of his experience and his

knowledge of the Book—though there also existed many learned autobiographers. With the stress on continuous self-examination, diaries
appear in great numbers. They were kept as though they were spiritual
ledgers. Their daily recordings of spiritual debit and credit nicely illustrate a mentality of serious accounting (what Weber called *Rechenhaftig-
keit*). A certain John Janeway "did write down every evening what the
frame of his spirit had been all the day long, especially in every duty. He
took notice what incomes and profit he received; in his spiritual
traffique; . . . this made him to retain a grateful rememberance of mercy,
and to live in constant admiring and adoring of divine goodness; this
brought to him a very intimate acquaintance with his own heart."[8] As
Richard Baxter said, without self-examination we can never know how it
is with us. While the diary form thus assisted some in a quest for certainty, the person who had found the infallible signs that saving grace
was working within him might feel the urge to compose an autobiographic account. By telling his life, he could also confess his life. And one
of the main benefits he could bestow on his fellow men was the summation of his own experience. By the story of his own trials and rescue he
could help others to recognize the hidden power of habitual sin and to
heed the miraculous signs of divine action within the soul of the sinner.
The story of a transformed life in its concrete experience could attest to
the glorious working of faith and give assurance and practical guidance
to the neighbor in need. Old hagiographic forms were revived by the
Puritan experience.

## JOHN BUNYAN
### (1628–88)

As every child knows—at least every Victorian child would have
known—John Bunyan was in prison when he wrote his autobiography
*Grace Abounding to the Chief of Sinners*. In 1666, he was thirty-eight years
old, and he was established as an irrepressible preacher of the Particular
Baptist community of Bedford. Since he had been unwilling to cease his
unlicensed open preaching, he was incarcerated in November 1660, and
was released only in 1672. A simple promise not to continue open preaching would have set him free, but as he thought that such cowardice
would be a discouragement to the community of believers, he preferred
to suffer for his Lord, and "go upon the forlorn hope in this country"
that "my imprisonment might be an awakening to the Saints in the
Country."[9] Prison life was not too severe. He was allowed visitors,
received support from alms, even traveled to London, made "many

hundred gross of long Tagg'd Lace" to support his family, and as the prison had at times as many as sixty dissenters, he could even continue preaching in jail. Above all he began to write and publish on an extensive scale: poetry—*Profitable Meditations* (1661), *One Thing is Needful* (1664), *Prison Meditations* (1665); numerous pamphlets such as *I Will Pray with the Spirit* (1663), or *A Defence of the Doctrine of Justification by Faith* (1672); and the books *Christian Behaviour* (1663) and *The Holy City* (1665). Upon his release in 1672 (he was briefly reincarcerated during 1677), he filled the remaining sixteen years of his life with active preaching and care for those in danger of straying from the truth. His writing continued unabated: *The Barren Fig Tree* (1673), *Light for Them that Sit in Darkness* (1675), *Instruction for the Ignorant* (1675), *The Strait Gate* (1675), *Pilgrim's Progress* (Part 1, 1678; Part 2, 1684), and *The Life and Death of Mr. Badman* (1680). The simple tinker had immortalized himself as a most effective interpreter of a major part of England's religious experience.

His life lay squarely embedded in the most tumultuous history of England. He was born at Elstow into the Midland yeomanry. His father Thomas was a tinsmith, but the family had a nine-acre farm. John Bunyan received an education in basic writing and reading, but probably not in Latin. He learned his father's trade. In early life, by his own account, he was "without God in the World"; fully conscious involvement in religion came to him only under the impact of the Puritan Revolution. In 1644, he lost both his mother and a younger sister. And in November of that year the sixteen-year-old joined a parliamentary levy. Although he spent most of his army service, which lasted until 1647, in the Newport garrison, he must have seen action (perhaps the siege of Leicester), since he reports in *Grace Abounding* how a fellow soldier, who had taken his own place briefly, was killed in his stead by a musket bullet. In the New Model Army's militant Puritanism, and increasingly also in his observations of the Quakers, Bunyan met a religious force different from the one with which he had grown up.

Upon his return to the Bedford region in 1647 (after having volunteered to go to Ireland, but not having been sent), Bunyan married a poor woman whose dowry consisted of two religious books. These, and the conversations with his wife, gradually led him to a more personal religious search. The decisive turn came after 1651, probably from his more intensive contact with the Particular Baptist congregation at Bedford. He formally joined this group in 1653, moved to Bedford in 1655, and one year later began to preach in public and wrote his first pamphlet against the Quakers. With the Restoration in 1660 began his "martyrdom" as a Nonconformist. His world underwent all the immense changes that flowed from the reign of Charles I, the Puritan Revolution, the Cromwell Commonwealth, the Restoration under Charles II and James II, and the Glorious Revolution. Next to nothing of all this appears in his personal account. The autobiography is the story of a private life.

Yet the public events were of immense importance to the life of this man. And they were important also in creating the atmosphere in which his type could function. Bunyan's life was an act of profession, of professing the message as he had come to understand it, helping others to find their way into it, defending the faith by speech, writing, and teaching. Profession is intensely public. But the autobiography concentrates on the internal drama of a private person. "I am here unfolding of my secret things."[10] It is the story of the very lonely struggle by which a man found the inner certainty of his calling as an instrument in the Work of the Lord. This struggle is fought not by a man isolated from the world, or indifferent to it; the account itself is explicitly written to affect the world by its didactic value. But the struggle is Bunyan's struggle with Bunyan; the great interlocutor is the Book; the great enemy is the Devil. There is no helping hand from a friend, no helping priest, no sustaining sacrament. Bunyan is alone with his despair, his hopes, his limited but growing understanding of his central experience, alone with his Bible, his God, and his Devil.

The basic structure of *Grace Abounding* is simple: it is dictated by the nature of the experience it narrates. Between a short preface and conclusion lie 339 paragraphs. In the first 35 of these Bunyan presents his early life of natural sinfulness and his turn to external religion. The last 100 paragraphs, not a particularly artful conglomerate, consist of sections in which he attempts to restate what happened to him and narrates some more experiences without integrating them with the central drama. A longer section describes his "Call To the Work of the Ministry," and contains a brief account of his imprisonment. Even in the first edition these last two sections were announced as "additions." The real heart of the book (paragraphs 36–235) is the dramatic account of his intense quest for certainty of salvation. Its beauty derives from its dramatic structure, and from Bunyan's skill in blending biblical language with an astounding simplicity of everyday speech and imagery.

The preface stresses the didactic intent of the work. Bunyan dedicated it "to those whom God hath counted him worthy to beget to the faith by his ministry in the Word." He addresses them as "my dear children." If he could be with them, he would preach; as he is "between the teeth of the lions in the wilderness," he offers them instead this "drop of that honey that I have taken out of the carcass of a lion." The purpose of the work is clearly meant to be the instruction and comfort which the account of a true Christian experience can have for its reader. It is thus entirely typical of that immense outpouring of "personal lives" and diaries and conversion accounts produced by English Puritans. Presumably, Bunyan rehearsed it in the oral account he gave the Bedford community when he joined it around 1655. He consciously wished to lay the thing down plain and simple: "God did not play in convincing me, the devil did not play in tempting of me, neither did I play when I sunk as into a bottomless pit. . . . Wherefore I may not play in my relating of them."

Like this traditional preface, the account of Bunyan's early life also has a common and schematic quality, despite all the revealing personal touches. As the central significance of the Puritan experience lies in the later growing consciousness of grace, the earlier phase of life is significant only as the contrasting image of the natural life. Its details have less weight, and a general description is thought to suffice.[11] Thus Bunyan is brief: as a young person he lived according to the course of this world; he was filled with all the means of unrighteousness. He cursed, swore, lied, and blasphemed; with vain companions he pursued vain sports and other vanities. He was greedy and lustful and delighted in transgressing the law of God. If there were a heaven and hell, and if hell was to be his likely place, then it would be better to be a devil, a tormentor rather than a tormented. His punishments for this unholy youthful life were fearful dreams and dreadful visions. And yet, even then the script required that he be allowed to discern the signs of future hope; so Bunyan dwells briefly on his miraculous escape from dangers, suggesting the presence of a providential hand. And he makes clear that even in his sinful state of nature he hated any form of hypocrisy.

In the autobiography Bunyan passes over the war experience and attributes his turn to religious interests to the more settled state of the married man. Reading the two books his wife brought to the marriage begot within him "some desires to religion." Characteristically, it was the external trappings of religion that fascinated him; he even admits to a kind of fetishism for the priests, their vestments, the material objects of the service. The intervention of a divine voice—while he was in "the midst of a game at cat" (22)—posed the question: "Wilt thou leave thy sins and go to heaven, or have thy sins and go to hell?" Reviewing his sinful past and despairing of pardon for such transgressions, he considered that he might as well be damned for many sins as for few. Only when the ungodliest woman of the village takes him to task for his awful swearing and cursing, does he feel ashamed. "How it came to pass, I know not," but Bunyan now began an "outward reformation." He gave up his swearing and his bell ringing; the neighbors began to look upon him as a very godly man. He reads the Bible, but concentrates on the historical parts—"yet I knew not Christ, nor grace, nor faith, nor hope" (31). His was the religion of the external law, "legal" religion, the personal attempt at righteousness, the creature adoring the creature instead of the Creator (a fine illustration of what Weber called *Kreaturvergöt-terung*, idolization of the creature).

The inward turn to his sense of calling was occasioned when his external calling, his tinker's trade, brought him to Bedford. There, by chance, he observed a group of old women sitting in the sun (the oft-repeated symbol when good things came to him), and heard them describe the new birth in their hearts by which God had given them the confident trust which Bunyan himself was missing (37). The heart of stone now "began to shake," the first sign that it was being turned into the heart of flesh belonging to the believer. The softening of the sin-hardened heart and the "great bending" in his mind toward continual meditation announce the beginning inner drama. Bunyan nicely suggests the growing inner loneliness by telling how he cut himself loose from the temptations of seductive companions: he forsakes his closest friend. Until the victory is won, the text will have very few references to the human world about him. The pilgrim is on his lonely pilgrimage. "His wife and children ... began to cry after him to return; but the man put his fingers in his ears, and ran on, crying, Life! Life! Eternal Life!"[12]

The immense theological proposition in which the entire quest rests is the Calvinist doctrine of a double decree of predestination; Bunyan does not doubt this doctrine. Quite in keeping with the spiritual advice so often given in Post-Calvin Calvinism, he begins his quest with the persuasion that he must assume himself to be among the elect so as to avoid the temptation of total despair (47 especially). The elect has faith: "though I am convinced that I am an ignorant sot ... I will conclude I am not altogether faithless, though I know not what faith is" (48). The question then becomes: "But how can you tell you have faith?" (49). The entire process is thus bent on acquiring *certitudo salutis*. "I could not rest content until I did now come to some certain knowledge whether I had faith or no" (49). A Christian has nothing but the promise of God's merciful acceptance; a promise cannot do its healing work unless you trust it completely.

The first step in the search for certainty proved to be a dangerous temptation. On the road between Elstow and Bedford, the tinker is tempted to try a proof of faith: if I have faith, I ought to be able to work a miracle. "I must say to the puddles that were in the horsepads, Be dry, and to the dry places, Be you the puddles" (51). At the very last moment he held back for fear of failing. The incident serves to remind one, however, of that powerful though only gradually developing process whereby, ever since the start of the Protestant Revolt, the miraculous becomes deemphasized, and the use of magic as a means of evoking divine help for the world gives way to the search for a rational control of this world. Max Weber gave the beautiful term *Entzauberung der Welt* to this process.[13] The magic is being taken out of the world, which, henceforth, submits to scientific explanation. Hereafter, Bunyan did not try to tempt God like this again; internal certainty had to be gained differently.

Instead, the whole struggle now becomes concentrated on a systematic testing of Scripture, especially the Gospels and the Pauline Letters. This testing has a remarkably systematic rigor. Every doubting question leads to a scriptural search for a reliable answer. When the meaning of a supportive biblical phrase is clear, the next doubt leads to a renewed search, until there is a coherent interpretation of all questions. Repeatedly, Bunyan will resort to thought experiments, testing whether his answer can be trusted. And as the intense motivation is the quest for personal certainty of salvation, every biblical statement must be shown to be pertinent to the personal situation. Only when the personal direct experience of the text is in keeping with the unalterable Sacred Word, only then will the inner peace have come.

Bunyan suggests that early on he knew salvation to be God's work, not man's: "It is neither in him that willeth, nor in him that runneth, but in God that showeth mercy" (58). But the text still perplexed him, and the Devil posed the logical question: if it is not up to you, why strive any further? Could it be that election discernibly manifests itself in the comforting of the elect? Did the Bible support this? "Look at the generations of old and see; did ever any trust in the Lord, and were confounded?" (62). Bunyan combed the text from Genesis to Revelation, and finally found that comfort. Then the thought immediately occurred to him: but all these biblical examples are past history! "How if the day of grace should be past and gone? How if you have overstood the time of mercy?" (66). The full horror of wasting and of trifling with time fell upon him. He wasted time and energy on unrelated distractions and trivia instead of concentrating his efforts on an essential task. This horror of wastefulness had always been one of the strongest forces driving men to the unification of their personality; Augustine had experienced it with immense forcefulness; it was to be a weighty factor in the Puritan personality, and, in totally secularized form, time would be money, in the life of the secularized Puritan.

Persuaded that men had formerly experienced effectual calling and that there was yet room in Christ's mansion, Bunyan faced the next assault of doubts. Would Christ call him? What if Christ had no liking for him? For Christ only called "whom he would" (75). It was clear to Bunyan that he could obtain God's acceptance only in Christ's acceptance of him. But what reason did Christ have to accept him? In this phase Bunyan was overcome by the sight of his own vileness: "I was thus troubled and tossed and afflicted with the sight and sense and terror of my own wickedness" (86). He could no longer bring himself to thank God for having made him a man since he hated the very thought of being a man. How could Christ love such a creature? Bunyan, in the grip of a Christian's most problematic experience, faced the true night of the soul, and was tempted by blasphemy. Was there any truth to this story of a loving God and a loving Son? Perhaps the Scriptures were but a fable. Jews, Moors, and Pagans all thought their religion to be true; the Scriptures might "be but a think-so too"! In deepest despair, when God for a few moments gave him leave to swallow his spittle, he knew that such blasphemy could not come from one who truly loved God. In the grip of his doubts he compared himself to the "child whom some gypsy hath by force took up under her apron and is carrying from friend and country" (102).

For a year Bunyan was in this despair. As many Christians had found before him: when man has reached the depths of hopelessness about himself, when he is willing to see himself as a totally worthless being, only then can the truly gratuitous, the undeserved nature of God's love and mercy be recognized. The vision of the merciful father begins to complement and to displace the frightening vision of the perfect judge. Slowly but persistently, Bunyan labored to compose his mind and fix it upon God (108). He read the Bible systematically; he was "orderly led into it" (120). He slowly perceived the order in God's manner of working on him: how He would suffer him to be afflicted with temptation, then reveal the meaning thereof; crush him to the ground, then show him the death of Christ. Bunyan found wonderful comfort in reading a tattered copy of Luther's *Commentary on Galatians;* here was a man of religion who knew nothing about the problems of today's Christians and yet had written as if his problem were Bunyan's problem. By and by Bunyan acquired the sense that God "had set me down so sweetly in the faith of his holy gospel" (132).

But the quest was not ended. Bunyan still had to face the weighty issue as to whether grace was amissible; could it be lost again? Or was it indefectible, and was effectual calling a permanent gift? This problem came to Bunyan with extraordinary force; almost a hundred paragraphs are given to it. It reopened many a question that had seemingly already been resolved.

With intense directness the matter pounced upon Bunyan in a devilish temptation to sell the Christ who had now been given to him in exchange for things of this world. He felt rent by a tug of war: "Sell Christ for this, or sell Christ for that; sell him, sell him" (135). "By the very force of my mind, in laboring to gainsay and resist this wickedness, my very body also would be put into action or motion by way of pushing or thrusting with my hands or elbows . . . . I will not, I will not, I will not; no, not for thousands, thousands, thousands of worlds" (137). Exhausted and out of breath, he finally gave in to the temptation: "Let him go, if he will" (139). The Devil had won this battle. "Down I fell, as a bird that is shot from the top of a tree, into great guilt and fearful despair" (140).

Bunyan felt like Esau: he had sold his birthright. Like Judas he had sold his Savior; like Peter he had denied him. God had loved these two, but he, Bunyan, "was gone" (156). He had committed the sin unpardonable. For days he would shake and totter under the sense of a dreadful judgment, feeling a clogging and heat at his stomach, as if his breastbone would split asunder, or all his bowels gush out. Would God mark him like Cain for his point-blank sin against Christ? Systematically comparing his sins to those of others, and seeing that where they had sinned against the Law he had sinned against the Holy Spirit, he found it impossible to pray for mercy from the Christ he had denied. He now verily felt the physical order turn against him: the sun seemed to grudge giving him her light, the stones in the street and the tiles on the houses bent themselves against him; creation itself seemed set upon driving out such a sinner (187). Where else but to this denied Christ could he turn in his need? The doubts now began to work the other way: how could he assume to be the exceptional case? Was Christ's love helpless against such a sin? Systematically, he again went over his experience by means of a systematic search of Scripture. The thought gradually grew stronger that "this sin is not unto death"; so did the sense of belonging to a brotherhood of sinners and, like them, of having a right to the Word. The comfort suddenly came in the thought that the Christ would say: "I loved thee whilst thou wast committing this sin, I loved thee before, I love thee still, and I will love thee forever" (191). Grace was indefectible; once given, it was a comfort forever. "My grace is sufficient" (204). Bunyan found profound hope in this—but not until the very personal assurance was added: "for thee." "My Grace is sufficient for thee." Bunyan now understood: he had fallen, but not fallen away. He had tempted the Christ: Let him go if he will! And the Christ had answered: But I will not leave thee.

In a way, the inner drama had now run its course. Its lasting effect was to have made the man an instrument for the Work of God. Bunyan gave himself wholly to the call of the ministry, speaking about his experience, ceaselessly attesting to the veracity of the Word. The lonely experience led back to powerful work in the world.

The message itself and the content of the experience repeated an age-old Christian theme. But the framework set by doctrinal detail and by the mentality of the Puritan gave a specific quality to the personal struggle and to the integration of the personality. Such a struggle is intensely personal; the end comes only when the general lesson has found application in the direct personal experience. As Bunyan permits the reader a look into his life struggle, he can be only a helpless witness, unable to help because he knows that each person must fight such a battle alone. No priest is there to help, there is no function for a mediator. There is no support in sacrament or sacramental act because the Puritan cannot allow for the mediating miracle, for institutionalized grace, for the "magical" call upon God. He cannot confess to a confessor who could, by imposition of a penitential act, give momentary relief from the oppressive guilt of sin. There is no confessor to provide an interpretation of a personal experience, no authoritative guidance to which one can submissively entrust oneself. The only authoritative guidance is in the systematic reading of Scripture. Literacy is an absolute necessity. Relentless and sober self-examination is the other compelling activity. For only by bringing about a concordance of the unalterable Word and the soberly assessed inner experience can the desired certainty be attained.

By almost every aspect of his realities the Puritan is driven to place a very high premium on system, on method, and on the creation of an internal order of the self as well as an external order of things. Very low value will be assigned to enthusiasm, spontaneity, or intense emotions—except insofar as they remain contained within the systematic frame. The remembrance of the earlier unredeemed state of nature reinforces the horror of a life dominated by wastefulness, moved by arbitrary whim or by seductive companions, a body that dictates to the soul, or feels helplessly delivered to external forces and circumstances. The horror is amplified by the horror of hypocrisy—the presentation of a deceptive external order to which no internal order corresponds. The instrument of God is a unified personality in whom the outer man is a true expression of the inner man. Bunyan, therefore, suggests that a saving grace was present within him even in his most godless phase of life. Even as a youth he hated the hypocrite (11). The turn to the Christian life is less a matter of a sudden conversion than of gaining inner illumination and finding certain signs of election within one. The danger is always self-deception, succumbing to illusion or seduction; the search requires an unrelenting process of testing, of experimenting, of amassing the clarified evidence: "What if . . .? Then . . ." One must methodically probe the only authority capable of corroborating the lonely experience: so, Scripture is combed from Genesis to Revelation. The illumination on any point of doubt may come suddenly—it is inspired and does not depend on human methodicalness. Yet is must be tested. Since the efficacy of the calling must express itself in the righteousness of the inner motivation for action, the total being must be kept under control. "I have been forced to stand as continually leaning and forcing my spirit against it, lest haply, before I were aware, some wicked thought might arise in my heart that might consent . . ." (136). There is no relief from this unceasing demand to unify the whole personality. And once the inner certainty is won, all energy is devoted to being a worthy instrument in the service of God; every act must have the single-minded motivation to labor *ad Maiorem Dei Gloriam*.

Once the inner struggle is won, when the intense work on unifying the personality, this absolute need to bring order and method and system into conduct, has been undertaken, attention is transferred to the creation of order in the surrounding world as well. It was thus with Benedictine monasticism, with Teresa's Discalced Carmelites; it was doubly the case in this Puritan "innerworldly asceticism." The only outlet for this intensely concentrated personal energy was in the orderly transformation of the surrounding world—for in this theology and theodicy there was no premium on mystical contemplation (to say nothing of a search for mystical union), or on spontaneous orgiastic enthusiasm or aesthetic enjoyment (to say nothing of a *dolce far niente*) in a magically controlled garden paradise, or on any nondirected useless activity. A compelling premium was placed instead on a sober rational assessment of the physical world that inculcated a preference for science over magic. A systematic and a calculable control of the social world could methodically be made to serve as the field in which man labored for God's glorification—hence the Puritan's preference for steady law and political principle rather than for the unpredictable personal political act. There was a premium on the rational pursuit of calculable ends, on methodical work and conduct, on the execution of a divinely assigned task. Personal fulfillment comes in one's profession, in the specified work to which one is called; here the expert wins over *l'uomo universale*. Methodical work has become a prime value; the aristocratic ideal of *otium cum dignitate* becomes suspect. And as the immediate hedonistic enjoyment of the fruits of one's labor is a surrender to temptation, reinvestment in future growth takes precedence over immoral consumption. Though some of these consequences were not yet to be seen in Bunyan, he illustrates so well the unrelenting religious motivation that drove men toward a new ideal of character and personality.

## RICHARD BAXTER
### (1615–91)

Richard Baxter was thirteen years older than Bunyan. He wrote the first part of his autobiography in 1665, one year before Bunyan wrote *Grace Abounding*, although Baxter added important parts only in 1681 and no part was published until 1696. Bunyan wrote a compact dramatic account in 80 pages; Baxter's *Reliquiae Baxterianae*, as edited posthumously by his friend Matthew Sylvester, was a huge folio volume of 800 pages, depicting the variegated life of a divine who was much more deeply involved in wide-ranging national affairs than was Bunyan. Although the *Reliquiae*[14] is a most interesting work, here attention is focused on a few select points only. Baxter has been included in this chapter because it seemed desirable to *suggest*, albeit in the sketchiest way, that inbetween the deeply committed religious Puritan personality type of Bunyan and the secularized Puritan personality of Franklin, there stands indeed a historical personality in whom one can detect some of the features explaining the transformation to the secularized type that the

Weber thesis implies. For this thesis maintains that a personality under-standable in terms of its intense religious motivation gradually turned into a human type whose basic personality traits and personal conduct were similar to those of the religious Puritan but whose motivations and world view had become secular. Even a full study of Baxter that included pastoral works such as his *Christian Directory* could not furnish a con-clusive "proof" of such a thesis, though it might suggest probable cause. All the matters in this essay are of such complexity that, at best, one can only make suggestions.

When Richard Baxter composed his autobiography he included in it not only the accounts of his inner life but also many observations of the interesting events in which he had participated. He gives us long sec-tions on his life with the New Model Army, and reflections on Cromwell and the Commonwealth period; in many of the long sections on his London life after 1660, he dwells on national religious questions and policies of the Restoration. In many respects this autobiography veers toward the genre of the memoir. Baxter tells us much less about "his work on himself" than about "his work on the world" as the concerned Christian pastor. He found his fulfillment in his ministry; he was one of the greatest preachers and theological writers of his age.

Baxter was born in 1615 near Shrewsbury in Shropshire. After having endangered the family estate with gambling debts, his father had ex-perienced a conversion. He was Richard's best teacher. The young boy desired a university education but did not obtain it. In most ways he was an autodidact, a voracious reader. At the age of nineteen he was or-dained by the bishop of Worcester, and in 1640 he was called to the parish church of Kidderminster as a lecturer. When the war broke out between king and Parliament, Baxter opted to support Parliament de-spite Royalist leanings. Cromwell invited him to become chaplain to his own regiment, but during the early phase of the strife Baxter preferred to stay out of the army. Only after having become deeply concerned about the growing religious radicalism in the New Model Army, did Baxter become chaplain in Colonel Whalley's regiment, where he served from 1645–47 until his failing health forced him to retire. From early in 1648 until 1660, Baxter became the successful "reformer" of Kiddermins-ter. On the whole, this was the most significant period of his life. While he himself was actively involved in restoring the monarchy in 1660, a Royalist lord at Kidderminster nonetheless deprived him of his position there. After settling in London, he was initially prominent in trying to work out the new church settlements, but after passage of the Act of

Uniformity in 1662 he left the Church of England. As one of the most eminent Nonconformists, refusing to give up his preaching, he was repeatedly in difficulties with the authorities. Several times he was in prison. He had a very happy late married life, but his old age was in general one of physical hardships and ill-health. Although he had already attracted attention as a writer during his Kidderminster period, most of his works were written during his Nonconformist days. Besides the many writings on questions of church governance, he wrote most eagerly on matters of pastoral care and guidance, on issues of Christian ethics and society, and never ceased writing and working for his great hope of Christian unity.

When Baxter wrote his personal account he quite consciously subordinated the discussion of his inner life to a description of the work he had done. The contrast to Bunyan is striking: the core of Bunyan's account is the drama of his private quest for certainty; even when, in the last sections, he tells of his work in the ministry, it is his inner state that he emphasizes. Of Baxter's inner religious experience we would not know much had he not inserted in 1681 an amazing section of "self-analysis" within the basic account written in 1665. At the beginning of that analysis, he states why he is reluctant to yield to requests for accounts of soul-experiments "and God's dealing with his soul." He is only willing to suggest wherein the older man differs from the youth. "And for any more particular account of heart-occurrences, and God's operations on me, I think it somewhat unsavoury to recite them, seeing God's dealings are much ... the same with all his servants in the main, and the points wherein he varieth are usually so small that I think not such fit to be repeated. Nor have I anything extraordinary to glory ..." (p. 103).

The description of his early religious life clearly suggests that Baxter did not experience the wrenching turn of conversion that so dramatically marked other Puritan lives. He quickly sketches the merry old England in which he grew into a boy: the widespread drunkenness and gambling, the dancing under a maypole, the court where on Sunday theater was to be had instead of sermons, and the public disdain for everything strict that might be called Puritan. He was aware of a personal Providence: "It pleased God to instruct and change my father by the bare reading of the Scriptures" (p. 4). "God made him the instrument of my first convictions." Richard became alarmed over his sinful inclinations: lying, the gluttonous eating of apples, the addiction to play, love of romances, pride in learning, and the waste of foolish chat. His conscience now stirred; the reading of a Jesuit text, *Bunny's Resolutions*, was the occasion, at age fifteen, for a more decisive religious turn. "It pleased God of his wonderful mercy to open my eyes with a clearer insight into the concerns and case of my own soul and to touch my heart with a livelier feeling of things spiritual" (p. 6). His frail health and expectations of early death drove him to systematic study. It seemed to him that the God who "breaketh not all men's heart alike" conveyed the sense of grace to him by means of an education.

Baxter did not claim the absolute certainty of salvation: "I could not distinctly trace the workings of the Spirit upon my heart ... nor knew the time of my conversion ... I was glad of probabilities instead of full undoubted certainties; and to this very day, though I have no such degree of doubtfulness as is any great trouble to my soul or procureth any great disquieting fears, yet I cannot say that I have such certainty of my own sincerity in grace as excludeth all doubts and fears of the contrary" (pp. 10–11). The later "life-review" in the self-analysis adds a series of general remarks about the frailty of our knowledge. We find ourselves in darkness about so many things. Baxter now declares it to be fruitless to study books on predestination and free will (p. 114). Early on, he had attributed his peace to God's Providence, which called him "to the comforting of many others that had the same complaint" (p. 11). To this he adds in the retrospective section on self-analysis that the earlier concern with his own sin had been replaced by an inward concern with failing to execute the vital duties of grace. Meditating on his own heart ("though I am greatly convinced of the need of heart-acquaintance") now seemed less important than recognizing the "need of a higher work" (p. 113).

The powerful psychological drive toward gaining knowledge of the certainty of salvation has thus been considerably weakened. The thought of early death partially takes its place. The impulse toward a rational understanding of religious verities is strengthened. The concern with work is the real driving force. Baxter's life has no noticeable turning point to which the miraculous sense of transformation attaches itself. In its place Baxter had an awareness of a continuous process whereby the boy had gradually turned into the man of fifty-five or sixty-five. This change becomes a conscious matter only from the self-reflective distance where all the results of the gradual inner change have accrued. Retrospective self-analysis thus takes the place of a dramatic step-by-step account.

For Baxter, the meaning of life lay in his calling to minister unto others. What counted were the results of devoted labor. His motivation is still entirely religious: the love of God, and the desire to do his assigned work. For this conception of the task Baxter is willing to give his life. The work itself—no longer the obsession with personal sin and salvation—demands the wholly committed man, the concentration of his will power. The life-style he imposes on himself and on his parishioners has all the marks of the Puritan's inner-worldly asceticism.

Baxter worked and preached as the dying man unto the dying; the urgency of the expected last minute stayed with him even as he grew to be very old. But his poor health never drove him to melancholy or to despair. Nor did he, not having experienced a dramatic religious turn himself, work to achieve sudden conversions in his flock. He lacked both the concentrated fanaticism of such Fifth Monarchy Men as Major-General Harrison, and the millenarian enthusiasm of the more radical sectarians who were prime movers in the rapidly progressing revolution. He thought that England had had a chance "to become a land of saints and a pattern of holiness to all the world." But the extremists on both sides of the spectrum, the prelatists on the one side and "the factions of the giddy and turbulent sectaries on the other side," had ruined that chance (p. 84). Ultimately he accepted this, as he accepted every historical outcome, as God's Will. The mark of the Christian was to endure suffering. Life on earth could indeed be sanctified, but heaven remained a world apart.

A persistent devotion to patient and disciplined work was Baxter's characteristic way of turning a community to a righteous life. He did not much like to count on sudden miraculous shifts produced by spontaneous inspiration and enthusiasm. He rather trusted the means that could produce lasting effects: reason, discipline, and day-to-day labor done with a practical sense for the possible. He had seen too many inspired men go wrong; he knew the common man, he knew the high and mighty too well to trust undisciplined human nature. He was a sober, practical soul. He saw the absolute need for pastoral guidance and sought to give it by concentrating on a workaday ethics. He wanted a practical, moderate form of episcopacy, not the older centralized type, but one that would assure the local communities devoted religious servants. Church discipline was for him an essential, practical tool. He wanted a unified Christianity concentrating upon the essentials men could agree upon, avoiding strife over the unknowables. "We must have unity in things necessary and liberty in things unnecessary, and charity in all" (p. 91). All his writings are reasoned attempts to accomplish the possible.

His success in the Kidderminster ministry became the badge of Baxter's aims and his powers of work. Here Baxter's personality put its stamp on a whole community. Kidderminster was a small town of some 1600 families, about 600–800 of whom became Baxter's followers. It was not a rich town; it was mostly populated by "stuff weavers" and small traders. Before Baxter's arrival, there had been no good preaching for a long, long time. "I came to a people that never had any awakening ministry before" (p. 79). The town's moral life showed the common defects of drunkenness, frivolous vanities, and sexual looseness. Baxter "had heard of its inhabitants as 'an ignorant rude and reveling People'; but found them worse than the report."[15]

His initial work was difficult, and the first brief period of his ministry was not marked by success. He was slandered and made the object of pranks. "Once all the ignorant were raging mad against me for preaching the doctrine of original sin to them" (p. 28). But after Baxter had returned from the army in 1647, he worked methodically for thirteen years to turn the community around. His main tool was preaching, once on Sundays and once every Thursday. His long sermons demanded many hours of studying and writing. "My public preaching met with an attentive diligent auditory.... The congregation was usually full, so that we were fain to build five galleries after my coming thither" (p. 79). On Sundays the streets were now orderly and psalm singing had displaced drunken shouting. Every Thursday night he received concerned families at his home, where they could sum up their understanding of the previous sermons and where Baxter resolved their doubts about "cases of conscience" (p. 77). The younger people met with him every Saturday night for a three-hour prayer session and a review of the essential points of the previous Sunday's sermon. Two days every week Baxter and an assistant would each take fourteen different families for private catechizing and conferences on practical ethical issues. Baxter thought it providential that most of his parishioners were weavers who had "time enough to read or talk of holy things ... as they stand in their loom they can set a book before them or edify one another" (p. 80). He thus saw the essence of his task in the patiently persistent and intensely methodical work of bringing the Word to people, explaining it, repeating it, systematically catechizing its essentials. His congregation saw much of their minister, even though he says that writing was his "chiefest labor" (p. 79); he had no family of his own to encroach on his time, though he did take care of his old parents. Having learned from his own illnesses, he also was very much in demand "to practise physic" and was overrun by patients. He distributed the income from his books as alms. His community began to live his way, and he did not hesitate to use its support to enforce church discipline against the inconvertible reprobate.

In this way the disciplined methodical work of a preacher affected thousands of simple men and women whose lives he turned toward greater literacy, greater self-discipline, greater consistency in work and conduct. Some of them had at least gained a chance to become unified persons; they could begin to take a step in the direction of forming themselves as self-motivated, autonomous persons. Their work flourished in sobriety and discipline. A hundred years later John Wesley would touch the same social stratum with very similar teachings and produce the same phenomenon of the disciplined working man.

What had happened at Kidderminster had also happened in Baxter. For when he later on sought to assess the meaning of his life, he found satisfaction in having expended his energy and talents in an active calling. By sober disciplined devotion to tasks demanding concentration of the whole unified person upon the objectives ahead, he had been spared the wastefulness marking many lives. He was less certain how to supply the theological foundations for such a notion, but he was certain about the cumulative effects of a life lived in a calling.

The intense rationalization of practical conduct, of the personality, and of life itself was in Baxter's case accompanied by important theological shifts. Bunyan's account is at all essential points vertebrated by Scripture; by comparison, Baxter's text is remarkably free of biblical citations. The Bible plays a different role: as a continuous support of his life but less as the exclusive proof of his convictions. The trust he had in his own experience as a life supported by God's spirit made the biblical message dear to Baxter because it also showed the motions of God's spirit in countless human lives. Baxter was less anxious about making his life fit an authoritative dogma. He sought a faith of his own. When younger, he seriously examined "the reasons of Christianity" and had tried to give "a hearing to all that could be said against it, that so my faith might be indeed my own" (pp. 26–27). Had he been void of internal experience, he would "certainly [have] apostasized to infidelity" (p. 110). The older man stated his hierarchically ordered certainties in an interesting way. He thinks it best to begin with "natural verities."

> My certainty that I am a man is before my certainty that there
> is a God .... my certainty that there is a God is greater than
> my certainty that he requireth love and holiness of his crea-
> ture; my certainty of *this* is greater than my certainty of the

life of reward and punishment thereafter; . . . my certainty of
the Deity is greater than my certainty of the Christian Faith;
my certainty of the Christian Faith in its essentials [Nota
Bene] is greater than my certainty of the perfection and infal-
libility of all the Holy Scriptures; my certainty of that is
greater than my certainty of the meaning of many particular
texts and so of the truth of many particular doctrines. [p. 111]

The love of God and the joy in His work diminish the weight of specific
doctrine. Baxter found it increasingly unprofitable to speculate about
such matters as predestination; he found less use in theological
controversy—"we are all yet in the dark" (p. 114). Later he considered
discussion of rituals a waste. He thought it wisest for Christians to agree
on the Creed, the Lord's Prayer, and the Decalogue and tolerate other
individual convictions. Divisive theology destroys charity.

  Though as a young man Baxter loved the scholastic writings, he begins now to turn away from theological speculation and metaphysics.
He quotes Bacon repeatedly. He becomes less concerned with sub-
stances but expresses a growing concern with effects. "Subjective certainty cannot go beyond the objective evidence" (p. 111). In a sense:
what is true is what works. "I value all things according to their use and
ends . . . . My meditations must be most upon the matters of my practice
and my interest" (p. 108). Dealing mostly "with ignorant miserable
people" (p. 108), he desires to work for them in terms of what is both
meaningful and helpful. Rather than dwelling on personal problems of
election, he suffers "with the thoughts of the miserable world," and is
interested in such missionary work as John Eliot's work among the
Indians. He finds it increasingly difficult to assume that God excluded
the heathen—what force can the notion of predestination have for such
a mind? He rests ever more securely in the comfort of the goodness of
creation and of God's ways with man. When he looks at history—and he
witnessed tumultuous times—he is gratified by discerning the magnificent concurrence of all the varied instruments of Providence (see especially p. 90). He puts his trust in nature. "And it is a marvellous great
help to my faith to find it built on so sure foundations and so consonant
to the law of nature" (p. 111). Yes, Christians, alas, are divisive quarrel-
ers, but he even considers Catholic errors "a conquerable dose of poison
which nature doth overcome" (p. 118). He deplores the lack of Christian
unity, and he suffers at the thought of a very wide, as yet unconverted,
world. But he trusts God's goodness to provide the solution. "And I can
never believe that a man may not be saved by that religion which doth

but bring him to the true love of God and to a heavenly mind and life, nor that God will ever cast a soul into hell that truly loveth him" (p. 118).

By thus cutting back the metaphysical speculation and the theological justification for the doctrine of the calling, by skeptical resignation to the thought that much darkness remains, by trusting the beneficial order of the world as seen in its beneficial results, Baxter throws the full weight of life into the work on the problems at hand. The value of life lies in the work that is done. Work is not done to support life; life is devoted to work. For the Puritan, work inside this world, whatever work the calling might imply, was sanctified to a degree it had never been before. Thus his inner urging to an inner-worldly asceticism completed a long cultural process for Western Man by which work gradually lost its curse and its banausic quality. No ancient aristocrat saw virtue in scrubbing around for an existence; the Benedictine monk worked with high discipline, but to banish temptation; modern man finds the fulfillment of his person in a profession, in a job well done—at least he tended to do so until recently. For Baxter, the ultimate motivations for such work lay in the psychological sanctions that rested in firm religious convictions. In the decades that followed the religious convictions atrophied, until for us moderns "the idea of duty in one's calling prowls about in our lives like the ghost of dead religious beliefs."[16]

To the Puritan, a job well done meant a job done with concentration, discipline, and method—without waste. Purpose-rationality asserted its hold over the individual; its concern is with the most efficient relation of ends and means, the least waste in means to obtain the desired end. It does not ask about the rationality of the objective itself. Indeed, from many a world view, it may seem irrational to devote life to making a profit, but whoever wishes to do so can rationalize life to attain this objective. Purpose-rationality puts a high premium on method and on the concerted effort. The unified personality "rationalizes" its life and the world in which it must act so that the job can be done.

This mentality expressed itself in Baxter through his concern with the useful, the realistically practical, and through his constant quest for evidence and his emphasis on results. He hated confusion, he hated waste. "I could never from my first studies endure confusion ... I never thought I understood anything till I could anatomise it and see the parts distinctly and the conjunction of the parts as they make up the whole. Distinction and method seemed to me of that necessity" (p. 10). Like several other statements (cf. pp. 26–27 and especially p. 111), this quotation could be taken from Descartes; it can easily be reconciled with purpose-rationality, though here rationality takes a new form. Baxter found comfort in the apparent compatibility of his faith and in the rationality of the natural law his God had built into His universe. For him, the world and its course had the rationality that man could discover in its manifest effects and results. His contemporary, Pascal, urged men to use reason so that they might perceive its inadequacy for human happiness and thus be convinced to take the leap into faith. Baxter thought such a prescription a trick of Popish deceivers (p. xxiii): it was in reason that he saw the full support of his faith. It is here that he stands as a link to the Enlightenment, a period in which faith lost much of its hold on men. The freshly perceived secular task of saving man by means of his civilizing work derived immense support, however, from a personality type that had been formed under quite different conditions.

## BENJAMIN FRANKLIN
### (1706–90)

More than any other American, Benjamin Franklin seems the likeliest candidate for patron saint. While he had no traces of old-fashioned saintliness, he was the quintessential American. He was not an irreligious man. He surely did not present himself as such. He classed himself with the Deists; their trust in God as the necessary Creator and their trust in a general beneficial providence belong quite properly (and not hypocritically) to his intellectual outlook. He could not have held the positions he maintained had he been moved by an agnostic doubt about a providentially ordered creation. But very little seems to be left of the stricter Christian commitment of his Puritan forebears; and he can hardly be thought of as a religiously driven man. Yet he makes such a Puritan impression! Many of his convictions and sayings could be inserted in Bunyan or Baxter; his conduct and his workaday ethics are so often the embodiment of the one they preached. He is the Puritan personality without the Puritan motivation and the Puritan objective.

Franklin wrote his autobiography in four separate spurts between 1771 and 1790; he never completed it. The intent throughout was highly didactic: this life was to be seen as an instructive one. While some interpreters—inordinately obsessed with a desire to prove the Puritan a hypocrite—will treat the literary self-presentation of Franklin as a theatrical performance, stressing his penchant for role-playing, or as an attempt to hide behind a mask, as the work of a *poseur* putting on hats, the assumption that Franklin consciously falsified the character he presented seems ungrounded.[17] The teaching is about character and what character can do in this world. The character seems to be much too coherent for contrived poses; it reveals itself in the many small textual elements that would have been impossible to manipulate purposefully, especially considering the haste with which each section of the book was written. The hypocrisy would, of course, have been glaring if the pretense of religious motives were assumed for religiously adiaphorous, or religiously indifferent, behavior; but the opposite argument is maintained here. Franklin pursued secular ends and had secular motivations.

The old Franklin clearly remembered the religious atmosphere in which he grew up. His father Josiah had left England so that he might practice his nonconformist religion in greater freedom; his mother Abiah came from good religious New England stock. Before the parents found such training too expensive for such a large family, they had wanted Benjamin to become a minister. Cotton Mather's presence touched their lives at numerous points. The boy liked *Pilgrim's Progress*, and the first books he acquired with his sparse savings were Bunyan's other works. But apparently he had no sensitive religious nerves which could be touched by such stimuli. He reveals his characteristic attitude in the story describing his frame of mind during family prayers: "At morning and evening prayers the restless apprentice taught himself geography from the four large maps which hung on the walls of the solemn rooms."[18]

The voraciously reading autodidact was as much stimulated by Plutarch's *Lives* as by Mather's *Essay To Do Good*. The more he reached the age at which young men consciously seek answers to the world's great questions, the more Franklin found catalysts for his own doubts in such modern "doubters" as Locke, Collins, and Shaftesbury. "My parents had early given me religious impressions and brought me through my childhood piously in the Dissenting way" (p. 71). "I had been religiously educated as a Presbyterian" (p. 100). But he knew he was no churchgoing man. At the age of fifteen he doubted—or at least found unintelligible—such a central dogma as predestination. "I began to doubt of Revelation itself" (p. 71). Deist arguments won him over easily. Yet he simply shows no sign of struggle in turning his back on his religion, nor any hint of a religious struggle later on. He remained a tepid Deist all his life. He was basically tolerant of the religious around him, for, like so many thoughful men of his age, he recognized the social usefulness of belief; he clearly preferred preachers who made good citizens to preachers who made good Presbyterians. But when he says of himself that he "never was without some religious principles" (p. 100), we should take him seriously. He believed in a God who had created this world, who governed it by His providence, and who demanded that man do good to his fellow men. Some such vague belief in the purposeful order of the world—not too deeply questioned, not too deeply thought out—was still a necessary supporting frame within which such a man had to function. For all the rest, he could afford to be religiously tone-deaf.

It was of the utmost importance, however, that the young man, though unaffected by the meaning of religion, had absorbed a life-style and workaday ethic created by religious impulses. In the world in which he moved, he found a deep respect for literacy and learning, for soberly rational intelligence and practical wisdom. Public spiritedness came early to Franklin. So did the appreciation of personal independence; a man was best off when he relied on himself. God helps those who help themselves. The command to take up a useful calling and the Gospel of Work entered his being as if by osmosis. The adventures of the sea or the charm of poetry might beckon briefly, but they had no force in the face of this demand to be practical and intensely active. With work taken this seriously came all the stress on traits that would make it rational and efficient: self-discipline, honest concentration of effort, ingenuity and self-help, persistence and consistency, soberness and frugality, simplicity and sincerity, punctuality and accountability. The emphasis was on systematic work for the sake of systematic, step-by-step advancement of the worker and his enterprise. For an eager young man the premium was on method—a term that appeared with much frequency on the pages of Franklin's young life. A young man might not understand what inner impulses drove his elders to such a rationalization of work and conduct, he might (if he did understand) develop doubts about the "irrational" ends to which such "means" were employed, but he could not help seeing that such lives were immensely effective. And he might very well come to understand that in colonial America you either managed to survive because of such values and such conduct, or you succumbed.

This work ethos, and the attributes of character it supported, must have entered young Franklin's very bones. He never lost it, though as an older man he was willing at times to give in to more pleasurable pursuits. He carried the ethos with him from Boston to London and Philadelphia. He developed it further—and to an exemplary degree. He systematized it with immense rational consistency.

When the old autobiographer looked back at his life, he presented, either wittingly or unwittingly, all the elements necessary for understanding the formation of his character as well as the world view consonant with it. The foundations that had already been laid, the new experiences that confirmed the value of efficiency, and the rational system that meshed character and convictions went nicely hand in hand. On leaving Boston there came an initial danger point: would the "want of religion" (p. 73), and now the loss of the supporting context of established tradition, lead to gross immorality and injustice? The old Franklin understood that the very values by which he had been living were potentially endangered as soon as the religious sanctions supporting them had lost their authority.[19] "Revelation had indeed no weight with me, as such; but I entertain'd an opinion that, though certain actions might not be bad *because* they were forbidden by it, or good *because* it commanded them, yet probably these actions might be forbidden *because* they were bad for us, or commanded *because* they were beneficial to us, in their own natures, all the circumstances of things considered" (pp. 72–73; the italics are Franklin's). Franklin thus saw no issue in doubting the validity of the specific norms of conduct he had inherited. The values he had absorbed in his character remained firm, and life did not have to become a troubled quest for the "proper" norms of action. The precious energy of the soul did not have to be expended in a search for values by which to live. All he needed was a new foundation for the values he already had, and he provided it himself: their justification lay in their usefulness. What is good is what works; what is true is what works. Only if life's experience were to contradict such propositions, would standards be called into question. If experience validated them again and again, they could consolidate into a consistent ethical system. As the adolescent began to doubt the justification usually given for the norms presented to him in childhood, he furnished himself with a new justification, for which life would provide the proof.

"I had therefore a tolerable character to begin the world with; I valued it properly, and determined to preserve it" (p. 73). On his own now, the young Franklin found the validation of the effectiveness of his character and his values in every experience he recounted. Life had left no doubt that methodical devotion to work was clearly the means for advancement. Those who looked for sudden windfalls (the adventure capitalists), those who merely trusted good fortune instead of their own consistent effort, came to no good. "Human felicity is produc'd not so much by great pieces of good fortune that seldom happen, as by little advantages that occur every day. Thus, if you teach a poor young man to shave himself, and keep his razor in order, you may contribute more to the happiness of his life than in giving him a thousand guineas" (p. 159). Experience upon experience showed that the cultivation of virtues contributing to effective work was most beneficial. Have a sober mind instead of a besotted head! Do not eat up the fruits of your labor, but let them work for you—money (as accumulated energy) is productive, so do not kill the capitalist embryo! Be prepared to account for the efficient use of your means! Be orderly (Franklin found it difficult, but his memory helped him when things became too disorderly) and consistent! Rely on yourself as much as you can! Know how to help yourself and cultivate habits that can lead to ingenious solutions for more effective use of your energy—read useful things, make sensible experiments! As you live with fellow men, coordinate your life effectively with theirs: clearly, relationships work best when founded on genuine mutual interest. Let the notion of friendship presented in the old Roman *amicitia*—relations based on mutually beneficial acts—displace the less trustworthy inclinations and infatuations of the heart: friends can so easily become burdens and obstacles! Have a clear understanding of what these interests are; it will save "friendships" for the future (cf. pp. 134–35 especially)! Be sincere and honest, but do not hide your virtues under a bushel! Let people know why they can trust you—do care for the effective appearance you make! Develop beneficial and useful institutions in a common effort, without entangling yourself disadvantageously!

Step by step, the vast experiment of life convinced this inveterate experimenter, in an age glorifying experimentation, that the old virtues had been proven effective. Where there is no question about the efficacy of virtues, where they are seen as the means for promoting the good life, there is an irrepressible urge to turn virtue into second nature. For the Puritan the need for method and system had flowed from his longing to assist the divine process in turning natural man into righteous man. The intense anxiety over God's acceptance furnished the energy for unifying the personality. Secularized man, without the comfort of believing that God was working the true transformation, had to set his own law and implement it. Franklin came to realize that the mere recognition of useful interest needed to be reinforced by habit. "I concluded, at length, that the mere speculative conviction that it was our interest to be completely virtuous, was not sufficient to prevent our slipping; and that the contrary habits must be broken and good ones acquired and established, before we can have any dependence on a steady, uniform rectitude of conduct" (p. 102). The fear of sanctions is replaced by the desire for habitual virtue, and the effort was secured by the power of a second nature.

A need for self-exploration is superseded by an urge toward self-perfection. The catalogue of virtues to which Franklin subscribed also prescribed the model for the personality. Henceforth the stress lies on the task of self-formation, on the realization of the ideal personality, a task that Franklin meant to attack with his usual methodical rigor and consistency. The key term is *method,* and it is predominant throughout Franklin's text. The fundamental drive to rationalize procedures so as to avoid waste is the concern for the most rational relation of means toward the desired ends. Devotion to method, methodicalness, and system are hallmarks of Franklin's character. Viewed from this vantage point Franklin's "project of arriving at moral perfection," as well as his intention to write an *Art of Virtue* as his most instructive work, should be seen as emanating directly from his personality and world view; to argue that this is the artful pose of a sophisticate presenting himself as the naïve philosophical Quaker to oversophisticated Frenchmen seems a perfect example of a view that puts the cart before the horse.[20] Like any scheme for moral perfection, Franklin's scheme is naïve, naïve in the sense of discounting the true complexity of life and the world. But Franklin did not remain oblivious to such complexities. He knew better than many a feckless reformer how to endure the imperfections of the world and of himself with tolerance, grace, charm, and wit (that key indicator suggesting awareness of imperfection). Yet the sincerity of the message describing his project for moral perfection need not be doubted.

A methodical training in the virtues was to be undertaken with all the qualities of craftsmanship bestowed on any productive enterprise. Know the objective clearly; subdivide the process into its most manageable steps; then work consistently; check and doublecheck, and keep your accounts straight. There is seriousness in the intention, in the persistent effort, and in the careful accounting. The whole scheme is set up so that careful record-keeping can reinforce the effort. The urge toward accountability is a key trait. Franklin always works with balance sheets: proudly recording deficits ("my errata") he managed to make up, he has a special word of praise for the Dutch-trained postmistress who knew how to keep books (p. 120). A man ought to know the state of his resources. The drive for rational efficiency applies above all to the personality. A person unified in his self-consciousness, a person whose intent and habit function in true unison, will work most effectively and efficiently. A life concentrated in its efforts will also be a successful life.

Even if the complexities of life itself deny perfection, the force of the message to the young seemed all-compelling to Franklin.

Character is effective in work; effective work inevitably leads to success; and individual success readily translates itself into social benefit. As soon as the individual has made an internal order of himself and his own life, the concentrated energy flows over into the effort to order his wider social world. After achieving success himself, he applies his talent for the benefit of his city and his country. He does not fight against his world like a Rousseau, but he works within and for it. He does not dream of a radically different world but has a sober realistic vision of practical reform. Fully in keeping with his character and experience, his efforts go toward the creation of instruments for self-improvement: libraries, discussion groups, academies for experimentation, schools, and universities. His "hygienically oriented utilitarianism"[21] results in projects for clean streets, hospitals, and better lighting and heating. The stress always lies on "enabling acts," on the cultivation of useful knowledge, the identification of the common interest, sound management, practical schemes like matching grants and sound investment. The objective always seems to be the creation of a world in which men can learn to be more productive and effective, a world in which those who want to help themselves can do so.

For Franklin, this work was never done, and he expended himself willingly. By his work he helped to shape a way of life and a utilitarian ethic. This ceaseless labor for a more ordered world found its justification, in part, in the self-fulfilling proposition: it works better that way! Franklin had a simple answer to the question: "Why work so hard for social reform?" "God's Law demands that man do good to his fellow men." The work Franklin chose to do still derives meaning from an unquestioning belief in God's meaningful order. For others, those who had lost belief in creation as a purposeful order designed for men, an order already endowed with meaning by its creator, the question was more troubling. Franklin's older contemporary, Voltaire, had discerned no evidence that a meaning had been written into the universe. No message came back when he peered into space. The eternal silence of the infinite spaces was frightening. For him there was only one conclusion: that man had to save himself by creating his own meaningful order. He could do so by working for the ideal of a decent secular civilization.

Since in Catholic mystics and Protestant Puritans the religious devotion burned with a particularly intense flame, the traits of the Christian person are strikingly highlighted in both groups. Both experiences accented again the convictions through which Christianity had a lasting effect on the formation of the Western personality: the high valuation of each human soul, its transcendent yearning, its inwardness and its search for inner coherence and harmony, its pervasive sense that life was a dramatic process and not simply a state of being, and its double ethical commitment to care for one's self and one's brother. But in their conceptions of dogma and institutional life the Catholic mystic and the Protestant Puritan presented different aspects of the basic Christian personality.

In his most basic experience and impulse, the mystic had to emphasize meditation and contemplation, even if orthodox mysticism also properly respected the absolute need to return from contemplation to caritative work. His pronounced sense of union with the Godhead and with all creation resonated in a wondrous sense of the soul as an immensely rich inner realm of experience. A powerful drive toward sensitive inward exploration permitted an interplay of reason, intense passion, imagination, and aesthetics. But the mystical quest and experience took men and women so dangerously close to the limits of the human range that they stood in special need of the authoritative guidance which a tested tradition of orthodoxy and the accumulated wisdom of an institutionalized Church could provide. Thus the backbone of the personality remained the grand model of the perfect Christian life, the *Imitatio Christi*.

The Puritan was the child of the Protestant Revolt which had broken so many of the retaining walls of tradition and of a binding institution. He was still on the leading-leash of the absolute authority of the Holy Word, but in the intense quest after the certainty of salvation he was thrown upon his own inner resources. Having denied the Catholic's valid distinction between two different ways to salvation, the way of the devoted ascetic and the way of the sacramentalized secular life, but recognizing in the ascetic the hallmarks of full religious devotion, the Puritan had to cultivate an inner-worldly asceticism. The powerful stress on an individual calling obliged the personality to order itself and its world for specific tasks that demanded the concentrated effort of the whole being. The premium thus came to lie on effective work; in turn, irrational pleasures, emotions, and aesthetic sensitivites became suspect (though a renewed justification for some of these human faculties reappeared in certain forms of Pietism). The intense unification of the personality was accomplished at the cost of a fuller human potential, one which would also admit the emotional and aesthetic needs that a personality dominated by its pursuit of purpose-rationality found it hard to fulfill.

The emergence of this Puritan personality was a fitting expression of far-reaching processes of differentiation in the social mass. Protestantism was part of a long process creating ever more centers of authority, foretelling a time when the autonomous individual became the ideal. Each has the right to his very own religion; personal experience is the ultimate ground of verity. The notion of the personal calling accelerates the processes of differentiation. The work of the world is efficiently subdivided into individual tasks. The Puritan could leave the rationale for this division of labor to the God who coordinated it all as a part of a whole design. Yet, secular minds, omitting the divine creator of a purposeful pattern, could readily secularize this conception: to them a totally differentiated social organism required many different talents; society would function optimally when everyone did best what he could best do. The social contribution of the individual coincides with the fulfillment of the individual calling. Franklin himself was a prime example: the well-being of society depends on the well-functioning individual. The individual makes himself a functional order; he can then become part of an orderly society; and a well-ordered society can make an orderly world.

The Puritan experience helped in many ways to prepare the ground in which the notion of individuality might arise. And yet this Puritan personality, especially in its secularized version, contributed more heavily to the growth of individualism than of individuality. It was a natural consonant of the social theory that the individual, as the primary constitutive element of society, functioned most effectively when social control was limited to the necessary minimum. When the individual is free to develop his potential, society profits from personal initiative, free motivation, personal responsibility; enlightened personal interest is ultimately harmonious with social interest. But such a social theory of individualism does not by itself predicate a preference for individuality. For all the free individuals may adhere to the same model of the personality—such as the ideal of the truly rational man. In the Puritan personality there were actually many barriers to individuality. Its religious version was still strongly affixed to the model of the hero of faith, and was thus only a variant of the basic Christian personality. Its powerful motivation, working *ad Maiorem Dei Gloriam*, is contained within scriptural prescriptions. Experience must still fit a script. The cultivation of emotional richness, the fulfillment of aesthetic needs, the opportunity for spontaneity and irrational urgings was sacrificed for the benefit of an extraordinarily efficient personality. Indeed, it was as a countervailing force to the restrictions imposed by the purpose-rational system of science, industrial-capitalism, and utilitarianism which the Puritan personality helped to create, that modern man came in time to invoke the ideal of individuality.

# 11
## Vico and Gibbon:
## The Historical Mode of
## Understanding Self-Development

 The views men have of their collective existence as peoples, nations, societies, or cultures are intrinsically related to their views of individual existence. The self-conception we call individuality came into prominence as a by-product of a profound change in Western man's historical outlook. During the eighteenth century a conception of historical consciousness emerged to which historiographers have given the ugly word *historicism* or *historism*. The age that is seen so often as a period dominated by the pursuits of uniform rationality, natural-law philosophy, and scientific modes of understanding reality was also the age in which a historicizing view of existence emerged that countermanded these very tendencies.

The mental turn toward historicism had decisive consequences. It was more than a change from one manner of accounting for the past to another, from a providential view of history to one of secular progress, for example. As part of the series of profound revolutionary changes that gave the eighteenth century such intellectual excitement came a fundamental awareness that human reality is profoundly historical. Life came to be seen as process; it was now to be understood as development.

The roots of such a historical approach reach far into the European past. Europe is a complex amalgam of different peoples and different traditions, a complicated fusion of classical, Judeo-Christian, Germanic, Celtic, and Slavic elements. It carries the memories of multiple heritages that are the stuff of cultural "renaissances." Renaissances have exceptional power to stimulate historical reflection. The faith of Jews and Christians in an inscrutable deity working out its will in history helped to develop their strong historical-mindedness. The expansion of European awareness through the geographical discoveries that continually widened world horizons, the need to align so many traditions (even in so banal a matter as chronology), stirred historical thought. The steadily advancing secularization that blocked out transcendental yearnings necessitated a rethinking of tradition; the rapid rise and sudden fall of states and dynasties, the growing fascination with such a notion as *raison d'état* or with law and constitutions as cumulative experience, raised historical questions. Quarrels over religious issues requiring the support of historical argument—and similarly those involving philosophical and aesthetic issues—sharpened historical wits.

All this, and much more, gradually prepared many thoughtful Europeans to look upon history as a form of knowledge peculiarly germane to the understanding of the human world. They became increasingly persuaded that the knowledge of things was essentially a knowledge of why things had become what they were. Knowledge appeared to be subject to the limitations of space and time. That this was a revolution in man's understanding of things in general, and not only in human affairs, is evident in the change in the age-old conception of a stable order of creation, the "Great Chain of Being," which gave way in the eighteenth century to the idea of the "temporalizing of nature."[1] The world of plants and animals came to be seen as an evolving world. The earth itself began to acquire a history explained in terms of geological processes. When the century had run its course, conceptions of an evolving nature, an evolving cosmos, an evolving reason or spirit (as in Hegel's system), and even the idea of the Deity as creative evolution, had begun to displace older notions of stable Being.

Man's self-conceptions were profoundly affected by these changes. This chapter restricts itself to the impact of a growing historical-mindedness on the human reality observed by a great historical thinker, the Neapolitan Vico, and a great historian, Edward Gibbon, as each turned to himself in his autobiographic writing. On closer inspection it will apear that Vico and Gibbon represent two different conceptions of historical growth which should be distinguished from each other.

Our inclination to view man and his works historically can rest on quite different assumptions which lead to quite different conclusions. It makes a difference, for instance, whether one thinks that every life, or even the complex life of a whole culture, is a process of *unfolding*, subject to the laws of a preformed destiny or nature; or whether one believes that something becomes what it is through an unpredictable, contingent interaction of diverse factors in a constantly *developing* configuration of reality. Where is the attention to be focused? On the idea that the acorn becomes the oak tree because its future lies already in the givens of the seed? If so, are the incidentals of soil and sunshine only to be seen as accidentals? Or does the story of a specific tree necessarily depend on the complex interaction of all the givens and all the unpredictable events? And is "accident," then, an integral and inextricable part of growth? That both notions can be combined by historians in a whole spectrum of differently balanced views complicates the matter even further. How much weight is placed on the effect of such an external cause as geography, or how much is placed on causation within the historical actor, by something, for instance, like Shaftesbury's "inner form," a spiritual power that gives shape to matter? Conceptions of historical subject matter affect these views as well. "What" is unfolding or developing? Empires and nations? The destiny of God's people? Or civilization and culture? Or even civilizations and cultures, in the plural? Is an unfolding culture, for instance, at the concrete historical moment one looks at it, an imperfect expression of the ideal nature toward which it is moving, and thus only a step on the road to indefinite perfectibility or eventual perfection? Is history, then, the story of progress? Or is every historical moment the manifestations of a value *sui generis*, not to be supplanted by ever better variants, but simply to be followed by ever new, ever different formulations of a human potential capable only of revealing itself *seriatim*? These and many other questions occupied historical thinkers in the eighteenth century, and a resolution, of sorts, led to a fuller historical view. One of its fruits was our self-conception as individualities.

The emergence of individuality, traced here in autobiographic consciousness, depended on the gradual fusion of two ideas: the idea of genuine historical development *and* the idea of individuality as a value. In their autobiographic view of themselves, or, for that matter, in their historical conceptions of man's general course, neither Vico nor Gibbon came to such a fusion. But both serve as signposts along the way. And, significantly, both historical minds turned to the writing of autobiography.

## GIAMBATTISTA VICO
### (1668–1744)

Great minds, busily teeming with ideas and plans, can often do no better than suggest certain intellectual tasks to others. In a letter of March 22, 1714, the ever busy Leibniz offered such a suggestion to one Louis Bourget. Leibniz was irritated by Descartes's habit of covering the tracks of his own development, especially where he might have revealed his debt to the work of others. Leibniz, therefore, thought it a good idea "to study the discoveries of others in a way that discloses to us the source of inventions and renders them in a sort our own. And I wish that authors would give us the history of their discoveries and the steps by which they arrived at them. When they neglect to do so, we must try to divine these steps, in order to profit the more from their works. If the critics would do this for us in reviewing books, they would render a great service to the public."[2] It is of interest that the great philosopher felt the urge to understand men's thoughts in terms of their gradual development, and not simply as the finished product on the printed page.

Leibniz's casually dropped suggestion became the indirect cause for Vico's autobiographical sketch. The Italian Count di Porcía, acquainted with Bourget, turned the suggestion after 1720 into a project that would serve the greater glory of Italy. As Vico tells it: the count "had conceived the idea of guiding young men with greater security in their course of study by setting before them the intellectual autobiographies of men celebrated for erudition and scholarship. Among the Neapolitans whom he considered worthy for this purpose, he deigned to include Vico" (p. 182). At this time, Vico was not yet known as the author of the *New Science*, the one work for which he wished recognition. But he was sufficiently known "for erudition and scholarship." To be included among a list of eight or nine professors from the University of Naples was perhaps no signal honor. For some time Vico was not sure that he would furnish the requested *vita*, "partly from modesty and partly because of his ill fortune" (p. 182). But in 1725 he sat down to write Part A of the autobiography, drafted Part B, which he revised in 1728, and continued in 1731 to bring the account up to the events of that year. A first version was published in 1728 in the *Raccolta d'opusculi scientifici e filologici* as a "model" for other contributors. But Vico's *Life* is the only survivor of Count di Porcía's entire project.

It is doubtful that this autobiography would have been written without insistent solicitation. When the request came, Vico's labors were being directed toward a new, a "positive" formulation of the *New Science* which he had "completed" in 1724 in *"forma negativa."* He was an obscure professor of rhetoric at the University of Naples. Having been born poor, he was struggling to supplement his miserable annual salary of 100 ducats by hiring out his versifying talents for the occasional wedding songs or funeral orations needed by high society. After two decades of faithful service his own university had not even taken seriously his application when he eagerly sought promotion to the "morning chair of law," which paid 600 ducats, an inferior chair to the "evening chair," which paid 1100. Before the first version of the *New Science* was printed in 1725, Vico had written orations delivered to Neapolitan students, panegyrics on diverse rulers and prominent men, a life of Marshall Antonio Caraffa (1716), a treatise "On Modern Methods of Study," and one on the "Wisdom of the Ancient Italians." However original some of these writings were, they did not make him a famous man. After 1719, he published, in rapid succession, a set of writings on the nature of universal law which did not help him to obtain the desired legal chair but which received recognition abroad. He found comfort in a letter of praise from Jean LeClerc, the editor of the well-known scholarly journal *Bibliothèque ancienne et moderne* (pp. 158–59). These minor writings were important works when seen in relation to the great work of the *New Science*, but it is doubtful that they could have supplied sufficiently interesting material for an intellectual autobiography.

It thus seems altogether providential that the solicitation for the autobiographic sketch came at the very time when Vico had given definitive form to his life's task in writing the *New Science*. Now a sketch of life could become as much the autobiography of a book as of its author. In some autobiographies a centrally important experience dictates the form of the presentation; in this case, form and structure were given as soon as the author perceived how all of life had tended toward the creation of a work that summed up his whole scholarly existence. Vico himself saw this clearly: "he [the whole work is written in the modest third person] wrote it as a philosopher, meditating the causes, natural and moral, and the occasions of fortune; why even from childhood he felt an inclination for certain studies and an aversion from others; what opportunities and obstacles had advanced or retarded his progress; and lastly the effect of his own exertions in right directions, which were destined later to bear fruit in those reflections on which he built his final work, the *New Science* which was to demonstrate that his intellectual life was bound to have been such as it was and not otherwise" (p. 182). Here his own phrasing suggests the presence of three different themes that are fused into the relatively short autobiography of some ninety printed pages. (1) The outer frame of life is presented in terms of traditional canons for describing a scholar's existence: parents, early omens concerning a future career, early training, memorable teachers, formative reading, university career, a summation of personal qualities, and the judgment of others. (2) The central line of presentation attempts to show the inner dynamics and lines of development of Vico's thought: how did the system of the *New Science* become a system? (3) The supporting link between matters discussed under (1) and (2) is Vico's strong belief that his life was in the hand of a personal providence; the peculiar facts of his professorial career and the pattern of his intellectual advance appeared to him to have been interlinked and mutually supportive in a miraculous way, even though only in time was this clear to him.

Lives of Scholars, Thinkers, Writers had been written since antiquity. They were a fairly standardized humanistic genre. In setting the external frame of the key events serving him as ready reference points, Vico had no reason to be innovative: he sticks to standard fare. He reports that he was born in Naples, which remained the setting for his entire life except for a stay of nine years (1686–95) in the country, at Vatolla, as tutor to a son of a noble family. Vico took pride in being a Neapolitan even if his own city failed to reward his contributions to her life and fame. He states the year of his birth, but incorrectly. He describes the character of his parents and assesses their effect on his own formation. When he was seven years old, he fell from a ladder in his father's small bookshop and split his cranium; the aiding surgeon prophesied that the boy "would either die of it or grow up to be an idiot" (p. 111). Instead of doing either, he grew up with "a melancholy and irritable temperament."

In somewhat lengthier sections Vico then deals with his education, tracing his developing intellectual interests, sketching his early teachers, his courses of study, and his encounters with formative books. The intent is to portray an autodidact who profited most from following his inner genius, even if he little understood the direction of its guidance. But though such subject matter can be found, for the most part, in books on other lives, Vico's discussion takes on an individualized coloration: he lets the reader know that all these diverse intellectual influences and pursuits will ultimately fuse in the work of a special genius. The more common aspects of his life gain significance in his references to the second stratum, the unfolding of his system of thought.

Vico saw the important formative phase of his youth in the nine-year stay with the Rocca family at Castle Cilento (Vatolla). Here he had time to read and reread texts—in particular, the texts of the ancients and the great Tuscan writers whom he knew so thoroughly and who gave him so many insights for his subsequent work. When he left Vatolla and returned to Naples, he failed to obtain a city clerkship, obtaining instead a lowly professorship in rhetoric. He uses the occasion of his return for a lengthy discussion of the intellectual atmosphere of Naples, which he found to be dominated by Cartesianism. The diverse structural elements fuse again at this point, for Vico believed his own achievements to have been the persistent and successful struggle against the implications of Descartes's rationalism. Henceforth, remarks about the "external" aspects of his life become more sparse. He reports his successful competition for the chair of rhetoric in 1697 and carefully lists the various orations he gave the entering students at Naples, year after year. He lists the various commissioned works of poetry and eloquence. But otherwise we learn little of his nonintellectual life during the first two decades of the new century.

Gradually Vico's hope for the better paying chair of law enters all his intellectual discussion. After 1717, he writes several legal treatises in preparation for the promotion. He competes with high hopes. He fails largely because he could not deal effectively with certain political maneuvers, some of which were entirely beyond his control. Part A of the life ends with his lamentations over the failure but also with the solace he found in LeClerc's favorable comments on one of the legal writings: an expert outside his own city had seen virtue in his work. Part B begins again with a reference to the professional failure which he now, however, sees as an extra incentive for completing his work on the *New Science*. The text then turns entirely to a discussion of the big book. The reports on its reception are typical humanist fare. And the end is also entirely in keeping with the standard form for presenting a professorial life: Vico sums up his character and his works. He is proud of his devotion to educating young people: he "lectured every day with as much elegance and profundity in various branches of scholarship as if famous men of letters had come from abroad to attend his classes and to hear him" (p. 199). In other words, he had been a most conscientious professor. From a postscript by the marquis of Villarosa, added in 1818, we learn that the last thirteen years of Vico's life were given to continuous correcting and amending of the *New Science*. For the most part, they were very hard years, filled with economic misery, sorrow over a good-for-nothing son, and worry over the poor health of his favorite daughter. He himself suffered from a dreadful cancer of the throat and the face which ultimately debilitated him completely. Even his burial was beset by trouble; as the two groups of men who acknowledged him as one of their own, the Confraternity of Santa Sophia and his university colleagues, were carrying the coffin, they began to quarrel so intensely that the funeral procession had to be interrupted and postponed to another day.

This not especially noteworthy account of the external trappings of a poor professor's life has the virtue of securely anchoring the truly noteworthy aspect of the life in a frame of events. Thus the very modest quality of the external life highlights the greatness of the life of the mind. Vico's triumph was an intellectual breakthrough. The value of the autobiography does not lie simply in the fact that it is the story of an important thinker; its greater significance comes from its story of a grandiose intellectual experiment.

The discussion here does not attempt to reconstruct the actual course of Vico's mental evolution; only a true Vico scholar could do this.[3] Our concern instead is with the view that Vico himself had of this development, though his often oblique and opaque formulations make even this more modest attempt difficult. As soon as he knew himself to be the writer of such a systematic work as the *New Science*, he also knew that it was his task to describe the formation of that system. His self-conception and the objectives Count di Porcía stated for his intended series meshed ideally.

From the first page onward Vico sets his own development apart. By his repeated use of such terms as ingenuity, *ingenium*, and genius (e.g., pp. 111, 114, 115, 133), he clearly suggests that a very special quality was responsible for the peculiarity of his work. This stress is all the more important because he insists on depicting himself as an autodidact. He never felt disposed to fit himself for long into any class; he was not subjected to periods of formal training in any one discipline; and he had no master to form him. The pupil acted from the start as his own teacher, roaming from book to book, from subject to subject, leaving those aside in which a mere youth could only get lost. Early leads brought him to a basic "realism," which he reconciled with a commitment to Platonic "ideas" and a fascination with Zeno's doctrine of "metaphysical points," which he understood as ultimate metaphysical powers belonging to the intelligible world of the mind, but which could also be used to account for the behavior of the physical world. These were positions to which he adhered all his life.[4] An "accidental" visit to a university lecture led to a long fascination with law as the study of particulars, which he hoped would supplement the development of "one who had already begun to acquire the universal mind from metaphysics and to reason of particulars by axiom or maxims" (p. 115). He had begun a lifelong attempt to unite in one intellectual vision the opposing tendencies of universalizing philosophy and particularizing philology, a project greatly strengthened by his growing interest in the analysis of legal terms. Listening to the tedious and seemingly unfounded theorizing of others made him "impatient for new knowledge" (p. 114). The young man understood, but not yet clearly, that comprehensive knowledge must indeed be coherent in all its parts. He thought that his intellectual formation was momentarily corrupted by a temporary infatuation with modern poetry; yet he considered even such a wasteful extravagance as but a proper diversion for a young mind needing to expand its imaginative powers.

The vast and self-directed reading program that Vico pursued for nine years at Vatolla reinforced most of these early tendencies. It opened new views through a better acquaintance with the poetry of the classical period and of the Tuscan Renaissance. Vico systematically studied the Latin language and worked toward a better understanding of the Catholic doctrine on Grace. Reflections on Greek ethical theories led him to reject Aristotle, Epicurus, and most of the Stoics. A growing knowledge of his favored Plato awakened a sense, "without his being aware of it" (p. 122), that the idea of an ideal commonwealth ultimately must be connected with the concrete particularized manifestation of such ideal principles in actual historical developments. Vico had "the thought of meditating an ideal eternal law that should be observed in a universal city after the idea of design of providence, upon which idea have since been founded all the commonwealths of all times and all nations" (p. 122). A brief excursion into geometry, and a return to the ever-growing delight he found in observing the rich interrelations of the human world depicted by poets and historians, convinced him that it was a mistake to overstress logic and abstract sciences in the training of young people. At this point of his autobiography Vico inserted passages from a later oration to his students in which he insists on the need to cultivate memory, perception, imagination, and judgment, as well as logical reasoning. In particular he pointed to the important old rhetorical art of "Topics" as the most suitable device for training young minds in invention.[5]

By inserting passages from a later oration, Vico elegantly makes the transition to his return to Naples and his struggle with the Cartesianism he found dominant there. The older Vico who wrote the autobiography wanted to see this early phase of life as one marked by his forceful opposition to Cartesianism. He passes over the fact that his own epistemological position was once very close to Descartes's, whose thought he knew mostly only at secondhand, and often in garbled versions. He expresses strong dissatisfaction with the purely deductive reasoning of the geometrical method, and again pleads for the inventive procedure of

"Topics." He laments the neglect of history and the surrender of the human sciences to physics and medicine. He cannot persuade himself to accept ideas about uncreated matter or about a world of vortexes moving by necessity. In that context he makes observations pointing to matters which developed into central lines of his later thought. Plato's doctrine of ideas seems to him the basis of knowledge and consciousness: our minds contain certain eternal truths not of our own making. But our minds also know things made by ourselves in time: "Images by imagination, recollections by memory, passions by appetites; smells, tastes, colors, sounds and touches by the senses; and all these things we contain within us" (p. 127). The distinction is thus drawn between what is divinely made (such as divine knowledge), and what is man-made (human knowledge). As Vico assesses the new fashions he found around him, he blesses the good fortune which deprived him of a teacher to whom he now would have to be bound, a fortune which kept him free from any one school and sectarian bias, and which permitted his genius to guide him out there in the woods of Vatolla without involving him in the falsehoods of the capital.

He begins the discussion of his professorial career with a condensed statement of his main interests. Two ancient authors symbolize these interests for him: Plato, who contemplates man as he should be according to the nobility of intellectual wisdom, and Tacitus, who contemplates man as he is, following the "counsels of utility, whereby, among the infinite irregular chances of malice and fortune, the man of practical wisdom brings things to good issue" (p. 138). The combined objectives of these two figures foreshadow "that plan on which he later worked out an ideal eternal history to be traversed by the universal [and factual] history of all times" (p. 139). To these older intellectual symbols, Vico now adds the figure of Bacon as the teacher who persistently suggested that there is much knowledge to be added and then unified in a system.

Vico uses an interesting device for compressing his subsequent intellectual evolution by inserting summaries of the various orations given to his students through the years "to propose universal arguments brought down from metaphysics and given social application" (pp. 139–40). He sees their themes in direct relation to his great work. Self-knowledge, he holds, should be based on a study of all branches of knowledge; it should develop all our faculties. "The human mind is by analogy the god of man, just as God is the mind" of all things (p. 140). By self-knowledge the mind thus ascends to the knowledge of God. Human

Wisdom is but the intellect's apprehension of divine reason, the reason manifest in the order of all things. Only a foolish man, warring against himself, will war against the constitution of things—it was on this thought that Vico based his later treatise on *Universal Law*. While some of the earlier orations had a more exhortatory character, addressing students just entering the university and often dwelling on methods of study, the later orations seem to introduce more historical matters. The fifth oration, for instance, works out the theme that periods of military and political strength coincide with the flourishing of letters, a hint of his later conviction that there is a general cultural unity to all periods of history. The sixth oration announces themes that will be prominent in the future: language is the most powerful instrumentality in forming societies; childhood is marked by memory, strong imagination, but weak reasoning; in early youth the senses prevail, etc. "It is evident ... that Vico was agitating in his mind a theme both new and grand, to unify in one principle all knowledge human and divine. But all these arguments of which he had discoursed fell too far short of it. He was therefore glad that he had not published these orations" (p. 146).

Between 1709 and 1722, the rate of writing increases considerably; the profusion may signify a growing confidence of theme. Older thoughts recur in surer formulations. Vico still attacks the modern insistence on absolute certainty of knowledge: it endangers our generalized powers of prehension and our need to weigh mere probabilities. Apprehension of reality, discovery of possibilities (therefore the need for "Topics") must precede judgment, and the critic cannot presume insight as if it were a matter of right given by judgment.[6] The fashionable fascination with a stable knowledge of the nature of physical things is driving man away from a concern with his human world, a world not to be known by such fixed and certain knowledge. During this period of his life Vico becomes steadily more preoccupied with the history of words as a possible clue to the history of peoples, with early poetry and mythology as a source for historical understanding. He perceives possibilities of correlating the history of Roman jurisprudence and Roman political institutions into a system. A concern for jurisprudence as the knowledge of things divine and things human, as a study which can unify all other branches of study, gains a prominent place in his intellectual development.

While engaged in a diversion—the commissioned biography of Caraffa—Vico encounters the last of the model authors who assumed symbolic importance for him: Grotius. Here was not merely the historian of factual man, like Tacitus, nor the thinker about ideal man, like

Plato, but a scholar who used all available knowledge in Hebrew, Greek, and Latin to embrace "in a system of universal law the whole of philosophy and philology" (p. 155). Grotius's *On the Law of War and Peace* preoccupied Vico's thought intensely; he considered publishing a rich set of annotations to the text but then abandoned the idea since he did not think it proper for a good Catholic scholar to annotate the work of a heretic. He also began to perceive that the model was flawed by Grotius's assumption of rationality as the cause of all law. But, in a way, the last of the necessary building blocks had now been acquired, and

> by these four authors [Plato, Tacitus, Bacon, Grotius] whom he admired above all others and desired to turn to the use of the Catholic religion, Vico finally came to perceive that there was not yet in the world of letters a system so devised as to bring the best philosophy, that of Plato made subordinate to the Christian faith, into harmony with a philology [i.e., knowledge of particulars] exhibiting scientific necessity in both its branches, that is, in the two histories, that of languages and that of things; to give certainty to the history of languages by reference to the history of things; and to bring into accord the maxims of the academic sages and the practices of the political sages. By this insight Vico's mind arrived at a clear conception of what it had been vaguely seeking. [pp. 155–56]

His metaphysical reflections had meanwhile reinforced his belief in the analogies between Divine and human reason: God is mind infinite in knowledge, will, and power; man is mind finite in knowledge, will, and power. All principles of understanding come from God, but man comes to fuller understanding only by a gradual process, and since he may lose his understanding again, he must periodically restart his advance from ignorant barbarism. Vico thought that it *must* be possible to discover a new science which could lay down the principles for understanding the various phases of such development in terms of their own germane expressions. Early societies simply were not understandable in rationalistic terms; they could become accessible only by means appropriate to their own stage of development. Thus language in its formation, the poetry of Homer, Roman law, Greek myth, and the ancient world, had to be studied in ways fundamentally different from contemporary institutions. Vico tried to find solutions to these problems in the work he was doing on jurisprudence and philology; these were the writings on which he had pinned his hope of gaining the more remunerative professorial chair.[7]

His hopes for advancement were dashed. The great work which would immortalize him was on the drawing boards, however. By 1724, he had completed what became known as the *Scienza nuova in forma negativa*. Vico was not satisfied to present his new ideas by interweaving them with his critiques of predecessors. Later on he was glad that a lack of funds had prevented publication of a premature work. But as a major step in his development this first version should not be discounted; it seems entirely reasonable for a breakthrough of such dimensions initially to have taken the form of a struggle against older ways of treating such subjects. Within a year Vico had reworked it by "a positive method" (p. 166) and the First (or Prima) version of the *Principles of a New Science of the Nature of Nations, from Which are Derived New Principles of the Natural Law of Peoples* was printed in 1725. In the Autobiography Vico still reports the publication of the corrected Second version of 1730, printed in a much better type than the one marring the readability of the First. The version read nowadays is the edition of 1744, incorporating all the changes made during the last thirteen years of Vico's life. Though it is no longer mentioned in the autobiographic account, in Part B of the autobiography at least the main lines of thought in his great work are discussed.

Vico's metaphysics had led him to the fundamental insight that man can best know what man has made, his whole social-cultural world. By using the right method the human mind is capable of recapturing what once was human. The scholars of rational ages had used false methods; they had erred in carrying their own rationality back into the origins of human things. To understand human beginnings it was best to replace the old adage *homo intelligendo fiat omnia* by the suggestion *homo non intelligendo fiat omnia*. Vico's triumph rests in his insight that man, after the Flood had delivered him over to raw nature again, began his history as a creature weak in reasoning but strong in the will to live, immensely stronger in the powers of sensation and imagination than modern rationalists can fathom. Early man was a dumb creature, beastlike, beset by fears, and nomadic. The terror of lightning and thunder set into motion a gradual development by which natural forces became personified in Jupiter and in other gods; through his consciousness of gods, man became conscious of himself. Gradually men settle down and harvest their crops. They regulate their sexual relations, they bury their dead. Ritual magic is expressed in formalistic poetry. The all-powerful fathers are priest and judge, ruling by divination and magic formula. A dumb language, expressible in hieroglyphs, is formed. This is the age of the gods, of poetry, and of myth. When godless nomads, in need of protection, now turn to these human gods, they are granted it but are not permitted to partake of religion, the sacred rites, property, monogamous relations, and burial rights. They have no legal personality, and as landless *famuli* they struggle to obtain legal status. In need of protection against such claims, the patrician heroes of this heroic age band together and create the first civil government. Writing and language develop; written law appears. The power of reasoning grows as a consequence of this strife between the classes. The landless class, with steady success, advances its claims for a more natural-reasonable law freed from ritual formalism, equality for all, and the rights to property, marriage, and burial. The gradual victory of the plebeians then gives rise to the third stage, a civic age. Confronted by advancing rationalism, the powers of imagination and of the senses grow weak; abstraction, prose, philosophic religion gain the upper hand. Finally, the hypertrophy of steadily growing egotistic interests, the craving for luxury, and the growing political disorder (only temporarily reordered by absolute monarchy), cause a gradual decline until man falls back onto barbarism.

The history of Roman law had, in essence, become for Vico the history of Rome, and the history of Rome furnished him his pattern for universal history. Only the history of the Hebrews departed from this pattern; it served him instead as the model of a development in which direct divine legislation had protected a chosen people from the deviations undergone by the gentiles. In the gentile sequence of the age of gods, the age of heroes, and the age of men Vico perceived a repeatable pattern of development; the West had repeated it in a dark age, a middle age, and modernity. Vico was convinced he had read off the pattern from the facts. But he was pleased to find that this supposedly factual pattern also coincided with his understanding of the ideal pattern proclaimed by philosophy and theology since Plato's time. He thus felt persuaded that fact and general truth, that philology and philosophy had now been shown to be convertible. The development of human nature and human history were the same. Man's life at any stage was an ordered cultural whole: states of mind corresponded to states of language, of law, of literature, of forms of knowing, and of institutions. Homeric poetry was not the creation of a single poet but the poetic accretion by which a people in two different phases of its development had expressed its experience. The Law of the Twelve Tables seemed to be the law that evolved with the Roman Quirites; it was not a garbled borrowing from Greek philosophers. As a convinced antidiffusionist, Vico saw the separate development of each nation as an inherently necessary one, executed by human means. Since men had free will, the necessary pattern was yet open to variations.

A critical method about origins of human things had led Vico to a system. In truth, it was a theology: for the discernible historical development was for limited man the readable version of God's providence. Vico was proud that a Catholic, in a Catholic land, had found the way to this new science.

In Vico's vision of his own life, providence had enabled him to find his way to the *New Science*. The double-tiered account of the autobiography, the life of the man and the unfolding of his intricate set of thoughts, rested for Vico in the third, but prime, stratum of a personal providence. Providence had coordinated the external events of the life and the course of the mind on its exploration. The seemingly unordered gropings of an autodidactic youth had all had their secret and gradually unveiled order. His *ingenium*, the surest means for aiming at divine intent, had guided him better than any teacher might have done. Where the scholar had mistakenly chased wrong objectives without obtaining them, adverse fortune saved him for his true work; the remunerative chair was denied to him, but his great work was thus saved, and the lack of funds, so much lamented at the time, had prevented the printing of a defective enterprise. Vico now understood the necessary sequential inner order of his life, and he seemed gratified. "He however blessed all these adversities as so many occasions for withdrawing to his desk as to his high impregnable citadel, to meditate and to write" (p. 200).

Vico had been asked to furnish an account of the evolution of his thought. He fulfilled this request magnificently, albeit that the autobiography often has, for a modern reader, an opaqueness paralleling the "baroque atmosphere ... covered with a cloud of impenetrability"[8] that makes the *New Science* also such a difficult book. In a way, Vico wrote *one* model for an intellectual autobiography. It was not the first of its genre; similar traits are to be found in Augustine's *Confessions*, Dante's *Vita Nuova*, and Descartes's *Discourse on Method*. That it was a type with a great future was shown by Gibbon, John Stuart Mill, Darwin, Newman, Collingwood, or, in sketchy form, even by Freud and Einstein. Its appeal, and its inner necessity, grew as it became more possible for certain Western men to equate their lives with their professional existence as thinkers. When Paul Arthur Schilpp asked Albert Einstein for an autobiographic sketch, the request for an answer to the essential question "Who are you?" was requited by a rendition of a life conceived exclusively as the evolution of the mathematician-physicist-cosmologist.

Such autobiographies are testimonials to the immense process of professionalization that has marked our Western lives since the time when some men began to insist on a special calling.

But this form of autobiography also has a problematic aspect. Vico does indeed tell us something about Vico the man. But what is overshadowing is the account of the evolution of Vico's thought, which, finally systematized in the *New Science,* has its own inner dynamics and follows its own inner laws of gradual clarification. The external facts and conditions of life function, at most, as catalysts speeding up or retarding the mental reactions. The reliance on providence, as the coordinating force of life and reason, strengthens the sense that all of life was so arranged as to permit the free unfolding of a train of thought into a system which, in turn, might help to explain the process typical of all human life. The personal life parallels in miniature the evolution of a humanity that also follows an inevitable course in unfolding its mental capacities.[9] A gifted human being, mysteriously aided by circumstances, enters through its groping intellectual efforts into the vast total structure of man's mental world, dimly aware that this world of mind must be a coherent one and that its order, tied into the order of a transcendent creator, must become visible from some vantage point. The mind, gradually finding the appropriate tools and methods, penetrates this mental world of man ever more deeply, gaining ever clearer sight of its structure, its cause, and its necessary being. It finally comes to rest with the remarkable sensation that the meanings of the world, of all human existence, and of the personal life are all in harmony. Vico does not present this process as one in which he, for specific reasons of his own existence, imposes his personal intellectual order on an otherwise unintelligible human chaos, a view that modern hermeneutics might be forced to have of this process. Instead it is seen as a process in which Vico's mind, by keeping true to its functions, is ever more forcefully being channeled into the flow of universal reason that is carrying him to the desired goal.

Such a historical vision of ideas unfolding according to inner necessities has a strangely "atemporal" aspect. The stress lies on a notion of a process having to run its course; a sequential unfolding must occur. Time seems to be of the essence. But what conception of time? Whether it is a millennium or a day seems irrelevant. The history of mathematics can be written (and perhaps it is most of the time) by concentrating on the logically necessary sequence of thought moving from problem to solution, problem to solution, etc. Whether this sequential unfolding took centuries or was accomplished within the life-span of one mathematical genius does not affect the sequential order. The specific process can be studied as though it occurred in "atmospheric isolation," that is, free from the effects of milieu and surrounding contingency (although it may be interesting for other reasons). All "disciplinary" history—the history of philosophy, of literature, of painting, etc.—tends toward such "atemporality," underemphasizing the vital importance of milieu and externally conditioning circumstance. Thematic history has a similar tendency—as the writer of this essay regretfully acknowledges. This tendency will have a special appeal for those who conceive of historical processes as movement toward predetermined destinies, as the gradual realization of final causes, or as the unfolding of the predetermined nature of things. It is an altogether reasonable element to expect in someone believing as firmly in a providential order as Vico did. It may have an appeal for the great systematizers, the minds who use the vicissitudinous character of history for discovering its hidden logic and universal order. This notion of unfolding flourished in the eighteenth century as long as the urge to extract the quintessential universal truth about the human condition was stronger than the fascination with a pluralistic and incomparable diversity of life. It remained important far beyond the Enlightenment. Ideas continued to have the force of their consequences, men continued to search the inner logic of things. Even the conception of historical individuality contained an element suggesting a necessary, internally dictated logic of development.

But the idea of an unfolding process was gradually challenged by a different notion of development. Men acquired habits of mind for thinking of life as the unpredictable product of an ever-changing interplay between an I and a world. "Accident" came to be seen as an integral building block of a life rather than as a discountable perturbation in a set course. The evolution of thought came to be perceived as the story of men thinking in the face of circumstances. A pronounced taste for fine nuances and a love for the specifically particular came to counterbalance the drive for uniformly intelligible order. And, interestingly enough, these tendencies appeared in the thought of the very eighteenth-century thinkers who adhered more strongly still to the notion of unfolding process.

Vico's own account leaves room for a consideration of the specificity of his circumstances. He, at least, faintly suggests that a providential timing permitted him to win these great insights for mankind at the very time and in the circumstances in which he did. But at the crucial moment he subordinates any such inclination on his part to consider the influence of external factors to his fascination with the unfolding inner dynamics of his system. In an analogous way, his conception of the historical evolution of humanity allowed for variations caused by different circumstances; yet these do not draw his loving attention. Instead he focused on the *typical* and the *necessary* course of this evolution. Yet, in his willingness to take a step away from the fixation on human nature as a static, an eternal given, he became one of the great teachers who stressed the imperative that man be understood as a historically evolving being.

The bearing of Vico's self-conception on his notion of individuality was thus limited to the degree to which he remained devoted to the idea of an unfolding order and captivated by the desire to find the all-explaining typical system. An overwhelming sense of the loneliness of his struggle and of the singularity of his fate pervaded the autobiography. He knew he was different, and he wanted to follow his own special course. But ultimately he did not place a high value on his uniqueness. He instead found inner peace and satisfaction in his final discovery that his life and his way of doing and seeing things were in full harmony with God's way for all men. When before him lay the great vision revealing all of human life to be a great universal order, Vico was ready to die. A life had fulfilled itself in its great task. "Vico had nothing further to hope for in this world; wherefore, an account of his advanced age, worn out as he was by so many labors, afflicted by so many domestic cares and suffering from spasmodic pains in the thighs and legs and from a strange disease devouring all the tissues between the palate and the lower bone of the head, he definitely abandoned his studies" (p. 198).

But even if he did not explicitly value it for himself, and even if his thought had not much *immediate* effect, he explored elements which later on contributed much to a positive valuation of individuality. He made his breakthrough when he understood that men of different ages could not be understood by the norms of his own time, that they had to be understood on their own terms, and that they deserved respect for their own manner of existence. He brought to this historicist understanding a remarkable sensitivity for total styles of life, perceiving the unique pattern created by putting a *this* with a *that*. The noteworthy aspect of all human beings was that they sought to live whole lives: their language, their artistic expression, their religion, their law, their institutions, and their entire mental make-up were cut from the same cloth. Though he may not have been particularly aware of doing so, "he did uncover a mode of perception, something entailed in the notion of understanding words, persons, outlooks, cultures, the past."[10] Once in the autobiography Vico declared his intention "to read the Latin authors completely free of notes, entering into their spirit by means of philosophical criticism" (p. 134). "Entering into their spirits"—the only way by which ineffable individuality can be understood, from the inside, so to speak, by empathy with the actor himself. Despite his pronounced love for the great universal truths, his feeling that truth could be discovered "by means of philosophical criticism," it was his great achievement to point out that understanding of the past comes through imaginative self-identification with the lives of those who had gone before.

## EDWARD GIBBON
### (1737–94)

Half a century after Vico, a great historian sat down to write the history of his own life. Death intervened before Gibbon could write the final version of the six different drafts he had made of his "memoirs." His friend Lord Sheffield put together a composite version by skillfully selecting from the various drafts. Since this literary executor listened too willingly to the moral sensitiveness of his strong-willed daughter Maria, he excised from the text those phrases potentially offensive to eighteenth-century ears but so delightful to ours.[11]

Perhaps, Gibbon's appetite for writing these memoirs was whetted by the gift of a book on heraldry written by his forebear John Gibbon.[12] But it is more tempting to find the reasons for his motive in undertaking the autobiographic effort in a few sentences of the memoir itself. In his first sentence he says: "In the fifty-second year of my age, after the completion of a toilsome and successful work, I now propose to employ some moments of my leisure in reviewing the simple transactions of a private and literary life" (p. 27). One is reminded of the sentences describing the scene during the late evening hours of June 27, 1787, when Gibbon had just completed the last paragraph of the *Decline and Fall*. Under the acacia trees above Lake Geneva, he took leave of the "old and agreeable companion" that had made him famous. "Whatsoever might be the future fate of my *History*, the life of the historian must be short and precarious" (p. 195). But was there not also a way to prolong the historian's life?

However much Gibbon enjoyed filling out the days and evenings by attending parties where he could be celebrated as "the" historian, life was somewhat empty once the great work had been completed. The work had had its roots in a very strong craving for fame, and his wish was answered. What was to follow? Indeed, there was some talk of a seventh volume perhaps, or of a series of portraits of famous Englishmen.[13] But ultimately the wisest and most tempting course was surely to fill the leisure hours of life's autumnal felicity by exploiting the fame of the history in behalf of the fame of the historian, and then to ensconce the history behind the author's autobiography. And so it went—if the guess is right that there are three readers of Gibbon's *Life* for every reader who plows through those "damned, fat, square, thick books" of the *Decline and Fall*.

Like Vico, Gibbon justified his life by the importance of his great work of scholarship. The autobiography seems to be written to answer the one important question: How did this particular man become the author of the *Decline and Fall*? The question itself obviously takes for granted the unquestioned value of the history. Gibbon never doubted that he had written a great book, and the judgments coming from the best men of his time confirmed his feelings. Thus, the autobiography had to be a success story from the outset. A reader comparing it to Vico's will note how much more Gibbon's autobiography is a narrative rather than an intricate analysis loosely affixed to story elements. As a historian Gibbon had acquired an expertly honed sensitivity for the dramatic quality of life, and for the fine interplay of an actor and his scene. He understood the rhythms that gave human life an appearance of a whole, though it was composed of successive phases each with its own inner coherence. He would not have denied that much about man could be explained by philosophical insights into his nature. But the peculiar whole constituting a life could be made intelligible only by drawing its dramatic lifeline, by telling its story by recording its unexpected turns. If at one of the soirees he liked to attend, one of his many lady friends had asked him the question "Who are you, Mr. Gibbon?" he would unquestionably have said, "I am the author of the *Decline and Fall*. And it is an interesting story how this came about. Twenty-five years ago I could not have answered your question, for the warm desires, the long expectations of youth are founded on the ignorance of themselves. So if you have a few hours to spare, my dear, let me take some snuff, tap my golden snuffbox until everyone listens attentively, and I shall tell you how I came to be what I now am." But as a man of a very elegant age, he would have responded much more elegantly.

Gibbon was very much a man of his own age, an age with a decidedly philosophical bent of mind. Even if the footnotes of the *Decline and Fall* quarrel more with Voltaire than with any other contemporary writer, Gibbon shared Voltaire's programmatic stance that history in such an age ought to be written *en philosophe*. He relished no other judgment more than David Hume's praise that the history of Rome had finally been written by a philosopher of man. But *écrire l'histoire en philosophe* did not mean fitting the facts of history into a philosophical scheme; the phrase merely exhorted the historian to take an enlightened stance in viewing the past course of human life. First of all, he must understand the doings of men not as the result of mysterious transcendent wills but as the result of intelligible human motivations. Men were the playwrights of their own drama. The explanations of their lives lay within themselves. The enlightened historian writes history to enlighten his fellow men. His enlightened perspective informs him of what ennobles man in his true humanity and what he must scorn and ridicule as uncivilized behavior. This kind of historian explains man to man; he instructs by holding up the standard of civilized conduct, regardless of whether he writes the story of humanity or of his own life.

Gibbon began the story of his own life by reaching far back into the past of his family. He could do so because he was the lucky possessor of John Gibbon's seventeenth-century heraldic treatise which permitted him a long historical perspective that no previous autobiographers enjoyed. They all had been restricted to "contemporary" history, sharing the limited vision of all historical work that preceded the great age of erudition in which comprehensive records were being compiled for a more extended view. John Gibbon himself was an exemplar of this erudition. Augustine, Guibert of Nogent, Giraldus Cambrensis, Abelard, Montaigne, Vico, even Cardinal de Retz—none could reach back further than to mother and father. Cellini, tongue in cheek, connects the immediate family to Caesar's captain, jumping back over intervening generations. Cardano strains hard for more precise data about an extended family but does not have the material for doing so, even if the motive is interesting. The exception is James I of Aragon, who, being a king, knows of a royal line of descent.

That Edward Gibbon had thus a headstart in a historically researched family tree, is less interesting, however, than his philosophical inclination to reflect about man's "lively desire of knowing and of recording our ancestors" as "some common principle in the minds of men" (pp. 27–28). He deems it an understandable prejudice on our part to seek this "ideal longevity" by enlarging "the narrow circle in which nature has confined us," thus filling "up the silent vacancy that precedes our birth." That such a longing for a backward extension of the self through one's forebears could be problematic, especially for an aristocracy steadily losing its social position, was suggested by Napoleon's great minister Talleyrand when he said that a certain duke, bragging about his fine ancestry, reminded him of the newly praised potato plant the best of which was also buried underground. Gibbon protected himself against any such charge by allying himself to those ancestors whose qualities "best promote the interests of society." He thought it would have been the greatest honor to be a descendant of Confucius; and after that it was surely better to "descend from Cicero than from Marius, from Chaucer than from one of the first Companions of the Garter" (p. 29). Thus biased toward the socially useful, Gibbon singles out the ancestors who built buildings, or supported good schools, or that alluring "martyr of learning" James Fiennes, or the Blue Mantle Poursuivant John Gibbon who left a useful record book.

The more Edward Gibbon nears his immediate ancestors, the more he meets the urbanized trader instead of the country gentlemen. The historian, struggling to keep the funds together that permitted him to write in leisure, had the utmost respect for the value of a penny; he looked with great favor at these useful ancestors who had made money and had proved by their very conduct that "gentility is not degraded by the exercise of trade" (p. 32). He gives a particularly prominent place to the paternal grandfather Edward, a genius at turning his deeds into useful gold—a very wealthy man, who, alas, suffered heavy losses as a director of the South Sea Company when the bubble burst. How suddenly the affairs of men could change! And this was an affair that hit home! For a moment Gibbon loses his customary equanimity and lashes out against Parliament and the treacherous lawyers who did not protect the investors and who thereby violated the high standards of their civilization, robbing honest men of the fruits of their labor. Such selfish disregard of politicians for civilized conduct had cost poor Edward Jr. the potential comfort of an additional £ 96,000!

In the same vein, Gibbon tells the story of his parents' romance. His grandfather had objected so vigorously to his son's choice that he spitefully left a much larger share of the inheritance to his daughter, at the cost of the ... grandson! Here is a well-told bit of history to which the historian skillfully ties his own lifeline. The lengthy discussion of his ancestry, fully an eighth of the book, is thus by no means the jocose rambling of a leisurely writer toying with the curiosa of a family emblem book. Gibbon not only sets the scene on which he was to appear but uses the account for a justification of his own career. He suggestively draws the contours of the civilization with which he identifies. He sketches the material conditions, an element of chance that always seemed to affect his career. This skillfully executed backward extension of the self not only reveals a heightened historical sense; it also shows his sensitivity for the interaction of general conditions and a specific personal development.

In the account of his early life Gibbon consistently notes the concatenation of a given setting, of developing character traits, and of the power of chance. He sees that, for the most part, man's fate is to be slave, savage, or peasant; it was his own good luck to be born "in a free and civilized country, in an age of science and philosophy, in a family of honorable rank and decently endowed with the gifts of fortune" (p. 49). But, despite the bad health threatening his entire youth, he was the sole survivor of seven children. He was tied to the home for much of his education. Had it not been for the loving care of his Aunt Catherine Porten, "the true mother of my mind as well as my health" (p. 61), he never might have survived. She was always near to nurse him, to lead him to books, and to discuss what he had read. The sickly boy, so poorly made for the role of heir to a country gentleman, turned to the world of books at an early age. He approached it with an "indiscriminate appetite," wandering without direction through ancient and modern authors. Yet it seemed to the historian in retrospect that this "free desultory reading" had "by degrees" subsided "in the historic line." Chance encounters led steadily deeper into the books on world history, especially the history of the Orient. An awakening critical sense drove him to the true sources, and the "indigested chaos" was given a backbone through his love for maps and chronologies, those basic tools of the historian most easily accessible to the young. However, this "stock of erudition that might have puzzled a doctor and a degree of ignorance of which a schoolboy would have been ashamed" (pp. 66–68), hardly constituted an adequate education.

Entering Oxford at the age of fourteen was supposed to remedy this, but, as the wonderfully witty indictment of academia in Chapter 3 explains, eighteenth-century Oxford provided no means for such improvement. Since the professors really did not want students, young Gibbon had the freedom he ardently desired. But, alas, he had no sensible sense of direction. The youngster turned his first independent act into a near disaster by converting to Catholicism. Later on he felt a bit ashamed for having once departed from the religion of his country. In retrospect it seemed incredible that he ever thought he could believe in transubstantiation! (P. 84.) But he does not apologize for his youthful error. Instead, he tells the story about Chillingworth and Bayle who, before him, had traveled the same precipitous road. The historian had learned to use historical parallels for his own apology and justification.

But by this peculiar turn of events the chances for an English education had now been diminished. His horrified father saw to it that the premature freedom was replaced by a Calvinist minister's strict tutelage in foreign Lausanne. The new life was less easy for young Gibbon, but the education more expertly planned. The historian later on acknowledged that under Monsieur Pavilliard's tutelage he had acquired scholarly habits and had learned how to form his own mind. The ardent interests in religion responsible for this transplantation to Swiss soil gave way to religious indifference. Having reverted to Protestantism, "I suspended my religious inquiries" (p. 97). But the workaday ethics of those Calvinist surroundings helped to make him more diligent, and he became as well a more unified personality. He uses the revealing terms "method" and "system." "The rigid course of discipline and abstinence to which I was condemned invigorated the constitution of my mind and body" (p. 110). "I felt myself invigorated by the habits of application and method . . . . As soon as I was confirmed in the habits of industry and temperance he [Pavilliard] gave the reins into my own hands" (p. 96). "He [who received an education] will not, like the fanatics of the last age, define the moment of grace, but he cannot forget the era of his life in which his mind has expanded to its proper form and dimensions" (p. 98).

In this setting there occurred the true miracle of education: that wondrous turn from merely executing a teacher's assigned lessons to that moment when voluntary labor spends itself on self-set tasks of cultivation. After having received solid training in languages, Gibbon "systematizes" his reading. He moves "methodically" through all the classics and acquires a vast acquaintance with ancient life. The great historical work would rest on this, but at Lausanne Gibbon had no idea what purpose the reading would serve. He tries his hand at working out contested points of scholarship, learning patiently to track down the evidence in scholarly reference works. He applies the same "methodical" rigor to cultivating his skills of expression by "systematic" labor of translation until he has "the command of at least a correct style" (p. 99). Like the reading, the translation is training for training's sake; Gibbon translates French into Latin and Latin into French. Later on in life Gibbon had to put himself through similar paces as he acquired his refined English style.

In that corner of Switzerland, he came in touch with the lively intellectual world of the eighteenth-century French Enlightenment. He delved into modern authors with the same systematic persistence he had applied to the ancients. Yet, he formed his own world view: a moderate deism, a fervent belief in the value of letters, fine taste, and civilized living, tempered by a forbearing ironic attitude toward human frailties, and an intense commitment to the virtue of a free life. Gibbon joined no "school of thought"; he was becoming his own man. His immense curiosity and love for books, which he had brought from England, had been strengthened and expanded by new skills. The always strong taste of his sedentary nature for pleasurable sociability and comfort had found a counterweight in self-disciplined working habits and in the necessary *Sitzfleisch* without which the vast labor of the *Decline and Fall* could never have been accomplished.

The return to England made very clear, however, that the established personality, tastes, and capacities had no object to which to apply themselves. Others of his age and class were taking the customary road to public office, the running of estates, and the absorbing social life of the metropolis; Gibbon had neither the inclination, the gifts, the opportunities, nor the funds for such career lines. And after he had once sighed as a lover over Susan Curchod, but had obeyed as a son awaiting his inheritance, he never returned to the idea of marriage and later lived out "the most strenuous part of his sex life in his footnotes."[14] He wanted to be economically independent, but until his father's death in 1770, Edward Jr. remained in modest dependence, reading and studying at home, worried that his father's hopeless mismanagement of the estate could deprive his heir of the necessary comfort needed for his work. But for a long time there was no clarity as to what this work was to be. Gibbon had a very strong ambition for fame and public recognition, but this too was checked by an uncanny sense for biding his time. Even later, when he had found his objective, he hid his work from public sight until it was ready for publication. The dramatic effect with which Gibbon suddenly appeared as "the" historian derived, in no small degree, from the fact that nothing had announced his coming.

For the time being, the *Essai sur l'étude de la littérature* (1761) was a modest outlet for his ambition; written in French, it did not establish him as a major English author. But his father, pleased with having a published writer in the family, promised Gibbon a Grand Tour of the Continent to round off his education. The Seven Years' War intervened, and both Gibbons served time with the Hampshire Grenadiers. Though Edward Jr. was a much more efficient and effective officer than he was willing to reveal in the autobiography, obviously these years of senseless bivouacking and riding a horse hardly fitted his conception of life. It remains a true mark of his self-conception, however, that, in retrospect, even this accidental interlude became for him a means for fashioning the historian: "the captain of the Hampshire Grenadiers (the reader may smile) has not been useless to the historian of the Roman Empire" (p. 134). As he compared ancient and modern military tactics, and read as much as duties permitted, Gibbon's awareness ripened to tell him that all the acts of his life had conspired to make him a historian. But by inserting some pages of his diary at this point in the autobiography he clearly suggests that he was only potentially a historian, still searching for a suitable subject. Which subject could gain him the fame he desired? The expedition of Charles VIII in Italy? A history of the Black Prince? A comparison of Henry V and Titus? A life of Sir Philip Sidney? Or a life of Sir Walter Raleigh? A history of Swiss liberty? Or the history of the Florentine republic under the house of Medici?

The steadily worsening economic condition of the family again threatened the Grand Tour, but when it finally took place Gibbon knew how to use it. He turned it into another one of those experiences for pulling together the varied strains of his being. An extended stay in Paris and the many occasions it gave him for mingling with the prominent French intellectuals assured Gibbon that he, with his stock of sound learning, his sane outlook on life, and his fine wit, could easily hold his own among the best minds of his time. Revisiting his friends at Lausanne showed him how much he had become his own man; the memories of the romance no longer hurt too badly. The Grand Tour had its climax in Rome. Although he was "by temper not very susceptible to enthusiasm" (p. 152), the impact of the Eternal City deeply stirred Gibbon's emotions. The miracle of Rome, where the presence of so many different layers of past life continuously feeds the historical consciousness of an observer, brought Gibbon to his topic. How did it come to pass that monks were to chant their Christian persuasions amid the still visible splendor of classical Rome? The scene on the Capitoline Hill and the date, October 15, 1764, remained forever present to him.

The autobiography depicts this as the turning point. In actual life almost a decade of "many distractions"[15] intervened before a brief reference in July 1773 suggests that Gibbon is at work on the *Decline and Fall*. He wrote more French *essais*. The interesting *Critical Observations of the Sixth Book of the Aeneid* established him at last as a respected English writer. When his father died in 1770, Gibbon gained his economic independence. He established a working home in London where he also found his way into English intellectual circles. His time was still misdirected toward the writing of a History of Swiss Liberties. Since he refused to learn that barbaric German language he had to ask his friend Deyverdun to translate the sources! The strange venture did not get far, but, by having tried his hand at the enterprise, he freed himself of his impulse to deal with the topic. An undistinguished parliamentary career, financed by a remote member of the family, and a sinecure on the Board of Trade, both coinciding with the American War of Independence, were further distractions, though they did not seriously retard his work. The parliamentary experience served him as a school of civil prudence, an essential tool for a historian. In general, Gibbon had fashioned a setting for himself in London that gave him stable conditions for sustained work on his immense topic.

His life was now fully centered in his work. It was a stupendous labor, even if no other topic in Western history had been as thoroughly prepared in the learned compendia as that of imperial Rome. It was the one great topic a single man could still hope to master. Gibbon's autobiography gives the reader glimpses of the historian's working problems, but it cannot fully show the historian at work. A part of the account dwells on the production of the great work, its publication, and reception. But the immense methodical labor, day in, day out, could not be reproduced and is elegantly hidden, reinforcing the impression that a great genius created it with typical aristocratic ease. Gibbon only vaguely suggests how he gradually imposed an order on the overwhelming mass of material or how he acquired that marvelously steady rhythm of his prose. The excellent footnotes to the History seem to be written as effortlessly and with the same elegant ease. Only a thoughtful analysis of the text, preferably with some knowledge of the sources underlying it, can give an adequate appreciation of the colossal achievement of giving form to so intractable a subject. Gibbon still belonged to that vanishing breed of historians who plainly take pride in the finished product and see no virtue in conducting the public through their workshop so that it may be properly impressed by the labor and skills displayed there. Thus the autobiography explains how this man became the historian of the *Decline and Fall*; it is very much less an account of how the work was executed.

Upon publication of the first volume in that memorable year 1776—which marked Adam Smith's *Wealth of Nations* and Goethe's first year in Weimar as well as American independence—Gibbon was famous at once. One recalls Tacitus's words about Seneca: that there was something about the man's bent of mind which was exactly suited to his age. Gibbon's greatest reward was the praise from men whom he himself admired—Hume and Robertson, for example. The general reading public was equally given to praise. Since the critical attacks were concentrated so heavily on Gibbon's treatment of Christianity, they made him a hero rather than a villain to the "enlightened" public he sought. After volumes 2 and 3 had appeared in 1781, and when his parliamentary career proved less and less gratifying, Gibbon gradually extricated himself from entangling political alliances. Volume 4 was published when he was still in London in 1783. But then he settled for his autumnal felicity in Lausanne, where volumes 5 and 6 were written between 1784 and 1787. The production of his great work had filled the prime of his manhood; he had six years left to bask in the glory he had gained by it.

The autobiographer employed the cultivated artistry he had made his own in writing the history. The *Life* is cast with the same narrative dramatic skill. Gibbon knows what is important and executes a main line of development; he indulges in side issues only when he has a good story. His highly refined sense for the sequential qualities of his personal development gives the book a vertebrated story line. But all forward-moving historical narrative must at times be interrupted for a description of conditions. Gibbon's sense of proportion for the synchronic and diachronic demands of all historical writing, so remarkably strong in the *Decline and Fall*, is also present in the *Life*. The story is arrested at appropriate points for a presentation of the general conditions of his life. He enriches the narrative by an understanding of the setting in which it occurs. He also reinforces the rhythm of the account by highlighting its phaselike structure. Such a method gives Gibbon an opportunity to insert the "philosophical" reflections on his life and his world and to present the judgments about persons and culture that are such a pronounced feature of the work.

Yet, for all his highly developed historical sensitivities, Gibbon wrote neither the History nor the Life from a "historicist point of view." He does not have the modern historian's relativized judgment. Gibbon's unquestioning belief in the superiority and universal validity of his own cultural norms stood in the way of such a modern perspective. He felt very much obligated to give an objective presentation of what he saw.

He was equally strongly inclined to pass judgment, and he fearlessly weighed past life against the model of his own contemporary civilization. Past reality was discerned as an interplay of self-willed men and the world in which they had to act. With wit and aloof irony, he castigated the follies of men who could not share the high civilization of his own day. To this one must add Gibbon's greatest but least fathomable talent: his immense power to give form and structural coherence to the near-chaotic complexity of massive historical data. The great achievement of the *Decline and Fall* is, after all, the ability of one mind to give intelligible and beautiful form to such an immense historical mass. The lesser task of giving form to the presentation of his own life profited from this talent as well.

Gibbon answered the question of who and what he was by telling a story of his growth. His autobiography had a central message: only my history can explain myself; and if you wish to understand this history, do not impose a teleological scheme on it. No prewritten script decreed that this man should present that work in this manner. There was no unfolding of a person toward a predestined end. To be sure, certain firm givens exerted their own influence and helped determine this life. Gibbon himself suggests certain indelible character traits: his "innate" curiosity, his penchants for ease, comfort, and sociability. He treats his thirst for fame, the strongest driving power of his life, as a universal motive in all men. But in most other respects Gibbon saw his developed character as a consequence and an expression of his circumstances, of his world, and the age in which he lived.

Despite all his flirtations with French culture, Gibbon wanted to see himself as an Englishman, albeit one with cosmopolitan awareness. "Britain is the free and fortunate island" (p. 201). He loved its freedoms. He identified with the nontheoretical, practical, and pragmatic compromises of English politics. How very revealing is his remark about his tutor Pavilliard: "He was rational because he was moderate" (p. 96). Gibbon understood the practical economic concerns of his nation of shopkeepers. Ultimately he is more in tune with an English-Scottish version of the Enlightenment than might be expected of such a French-ified and foreign-educated man. He had the tastes and the prejudices of an English aristocrat, albeit that he, like many others, transformed the ideal into an aristocracy of the mind, of taste, and of cultured behavior. All in all, he felt comfortable with the tastes, the values, and the habits of his world and his age. The self-assured quality of all his judgments rests on this absolute trust in the values of civilized humanity, moderated by an ironic stance toward any claims of man's indefinite perfectibility. Gibbon could not follow the turn to the modern world of mass man. He could not cope with the implications of the French Revolution; and he was apparently as unaware of the beginning effects of that still more portentous Industrial Revolution as was his compatriot Edmund Burke.

Gibbon was aware that his own development resulted from an interaction of a developing self with often unpredictable events and circumstances. Accident had played a great role in shaping him: his youthful illnesses, the chance encounters with certain books, the sudden flirtation with Catholicism, the abrupt transplantation to Lausanne, the Hampshire Grenadiers, or the illuminating moment on the Capitoline steps. In such moments an unforeseeable "accidental" factor intrudes into his life. Since he had no use whatever for providential explanation, he could only deal with these facts as unaccountable occurrences. What he could do, however, and what he did do in such excellent fashion, was to show how he integrated the unexpected into his lifeline, how he made use of such accidental events, how they became constitutive building blocks of this very being he knew as Edward Gibbon. The inner dynamics, a set of given facts, and the pursuit of a certain objective were thus inseparably intertwined with the power of the fortuitous. Only a history interweaving all the significant givens, conditions, and changing events in their proper sequential order could account for his life.

This deep-seated historical mentality, concerned with the interplay between self and world, drove man toward a view of life as an individuality, explained only by a unique constellation of temporal-spatial factors. But though Gibbon is in that sense a witness of a strong shift toward the historicized vision of life, he is not someone to whom the notion of individuality was important.

In his own way, Vico and Gibbon each advocated the nobility of history. Gibbon "philosophized" little about the historical activity, and wrote wonderfully effective history. He enjoyed immediate success. Vico wrote history in a frequently baffling, and often unintelligible way, but he "philosophized" about history in a fascinating manner. He had no immediate success, and it took almost a century until a wider group of readers discovered the depth of his thought. At the very beginning of the eighteenth century this little noticed Neapolitan professor formed a passionate conviction that we have in our historical understanding a powerful, a necessary, and a noble means for explaining our lives and our world. In his view historical knowledge was surer and more suitable for us than the dominant scientific or natural-philosophical knowledge with which his views clashed. Yet it seems doubtful that Vico meant to substitute a historical mode of understanding for a philosophical one. He desired to unify philology and philosophy, a knowledge of the particular and a knowledge of the universal. And in the end he perhaps became more interested in the universal patterns of developments, in historical morphology, than in the individual fact, or in the reconstruction of irrepeatable history.

Throughout most of the eighteenth century the universalizing tendencies of philosophy and science remained very strong. And yet this was a century in which history also claimed more and more of men's attentions. Philosophers, theologians, critics, and aestheticians increasingly pointed in their own disciplines to a genetic mode of understanding, or, at least, they prepared the ground in which such understanding might flourish. They promoted a growing awareness, sometimes only a suspicion, that motion and change might be as characteristic, or even more characteristic, of matter and of spirit, of human fate and of the creations of the human mind, than permanence and eternal order. The more continuing process was stressed, the more a premium was placed on a genetic mode of understanding. If you wish to know why a thing is what it is, try to discern how it came to be what it is. It takes time for things to become what they are.

Descartes, with a mathematical-logical notion of rationality, started with a plan: wipe out the accumulated errors of past thought, and on this *tabula rasa* construct the total tree of knowledge by means of absolutely certain rational propositions. He fervently dreamt of doing this by himself in his lifetime—until he ran into the perverse multiplicity of things that could only be sorted out by experiments designed to establish the adequate cause of a thing. When empiricist thinkers, like John Locke, undermined the notion of innate ideas and insisted on experience and sensation as a necessary foundation of knowledge, they also implied that the growth of our knowledge is dependent upon processes requiring time. A much more time-bound vision of human knowledge than Descartes desired emerged from this. By the end of the eighteenth century, Condorcet, the last of the great *philosophes*, took it for granted that Locke was right: man is a sensate being, ordering sense data by means of his rational categories, building coherent systems of knowledge through time. Condorcet perceived the necessity of tracing the long history of the progress of the human mind. It took time to establish sound conceptions of reality; it took time to disseminate these among men so that they might live rational lives. It took time to correct the errors which men at any time committed because they could not free themselves from prejudice. The history of all knowledge was thus a history of indefinite progress, of indefinite perfectibility—at least, as long as the sun shone to sustain human life. Yet, this historicized view of knowledge did not prevent Condorcet from trying to use the historical data for discovering the stable laws of a social science, on the model of the physical science, by which men might plan their progress.

Voltaire, a more skeptical mind than Condorcet, had worked as hard as anyone to promote a world view consonant with Newtonian science. But he also understood the power of historical explanations. He felt driven to criticize his contemporaries who thought that everything could be explained scientifically or by philosophical constructs. He was very aware of the dilemma that the strange vicissitudes of human life, even if they were perversions of the life that should be, were nonetheless facts. The past could be explained only by telling its story. No simple rational proposition could explain why a Turkish Sultan, like Mohammed II, came to rule in Constantine the Great's city, or why the Spaniards were not ruling in Amsterdam. Voltaire used a sober historical mentality to attack cherished beliefs. How great a leader of men was Moses when the historical evidence suggested that he could not find his way out of forty square miles of desert in less than forty years? Voltaire noticed that the English had made their island inhabitable by wiping out all wolves and bears. What would happen to a cherished standing belief in a fixed creation, a permanent Great Chain of Being, if all other nations were to follow the English example? A man had to resort to history to deal with the implications of time on human affairs.

The evidence of history pointed strongly to the vast diversity in human reality, a view that potentially had the power to relativize knowledge. This new outlook can be partially seen in England, and in Germany, especially toward the end of the century, when the fascination with the singular and unique aspect of all reality became wedded to a genetic mode of understanding. In the French Enlightenment, which dominated so much of the century by its powerful intellectual positions, the awareness of the manifold richness and perplexing complexity of reality was still reined in by a vigorous tendency to discover the uniform laws and stable patterns beneath all such diversity. The belief in absolute norms, often in natural-law tenets, in the virtue of uniformity, in ideal patterns, and in models of perfection was in many thinkers a good deal stronger than their willingness to attribute prime value to unique specificity and manifold diversity. Beneath all the rich creations of the law it ought to be possible to discern a permanent spirit of the laws. And amid all the unsuccessful and the partially successful human attempts to create civilized life it ought to be possible to find the one true model of a perfect civilization.

# 12

# Jean-Jacques Rousseau: A Self Confronts the World

Western man's growing awareness of the historical dimension of life also expressed itself in an increasing recognition of society as the great human variable. As life came to be seen as a process, men also moved away from a static view of the social order as a fixed fact and function within the great natural order of things. Since the waning of the Middle Ages diverse processes of secularization had eroded the belief that society was the inevitable God-willed condition willingly accepted by a good pilgrim on his passage through this world. By the eighteenth century such secularization had proceeded to the point where a growing number of Europeans found it impossible to conserve any part of the older providential view. The Heavens, in their infinite spaciousness and eternal silence, gave no answers to the human whys and wherefores. Earthbound man faced an earthly life as the only one to be had. Such a life would have meaning only if man endowed it with meaning. Voltaire, the spokesman for many aspects of the new world view, saw this meaning in man's cultivation of a decent civilized existence. Whatever else the Enlightenment was, it surely was also the moment when Western man, for the first time since antiquity, fully faced up to the tremendous task of justifying his existence by creating a secular civilization.

In this climate of opinion, society seemed to be a matter of human will and intention. Man was the maker and the breaker of social institutions. The little demiurge made his own world, either by contracting with others on a common goal, or by seeking to form a social world to fit his nature. The older belief in man's original sin had checked exaggerated ideas about man-made progress; an ineradicable defect in human nature stood forever in the way of perfection. When men lost the sense of their sinful inadequacy they thought they might be destined to progress to a state where the ideal social realities could guarantee an ideal life. In "society-building," man seemed to have a wand for bringing about paradise. Some saw a promise, so great that it was surely pointing toward impending perfection, in the great advance Europeans had made beyond the barbarism still engulfing so much of mankind. But there was a powerful dissenter from this view: Rousseau. Though he often stood on the same ground as his enlightened colleagues, he thought radically different thoughts on how much value the present civilization had. Man needed a decent society, but surely only very little civilization. Indeed, to Rousseau, the present society and civilization had become man's worst enemy and his greatest problem.

When this great questioner of society, and even more of civilization, turned autobiographer, he was destined to view his remarkable life as an exemplification of the problematic encounter between man and society. The autobiography became a link in his system of reflections and teachings; in one sense it is the thread tying the diverse parts of his vision together.

Rousseau's *Confessions* are of particular value for this study because Rousseau evokes one of the key questions of the autobiographic venture in such an exemplary manner: how should the relation between the self-reflecting self and the world be conceived? Can a human being have a viable conception of self when its encounter with the world is experienced as a hostile one? Does the notion of individuality make sense when it is not conceived as the fruitful interaction of a self and its world? When one accepts one's own personality as a valuable thing deserving of cultivation, must one not also accept with trust and even love whatever constitutes "one's own world"? These problems do not arise for the first time in Rousseau: they have accompanied us throughout this study. How men conceive of the interplay between an I and its world has been a factor in all self-presentations. But in Rousseau this problem constitutes the key issue of his autobiographic awareness.

In their classical formulations, Rousseau in the *Confessions* and Goethe in *Dichtung and Wahrheit* circumscribe the central problem in our commitment to the notion of individuality. To struggle with the two greatest modern autobiographies is the most rewarding way of exploring our subject. But it is a wrestling with two geniuses, undertaken with some hesitation. Both writers have dimensions and complexities (not unlike Augustine and Montaigne) that cannot adequately be dealt with in the inevitable compression of these chapters. Rousseau has proven himself to be so recalcitrant to a unified interpretation that in every generation of Rousseau scholars someone had to exclaim: but there must be some ultimate coherence![1] The *Confessions* suggest that Rousseau himself believed in such coherence, and it is this unifying thread that is so crucial to any study of autobiographic self-awareness.

Rousseau came to write autobiographic books under trying circumstances. The *Confessions* were written between December 1764 and December 1770. These years were the most deeply perturbed period of his life. He seemed to belong nowhere. When officials were not chasing him from his latest abode, his own fears and distrust of his fellow men drove him from refuge to refuge. Serenity had rarely been his good fortune, but a very special curse seemed to hang over these years. The miseries of the sixties were perhaps even heightened by the fact that the past decade had been filled with enormous achievements. The years between October 1749 and the middle of 1762 had not been tranquil; they had been tumultuous. But this central segment of Rousseau's manhood, from his thirty-seventh to his fiftieth year, had been a period of exceptional productivity, yielding books destined to change the life of Western man. Late in 1749, he had formed his vision of what he had to do as a writer. First he tried to give expression to this vision in the two discourses, one on the arts and sciences, and one on the problem of inequality. Then, in incredibly rapid succession, came the three master works *La Nouvelle Héloïse*, the *Social Contract*, and *Emile*. Even the deeply disturbing break with Madame d'Epinay and Baron Grimm, which had driven him from the beloved retreat at the Ermitage into his resettlement on the Luxembourg estate at Montmorency, had not broken the productive fever. But the official condemnation of *Emile* and the *Social Contract*, and the necessary flight from France during the early summer of 1762, had completely uprooted him.

It seemed to Rousseau that his reluctant choice of a role as reformer and writer had turned the world against him. His hometown of Geneva was closed to him, and his badly tempered *Lettres écrites de la Montagne* led to a complete break with the leading circles of Geneva. "It is as if, for me, Geneva no longer existed."[2] Plans for going to Corsica as a sort of Solonic legislator had evaporated. The best available refuge was in the Prussian enclave at Neuchâtel, in the Swiss Jura. With Thérèse, Rousseau settled there in the Val de Traverse at Motiers, where he was temporarily protected by its remarkable governor, George Keith, the Scottish marshal in Prussian service. But Rousseau, who thought of himself as a man of the people, living with a true daughter of the people, did not manage to come to a living accommodation with his neighbors in

Motiers. Difficulties arose with the Protestant consistory and its ministers. Rousseau, now usually attired in the exotic Armenian dress which gave him relief from the pains of the catheters and the urinary ailment that had already plagued him for a long time, remained an odd man out. In the summer nights of 1765, his house was stoned several times. Once again he went in search of a suitable exile. Finally he thought he had found the place where he might eventually die, out on the small island of St. Pierre in the lake of Biel. But after a short month, the Council of Bern chased him from there as well. Only now did he fall back on older plans of seeking refuge in the British Isles. During January 1766, in David Hume's company, he passed over to England.

At the very end of 1764, Rousseau had meanwhile received a copy of an anonymous pamphlet answering the charges he had leveled against Geneva in the *Lettres écrites de la Montagne.* He labored under the illusion that the pamphlet *Sentiment des citoyens* had been written by the same Genevan minister, Jacob Vernes, who had annoyed Rousseau in 1762 by asking him to disavow the authorship of the "profession of Faith of the Savoyard Vicar."[3] Actually the pamphlet had come from the pen of the mightiest and the most dangerous of all propagandists, Voltaire, who had learned Rousseau's most haunting secret. Voltaire had long since been convinced that Rousseau was an outright fool, even a dangerous one. "On a pitié d'un fou ...," but then, without pity, Voltaire hit Rousseau where it had to hurt most. "We must admit blushingly and with pain that this is a man, who, marked dreadfully by his own debaucheries and dressed like a circus clown, drags with him from village to village, over every mountain, the luckless woman [Thérèse] whose old mother died because of him, and whose children he left at the door of an orphanage, rejecting the kind offer of a charitable person to take care of them, abjuring all natural sentiments, just as he has stripped himself of those toward honor and religion.... Such is he who dares give advice to our citizens ...! Such a one speaks of the duties of society."[4] Rousseau had told this secret of the five exposed infants to very few intimates; here it appeared now in a widely distributed vicious pamphlet. The image of the virtuous reformer of the past fifteen years seemed about to be destroyed. Rousseau clearly understood: it was best that he tell his own story.

So the little pamphlet, on the very last day of the year 1764, made Rousseau return to older plans of writing his autobiography. Exactly three years earlier, his Dutch pubisher Rey had asked him to append it to the new edition of the *Oeuvres diverses.* The four self-revealing letters to the French censor Malesherbes had been autobiography *in nuce*.[5] At one point, difficult to date precisely, Rousseau had tried his hand at writing a self-portrait (*Mon portrait*).[6] But mere portraiture surely could not equal the fuller life history of a man who knew himself to be innocent. More recently Rousseau had set out several times to visit the regions of his youth, but he had always interrupted the trips; yet the planning had stirred memories of a better world that stimulated his pen. The accusations of the *Sentiment des citoyens* could best be countered by attempts to show how this man had come to be what he was. By the last day of 1764, Rousseau was resolved to write confessions showing a man *intus et in cute*,[7] as he was and had been in all his complex truth. When Rousseau began this work he hoped that posterity would come to understand him and even to love him once the veils were lifted from his troubled life.[8]

The year 1765 was the year of the flight from Motiers and St. Pierre and finally the departure for England. The writing of the *Confessions* had not advanced much. The bulk of the first six books was written during the months from March 1766 to May 1767 at Wooton, in Derbyshire, despite Rousseau's inner agitation over that "infernal business" with Hume and the matter of a royal pension. He grew more suspicious that Jean-Jacques was becoming the victim of a conspiracy. In 1767, he abruptly left England and resettled secretly in France at the Château Trye, owned by his protector the Prince de Conti. He gained no greater inner peace, and at times his suspiciousness totally absorbed him. But Rousseau, now hidden as Jean Joseph Renou, was able somehow to complete Book 6, thus bringing his life's story to the permanent departure from Les Charmettes, that long-remembered paradise of his youth.

The next two years were a dreadfully confused period, as Rousseau wandered about in the southwestern part of France around Grenoble. His biographer fittingly entitles the chapter on these years "The Shattered Consciousness." The fits of madness over the suspected conspiracy grew worse. And yet, his very obsession aroused Rousseau to such a burst of activity that he almost completed the *Confessions*, certainly Books 7 to 11, and probably also most of Book 12. By December 1770, the book had attained its final form, bringing the story down to the moment of departure for England. Rousseau, again under his true name, had returned to Paris in June 1770 and stayed there quietly in a small apartment until 1778. His deep urge for self-justification, and the frantic desire to break out of the conspiratorial nets in which he believed himself to be trapped—the very same forces that had driven him to resume the *Confessions*—impelled him to produce further autobiographic writings. In between his music copying and botanical field trips, he wrote three long dialogues, *Rousseau juge de Jean-Jacques*. He formally wished to deposit these into God's hands by placing them on the altar of Notre Dame. But when he tried to do this on February 24, 1776, he found himself unexpectedly cut off from the altar by a closed grillwork which he had not noticed on previous reconnoiters. This blow was at first terrible—even God seemed to reject his explanations. Its impact drove him out into the streets where he handed out a proclamation to any of the incredulous passers-by upon whom he could press a copy.[9] But after this extraordinary episode, a greater measure of inner peace must have come to Rousseau. Dark shadows continued to cover his mind; the strong feeling that he was a human outcast never left him. But the sensitive beauty of the *Rêveries du promeneur solitaire*, written between the fall of 1776 and the early spring of 1778, suggests a mind that, partially at least, was coming to peace with itself and the world of nature. In May 1778, Rousseau and Thérèse accepted the hospitality of the Marquis de Girardin to stay at his estate at Ermenonville. There, on July 2, 1778, Rousseau died.

During the last fifteen years of his life Rousseau had thus turned most of his writing toward the autobiographic genre. How did he conceive of the autobiographic task?

The key work is the *Confessions*, a rich book with many problems, which reflects the author's current self-conception. If one reads the letters written at the time of some of the episodes reported in the *Confessions*, the earlier writings often read very differently. Modern scholars have shown that certain key scenes in the *Confessions* are distorted when they are contrasted to the historical reconstruction from other evidence.[10] But if one takes the self-conception presented as "autobiographic truth," then Rousseau's intentions as autobiographer must be understood before one turns to an assessment of the self-characterization he presented.

By his choice of title Rousseau evokes comparison with the Augustinian confessional model. But in the first sentence, whichever of the two different preambles one takes, Rousseau seems to deny the validity of any comparison. He was convinced he had written a totally unique work. Such a truthful portrait of a man has never existed before and will never exist again. Yet, the comparison is inviting, if to show only how much the world has changed from Augustine to Rousseau.[11] Rousseau is genuinely involved in the activity of confessing. But while

Augustine, befitting a God-centered view, confesses his soul to God and only incidentally to his fellow men, Rousseau, as a measure of the degree to which the world had become secularized, has nothing to confess to God, but everything to his fellow men. While God, as so often in Rousseau, is witness to the act, His function is restricted to that of arbiter in Rousseau's quarrels with his fellow men. Rousseau has the inner certainty that God is on his side. Augustine confessed sins; his soul thus gained a measure of relief; but he never meant to put more stress on the *confessio peccati* than on the *confessio laudis*, praising his God for His mercy. His presence before God made him scrupulously honest with himself. Rousseau indeed made a cult of truthfulness; he repeatedly assures his reader that he will reveal more about himself, many more seemingly despicable acts, than any man before or after him.[12] But he never seems to be driven to such veracity by heeding the watchful eye and ear of God.

Rousseau gains relief from revealing the sins he had secreted away in his own consciousness; in one instance, recounting the famous episode when he falsely accused the innocent servant girl Marion of a crime he himself had committed in stealing a velvet ribbon, he even states that his desire to rid himself of this horrible memory greatly contributed to the resolution to write the *Confessions*.[13] But whenever Rousseau confesses a sin, he adds an element missing in Augustine. He first confesses an act as a despicable one. He next wishes to be credited for telling such bad things about himself. And then inevitably comes an explanation making it clear that Rousseau does not hold himself responsible for the act. When Augustine confesses sins, he knows himself to be sinful and in dire need of divine mercy. In his heart of hearts Rousseau knows himself to be good. He dares his fellow men to judge him without thereby judging themselves: "And let any one who dares, say 'I was better than this man there' " (p. 5). He is certain that by revealing his secrets he will lead others to the truths of his heart; when they can thus understand him, they will also love him.[14] Confession thus merges with self-justification.

Augustine's psalmodic *confessio laudis* became in Rousseau's version *apologia pro vita sua*. Augustine was preoccupied with the right relation between his soul and the infinity of God; his book had to be *exercitatio animi*, the constant self-testing, searching, and conditioning of a soul and mind trying to find their way back to God's loving acceptance. Rousseau had no problem with God or with Nature; his quarrel was with Society. Secularized man, now without a sense of original sin, had to justify himself to his equals. He also wanted love, but he wanted the love of men. Confession to a higher Being had totally lost its meaning. Rousseau very intensely experienced the presence of evil, and he needed new formulations, in most ways untried ones, to account for it. The central human problem of theodicy, an explanation of the origin of evil and the justice of God in tolerating it, a problem as old as man, as new as each individual effort of coping with it, came to lie at the very heart of the *Confessions*.

To meet his new task, the writer has to find a new form. Neither the form nor the literary frame which Augustine and others had been able to use for their self-revelations could serve Rousseau. When preoccupied with the question of an autobiographer's sincerity, Rousseau briefly speaks of the models presented by Montaigne and Cardano; but the former was a model of the "falsely sincere ones," and the latter was too crazy.[15] Rousseau knows instinctively that self-portraiture or topical self-analysis cannot adequately serve him. He somehow understood that he could only persuade men of his case by telling the story of his soul struggling with the concrete circumstances it was condemned to experience. At times he was aware that the artistic solution of the task was difficult; he hurriedly leaves the reader with the admonition: here are my facts, you must do the work of relating and interpreting them.[16] The basic form had to be a story form. For Rousseau could justify himself only by showing that a truly moral man had lived continuously throughout all the strange and deplorable turns of his life.

As a history of a self the *Confessions* are marked by the writer's consciousness that his life had had a most important turning point. Thus the autobiographer had, in part at least, come to understand the over-all structure of his life by reference to a nodal experience. He had gained true insight into the nature and the function of his life during one illuminating moment, which provided the long-sought meaning and interpretation. For Rousseau this turn came on a day early in October 1749, when he walked the chaussée from Paris to Vincennes in order to visit his friend Diderot who was under house arrest in the huge fortress prison. Rousseau later on told the story of that day with wonderful persuasiveness at the beginning of Book 8. Exhausted by the sun, he sat down under a tree, reading by chance of the prize essay contest announced by the Academy of Dijon: Had the progress of the arts and the sciences contributed more to the corruption or to the purification of morals? "In that instance ... I saw another universe and became another man."[17] The reader must take this judgment with some care.

Rousseau often talks about "crucial" turning points in his life. Yet the experience on the road to Vincennes was obviously a special moment with profound implications for the structural pattern of his life.[18]

While to a modern reader the academy question may not seem sufficiently profound to signal a significant turning point, the compact and challenging formulation of the essay question functioned for Rousseau as a catalyst accelerating an intellectual process that forced him to confront a subject for which his preceding struggle with life had prepared him. The issues of this academic question surely cut through to the quick—and in a manner totally different from the intellectual matters that had currently preoccupied him: revolutionizing the system of musical annotation or composing fashionable light opera, for example.[19] For seven years Rousseau had sought to make his way in that sophisticated Parisian world of young intellectuals, musicians, and salons. He had tried to adapt himself to its standards—at least, to the best of his limited fashion. He had sought to "fit in," and still heed somehow the voice of his genius, without clearly understanding it. He had tried to be sociable in a society which always made men like him dependent on prominent ladies and gentlemen. At the very least, the academy question raised doubts as to whether all these efforts at socially acceptable conduct had been worth the effort. Deeper still lay the question as to whether the values this sophisticated world meant him to live by were in accord with the values he had developed in his youth. And on the most fundamental level the question seemed to ask Jean-Jacques to confront his own system of values with that of the social and intellectual world in which he now moved. As the implications of the academy question became gradually clearer, Rousseau had to think through all the problems that had been stirred up in him by his problematic encounters with the world.[20]

Now a distinctively different phase of life opened up. It was unlike his life up to October 1749 or after 1762. Now a man with a vision assumed the role of writer and reformer. Later on Rousseau believed that this role, to which he was not drawn by his nature, ruined his life. Without it, however, nobody nowadays would know much about his existence.

Obviously stimulated by the academy question, he wrote his *First Discourse* as a thought experiment exploring man's strength as a natural, uncivilized, unsocialized creature and the positive and negative effects on him of instruments of civilization. He won the prize—and now he felt compelled to live a life in accord with the position of a thinker who had drawn public attention upon himself by questioning the value of contemporary civilization in such a fundamental fashion. He entered upon the reform period of his life, as he was to call it later when he looked back on it as autobiographer. The controversies surrounding his first major publication, the exchange of views with critics, further sharpened his own views and strengthened his intention to live by his philosophy. So did his next attempt to enter deeper into the problems that had opened up, the second *Discourse on the Origins of Inequality among Men* (1754). He reverted to his Calvinist faith. He gradually sought to free himself from those external influences that he considered falsifications of his life. In 1756, Madame d'Epinay offered him and Thérèse (his partner in a liaison dating back to 1745) residence at the Ermitage, her small country house. There, and then after December 1757, at the Luxembourg estate of Montmorency, the great works were written in the amazingly brief span of five or six years. His life-style at that time separated him from his *philosophe* brethren. His literary skirmishes with them, resulting in such forceful shorter pieces as the *Lettre sur la Providence*[21] and the *Lettre à d'Alembert sur les spectacles*, [22] ever more sharply pointed to the line dividing his own thought from the intellectual mainstream of the Enlightenment.

The grandest of his thought experiments, the *Nouvelle Héloïse*, the *Social Contract*, and the *Emile*, were, if nothing else, attempts to answer the enormous questions evoked by the crisis on the road to Vincennes. What, ideally speaking, would have to be the nature of the smallest social circle of life, the family and the extended household, in order for man's unfalsified natural goodness to also express itself as a social good? What qualifications would men's more extended association in society and state have to meet for the good natural man to perceive in them the instruments for fulfilling his human potential without falsifying it? How could natural man become both moral and a true citizen? And the key question perhaps: how could an educator form the individual human being so that its growth would be natural, so that it could conserve its natural strengths and yet gradually become socialized? Rousseau applied his own characteristic method to these inevitably interrelated questions and tasks: he construed the ideal imaginary conditions that could lead to the desired objectives. This repeated quest for the conditions that would make social realities at least bearable required immense labor on the part of a writer who knew himself to be too lazy by nature for such tasks.

These books brought on the catastrophe. They marked Rousseau as a man opposed to unnatural society and civilization. It became a part of the autobiographic problem, however, that Rousseau could not perceive this reason for the estrangement between himself and his world. He instinctively understood that his life as a writer had brought him havoc, but he felt hard put to explain what had gone wrong with his noble urge to reform. So he had to look for other reasons than the nature of his message.

In part Rousseau was right: the questions he had asked could also have been asked by other members of the confraternity of *philosophes*. It was a daring intellectual age, in which daring intellectual questions were raised, though they were usually couched in more sophisticated terms than the cultivated bluntness to which Rousseau felt entitled. In many ways his thought accords with the more common outlook of his age. After all, the enthusiastic acceptance of his great works did not come from a public out of tune with the Enlightenment. And Rousseau was generally so convinced of the basic nobility of his thought that he considered himself as a prophet of self-evident, though alas forgotten, truth. When the government's blows against the *Emile* and the *Social Contract* fell in rapid succession during the summer of 1762, Rousseau's first reaction was to look for the cause in a few very specific passages of his writings that might be considered critical of France. He wondered, too, whether his astonishing life-style as a reformer had perhaps aroused others who were either jealous or convention-ridden against him. As his misfortunes multiplied, partially as the result of his own touchiness and growing suspicions, the wish to understand the reasons for his often intolerable fate led him ever deeper into the morass of suspected conspiracies and evil behind-the-scenes manipulators.

However, another web of reasons more clearly suggests that the specific occasions for conflict after the disastrous summer of 1762 indeed rested in a fundamental confrontation, perhaps the most fundamental conflict imaginable, between man and culture. If Rousseau stood with his age and with the *philosophes* in numerous matters, he stood against them in some very crucial matters as well. As his fellow Genevan, Henri Frédéric Amiel, saw, more than a century ago, on certain key matters Rousseau was in outright conflict with the *philosophes:* "He was for God against d'Holbach, he was for Providence against Voltaire, he was for a soul in man against La Méttrie, he was for moral freedom against Diderot, for disinterested virtue against Helvétius, for spontaneity against Condillac, for the rights of the heart against Maupertuis, against the communism of Morelly."[23] Rousseau vigorously came to

oppose the belief in a steadily progressing civilization in which his contemporaries had placed their trust for human betterment. In some sense
Rousseau is already tied to the romantic reaction against the Enlightenment. But most important: while he participated in some of the work of
the *philosophes*, he opposed much of it by basic misgivings and the full
force of his genius. A large part of his nature and his experience war-
ranted his hostile stance; at least, he thought it did, and this conviction
became an important part of his self-conception and a key to his crucial
self-image as a writer, the very activity on which his fame rests.

The account of the crisis on the road to Vincennes very clearly implies
that Rousseau then and there found his "calling" as a writer. He formed
a vision which he thought to be the self-evident solution to man's basic
problems. His perception of a coherent message, even if it only
gradually grew in detail, set him to work with a prophet's zeal. With the
absolute certainty of his convictions he undertook his mission to
enlighten mankind by his great works. He thought they all involved the
same basic subject, and he spoke of "his system."[24] As the pressures of
the work grew and he perceived the hostile reactions it seemed to evoke,
he cut the scope of some of the planned works. The intended work on
"Political Institutions" became the abbreviated *Social Contract*. He gave
up entirely the plans for a "Morals of Sensibility" which very well might
have been a literary milestone. Meanwhile he strove to buttress the
writer's mission by reforming his personal life-style so that the verbal
message would be reinforced by the model of a philosopher living his
own philosophy. "To gain a hearing I must reconcile my actions to my
principles. . . . I had been good . . . I became virtuous . . . I became indeed what I appeared . . . I was truly transformed" (pp. 416–17). But as
he himself wanted to see the situation (p. 362): this reformed life-style,
more than his literary fame, occasioned the increasing frictions with his
former colleagues and his new patrons. It led to the crisis at the Ermitage. The letters of early 1762 in which he tries to explain himself to the
censor Malesherbes still dwell heavily on the conflicts inherent in his
life-style. But he now persuades himself that a genuine plot is brewing
against his books as well.

The disastrous turn of events that came in the summer of 1762 radically changed Rousseau's conception of his life and his tasks. He did not
much change his adopted life-style, but he now assigned it a different
function. He adhered to it even in his lonely life because it had come to
suit his personal taste, but he no longer felt he needed to serve as an
example. Rejected by the social world around him, he felt restored to

nature, the true realm for his natural self. "Circumstances put an end [to my reform] and restored me to Nature, out of whose realm I had been trying to soar" (p. 417). By his own choice he abdicated the role of the reforming writer. Rousseau published more after 1762, but aside from the autobiographic writings, his later works were totally different from those of the reform period. The *Lettres écrites de la Montagne* (1764) were polemics occasioned by a specific situation; the *Considérations sur le gouvernement de Pologne* (1771–72) were in a sense a solicited work; and the *Dictionnaire de musique* (1767) and the *Dictionnaire des termes d'usage en botanique* (for which he wrote the introduction in 1774) resulted from his music copying (by which he earned a meager support) and his studies of plants in the woods. He had once given himself to the great task of teaching men how they might produce a better society by remaining true to their nature, but this subject did not occupy him after 1762. The more distance he gained from it, the more it seemed to him that a perverse fate had afterward readmitted him to the life for which nature had meant him. The experience on the road to Vincennes burdened him with a task he had not really wanted and which conflicted with his nature. Only the inspiration of his vision had enabled him to be the writer. By renouncing the role of the author, *auteur presque malgré moi*,[25] Rousseau gave himself back to himself.[26]

From this point of view the *Confessions* are fully imprinted with the curve which Rousseau perceived in his life. His life had been composed of blocks of different realities. The young Rousseau, unaffected by the vision of a specific life task, was at a crucial moment thrust into it; his very success called forth forces in his surrounding world that drove him back again upon a life he now perceived as the fitting one for his nature, a life he never should have abandoned. Life had thus been cut by two caesuras. The middle block carved out in this way had placed him in the limelight.

In one sense the *Confessions* had to explain this strange turn in his life and correct the impressions others had formed of a publicly maligned figure. Rousseau needed to reveal his true self as only he could know and reveal it. Together with these justificatory functions another should be considered, admittedly a much more speculative one. Rousseau had planned to include in the system of his works a book on "Morals of Sensibility." When he speaks of it in the *Confessions* he says: "I had derived the idea for it from some observations made on myself . . . the book I would write would be truly useful to mankind, indeed one of the most useful to present. . . . It was meant to trace the causes explaining why men were in the course of their lives so often unlike themselves. ... Looking within myself and seeking the cause in others.... But it remained unwritten.... Distractions of which the cause will soon be learned prevented me from occupying myself with it and it will also become clear what the fate of my outline was which is more closely connected with my own fate than may appear."[27] When Rousseau, a hundred pages later, reports his resolve to end his writing career, he remarks that he abandoned the "Morals of Sensibility" altogether. But in the paragraph immediately following, he speaks of his intention to write the *Confessions:* "and I resolved to make it a unique work by virtue of its unparalleled veracity so that in one instance at least one might see a man as he was inside" (pp. 516–17).

The same intention was stressed in both preambles to the *Confessions,* the first one adding that thus for the first time men, who until now could know only themselves, might have for comparative reference the truthful self presented by this man.[28] In a sense then, the *Confessions* enabled Rousseau to present much of the subject matter once intended for the "Morals of Sensibility." He had substituted a concretely detailed description of his own inner moral life for a more theoretical synthesis. When the *Confessions* and the other autobiographical writings are assigned such a function, then, they are also part of his system. They are the parts which show how his philosophy rested on his experience and was fed by his own life.

With so many diverse functions, the *Confessions* was bound to be a many-layered book. Rousseau wanted to correct rumors about deeds that would be forgiven only when his intentions were understood. The book was meant to present the true Rousseau so that the truth about the man might accompany the truths of the works which had made his name destined to live forever. The image of the man should illuminate the image of the writer, and the correctly understood writer could then further illuminate the man. Although the book is so different from Cardano's or Montaigne's, like most autobiographic writing, the *Confessions* would inevitably aid this writer too in coming to understand more of the dark mysteries of his own character. Rousseau was not all that certain of himself. The very last work, the *Rêveries,* shows that he continued to ask himself about himself: "Que suis-je moi-même? Voilà ce qui me resta à chercher."[29] The closer he came to the writing of Books 7–9, the more the nightmare of the suspected conspiracy closed in upon him. As the course of his life became less intelligible to himself, he hoped the book would provide the clues to others from which they, perhaps, might be able to discover how the curse of the conspiracy could be lifted. Rousseau certainly intended to supply the apology for the life of a man deeply convinced that, despite all false appearances, he was a good man always working for the best interests of mankind. The autobiography also had to establish its author as a reformer. It had an intensely didactic purpose, almost the function of a scientific work: take this one unique model you are being given by a truly sincere man so that you may understand yourself better through the comparison. It would have required an even greater artist than Rousseau to give artistic unity to so many diverse tasks, and to succeed under conditions that were as haunting as those that shaped Rousseau's life after 1762

Two levels of meaning will be of special interest here. On one level, this work is the self-representation of a man, deeply conscious of his unique individuality, desiring to be understood in his very own specificity. On another level, still more important to Rousseau, this is a book of lessons. The man who revealed himself in this book is not an oddity unto himself, but is the very man destined to teach other men how to fulfill the human potential by grasping the chance to be their natural selves. But the wish to be an individuality *and* a general model for man will inevitably subject an author to unbearable tension. Yet, this strange genius sought to forge a unity that encompassed both objectives, and with their tensions, in his life and work.

Rousseau had a highly developed sense of his uniqueness. He tells his readers at the very outset that he is unlike anyone else he has seen. Nature broke the molds in which she made him. "I would prefer being forgotten by the entire human race than being looked upon as an ordinary man."[30] He thought that his "position was without parallel; since the world began there never was another case"[31] like his own. At one point he declared that he would have to invent a new language for presenting his unique sentiments.[32] Others had made the repeated mistake of judging him, who was so different, by their own corrupt standards. He sent his first great writing, *Discourse on the Arts and Sciences*, into the world under a motto stressing that others take him for a barbarian simply because they do not understand him. He often uses a tone of pride in stressing this singularity, but he also despaired over it. "Ah! Moultou!" he wrote to his Genevan confidant, "Providence has erred; why did it decree that I should be born among men, yet made of different species from the rest of mankind?"[33] In the first promenade of the *Rêveries* Rousseau is haunted by being alone on the earth, without brother or near ones, living as if on a strange planet.[34] There were profound reasons for this ambivalence toward his uniqueness. But Rousseau could not render the story of his remarkable life without making it the story of an incomparable individual.

The first six books of the *Confessions*, written at Wooton and Château Trye, deal with the first thirty years of his life. These artistically unified books of his youth are the most immediate evidence that Rousseau could explain himself only by narrating his life: "to know me in my later years it is necessary to have known me in my youth" (p. 174). He was the first among the great autobiographers who took childhood and youth seriously as the formative phases in a man's life. He had a most sensitive understanding of childhood, perceiving that this age had to be understood on its very own terms. As an educational writer, he could translate this into a revolutionary program of education. That he never lost his childhood remained fateful for his outlook on life. "Although in certain respects I have been a man since birth, I was for a long time, and still am, a child in so many others" (p. 174; cf. also p. 62). By drawing attention to the details of his own life, he was the first to suggest the way in which a personality in its essential traits is formed by the time it reaches the age of twenty-five. Later autobiographers restricted their accounts entirely to this early formative phase as if to say: and what beyond this point might be of true importance for understanding me? To the end Rousseau cherished some of the moments of his youth; they sustained him in times of difficulty and gave him the texts for the lesson he meant to preach. And yet he says that "in certain respects I have been a man since birth." He could never view his young life as a regular or modular one; it radically departed from the normative youth and adolescence he drew in the *Emile*. The exclamation with which he repeatedly concludes scenes in the first six books is a key to the theme of his entire account: if only at this point things had developed differently, I might have been spared the irregularities of my existence!

The man who belonged nowhere, who dreamt so many fine dreams about true citizenship, reports with pride that he was born in 1712 in Geneva of a *Citoyen* (spelled in capitals) and a *Citoyenne*. His father had to leave Geneva in 1722 and resettled in Noyon. Jean-Jacques lived in Geneva for only fourteen years, but it remained, despite the disappointments of his later conflicts with the city, the focus of his political dreams. By idealizing this small polis, and reinforcing it by images of polis life drawn from ancient authors, this eternal outsider saw Geneva as the home in the distance to which he could point with pride and through which he could blunt the painful awareness of being a rootless bastard of humanity. He had a moral earnestness, an almost humorless seriousness, that may very well have been shaped by the life-style of that Calvinistic center. That his pride of citizenship went along with pride in lower-class descent may have made it particularly important; it was after all a psychic trump card to be played amid aristocratic and upper bourgeois Frenchmen who had no sense of active citizenship.

"My birth was the first of my misfortunes" (p. 7). This statement was for Rousseau no affectation of world-weariness, but a reflection of a real problem. His birth cost his mother's life; his father never let him forget it. Rousseau does not make much of the motif subsequently; but how can a life be free of a fundamental sense of guilt when it has such an awareness of its origins? From his parents he inherited a sensitive heart, "the cause of all the misfortunes of my life"—but surely also the source of his great accomplishments. He had, as he often says, an expansive soul, apt to flow over into its surroundings, as it tried to make the world around him one with himself. He longed for acceptance by humans in return. "My strongest desire was to be loved by everyone who came near me" (p. 14). Meanwhile he was not subjected to any coherent or disciplined education. His father's tastes provided the early intellectual stimulation, and he was introduced to many important books, especially those of his beloved Plutarch. But his father's habits also endangered him for the rest of his life: together they read sentimental novels, staying up through the night, a seven-year-old child and a father who knew himself to be a bigger child yet than his son. "I had grasped nothing; I had sensed everything ... giving me the most bizarre and romanesque notions of which neither experience nor reflection has ever been able to cure me" (p. 8). When Isaac Rousseau could no longer take care of the boy or the household, Jean-Jacques made his first acquaintance with rural life at Bossey outside of Geneva. He remembered it always as a free, joyous life of friendship and play in a bucolic setting.

But here Rousseau's account also begins to turn to the first problematic encounters with society. He becomes vaguely aware of his complex sexual stirrings, and he makes much of the mixture of pain and pleasure he experienced when being beaten by a woman. He is unjustly punished for an offense he did not commit; his pulse races at the memory of the affair of the broken comb even fifty years later. "There ended the serenity of my childhood. From that moment on I have been unable to enjoy pure happiness ... the vices of our years began to corrupt our innocence" (pp. 20–21). An unhappy apprenticeship to a tyrannical master engraver turned Rousseau to a state of silent rebellion in which he began to steal, mainly foodstuffs. At almost the age of sixteen he had gone for a walk one day outside the city gates; upon returning he found to his utter horror that an over-eager official had closed the gates and drawn up the bridge too early. Rousseau felt himself locked out from his city. He dramatically turns the event into a major turning point in his life by wandering away for good from Geneva. He ends his later reflections on the scene with words and feelings that are purest Rousseau: what would life have been like had I had a better master? All I wanted was the chance for a calm and uneventful existence as a Genevan citizen, "a life spent in the uniform pursuit of a trade ... in a society after my own heart. I should have been a good Christian, a good citizen, a good father, a good friend, a good workman, a good man in every respect" (p. 43). If only reality could have been different.

In the concrete experiences of his earliest life in Book 1, Rousseau most skillfully placed before the reader the main traits of the peculiar hero of all the books of the *Confessions*. A highly sensitive boy, forever rating the stirrings of his heart above all else, a strong imaginative mind filled with everlasting dreams about castles in Spain, a human being forever prepared to move from the real world into its idealization. He depicts a youth wanting friends and hungering to be loved, timid, often awkward and submissive, aware already of a peculiar sexuality, always internally impeded from reaching out for love. He portrays an autodidact, never systematically trained in anything nor able to derive the benefits of disciplined labor, one who prefers to work only when his moods impel him to some activity, one who lacks the sureness of genuine education, but is forever convinced of his own convictions. The essential marks are on the personality, grafted onto it like the cuttings in the bark of a young tree that enlarge with growth, expanding and reinforcing all the tendencies during the strangely adventurous life that was to come.

The story line of the next few books is almost that of a picaresque novel. It is the story of a youth, rarely settled for long, wandering about in search of life and himself. Once outside Geneva, he was drawn into the complicated machinery of Counter-Reformation Catholicism which in that region had its heart set on bringing errant Calvinists back into the fold (as we saw in the earlier case of Madame Guyon). Rousseau thus became the son, friend, lover, and admirer of Madame de Warens, a woman whom only a highly imaginative novelist could have invented— if Rousseau had not first rendered her for the world. Before he was allowed to settle in her home, he was sent off across the Alps to Turin so that there he might be retrained enough to be a good Catholic. The task was undertaken in a cloister for boys that was hardly conducive to making the true religious out of the young. After that, he sought to make his way as best as he could, as clerk, servant, or secretary. He does not succeed in anything for very long. Here and there he falls in love without really knowing what to do with his sexuality.

And yet, as Rousseau reports it, amid utterly precarious conditions that easily could have broken any sensitive soul, he retained the purity of his heart. He found a mentor for his moral life in the Abbé Gaime, whom he later immortalized in the figure of the Savoyard Vicar. This man "planted a seed of virtue and religion in my heart which has never been choked and which merely needed the tending of a more beloved hand to produce fruit" (p. 92). Many of the scenes depicting his north Italian wanderings set up this complex juxtaposition: a totally insecure existence, maintained by servile labor, and yet an inner independence, slippery temptations to get involved with married women and girls above his station, anxious moments of exhibitionism, small thefts—a being enveloped by a world where the mere struggle for existence brings out all the cruder instincts, and yet a youth continuing to dream noble dreams and somehow holding on to what he later always saw as his self-sustaining moral sensibility. But this life ends rather abruptly, just as it had begun. Joining another youth, Rousseau sets out on new wanderings, fully expecting to make a living by exhibiting a toy fountain.

When the fountain broke, Rousseau took the way back to Annecy and to Madame de Warens. For about a dozen years, from eighteen to thirty-one, life with this extraordinary woman stood at the center of his adolescence and early manhood. From the distance of memory, he saw her household at Chambéry and above all the pastoral idyll of Les Charmettes as the real anchorage in his restless life. With her he had the human relation he was ever given to idealize: two souls communing without many words, preferably in the all-conducive setting of a friendly nature. In a way she sought to form him or, at least, she gave him the opportunity to follow his own instincts in reading, experimenting, learning, and dreaming. In a free autodidact fashion he laid up there that basic store of knowledge, impressions, skills, and ideas on which he drew later on. In retrospect, the fine moments of that period seemed to entitle him to say: yes, indeed, I have lived!

And yet, his own descriptions of the idyll make it both a troubled relation and a troubled time. For much of the time it was a *ménage à trois*, a setup for which Rousseau had a certain liking as long as he did not feel threatened. He felt secure with the older Claude Anet, but when the young robust Wintzenried took Anet's place, Rousseau could no longer bear it. How could he live as a stranger in the house of his own mother? (p. 92; cf. also p. 270). Even before this, the idyll was always endangered by Madame's total inability to manage her financial affairs. One scheme after another was tried to set up Rousseau in a career that would bring in some funds. None worked out, none was to the liking of a young man permitted to indulge his own fancies. He dabbled in chemistry—as did she with her endless schemes to invent a cure-all salve—until he almost blinded himself. Above all he dabbled in music. Without any real training, but with obvious talent, he gave music lessons. He gives us one unforgettable scene in which he is trying to conduct an orchestra although he was unable to "score the simplest drinking song.... Never in all the history of French opera was there to be heard such a discordant row" (pp. 148–49). However idyllic his life at Les Charmettes was, several times Rousseau suffered from serious illness.

Though his life now seemed quiet and settled, this was also a period of strange wandering about. Twice Rousseau accompanied some of Madame's servants to their far-off homes. On one of these trips he committed one of his extraordinary moral lapses when he abandoned the old servant Le Maistre in the streets of Lyons while the man had an epileptic fit. Upon his return to Les Charmettes, Rousseau found that Madame de Warens had left for an unexplained trip to Paris; so Rousseau set out on a series of strange adventures, living for a short while as a music teacher, then becoming the assistant of a fake Archimandrite priest who collected money for restoring the Holy Sepulcher, and finally making a useless trip to Paris in the company of a Swiss colonel. In search of romance, he went on a trip with two charming young ladies. He recounted the whole outing as an enchanting experience, but then confesses, "I did not exactly know what I wanted from these two charming girls" (p. 138). When he traveled to Montpellier to see a doctor, he got involved on the coach with a sensuous older woman to whom he passed himself off as a Scottish Jacobite emigrant called Dudding; but when the play threatened to become earnest, he again ran. When he returned to Les Charmettes, he found that the young Wintzenried had joined the household. Unable to put up with this competitor, he left for Lyons to earn a living as a tutor in the Mably home, where he made his first plans for an educational reform program. He again returned to his Alpine idyll, became seriously ill, but finally made up his mind to go out into the world to make a fortune which he then would lay at "Maman's" feet. The wonder fountain by which he meant to conquer the world this time was a new scheme of musical notation that he had invented.

Rousseau had reached the age of thirty. He had done everything and nothing. He was entirely self-taught. He had enjoyed the perhaps questionable privilege of indulging his wanderlust and dreaming away his young life. What was to be expected when a creature thus prepared, or unprepared, entered the kind of world in which men had to justify their existence?

When Rousseau had reached this point in his story he temporarily closed it there. The turmoil of early 1768 proved totally disabling; Rousseau added nothing to the manuscript. But obviously, the account could not be left here. However much the story of his youth might explain, it had to be understood in relation to, and in juxtaposition to, the subsequent life of the author and reformer. When he resumed the work on his story, after two years of wild migrations in southwestern France, he drew the contrast. "What a different tableau will I now have to develop! After fate had favored my tendencies [*penchans*] for thirty years, it was to oppose them for the next thirty and from this continuous opposition between my situation and my inclinations one will see born enormous mistakes, unheard-of misfortunes as well as all the virtues, except strength of character, which can do credit to adversity" (p. 277). The last six books, a good bit longer than the story of his youth, dwell in essence on the course of events that made Rousseau the famous writer who became a human outcast through his writing and his attempt to lead a model life. It is, in many ways, a heart-rending story, artistically less unified than the previous books, but still filled with descriptive scenes of extraordinary accomplishment. This part of his life also had to be a history of his experience. The concrete details of life and circumstance would mirror a complex and exceptional individuality.

Rousseau entered the world at its very center, the Parisian life of the middle of the eighteenth century. He came with good introductions, and he always found highly placed persons who lent him a hand. For years now we hear very little about "the life for which he was truly meant." Descriptions of nature recede into the background. He had set out to make his way in that world, he desired a glorious name and position, and, all in all, he tried to adapt to the social and cultural game as best as he could. He found no acceptance for his musical scheme, but by and by he gained recognition as a writer on music and as a composer of operas. Diderot entrusted to him the Encyclopedia articles on music. Had it not been for the fame he had gained by the publication of the first *Discourse*, anyone looking at Rousseau's situation prior to 1754 would have concluded that his future lay in his musical talent. His light opera, *Le Devin du village* (1752), brought him a striking success, and he attracted further attention with his startling behavior of not appearing at a royal audience where he might have received a royal pension. He seemed to have merged with that circle of young intellectuals surrounding Diderot, and, at that point, it is hard to conceive of him as a man destined to be an odd man out. A brief interlude had taken him to Venice as secretary to the French ambassador; but this venture had not proven to signal a promising career line, though it did incidentally stimulate his future political thought. The first conception of his intended work on "Political Institutions" goes back to this time. On the whole, the main thrust of some dozen years seems to be in the direction of success as musician and *philosophe*.

But while the story in one way conveys the impression that this life, measured by its successes, was on an upward turn, Rousseau wove into this account much that presaged the troubled conflicts that were to follow. Later he saw the illumination on the road to Vincennes as the dramatic turning point. But since it was really the moment at which he was able to confront his civilization with a clearly conceived critique and plan for reform, this moment of crisis only placed into clearer light a long series of prior experiences and questions that had troubled him. However much Rousseau's ambitions told him to be clever and play the social game, there was a basic part of him that was chafing under its rules, that made him occasionally rebel, or that led him into actions which, in the long run, were to have explosive consequences. "The more I have seen of the world, the less I have been able to conform to its manners" (p. 156).

As he describes his life in Book 7, the book covering his Parisian and his Venetian experience up to 1749, he inserts references to the hidden and open difficulties of living in society. At times he blames his natural penchant toward laziness for his failure to make use of great opportunities coming his way, but often his omissions indicate only that he is disinclined to work at the behest of others and during hours determined by them. He considered himself dull-witted for certain occupations. Each experience of being subject to the commands of others reminds Rousseau that he simply cannot bear such a sense of dependence. He is incensed over the injustice of a superior like his ambassador who will permit him to do all the work but is not willing to grant him the social recognition to which he is entitled by doing his job well. A supercilious

noble misusing both his power and position is always a red flag for
Rousseau. He is forever falling for the offered charms of a lady, only to
be held at a distance when his romantic feelings are awakened. He has
to face his social awkwardness in many situations. He is not good at
small talk or quick repartee; he states bluntly what he feels. He has never
learned the *politesse* so highly valued in the society of his day. And as his
incurable urinary ailment asserts itself with increasing painfulness, his
social awkwardness becomes ever more pronounced. He is best off
alone.

Rousseau's famous letter to Mirabeau, though written at a later time
(1767), summed up the torment that had been building for years.

> I feel myself obliged to talk when I have nothing to say; to
> stay in one place when I would like to walk; to remain seated
> when I would like to stand up ... to eat at times fixed by
> other people, to walk at their pace, to repay their compli-
> ments or sarcastic remarks ... to reason with "reasoners"
> and follow the conceit of wits; to make insipid conversation
> with women; in short to spend the whole day doing those
> things at which I am the least competent ... while being de-
> prived of not only doing those things I should like to do but
> also those that nature and the most pressing needs impose on
> me, in the first place the need to urinate which in my case is
> more pressing and harassing than any other.

What was he supposed to do in a society where you never could get
away from people and servants? "Urinate ... in full view of everybody
and onto some noble, whitestockinged leg?"[35] He felt as if the world of
appearances was closing in on him. He abhorred the society dominated
by *amour-propre*, which he deemed an utter perversion of beneficial self-
love (*amour de soi-même*). He had meanwhile entered upon his relation
with Thérèse Le Vasseur, enjoying her company but beginning to suffer
from her greedy family. The children were coming, and not knowing
what to do or fully understanding what he was doing, he met the situation by the convenience of placing the nameless infants one after the
other, five in all, at the door of the orphanage. When one reads all these
things spread out through the accounts of his growing success as a
musician and a writer, it is as if one hears a time bomb ticking.

The long Books 7 to 11 deal with the thirteen years from 1749 to 1762,
the time in which Rousseau became the famous writer and reformer.
During this phase he comes to stand out more and more in his uniqueness. In the earlier years of this period, say until 1754, he continued to

live, on the whole, in the style of the preceding years. His greatest musical successes came during that time, as did the fame brought to him by the first *Discourse*. As the consequences of his own thought became clearer to himself, and as his "system" took hold of his mind, he grew determined to fit his life to his thought.

The reform had strange aspects. While the abandoning of the first child had been presented as the act of a man who too readily adapts to the less scrupulous mores of his surroundings, the second instance of the same act is reported almost glibly: "In the following year the same inconvenience was removed by the same expedient."[36] When he comes to report the abandoning of the third child in 1751, he indulges in a philosophical *raisonnement* as to why the children would be better off being educated by the state rather than the father. Despite all the basic satisfaction he drew from his relation with that child of the people, Thérèse, he did not deign to marry her until 1768. Despite the importance to him of good and active citizenship, in one way or another he let all the chances to live as a citizen of Geneva drift by and instead paraded his pride in citizenship around only in the distance.

Other aspects of his effort to change were more harmoniously in keeping with his philosophy and his truest penchants. He willingly abandoned the hope of any career that might have made him wealthy, settling down instead to a modest life of music copying (in his later life he copied as many as 11,185 pages of music),[37] and he also earned some money by his writings. He gave up his refined clothes—the forty Venetian silk shirts were stolen anyway by Thérèse's brother. In general, he sought the appearance of a simple man of the people. Resentful of any instrument that imposed discipline on him, he joyfully surrendered his watch: "Heaven be praised, I shall not need to know the time anymore!"[38] He describes his little apartment with its flower boxes in the window as a poor man's idyll. But the really important change came only when some noble sponsors, such as Madame d'Epinay and, later on, the Luxembourgs, offered him a residence in the country. Only there could a fusion with nature occur, an existence for which Rousseau longed with an extraordinary craving.

For Rousseau the essential completion of his efforts at self-reform meant life in the bosom of nature. It worked as the catalyst for his writing; it was the fount that gave him the strength and assuredness to speak to his fellow men about the virtue that welled up in man when he relied on his natural foundations. But even there Rousseau could not escape the most critical problem of all: the ever complicated and often unmanageable relations with his fellow human beings. The relations with his *philosophe* brethren deteriorated steadily. Annoying problems arose over the position of Thérèse's mother in the house. He was forever irritated by the haughty behavior of Madame D'Epinay's servants. And the ties between him and her, and her entire entourage, were broken by a violent explosion of temper after only a year and a half of residing at the Ermitage. He misread others' intentions, he often was irritable because of his ailment, he was suspicious and touchy. His principled desire for personal independence sometimes involved him in the most ridiculous situations. What a dreadful fuss he made over a few partridges sent to him by an admiring nobleman! In the face of "Principle," gracious acceptance of a well-meant kindness seemed out of the question (p. 502).

There were even tensions in his relations with Thérèse, the one loyal human being with whom, on the whole, he managed to live most peacefully. Permitting his expansive heart to commune freely with nature, he was overcome with a longing for the love he thought he had never found. In the process of composing the *Nouvelle Héloïse,* he began to fuse his imaginary and literary life. His dream world, populated by ideal houris of Paradise, became intermingled with his love and admiration for a real woman, Madame d'Houdetot. He became trapped in a disastrously unmanageable situation. She, a married woman talking about her love for another man away on a campaign, listens to Rousseau lying out there in the park at her knees trying to tell her about his love for her! It is bad enough to invent such scenes; Rousseau thought he could live them. Except for short moments, there was no viable way for him to merge his dreams about man with actual human beings. By some extraordinary literary activity he could deposit such dreams in his great works. But the real human world around him collapsed. The condemnation of his books finally brought an end to this whole phase of existence and turned him, with his own assistance, into a human outcast.

Thus Rousseau's autobiography tells the story as Rousseau wanted to see it: an extraordinary story about the extraordinary life of an extraordinary man. No model existed for depicting such a personality; there was no given literary frame in which to place such a life. The history of his experiences was put down in terms of their meaning for him. In this sense the conditions for self-consciously presenting an individuality were fulfilled. But the key question arises: did Rousseau mean to place a positive value on individuality; did he seek to cultivate himself as such?

The answer will lead to some speculations which, at best, can end only in a series of suggestions.

Rousseau had many diverse intentions in writing the *Confessions*. The multitiered objectives and character of the book served him well in portraying a multilayered personality. Beneath the ever-changing and turbulent life of the man of appearances, the part of life most readily visible to others, Rousseau discerned the true Rousseau known only to him—it persisted throughout all the turmoil, though it was hidden behind the impressions of the fluctuating images his figure cast upon the world. The man who had been formed and misformed by the forces of society knew of a true self which had not been dislodged by the idiocies of his fate, or by the pressures of the world responsible for that fate. Others erred in trying to read off his character from his visible conduct in the world. Much that seemed to be singular was singular only in that it so often departed from fashionable norms. Why would nobody question whether these norms were fit for a man? The world always seemed to play a silly and a disastrous game in its eagerness to take appearances for reality. Rousseau felt sure that he was the one man who, beneath a false appearance, had preserved his true nature. He saw himself as a man who, more than anyone else, had somehow succeeded in sustaining this true self by keeping it in close touch with nature, the foundation of all existence. Rousseau knew that he could make others understand this "natural Rousseau" only if he could show them the genuine motions of his heart and of his sentiments, his natural inclinations, and the steadfastness of his conscience. The vision of this true inner man would be his greatest gift to his fellowmen: he alone would point them to the ultimate human reality. Rousseau wrote the *Confessions* so that this man might become visible, so that, for once, men might find in an individualized human truth the path to the general human verities.[39] Only by revealing the truth of his heart could the autobiography perform its other function—to justify Rousseau.

Thus Rousseau clearly implies that his uniqueness, and the value of such uniqueness, was not really to be found in the apparent course of life or in the extraordinarily fascinating individual fate. It lay, rather, in his special ability to remain close to man in his primary natural essence. This gift made him unique in a world of overcivilized beings; it entitled him to an extraordinary role as a preacher offering a new vision of human life. He would serve as the only available standard for others in their own search. But the more he stressed *this* aspect of his uniqueness, the more he pointed also to what he thought to be the common, the truer human element. There was a paradox: the more he presents himself as a unique individuality the more he devalues individuality as a general human object of cultivation.

"From time to time a soul is born whose privilege it is to perpetuate throughout the world the idea of what nature was like in her pure state."[40] Rousseau had no doubt that he was this privileged soul. His heart told him so. If he knew one thing well, it was his sensitive heart. It was his best guide to the truest stirrings within him: genuine love of self and sympathy for other creatures. His heart was the surest link to the order of nature in which his true being rested; it motioned toward oneness with nature, with love, admiration, gratitude for this life-sustaining order. Nature was good, and the heart, as a part of nature, was good. When listening to it with sensitivity, you could not go wrong. And when the heart guided reason, when reason refrained from being merely *raisonnement* and from dictating terms to life, when it was satisfied instead with being the sensitive interpreter of the natural order, when the "heart gave shape to understanding" (p. 123), then, in unison, heart and reason could steer man toward the self-fulfillment that was his by nature. Then love of self and sympathy could be turned into virtue. The unimpeded vision of the good, as nature's law, could function as man's conscience. "Virtue is won by embracing the law with the will, and consists in conformity with its spirit."[41] In this lay man's hope of becoming a virtuous social being while yet remaining true to his own nature. Rousseau's key works are the elaboration of this message.

He supported the same essential vision, moreover, by making the *Confessions* the revelation of this very reality within him. The book is nothing so much as it is a confessing of the truest stirrings of his sensitive heart (by which he never means passion, a negative quantity in his opinion). It is an expression of his need to love and to be loved in return, his need for all-fulfilling, all-trusting friendships, his need for true communion with others. He wishes to be able to read the hearts of his fellow human beings. In return he wants to make his soul transparent to the reader's eye. A man ought "to show his heart upon his face."[42] That throughout the course of life his heart has been "as transparent as a crystal" is, in his view, his finest attribute.[43] He wanted to achieve that ecstasy of unmediated, immediate, unobstructed communing with men, and above all with women, which he, at times, was privileged to have with nature.[44] The richness of Rousseau's descriptions of nature were

not to be found prior to him. They resulted from his full sense of existence during those privileged moments at Les Charmettes, in the woods
around the Ermitage, or on the island of St. Pierre in Lake Biel, when the
peace of nature filled him and his expansive heart could flow back out
and over into nature. At such times he felt himself to be whole, to be a
harmonious part of a larger whole. At such moments he needed nothing, not even words; the fewer, the better. A simple exclamation "Oh!
Oh Nature! Oh Mother!" (pp. 643–44) was the fully adequate expression
of his overflowing heart. No specific activity was needed; there was no
room for any mediator. The self communed with nature from which,
Antaeus-like, it drew its strength.

Why could such immediate happiness not be made to last a lifetime?
Why did men not strive for such crystallike unobstructed reflection in
one another? Why could they not have social communion in which each,
as a part of the whole, would be in harmony with the whole? Why should
appearance and reality not be permitted to be one? The Rousseau for
whom such desires were the reality in which his true self rested is
presented in the *Confessions* as the constant that persisted through all the
turmoil of life. From this point of view the unity of the *Confessions* came
to lie in the unity of his sentiments, the unalterable rightness of his
feelings. "I have but one faithful guide on which I may count: the chain
of sentiments [*la chaine des sentimens*] which have marked the succession
of my being ... I cannot be wrong about what I have felt and what these
sentiments made me do.... The true object of my confessions is to
reveal my inner self [*mon intérieur*] in all the situations of my life....
[For] the history of my soul ... it is sufficient that I reenter myself as I
have done all along" (p. 278). But the problem was that this pure, this
natural Rousseau could rarely dominate the page; it could emerge only
in compressed form in the descriptions of the idyllic scenes of Les
Charmettes, the Ermitage, St. Pierre's island. They might clearly signal
the life for which he had been meant; they represent the moments of
bliss which entitle him to say that he has lived, the moments to which
one might say, like Faust: Stay, last forever! This Rousseau of the heart
was, of course, never really absent, not even in the most despicable
scenes. But most of the time in the *Confessions* the Rousseau of the heart
and the socially misformed Rousseau are made to lie like double layers
over each other. Reality and appearance were not congruent. The vision
of reality was distorted.

Why did his life have to be marked by this cursed discontinuity between appearance and reality? "It has been observed that the majority of

men are often in the course of life so unlike themselves and transform themselves into quite different men." The projected aim of the "Morals of Sensibility" was "to trace the causes of these changes, putting my finger on those that depend on us so that I might show how these might be controlled by us and we thus become better men and surer of ourselves."[45] He thought that the cause of these different states of being was in the modification of our impressions of external reality worked by the interference of our sense organs.

> We are unconsciously affected in our thoughts, in our feelings and also our actions by the impact of these slight changes upon us. . . . From what errors would reason be preserved, and vices could be prevented from being born if one knew how to force these animal functions [*économie animale*] to favor the moral order which they did disturb so often! Climates, seasons, sounds, colors, darkness, light, the elements, the aliments [*les elemens, les alimens*], noise, silence, motion, rest they all act on our machine and consequently on our soul; they all offer us a thousand almost certain means for controlling the sentiments in their origins by which we let ourselves be dominated.

In other words, sentiments are shaped and distorted by external stimuli which you must control if you wish to retain them in their purer form. Even if Rousseau did not hold to this notion in its cruder materialistic form, it still contains the root thought for all his dreams of social reform. It also gives us a clue to an important aspect of the *Confessions*.

Again and again, the confessional account comes to scenes about which Rousseau exclaims: if only this or that had not happened, or if it had been handled differently by those in control of the situation, then my existence could have been different. This element of chance can be seen even in the very early scenes of his life. Too early an exposure to literary romances misdirected his development toward romantic notions about life (p. 8); the wrong kind of punishment awakened the wrong kind of sexual stirrings in him—and there are many other scenes alluding to premature sexual contacts which ultimately had serious consequences (pp. 14–18); an unjust punishment turns him to lying (pp. 20–21); a brutal master, denying him the gratification of natural desires, turns the young Rousseau to crime (pp. 31–32); shame turns him to simulation, thus converting the good love of self into the evil *amour-propre* (pp. 36, 39–40); the wrong kind of reading stimulates the imagination too strongly; an unscrupulous guard, closing the city gates too early, deprives Rousseau of a future in his own city (pp. 42–44). From his surroundings, unprotected by better knowledge, he absorbs ambitious yearnings and a false conception of needs. Sophistry involves him with the wrong religion. Malicious intrigues prevent him from being true to himself.

But while he considered himself misformed and falsified by many of the circumstances of his life, he also consciously kept track of the positive influences that returned him to his good self or permitted its continued existence underneath the false overlay. In some ways his father and aunt gave him a good education; he drew much from the spirit of Geneva that later was supportive of his good self; the Abbé Gaime steered him to the correct notion of virtue and the right sense of moral action; and, above all, Madame de Warens gave him the kind of home and the kind of love that was conducive to his full growth. Thus he renders an account of his life that constantly interlinks the developing self and its circumstances. What results is the view of a double-layered personality in which the man of appearance is superimposed upon the man with the pure heart.

An analysis of the great moral dilemmas Rousseau faced provides the clearest sense of the problematics of such a view of self and circumstance. Suggestions must suffice here. In the account he makes it clear that handing his five children over to the orphanage was done against Thérèse's wish. It was an action that obviously left him with the worst guilt feelings throughout life. When the narrative reaches the point of the first infant's exposure, Rousseau had not yet started his reform. He describes his motivation entirely as that of a man who, pressed by an unexpected social embarrassment, too willingly picks up a suggestion from unscrupulous men that it would be a socially accepted custom to lay the infants at the door of a foundling home. "The man who best helped to stock the Foundling Hospital was always the most applauded.... Since it is the custom of the country, I told myself, if one lives there, one must adopt it" (p. 344). But then he makes a distinction. "Gradually indeed I adopted, not thank Heaven, the morals but only the maxims I found accepted here." The maxim by which he acted was wrong, but it left his true moral sense unimpaired. But by the time he abandons the third child, the period of self-reform has clearly begun. He mixes general reflections on morality with the narrative. The dominant remarks are about "false shame and fear of opprobrium" as the false motives still delaying his reform. Civilization and its concerns are still too much with him. He places his ultimate justification in his *raisonne-*

*ment* about how much better it is to let the state educate the children and how much this is in accord with Plato's teachings. But underneath all of this are the stirrings of the truly moral Rousseau. He wonders: is it really possible that a man with a heart like mine can be said to have been immoral at that moment? "No, I feel it and boldly declare, that is not possible. Never, for a single instant of life, could J. J. [*sic*] have been a man without feeling, without compassion [*sans entrailles*], an unnatural father. I may havè deceived myself, but could not be callous."[46] The act may have been wrong, but his ultimate moral worth depends only on the inner state of his heart during the act. He looked at Madame de Warens's actions in the self-same way: "Her motives were praiseworthy, even in her errors; she could have slept with twenty men a day" and still would have kept her clear conscience (p. 230).

Another example may make clearer still the way in which the two Rousseaus were superimposed upon each other. In one of the most famous scenes[47] of the *Confessions*, Jean-Jacques unburdens himself of the "unbearable remorse" he felt over the youthful crime of having shifted the blame for a stolen ribbon onto a totally innocent servant girl. He insists on the absolute criminality of the act. "I may have ruined an . . . honest and decent girl." But the confession of the despicable act is followed by an analysis of motives that suggests that two layers of his person interfered with one another. His liking for the girl was the truest intention behind the theft. He had wanted to give the ribbon to her. So she was on his mind at the very moment when he, under public pressure, was asked to account for the theft. "I threw the blame on the first person who occurred to me." He asserts firmly that his intentions were morally correct: "never was deliberate wickedness further from my intention than at that cruel moment." And yet his visible behavior departed so radically from his intentions. The other actors in the little drama worked on the deformed part of Rousseau's personality, making it too difficult for the good intentions of the heart to assert themselves against the perverting social pressures. His sense of shame, his fear of disgrace and losing face, all the bad inclinations of his *amour-propre*, gained the upper hand in the artificial public situation.[48] "It was my shame that made me impudent. . . . If the head of the household had taken me aside and said 'Do not ruin that poor girl, if you are guilty tell me so,' I would immediately have thrown myself at his feet, I am perfectly sure. But all they did was frighten me, when what I needed was encouragement." In addition, of course, the reader is asked to give weight to the fact that Rousseau was so young. Thus, a goodhearted person, wanting to please someone he liked, feels driven by the pressures of the social situation to defend his appearance by the false means offered by a society that makes false demands. How can he now judge himself? Since he knows his own motives to be pure, the blame must fall on society. With this kind of situational ethics as a yardstick, Rousseau feels positively sure about the goodness of his intentions: the strongly lamented crime apparently amounted to no more that temporary weakness. But he cannot explain at all why his sense of guilt remains.

Such ethical dilemmas arise continually for Rousseau. He trusts his heart, and is certain that he can do no wrong. Yet he finds himself to be guilty of crimes and despicable acts. The fault, then, must lie outside him, in anything that prevents the goodness of nature from functioning unimpeded. A full explanation of the circumstances ought to make clear that the fault is not really in him. He concludes from all his reflections on this matter that it is necessary to bring external circumstances under his control. That is not only his hope for his own life; it is his dream for a better mankind. It is important "to avoid situations that place our duties in opposition to our interests."[49] Rousseau invariably perceives his life as the encounter between a basically good self ("I who believe and always have believed that I am on the whole the best of men" [p. 517]) and a civilization that prevents men from being good. The middle period of his life he turned into an attack on the surfeit of civilization, all those external arrangements that were not reconcilable with natural motions and their potential transformation into virtue and true citizenship. But he never meant this to be an attack on everything that made man civilized,[50] though he had come to hate civilization whenever it thwarted the development of the natural human being. He could only present his life as the dramatic struggle of a self wanting to fulfill its self-hood in spite of a hostile surrounding world. And in that vision of an unreconcilable confrontation of the individual self and society lay a fundamental dilemma from which our thinking about the notion of individuality has suffered ever since.

Rousseau stands at a point in our history where general cultural developments had made it easier for some men to turn to the ideal of individuality. Many of the older personality conceptions, especially those fitting a Christian culture, had begun to lose their hold. Many of the caste distinctions were giving way to an egalitarian conception of society that made it incumbent on individuals to define themselves on their own. Thoughts about society had become relativized by a penchant for explaining it in terms of diversified geography and history, and certain strains in Rousseau's thought suggest that he gave weight to all such differentiating factors in trying to understand the human condition. He adhered to the notion of geographical determinism. He had a sense of the difference in the various stages of individual development and growth—his educational theory gives evidence of this. And he relied very much on a situational ethical casuistry.[51] Not only did he teach us to understand childhood on its own terms, but he himself wanted to be understood on his own terms. And he knew that such an understanding of himself could only be had from the individualized historical account. Hence the *Confessions.*

But a genuinely historical understanding of the individual must ultimately rest in the awareness of a fruitful interplay between a self and the world it experiences. In a sense the individual must come to perceive itself as the product of such an interplay. To value itself, it must also value its world. And it was this that Rousseau was not able to do. The world view and the social theories he developed in response to his conflict with civilization did not bring him to value individuality highly. He was a genius, he influenced the modern world, and he thus left us a dilemma.

From his own experience Rousseau was certain of some absolute given facts. Nature gave to man his powers as a sensitive being. Man was a creature meant to have the intense pleasure of a pure sense of existence, the pleasure Rousseau could find in letting the drifting boat carry him over the waters of Lake Biel, that bliss when the whole being feels in full harmony with those parts of creation to which it corresponds. Then the self can enjoy the incomparable feeling of the inner connectedness of all life. Then it can say: I live, I exist. It strives for the permanent possession of such happiness, wanting to exist as a whole being without pain and conflict.[52] The very stress on this wholeness of experience precluded Rousseau from seeing man's "salvation" in the overcultivation of any single aspect of the human potential, such as his rationality; on this point a conflict with certain tendencies of the Enlightenment was inevitable. All human pursuits are directed toward achieving this sense of existing as a whole; and insofar as this is true, all morality is based on genuine self-interest.

But our sensibilities will not develop unless they are stimulated. We must, therefore, cope with two sorts of dependencies: we are dependent on nature, and we are dependent on man. Dependency on nature is morally a neutral, an adiaphorous matter; strictly speaking, no moral issue is involved since there is no intention in nature, but only necessity. Morality is not at issue in the case of the falling stone which hurts me. Morality is very much at issue when the stone is thrown at me. Much of our dependence upon things is like our dependence upon nature. Man is not to be shielded from this dependence; as the teachings of the *Emile* make clear, most of our human growth consists in learning to live with our dependence on nature. If it causes us pain, then we must learn to resign ourselves to such pain, much as Rousseau learned to bear his ailment.[53] Our search for the natural idyll in which our being can blend with nature is an appropriate response to our search for the happiness we are meant to have as men. And by modest and simple lives we can also free ourselves from an unnecessary dependence upon things. The moral stance involved is neither a monk's ascetic denial of things nor the Stoic's ataraxy, his unshakability in the face of vicissitude. It is the sense of well-being of the true sage, the "Epicureanism of reason": abstain, in order to enjoy yourself![54] Such a position carries with it the implication that we are better off in reducing the accouterments of civilization to a minimum.

Morality comes fully into play in our dependence upon our fellow men. In this dependence on them we also strive for a sense of well-being preserving the natural strength of the whole self. We seek the human idyll as much as we seek the natural idyll. We desire an untroubled coexistence with others when each self can be true to its self. We yearn for that mutual acceptance capable of satisfying our need for loving and being loved. We look for a togetherness with a total understanding of human beings whose hearts are transparent crystals to one another. But civilization, as Rousseau knew it, attested to man's utter failure to manage the dependency between man and man. Love of self had turned to *amour-propre*; appearance had become more important than reality. Society and civilization had become man's most dreadful problem.

Rousseau saw only two possible solutions: to reform society so that the morality of virtue and conscience would be the improved condition of our natural potential, or to withdraw from society to a life in nature. Rousseau tried to teach men about the first solution; he himself felt forced to live by the latter one.

If we can reform society, we will, in a sense, make our dependence upon man similar to our dependence upon things. In the thought experiments of his three great works, Rousseau meant to state the conditions which would have to be met if society were to fit the realities of our nature. What would an association among men have to be to permit the free individual to pursue his natural self-interest and optimize his own development to its full potential set by nature? It must allow men to associate as absolute equals; all must submit themselves to the same law expressing the general will, the true interest of the whole association. Voluntarily accepted, the law functions as the great educator of all associates; it makes them virtuous, it hones their conscience. When virtue has become a second, an improved nature, when true self-interest and the interest of the whole entirely coincide, when mores, customs, opinions, the laws written upon men's hearts, are fully congruent with men's truest sentiments, only then will man's moral and rational potential be fulfilled. He will experience no conflict between self and society, between inclination and duty. Equals, governed by what is crystal clear to each one, will have pellucid hearts for the benefit of all others. Appearance and reality will have become one. Such is the dream of the *Social Contract*. But there is an implicit distinction between the formal and the substantive levels of the argument; Rousseau leaves room for the possibility of distinctly different associations, distinctively different collective individualities. But what significance can individuality have within the association?

In Rousseau's vision of the *Nouvelle Héloïse* the more intimate and smaller society at Clarens aims at the same optimal development of our natural potential amid social relations marked by love, resignation to duty, and genuine respect for one another. Rousseau stresses the virtues of the simple life, the life free of unnecessary temptations. Here also man will become virtuous and civilized only to the degree to which his nature permits. The variations among the key characters of the novel might suggest that Rousseau wanted to emphasize that there was room for the cultivation of individuality. Until one remembers his old dream: "I observe that in a very intimate society the styles approach to one another as do the characters, and that the friends blending their souls also blend their manner of thinking, of feeling, and of speaking."[55] As in the vision of the *Social Contract*, long processes of socialization reduce our differences.

And in *Emile* he undertakes to investigate how, through both manipulation of the surroundings and the careful control of possible experiences, an ordinary young man can develop in accord with the natural phases of a child's growth; at the point of entering a world he has not made, he can survive by virtue of his natural potential as fulfilled in virtue and guided by conscience. Here also, the emphasis lies on the elements of a *general* anthropology and the *typical* aspects of man.

Rousseau's attempts at personal reform in the middle of his life, as described in the *Confessions*, were meant to show the world that one man, seeking to recover, to hold on to, and to cultivate the natural stirrings of his heart, could take at least the beginning steps toward virtue. But Rousseau could not manipulate the realities of his real surroundings as he could the conditions within his thought experiments. As he saw it: the world undid his reform. Now he must resort to the only other solution left in the conflict with civilization: withdraw from it, as best as you can. Turn to the natural foundations within you and try to attain an existence that permits your self to live in harmony with nature. You must surrender the search for love and resign yourself to the virtue fit for a single man whom others did not grant the right of true citizenship. The *Confessions*, the *Dialogues*, and the *Rêveries* show how Rousseau tried this, and what a bitter conflict it was.

The fundamental longing for an untroubled blissful harmony of the self with all the surroundings on which it depended forever led Rousseau to flee into fantasy worlds. The very conception that the evils of the existing society meant an inevitable conflict between a good self and a world bent upon falsifying it permitted Rousseau to forge only a radical solution to the problem of personal growth. Since he was so concerned with moral issues, he entangled himself in the basic conflict between two different ethical positions. The ethics he represents as his own has all the earmarks of what Max Weber called a *Gesinnungsethik*, an ethics of intentions and absolute commandments. The moral law itself is clear; man does not have to engage in a lifelong struggle to determine his ethical code. He is to be judged by the intensity and sincerity of his intentions. Thus his primary responsibility is for the purity of his ethical intention and not for the consequences of his action. Such an ethical attitude is typically unconcerned, even adverse, to considering the most serious problem of how means should be related to ends. Rousseau was naturally drawn to this ethical stance. He had an exceptionally strong aversion to "the mediate" and an intense longing for "the immediate." He had a characteristic distaste for money. "I am less tempted by money than by things, because between money and the desired object there is always an intermediary, whereas between a thing and its enjoyment there is none."[56] He distrusted the transformation of immediate experience into knowledge through the mediation of concepts; he yearned instead for the un-mediated and direct communing with nature. He hated the dependencies that stood between men. Above all, he distrusted the word as a necessary mediator between men. He coined a

profoundly revealing term for his attitude when he spoke of his desire
for crystal-clear hearts.

But his psychological "theory" predicated the necessity of external
stimulation of varied situations for the development of our sensibilities.
"Lacking the right circumstances [les causes occasionelles] a man born with
great sensibility would feel nothing and would die without having
known his being."[57] But then the urge to control circumstances becomes
irresistible. This desire had to involve Rousseau deeply in the question
of how to relate means to ends, the characteristic problem of a fundamentally different ethical position, an ethics of responsibility, what Max
Weber called a Verantwortungsethik. Judging by this ethical position, a
man asks what he objectively desires to obtain (and this may, of course,
be an absolute moral value) and what means will lead to the objective
most efficiently. Concerned with the efficient use of means, he is less
concerned with the moral quality of the means employed to reach the
stated end. You compromise, and if necessary you make a pact with the
Devil. There is no room here for being overly preoccupied with the
purity of intentions of every act undertaken. This is an intensely ma-
nipulative ethics. A willingness to take responsibility for the best possible
act in an immensely complex world engages man in the everlasting
weighing and accommodating of many values to one another. The desire for his own reform in a real world forced this ethics on Rousseau; it
was difficult for him to reconcile it with his penchant for an absolute
ethics. When in his mind he was busily creating ideal worlds, he had to
resort every time to the purest conceivable type of the manipulator. The
figure of the Great Legislator (a role that perhaps could only be filled by
a God, as he says) so completely manipulates the laws of the association
in secret, that they can accomplish the desired objective of making self-
interest and general will identical. Woldemar, as the rational designer of
Clarens, is an arch-manipulator. And Emile's educator totally manages
Emile's surroundings. If all circumstances must be thus arranged and
manipulated for the sake of man's fulfillment, if such a belief is not the
ultimate seedbed for our totalitarian tendencies, then, pray, what is?
Where in that vision of the perfectly modulated and manipulated production of the ideal self is there room for the notion of individuality?
Many desires genuinely alive in Rousseau—his love for freedom, his
attachment to his unique self, his devotion to spontaneity—stood in
basic conflict to such arch-acts of manipulation. A great paradox remained. This man longed for the unmediated communing with nature;
simply exclaiming "Oh!" when overcome by his admiration for nature

was already to use one word too many. This same man had to turn to the mysterious mediation of language to make himself understood. He had to be a writer in an age of writers. In most of his writings he asks at some point: Why do I have to live in an age when it is necessary for me to write? He sensed the nature of his dilemma very well. Writing, which was in a sense a sacrifice of his true self, brought him suffering. He felt misunderstood and could only hope for understanding from coming generations. So he spent the last decades of his life trying to explain himself to the world so that knowledge of the author's intentions might redeem the works.

He never found an adequate explanation for the presence of evil in this world. Whether he ever understood that his ultimate dilemma was the total inadequacy of his theodicy, seems doubtful. He wanted to live by the intentional *Gesinnungsethik* of saints, but he had lost the world view of the saint who believed in a world as something to be borne as a pilgrim, something of lesser value than the world toward which he moved, and something he could leave to the care of the Creator on whom he depended for grace. As a man of a secularized age Rousseau wanted men to take responsibility for their lives and their world, at least their social world. But rather than struggle day in, day out with this damnably complicated existence, he began to dream of a simpler world in which evil could be made to disappear, of a nature in which spiders do not eat flies. He wanted a world in which God is good, nature is good, man is good; a world where it is true that from good only good can come. But this, as Max Weber has said, is the ethics of a childlike mind which has not learned to live responsibly with the tragic dilemma of the inherent conflict between all our values. The very fact that Weber had to repeat this point in the twentieth century points to the persistence of Rousseau's heritage.

Rousseau possessed a strongly developed genetic sense; he understood that the man develops from the child. He pleaded for treating the child as child and not as adult. He envisaged natural man as transformed over time into citizen. He instinctively must have felt that only his story could explain how he came to be what he was. And yet he yearned with his whole being for permanent states of being, not for everlasting change. In other words, he did not truly care for the historical quality of our existence and placed no ultimate value on it. He was genuinely aware of being a unique and singular person. Though at moments he took pride in his singularity, ultimately he found it a cruel fate. Though he allowed for the differentiations among us, the stronger urge led him to bury these in our common nature, recapturing it from what divides us. In his hope of creating societies in which there was no real use for individuality, he ultimately valued it as little as our historicity.

Our modern sense of history and of individuality grew from the fusion of an emergent genetic sense and a growing concern for singularity. For part of the way it was possible for these two ideas to have independent careers. With Vico and Gibbon, it was possible to cultivate a sense of historical development without yet stressing the singularity and diversity of historical moments as a matter of value. And with Montaigne as well, it was possible to value particularity without connecting it to a historical sensibility.

In the thought of some eighteenth-century minds the balance gradually tilted toward a growing preoccupation with the manifold richness of this world. The *res singularis* was given loving attention. The differences between phenomena seemed to become a matter of importance. Subtle nuances were really more captivating than discernible uniformities. It had long been known that it was logically difficult fully to subordinate any particular fact under a comprehensive general formulation; just as men were never really blind to the fact that there was so much diversity in things. But now there was a different question: on what do men fasten their attention, and more important still, to what do they affix prime worth? A scholastic logician may rightfully conclude that he cannot fully define any particularized fact in terms of general categories and that some ineffable quality continues to elude his definition. He may see his problem, and yet not assign great value to the unutterable remainder. Something quite different happens when in 1780 the young Goethe suddenly sees cosmic significance in cultivating the ineffable individuum.

That something was changing in the eighteenth-century mentality is nicely illustrated by Leibniz's story about Princess Sophie Charlotte. Walking in the palace gardens she philosophically reflected on the "fact" that no two leaves in that garden could be found to be alike. One of her courtiers, unwilling to believe her, started to compare leaf with leaf. The story does not say whether he is still doing so. The fascinating aspect of this story is how Sophie Charlotte knew for a fact that all these leaves were different? To believe in the indefinite variation was for her important. And this is the significant issue. As such attitudes became more prominent throughout the course of the century, as the fascination with the immensely rich manifoldness of nature and of human creativity gained the upper hand over an instinct searching for uniformity (or became at least as strong), a profound change occurred in the outlook of the Western world. "There have, in the entire history of thought, been few changes in standards of value more profound and more momentous than that which took place ... when it came to be believed not only that in many, or in all, phases of human life there are diverse excellences, but that diversity itself is of the essence of excellence."[58] Individuality was not only accepted as a fact but had become a matter of great value. It led to much good and in its train it brought much evil. "The discovery of the intrinsic worth of diversity was ... with all of the perils latent in it, one of the great discoveries of the human mind; and the fact that it, like so many other of his discoveries has been turned by man to ruinous uses, is no evidence that it is in itself without value."[59]

These two different strains—the idea of development and the idea of individuality—eventually merged and interpenetrated one another. The revolution in our Western world view that resulted was potentially greater than the one celebrated in Lovejoy's thesis.[60] The idea of development has an elective affinity for the idea of individuality. For he who traces a historical development has an implicit interest in the precise moment, the constellation, the specific way in which specific factors interact and result in a new configuration of factors. In the idea of development the idea of individuality found an agency of explanation. For only by telling the story could one account for the continuous differentiation of reality into viable specifications of unique value, a logically undefinable quantity and quality. The two notions interacted, interpenetrated, and in their fusion reinforced one another. The historical way of looking at the world acquired a profound respect for the value of the specified particularity of every historical moment; the specificity of individuality could be made intelligible as a historical phenomenon. The willingness to understand each specific part of reality as qualified by its setting and moment meant an enormous refinement in our awareness of human realities—it also created enormous problems. These have now become a basic ingredient of our Western mind.

The most powerful early formulations of this combined fascination with individuality and history came from some German thinkers. Probably with good cause. Germany was a weak, or even nonexistent, national quantity in a world of nation-states in which the power of the state could buttress a culture. Language, art, culture, and memories of a great past were the only means of German self-identification. But even these were threatened by the fascination of German intellectuals and princes with the spectacular brilliance of the great model of civilized life her western neighbor France had evolved. The defense of "their own" became for some Germans the defense of everything that differed from this powerful model that claimed universality. That they reached for and found support in English artists and English thinkers is an interesting matter.

The young Herder—in an early writing of such vigor and explosive passion that he does not know where to place all the exclamation marks, rhetorical questions, exclamations, and fireworks of metaphors— inveighs against the universal claims of the French historian Voltaire. Who do you think you are claiming the right and the power to stand there, with these "toy scales" in your hand? On the one scale you place the weight of your own civilization as if it were the only gold by which to balance; on the other scale you place, one after another, all of man's diverse efforts through the historical ages; weighing by your own standards, you also find them all wanting, and thus you condemn them! How can a man condemn the honest strivings of other men who differ? If we need different standards for different forms of life, then let us have many yardsticks. Other men deserve to be taken as seriously, on their terms, as I want to be taken myself. No form of life possesses a universal perfection; each has only the limited perfection specifically its own. Since men are limited vessels, incapable of comprising all potential human worth, each group and each age of men can but represent one of the many specific formulations of which this potential is capable. Each has value by virtue of being the one form of the humanly possible that could be actualized at its own time. This specific form will never recur; but had it not been actualized, then one possible form of being human would have been lost forever. Thus the richness of humanity lies in its indefinite manifold variability. A man like Herder was, in a sense, over- come by the vision of an immensely rich humanity. God had created many peoples so that Man's Protean character could be expressed in every further specifications of a basic human nature. History, for Herder (at least in his pre-Kantian phase) was the awesomely inspiring specta- cle of humanity showing its variable capacity in temporal successions. Each people, each age had its own form of happiness, its own form of excellence, its very own aspirations. Each of these could only be under- stood on its own terms, its specific conditions through time—that is, its history.

Such a generalized "poetic" vision of the passing panorama of collec- tive individualities of peoples had its concrete companion piece in the history of the town and land of Osnabrück by Justus Möser. This out-of-the-way part of Westphalia—with its old peasant customs, its complex constitution balancing urban and landed interests, its mixture of feudal and modern customs, Catholic and Protestant persuasions (Protestant and Catholic bishops succeeded each other in a fixed pattern of rule), its complex overlay of altered legal traditions—proved to the civilized Voltaire the very idiocy of history. A civilized people listening to the demands of universal rationality would, long ago, have "straightened out such a mess" through rational reforms. But what seemed to be a demand of reasonable simplicity to Voltaire seemed unreasonable to Möser. He loved his small land for what it was. Having served it as a lawyer and administrator for decades, he was persuaded that all the complexity constituted a good working order, harmonizing many differing interests. It was lovable in its own right. The system worked, and had its viable reason in that whole long series of accommodations whereby this specific community of men had sought to express its specific commitment to the human tasks. Its explanation lay in its accumulated experience, which also provided its justification. Thus History had its reasons where Reason did not.

In such positions, celebrating both the wonder of unique individuality and the long dimension of life that is history, lay the potentials for much rich thought. Herder and Möser were captivated by the spectacle of "collective individuality," that of peoples, of whole styles of life, of styles of art, of traditions of poetry and languages. It would not take long until individual men and women, in seeing that their task was to cultivate their personal individuality, would thus discover the historical dimension of their own lives.

# 13

# Johann Wolfgang von Goethe:
## A Self and Its World

The historical quest of this essay comes to rest with the consideration of Goethe's autobiography, *Dichtung und Wahrheit*. Autobiography and the personality conception of individuality flourish after him. In our effort to trace the gradual emergence of individuality, Goethe's autobiography is important as a work in which the diverse elements which must unite to produce the notion of individuality converge. Here was a man who took life as a value, in itself and for itself; its purpose lay simply in "existing" and "fulfilling" its potential. Goethe looked with respect and wonder upon the ineffable quality of an individual existence. He possessed a clear sense of his own individuality, and was highly conscious of its effect on the surrounding world. He thought of nature as a ceaselessly pulsating reality, an order of creation constantly transforming itself; he thought of individuality as an evolving part of the natural realm. The never-resting process of individuation inevitably meant a ceaseless interaction of a growing self with an ever-different world configuration. To experience such an interlinked coexistence of a forming self and a changing world was to experience history. A self could not value itself apart from its world; a love of self includes the love of its circumstances. Goethe did not set the self and the world against each other; he did not think well of self-cultivation at the cost of the world. He thus warned against the false cult of self-idolization which threatened the commitment to individuality when it became fashionable.

Goethe could draw on many elements of eighteenth-century German culture for sustaining his conception of individuality. *Dichtung und Wahrheit* itself tells the story. The book is a key document for understanding the German history of its time. In the confines of this chapter it is possible neither to compress its historical content nor to provide a fuller historical context for understanding the personal story. Suffice it to enumerate the most essential factors of the historical setting.

Until the nineteenth century, Germany was a cultural rather than a political totality. Neither the Germans, nor the Italians for that matter, had been able to achieve that congruence of nationhood and national culture so characteristic of the dominant European pattern set by the great Western nations. The Empire meant very little; its institutions hardly functioned as Goethe, the young lawyer at the *Reichskammergericht* at Wetzlar, himself observed.[1] Literally hundreds of the most diverse political units existed in greater or lesser political independence. Aside from Prussia, Bavaria, and Saxony (not counting Austria), none of these states had populations over 1,000,000 inhabitants, and scores had fewer than 50,000. Sachsen-Weimar and Eisenach, which Goethe for fifty years helped to govern as minister of state, had 765 square miles (i.e., an area one-third the size of Delaware), 106,000 inhabitants (the size of Hammond, Indiana), and a capital city of 7,000. Only Berlin and Hamburg, among the numerous German towns, exceeded 100,000 souls. Even though it was a town of 50,000 inhabitants, Goethe's birthplace, the Freie Reichstadt Frankfurt, had more people within its town walls than the total population of any number of independent principalities. Political systems varied from the patrician rule of free towns to the rule of *Reichsgrafen*, prince-abbots, archbishops, and the "benevolent" despotism of some principalities and kingdoms. It was not a world in which one could fill life with meaning if one sought this in the role of the citizen. A pattern of different religious loyalties cut into and across this excessive political fragmentation; only a century earlier it had involved frightful bloodshed. A city like Möser's Osnabrück had achieved religious peace only by alternately electing a Catholic and a Protestant bishop. Only peculiar practices of toleration could assure a semblance of peaceful coexistence in such a diversified land.

Only ties of a common culture, a few cherished historical memories, and the always-present threats from "abroad" served as countervailing forces against this extraordinarily advanced political particularism. The educated classes had at least a common written language, though it had by no means become as standardized as had others of the European continent. They all knew Latin and the number who knew French was increasing—in itself a mark of a cultural dilemma. Few thoughtful Germans of Goethe's generation could afford to be indifferent to the threat posed by the high French culture in matters of language, art, and general cultural affairs. Frederick the Great, the only possible candidate for

German hero worship at the time, preferred the French models; but then Goethe knew from his family experience—where one half was "fritzisch" and the other "pro-Hapsburg"—that even "der grosse Friedrich" could only be a hero to half of the land. It was the same with most other candidates for the role of all-German hero—Luther being the outstanding example. There was, of course, Arminius (typically enough better known by his Latinized name than by the German, Hermann der Cherusker); but how much loyalty could educated men master for the victor over the Romans who had kept most of Germany outside the reach of civilization?[2] The young Goethe often lamented the lack of national themes on which the French, English, Italians, and Spaniards could draw for their poetic inspiration. Only his own and subsequent generations recovered the elements that later on could form a national culture, especially the medieval inheritance of folktales and folksongs. The high culture of modern Germany was in many ways the work of the very group of poets and thinkers among which Goethe himself stood. Weimar was Germany, and Goethe was Weimar. The great English cultural models, as counterweights to the all-engulfing French culture, had a growing appeal for these Germans searching their own cultural ground. Especially during the formative period at Strassburg, English writers are Goethe's constant companions. The influence of Shaftesbury's formulations of Neoplatonism on German aesthetics was very strong. In the long run, Shakespeare became the most powerful antidote to French classicism; the old Voltaire knew very well why he feared this "barbaric genius."

Certain indigenous German cultural strains had particular importance in conditioning the outlook of men who now more readily inclined toward the ideal of individuality. Much in Leibniz's thought, however arch-rationalistic he was, prepared the ground. The very notion of the monad, with its implied perspectivism and its teleology of self-fulfillment, was useful to those who came to think of the world as a highly differentiated order of reality. Every part of this philosophy pointed toward the "temporalizing of the Great Chain of Being," as Lovejoy termed it—in other words, toward conceiving of nature as a continuous process. The thought of the cosmopolitan Leibniz should not be seen as typically German, but, if Germans had a "national" philosophy on which to try their teeth, it was that of his "systematizer" Christian Wolff. Few mid-century intellectuals could escape its influence. Fewer still escaped the effects of German pietism with its extreme stress on man's inner self-cultivation,[3] and its impact was anything but lost on the young Goethe. He found a very persuasive living example of it in his personal friend Fräulein von Klettenberg. It came to him through the influences of Klopstock's poetry. He discerned the force of a pietistic interpretation of Christian history in his reading of the church historian Arnold.

Many an aspect of pietism blended nicely with the exaltation of simple life and the veneration of local tradition. Goethe was receptive to the charms of local variation and particularism, both through his hometown and his love of wandering and travel. He had an instinctive respect for any genuine human effort. He was fascinated by the rich diversity of man's work. Herder reinforced these inclinations in Goethe by teaching him to place a high value on every individualized form of human experience. From Justus Möser, "this incomparable man,"[4] Goethe had learned early in life that the particularity of local traditions could be understood by a historical, a genetic method. But Goethe and his contemporaries derived an equally powerful, though different, strain of historical understanding from the art historian Winckelmann. This strange man, having seen little more than copies of Greek sculpture, awakened a passion for Greek art and Greek beauty by his *Geschichte der Kunst des klassischen Altertums* (1764). Here a profound sense for historical development of a style of art was blended with a strong penchant toward a normative classicism, a blend which, in the long run, proved to be of exceptional importance for Goethe and German culture.

Thus the characteristic quality of Goethe's own formation, and of much of Weimar culture, was the specific blend of a loving cultivation of particularity and of a commitment to common ideals of humanity as these were stressed by the Enlightenment. Genuine cosmopolitanism and individualistic particularism belonged together. A living relation to the Bible and to Homer, to Jerusalem and to Athens, was as essential to Goethe's growth as his German setting. He thought of his individuality as a highly specified and unique form of existence. And yet he thought of it as an inextricable piece of reality completely embedded in a pantheistic nature and in the total cultural inheritance of Western man. Goethe was a very conscious heir of this past. He was equally aware of his role in shaping a culture by means of his own personal transformation of this inheritance.

When Goethe, in the first decade of the nineteenth century, turned to the autobiographic task, he was fully aware that the world which had helped to form him had passed, and that he himself had helped to transform it. The events of the Great Revolution, the dissolution of the Holy Roman Empire, and the battle of Jena, with Sachsen-Weimar on the losing side, had deeply cut into German history.[5] During that very decade Goethe lost the companionship of many who represented ties to the older world: in 1808 his mother had passed away; the Grand Duchess Anna Amalia, who had done so much to make Weimar the special place it was, had died in 1807; the loss of Schiller in 1805 had deprived Goethe of the intellectual and literary exchanges that had meant so much to both men; in 1803 Herder had died; and in 1801 he himself had been so ill that the Viennese newspapers prematurely announced his death. He did not personally identify with the political movements stirring in the German lands now subject to French political dominance. He had a venerable status; thousands of educated men made literary pilgrimages to Weimar. But Goethe did not set the tone for the literary magazines, and he more often scorned than praised the aesthetic tendencies of the younger generation of writers. His extraordinary inner drive for continuous development, both as a man and as an artist, had left him with the sense that large segments of his life lay in the past, "done with." In earlier days this sense had led to periodic autos-da-fé of his works. This sense of detachment now also embraced that whole phase of life that had made him the world-famous author of *Werther*. Like any man, he had had thoughtful moments about his past life; but he had never indulged in extensive retrospection. He was to do much more of this as he came to his seventh decade. And most of this retrospective activity was born of a simple wish to present the youth of the early nineteenth century with a clear impression of what it had meant to live earlier—as best as such history could be given through the mind of one who had experienced it.

In the introductory letter to *Dichtung und Wahrheit* Goethe implies that the impulse for writing came from a request for explanatory notes for the new edition of his collected works. Many an autobiographic enterprise has originated in the desire to illuminate an author's works by insights into his personal life. Such a purpose was the recurring link in such eighteenth-century writers as Vico, Gibbon, Rousseau, Alfieri, Coleridge, and Goldoni. Goethe says that he had "an immediate desire" (p. 12) to fulfill this request. There is some question as to how one should take his statement. For, on the one hand, Goethe evinced throughout his life a pronounced aversion to explaining either himself or his writings. He forever stunned inquirers either by abrupt changes in the topic of conversation, or by mystifying propositions, or by remarks that more or less said: well, I did not advise you to read *Faust*; now that you have engaged upon it, see how you can make out on your own![6] What business had a poet to explain the very words by which he had said what he had to say? The aversion was deep-seated; it had nothing to do with false public modesty or with a penchant for obfuscation.[7] On the other hand, Goethe understood, better than anyone else, that his poetry was *"gegenständlich,"* that it was in a marked manner tied to specific persons, specific events, specific occasions. It possessed an extraordinary concreteness and always a highly specific experiential content. As a true poet, he was convinced that the fleeting moment had been both subsumed and clarified in the poetic expression—thus making any further explanation of the text redundant. Yet such a poet had reason to throw some light on the circumstances in which the work was anchored. In part *Dichtung und Wahrheit* subsequently fulfilled such a function, striking as it is that there are hardly any references in it to such a life-absorbing work as *Faust*.

Still weightier than the felt need to provide contexts for specific works was the poet's own sense that his writings were "fragments of a great Confession." Lyric poetry always has an intensely autobiographic core; for him, his own poetry was autobiography.[8] But it was fragmentary, especially for all who missed the incomplete and unpublished writings which in his mind at least provided a greater cohesion of all the fragments. His introduction clearly alludes to this: "all my earliest efforts were missing; much that had barely been begun or that had never been completed was missing; yes even much that had been completed and lost its original external form [*Gestalt*] having later been totally reworked and cast in another form" (p. 13). And most of his scientific investigations and writings really stood outside these confessional fragments. If the autobiography could then be conceived in an appropriate manner it might well serve an explanatory role which the poet was otherwise instinctively inclined to reject. In some sense, then, the enterprise may well have originated in the stimulus of the new edition of the works.

But other grounds also underlay this great autobiographic undertaking. In more ways than one Goethe was being drawn at the time into historical matters. The events of the day led to meetings with the current shapers of history: the French marshals Lannes and Augereau had been billeted in his home after the Battle of Jena. In 1807, he had a meeting with Freiherr vom Stein, the great Prussian minister. In 1808, Goethe had three separate meetings with Napoleon, for Goethe the prime living exemplar of the "daemonic" in history. Goethe raised some fundamental questions about the nature of historical work in a series of conversations held at this time with the historian Luden. More important, Goethe was increasingly engaged in writing works which decidedly had historical dimensions. Since 1798, he had actively been thinking about the historical segment of his theory of color;[9] the years 1809 and 1810 deeply involved him in preparatory work for this. Since 1799, he had, off and on, been preoccupied with a historical assessment of the life of Winckelmann. The art historian's letters to a friend, Hieronymus Berendis, had passed into the possession of the Duchess Anna Amalia, who in turn had asked Goethe to publish them with an introduction. In 1805, Goethe published *Winckelmann und sein Jahrhundert*.[10] This neglected but precious book of Goethe was a stimulant in several regards: it made him think about the formal problems of biography and the way in which a biographer might soberly assess a man's historical significance; the subject itself drew Goethe back to his own Italian journey so that the little book reads in places like an announcement of his later work. Most importantly perhaps, by presenting Winckelmann Goethe could oppose the classical milieu of his own youth to the lamentable new fashion of idolizing everything medieval and the turn against classical norms he found so perturbing in the Romantics. It was a way of rescuing a major historical "value" of his youth. He was very ill when he put his finishing touches to it, but the words with which he sent the manuscript to Schiller—*in doloribus pinxit* (painted while in pains)—may not have alluded to a physical state only.

A few years later another biographic task came his way when the painter Phillip Hackert, a friend from the days of the Italian journey, shortly before his death in 1807, sent his autobiographic notes to Goethe with the request to publish them. Hackert had been deeply impressed by the work on Winckelmann and may well have wished for such an exceptional biographer for himself. Goethe sat down to work on this material, incorporating in the text his own translation of a travel diary by Henry Knight who had accompanied Hackert to the island of Sicily.[11] Thus Hackert, a much lesser figure than Winckelmann, gave Goethe the same opportunity for presenting an age, important to himself, through the lifelines of a specific person. And again: he could thereby juxtapose an older style of art, especially landscape painting, to more modern trends. The writing was in many ways a nuisance for Goethe; there were troubling interferences from heirs; and the banal observations of Knight must have suggested to Goethe how much more he himself had to say about his own travels to Sicily. The annalistic entry for the year 1811 (written after 1817) states immediately following a note on completing the work on Hackert: "Through this work I was pulled back to the south [events] came alive in my imagination; I had cause to ask myself why I was not undertaking for myself what I was doing for another."[12]

Such interest in his own past had been evoked by another series of events. After April 1807, Goethe received several visits from Bettina Brentano, who later became the wife of Achim von Arnim. She was a daughter of Frankfurt friends of the Goethes. During the preceding year she had written down the stories about the young Goethe as his mother lovingly told them. Thus Bettina came to him as the most recent link to his deceased mother, and she presented him with material that he, no doubt, had mostly forgotten. He later asked her for the record. But meanwhile the stories he had heard put him in a reminiscing mood, and he regaled members of his household with many previously untold experiences. Their appetite was whetted, and Riemer, his amanuensis, more and more frequently urged Goethe to undertake an autobiography. Goethe, no doubt, was becoming fascinated by himself as an interesting historical phenomenon. He was not bashful in admitting to himself that he had become a very noteworthy subject.[13] The immense richness of his experiences must have contrasted most favorably with the meagerness of the autobiographic and biographic works he had been reading, reviewing, and writing.

When all the various impulses to write his own life had interlocked, Goethe entered upon the project with considerable vigor. He set down in dry chronicle style a year-by-year listing of events, extending from 1742, when his father had been named imperial councilor, to 1809, when his own son August returned from the University of Heidelberg. This rough biographic schema made him turn to an intensive study of town histories, memoirs, literary handbooks, etc.[14] By January 1811, Goethe had started to write the text. Books 1–5 were printed in October 1811; Books 6–10 were ready for printing in October 1812; Books 11–15 were available for printing in May 1814; and Books 16–19 were at least sketched out between 1813 and 1816. But this last part of *Dichtung und Wahrheit* was to be completed only very late in life and was published posthumously. The most probable reason for the delay was Goethe's scruple in writing about Lili Schönemann, the great love of Part IV, while she was still alive. But all sorts of other work had also begun to interfere.

For several years, however, Goethe was intensely involved in the recovery of his own past. "This undertaking, in as much as I had to invest much time in historical studies and attempts to make present all sorts of localities and persons, kept me busy where I went and stood, at home and abroad, so that my actual condition took on the characteristics of a by-matter [*Nebensache*]."[15] The man who thought poorly of historians, who had such aversion to history as a discipline, confessed with surprise that late in life he had turned to historical labors. And the poet who had little interest in adding self-explanations to the sufficiency of his poetry published a substantial body of autobiographic writing in the last two decades of his life. For, although *Dichtung und Wahrheit* was left uncompleted until just before his death, other autobiographic material appeared to supplement it. The *Italienische Reise*, covering the years from September 1786 to June 1788, was published in 1816–17 with the subtitle: *Aus meinem Leben. Zweite Abteilung*, thus linking it directly to *Aus meinem Leben. Dichtung und Wahrheit*. In 1822, he published the *Campagne in Frankreich*, and in 1829 the *Belagerung von Mainz*, both representing his experiences during the war of 1792. The correspondence with Schiller, which Goethe considered an essential part of his life, appeared in print in 1828–29. And the *Annalen*, or *Tag- und Jahreshefte als Ergänzung meiner sonstigen Bekenntnisse*, written between 1817 and 1822, covering the years from 1790 to 1822 most intensively, appeared in 1830. The conversations between himself and his secretary Eckermann belong to the years 1823–32; Goethe probably suspected that Eckermann would publish these later on. To all such material one can apply the phrase he had used for his poetry before: "Bruchstücke einer grossen Konfession"—fragments of a great confession. He revealed more about himself than any other great writer.

Goethe read much history, but he was not much drawn to the discipline of history or to its practitioners. The cult of facts meant nothing to him; the history of institutions and abstractions had no appeal; mere events left him uninterested; the cadaverous smell of the sepulcher that clung to all history held him off. Only as a human life drew the world and its development into its own orbit, endowing it with the meaning of a personal experience, feeding it with the lifeblood of a human existence, was Goethe's, then very strong, interest awakened. Autobiography was thus a very important genre for him, and he was well read in it. There is no evidence of a thorough reading of Augustine's *Confessions*, but Cardano and Montaigne Goethe read more than once; he knew the work of Alfieri, of his own youthful companion Jung-Stilling, and he reviewed the autobiography of Johannes Müller. He himself translated Cellini; he personally knew Philip Moritz and read his *Anton Reiser*; Rousseau's *Confessions*, despite having made a strong first impression, remained for Goethe the problematic autobiography par excellence.

When Goethe decided to write his own life, he had already developed definite ideas about the autobiographic genre. He saw himself as the center of his life and his surrounding world; he could not write a God-centered Augustinian confession. He felt no need to justify his life or work since they were their own justification. A history of his calamities was totally unnecessary. He knew what he had been, and he had done with it; autobiography as self-discovery was of very little importance. Goethe clearly directed his autobiography at a public; indeed, it was as intensely public as any autobiography could be. It had to have a cohesive form and could not model itself on Cardano or Montaigne. No central crisis had suddenly illuminated his existence for him; the autobiographic pattern for religious persons having experienced conversions was thus of no use. Unlike Vico or Gibbon, Goethe had not produced a single work commanding such central attention that all of life had to be viewed in relation to its creation—although for him the autobiographic task had similar objectives in that it did require a man to explain himself in relation to his works. The drive for self-aggrandizement and personal *virtù* leading a Cellini to build another monument for himself in his autobiography did not impel Goethe. He was most troubled, however, by the problems posed in two fashionable autobiographies, Moritz's *Anton Reiser* and Rousseau's *Confessions*. The one, in its pietistic mold, represented a model of sentimental self-indulging and self-slashing by a never-ending inward self-analysis which Goethe deemed a disastrous modern tendency. The other, though at first admired,[16] unnecessarily offended sensibilities, pursued a false objective in claiming to reveal everything, and erred in making sentiments its linking thread. The confessional mode itself seemed dangerous to Goethe: "Anyone writing confessions, is in peril of becoming lamentable."[17] Self-pitying lamentation was an unsuitable conception of the poet's task. A poet should use the gift entrusted to him for comforting, elevating, and enriching human life. Goethe admonished an ever-dissatisfied, ever-complaining friend: "It is always better to enchant friends a little with the results of our existence than to sadden or to worry them with confessions of how we feel."[18]

Merely to report facts, because they were there, and then to take inordinate pride in one's truthfulness, did not impress Goethe at all.

When the writer Jean Paul sneered at the title of Goethe's *Dichtung und Wahrheit* and then ostentatiously published his own autobiography under the title *Wahrheit aus Jean Paul's Leben,* Goethe made the cutting remark: "As if the truth from the life of such a man could be anything else but that the author was a philistine."[19] His rejection of the confessional mode and confessional mood had deeper roots than personal aversion. For Goethe was deeply convinced that intense staring into the soul to recall and register all its moods and twitters would not make us wiser about the self. Introspection was not the royal road to self-knowledge. And, as will be seen, an individuality was not to be found in isolation from the world in which it moved.

All life was for Goethe an objective given that adhered to the laws of living nature. It was to be known objectively. In the metamorphoses of plants, that lifelong object of study, he saw the basic processes of nature of which human life was also a part. Though he later discarded the idea, it had been his original intention to write his life as if it followed a plantlike growth. The first part might show a child stretching out delicate roots in all directions, not yet showing many buds. In the second part the boy, now appearing as a much more thriving green plant, would push out, level by level, different sorts of branches, and then in the third plot of ground this living stem would be seen to develop quickly the blossoms, arranged like full ears of grain or clusters, representing the young man now filled with many hopes.[20] Such a botanical scheme can still be used in part to explain the structure of the work, though it hardly fits the whole. It places too heavy a stress on the inner unfolding nature and not enough on the impact of the conditioning circumstances.

Indeed, man was a nature, and as such metamorphosis was his lot and he was intelligible only in genetic terms. But even if Goethe was partially inclined to see his life as a lawful fulfillment of general natural processes, he also was sure that the general law reveals itself only in the individually particularized phenomenon. *This* he must present in presenting himself. His proper subject was what Burckhardt later on called *ein geistiges Individuum:* a being forever forming and transforming itself in a never-ceasing interaction between itself and its sustaining natural ground and social world, a being individualized only by its mental awareness of continuous experience. Along the road he had traveled as a poet he had left the lasting embodiments of moments of experience in his poetry, drama, and prose. These poetic transformations of experience had their own life now and could speak for themselves; at most they required some explanation of the circumstances surrounding their creation. Goethe knew that he had made an impact on his world with these writings, and that he had participated with others in shaping a culture. Thus the great subject he saw in his autobiography was the story of an individuality formed within the conditions of its day, absorbing food for its growth from these conditions, and returning its creations to a world that was changed in the process. The individuality was not to be known without the world with which, in which, by which it was coming to be and into which it constantly reentered by its own activity. A man knows himself insofar as he knows his world; he is aware of this world only within himself, and he is aware of himself only in this world—"*Der Mensch kennt nur sich selbst insofern er die Welt kennt, die er nur in sich und sich nur in ihr gewahr wird.*"[21] Ideally conceived, the autobiography would have to be the story of the gradual formation of that very specific phenomenon Johann Wolfgang Goethe within the context of a very specific historical development, a development which was but a phase in a long-lived civilization, a civilization which was but one specific way of expressing our common humanity. The figure he would make visible was at the same time a unique individuality, a representative of his time, a European, and a Man.

It was clear from the outset that the guiding ideal was an unattainable ideal, "*ein kaum Erreichbares*" (p. 131): to write biography as if it were cultural history. Who knows himself well enough for doing this? Who sufficiently knows his age? Goethe was diligent in reading sources; he sought to collect data as best he could. For many matters he could only rely on his memory; needless to say, it occasionally failed him. The chosen title is the most self-evident hint of Goethe's awareness of the problematics. *Aus meinem Leben. Dichtung und Wahrheit.* The first part clearly states that no full life was to be expected. The customary *vita* or life promised too much. But this was not simply a hedge against expected methodological difficulties. Goethe rejected the very idea of undressing in public as Rousseau so unabashedly did. Goethe had no intention to tell it all. He had a clear sense of the limitations upon self-knowledge, and he had a pronounced sense of propriety. Above all: his sense of proportion instructed him to distinguish the significant fact from the others. "A fact of our life counts, not insofar as it is true, but insofar as it means something."[22] The fact bearing fruit is truer, by being more significant, than the merely corroborated fact. The didactic purpose of the whole enterprise was always on Goethe's mind. How often does he not begin or end the detailed accounts with a generalized lesson? This book was meant to give present-day youth a useful picture of an important past. The chosen term *"Aus meinem Leben"* reveals above all else Goethe's sense of proportion.

That wonderful puzzler *Dichtung und Wahrheit* has intrigued readers and has pushed the phrase *Aus meinem Leben* into the background (if indeed, it is remembered at all!). It is perhaps the most apt of all autobiographic titles. One can forever play around with its potential meanings; in part because there is no way of capturing the full meaning of that broadly penumbrous word *Dichtung*. Even Goethe's own hints about the use of the word do not exhaust the possibilities.[23] On the most superficial level, he directed the term *Dichtung* as a plain warning to a somewhat philistine German public: do not expect that kind of naked truth you commonly demand from such biographic revelations and then forever assert you cannot find! The coupling of the two terms, of course, suggests that there is truth and—something else: fiction? poetry? that which is not historical truth? This ambiguity frequently leads to the conclusion that the author told the truth insofar as he could and then supplemented the whole by his imagination. And occasionally a critic even suggests that putting the term *Dichtung* first implies an intended preponderance of the imaginative component.[24] But the title was originally *Wahrheit und Dichtung;*[25] Goethe interchanged the words because the double d-sound offended his poetic sensitivities. And he made a very clear distinction between *Dichtung* and *Erdichtung,*[26] between the poetic formulation that lifts the truth of an experience onto a different, for him a higher, level of truth and simple poetic invention. *Dichtung* does not stand opposed to *Wahrheit,* but is intricately entwined with the attempt to give *Wahrheit.*[27]

Nor does the use of the two words imply the customary distinction between invented and tested historical fact. Rather: the subtitle expresses Goethe's awareness of the immensely fruitful tension any autobiographer, and ultimately any historian, experiences—the tension between the truth of facts in their strictly chronological occurrence at the time and the truth of the meaningful relations between facts as seen from the current retrospective position. Goethe opted for the latter as the higher truth. He intended to render a view of the world of his youth as it seemed important to him, and as he saw it filled with fruitful meaning when viewing it from his sixty-year-old perspective. The activity implied in *Dichtung* is the act of placing isolated facts in relation to others which they then join in a meaning that is wider than any single component part possesses. Factual *results* of life are thus used to convey a truth lying beyond the chronological fact. Goethe arranged the facts of his life to fit his understanding of the meaningful patterns of his life. All historical reconstruction is an immense act of telescoping, of compressing,[28] of rearranging *selected* facts. The reconstruction of his life was no arbitrary construction on Goethe's part; it was rather a reproduction of a life pattern already partially settled in his mind. Experience, the conscious precipitate of what he had undergone, had been sorted by a lifetime of reflection on its meaning. The basic network of meaning was part of the old man's consciousness; as with all autobiographers (and what historian's work is free of it?) this truth was superimposed on the truth of past events. Goethe stated this fact clearly; just as he sought to suggest to the reader that narration of a whole necessarily modifies narration of parts. That within these confines he strove for factual accuracy was a self-understood matter for him; aside from chronological errors, critics have not been very successful in proving alleged "falsifications."[29]

An excellent example of Goethe's working habit in all these respects is furnished by the fairytale "The New Paris: A Boy's Fairytale" in Book 2. Every reader of *Dichtung und Wahrheit* must have wondered about that insertion. It occurs at a point when Goethe is writing about his earliest awareness of his imaginative and narrative powers. He suggests how his activities with a puppet theater and the spinning out of motifs taken from his readings had made him a popular storyteller among his young playmates. He tells a fairytale about himself as a Paris who must choose among three apples offered by goddesslike creatures, and then becomes involved in all sorts of adventures that finally end with a miniature of the battle between Achilles and the Amazons. This plot has all the involuted qualities of a boyish imagination. Yet the narrative language is exquisitely polished and the built-in symbolism and allegory are of the subtlest nature.[30] On closer inspection one finds clear parallels to "later" works by Goethe: the Achilles poem/epic of which only a fragment was published but for which the schemata for the planned whole were later found, and especially the important Helena theme in *Faust*. When the little boy Goethe reaches for the beautiful little girl Alerte, he has exactly the same experience as Faust has when he reaches for Helena: both fall down as if struck by an invisible hand, and then pass out. The youngster's guide bears resemblances to the chastelain projected in the 1816 draft for a part of *Faust*. The symbolism of the colored garments is one Goethe used often. The key adjectives used in describing the miniature Greek soldiers in the Amazon battle are the very adjectives the old

Goethe used in characterizing the essential Greek traits. The little fairytale is filled with matters clearly belonging to the consciousness of the sixty-year-old poet who dictated it on July 3, 1811. And yet detailed research has shown that the story is full as well of elements from his childhood. Among his earliest attested readings was a children's version of the Homeric Paris theme. A scene of Greek horsemen fighting over a bridge and an old man in the same Oriental costume as the youngster's guide had appeared on the wallpaper which the French Count de Thoranc, who was lodged in the Goethe house during part of the Seven Years' War, had Frankfurt artists paint for his Provençal mansion. In a letter of 1773, Goethe refers to a boy's tale he says he told and which clearly contains the themes of the finished story. There is thus no real reason to doubt that the story is a most elegant merging of early and later elements.

The matter becomes more interesting still when one looks into the intended meaning of the story. It clearly contains the earliest appearance of a dominant and constantly repeated theme of *Dichtung und Wahrheit,* and indeed of Goethe's whole life: his gradual appropriation of the Greek, i.e., the classical world. The detailed elements clearly indicate that his first contact with that Greek world came through the rococo transformation of the Hellenic, a rococo antiquity he even later claimed to find in Wieland. Goethe himself shed it to gain the fresher vision emanating from Winckelmann's work and from his own experience during the Italian journey. Only after shedding his rococo wig and dress is the boy in the fairytale admitted to the sanctuary where he may play with naked, fully bodied Greeks—only to lose them again. The entire symbolism is executed with magnificent consistency. And the effect is heightened by insisting on a continuous process of miniaturizing everything to fit it to a child's reality. The total story was thus turned into a truly exquisite mixture of youthful inventiveness, details remembered, riper experience, childish naïveté, and refined symbolic use. It recalls a moment in Goethe's early youth while at the same time explaining his lasting qualities. It also has the function of assigning significance to a momentary activity which has symbolic value as a phase in a lifelong process of *Bildung.* Anyone willing to take the trouble of working his way through these fifteen pages of text will encounter unsurpassable autobiographic artistry—except insofar as Goethe himself surpassed it later on in *Dichtung und Wahrheit* with the Sesenheim story of his love for Friederike Brion.

The very fusion of *Dichtung* and of *Wahrheit* enabled Goethe to achieve his objective of writing his life as "irony in a higher sense" (*Ironie im höheren Sinne*). As the ripe man of sixty he could not and would not identify with his youth; he distrusted a Rousseau-like manner of recapturing sentiments. If Goethe wanted to relive past moments, he could turn back to his poetry, which "eternalized" and enshrined the particular sentiments of the past. True, he loved the optical game of reviewing past scenes as if he were standing between mirrors giving reflection upon reflection. But he never lost sight of the fact that it was an older man who was viewing such moments. For the detailed recovery of what the days had been he had his *Tagebücher*, his diary entries; but in *Dichtung und Wahrheit* he rose above the chronistic limitation. Diary, poetry, letters—all were fragments of an autobiographic confession. In *Dichtung und Wahrheit* he meant to give the inner connectedness of his life and a vision of a past world as it had meaning for a man who had experienced it and had the artistic power to communicate it to the youth of his day. He thus could draw universal lessons from a specific existence. And because he stood removed from the very self and its world that he depicted with ironic detachment in the truest sense, he could create the artistry of *Dichtung und Wahrheit*. It is this detachment that endowed the work with its curative value and gave it its solacing style, for it is a book that reconciles man with Man.

The desire to show the formation of the person in the interplay with his world led Goethe to weave the presentation of his developing self into the narration of his life. A closer look at the content and the structure of this book is, therefore, also a closer look at Goethe's self-conception and his view of how this self grew.

*Dichtung und Wahrheit* consists of twenty books. Units of five books are pulled together into four distinctive parts, each with a unifying motto. The whole work covers only the first twenty-six years of Goethe's life and ends with his departure for Weimar late in 1775. Part 1 (Books 1–5) deals with his youthful experience in Frankfurt until, at the age of 16, he sets off to study at Leipzig (1765). Its motto was taken from Menander: "Man will not learn if it is not painful." Part 2 (Books 6–10) carries the development through his Leipzig experience, his return to Frankfurt and his illness, his departure for Strassburg, and his encounter with Herder, and ends with the idyll of Sesenheim. For this part, Goethe coined his own motto: "What you desire as a youth, you have in abundance in old age." Part 3 (Books 11–15), prefaced by the proverb "Care is taken that the trees do not grow into the sky," covers the period from midsummer 1771 to the end of 1774, the break with Friederike, the departure from Strassburg, an unsettled period of life at Frankfurt, the legal career at Wetzlar and his love for Charlotte Buff, and then the composition of *Werther*. The whole part is centered on Goethe's first great productive period as a poet. Part 4 (Books 16–20) was finished only at the very end of Goethe's life; it is prominently highlighted by his love for and engagement to Lili Schönemann and the events leading up to his departure for Weimar. Its pivot is in the tension between poetic calling and acceptance of social obligation, and it is headed by the mysterious Latin motto *"Nemo contra deum nisi deus ipse"*—no one can oppose God except God himself. The entire autobiography is thus focused on the formative period of the youth and young man. And the heart of this formative process is the forming of the poet.

*Dichtung und Wahrheit* opens with a view of the stars: what was their constellation at noon on August 28, 1749, the day and hour of Goethe's birth? It closes within the context of a discussion of the forces moving the universe, especially of that incalculable "daemonic" force which could cut so decisively into a man's course and plans of life. But though the look at the planets and stars opens worldwide vistas in the first paragraph, the immediate setting for the following paragraph is a much narrower circle, the parental house. Thereafter, the reader accompanies the growth of a young man as he moves into an ever more widely opening world. Goethe evidently borrowed the theme of the horoscope from Cardano who indeed believed in the power of the stars. Goethe simply employs symbolism to underline at once his deep conviction that an individual fate is jointed into the juncture of a moving world. Here finally is the autobiographer who is fully aware of the fact that "being born ten years earlier or later . . . he would have become quite another" (p. 14). The very specificity of an individuality is tied to the unrepeatable uniqueness of a spatial-temporal point. And he mingles a concern with the self and a concern with the social world right at the beginning of the story: the birth was very difficult, the child was almost left for dead by the clumsiness of the midwife, with the result that Grandfather Textor, one of Frankfurt's highest officials, immediately decreed to institute better training for midwives—"which may have done good for many of those born after me" (p. 15).

The world presented in Book 1 is the narrow world of a youngster's awareness. Goethe skillfully depicts the world as the boy found it and also as it changed while the boy looked at it. The old-fashioned house from which he first gazes out at the nearest surroundings, especially the sunsets, was rebuilt to suit his father's more modern, perhaps more Italian taste. This project was one of the young boy's great excitements. When the family is temporarily displaced from the house, Goethe uses this moment to show his growing awareness of the town outside. His description of Frankfurt has all the qualities Goethe always gave to such descriptions. Visual observations predominate. His strongly developed sense for graphic concreteness (or *Anschaulichkeit*) leads him to deduce the institutional functions of the town hall, the famous Römer, from its physical arrangements. He shows how well he understood that things having their origin in peculiar historical accidents could eventually function as beneficial institutions. He clearly perceives the layout of buildings in relation to their natural surroundings and always also in relation to the human activity for which they were meant. And in this passage he already uses his favorite device of analyzing festivals and prominent social events in order to characterize the social customs and atmosphere of a place. Short commentaries about the symbolic value of such social realities, or brief references to his personal reactions, immediately clarify the meaning of such experiences for his own development.

Goethe uses the end of this walk through Frankfurt as the occasion for returning the family to the remodeled house which he describes in turn, with particular attention now to those furnishings, art objects, books, etc., that played a role in his "education" under his father's demanding but unorthodox training program. The tension between the taskmaster and the son can be sensed, a tension modified by the double-layered awareness of the old Goethe that though he owed much to his father he must still do justice to the independent urgings of the boy. The father-son relation is amplified into an extended generational context by the fine portrait of Grandfather Textor, the high town official. He represented the old world the young Goethe still knew, a world he respected but experienced only from a distance, a world which was not immediately "his own," and which was unproblematic by its greater distance.[31] Finally there was the world of Goethe's books: the Bible, especially the Old Testament, classical stories in children's versions, *Robinson Crusoe*, reports of Lord Anson's travels around the world, and the store of German *Volksbücher* (in very cheap editions), the stories of the Haimon's children, Eulenspiegel, the beautiful Melusine, and others which forever recurred as themes during his later life. In this very first book the significant motif is established: Goethe absorbs what is offered by books and the world around him, and then he reworks such stimulations into his own creations. He had already started versifying; by comparing his creations to those of other boys he quickly developed a sense of his own worth. The book ends with an account of his boyish attempt to give thanks to his version of the Deity by building him an altar of fruits and diverse offerings. He burned holes in the music stand that had served as altar. The "young priest was extremely embarrassed"; the old biographer observes the warning in this event: do not approach God in such a casual fashion.

All the essential themes for the entire work are set down in Book 1: the ever-recurring thoughtful observation of surroundings, the influences of specific persons, the objects and artworks to which he developed a personal relation, the books and literary themes, their meaning at that specific time as well as their enduring effects (the list of these books already suggests the key elements of the biblical, the classic, and the German *Volk* tradition), and always the transformation of all such data and experiences into Goethe's own active pursuits and creations. Goethe sets a tone which he holds throughout: a deep respect for all that he encounters, a gratefulness for what is given (without hiding the problematic), a clear recognition of his own value, and a desire to tie the specific particular to a universal symbol or a "moral" lesson. A human being grows in and with its world.

Only once in Book 1 do world events reach into the Goethe house. The earthquake at Lisbon led the six-year-old boy to reflect on God's "unfatherly" behavior. Why did He not at least save women and children? Book 2 is much more open to world events: the Seven Years' War, the conflict between the Prussian Frederick and the Hapsburgs, the intervention of the French. But while the autobiographer makes such openings to the wider outside world, he deals with them by showing the effects of world events on the Goethe house, the quarrels between the "fritzisch" part of the family and the Hapsburg loyalists, and especially the impact of the French occupation on Frankfurt itself. The circle of the world is thus drawn a little wider; throughout this Book the cultural, moral, and literary world of the boy also widens in parallel. The puppet theater, a gift from his grandmother, becomes an outlet for invention, and so does the storytelling of which the "New Paris" is a sample. The young "poet" increasingly begins to deal with questions of a public. Moral issues stand out more clearly; self-training (in this case by stoical experiments) becomes a more self-conscious objective. Goethe's descriptions of such issues as the potential conflict between nature and civilization show the boy's growing awareness of the complex relation among the various formative forces in his life. Systematic attention is again given to men and artists who appeared within the horizon in which he was being formed. Klopstock now begins to loom larger in the boy's reading; Klopstock's *Messias* was being enthusiastically received at this time, but father Goethe detested his rhymeless pietistic poetry so much that the rest of the family had to indulge secretly. Yet Goethe knew: this was *the* German poet before he himself came along.

In Book 3 the writer recounts events that diverted young Goethe's attention to a more powerful cultural influence. Frankfurt was occupied by the French; the king's lieutenant, de Thoranc, as we have seen, was quartered in the Goethe home. This highly civilized aristocrat made an impression on the young man; he had many artworks made for himself by local craftsmen and artists, and he involved the boy in his commissions. The deepest influence, however, came from the French theatrical troupe that performed in Frankfurt. Goethe fell under the spell of French drama and all that it symbolized and reflected of the high French culture. The imitation of these models became a passion for him; he tried his own hand at the genre, but failed miserably. When he then steeped himself in the critical literature, reading the great dramatists' own intentions so that he might discover where he had failed, he became confused. The immediate impact of the high culture from the west had been overwhelming, but it also left the young Goethe with a strong feeling, if only a vague understanding, that the groping young poet and his recent models were not attuned to each other. "Ich eilte wieder zu dem lebendig Vorhandenen" (I hastened back to that which could serve me as a viable reality [p. 123]).

In Book 4 the author gives a beautiful account of the steadily proceeding parental plan of education, the music lessons, the early scientific experiments and observations, the youngster's inquisitive visits to Frankfurt's craftshops. The text thus conveys a view of day-to-day scenes in which the various educational tasks do their quiet work in forming the boy. The uneventful Book 4 thus nicely functions as a counterweight to the impact of the eventful third book. The pedagogic stress still lies on learning languages: Latin, Greek, French, English, and Italian. The boy turned his exercises into a literary game, inventing a novel in which each national character wrote letters in a different language, to which Goethe added geographic studies so that he might better understand the diverse settings of his imaginary correspondents. He now persuaded his father that the study of Hebrew was essential.

The real weight of the fourth book thus came to be placed on a long section in which the old Goethe seeks to restate what the world of the Old Testament had meant to him in his youth. It seemed to him that he had his roots in that faraway world of patriarchs and prophets; it was his quiet port amid the dissipations of a young life. Here his world view was anchored, and here he found the first great themes on which he wanted to try himself as a poet—for, while he was thinking of alternative careers, the poet's glory seemed even then the strongest magnet.

Book 5, one of Goethe's most glorious achievements in prose, merges a detailed epic account of Joseph II's coronation at Frankfurt in April 1764 with the story of his own first great love affair. Each of the four parts of Dichtung und Wahrheit is centered on a great love of his youth; obviously, these were among his most significant formative experiences. His loves were the occasion for great poetic creation. Thus life found its second level of existence in the concentration of poetry.[32] His first love with the simple Gretchen opened "a new world of the beautiful and the excellent" (p. 189). This experience of confused bliss, mingling private happiness with the commonly shared excitement of public ceremonies, also led the young Goethe into bad company. His skills and connections were unscrupulously exploited for the devious purposes of others whom he did not understand. It was the first of the great lessons: how one becomes guilty without guilt (das schuldlos schuldig werden).

Early education in the protective shell of the home now came to an end, and the young man entered a wider world of influences. Books 6–7, and most of Book 8, are concentrated on the experiences at Leipzig where Goethe had gone to study law, as his father wanted him to do. Leipzig was a more modern world than the old-fashioned Frankfurt. Self-conscious about his hometown speech, he sought to adapt to the more fashionable world around him, and in more than one way he became a dandy. In retrospect the autobiographer depicts this whole phase of his life as one in which a myriad of fresh influences often disoriented an adolescent who at the same time was quietly experiencing formative processes that accented the qualities and views of his developing personality. The accounts of an exuberant social life, of intense student friendships, of a love affair that found poetic expression in Anacreontic verse—all of this is spread out in these books. But the autobiographer now sees as his main task a discussion of the cultural situation in which the young man had sought his own orientation.

Two matters stand out: the condition of German literature and the condition of the fine arts. Book 7, which has been called the first real history of German literature, depicts the young poet trying to find his bearing within the German literary tradition of his day. Through his vignettes of various writers, in which their achievements and the reasons for their failure are continuously assessed, Goethe describes the hopeless condition of a young poet in search of models and a meaningful tradition. There was no lack of talent, but neither was there national content;[33] the insufficient human substance ran thin in idyllic anacreontism. The poet-to-be was in search of substance that he might convert into poetry; no wonder that the discussions about experience (*Erfahrung*) suggest an *idée fixe* of the time.[34] All that seemed left was Klopstock's biblical pietism. It was not surprising that Goethe experienced instead a strong attraction to the fine arts at Leipzig. In Friedrich Oeser, the academy director and teacher of Winckelmann, Goethe encountered fresh aesthetic currents coming from Winckelmann and from Lessing. In his pictorial taste he remained, for the time being, loyal to his great love for the Dutch school which had formed the Frankfurt artists of his youth; but through the new aesthetic theories the pull toward classical form asserted itself. Goethe strategically placed throughout *Dichtung und Wahrheit* the events and the reflections by which he could show how he as a young man sought his own stance toward the entire inheritance of the biblical world, the classical world, and the German folk tradition.

Study at Leipzig ended when Goethe became seriously ill and returned home for recovery. Distance had given him a critical view of the parental home and of Frankfurt; now the tension with his father deepened. At this time Goethe developed a particularly strong interest in pietism, in Neoplatonic philosophy, in alchemy and other mysterious matters. Was he looking for magical answers? All the activity only drove him back to his nature studies and his growing conviction that he would have to form for himself the religious view that fitted him personally. The end of Book 8 is dominated by this religious testimonial and references to the auto-da-fé of most of the poetry he had written in Leipzig.

Books 9–11, overlapping the division into parts, are the heart of the matter. The account of Goethe's Strassburg period (1770–71) is the story of the poet gaining his inner freedom to be the poet and of the man striving to be himself. It was the crucial period of maturation. The very setting seemed to have been provided by Providence (a remark Goethe himself would not make): a town situated between two "cultures," in a beautiful landscape (at least for Goethe it was *"eine schöne Gegend"*), a university that attracted a diverse student body, a cathedral posing questions about the beauty of Gothic to tastes molded by the rococo. Goethe acquired an aesthetic love for the Gothic, understanding that it was an individual art style which deserved to be judged in its own right. In his discovery of English literature, especially through the works of Shakespeare, Goldsmith, Sterne, and the false Ossian, he found a valued counterweight to the French classics and *philosophes*. Now the more pronouncedly German themes of Faust and Goetz von Berlichingen began to occupy Goethe. In a not easy, indeed somewhat strained relationship, the slightly older, somewhat prickly Herder worked like a catalyst on him. Herder rarely approved of the young man, but through his suggestions and criticism he urged Goethe to move in the direction of a course already set. He showed Goethe how languages, poetry, and literatures might be understood as the collective expressions of historical individuality and how to value the manifold diversity of all such expressions. But the autobiographer does not present all these centrally important inner developments *en bloc;* instead he weaves them into the panorama of life as small significant sections made up of talk at the dinner table, encounters with new acquaintances and new books, the festival staged for Marie Antoinette as she passed through town as the young bride of the future Louis XVI, work on his habilitation as a lawyer, and excursions along the Rhine. As the introduction to Book 9 suggests: our true growth occurs when most of the powers of our soul (*eine Menge Seelenkräfte*)—our heart, our mind, our imagination, our sensitivities, our passions, and our diverse leanings—are all cultivated and made to function in harmonious interplay. All the details of these books serve to interlink the various formative processes of this period. And as the captivating centerpiece of this intricate weave Goethe gave himself and his reader the present of the idyll of Sesenheim. The description of the love affair with Friederike Brion elegantly ties together all the other strands of the Strassburg stay: reading the *Vicar of Wakefield*, exploring the Rhenish landscape and the town, fretting over the curse uttered by the dancing master's daughter, and reflecting on nature and art. In some ways Goethe here offers an idyllic prose version of some of the early poetry to which his fame was tied. It is so persuasive a piece of art that young men, with the text in hand, later set out to rediscover the enchanted place.[35]

Goethe ended Book 10, and thus Part 2, at the high point of the love affair, leaving the denouement of the entire Strassburg episode for Part 3. The central unifying aspect of the entire Part 3 now becomes Goethe, the writer of his first great works, the poet in the midst of a "German literary revolution" (p. 536). Book 11, as the first one of Part 3, seems to be conceived as a settling of accounts. Though the idyll is in part continued through the book, Goethe leaves Friederike at the end because there was no way of reconciling a life by the side of this woman with the life he vaguely envisaged for himself. He brings his studies to a conclusion by writing a dissertation on the legal rights of a state to regulate cults, but when the faculty advises him of difficulties in having it accepted, he settles for a licentiate in laws, at that time almost a doctor's equivalent. He had paid his debt to his father.

But the core of Book 11 turns to matters of general cultural and literary reorientation. Goethe argues his case against Voltaire and the French writers. Obviously, only through a great inner struggle could he free himself from the literary giants of his youth, and the effort was even more difficult than the autobiographic account makes clear. "My biography does not make clear enough what influence these men [Voltaire and his contemporaries] had on my youth, and what it cost me to defend myself against them and to find my own ground under my feet and my right relation to nature."[36] Goethe most vehemently rejects Holbach and everything that tends toward an atheistic, materialistic view of nature. But the attack involves all of French culture. "We found the French way of life too defined and genteel, their poetry cold, their criticism annihilating, their philosophy abstruse and yet insufficient" (p. 539). The defensive stance against everything French, right at the borders of France, is at once counterbalanced by an admission of deepest gratitude to Shakespeare for guiding him to a much richer notion of nature and art, to a freer view of man. Within such a settling of accounts lay the announcement of a future course: a search for a different idea of the relation between nature and God, nature and man, nature and art. "We stood at the point of giving ourselves to nature pure and simple [*rohe Natur*], at least by way of experiment." But while thus suggesting the coming age of *Sturm und Drang*, Goethe adds an account of his visit to Mannheim and its collection of classical sculpture. As so often in his autobiography, he points to the classical influences that always worked on him even though they were to have their full effects only later in life.

The momentous inner turn at Strassburg had led Goethe to the declaration: right and fitting is that which expresses the proper nature of a person—"*das Rechte sei was ihm gemäss*" (p. 508). A man is rightfully entitled to his nature. Goethe now entered a phase of life, depicted in Books 12–15, when he experimented in letting his nature expand, expressing its experience and its longing (*Sehnsucht*) in verse and prose. This was no radical departure, but it was now a much more self-conscious and resolute turn to his individuality. Much of the text is very similar to the earlier section in its wondrous blending of concrete life conditions at Frankfurt, Wetzlar, Darmstadt, the Rhineland (the greater diversity of locale being a reflection of the restlessness of the Wanderer), its depiction of the interesting men in life, its reflections on historical events, and reports of a lively social life. But the emphasis now lies differently. Much more light falls on the productive artist writing the youthful works that made him a world figure in literature, *Goetz*, *Werther*, and the great poetry of his youth. Goethe is fully conscious of his creative role; he knows that at a particular point he began to affect the world around him. The autobiographic intent to illuminate his art by the contexts of its creation becomes important. Events surrounding the reception of the works are given more room, and the problem of the relation of a writer to his public looms larger.

It was hard to find the appropriate autobiographic technique for this part. For certain sections it is now necessary that one know the works to which Goethe alludes. He disposes more freely of chronological fact. He modestly tones down the presentation of his passion for Charlotte Buff and gives only the rough outlines of the most necessary context for understanding how he came to write *Werther*. With extraordinary skill Goethe presents the mood in which he converted this affair into the *Werther*, and thus regained his emotional "health." The portrait of the writer at work is much more powerful than the description of the background events, and the discussion of the public effect that the work had is lively. It is a very interesting and fitting aspect of this Part that considerable space is given to the sketching of plans for works so grandiose in conception that only fragments remained: "Mahomet," "The Eternal Jew," "Prometheus." The titanic urge to create reached high for momentous themes, but as the motto for this book stressed, "Care is taken that the trees do not grow into the sky." Of *Faust* we hear next to nothing, except for references to actual events that were eventually made part of it; the poem was only a fragment and was completed only with a lifetime of experience and work. The other noteworthy aspect of these parts of the autobiography is the heightened use Goethe now makes of a favorite device. All through the work he lovingly draws the characters with whom he lived and who affected his development. Some of these sketches now become even more pronounced and even lengthier. It is as if in this phase in which he pursued a more unrestrained expression of his own nature, he saw the real counterweight to his own individuality in the individualities of others: his sister Cornelia, his friends Merck, Herder, Lavater, Basedow, LaRoche, Lenz, Zimmermann, Jacobi, and others. In subtle references spread throughout this Book Goethe suggests his growing awareness that a genuine individuality accepts the necessity of self-limitation and his perception that a voluntary acceptance of social necessities is indeed an integral part of achieving selfhood. Thus the great theme of Part 4 is being fully prepared.

The final version of Part 4, Books 16–20, was dictated when Goethe was over eighty years old; his last testament had been made and he sought to complete that lifelong work *Faust*. He now cut his own life story from shorter cloth; he resorted to devices he otherwise might have shunned: more readily extracting from his older travel diaries and inserting several of his poems. The number of themes and the array of personages are more limited than in the preceding books. The story element has a certain dramatic quality: Goethe was waiting for what life might bring; the first contacts with the Weimar court had been made; but who knew what would come of them and whether he himself was really ready to tie his fate to a court? His great love for Lili Schönemann grew in this period; the couple got engaged, and mother Goethe was already looking at the cradle stored in the attic. Would he settle down in Frankfurt? Awaiting events, Goethe took a lengthy trip to Switzerland; from the Gotthard Pass he looked down to Italy. Should he go? Should he return? The memory of Lili drew him back, but the relationship met with family obstacles. The emissary from Weimar had not come, and Goethe set out for Italy again only to be overtaken at Heidelberg by the arrival of a firm offer from Weimar. He changed the course of the horses to Weimar—to stay a lifetime.

The narrative of these events is still heavily interspersed with accounts of Goethe's literary activities and concerns, contact with the people who interested him, reflections on the condition of Germany, and especially assessments of the role of burgher and noble in that world. But the main accent lies on an ethical matter: a growing recognition of individual limitation and a voluntary submission to norm and rule (*Gesetz und Regel*). Now there is a turn from lonely wandering to willing acceptance of the common social tasks. Goethe had long had a sense of the danger that an unbound self might capsize in unbridled subjectivism. He had had this even in his most titanic period, when Prometheus, Sisyphus, Ixion, and Tantalus were his "saints" (p. 700), and when the awakened sense of his own poetic powers filled him to the bursting point. He vaguely must have felt the imperative of self-limitation even at the age when youth, driven by its limitless yearning (*Sehnsucht*) for an unreachable beyond, wants to give in to all the inner stirrings and whims (*Grillen*) and claims a "right" to be a natural self. For Werther there was no solution but suicide; Goethe lived for a while with the dagger under the pillow (the old autobiographer considered this a hypochondriac grimace—*hypochondrische Fratze* [p. 639]), but he had cured himself by writing the *Werther*. Many formative powers of his past, such as his youthful stoicism, his deep knowledge of the Bible, and ultimately his feeling for the power of classical form, worked within him as a counterweight to excessive self-indulgence.

But, he found himself in a world, one he himself had helped to create, where men with exaggerated notions of self-fulfillment promoted a cult of the natural genius.[37] "Another world seemed to open up; genius was demanded [not only from the poets but] from the medical man, the field commander, the statesman and soon from all who intended to prove themselves in theoretical or practical work." "When someone on foot ran into the world without a clear sense of knowing why and whereto, it was called the travel of a genius [*Geniereise*], and when someone undertook a wrong thing without purpose or usefulness, it was called a stroke of genius [*Geniestreich*]. Young lively men, and often truly gifted ones, lost themselves in the limitless." "We were still far from the time at which it would be said: genius is that force in man which sets norms and rules by its actions. At that time it manifested itself only by transgressing the existing laws, overturning the given rules, and declaring itself unbound [*grenzenlos*]."

Goethe had turned off the road leading to the excesses he now saw around him. At the beginning of Book 16 the autobiographer placed a powerful description of Spinoza's world view. A conception of world and nature bound by laws of necessity thus confronted the freely striving individual with an exhortation to resign himself to his appropriate place within an orderly nature. Goethe never became a totally resigned Spinozist, but he found peace in reading him. Above all he had reached a riper and fuller conception of individuality than lay in the unbounded cult of genius. A self was a self only in its fruitful interplay with its world; it was a self by making its world a part of itself and itself a part of its world. The value of individuality lay less in its separate uniqueness than in its unique way of making itself a part of its world.

The richness of his own nature led Goethe to search for a life in which he could combine his natural power for transforming the world by poetry with an appropriate social role. "But as this nature, capable of evoking from me such greater and smaller works without call [*unaufgefordert*], would rest in great pauses so that I could not produce anything even when I willed it, and thus found myself bored at times: then the thought came to face me with strong force whether I should not employ my other abilities and use what was human, reasonable, and sensible in me for my own and others' benefit thus to dedicate the meantime, as I had done already and was steadily more forcefully asked to do, to the affairs of the world, thus not leaving any of my powers unused" (pp. 736–37). What work this was to be meanwhile rested undisclosed in the lap of fate. More of life seemed to get organized around the impending homelife of a bridegroom. But then came the turn to Weimar. The autobiographer felt his last task was to explain this turn. But what ways were there to account for the turns in an individual life that were and at the same time were not accident, that were and were not the expression of a being's own inner law, that were and were not the result of external necessity? In all of this one touched the unspeakable, ungraspable, ineffable aspect of an individuality's existence. The aged autobiographer borrowed from his youthful creative work, the *Egmont* on which he had been working while waiting for the offer from Weimar. Both the drama's hero and the autobiographic subject seemed to have encountered a force of the universe which Goethe called the *daemonic*. It was a strange cosmic force no definition could properly capture. "It was not divine, for it seemed unreasonable; not human, for it had no reason [*Verstand*]; not satanic, for it was beneficent; not angelic, for it seemed to enjoy the mishaps of others. It seemed somewhat like accident, for it showed no concern for consequence; it resembled Providence, for it pointed toward an inner connectedness" (pp. 839–40). But by the title he gave the first stanza of the *Urworte. Orphisch*—"Daimon" —Goethe suggested that individuality was tied to the unaccountable intervention of this force.

A noteworthy aspect of this self-presentation is that its forward movement is not a linear one. Goethe did not perceive his self-formation as a sequential process in which preceding events become the cause of that which follows. Nor could he present it as the story of an entelechy unfolding its own natural potential by straightforward, innately necessitated steps—although there are hints of such an element. Growth is not simply an unfolding (p. 82). The form of the presentation itself denies a simple forward movement. The whole text is woven of many threads, any one of which may be dropped for a while, only to be taken up later on. Goethe aimed at *Bildungsgeschichte*, the story of a formation, or an "education," if the term is taken in a wide sense. But he never stays with any one formative element for very long; he constantly moves back and forth from books to men, to events, to his own activity, and so on, and never in a simple order. Hardly any statement suggests that after this or that experience he was such and such, that he then moved inevitably to the next phase of development. Goethe rarely compresses in one single description any notion of the way in which the important persons he met exerted their formative influence on his life; they appear and reappear and their effects on him seem to be gradual and cumulative. The figure of his father moves in and out of the narrative, and his power is summed up only in relation to the specific matter under discussion. Even when a love affair is presented as a magnificent idyll, as the Friederike story is, it is broken into separate segments; that it comes off as a whole, leaving an indelible impression of coherence, attests to Goethe's magnificent artistry, which also can be tested in the artfulness of his transitions.[38] But that is not the present point. As one enters deeper into the book, it is obvious that the same elements return again and again. The Bible and questions of the deity, the classical inheritance and problems of form, relations to the fine arts, Goethe's growing awareness of his poetic power, questions of morality, a writer's relations to a public, and many more such matters recur. One feels oneself being taken over the same substantive ground in book after book. But the same basic subject matter is always encountered next at a higher level of development—there is an upward-moving spiral.

Goethe's basic world view silently directed the presentation of his own life. The autobiographer's hand is guided by the key concepts of his convictions, now explicitly, then implicitly, but never in the form of a rigid conceptual schema that might have deformed the actuality of remembered experience. Goethe's notions of nature, metamorphosis, polarity, "heightening" (Steigerung), the drive toward specification, the capacity to persist (das zähe Beharrlichkeitsvermögen), or the terms from the Urworte. Orphisch: "Daimon," "Tyche," "Anagke," "Eros," "Elpis"— an understanding of all such notions could add much to our exploration here if space permitted more than a suggestion of the barest outlines.

In whatever way culture may determine our being, we remain creatures of nature.

> We are surrounded and embraced by her—incapable of stepping out of her, incapable of penetrating deeper into her.... She eternally creates new forms [Gestalten]; what there is, has never been, what there was, does not return—all

is new and always the old.... She seems to have placed every premium on individuality and does not care one bit about individuals.... Each one of her creations has its own character [*Wesen*] ... and yet all together make one.... She transforms herself eternally and knows no moment of standing still. For permanence she has no use, and puts her curse on all that stands still.... She spits forth her creatures out of the Nothing and does not tell them whence they come and whither they go. Let them run; she knows the course. ... Life is her most beautiful invention and death is her artifice for assuring much life, she clothes man in darkness and yet spurs him on towards the light.[39]

Polarity and a process of "heightening" (*Steigerung*) are the powerful driving wheels: life is breathing in, breathing out, systole and diastole, night and day, *stirb und werde*; life exists for more life, for its very intensification or heightening. "The animal quality [*das Tierische*] is heightened in Man for higher purposes."[40] Constant development to a higher level of existence is a law of our existence; as the angels say at the end of *Faust*. "Nur den der ewigstrebend sich bemüht, den können wir erlösen." Only he who seeks to strive eternally can be saved by us. We can understand life best by means of the genetic mode. We need to train the eye to see the flower already in the leaf's structure. We must cultivate a power of perception capable of tying past, present, and future into one. The never-resting drive toward specification, always counteracted by the drive toward persistence on the part of that which has already been attained, is an ever-present aspect of our reality—though it is difficult to express in words as one process, even for the poet.

Goethe transferred such organistic, naturalistic notions to the presentation of his own formation. He saw his life as a slow but steady development, or *Steigerung*, to an ever more enriched, ever more clarified, and ever more highly specified existence. The continuous adventure of life consisted of constant change—while "something" recognizable as a changing persistence was yet maintained. Life starts with an unaccountable occurrence, the play of the *daimon*.[41] At a most highly specified spot, at a precise moment in the world's constellation, nature has specified another creature. From what was then given, it can never escape. No power can break such "specified form developing while living" (*geprägte Form, die lebend sich entwickelt*). How to express this except in paradoxical terms? A form, already marked like the coin by the die from which it is cast, attains its full form only by a continuous process of living. Our difficulty, as Goethe says in trying to fathom the individuality of his sister Cornelia, is that we can think of the source only insofar as it flows (*denn die Quelle kann nur gedacht werden insofern sie fliesst*) (p. 253). Thus there is something in this notion of individuality that resembles Aristotle's idea of an entelechy or Leibniz's idea of a monad. But Goethe could not *identify* individuality with such a core; becoming an individuality could not be equated with a process of unfolding, the mere attainment of a given nature. For what was given was a coexistence with *Tyche*, a very specified world, "a moving something, moving with us and around us." A house on the Stag Ditch, a specific family, a Frankfurt, a Germany, an Athens and a Jerusalem, world and nature were continuously to be met, and many were to be constantly remet, and they in turn were to be affected by your own developing presence amid them, as you were perpetually being shaped by their own development.

For Goethe this coexistence stood under the symbol of Eros. A loving acceptance of the world is a fundamental virtue. With a basic willingness Goethe takes the world on its own terms, just as he, valuing his own individuality, was always prepared to accept others in their pronounced individuality. What is has its own value, and what is your world has its specific value for you. Thus Eros assists in the process of specification whereby you turn what is given by *Tyche* into that form uniquely befitting the *Daimon*. The self must not dissolve in an undifferentiated surrounding. Many a heart abandons itself with such fascination to unspecified and general matters that it loses itself entirely; the noblest dedicates itself to the One—"*Gar manches Herz verschwebt im Allgemeinen, / Doch widmet sich das Edelste dem Einen.*"

In one sense, the core element of Goethe's autobiographic effort lies in the attempt to depict this breathing-in and breathing-out process whereby his evolving self makes its choice from what the world offers, appropriating it and working it into its own fitting form, which he, as the poet, returns to the world, firmly putting his stamp on it. At the very end of the thirteenth book he bunches up the characteristic terms: *das was wir schätzen und verehren, uns auch wo möglich zu eignen, ja aus uns selbst hervorbringen und darstellen* . . . to value and to honor—to make our own—to externalize and to give it form.[42] By its very specificity the developing self makes the world around it its own specific world, just as the surrounding world helps to create the specificity of the self. As Hegel put this cryptically but most succinctly: *Die Individualität ist, was ihre Welt als die Ihrige ist.*[43] Individuality is what in its world is truly its own. As this process of self-formation, as an interplay with the world, advances, *Anagke*, Necessity, exerts her power in social demands, in the lawfulness of the world, and also in the lawfulness of the developing self. And the true individuality will learn how to turn the "oughts" of the world into laws it wills itself, so that the willfulness of individuality is not arbitrary whim. (*"Aller Wille / ist nur ein Wollen, weil wir eben sollten, und vor dem Willen schweigt die Willkür stille"*). In this sense individuality sets itself the law. A man becomes an autonomous person. Our irrepressible yearning to transcend necessity and individual limitation finds comfort in our ability to hope, *Elpis*.

This whole process whereby an individuality comes to be a unique self and at the same time a representative of its world, was for Goethe one that consumed a lifetime. But by the age of twenty-five enough of the process has occurred to suggest a clearly recognizable being. The formative process can only be given as the interplay of a self and its world, that is to say: as history. Goethe, paradoxically, solved the problem of autobiography by solving the problem of biography. "For it seems the main task of biography to present a human being in the context of his time, and to show in how far he strives against the whole, in how far it favors him, how he forms for himself from this a view of the world and of man, and how he reflects this outward again when he is an artist, poet, or writer" (p. 13). This biographic/autobiographic task cannot be solved by a deterministic sociological view: here is the social world, these were its effects on this man—certainly, the given social world has the quality of fate, but what is to be taken from it is unpredictable, how it is reworked is unpredictable, and how this works back on that world is unpredictable. The social world itself is a constantly evolving one. The task cannot be solved by an organistic notion of a nature unfolding. "There are few biographies which can present a pure, quiet, steady progress of the individual. Our life, as well as the whole of which we are a part, is, in an incomprehensible manner, composed of freedom and necessity. That which we would do is a prefiguration of what we shall do under all circumstances. But these circumstances lay hold on us in their own ways. The *What* lies in us, the *How* seldom depends on us, ... for the *Why* we are not permitted to ask, and on this account we are rightly referred to the *Quia* [Because]" (p. 524). A general anthropology or philosophy may help us to understand the specificity of our existence, but it is at best the outgrowth of our accumulated experience. Only the historical, the genetic view is left for an understanding and a presentation of this experience of a changing but persisting self in a given but changing world.

The very elements Goethe employs in speaking of his own development and individuality are indeed the key elements as well of modern historicism: a fascination with diversity, a sense of the unique value of each moment, a love for distinctive styles of being as a harmonious blending of diverse givens, an emphasis on process (albeit in his case organistically colored), a perspectivist viewpoint, the historical interconnectedness of all existence, and a genetic mode of understanding human reality.[44] *Dichtung und Wahrheit* thus represents the moment in the history of autobiography when the self-understanding and presentation of an individual parallels the emerging historicist mode of understanding human life. Winckelmann, Herder, Möser, and others had begun to teach that such "collective individualities" as peoples, literatures, art styles, etc., could best be understood by the light of the historical dimension. That their "pupil" transferred this manner to the presentation of an "individual individuality" was only fitting. Despite all his critique of historians and histories, Goethe reflects in his own autobiography how much he was a part of the intellectual revolution, then so strong in Germany, which made for the turn to a historicist view of life.

Goethe's view of individuality was a fitting part of this turn. So was his manner of presenting it. *Individuum est ineffabile.* Goethe knew of no way to fathom the depth of real being. In general he took a stance of epistemological modesty: try to perceive phenomena in their interrelations; if you do that with objective care, you may at times be privileged to "guess" (*ahnen*) the reality of which they are an expression; only by cultivation of such careful viewing are we occasionally permitted to construct general theories.[45] Goethe's favored manner of cognition was what he called *Anschauung*, a manner of viewing phenomena in their interrelated contexts. It is a visual approach to reality, resulting for him in a descriptive mode of presentation.[46] It comes close to what Whitehead later called prehension.

Light itself we cannot see; but we perceive it in its reflections. Similarly we have life only in its colorful resplendence—*Am farbigen Abglanz haben wir das Leben.*[47] There surely was no way of getting a hold of so elusive and so ineffable a reality as an individuality. Goethe did not see fit to present it as an abstraction, in summation, or in analytically probed isolation. If it was accessible at all, it was traceable in its effects on action, feeling, and thought; it might be detected in the specific manner in which it was reflected in the human beings and things around it. Only by becoming focused a thousandfold in the mirror of circumstance did its reflections hint at the presence of an organizing center somewhere. When Wilhelm Meister looks at the sky through a telescope, he reflects in awe: "What am I in the face of this universe? . . . How can man place himself in the Infinite except by gathering in his inmost being all the mental powers being pulled in so many directions? How can he do this except by asking himself: How can you even think yourself in the midst of such an eternal living order without if you find not in yourself also a persistent moving entity, circling around a true midpoint? And even if it were difficult for you to discover this center in your bosom, you may yet recognize it by the beneficial effect emerging from it and attesting to it."[48]

Goethe had come to know the presence of such a center within him. In *Dichtung und Wahrheit* he presents it to the reader by showing its resplendence in the things around him, its reflections in other people. His self is known by its effects in his actions, his choices, his developing viewpoint. He reveals as much of the subject as can be revealed by presenting the objects from which it is reflected. He thought of his poetry as *"gegenständliche Dichtung,"* a poetry never detached from the objects he is viewing. He was pleased when reviewers found that his "thinking never became separated from the objects." As scientist he had tried "to say how I view [*anschaue*] nature, but at the same time to reveal insofar as was possible, myself, my inner life, my manner of being."[49] As autobiographer he equally presented himself in his world. In few other autobiographies does the subject itself thus tend to disappear in its world while every object-reflection yet returns to the experiencing center. The role and the description of other human beings are thus particularly important in this regard. "Our fellow men serve us best as they have the advantage of comparing us with the world from their perspective, thus being able to obtain closer knowledge of us than we can gain. In riper years I have therefore attended carefully to the manner in which others may see me, so that I might gain clarity about myself and my inner part through and in these others, as in so many mirrors."[50]

*Dichtung und Wahrheit* thus became that magnificent collection of interesting and significant people in whom Goethe learned to know the world, in whom Goethe recognized effects on himself and his effects on them, in whom he recognized himself both by identification as well as by contrast. What pietism was for him he could best show in giving us his vision of Lavater or of Fräulein von Klettenberg (although he drew a more elaborate portrait of her in the *Bekenntnisse einer schönen Seele,* Book 6 of *Wilhelm Meister's Lehrjahre,* than in *Dichtung und Wahrheit*). The indefinable quality of an individuality directly faced him in his sister Cornelia, and he presents the problem to us by showing how and why he failed in drawing her portrait. Goethe drew a sharp picture of the critic who never could produce anything himself, and, by contrast to this recurring type of person, he also shows how his own productive strength lay in a loving acceptance of things. We very early meet this type in the little Derones, criticizing Goethe's drama in the French mode; as a heightened version there is Berisch in the Leipzig phase; then Herder at Strassburg who upset Goethe's world and yet furthered it, even if Goethe was unwilling to expose his poetry to this powerful critic; and lastly we come to Merck, the arch-critic who could never write a line himself and whom Goethe, in a way, eternalized in Mephisto, that spirit of negation.

Goethe reflects in and on such figures—such real, alive, complicated human creatures—the problems with which he is concerned. He gives us a more direct access to himself and his experience—and by placing them successively, he also gives us fuller access to his growth—than if he had resorted to self-analytical abstraction. One powerful effect of the book emerges from this wondrous manner of objectifying himself in the persons and things and circumstances around him while at the same time endowing them with the reflecting light of his own self and making them serve his life. Another effect comes from the skillful interlacing of general "teaching" observations about the human existence. Goethe's intense didactic leaning and intent made this a book of general human wisdom. He could do so the more he was a "natural object" to himself. Although he saw himself as an ineffable individuality, there were lessons to be drawn nevertheless, inasmuch as an individuality was a specific manifestation of something general, a representative of a larger human world.

Nature, the great All resting in God's lap, seemed forever to be fashioning individuality in her grand workshop and, by the artifice of death, to be making room for continuous new experiments in specification. Goethe, therefore, thought it a natural right to claim one's own individuality, to cultivate it, to value it, and to be responsible to it.[51] It is never easy to recognize one's individuality because it is forever in a process of formation.[52] In our youth especially we err, pulled here, pulled there, until we gradually learn to heed the inner law of our own being. The attractive power of other individualities and the myriad claims the world presents us mislead us. Many a human being is incapable of saving itself. The great art of education, which father Kaspar

Goethe understood only in part, was thus to present possibilities for growth, to stimulate more than to train.[53] It took the young Goethe a while to learn to trust his individuality; the more he learned to do so, the less he was inclined to force it—he let it guide his course even when he was in the dark. From his retrospective viewpoint the old man marveled at its secret working: how uncannily our strong wishes express our potential which is secretly translating itself into our actuality![54] What the young man had thus learned became the basic trust on which God Himself relied when He accepted the wager with Mephisto: *"Ein guter Mensch, in seinem dunklen Drange, ist sich des rechten Weges wohl bewusst"*—a good man striving darkly is still aware of the right course.[55] Gradually, you learn to make more conscious use of the richness the world offers. Letting yourself be guided by your own inner law goes hand in hand with recognizing your own limitations, finding the horizon of your own life, and learning to leave aside what cannot be saved for your individuality (p. 379).

The great strength of Goethe's personality, reflecting itself with such power in self-representation, came from his loving acceptance of his own individuality and of the world in which it thrived. He had such deep trust in the basic order of the world and in the natural goodness of life that his wonderment over the given reality and his awe for the potential of life always held an upper hand over all pathological drives. Perhaps there is no stronger proof of such trust than being able to hold that life exists for life's sake, that life justifies itself. A characteristic awe and respect (*Ehrfurcht*) for everything above us, beside us, and below us[56] is itself an expression of the loving acceptance of things. In it Goethe found the strength to live with the world as it was, and with himself as he was. When, in *Dichtung und Wahrheit*, he came to speak of Spinoza's significance for his own development, he says in an aside that he "always preferred to learn from a man how and what he thought rather than hear from another how he should have thought."[57] With the very same attitude he took himself for what he was, and so he took others as individualities to be respected in their own right. He cherished an ability to "find my way into the condition of others, to sense the specific mode of any human existence and to partake of it with pleasure" (p. 168). His utter fascination with the rich diversity of human existence was but the other side of his fascination with his own individuality. And the very specificity of the individuality would also protect it against the danger that a too willing surrender to the other being or to the endless wonder of the world would dissolve the self in its outward expansion.

The most powerful love cannot resist the demands of the inner law of an individuality. "Und keine Zeit und keine Macht zerstückelt, Geprägte Form die lebend sich entwickelt." To Goethe, our individuality is the firm reality on which we rest and depend, no matter how much it eludes our perception.

Its ineffable quality is in part the consequence of its unfathomable complexity and richness. Living in constant interaction with a vastly diversified and rich surrounding, an individuality is an ever developing "thing," a form forever clarifying itself more fully. It continually appropriates from the world moving along with it; it makes its own whatever fits its own character. What was not marked by it? Goethe found its presence in the dialect and speech of a man as well as in such a seemingly insignificant matter as a name: when Herder took the liberty of making puns with Goethe's name, Goethe objected: "For the name of a man is not just a coat which merely hangs about him and which you can twitch and pull as you like, but is a perfectly fitting garment, grown on him like his very skin which one cannot scratch and scrape without wounding the man himself" (p. 447).

The more deeply the individuality reached into the world, the more comprehensive its own inclinations, the more problematic became its unity. Finding the fitting horizon and limitation was not easy for a richly endowed person like Goethe. How long did he not live in a quandary as to whether he should be a painter or a poet? And how strangely self-deluding the old man sounds at times when his words seem to imply that he made a greater contribution as a scientist than as a writer! Among the vast gallery of interesting personages incorporated in *Dichtung und Wahrheit* he also saw "failed" individualities before him: the tragedy of his sister Cornelia, suffering under her father's idea of education, never reconciled to what she considered an unattractive face, failing totally as a married woman; or Lavater, always heaping up more experience than he could digest, having the power of neither art nor thought for creating an inner unity of self; and there were so many others who were more given to plucking themselves apart than learning to live with themselves.

But Goethe learned to live within his horizon, a horizon so much wider than for most. His poetic power helped him to do this by enabling him to lift accumulated and momentary experiences out onto a second "level of life."[58] He could thus create breathing space for himself, and rid himself of the "pathological" drives by placing them outside of himself in such art works as *The Sufferings of the Young Werther*. The very process of living and writing was a process of continuing inner "clarifica-tion."

And what could not be done by writing, could often be done by steeping oneself in activity of one sort or another. It is not surprising that Goethe always insisted, for himself and for others: be busy with something—not with yourself! He marveled at the steady growth of a self's inner harmony in the very process of active living. Thus the key to the unification of the personality did not lie in the Puritan's willful shaping of self and surrounding world. It was wiser by far to let the harmonious orchestration of the self occur in the interplay with the world, an interplay itself constituting active living. The many pow-ers of the soul gradually become attuned to one another; a man learns to pull to him what is appropriate to him (*das was zusammen gehört an sich heranzuziehen*) (p. 730). Gradually it appears that in the real world the things that are "compossible" stand together; what can coexist with another will also find this other. All the manifold diversity can be seen to have its fitting order (p. 673). The more an individuality "clarified" itself, the more were all its expressions also its own. Goethe found that he had his own way of speaking, his own way of dressing, as he had his own way of loving, and as he had his very own religion. No single element coming to him from the world was accessible only to him and not acces-sible to others; it might just as equally be building material for another. Every object "appropriated" became marked, however, by the specific-ity of his individual style.

Harmony and style are in a sense the key words, the only concepts for coordinating manifold diversity into a whole. Goethe himself suggests in *Dichtung und Wahrheit* how a genuine work of art is to be understood as such a unity of style, as a harmonious blending of a diverse manifold-ness of elements. It is most proper and most fitting that the example of the Strassburg cathedral coincides with Goethe's treatment of the phase of his own life when he more consciously began to understand the characteristics of individuality in himself. A recognition of the historical individuality of a specific style, that Gothic which in his own days was not much honored, belonged together with Herder's lessons about the collective individuality of "national" literatures, and the more conscious acceptance of Goethe's personal individuality.

In his description of the Strassburg minster church Goethe speaks repeatedly of the implausible but harmonious joining of diverse ele-ments.[59] In the façade "the sublime has entered into alliance with the pleasing." Vastness of mass and detail blend; "incompatible elements are united." "Contradictory elements could peaceably interpenetrate and unite themselves." In the colossal walls "the height bears an advantageous proportion to the breadth"; "the openings of this immense surface hint at internal necessities"; "at the same time light and graceful, and, though pierced through in a thousand places, giving the idea of indestructible firmness. The riddle is solved in the happiest manner. The openings in the wall, its solid parts, the pillars, everything has its peculiar character which proceeds from its own special function." "Everything is adorned with proportionate taste, and the great as well as the small is in the right place." "The right proportion of the larger divisions, the ornamental work, [was] as judiciously chosen as it was rich, down to the minutest part." "The connection of these manifold ornaments among each other, the transition from one leading part to another, the enclosing of details, homogenous indeed, yet greatly varying in form, ... are remarkable.... The ornaments [are] fully suited to every part ... subordinate to it, they seem to have grown out of it. Such a manifoldness always gives great pleasure since it flows of its own accord from 'the suitable' and, therefore, at the same time awakens the feeling of unity." "For a work of art that can be taken in as a whole of simple, harmonious parts, makes indeed a noble and dignified impression; but the true enjoyment which the pleasing produces can only find place in the consonance of all developed details." "The more I investigated, the more I was astonished." The very same astonishment overcomes us in the presence of a true individuality when diverse richness seems unified in a personal style. "Man effects all he can upon man by his personality" (p. 489).

By portraying his own powerful youthful personality as an individuality, Goethe certainly glorified this personality conception. But he placed a warning against the false aspects of individuality into this portrayal, as he did into almost everything he wrote during his Weimar period. He knew exactly why he did it. The youth around him, and then the whole generation of German "romantic poets" with whom he had to contend, had begun to turn the fascination with individuality into a cult of the personality. Goethe abhorred this cult. His warning contains almost all the ammunition we need if we, moving close to the twenty-first century, in any way care to preserve a healthy dedication to individuality.

The attractive power of individuality, the realization of the unique cosmic potential that each one alone can represent, is enormous. My mind may reel at the very suggestion that I present a one-time potential expression of what man can be which will be irretrievably lost if I fail to actualize it. It is an anxious thought that I may impoverish the human cosmos by not being true to my individuality. When one assigns so high a value to the self, egocentrism of such dimensions may result that the very social conditions which can allow for a culture of self-fulfillment are sapped. Anyone can so easily misuse the right to be himself and the freedom that he deserves to accomplish this, by falsely justifying arbitrary whim and the silliest idiosyncratic pursuits. It is by no means as easy to "do one's own thing" as most of those who use this modern vulgarization of a fruitful idea may think. To know one's individuality is a very hard thing. Such knowledge does not come by ceaselessly staring into one's soul. Twice, at least, Goethe took on that famous old phrase: Know thyself! (which over the centuries had come to mean something quite different from what the inscription at Delphi meant to say!). "If we then take that significant phrase: Know thyself, we should not interpret it in the ascetic sense ... it very simply says: do take some care of yourself, take note of yourself, so that you may obtain a sense of how you stand towards your equals and towards the world."[60] "In this context I confess that from early on I have suspected that the so important sounding task: «Know thyself» is a ruse of a cabal of priests trying to seduce man by distracting him with impossible demands from activity in the outside world, thus drawing him into a false inner contemplation. Man only knows himself in so far as he knows the world which he only comes to know in himself and himself only in it. Every new object, viewed carefully, opens up a new organ in us. And most helpful are our fellow human beings ..."[61]

Goethe inveighed against a sickly modern obsession with self-knowledge, or as he called it, the "heautognosy of these modern hypochondriacs."[62] Excessive demands for self-knowledge overburden the ordinary human being, throwing him upon personal resources which an individual, in isolation from the world, does not have. When such pathological preoccupation with the subjective self gets out of hand, an age becomes retrogressive; progressive ages, according to Goethe, involve men in objective tasks.[63] All these "modern" poets taking their subjective sensations as sufficient substance were no poets; "but if any one knows how to take in the world and then 'to speak it' [auszusprechen], then he is a poet." Even as a young man Goethe had discerned this error in Lavater's belief "that without help from many external means, one had enough substance and content in oneself, so that everything depends solely on unfolding this properly" (p. 664). Quite to the contrary, Goethe's own experience had taught him that "man needs endlessly many external pre-effects and co-effects [*Vor- und Mitwirkungen*] for a tolerable existence" (p. 450). The world furnishes us the material to form; it is the store from which we should take (p. 738). He had learned that even "the best of man only lives of the day, enjoying only a poor sustenance when he throws himself too much upon himself, and neglects to reach into the fullness of the external world where alone he can find food for his growth and simultaneously a measure of his growth" (p. 440).

The growth of an individuality is possible only in this coexistence with a world. An individuality forms itself only by the active process of making the continuous encounter with the world an individualized experience. Only by continuously accepting and forming one's world can one be forming oneself. Goethe saw this as a pulsating process of *"verselbsten"* and *"entselbstigen"* (p. 388), an oscillating between "making a self" and "unmaking a self." It is much wiser to come to see oneself move as an interesting object among other interesting objects than to place an unbearable weight of continual introspection on the fragile subject. The question whether we ourselves or the world contribute more to what we are is a silly question; Goethe had never thought of separating the two from one another.

The cure against the dangerous excesses of individuality thus lay in Goethe's fundamental experience and poetic lesson of the undissolvable nexus of self and world. The wisdom lay not in perpetual self-searching and preoccupation with the self but in active involvement in the world. Salvation was only to be found in an active life, and only he who "loses" himself finds himself. It was an old lesson. Augustine had learned to find his soul by surrender to God and in contemplating Him; Goethe discovered the same wisdom in relation to a historical social world and a pantheistic conception of ever-evolving Nature. Only life itself could teach each man what he really was—*"Das Leben lehret jeden, was er sei."*[64] Having lived by having given himself to his world, Goethe had also gained "that beautiful feeling that only mankind together is the true man, and that the single individual can be joyful and happy only when it has the courage to feel itself as a part of one" (p. 425). And his exceptionally strong belief in the saving power of active involvement in life and in work enabled him to make that stunning remark whereby individuality was preserved and transcended in yet another way: "The conviction of an afterlife springs for me from the idea of active life; for if I am restlessly active to my end, then nature is obliged to assign me another form of existence when my present one can no longer contend with my spirit."[65]

# Postscript

Goethe succeeded in weaving together the many fibers, often stretching far into the past, that constitute our notion of individuality. He came to understand its glory and its misery. He found a balanced and sane view of the self. He presented his vision with incomparable artistry. It is fitting that this search for some insight into the gradual emergence of this modern self-conception ends with his achievement. But with him does not end the story of modern man's fascination and problems with this ideal of the self.

The historian who will write this subsequent history will face a formidable task. He will find that his source material has grown to such a volume that no one mind can master it. Since 1800, autobiography has been written with growing frequency; it often consists of multiple tomes. The need to differentiate its various subgenres becomes much more pronounced; the problems posed by such a form as the autobiographic novel are weighty. The spread of autobiography to non-Western cultures poses its own dilemmas.

Under which perspective such a history might be written obviously depends upon the individual historian's outlook. A few key matters seem to invite special attention—they are, perhaps, unavoidable aspects of individuality's fate in the modern world.

In such an immensely variegated civilization as ours, it was seldom possible for the commitment to individuality to proceed to stand on its own. It usually had to go hand in hand with other conceptions of the self. The ideal of the rationally motivated man in an age of science, industrial capitalism, "scientific" socialism, and bureaucratic management asserted its own claims. So did the ideal of the professional man, even in that peculiar lasting version of what presumably should be a temporary vocation, the "professional revolutionary" of modern times. Our self-conceptions have been influenced by new conceptions of the "normal person," proclaimed by various brands of psychology, various psychoanalytical schools, and so on. Each attempt by modern men and women to coordinate the claims of such diverse callings for their selves with their wish to cultivate a specific individuality is a story of tension and inner dramatics worthy of study: we have only to look at a Mill, a Freud or Jung, an Owen, a Trotsky or Beatrice Webb, and many others. Our magnetic attraction to many different self-conceptions and tasks of life has remained one of our great problems, and we find it difficult to create our own inner harmony.

Since self-conceptions are rarely detached from men's vision of the desired society, it would be a major task to trace the modern fate of individuality in a world where so many seem to feel the urge to create and to proclaim their own utopian blueprints. The great age of liberalism and individualism had an affinity for this personality ideal which perhaps will never exist again. Does the disenchantment some feel with that world also mean a disenchantment with individuality? If so, what is to be put in its place? Or have the seemingly endless plans for ideal societies since Rousseau and the French Revolution been designed to assure the attainment of individuality for all? If so, what happens to that self-conception in a world of manipulated "ideal" conditions? Half the world has been yoked to the implementation of social theories which either seem to say nothing about ideals of self or seem to be bent on eradicating any concern with the person as a selfish perversion. Do men then make revolutions to attain the ideal of the perfectly functioning anthill? Shall man have no other function than the social one? How will the personal needs of a man take their revenge on such doctrines? Was the "revolt" of the individual against the species, which has marked so much of our Western tradition, indeed a perverse error? Our lives seem beset by the implications of social theories. The study of autobiography might provide some insights to help us cope with our problem.

The momentous realities of our modern world crisscross and interpenetrate both the ideals of self and the ideals of society. With these we have to live, whatever the role and force of the vision of ideal worlds may be. The ideal of individuality came into its own before an industrialized and intensely bureaucratic world affected it. A study of individuality since 1800 would have to show what viability it has under these modern conditions. Though modern conditions seem to have thoroughly disoriented a Henry Adams, do they necessarily do so? Added to the canvas is the great power of immense mass societies to foster the loss of genuine self-direction. Are these forces indeed such disabling powers that we can be only denied the possibility of our individuality? Or are the dreadful deluge of lamentations about "alienation" and the flight into atmospheric isolation in the hopes of giving the self its chance to survive away from troublesome society only based on totally mistaken notions of individuality? The dangerous dreams of Rousseau seem to reap a tremendous harvest. But does not Goethe's vision of the self as the simultaneously loving cultivation of one's world and one's self, inextricably intertwining both, grant us a healthier view?

In the outlook of historicism and in the ideal of individuality Western man obtained matters of very high value. When understood in the best terms, a view of life resting on a loving admiration for the diversity and the manifold richness of life is a magnificent one. It embodies the deepest respect for the formative powers of man. Even if we can know nothing about ultimate human purpose and the end objectives of this mysterious process of life, we can derive gratification and hope from a conception of cosmic order where creative individuality adds forever to the growing richness of the world. There is nobility in our willingness to understand men on their own terms and to complicate our judgments by giving each man his due. There is a refinement of knowledge in a perspectivist understanding of reality. All matters of great value exact their price. We pay for our commitment to individuality by incurring the dangers of lives floundering in capricious subjectivism, the pursuit of arbitrary whims, the loss of real selves in unrealistic dreams, and by cutting mistakenly the lifegiving interaction between self-formation and responsible cultivation of our given social and cultural world. Only the future can show whether the price is too high and whether we can live responsibly with such an ideal of the self. Perhaps those are right who say that history has no lessons. But historical contemplation may, at least, help us to be wiser. The only admonition that the historian gives us that is worth repeating may well be that, whatever else we do, we ought to live our lives as responsible heirs.

# Notes

### Introduction
1. Karl J. Weintraub, "Autobiography and Historical Consciousness," in *Critical Inquiry*, 1, no. 4 (June 1975): 821–48.
2. Georg Misch, *Geschichte der Autobiographie*, 4 vols. (vol. 1 in 2 parts, Bern: A. Francke, 1949–50; vols. 2–4 in 6 parts, Frankfurt: Schulte-Bulmke, 1955–69).

### Chapter One
1. Georg Misch devoted a double volume of his *Geschichte der Autobiographie*, 4 vols. in 8 (Bern and Frankfurt: 1907–69) to a discussion of the problem in antiquity; much learned detail and bibliographic information on the development of autobiography, in the context of the development of biography, is to be found in Arnaldo Momigliano, *The Development of Greek Biography, Four Lectures* (Cambridge, Mass.: Harvard University Press, 1971). Cf. also Ulrich von Wilamowitz-Moellendorff, "Die Autobiographie im Altertum," *Internationale Wochenschrift für Wissenschaft, Kunst und Technik* (1907): 1105–14.
2. Misch noted a similar phenomenon later on in the developments of the twelfth century A.D.: a certain loosening of older ties before a more dominant order asserts itself; he spoke of this as "a people's springtime." Victor Ehrenberg similarly spoke of "the rise of the individual" in the sixth century B.C. in "Epochs of Greek History," *Greece and Rome*, ser. 2, 7 (1960): 108.
3. Georg Misch, "Von den Gestaltungen der Persönlichkeit," in *Weltanschaung: Philosophie und Religion in Darstellungen*, ed. Max Frischeisen-Köhler (Berlin: Reichl & Co., 1911), p. 119. The article has particular interest in its discussion of why the conditions of the great Asiatic cultures were unfavorable to the emergence of individuality. It resulted from Misch's visit to Asia during the first decade of this century.
4. Might it be that with the appearance of some of the mystery religions the ideal of the wise man was retained—a man wise not in the rational knowledge of the everyday world but in the esoteric suprarational knowledge necessary for a life in harmony with a divine order that surpassed human forms of rationality?
5. There is a substantial problem involved in this assertion which ought to be worked out more fully in respect to all ancient forms of history and drama. Misch, *Autobiographie*, discusses it in relation to autobiographic literature; see especially 1:194, n. 4. Two of his own formulations sum up the problem: (1) "die uns so ins Blut übergegangene Wertschätzung der lauteren geschichtlichen Wahrheit ist im Altertum nicht zum Durchbruch gekommen, entsprechend der damaligen Lage der wissenschaftlichen Kultur, die das volle historische Wirklichkeitsbewusstsein nicht besass, das mit der Vertiefung in die innere Erfahrung zusammen anwächst" (p. 194). (2) "So blieb die wesentliche Aufgabe einer Entwicklungsgeschichte—zu erfassen, wie die Einheit der Persönlichkeit

im Verlauf des Lebens, in der Auseinandersetzung des Individuums mit der Umwelt sich bildet—im Grunde ausserhalb des Horizontes dieser antiken Biographie" (p. 303). Cf. also 2:10. Other arguments can be found in Erich Auerbach's *Mimesis*, trans. W. Trask (Princeton, N.J.: Princeton University Press, 1953), especially chaps. 1–3, 17–18. The apparent counterargument in Robert A. Nisbet, *Social Change and History: Aspects of the Western Theory of Development* (New York: Oxford University Press, 1969), pp. 15–61, dwells on the ancients' notion of growth as a notion of development; but the growth of an organism is difficult to equate with historical development.

6. A detailed survey, of 700 pages, is available to the reader of Misch's first two half-volumes.

7. Momigliano, *Greek Biography*, pp. 28–38, effectively deals with all the evidence we have for biographic and autobiographic material in the fifth century, drawing attention especially to the potential influence of autobiographically colored travel accounts; and he suggests the power of Persian influences— "Autobiography was in the air in the Persian Empire of the early fifth century, and both Jews and Greeks may have been stimulated by Persian and other oriental models to create something of their own" (p. 37).

8. Misch, Momigliano, and Wilamowitz-Moellendorff accept it as genuinely autobiographical.

9. Misch is particularly damning: "Sie zeigt ein solches Unvermögen, die eigene Individualität aufzufassen, oder wohl richtiger einen solchen Mangel an Interesse dafür, wie man es in diesem Zeitalter des Individualismus kaum für möglich halten würde; aber es ist die einzige in grossen Stücken uns erhaltene Schrift ihrer Art..." (1:321).

10. Misch, *Autobiographie*, 1:505.

11. I borrow this term from my former colleague Christian W. Mackauer, to whom I owe many insights. Misch, who, on the whole, treats Marcus's book as one of the major autobiographies in antiquity, employs the notion of the diary as well; cf. 1:463, 480.

CHAPTER TWO

1. Cf. also the *Epistle* 231 to Darius.

2. This suspicion has been discussed, it seems to me, with most insight in the fine book (which has greatly influenced me) by Henri-Irénée Marrou, *Saint Augustin et la fin de la culture antique*, 4th ed. (Paris: E. de Boccard, 1958), pp. 61–71 especially; this book, originally published in 1939, must be read with the "Retractatio" Marrou added in 1949. For other references see Pierre Courcelle, *Recherches sur les Confessions de Saint-Augustin* (Paris: E. de Boccard, 1950), p. 20.

3. Other clear examples of this type are Descartes's *Discourse on Method* and Rousseau's *Confessions*, to name but two in which such a dramatic turn was not associated with the more typical Christian conversion experience.

4. There are two aspects to the argument concerning Augustine's representativeness: he can be claimed as a product of the phase of culture that helped to shape him; but what is more, through his own gradual, though in parts highly dramatic transformation of that culture, he becomes representative as well of the changed culture pattern he himself helped to create. As will be seen, the latter aspect is one he never discusses. All of this is the theme of Marrou's great book.

5. Augustine later viewed his adherence to Manichaean gnosticism as an adherence to a heretical form of Christianity. He continued to consider himself to be a Christian catechumen; his real conversion, of course, was eventually to orthodox Catholicism. Even at a time when his religion was not his main con-

cern, he tended to be in a quandary about such a book as the *Hortensius* because it did not mention the name of Christ (*Confessions* 3.4).

6. Anyone acquainted with the immense literature produced on the meaning of conversion within the last sixty to seventy years will know that I stick out my neck perilously in these formulations. There has been an ongoing debate as to whether Augustine was converted in 386 to Catholicism or to Neoplatonism. The difficulty lies in the writings he produced between 387 and 391. The debate, which has illuminated many details, is beyond my competence. I still prefer to respect the Augustinian version in the *Confessions* which implies a conversion to religion instead of philosophy; that it may have taken the next decades, with its priestly functions, to clarify completely for Augustine what had actually happened, is another matter. For further guidance to the literature see Pierre Courcelle, *Les Confessions de Saint Augustin dans la tradition littéraire* (Paris: Etudes Augustiniennes, 1963), and Carl Andresen, ed., *Zum Augustin-Gespräch der Gegenwart* (Darmstadt: Wissenschaftliche Buchgesellschaft, 1962), pp. 480–85.

7. Augustine maintained that it was the crucial turning point, and this is what is significant for the autobiographic consideration. That the fuller formulation of the understanding of what had happened may have required further years to mature is another matter, a matter of great interest as soon as the question is raised about "truth" in autobiography versus the truth of historical reconstruction. But even if it can be shown that the explanations suggested by the works most immediate to the Milan experience are not quite those at which he arrived later, the truth of the later explanation does not thereby become the lesser one. Thus the problem of truth in autobiography is different from the historian's objective of showing "wie es eigentlich gewesen" (which also is not so simple a matter when one thinks through what is meant by *eigentlich* or by *es*).

8. The imagery of weight is pervasively used and is a derivation from Plotinian thought. Similarly, Augustine has an extraordinary preference for all terms having to do with a change in direction.

9. *Confessions* 2:4–9. The lack of understanding in the remark by Oliver Wendell Holmes to Harold Laski, cited in the fine biography by Peter Brown, *Augustine of Hippo* (London: Faber & Faber, 1967), p. 172, is too precious not to be remembered: "Rum thing to see a man making a mountain out of robbing a peartree in his teens."

10. Etienne Gilson, *The Christian Philosophy of Saint Augustine*, trans. L. E. M. Lynch (New York: Vintage Books, 1967), p. 32.

11. Cf. Robert O'Connell, *St. Augustine's Confessions: The Odyssey of Soul* (Cambridge, Mass.: Harvard University Press, 1969). This is the closest study known to me of such an exercise, but it has additional objectives that limit its value in this connection. Also useful is G. Nico Knauer, "Peregrinatio Animae: Zur Frage der Einheit der augustinischen Konfessionen," *Hermes*, 85 (1957): 216–48.

12. This remains true, in my opinion, even if the argument that Book 10 is a later insertion has validity; cf. Courcelle, *Recherches sur les Confessions*, p. 25.

13. What this meant in terms of day-in, day-out labor for almost four decades has been presented excellently in F. van der Meer, *Augustine the Bishop: Religion and Society at the Dawn of the Middle Ages* (New York: Harper & Row, 1965), trans. from *Augustinus de Zielzorger* by Brian Battershaw.

## CHAPTER THREE

1. Georg Misch, *Autobiographie*. In such a simple counting of pages one is, however, victimized by an obvious optical illusion. Misch began his work around 1900. The second half of volume 4, covering the entire period from Dante

to Fontane, is a reprint of the original draft Misch submitted for the prize of the Prussian Academy before 1904; it has not been rethought or redone in terms of the lines of argument gradually developed in the other volumes. Until Misch's death in 1965, at the age of eighty-seven, the elaboration of the study submitted to the academy had grown immensely, but in its coverage it had only reached the time of Dante. It had by now been extended to Icelandic poetry, Arabic poetry and autobiography, Byzantine autobiography. The work on the Middle Ages is thus the work of a lifetime; it has extraordinary richness, it is a monument to good German scholarship in the twentieth century—but it hardly reaches the period after which autobiography came into its own.

2. It, of course, always depends on how one counts these. For the period from the sixth century to 1500 (ca. 1350 in Italy), Misch himself treats only the following as full-fledged, self-contained autobiographies: Guibert of Nogent's *Vita*, Abelard's *History of My Calamities*, Coelestine V's *Vita*, Ulrich von Lichtenstein's *Frauendienst*, Seuse's *Das Buch das da heisst der Seuse*, Dante's *Vita Nuova*, the *Commentari del feyts* of James I of Aragon.

3. This chapter obviously owes an immense debt to the fundamental work of Misch. I accept his survey of the genre, and I was influenced by many of his insights and judgments. Except for Guibert, Suger, Abelard, Dante, I have not studied the texts he has discussed with anything like the intensity bestowed on others in this book.

4. The question of authorship is discussed by Misch, *Autobiographie*, 1:689, and by F. von Bezold, "Über die Anfänge der Selbstbiographie und ihre Entwicklung im Mittelalter," in *Aus Mittelalter und Renaissance* (Munich: Oldenbourg, 1918), pp. 208, 414.

5. These studies take up all of vol. 2, pt. 1.

6. Misch, vol. 2, pt. 1, pp. 46, 92.

7. A fine example of this is H. E. Butler, *The Autobiography of Giraldus Cambrensis* (London: Cape, 1937).

8. For this situation Misch developed the notion of a "morphological individual" (as against an "organic individual"), borrowing the former term from biologists; cf. the systematic discussion of this in *Autobiographie*, vol. 2, pt. 1, pp. 16–24.

9. Ibid., vol. 3, pt. 1, p. 91.

10. Ibid., p. 88.

11. Ibid., vol. 3, pt. 2, p. 1134.

12. As Misch said at one point: "Der Mensch hat es nicht nötig, sich zu stilisieren, wo das gesamte Leben einen einheitlichen Stil hat." Ibid., vol. 2, pt. 1, p. 141.

13. Ibid., vol. 3, pt. 1, pp. 283–387, under the rubric "Kirchliche Ortsgeschichte und Autobiographie," discusses a series of authors making this identification between local institutional history and their own story: Gyso of Somerset, Marquard of Fulda, Hermann of Nieder-Altaich, Guillaume Le Maire of Angers, Bernward of Hildesheim, and ultimately also Sugerius.

14. It is suggestive that a paperback has appeared under the title: *Self and Society in Medieval France: The Memoirs of Abbot Guibert of Nogent*, ed. John F. Benton (New York: Harper Torchbooks, 1970).

15. Misch, *Autobiographie*, 3:168–214, reinforces this by an analysis of a near-contemporary *biography*, Adam of Bremen's *Life of Archbishop Adalbert of Hamburg*, in which the central issue becomes the biographer's inability to maintain a unified view of Adalbert's personality. The churchman from Bremen understands Adalbert the archbishop, but he fails as soon as he has to account for that

part of Adalbert's life which was spent as imperial regent and tutor during Henry IV's infancy. The shift from one sphere of life to another was difficult to handle for a biographer who neither understood nor had sympathy for political reality.

16. Quoted from the document printed in Butler, *Giraldus Cambrensis*, pp. 358–59.

17. Dante, trans. with a preface by Barbara Reynolds, *La Vita Nuova* (Baltimore, Md.: Penguin Books, 1969), p. 11.

18. Leopold von Ranke, *Französische Geschichte*, 5 vols. (Stuttgart: Cotta, 1856), 1:32.

19. Suger, ed. and trans. Erwin Panofsky, *Abbot Suger on the Abbey Church of St. Denis and Its Art Treasures* (Princeton, N. J.: Princeton University Press, 1946), pp. 29–31.

20. Misch, *Autobiographie*, vol. 3, pt. 1, pp. 386–87.

## CHAPTER FOUR

1. The edition quoted here is the new translation by J. T. Muckle (Toronto: Pontifical Institute of Medieval Studies, 1964). Page references to this edition are found in parentheses in the text.

2. Mary M. McLaughlin, "Abelard as Autobiographer: The Motives and Meaning of his *Story of Calamities*," *Speculum*, 42 (1967): 487–88.

3. *Verzamelde Werken*, 4:104–22 and 4:231–75. The two articles can also be found in an English translation of essays: *Men and Ideas* (New York: Meridian Books, 1959). There is, alas, the everlasting confusion between individuality and individualism.

4. Etienne Gilson, *Heloïse and Abelard* (Ann Arbor: University of Michigan Press, 1960), p. 134 and p. v. Chapter 8 is entirely devoted to this periodization problem and is, at times, quite vitriolic in its attacks on "Renaissancists," occasionally without a fair attempt to understand their arguments. Gilson's analysis of the Abelard texts has greatly influenced me.

5. Cf. Gilson, *Heloïse and Abelard*, pp. 126–27, where he sneeringly suggests that the problem could be done away with by "a simple comparison between the Renaissance of the professors and the facts"—he alludes frequently to this idea that Renaissance historians do not respect facts. On pp. 143–44 he makes clear that he has no taste for periodization. One must wonder, however, what he can mean by such remarks as: "Could we ask for anything more characteristic of the Middle Ages?" (p. 131), or "Let them remember too that this impassioned drama ... is very much a story of the twelfth century" (p. 141).

6. McLaughlin, "Abelard," pp. 467–68, and Arno Borst, "Abälard und Bernhard," *Historische Zeitschrift*, 186 (1958): 512.

7. There has been an extended controversy as to whether Bernard could have been the second one implied here; McLaughlin, "Abelard," pp. 464–65, the latest account, sides with the belief that it was Bernard; Borst, "Abälard," pp. 502–3, and Misch, *Autobiographie*, 3:621–23, leave me with the stronger feeling that it most likely was not Bernard.

8. There is a most excellent treatment of the whole episode in Borst's article.

9. Otto of Freising, *The Deeds of Frederick Barbarossa* (New York: W. W. Norton & Co., 1966), p. 87.

10. In his memoirs (3:19) Guibert of Nogent, a near contemporary, analyzes a similar case. Guibert himself had to flee twice before his unruly monks.

11. Gilson, *Heloïse and Abelard*, p. 68.

12. *Epistle 4 to Heloïse* (Migne, PL 189. 350d–352d).

13. For an account of Soissons (1121) one can read what is customarily given as section 9 of Abelard's *History of My Calamities;* the scene at Sens (1141) can be recaptured in the description of Borst.

14. To me this is the fundamental weakness in Misch's analysis of Abelard. His notion of a *"Völkerfrühling"* in the twelfth century, a period in which individual freedom of expression results from looser social and cultural (i.e., Church) control, a fresh cultural moment of which Abelard was to be seen as a typical representative, which then was "killed" by the Albigensian crusade, etc., seems to me to falsify the Abelard problem.

15. One of the great virtues of Borst's careful argument seems to me that it blunts this "world historical" conflict between rationalism and fideism and brings to the fore instead the extent to which the clash between Bernard and Abelard was a clash between two strong temperaments and personalities.

16. Again: I part company with Misch where he implies such literary manipulation or ironic role playing.

17. Gilson, *Heloïse and Abelard,* pp. 9–19 especially, has, I think, clearly shown that it was, at that time, not impossible for a clerk and canon to obtain ecclesiastical consent for marriage.

CHAPTER FIVE

1. The *Kultur der Renaissance in Italien,* central to my thesis as well as to my historical outlook, is being cited from the Phaidon edition published in Vienna (n.d.).

2. Ernst Troeltsch, "Renaissance und Reformation" (1913), in *Gesammelte Schriften,* ed. Hans Baron, vol. 4: *Aufsätze zur Geistesgeschichte und Religionssoziologie* (Tübingen: J. D. B. Mohr, 1925), pp. 261–96, especially 276–94.

3. The English translation, even the "corrected" translation by Irene Gordon (New York: Mentor Books, 1960), simply says "free personality," which may be all right if it is understood that this "freedom" presents frightful anxieties and burdens as well as opportunities.

4. Unfortunately, the term *Renaissance man* is too frequently restricted to this human type only; this is, of course, not Burckhardt's understanding of the term.

5. Ernest Hatch Wilkins, *Life of Petrarch* (Chicago: University of Chicago Press, 1961), p. 261.

6. There are excellent discussions and illustrations of this problem in Hans Baron, "The Evolution of Petrarch's Thought: Reflections on the State of Petrarch Studies," and in "Petrarch's *Secretum:* Was It Revised and Why?," both in *From Petrarch to Leonardi Bruni: Studies in Humanistic and Political Literature* (Chicago: University of Chicago Press, 1968), pp. 7–50 and 51–101.

7. Cf. Baron, "Petrarch's *Secretum.*" It is now generally assumed that the final copy was made as late as 1358.

8. There is a fine description of the ceremony in Wilkins, *Petrarch,* pp. 24–29, a very sober but very instructive biography from a great Petrarch scholar.

9. The English quotations are from William H. Draper's translation, published by Chatto & Windus, London, in 1911. For the Latin text cf. Francesco Petrarca, *Prose,* ed. G. Martellotti et al. (Milan: Ricciardi, 1955). Page references set in the text refer to the translation.

10. In the very late *On His Own Ignorance* he said: "There is no way of learning to understand a thing more clearly except by comparing it to its contrasts."

11. The summary here does not follow the order of discussion in the dialogue.

12. Baron has argued that this is an insertion from the later forties and fifties, as may also be true of certain passages on *accidia.*

13. There is an interesting discussion of the theories about melancholia as a temperament in an article by Erwin Panofsky and Fritz Saxl, "Dürer's 'Melencolia I': eine quellen- und typengeschichtliche Untersuchung," in *Studien der Bibliothek Warburg* (Berlin: Teubner, 1923), vol. 2.

14. "Padre del ciel," written for Easter Friday, 1338, cited here from Wilkins, *Petrarch*, p. 22

15. Wilkins, *Petrarch*, p. 255.

16. One of my closest colleagues once had the intention of working this all out in psychoanalytical terms; it would have made him famous!

17. The Latin text in Petrarca, *Prose*, p. 68.

18. E.g., August Buck, "Das Lebensgefühl der Renaissance im Spiegel der Selbstdarstellungen Petrarcas und Cardanos," in *Formen der Selbstdarstellung; Analekten zu einer Geschichte des literarischen Selbstporträts: Festgabe für Fritz Neubert* (Berlin: Duncker & Humblot, 1956), pp. 35–52, especially p. 42, and also in Ernst Cassirer, *Individuum und Kosmos in der Philosophie der Renaissance* (Darmstadt: Wissenschaftliche Buchgesellschaft, 1963), p. 136.

19. Cf. Eugen Wolf, *Petrarca: Darstellung seines Lebensgefühls*, Beiträge zur Kulturgeschichte des Mittelalters und der Renaissance (Leipzig: Teubner, 1926), 28:52.

20. The letter is cited from Wilkins, *Petrarch*, pp. 239–40, but for the translation of *vita per acta iuvenem* I am following a suggestion of my former colleague C. W. Mackauer, from whom I first learned how to read Petrarch.

CHAPTER SIX

1. *Kultur der Renaissance in Italien* (Vienna: Phaidon, n.d.), p. 192.

2. See the *Oxford English Dictionary*, which shows that Carlyle, at least, considered this to be an English word.

3. Goethe, Supplement to the Cellini translation, *Gedenkausgabe der Werke* ed. Ernst Beutler (Zurich: Artemis, 1939), 15:894.

4. Cf. the Doubleday Dolphin Books edition.

5. Except where otherwise indicated, all citations come from Benvenuto Cellini, *Memoirs*, trans. Anne MacDonell (1903), Everyman's Library, (London: Dent, 1952). The numbers in brackets or parentheses following the page numbers indicate book and chapter in any edition. The present citation is p. 3 (1:1).

6. Letter to the historian Benedetto Varchi of May 22, 1559, who advised him, on inspection of the then available manuscript, not to polish and change too much.

7. Burckhardt, *Renaissance*, p. 192.

8. P. 37 (1:26); p. 64 (1:40); p. 66 (1:41); p. 71 (1:44); p. 91 (1:59); p. 203 (2:2); p. 242 (2:31); p. 290 (2:71).

9. P. 104 (1:67), "But I answered: 'God willing, I shall help myself' "; p. 171 (1:109), "I turned my face to God, and said, 'O Lord my God, defend my cause! For thou knowest it is good; and that I help myself.' "; p. 244 (2:32), "Otherwise it's war between us. And God, who always helps the right, and I who know how to help myself, will prove to you your great mistake." Also p. 118 (1:77); p. 254 (2:42); p. 267 (2:51).

10. Among many relevant passages see: p. 23 (1:17); p. 109 (1:71); p. 157 (1:101); p. 178 (1:113); p. 194 (1:125); p. 240 (2:30); p. 242 (2:31); p. 274 (2:59); p. 279 (2:62); p. 304 (2:82); p. 307 (2:84).

11. Burckhardt, *Renaissance*, p. 246, the English cited is from Mentor Books, p. 304.

CHAPTER SEVEN

1. All citations refer by page to the Jean Stoner translation of 1930, as reprinted in a Dover Publication of 1962; the citations in brackets refer to the customary chapter division of the *Vita*.

2. For details of this, cf. Lynn Thorndike, *A History of Magic and Experimental Science*, 8 vols. (New York: Columbia University Press, 1941), 6:152–53.

3. Cf. Oystein Ore, *Cardano the Gambling Scholar* (Princeton, N.J.: Princeton University Press, 1953), p. 23.

4. Cf. pp. 64 (15), 141 (33), 186 (40), 214 (43).

5. Cf. the citation from *De subtilitate rerum* in Thaddäus A. Rixner and Thaddäus Siber, *Leben und Lehrmeinungen berühmter Physiker*, Part II: *Hieronymus Cardano* (Sulzbach: Seidel, 1820), pp. 36–37.

6. Ibid., pp. 33 ff.

7. Ibid., pp. 123–26.

8. Ibid., pp. 134–35.

9. Thorndike, *History of Magic*, 5:520.

10. Rixner, *Leben und Lehrmeinungen*, p. 191.

11. These are the dates given in *De consolatione*, *De geniturarum*, and other places; in the first Parisian edition of the *Vita*, 1500 was substituted, and that date has stuck with subsequent editons, but it seems to be erroneous. Cf. Jean Dayre, "Jérôme Cardan (1501–1576). Esquisse biographique," *Annales de l'Université de Grenoble*, n.s. 4 (1927): 250.

12. Cf. also p. 277 (51).

13. Cf. p. 54 (13).

14. Rixner, *Leben und Lehrmeinungen*, p. 190, cited from *De subtilitate rerum*, Book 11.

15. Cf. the references in Dayre, "Cardan," p. 313.

16. P. 190 (41). Cf. also pp. 254 (48) and 286 (53).

17. For a useful discussion of these "battles of the scholars" see Ore, *Cardano*, pp. 53–107.

18. For support of this judgment cf. Dayre, "Cardan," pp. 298, 300, 309.

19. Misch, *Autobiographie*, 4:706. Following the interests of his teacher Wilhelm Dilthey, the young Misch, when he set out on his vast study of autobiography, became especially interested in Cardano. It is most regrettable that we have only his very early thoughts on that figure.

20. Rixner, *Leben und Lehrmeinungen*, p. 186. Cf. also W. Dilthey, *Die Funktion der Anthropologie in der Kultur des 16. und 17. Jahrhunderts* in *Gesammelte Schriften*, 2:430 ff.

21. He gives as the explicit reason for writing his *Liber de ludo aleae* (The Book on Games of Chance) the imperative that a medical doctor deal with such an incurable disease and with "natural" evil. Cf. Ore, *Cardano*, p. 189; Ore's book contains an English translation of this precursor of probability theory.

CHAPTER EIGHT

1. Quotations from the *Essais* are taken from *Oeuvres complètes*, ed. Albert Thibaudet and Maurice Rat (Paris: Bibliothèque de la Pléiade, 1962), p. xvi. Page numbers refer to this edition. I have used two different English translations: (1) *The Essays of Montaigne*, trans. E. J. Trenchman, 2 vols. in 1 (London: Oxford University Press, 1927); and (2) *The Complete Essays of Montaigne*, trans. Donald M. Frame (Stanford, Calif.: Stanford University Press Paperback, 1965). In most respects the Frame translation is the more fluent one.

2. The fundamental study for insights into the most likely sequence in which the *Essais* were written is Pierre Villey, *Les Sources et l'évolution des Essais de Montaigne*, 2 vols., 2d rev. ed. (Paris: Hachette, 1933). The Frame translation kindly provides, on the title page, the likely dates for each essay. The analysis of the first essay is drawn from Hugo Friedrich, *Montaigne*, rev. ed. (Bern: Francke, 1967), which I found to be one of the most interesting books on Montaigne.

3. In reference to the so-called Bordeaux edition, it has now become customary to identify, by marginal capitals, the material Montaigne inserted later in the *Essais* already published: A= material generally published in the 1580 edition; B= material added for the new edition (now including Book 3) of 1588; and C= material added after 1588.

4. *Essais*, ed. Thibaudet and Rat, p. 87.

5. The subsequent impact of Montaigne's skepticism has been dealt with by Richard H. Popkin, *The History of Scepticism from Erasmus to Descartes* (New York: Harper Torchbooks, 1968). Treatments of Montaigne's own development can be found in Donald Frame, *Montaigne's Discovery of Man: The Humanization of a Humanist* (New York: Columbia University Press, 1955), and *Montaigne's Essays: A Study* (Englewood Cliffs, N.J.: Prentice-Hall, 1969), two excellent books; and also in Friedrich, *Montaigne*, and especially in Villey, *Des Essais*, 2:182–235.

6. Popkin, *Scepticism*, pp. 56 ff., gives interesting examples of seventeenth-century Catholics who saw great value in Montaigne's fideism; but one may wonder about the assertion (p. 49) that "The marriage of the Cross of Christ and the doubts of Pyrrho was the perfect combination to provide the ideology of the French Counter Reformation." It is not easy to see Montaigne as an agent of the Counter Reformation.

7. They appeared in all editions of the *Essais* published in Montaigne's lifetime; the short preface to them, now essay no. 29 of Book 1, is all that is left of them in modern editions. The Pléiade edition reprints them in the Notes, pp. 1480–92.

8. Erich Auerbach, *Mimesis: The Representation of Reality in Western Literature*, trans. Willard R. Trask (Princeton, N.J.: Princeton University Press, 1953), pp. 291, 297.

9. But the most notoriously irrelevant one, "On Coaches," is essay no. 6 of Book 3. Montaigne was not bothered: "The headings of my chapters do not always embrace the matter of them ... I love the poetic gait, by leaps and bounds ... a light, fleetfooted, divinely inspired art" (p. 973).

10. Cf. also pp. 290–91.

11. Cf. Pascal, *Pensées* nos. 76–79, ed. Jacques Chevalier (Paris: Bibliothèque de la Pléiade, 1954), pp. 1103–4 ("la confusion de Montaigne ... le sot projet qu'il a de se peindre"); and Rousseau, *Confessions* (Paris: Bibliothèque de la Pléiade, 1959), pp. 516 ff. and p. 1524, n.3: "J'avais toujours ri de la fausse naïveté de Montagne [*sic*]...."

12. Auerbach, *Mimesis*, p. 276. The idea of the creatural (*das Kreatürliche*) was a major theme of his book, especially the central chapters—highly recommended reading.

13. Arthur O. Lovejoy, *The Great Chain of Being: A Study of the History of an Idea* (New York: Harper Torchbooks, 1960), pp. 142–43.

14. Marvin Lowenthal, ed., *The Autobiography of Michel de Montaigne* ... (Boston: Houghton Mifflin, 1935), p. lvi.

15. It was very characteristic that such words as *vulgaire* began to have more positive connotations in the later additions to the *Essais*. Montaigne's gradual

turn toward this acceptance of the common in him and toward the praise of the common people around him, has been traced in a beautiful fashion in the two books by Donald Frame; cf. above n. 5.

16. The extensive involvement of Montaigne in public life has been shown in Fortunat J. Strowski, *Montaigne, sa vie publique et privée*. Paris: Nouvelle Revue Critique, 1938, and in an old, and partially unreliable, book by Alphonse Grün, *La Vie publique de Michel Montaigne* (1855; Geneva: Slatkine Reprints, 1970).

17. Much of the value of Villey, *Des Essais;* Frame, *Montaigne's Essais;* and Fortunat Strowski, ed., *Essais de Montaigne*, 5 vols. (Bordeaux: Pech, 1906–33) lies exactly in this dimension.

18. *Correspondance de Bossuet,* ed. Charles Urbain et al. (Paris: Hachette, 1910), 3:371–74.

### CHAPTER NINE

1. The so-called *Exemplar* contained a Prologue, a two-part *vita* of Seuse, the *Little Book of Eternal Wisdom*, the *Little Book of Truth*, and the *Pastoral Letters*. The text used here is Heinrich Seuse, *Deutsche Schriften*, ed. Karl Bihlmeyer (Stuttgart: W. Kohlhammer, 1907), which gives the text in the original older High German, and *Das Leben des Seligen Heinrich Seuse*, trans. Georg Hofman (Düsseldorf: Patmos, 1966). The discussion of Seuse by Misch, *Autobiographie,* vol. 4, pt. 1, pp. 91–130, is excellent, and I do rely very much on it.

2. I follow Bihlmeyer and Misch in accepting the genuineness of Seuse's final authorship; the Hofman edition does not—it attributes the *Life* to Elsbeth Stagelin.

3. All references are to the Bihlmeyer edition by page and line.

4. See especially Chapter 19.

5. Seuse took the distinction between *Gott* and *Gottheit* from his master Eckehart.

6. Dom Cuthbert Butler, *Western Mysticism* (New York: Harper Torchbooks, 1966), originally published in 1922, presents a particularly strong analysis of this central issue.

7. Misch concludes: "Aber das Heterogene, das er nicht konsequent zusammenzudenken vermochte, hat er zusammen*gelebt*" (his underlining) and speaks of "diese irrationale Synthese." *Autobiographie*, vol. 4, pt. 1, p. 255.

8. See Bihlmeyer, *Deutsche Schriften*, pp. 144 ff.

9. *Life*, 10:11 and also 14:12. The quotation, by chapter and paragraph, as is customary with her writings, is taken from *The Life of St. Teresa of Avila* ..., trans. David Lewis, with an Introduction by David Knowles (London: Burns & Oates, 1962).

10. Prologue.

11. A clear account of the very involved history of the reform is to be found in Edgar Allison Peers, *Handbook of the Life and Times of St. Teresa and St. John of the Cross* (London: Burns & Oates, 1954), pt. 1.

12. A very intensive study of the nature of the problem, especially on the issue of discursive prayer, can be found in E. W. Trueman Dicken, *The Crucible of Love: A Study of the Mysticism of St. Teresa of Jesus and St. John of the Cross* (New York: Sheed and Ward, 1963), and also in several of the essays in Father Thomas O.D.C., ed., *St. Teresa of Avila: Studies in Her Life, Doctrine and Times* (Dublin: Clonmore & Reynolds, 1963).

13. Quoted here from the Appendix in the *Life*, pp. 400–401.

14. *Life*, 29:7, and cf. 26:6: "His Majesty afterwards would change the mind of that confessor."

15. *Life*, 11:24. Cf. also 30:25 and 40:25.
16. *Life*, 8:15–16; 20:28; 23:8–9.
17. *Life*, 26:4–6; 28:19–24; 29:4–9; 33:4–5; 37:6; 38:20.
18. The relationship to Molinos is unclear. Madame Guyon herself maintained firmly that she knew nothing about him until she was accused of his errors; her close associate Father La Combe was more likely influenced by Molinos. But in view of the appearance of many such teachings resembling Quietism (itself a vague term) in the second half of the century, it seems plausible that there was much independent movement in similar directions. The parallelism of Protestant Holland, with its Labadists and Collegianten, with a Schuerman, a Plockhoy, or a Bourignon, has been worked out in such books as Cornelia W. Roldanus, *Zeventiende Eeuwse Geestesbloei* (Utrecht: Het Spectrum, 1961). Any number of books on German pietism or English nonconformism have to touch on very similar phenomena.
19. Quotations are given from an abridged version, *The Life and Religious Experience of the Celebrated Lady Guion* (New York: Hoyt & Bolmore, 1820).
20. The most readable account of the controversy is Michael de la Bedoyere, *The Archbishop and the Lady: The Story of Fénelon and Madame Guyon* (London: Collins, 1956); other accounts are available in Emmanuel Aegerter, *Madame Guyon, une aventurière mystique* (Paris: Hachette, 1941); L. Guerrier, *Madame Guyon: Sa vie, sa doctrine et son influence* (Paris: Didier, 1881), and Henri Delacroix, *Etudes d'histoire et de psychologie du Mysticisme* (Paris: Alcan, 1908).
21 Quoted in Bedoyere, *Archbishop and the Lady*, p. 87.
22. Ibid., p. 43.
23. Cf. *Life of Lady Guion*, pp. 24, 29, 52–53, 72, 82, 90, 133, 138, 143, 155, 202, 238, among others.

CHAPTER TEN

1. My interpretation of this has been most heavily influenced by Max Weber's thesis on the Protestant Ethic, and by the fascination that this thesis had for my former colleague Christian Mackauer. A very helpful book, quoting a vast number of excellent sources, is Owen C. Watkins, *The Puritan Experience* (London: Routledge & Kegan Paul, 1972); his interpretation does not seem to be influenced by Weber, who is not even mentioned in the Index. Paul Delany, *British Autobiography in the Seventeenth Century* (London: Routledge & Kegan Paul, 1969), gives an extensive listing of autobiographic writings.
2. Calvin, *Institutes*, ed. John T. McNeill, 2 vols. (Philadelphia: Westminster Press, 1960), 3.21.2.
3. For a definition of Effectual Calling, Weber quoted Chapter X from the *Westminster Confession*: "All those whom God hath predestinated unto life, and those only, He is pleased in His appointed and accepted time effectually to call, by His word and spirit (out of that state of sin and death, in which they are by nature) ... taking away their heart of stone, and giving unto them an heart of flesh; renewing their wills, and by His almighty power determining them to that which is good." Cf. Max Weber, *The Protestant Ethic and the Spirit of Capitalism*, trans. Talcott Parsons (New York: Scribner, 1958), p. 100.
4. Weber, *Protestant Ethic*, p. 104.
5. Ibid., p. 106.
6. Ibid., p. 115.
7. Ibid., p. 117. See also the statement from Max Weber, *Wirtschaft und Gesellschaft*, Studienausgabe ed. J. Winckelmann, 2 vols. (Cologne: Kiepenheuer & Witsch, 1956), 1:446–47: "Denn unter allen Umständen war der Prädes-

tinationsdeterminismus ein Mittel der denkbar intensivesten systematischen Zentralisierung der Gesinnungsethik. Die Gesammtpersönlichkeit, wie wir heute sagen würden, ist durch göttliche Wahl mit dem Ewigkeitswertakzent versehen, nicht irgendeine einzelne Handlung." Which, perhaps, can be translated thus: "For the determinism of predestination was, in any case, a means for the most intensive imaginable centralization of an ethics of absolute values. The total personality, as we would say nowadays, and not simply any kind of single action, has been marked with the accent of eternal value by divine election."

8. James Janeway's life of his brother John is cited in Watkins, *Puritan Experience*, pp. 20–21. Watkins cites an anonymous MS. from 1693, in addition, which shows the "natural" ease with which spiritual accounting and fiscal accountings could interpenetrate: "31 day spent in seeking to cast up my accounts with God and to see all ye debt discharged by ye full satisfaction allready made by my ... blessed Savior Jesu Xt. I have considered my concerns ys moneth and find yt my Recepts have been 10£ 3s. 6: and have disburst and payd 9£4s. 6: Blessed by ye God of my mercys that sends me Recepts answerable to my charges and disbursms. Amen."

9. Roger Sharrock, *John Bunyan* (London: Hutchinson's University Library, 1954), p. 41. This is the most useful biography available.

10. *Grace Abounding*, par. 174; all citations refer to the customary subdivision into paragraphs. The edition used is the one by James Thorpe, ed., *The Pilgrim's Progress from this World to that which is to Come and–Grace Abounding to the Chief of Sinners* (New York: Houghton Mifflin, 1969).

11. Watkins, *Puritan Experience*, has useful examples of this technique in his analysis of the genre.

12. *Pilgrim's Progress*, p. 94.

13. I do not imply that this process has totally won out in the case of Bunyan; but his use of the Devil and of visions, interventions in the regular order of the world's course, has a tendency to be transmuted into allegory.

14. The text used here is the abbreviated edition made by J. M. Lloyd Thomas for the Everyman's Library in 1925, the only really readable edition of this huge ragbag of a book. Of biographical value are the two volumes by Frederick J. Powicke, *A Life of Reverend Richard Baxter 1615–1691* (Boston: Houghton Mifflin, 1924), which concentrates on the period up to 1660, and *The Reverend Richard Baxter Under the Cross (1662–1691)* (London: Jonathan Cape, 1927). The study by Hugh Martin, *Puritanism and Richard Baxter* (London: SCM Press, 1954), gives a good overview of Baxter's position within Puritanism.

15. Powicke, *Life of Baxter*, p. 41.

16. Weber, *Protestant Ethic*, p. 182.

17. The edition of the *Autobiography* used here is the Washington Square Press Collateral Classic (1966). For biographical data I have relied on Carl Van Doren, *Benjamin Franklin* (New York: Viking Press, 1964); a very useful collection of essays is Esmond Wright, ed., *Benjamin Franklin: A Profile* (New York: Hill & Wang, 1970), especially those by David Levin and I. Bernard Cohen. Robert F. Sayre wrote a book with a fine title, *The Examined Self: Benjamin Franklin, Henry Adams, Henry James* (Princeton, N.J.: Princeton University Press, 1964), but its argument puzzles me—it strongly stresses Franklin's role as poseur.

18. Van Doren, *Franklin*, p. 17. Cf. also *Autobiography*, p. 21: "evading as much as I could the common attendance on public worship which my father used to exact..."

19. This, of course, is one of Max Weber's key points.

20. Cf. Sayre, *Examined Self*, pp. 26–31.

21. Weber, *Protestant Ethic*, p. 263.

## CHAPTER ELEVEN

1. This is the main theme of Arthur O. Lovejoy's fine book *The Great Chain of Being*. Of particular interest are the two chapters on Leibniz in which he analyzes the philosopher's dilemma in trying to reconcile a deep commitment to eternal reason with an evolutionary tendency or thrust in the world of monads.

2. *Philosophische Schriften*, ed. Gerhardt, 7 vols. (Berlin: Weidmann, 1875–90), 3:567 ff. The above is quoted from the translation in the best piece of writing on Vico's autobiography, the "Introduction" by Max H. Fisch, *The Autobiography of Giambattista Vico*, trans. Max H. Fisch and Thomas G. Bergin (Ithaca, N.Y.: Cornell University Press, 1944), p. 5. All references to the autobiography are to this edition.

3. One very readable attempt to do this in English may still be Robert Flint, *Vico*, Philosophical Classics for English Readers (Edinburgh, 1884), cited from an undated edition by Lippincott, Philadelphia. Also useful are B. Croce, *The Philosophy of Giambattista Vico* (London, 1913); A. Robert Caponigri, *Time and Idea: The Theory of History in Giambattista Vico* (Chicago: H. Regnery, 1953); and several essays in Giorgio Tagliacozzo, ed., *Giambattista Vico: An International Symposium* (Baltimore, Md.: Johns Hopkins Press, 1969). The scholarly literature in Italian, most notably by Fausto Nicolini and Franco Amerio, has not been consulted.

4. Flint, *Vico*, pp. 19, 112–35, tries to show that Vico had some peculiarly confused notions of the derivation of such philosophic positions.

5. Cf. the interesting article by Ernesto Grassi in Tagliacozzo, *Vico*.

6. *De nostri temporis studiorum ratione* (1709) includes epistemological statements antedating many an aspect of historism.

7. *Inaugural Oration on Universal Law* (1719), *Sinopsi del Diritto Universale* (1720), *De uno universi iuris principio et fine uno* (1720), *De constantia iuris prudentis* (1721), and later, *Origine, progresso e caduta della poesia italiana* (1723).

8. Erich Auerbach, "Vico and Aesthetic Historism," in *Scenes from the Drama of European Literature* (New York: Meridian Books, 1959), p. 188.

9. This is not meant to say that Vico suggests that the phases of humanity's history are exactly reflected in the course of his own life.

10. Isaiah Berlin, "A Note on Vico's Concept of Knowledge," in Tagliacozzo, *Vico*, p. 376 ff., a particularly lucid article on a difficult point in Vico.

11. The "unbowdlerized" text was only made available in the last two decades. The text used here, in its footnotes and introduction, gives a good account of the process of reinstituting the full text, and also nicely illustrates Sheffield's great editorial skills. *The Autobiography of Edward Gibbon*, ed. Dero A. Saunders (New York: Meridian Books, 1961).

12. Much is made of this by Joseph W. Swain, *Edward Gibbon, the Historian* (London: Macmillan, 1966), pp. 3 ff. Gibbon received the *Introductio ad Latinam Blasoniam* in 1786; it contained the family tree on which he based the initial section of the autobiography.

13. David Morrice Low, *Edward Gibbon, 1737–1794* (New York: Random House, 1937), pp. 340 ff., has a wonderful account of the shenanigans in which Gibbon engaged to create the impression that the publishers were eagerly soliciting the "unwilling" author to write a seventh volume.

14. Philip Guedalla, in "A Letter to the Reader," prefacing *The History of the Decline and Fall of the Roman Empire*, 3 vols. (New York: Heritage Press, 1946), 1:xv.

15. The title that Low gave to the chapter on this phase of the life; cf. *Gibbon*, pp. 194–207.

CHAPTER TWELVE

1. Ernst Cassirer's *Das Problem Jean-Jacques Rousseau* still raises the issue most succinctly; this is available in English: Peter Gay, trans., *The Question of Jean-Jacques Rousseau* (Bloomington: Indiana University Press, 1963).

2. Jean Guéhenno, *Jean-Jacques Rousseau*, trans. J. and D. Weightman, 2 vols. (London: Routledge & Kegan Paul, 1966), 2:128, an indispensable work for placing the accounts of the *Confessions* in proper historical perspective.

3. .*Ebauches des Confessions*, in Jean-Jacques Rousseau, *Oeuvres complètes*. Vol. 1: *Les Confessions et autres textes autobiographiques* (Paris: Bibliothèque de la Pléiade, 1959), p. 1163. *Oeuvres complètes* is henceforth abbreviated as *O.C.* References in parenthesis refer to the page numbers of the *Confessions*.

4. "Sentiment des citoyens," in Voltaire, *Mélanges*, ed. Jacques van den Heuvel (Paris: Bibliothèque de la Pléiade, 1961), p. 717.

5. "Quatre Lettres à M. le Président de Malesherbes contenant le vrai tableau de mon caractère et les vrais motifs de toute ma conduit" (January 4, 12, 25, and 28, 1762), in *O.C.*, 1:1130–47. Cf. also *Confessions*, p. 569 for a statement of the intention to substitute these letters for memoirs.

6. *Mon portrait*, in *O.C.*, 1:1120–29.

7. The phrase from Persius's *Satires* ("inwardly and under the skin") was placed, as the motto, at the beginning of Book 1.

8. Cf. *Rousseau juge de Jean-Jacques*, in *O.C.*, 1:974, 976.

9. The little pamphlet "A tout François aimant encor la justice et la vérité," of April 1776, in *O.C.*, 1:990–92. That closed metal gates were a horror for Rousseau is also shown in *Confessions*, pp. 42, 60.

10. The eminent virtue of Guéhenno's biography is that it places the account of the *Confessions* in and against the context of Rousseau's life as this can be determined from other evidence. An interesting corrective study on one of the many episodes that have been investigated in detail is Henri Guillemin, *Rousseau à l'Ermitage* (1756–57) (Geneva: Milieu du Monde, n.d.), based on his detailed study "Les Affaires de l'Ermitage (1756–57); examen critique des documents" in *Annales de la Société Jean-Jacques Rousseau* 29 (1941–42): 59–258.

11. The standard work of Pierre Courcelle, *Les Confessions de St. Augustin dans la tradition littéraire* (Paris: Etudes Augustiniennes, 1963), pp. 459–60, borders on the incredible, as far as Rousseau is concerned, in the brevity and in the cavalier manner in which it speaks to this point.

12. Cf. especially the accusations against Montaigne that he only revealed those faults that he found it convenient to admit, *Confessions*, pp. 516–17, and *Ebauches*, p. 1150.

13. *Confessions*, p. 86, for another such remembered sin involving LeMaistre; cf. p. 128.

14. "I couild not help benefiting from showing myself as I was," ibid., p. 517.

15. *Ebauches*, pp. 1149–50.

16. Cf. especially *Confessions*, p. 175.

17. Ibid., p. 351; cf. also *Lettres à Malesherbes*, p. 1135.

18. This is, of course, no new thesis at all; many interpreters of Rousseau have believed in it. The strongest formulation of it may still be: Gerhard Gran, "La Crise de Vincennes," in *Annales de la Société Jean-Jacques Rousseau* 7 (1911), 1–17, especially pp. 14–15. "La question de l'Académie de Dijon agit comme un choc sur le 'seuil,' y fit une brèche, et par cette brèche se precipita soudain un flot fait des souvenirs des indignations, des impressions, bref, de toute la matière psychique venue de l'hérédité, de la race, des expériences antérieures, qui s'était accumulée dans son subconscient. Il s'établit, entre les sphères psychiques situées des deux côtés du seuil, une nouvelle voie de communication, grace à

laquelle il prit possession de lui-même, de sa personnalité, il devint le propriétaire conscient de ses instinct, qu'il put dorénavant suivre en toute sécurité. En d'autres termes, il passa par une crise qui fut décisive pour sa personnalité, sa vie, ses actes, ses oeuvres ... d'une grand conséquence pour l'histoire de l'esprit humaine. Cette crise de Rousseau fut en effet décisive à bien des égards pour le cours de la vie intellectuelle de sa génération et, plus encore, des générations suivantes."

19. Since coming to Paris in 1742, driven from his Swiss Eden by his jealousy of Madame de Warens's new lover, Rousseau had also spent a little over a year as the main assistant to the French ambassador in Venice (July 1743–August 1744).

20. Cf. especially *Rousseau juge*, p. 828, where he explains how the implications of the question gradually turned his life in a new direction.

21. Rousseau's restated trust in Providence, answering.the questions raised in Voltaire's poem of 1756 on the Lisbon earthquake of 1755; Voltaire answered Rousseau in *Candide* (1759).

22. Rousseau's misgivings about d'Alembert's article on Geneva in the *Encyclopédie* (1758).

23. Cited here from Mario Einaudi, *The Early Rousseau* (Ithaca, N.Y.: Cornell University Press, 1967), pp. 55–56.

24. *Confessions*, p. 368, and *Lettres à Malesherbes*, p. 1136.

25. *Lettres à Malesherbes*, ibid.

26. For support of this argument see: *Confessions*, p. 513; *Rousseau juge*, pp. 673, 676, 791, 810, 829 (esp), 843; *Rêveries*, *O.C.*, 1:1134–36, 1151; and *Art de jouir*, *O.C.*, 1:1173. It is, of course, interesting that this argument grew stronger in the later writings.

27. *Confessions*, pp. 408–9, pp. 1469–70 (n. 1), lists a number of scholarly works that try to trace the psychological theories Rousseau had intended to incorporate in this book, but apparently this was not done for the autobiographical material where, one would assume, it would be most rewarding.

28. Cf. also *Ebauches*, p. 1158.

29. *Rêveries*, p. 995.

30. *Mon portrait*, p. 1123. Late in 1770, Rousseau read the *Confessions* to a group of Parisian confidants; in the note introducing this reading, he stresses his singularity: "Il serait important, pour bien juger de ma conduite, de connaitre à fond mon tempérament, mon naturel, mon caractère, qui, par une singularité de la nature, ne ressemblent point à ceux des autres hommes..." In "Discours projeté ou prononcé pour introduire la lecture des Confessions," *O.C.*, 1:1185.

31. Guéhenno, *Rousseau*, 2:236.

32. *Ebauches*, p. 1153.

33. Cited from Guéhenno, *Rousseau*, 2:89.

34. *Rêveries*, pp. 995, 999.

35. Quoted by Guéhenno, *Rousseau*, 2:200. Cf. also the passage in *Confessions*, pp. 640–41.

36. *Confessions*, pp. 343–45; quotation is on p. 345.

37. Guéhenno, *Rousseau*, 2:265.

38. *Confessions*, p. 363; the phrase was important to Rousseau—he repeated it verbatim in *Rousseau juge*, p. 846.

39. Cf. first preamble and also *Ebauches*, p. 1154: "by its objective this will always be a precious book for the thinking men [*les philosophes*]: it is, I repeat, a piece of comparison for the study of the human heart, and it is the only one in existence."

40. The sentence comes from Maitre de Claville's *Traité du vrai mérite* (1742), a

very popular book in Rousseau's early years. It is here quoted from Guéhenno, *Rousseau*, 1:64, who credits Masson for finding it. It is too irresistible a quotation not to be pilfered in turn.

41. M. B. Ellis, *Julie or La Nouvelle Héloïse: A Synthesis of Rousseau's Thought 1749–59* (Toronto: University of Toronto Press, 1949), p. 80, an excellent book on the basic consistencies in Rousseau's intellectual outlook.

42. *Confessions*, p. 468, where Rousseau reacts to the code of morality of his one-time friend and later enemy, Grimm. Cf. also ibid., p. 91, 175, and *Rêveries*, p. 1058.

43. *Confessions*, p. 446; the phrase is repeated in *Rousseau juge*, p. 860. To obtain a fuller sense of what this great theme meant for Rousseau, the reader should read the magnificent book by Jean Starobinski, *J. -J. Rousseau: La Transparence et l'obstacle* (Paris: Gallimard, 1971).

44. Cf. *Lettres à Malesherbes*, p. 1132: "On suit son coeur et tout est fait."

45. *Confessions*, p. 408; pp. 408–9, contain the subsequent citations. Cf. also pp. 174–75.

46. Ibid., pp. 356–59, for the whole painful analysis of his deed.

47. Ibid., pp. 84–87, from which all the quotations are taken.

48. Cf. the parallels in ibid., pp. 462, 473, 535.

49. Ibid., p. 56. Cf. also *Rêveries*, p. 1053.

50. Rousseau directly confronts this "accusation" in *Rousseau juge*, p. 887, by saying that he had not sought to overturn all existing institutions.

51. Perhaps one of his strongest statements showing the importance of individual differences is in *La Nouvelle Héloïse*, letter no. 3, part 5, *O.C.*, 2:562: "Outre la constitution commune à l'espèce chacun apporte en naissant un tempérament particulier qui détermine son génie et son caractère, et qu'il ne s'agit ni de changer ni de contraindre, mais de former et de perfectionner." On the differences among peoples, see the *Lettre à Philopolis*, *O.C.*, 3:234.

52. Cf. *Rêveries*, p. 1047, for a strong statement.

53. Cf. *Rousseau juge*, p. 845: "Il porte sans peine le joug de la necessité des choses, mais non celui de la volonté des hommes," and also *Rêveries*, p. 1078.

54. Cf. Claire's letter to Julie, *La Nouvelle Héloïse*, letter no. 5, part 6, p. 662: "Ainsi s'aiguise la volupté du sage: s'abstenir pour jouir c'est ta philosophie; c'est l'epicureïsme de la raison."

55. Second Preface, ibid., p. 28.

56. See the discussion of this issue in *Confessions*, pp. 35–38, and the discussion in Starobinski, *Rousseau*, pp. 130 ff.

57. *Confessions*, p. 104; cf. also pp. 162, 178–79, 426, 428, 521.

58. Lovejoy, *The Great Chain of Being* (New York: Harper & Row, 1960), p. 293.

59. Ibid., p. 313.

60. "the emergence of Historism was, as is to be shown in this book, one of the greatest revolutions of the mind experienced by the Western intellectual tradition" [Und das Aufkommen des Historismus war, was in diesem Buche gezeigt werden soll, eine der grössten geistigen Revolutionen, die das abendländische Denken erlebt hat]: Friedrich Meinecke, *Die Entstehung des Historismus* (Munich: R. Oldenbourg, 1965), p. 1. An English translation of this has been published by Routledge and Kegan Paul.

## CHAPTER THIRTEEN

1. "Deutschland hatte eigentlich keine Verfassung. Es war vielmehr ein blosser Zustand, in welchem zur Friedenszeit sich jederman wohlbefinden konnte." Quoted by Ernst Beutler in the *Einführung* to *Dichtung und Wahrheit* (Zurich & Stuttgart: Artemis Verlag, 1948), p. 939.

2. In the seventeenth century Casper von Lohenstein had written a long epic novel about Arminius; Klopstock wrote on him in the eighteenth century; in the nineteenth century Heinrich Heine made devastating fun of the whole cult: "Das ist der Teutoburger Wald, den Tacitus beschrieben, das ist der klassische Morast wo Varus stecken geblieben. Hier schlug ihn der Cheruskerfürst, der Hermann der edle Recke; die deutsche Nationalität, die siegte in diesem Drecke." *Deutschland, ein Wintermärchen,* chap. 11.

3. For some of the most incisive remarks about this influence of pietism, see Ernst Troeltsch, "Er [der Pietismus] hat ... mit der Aufklärung zusammen den neuen Stand des gebildeten Bürgertums, der selbständigen Individualitäten schaffen helfen, der dann das Zentrum der deutschen Kultur geworden ist." In "Leibniz und die Anfänge des Pietismus," *Gesammelte Schriften,* Vol. 4: *Aufsätze zur Geistesgeschichte und Religionssoziologie,* ed. Hans Baron (Tübingen: Mohr, 1925), p. 530.

4. *Dichtung und Wahrheit,* ed. Ernst Beutler (Zurich: Artemis Verlag, 1948), p. 651, and see also p. 703. All subsequent citations are from this edition, which is referred to as *D & W.* Only very recently an English edition of the text has again become available, Goethe, *The Autobiography,* trans. John Oxenford (Chicago: University of Chicago Press, 1974). Of all the greatest figures of world literature, Goethe seems, strangely, to be one of the least known to the English-speaking world. Academics, of course, meet dutifully for anniversary celebrations such as those in 1932 or 1949, usually assessing the relevance of Goethe to our own age; cf. the listings in Heinz Kindermann, *Das Goethebild des 20. Jahrhunderts* (Darmstadt: Wissenschaftliche Buchgesellschaft, 1966), pp. 466 ff., 678 ff., in which he makes strangely optimistic remarks about Goethe's popularity. Meanwhile, the ordinary mortal has difficulty in getting a paperback copy of one of the greatest autobiographies!

5. "Europa hatte eine andere Gestalt angenommen," in *Tag- und Jahreshefte oder Annalen als Ergänzung meiner sonstigen Bekenntnisse,* ed. Beutler (Zurich: Artemis Verlag, 1950), p. 785. (Hereafter cited as *Annalen*).

6. To Holtei, January–February, 1828, "Ja, ja ihr guten Kinder, wenn ihr nur nicht so dumm wäret."

7. One of the exceptions to this are the introductory and explanatory notes Goethe wrote to the *Urworte. Orphisch,* a poem quoted and reproduced below.

8. Some of the books with the most rewarding insights into Goethe concentrate very much on this task of understanding him by the concretizations of his experience in the poetic works themselves, and give very little weight to his own reflections about his life and works; one of the most fascinating of these is the work by Friedrich Gundolf, *Goethe* (Berlin: Bondi, 1920), who introduces his intention thus: "Die Werke sind dann nicht die Zeichen welche ein Leben bedeuten, sondern die Körper welche es enthalten. Der Künstler existiert nur insofern er sich im Kunstwerk ausdrückt" (p. 2). Somewhat different in method, but parallel in intent, is the very interesting book by Georg Simmel, *Goethe* (Leipzig: Klinckhardt, 1913).

9. See the reference in *Annalen,* pp. 67 ff.

10. As the book appeared originally in Cotta's edition, it also contained letters by Winckelmann and, in addition to Goethe's biography, writings by Heinrich Mayer and Friedrich August Wolf; the edition used here is Beutler's *Gedenkausgabe,* Vol. 13: *Schriften zur Kunst* (Zurich: Artemis Verlag, 1954), 407–50.

11. The book on "Philipp Hackert, eine biographische Skizze" can be found in *Schriften zur Kunst,* pp. 459–627.

12. *Annalen,* p. 846.

13. See, for instance, ibid.: "Ich hatte die Entwicklung eines bedeutend gewordenen Kindes ... darzustellen."

14. Cf. the addendum to Carl Alt, *Studien zur Entstehungsgeschichte von Goethes Dichtung und Wahrheit*, Forschungen zur neuren Litteraturgeschichte, no. 5 (Munich, 1898).

15. *Annalen*, p. 846.

16. Goethe, like so many of his generation, actually made a trip to visit Rousseau's favorite haunt, the Isle of St. Peter in Lake Biel; later on, the most favorable remarks on Rousseau are usually the ones about his herbarizing.

17. Entry from *Tagebuch*, May 18, 1810; cf. also Emil Staiger, *Goethe*, 3 vols. (Zurich: Artemis Verlag, 1959), 3:255.

18. Letter to Knebel, April 23, 1790: "Besser ist es immer, mit den Resultaten unseres Daseins die Freunde ein wenig zu ergötzen, als sie mit Konfessionen, wie es uns zumute ist, wo nicht traurig, so doch nachdenklich zu machen."

19. *Gespräche mit Eckermann*, March 30, 1831.

20. Quoted in Karl Viëtor, *Goethe; Dichtung, Wissenschaft, Weltbild* (Bern: Francke, 1949), p. 220.

21. "Bedeutende Fördernis durch ein einziges geistreiches Wort," in *Naturwissenschaftliche Schriften*, ed. Beutler, 2 vols. (Zurich: Artemis Verlag, 1949), 1:880.

22. *Gespräche mit Eckermann*, March 30, 1831: "Ein Faktum unseres Lebens gilt nicht, insofern es wahr ist, sondern insofern es etwas zu bedeuten hat." Cf. also the letter to Zelter, December 31, 1829: "Ich habe bemerkt, dass ich den Gedanken für wahr halte, der für mich fruchtbar ist, sich an mein übriges Denken anschliesst und zugleich mich fördert."

23. Cf. especially the letter to King Ludwig of Bavaria, extant as an addendum to a letter to Zelter, February 15, 1830.

24. Cf. Derek Bowman, *Life into Autobiography: A Study of Goethe's Dichtung und Wahrheit*, German Studies in America, no. 5 (Bern: Lang, 1971), p. 99; this is, on the whole, a very refreshing recent study, especially in the analysis of literary techniques.

25. Momme Mommsen et al., *Die Entstehung von Goethes Werken; in Dokumenten*, Vol. 2: *Cäcilia bis Dichtung und Wahrheit* (Berlin: Akademie Verlag, 1958), pp. 396, 524.

26. On this see the excellent section in Staiger, *Goethe*, 3:248–49.

27. Kurt Jahn, *Goethes Dichtung und Wahrheit* (Halle: Max Niemeyer, 1908), p. 328: "Wahrheit war also das letzte Ziel der Autobiographie, Dichtung nur ein Mittel sie zu realisieren."

28. I have long felt sorely tempted to play on that aspect of the German word *dichten*, but I see no single passage where Goethe would have "misused" the term thus.

29. Cf. Staiger, *Goethe*, 3:248 and Beutler's *Einführung*.

30. The most successful attempt known to me to explain this symbolism, is in Wolfgang Schadewaldt, *Goethestudien: Natur und Altertum* (Zurich: Artemis, 1963), pp. 263–82.

31. *D & W*, pp. 46–47: "Alles was ihn umgab war altertümlich.... Überhaupt erinnere ich mich keines Zustandes, der so wie dieser das Gefühl eines unverbrüchlichen Friedens und einer ewigen Dauer gegeben hätte."

32. Note the phrase he uses later on in discussing the qualities of the poet Günther, *D & W*, p. 292: "alles was dazu gehört, im Leben ein zweites Leben durch Poesie hervorzubringen."

33. *D & W*, p. 292: "was der deutschen Poesie fehlte, ... war ein Gehalt, und zwar ein nationeller ..."; p. 300: " ... sie hatte wenig oder keine Nationalgegenstände ... die idyllische Tendenz verbreitete sich unendlich."

34. Cf. Berisch's jocular thesis: "die wahre Erfahrung sei ganz eigentlich, wenn man erfahre, wie ein Erfahrener die Erfahrung erfahrend erfahren müsse" (*D & W*, p. 337)—that the sign of true experience was properly when one experiences what an experienced man must experience in experiencing his experience.

35. An excellent analysis of Goethe's own re-viewing of the scene, long after he had written it, under the impact of reading the account of Ferdinand Näke's visit to Sesenheim in 1822, can be found in L. A. Willoughby, "Literary Relations in the Light of Goethe's Principle of 'Wiederholte Spiegelungen'," in Elizabeth M. Wilkinson and L. A. Willoughby, *Goethe, Poet and Thinker* (London: E. Arnold, 1962), a book with very illuminating studies.

36. In a conversation with Eckermann, January 3, 1830, when he held a copy of Gérard's translation of his *Faust* in his hand and reflected on the wondrous thought that his own book seemed readable to Frenchmen whose language and literary taste had been dominated by that of Voltaire not more than fifty years before.

37. See especially the compact summary of this *D & W*, Book 19: 822–23.

38. The book that does this ought to be written; short attempts at it are in Bowman, *Life into Autobiography*.

39. From the fragment "Die Natur," as taken down by Christof Tobler, in *Naturwissenschaftlich Schriften*, 1:921–23. To this writing Sigmund Freud attributed his turn to science.

40. Quoted from Elizabeth M. Wilkinson, "Tasso—ein gesteigerter Werther in the Light of Goethe's Principle of 'Steigerung'," in Wilkinson and Willoughby, *Goethe*, p. 195, an excellent article on this principle in its aesthetic function.

41. Since Goethe's great poem *Urworte. Orphisch*, written several years after the first books of *Dichtung und Wahrheit* had been completed, is of such importance for the following interpretation, it is here reprinted. *Goethe's Lyrische und Epische Dichtungen*, 2 vols. (Leipzig: Insel Verlag, 1920), 2:180–81.

DAIMON   Wie an dem Tag, der dich der Welt verliehen,
Die Sonne stand zum Grusse der Planeten,
Bist also bald und fort und fort gediehen
Nach dem Gesetz, wonach du angetreten.
So musst du sein, dir kannst du nicht entfliehen,
So sagten schon Sibyllen, so Propheten,
Und keine Zeit und keine Macht zerstueckelt
Gepraegte Form, die lebend sich entwickelt.

TYCHE   Die strenge Grenze doch umgeht gefaellig
Ein Wandelndes, das mit und um uns wandelt;
Nicht einsam bleibst du, bildest dich gesellig,
Und handelst wohl so, wie ein andrer handelt.
Im Leben ists bald hin-, bald widerfaellig,
Es ist ein Tand und wird so durchgetandelt.
Schon hat sich still der Jahre Kreis geruendet:
Die Lampe harrt der Flamme, die entzuendet.

EROS   Die bleibt nicht aus!—Er stuerzt vom Himmel nieder,
Wohin er sich aus alter Oede schwang,
Er schwebt heran auf luftigem Gefieder
Um Stirn und Brust den Fruehlingstag entlang,
Scheint jetzt zu fliehn, vom Fliehen kehrt er wieder:
Da wird ein Wohl im Weh, so suess und bang.
Gar manches Herz verschwebt im Allgemeinen;
Doch widmet sich das Edelste dem Einen.

ANAGKE    Da ists denn wieder wie die Sterne wollten:
          Bedingung und Gesetz, und aller Wille
          Ist nur ein Wollen, weil wir eben sollten,
          Und vor dem Willen schweigt die Willkuer stille.
          Das Liebste wird vom Herzen weggescholten,
          Dem harten Muss bequemt sich Will und Grille.
          So sind wir scheinfrei denn, nach manchen Jahren
          Nur enger dran, als wir am Anfang waren.

ELPIS     Doch solcher Grenze, solcher ehrnen Mauer
          Hoechst widerwaertge Pforte wird entriegelt,
          Sie stehe nur mit alter Felsendauer!
          Ein Wesen regt sich leicht und ungezuegelt:
          Aus Wolkendecke, Nebel, Regenschauer
          Erhebt sie uns, mit ihr, durch sie befluegelt.
          Ihr kennt sie wohl, sie schwaermt durch alle Zonen:
          Ein Fluegelschlag, und hinter uns Aeonen!

42. *D & W*, p. 653, italics mine. See also p. 39: "Ergreifen-verarbeiten-festhalten"; p. 42: "beschäftigen-verarbeiten-wiederholen-wiederhervorbringen"; and p. 742: "Meine Richtung, die immer darauf hinging, das Höhere gewahr zu werden, es zu erkennen, es zu fördern und womöglich solches nachbildend zu gestalten."

43. Hegel, *Phaenomenologie des Geistes, Sämmtliche Werke* (Stuttgart: Jubilaeumsausgabe, 1927), 2:239.

44. Anyone interested in the fuller elaboration of this will not find a better source than the chapter on Goethe in Friedrich Meinecke, *Die Enstehung des Historismus* (Munich: Oldenbourg, 1965).

45. "Das reine Phaenomen steht nun zuletzt als Resultat aller Erfahrungen und Versuche da. Es kann nie isoliert werden." *Erfahrung und Wissenschaft,* in *Naturwissenschaftliche Schriften,* 1:871. "So kann man von einem Phaenomen sagen, dass es mit unzähligen anderen in Verbindung stehe, wie wir von einem freischwebenden leuchtenden Punkt sagen, dass er seine Strahlen nach allen Seiten aussende." *Der Versuch als Vermittler von Objekt und Subjekt,* ibid., pp. 851 ff. "Ein Phaenomen, ein Versuch, kann nichts beweisen, es ist das Glied einer grossten Kette, das erst im Zusammenhang gilt." *Maximen und Reflexionen,* ed. Beutler, p. 513. "Kein Phaenomen erklärt sich aus sich selbst; nur viele zusammen überschaut, methodisch geordnet, geben zuletzt etwas, was für Theorie gelten könnte." ibid., p. 654.

46. Cf. "Man habe auch tausendmal von einem Gegenstande gehört, das Eigentümliche desselben spricht nur zu uns aus dem unmittelbaren Anschauen," *Italienische Reise,* ed. Beutler, p. 235—"Du weisst wie ich im Anschauen lebe," letter to Merck, August 5, 1778—and "Das unmittelbare Anschauen der Dinge ist mir alles," letter to S. Boisserée, March 22, 1831.

47. *Faust,* Part 2, Act 1, end of "Anmutige Gegend."

48. *Wilhelm Meister's Wanderjahre,* ed. Beutler, p. 131. Cf. also Goethe's review of Stiedenroth in *Naturwissenschaftliche Schriften,* 1:884: "In dem menschlichen Geiste sowie im Universum ist nichts oben noch unten, alles fordert gleiche Rechte an einen gemeinsamen Mittelpunkt, der sein geheimes Dasein eben durch das harmonische Verhältnis allter Teile zu ihm manifestiert."

49. "Bedeutende Fördernis durch ein einziges geistreiches Wort," in *Naturwissenschaftliche Schriften,* 1:879–80.

50. Ibid., p. 880.

51. *D & W*, p. 268: "für sein eigenes Selbst zu leben . . . ist immer dem Willen der Natur gemäss." Cf. also p. 591.

52. *D & W*, pp. 144, 716, 732.

53. Cf. *D & W*, p. 361, and also *Lehrjahre*, p. 46: "Mann kann einem jungen Menschen keine grössere Wohltat erweisen, als wenn man ihn zeitig in die Bestimmung seines Lebens einweiht."

54. Cf. especially *D & W*, p. 424, "Unsere Wünsche sind Vorgefühle der Fähigkeiten."

55. *Faust*, Part 1, Prologue.

56. This is the great educational principle of the "Educational Province" in *Wilhelm Meisters Wanderjahre*, Book 2, chap. 1. See also *D & W*, p. 56: "Mein Gemüt war von Natur zur Ehrerbietung geneigt."

57. *D & W*, p. 730; cf. also pp. 406, 644.

58. *Ibid.*, pp. 292, 312, 402.

59. *Ibid.*, pp. 420–23, not quoted here in the order of the text.

60. *Maximen und Reflexionen*, p. 586.

61. "Bedeutende Fördernis . . . ," in *Naturwissenschaftliche Schriften*, 1:879–80.

62. As he said in a conversation with Riemer on May 3, 1814: "Hypochondrisch sein heisst nichts anderes als ins Subjekt versinken."

63. Cf. the famous remark in a conversation with Eckermann, January 29, 1826, about progressive ages as objective, and retrogressive ones as subjective.

64. *Tasso*, Act 2, scene 3.

65. In a conversation with Eckermann, February 4, 1829. "Die Überzeugung unserer Fortdauer entspringt mir aus dem Begriff der Tätigkeit; denn wenn ich bis an mein Ende rastlos wirke, so ist die Natur verpflichtet, mir eine andere Form des Daseins anzuweisen, wenn die jetzige meinen Geist nicht ferner auszuhalten vermag."

# Bibliography

This selected bibliography lists the major autobiographies prior to 1800 A.D. which form the core of this work; only a few are listed for the period after 1800. The scholarly writings that were most helpful to me in studying the autobiographies treated here are also listed, and a few general works on autobiography as a genre are included. Since the theme of historicism is central to my thesis, I have listed some essential treatises on that topic. With regard to the general cultural background, I have included only those books which over many years have done the most to shape my understanding of our Western civilization.

Abelard, Peter. *Opera Omnia.* Migne, *PL* 178. Paris: Garnier, 1885. (Based on the Paris 1626 edition).
———. *Epistolae duorum amantium: Briefe Abelards und Heloises?* Edited by Ewald Könsgen. Mittellateinische Studien und Texte, vol. 8. Leiden: Brill, 1974.
———. *Brieven van Abelard en Heloize.* Translated by O. Noordenbos et al. Rotterdam: Brusse, 1929.
———. *Ouvrages inédits d'Abelard pour servir à l'histoire de la philosophie scholastique en France.* Edited by Victor Cousin. Paris: Impr. Royale, 1836.
———. *Peter Abelard's Ethics.* An edition with introduction, English translation, and notes by David E. Luscombe. Oxford Medieval Texts. Oxford: Clarendon Press, 1971.
———. *The Letters of Abelard and Heloise.* Translated by Charles K. Scott-Moncrieff. London: Chapman, 1925.
———. *The Story of Abelard's Adversities: A Translation with Notes of the Historia Calamitatum.* Edited by J. T. Muckle. Toronto: Pontifical Institute of Medieval Studies, 1964.
Adams, Henry. *The Education Of Henry Adams.* New York: Random House, 1931.
Adamus Bremensis, (11th century). *Adami Gesta hammaburgensis ecclesiae pontificum ex recensione Lappenbergii.* Edited by G. Waitz. Scriptores rerum germanicarum. Hanover: Hahn, 1876.
———. *History of the Archbishops of Hamburg-Bremen.* Translated with an introduction and notes by Francis J. Tschan. Records of Civilization: Sources and Studies, no. 53. New York: Columbia University Press, 1959.
Adelardus of Bath (12th century). *Des Adelard von Bath Traktat De eodem et diverso . . .* historisch-kritisch untersucht von Hans Willner. Beiträge zur Geschichte der Philosophie des Mittelalters. Text and analyses, vol. 4, fasc. 1. Münster: Aschendorff, 1903.
Adkins, Arthur W. H. *From the Many to The One: A Study of Personality and Views of Human Nature in The Context of Ancient Greek Society, Values, and Beliefs.* London: Constable, 1970.

Aegerter, Emmanuel. *Madame Guyon, une aventurière mystique*. Paris: Hachette, 1941.

Aiken, Conrad. *U Shant: An Autobiographical Narrative*. Cleveland, O.: Meridian Books, 1962.

Ailred de Rievaulx [Saint Ethelred]. *La Vie de recluse: La Prière pastorale*. Latin text. Introduction and translation into French by Charles Dumont. Sources chretiennes, no. 76. Serie des textes monastiques d'occident, no. 6. Paris: Editions du cerf, 1961.

Alfaric, Prosper. *L'Evolution intellectuelle de St. Augustin*. Vol. 1: *Du Manichéisme au néo-platonisme*. (Only part published.) Paris: E. Nourry, 1918.

Alfieri, Vittorio. *Mein Leben*. Edited by G. Zoppi. Zurich: Manesse Verlag, 1949.

Alt, Carl. *Studien zur Enstehungsgeschichte von Goethes Dichtung und Wahrheit*. Forschungen zur neuren Literaturgeschichte, no. 5. Munich: 1898.

Amiel, Henri-Frédéric. "Charactéristique générale de Rousseau." In *Jean-Jacques Rousseau jugé par les genevois d'aujord'hui*, pp. 3–65. Geneva: n.p., 1879.

Ammianus Marcellinus. *The Roman History*. Translated by C. D. Yonge. Bohn's Classical Library. London: George Bell & Sons, 1887.

Andreas Cappellanus. *The Art of Courtly Love*. Translated, with an introduction and notes by John Parry. Records of Civilization: Sources and Studies. New York: W. W. Norton, 1969.

Andresen, Carl, ed. *Zum Augustin-Gespräch der Gegenwart*. Wege der Forschung, vol. 5. Darmstadt: Wissenschaftliche Buchgesellschaft, 1962.

Anselm, St. *Basic Writings*. Translated by S. N. Deane. LaSalle, Ill.: Open Court Publishing Co., 1962.

Antoniade, Constantin. *Trois figures de la Renaissance: Pierre Arétin-Guichardin-Benvenuto Cellini*. Paris: Desclée de Brouwer, 1937.

Aristides, Aelius. *Aristides*. Edited by C. A. Behr. 4 vols. Loeb Classical Library. Cambridge, Mass.: Harvard University Press, 1973–.

———. *Aristides*. Edited by W. Dindorf. 3 vols. Leipzig: Weidmann, 1829.

Aristotle. *The Nichomachean Ethics*. Loeb Classical Library. Cambridge, Mass.: Harvard University Press, 1962.

Arneth, Joseph Calasanza. "Studien über Benvenuto Cellini." *Akademie der Wissenschaften, Vienna. Philosophisch-historisch Klasse. Denkschriften*, 9 (1859): 99–134.

Auerbach, Erich. *Dante als Dichter der irdischen Welt*. Berlin: de Gruyter, 1929.

———. *Literary Language and Its Public in Late Antiquity and in the Middle Ages*. Translated by Ralph Mannheim. New York: Bollingen Foundation, 1965.

———. *Mimesis: The Representation of Reality in Western Literature*. Translated by Willard R. Trask. Princeton, N.J.: Princeton University Press, 1953.

———. *Scenes from the Drama of European Literature: Six Essays*. New York: Meridian Books, 1959.

———. "Vico and Herder." *Deutsche Vierteljahrsschrift*, 10 (1932): 671–86.

Augustinus, Aurelius, St. *Opera Omnia*. Louvain Edition. 47 vols. Paris: Gaume & Migne, 1835–77.

———. *Writings of Saint Augustine*. The Fathers of the Church, a new translation. vol. 1–. New York: Cima, 1947–.

———. *Select Letters*. With a translation by James H. Baxter. Loeb Classical Library. London: Heinemann, 1953.

———. *The Confessions*. Edited by John Gibb and William Montgomery. Cambridge Patristic Texts. Cambridge: At the University Press, 1908.

———. *Confessions*. Translated by R. S. Pine-Coffin. Baltimore, Md.: Penguin Books, 1961.

———. *Confessions*. With an English translation by William Watts (1631). 2 vols. Loeb Classical Library. London: Heinemann, 1946.

———. *On Christian Doctrine*. Translated by D. W. Robertson. Indianapolis, Ind.: Bobbs-Merrill, 1958.

———. *On Free Choice of the Will*. Translated by Anna S. Benjamin et al. Indianapolis, Ind.: Bobbs-Merrill, 1964.

———. *Vom Gottesstaat*. Translated by Wilhelm Thimme. 2 vols. Zurich: Artemis, 1955.

*Augustinus Magister. Congrès International Augustinien, Paris, 21–24 Septembre 1954. Actes.* 3 vols. Supplément à l'année théologique Augustinienne. Paris: Etudes Augustiniennes, 1954.

Augustus, Emperor of Rome. *The Monumentum ancyranum*. Edited by E. G. Hardy. Oxford: Clarendon Press, 1923.

———. *Res gestae divi Augusti: The Achievements of the Divine Augustus*. Commentary by P. A. Brunt, et al. London: Oxford University Press, 1967. (Parallel Latin and English texts)

Baethgen, Friedrich. *Beiträge zur Geschichte Coelestinus V. Schriften der Königsberger gelehrten Gesellschaft*. Geisteswissenschaftliche Klasse. 10th year, fasc. 4. Halle: Niemeyer, 1934.

———. *Der Engelpapst: Idee und Erscheinung*. Leipzig: Köhler & Amelang, 1943.

Baron, Hans. *From Petrarch to Leonardi Bruni: Studies in Humanistic and Political Literature*. Chicago: University of Chicago Press, 1968.

Bates, E. Stuart. *Inside Out: An Introduction to Autobiography*. New York: Sheridan House, 1937.

Baxter, Richard. *The Reformed Pastor*. Edited by Hugh Martin. London: SCM Press, 1963.

———. *Reliquiae Baxterianae: or Mr. Richard Baxter's Narrative of the Most Memorable Passages of His Life and Times. . . . from His Own Original Manuscript by Matthew Sylvester*. London: Parkhurst, 1696.

Becker, Hans. *Augustin: Studien zur seiner geistigen Entwicklung*. Leipzig: J. C. Hinricks, 1908.

Becker, Reinhold. *Wahrheit und Dichtung in Ulrich von Lichtenstein's Frauendienst*. Halle: Niemeyer, 1888.

Behr, Charles Allison. *Aelius Aristides and the Sacred Tales*. Amsterdam: Hakkert, 1968.

Bénichou, Paul. *Man and Ethics: Studies in French Classicism*. Translated by Elizabeth Hughes. Garden City, N.Y.: Anchor Books, 1971.

Bercovitch, Sacvan. *The Puritan Origins of the American Self*. New Haven, Conn.: Yale University Press, 1975.

Bergstraesser, Arnold. *Goethe's Image of Man and Society*. Chicago: H. Regnery, 1949.

Berlin, Isaiah. *Vico and Herder: Two Studies in the History of Ideas*. New York: Viking Press, 1976.

Bernard of Clairvaux. *The Letters of St. Bernard of Clairvaux*. Translated by Bruno S. James. London: Burns Oates, 1953.

Beutler, Ernst Rudolf. *Essays um Goethe*. 4th ed. 2 vols. Wiesbaden: Dieterich, 1947.

Beyer-Fröhlich, Marianne. *Aus dem Zeitalter der Reformation und der Gegenreforma-*

*tion.* Reihe Deutsche Selbstzeugnisse, vol. 5. Darmstadt: Wissenschaftliche Buchgesellschaft, 1964.

————. *Die Entwicklung der deutschen Selbstzeugnisse.* Leipzig: Reclam, 1930.

Beyle, Henri [Stendahl]. *Oeuvres intimes.* Edited by Henri Martineau. Paris: Bibliothèque de la Pleïade, 1955.

Bezold, Friedrich von. "Über die Anfänge der Selbstbiographie und ihre Entwicklung im Mittelalter." *Aus Mittelalter und Renaissance.* Munich: Oldenburg, 1918.

Bielschowsky, Albert. *Goethe, sein Leben und seine Werke.* 2 vols. Munich: Beck, 1910.

Bizet, Jules-Augustin. *Le Mystique allemand Henri Suso et la déclin de la scholastique.* Diss. Paris. Paris: Ed. Montaigne, 1946.

Bliemetzrieder, Franz Plazidus. *Adelhard von Bath, Blätter aus dem Leben eines englischen Natur-philosophen des 12. Jahrhunderts und Bahnbrechers einer Wiederverweckung der griechischen Antike.* Munich: Hueber, 1935.

Böhm, Benno. *Sokrates im achtzehnten Jahrhundert: Studien zum Werdegange des modernen Persönlichkeitsbewusstseins.* Neumünster: Wachholtz, 1966

Boethius. *The Consolation of Philosophy.* With an English translation by H. F. Stewart. Loeb Classical Library. London: Heinemann, 1946.

Bonaventura, St. *Itinerarium mentis in deum.* Darmstadt: Wissenschaftliche Buchgesellschaft, 1961.

Borst, Arno. "Abälard und Bernhard." *Historische Zeitschrift* 186 (1958): 497–526.

Bossenbrook, William John. *Justus Möser's Approach to History.* Diss., Chicago. Chicago, 1938.

Bossuet, Jacques-Benigne. *Oeuvres complètes.* 12 vols. Nancy: Thomas et Pierron, 1862–63.

————. *Correspondance de Bossuet.* Edited by Charles Urbain et al. 15 vols. Paris: Hachette, 1900–25.

————. *Oraisons funèbres, Discours sur l'histoire universelle, Relation sur le quiétisme,* in *Oeuvres.* Edited by Velat & Champailler. Paris: Bibliothèque de la Pleïade, 1961.

Bowen, Merlin. *The Long Encounter: Self and Experience in the Writings of Herman Melville.* Chicago: University of Chicago Press, 1963.

Bowman, Derek. *Life into Autobiography: A Study of Goethe's Dichtung und Wahrheit.* German Studies in America, no. 5. Bern: Lang, 1971.

Bowra, Cecil Maurice. *The Greek Experience.* New York: Mentor Books, 1959.

————. *Periclean Athens.* London: Weidenfeld & Nicolson, 1971.

————. *The Romantic Imagination.* New York: Oxford University Press, 1969.

Brandes, Georg. *Goethe.* Berlin: Reiss, 1922.

Bremond, Henri. *Apologie pour Fénelon.* Paris: Perrin, 1910.

————. *Histoire littéraire du sentiment religieux en France depuis la fin des guerres de religion jusqu'à nos jours.* Paris: Bloud et Gay, 1916–33.

Brown, Peter. *Augustine of Hippo: A Biography.* London: Faber & Faber, 1967.

Brucker, Gene, ed. *Two Memoirs of Renaissance Florence: The Diaries of Buonaccorso Pitti and Gregorio Dati.* Translated by Julia Martines. New York: Harper Torchbooks, 1967.

Bruford, Walter Horace. *Culture and Society in Classical Weimar, 1775–1806.* London: Cambridge University Press, 1962.

————. *Germany in the Eighteenth Century: The Social Background of the Literary Revival.* Cambridge: At the University Press, 1965.

Büchner, Karl, ed. *Das neue Cicerobild*. Darmstadt: Wissenschaftliche Buchgesellschaft, 1971.

Buck, August. "Das Lebensgefühl der Renaissance im Spiegel der Selbstdarstellungen Petrarcas und Cardanos." In *Formen der Selbstdarstellungen; Analekten zu einer Geschichte des literarischen Selbstporträts: Festgabe für Fritz Neubert*. Berlin: Duncker & Humblot, 1956.

———. *Zu Begriff- und Problem der Renaissance*. Darmstadt: Wissenschaftliche Buchgesellschaft, 1969.

Buffum, Imbrie. *Studies in the Baroque from Montaigne to Rotrou*. New Haven, Conn.: Yale University Press, 1957.

Bunyan, John. *The Complete Works of John Bunyan*. Edited by Henry Stebbing. 4 vols. London: Virtue and Yorston, 1859.

———. *The Heavenly Footman: Or, a Description of the Man that Gets to Heaven: With Directions How To Run So as To Obtain*. Philadelphia: American Baptist Publication Society, 1851.

———. *Grace Abounding and the Life and Death of Mr. Badman*. Introduction by G. B. Harrison. New York: Dutton, 1969.

———. *The Pilgrim's Progress and Grace Abounding to the Chief of Sinners*. Edited by James Thorpe. Boston: Houghton Mifflin, 1969.

Burck, Erich. "Die altrömische Familie." In *Römertum*, edited by Hans Oppermann, pp. 87–141. Darmstadt: Wissenschaftliche Buchgesellschaft, 1962.

Burckhardt, Jacob C. *Civilization of the Renaissance in Italy*. Translated by Irene Gordon. New York: Mentor Books, 1960.

———. *Griechische Kulturgeschichte*. 3 vols. Leipzig: Kröner, n.d.

———. *Die Kultur der Renaissance in Italien*. Vienna: Phaidon, n.d.

Burgelin, Pierre. *La Philosophie de l'existence de J. -J. Rousseau*. Paris: Presses Universitaires, 1952.

Burr, Anna Robeson. *The Autobiography: A Critical and Comparative Study*. Boston: Houghton Mifflin, 1909.

Butler, Cuthbert (Dom). *Western Mysticism: The Teaching of Augustine, Gregory, and Bernard on Contemplation and the Contemplative Life*. 2d. ed. New York: Harper Torchbooks, 1966.

Butor, Michel. *Essais sur les Essais*. Paris: Gallimard, 1968.

Caesar, C. Julius. *C. Iuli Caesaris Comentarii*. Edited by Alfred Klotz. 3 vols. Leipzig: Teubner, 1926–27.

———. *C. Iuli Caesaris Commentariorum pars prior et pars posterior*. Edited by Renatus du Pontet. Oxford: Clarendon Press, 1900–1901.

———. *Caesar*. Translated by William Duncan. 2 vols. London: Valpy, 1832.

Calvin, Jean. *Institutes of the Christian Religion*. Edited by John T. McNeill. 2 vols. Library of Christian Classics, vols. 20–21. Philadelphia: Westminster Press, 1960.

Cantor, Mortiz. "Hieronymus Cardanus; ein wissenschaftliches Lebensbild aus dem XVI. Jahrhundert." *Neue Heidelberger Jahrbücher*, 13 (1905): 131–43.

Caponigri, A. Robert. *Time and Idea: The Theory of History in Giambattista Vico*. Chicago: H. Regnery, 1953.

Cardano, Girolamo. *Opera Omnia: The 1662 Lugduni Edition with an Introduction by August Buck*. 10 vols. New York: Johnson Reprint, 1967.

———. *The Book of My Life. (De vita propria liber)*. Translated by Jean Stoner. New York: Dover, 1962.

———. *Offenbarung der Natur und natürlicher Dingen auch mancherley subtiler*

*Würckungen.* Translated by Heinrich Pantaleon. Basel: Petri, 1559. (Translation of *De rerum varietate.*)

Carlyle, Thomas. *Reminiscences.* New York: C. Scribner's, 1881.

Cartellieri, Otto. *Abt Suger von Saint-Denis, 1081–1151.* Historische Studien, vol. 11. Berlin, 1898.

Cassirer, Ernst. *Individuum und Kosmos in der Philosophie der Renaissance.* Darmstadt: Wissenschaftliche Buchgesellschaft, 1963.

―――. *The Question of Jean-Jacques Rousseau.* Translated and edited by Peter Gay. Bloomington: Indiana University Press, 1963.

―――. *Rousseau, Kant and Goethe.* Translated by James Gutmann, Paul Oskar Kristeller, and John Herman Randall, Jr. New York: Harper & Row, 1965.

Cayre, Fulbert. "Le Sens et l'unité des Confessions." *Année théologique Augustinienne,* 4 (1953): 13–32.

Cellini, Benvenuto. *Autobiography.* Translated by John Addington Symonds. Garden City, N.Y.: Dolphin Books, 1961.

―――. *Memoirs.* Translated by Anne MacDonell. Everyman's Library. London: Dent, 1907.

―――. *Vita di Benvenuto Cellini: Testo critico.* Edited by Orazio Bacci. Florence: Sansoni, 1901.

Charrier, Charlotte. *Heloïse dans l'histoire et dans la legende.* Paris: Champion, 1933.

Chateaubriand, Francois A. R. *Mémoires d'outre-Tombe.* 2 vols. Edited by Maurice Levaillant, et al. Paris: Bibliothèque de la Pleïade, 1951.

Chroust, Anton Hermann. *Socrates: Man and Myth: The Two Socratic Apologies of Xenophon.* London: Routledge, 1957.

Cicero, Marcus T. *Brutus.* With an English translation by G. L. Hendrickson. Loeb Classical Library. London: Heinemann, 1939.

―――. *Letters to Atticus.* With an English translation by E. O. Winstedt. 3 vols. Loeb Classical Library. London: Heinemann, 1928.

―――. *Letters to his Friends.* With an English translation by W. Glynn Williams. 3 vols. Loeb Classical Library. London: Heinemann, 1958–72.

―――. *De oratore.* With an English translation by E. W. Sutton. 2 vols. Loeb Classical Library. London: Heinemann, 1967–68.

―――. *De senectute, de amicitia, de divinatione.* Translated by W. A. Falconer. Loeb Classical Library. London: Heinemann, 1923.

Claesen, A. "Augustinus en Cicero's Hortensius." *Miscellanea Augustiniana,* 5:391–417.

Clark, Arthur Melville. *Autobiography, Its Genesis and Phases.* Edinburgh: Oliver & Boyd, 1935.

Cochrane, Charles N. *Christianity and Classical Culture.* New York: Oxford University Press, 1957.

Coleridge, Samuel T. "From Bigraphia Literaria." in *The Portable Coleridge,* pp. 432–628. Edited by I. A. Richards. New York: Viking Press, 1950.

Collingwood, Robin George. *An Autobiography.* London: Oxford University Press, 1939.

Collins, Joseph. *The Doctor Looks at Biography: Psychological Studies of Life and Letters.* New York: Doran, 1925.

Comité national pour la commémoration de J.-J. Rousseau. Colloque, Paris, 1962. *Jean-Jacques Rousseau et son oeuvre: Problèmes et recherches; Commémoration et colloque de Paris (16–20 Octobre 1962).* Paris: Klincksieck, 1964.

Compayré, Gabriel. *Abelard and the Origin and Early History of Universities*. New York: Greenwood, 1969.

Condorcet, Antoine-Nicolas de. *Esquisse d'un tableau historique des progrès de l'esprit humain*. Edited by Belaval. Paris: J. Vrin, 1970.

―――. *Sketch for a Historical Picture of the Progress of the Human Mind*. Translated by J. Barraclough. New York: Noonday Press, 1955.

Contreras, Alonso de. *Das Leben des Capitan Alonso de Contreras von ihm selbst erzählt*. Translated by A. Steiger. Zurich: Manesse Verlag, 1961.

Cottiaux, Jean. "La Conception de la théologie chez Abelard." *Revue d'histoire ecclésiastique*, 27 (1932): 247-95.

Cottrell, Robert D. *Brantôme: The Writer as Portraitist of His Age*. Geneva: Droz, 1970.

Courcelle, Pierre. *Les Confessions de St. Augustin dans la tradition littéraire*. Paris: Etudes Augustiniennes, 1963.

―――. *Recherches sur les Confessions de Saint-Augustin*. Paris: E. de Boccard, 1950.

Cowdrey, Herbert Edward John. *The Cluniacs and the Gregorian Reform*. Oxford: Clarendon Press, 1970.

Cresson, André. *Socrate: Sa vie, son oeuvre avec un exposé de sa philosophie*. Paris: Presses Universitaires, 1947.

Croce, Benedetto. *An Autobiography*. Translated by Robin G. Collingwood. Oxford: Oxford University Press, 1927.

―――. *Goethe*. Translated by Emily Anderson. New York: Knopf, 1923.

―――. *The Philosophy of Giambattista Vico*. Translated by Robin G. Collingwood. London: Latimer, 1913.

Crouslé, Léon. *Fénelon et Bossuet, études morales et littéraires*. Paris: H. Champion, 1894-95.

Curtius, Ernst Robert. *European Literature and the Latin Middle Ages*. Translated by Willard Trask. New York: Harper & Row, 1953.

D'Arcy, M. C. et al., eds. *Saint Augustine*. New York: Meridian Books, 1957.

Dante. *La Vita Nuova (Poems of Youth)*. Translated by Barbara Reynolds. Baltimore, Md.: Penguin Books, 1969.

―――. *Vita nuova [e] Rime*. Edited by Fredi Chiappelli. Milan: Mursia, 1965.

Darwin, Charles. *The Autobiography of Charles Darwin, 1809-1882*. With original omissions restored and edited by Nora Barlow. New York: Harcourt, Brace, 1959.

Daus, Hans-Jürgen. *Selbstverständnis und Menschenbild in den Selbstdarstellungen Giambattista Vicos und Pietro Giannones; ein Beitrag zur Geschichte der italienischen Autobiographie*. Kölner Romantistische Arbeiten; n.s., vol. 20. Geneva: Droz, 1962.

Dayre, Jean. "Jérôme Cardan (1501-1576): Esquisse biographique." *Annales de l'Université de Grenoble*, n.s. 4 (1927): 245-355.

DeBeer, Gavin. *Gibbon and His World*. London: Thames & Hudson, 1968.

Delacroix, Henri. *Etudes d'histoire et de psychologie du Mysticisme: Les grands mystiques chrétiens*. Paris: Alcan, 1908.

Delany, Paul. *British Autobiography in the Seventeenth Century*. London: Routledge & Kegan Paul, 1969.

Demole, V. "Analyse psychiatrique des Confessions de J.-J. Rousseau." *Schweizer Archiv für Neurologie und Psychiatrie*, 2 (1918): 270-304.

Demosthenes. *The Oration of Demosthenes upon the Crown*. Translated into English, with notes, and the Greek text ... by Henry Lord Brougham. London: Knight, 1840.

Derathé, Robert. *Jean-Jacques Rousseau et le science politique de son temps.* Paris: Vrin, 1970.

———. "Les Rapports de la morale et de la religion chez Jean-Jacques Rousseau." *Revue Philosophique,* 139 (1949): 143–73.

Descartes, René. *Oeuvres et lettres.* Edited by André Bridoux. Paris: Bibliothèque de la Pleïade, 1953.

Dicken, E. W. Trueman. *The Crucible of Love: A Study of the Mysticism of St. Teresa of Jesus and St. John of the Cross.* New York: Sheed & Ward, 1963.

Dilthey, Wilhelm. *Gesammelte Schriften.* 17 vols. (to date). Stuttgart: Teubner, 1957–.

Vol. 2: *Weltanschauung und Analyse des Menschen seit Renaissance und Reformation.*

Vol. 3: *Studien zur Geschichte des deutschen Geistes.*

Vol. 5: "[Über vergleichende Psychologie] Beiträge zum Studium der Individualität." In *Die Geistige Welt,* pp. 241–316.

Vol. 7: *Der Aufbau der geschichtlichen Welt in den Geisteswissenschaften.*

Vol. 8: *Weltanschauungslehre; Abhandlungen zur Philosophie der Philosophie.*

Vol. 9: *Pädagogik; Geschichte und Grundlinien des Systems.*

Vols. 13–14: *Leben Schleiermachers.*

Dimier, Louis. "Benvenuto Cellini à la cour de France." *Revue archéologique,* 3d ser., 32 (1898): 241–76.

Dodds, Eric Robertson. *The Greeks and the Irrational.* Berkeley: University of California Press, 1964.

———. *Pagan and Christian in an Age of Anxiety: Some Aspects of Religious Experience from Marcus Aurelius to Constantine.* New York: W. W. Norton, 1965.

Dollard, John. *Criteria for the Life History.* New Haven, Conn.: Published for the Institute of Human Relations, by Yale University Press, 1935.

Duckett, Eleanor Shipley. *Carolingian Portraits: A Study in the Ninth Century.* Ann Arbor: University of Michigan Press, 1969.

Dudden, F. Holmes. *The Life and Times of St. Ambrose.* 2 vols. Oxford: Oxford University Press, 1935.

Düntzer, Heinrich. *Goethe's Dichtung und Wahrheit: Erläutert von Heinrich Düntzer.* 2 vols. Leipzig: Wartig, 1881.

Dunn, Waldo Hilary. *English Biography.* London: Dent, 1916.

Dunne, John S. *A Search for God in Time and Memory.* New York: Macmillan, 1969.

Eckermann, Johann Peter. *Gespräche mit Goethe in den letzten Jahren seines Lebens.* Edited by Adolf Bartels. 2 vols. Jena: Diederich, 1905.

Ehrenberg, Victor. *Aspects of the Ancient World: Essays and Reviews.* Oxford: Basil Blackwell, 1946.

———. "Epochs of Greek History." *Greece and Rome,* ser. 2, vol. 7 (1960): 100–13.

———. *The Greek State.* New York: W. W. Norton, 1964.

———. *From Solon to Socrates.* London: Methuen, 1967.

Einaudi, Mario. *The Early Rousseau.* Ithaca, N.Y.: Cornell University Press, 1967.

Einstein, Albert. "Autobiographisches." In *Albert Einstein: Philosopher-Scientist,* pp. 2–94. Edited by Paul A. Schilpp. 2 vols. New York: Harper Torchbooks, 1959.

Ellis, Madeline B. *Julie or La Nouvelle Heloïse: A Synthesis of Rousseau's Thought: 1749–1759.* Toronto: University of Toronto Press, 1949.

Emerson, Ralph Waldo. *The Journals.* Abridged and edited by Robert N. Linscott. New York: Random House, 1960.

Epictetus. *The Works of Epictetus, Consisting of His Discourses, in Four Books, the*

*Enchiridion, and Fragments.* Translated by Thomas W. Higginson. Rev. ed. 2 vols. Boston: Little Brown, 1890.

Eynde, P. Damien van den. "Details biographiques sur Pierre Abélard." *Antonianum*, 38 (1963): 217–23.

Fabre, Jean. "Deux frères ennemis, Diderot et Jean-Jacques." *Diderot Studies*, 3 (1961): 155–213.

Fabre, Joseph. *La Pensée Moderne (de Luther à Leibniz).* Paris, 1908. Repr., Geneva: Slatkine Reprints, 1970.

Faculté de L'université de Dijon. *Etudes sur le Contrat Social de Jean-Jacques Rousseau.* Actes des journées d'études tennés à Dijon les 3, 4, 5, et 6 Mai 1962. Paris: Société Les Belles Lettres, 1964.

Ferrero, Guglielmo. *The Life of Caesar.* Translated by A. E. Zimmern. New York: W. W. Norton, 1962.

Festugière, André Marie Jean. *Socrate.* Paris: Fuseau, 1966.

Fierz, Jürg. *Goethes Porträtierungskunst in Dichtung und Wahrheit.* Wege zur Dichtung. Züricher Schriften zur Literaturwissenschaft, vol. 48. Frauenfeld: Huber, 1945.

Flach, Werner. "Die wissenschaftstheoretische Einschätzung der Selbstbiographie bei Dilthey." *Archiv für Geschichte der Philosophie*, 52 (1970): 172–86.

Fleming, Willi. "Die Auffassung des Menschen im 17. Jahrhundert." *Deutsche Vierteljahrsschrift*, 6 (1928): 403–46.

Flint, Robert. *Vico.* Edinburgh: Blackwood, 1884.

Flitner, Wilhelm. *Europäische Gesittung; Ursprung und Aufbau abendländischer Lebensformen.* Zurich: Artemis, 1961.

Fox, George. *The Journal.* Edited by Rufus Jones. New York: Capricorn Books, 1963.

Frame, Donald. *Montaigne's Discovery of Man: The Humanization of a Humanist.* New York: Columbia University Press, 1955.

———. *Montaigne's Essais: A Study.* Englewood Cliffs, N.J.: Prentice-Hall, 1969.

Françon, Marcel. "La Condemnation de L'Emile." *Annales de la Société Jean-Jacques Rousseau*, 31 (1946–49): 209–45.

Franklin, Benjamin. *The Autobiography.* New York: Washington Square Press, 1966.

———. *The Autobiography of Benjamin Franklin.* Edited by Leonard W. Labaree et al. New Haven, Conn.: Yale University Press, 1964.

———. *Papers.* Edited by Leonard W. Labaree. Vol. 1–. New Haven, Conn.: Yale University Press, 1959–.

Franklin, Phyllis. *Show Thyself a Man: A Comparison of Benjamin Franklin and Cotton Mather.* The Hague: Mouton, 1969.

Franz, Arthur. "Die literarische Porträtzeichnung in Goethes Dichtung und Wahrheit und in Rousseaus Confessions." *Deutsche Vierteljahrsschrift*, 6 (1928): 492–512.

Frässdorf, Walter. *Die psychologischen Anschauungen J. J. Rousseaus.* Langensalza: Beyer, 1929.

Freud, Sigmund. *An Autobiographical Study.* Translated by James Strachey. New York: Norton, 1963.

———. *The Origin and Development of Psychoanalysis.* Introduction by Eliseo Vivas. Chicago, H. Regnery, 1965. (Reprinted from the *American Journal of Psychiatry*, 21 [1910]).

Freyer, Ilse. *Erlebte und systematische Gestaltung in Augustins Konfessionen; Versuch einer Analyse ihrer inneren Form.* Berlin: Junker & Dünnhaupt, 1937.

Friedenthal, Richard. *Goethe: Sein Leben und seine Zeit*. Munich: Piper, 1963.
————. *Entdecker des Ich: Montaigne-Pascal-Diderot*. Munich: Piper, 1969.
Friedrich, Hugo. *Montaigne*. 2nd ed. Bern: Francke, 1967.
————. "Montaigne über Glauben und Wissen." *Deutsche Vierteljahrsschrift*, 10 (1932): 412–35.
Fromm, Hans. *Der Deutsche Minnesang*. Wege der Forschung, vol. 15. Darmstadt: Wissenschaftliche Buchgesellschaft, 1961.
Fulgum, Per. *Edward Gibbon: His View of Life and Conception of History*. Oslo Studies in English. Oslo: 1953.
Fukuzawa, Yukichi. *The Autobiography of Yukichi Fukuzawa*. Translated by Eiichi Kiyooka. New York: Columbia University Press, 1966.
Fülop-Miller, René. *The Saints that Moved the World; Anthony-Augustine-Francis-Ignatius-Theresa*. New York: Crowell, 1945.
Gallay, Paul. *La Vie de Saint Grégoire de Nazianze*. Lyon: Vitte, 1943.
Gandhi, Mohandas. *Mahatma Gandhi: His Own Story*. New York: Macmillan, 1930.
Garraty, John Arthur. *The Nature of Biography*. London: Cape, 1958.
Germain, Gabriel. *Epictète et la spiritualité stoicienne*. Paris: Seuil, 1964.
Gibbon, Edward. *The Autobiography of Edward Gibbon*. Edited by Dero A. Saunders. New York: Meridian Books, 1961.
————. *The English Essays of Edward Gibbon*. Edited by Patricia B. Craddock. Oxford: Clarendon Press, 1972.
————. *Essai sur l'étude de la littérature*. London: Becket, 1761.
————. *Gibbon's Journal to January 28th 1763, My Journal I, II, III, and Ephemerides*. Edited by D. M. Low. London: Chatto, 1929.
————. *The History of the Decline and Fall of the Roman Empire*. Edited by J. B. Bury. 3 vols. New York: Heritage Press, 1946.
————. *The Letters of Edward Gibbon*. Edited by J. F. Norton. London: Cassell, 1956.
Gide, Andre. *If It Die . . . an Autobiography*. Translated by Dorothy Bussy. New York: Vintage, 1963.
————. *The Journals*. Edited by Justin O'Brien. 2 vols. New York: Vintage Books, 1956.
————. *Madeleine (Et Nunc Manet In Te)*. Translated by Justin O'Brien. New York: Bantam Books, 1968.
————. "Presenting Montaigne." in *The Living Thoughts of Montaigne*, pp. 1–27. Philadelphia: McKay, n.d.
————. *Return from the USSR*. Translated by Dorothy Bussy. New York: McGraw-Hill, 1964.
————. *The White Notebook*. Translated by Wade Baskin. New York: Citadel Press, 1965.
Gilson, Etienne. *The Christian Philosophy of Saint Augustine*. Translated by L. E. M. Lynch. New York: Vintage Books, 1967.
————. *Dante and Philosophy*. Translated by David Moore. New York: Harper & Row, 1963.
————. *L'Esprit de la philosophie médiévale*. Gifford Lectures: 1931–32. 2 vols. Paris: Vrin, 1932.
————. *Heloïse and Abelard*. Translated by L. K. Shook. Ann Arbor: University of Michigan Press, 1960.
Giraldus Cambrensis. *Opera*. Edited by J. S. Brewer. 8 vols. Rerum britannicarum medii aevi scriptores, no. 21. London: Longmans, 1861–91.

———. *The Autobiography of Giraldus Cambrensis.* Edited and translated by H. E. Butler. London: Jonathan Cape, 1937.

———. *The Historical Works.* Rev. ed. by Thomas Wright. London: Bell, 1913.

Glover, Terrot Reaveley. *Life and Letters in the Fourth Century.* Cambridge: At the University Press, 1901.

Goethe, Johann Wolfgang von. *Werke, Briefe und Gespräche. Gedenkausgabe.* Edited by Ernst Beutler. 24 vols. Zurich: Artemis Verlag, 1948–53.

Vol. 6: *Weimarer Dramen.*

Vol. 7: *Wilhelm Meisters Lehrjahre.*

Vol. 8: *Wilhelm Meisters Wanderjahre.*

Vol. 9: *Wahlverwandschaften-Novellen-Maximen und Reflexionen.*

Vol. 10: *Dichtung und Wahrheit.*

Vol. 11: *Italienische Reise-Annalen.*

Vol. 12: *Biographische Einzelschriften.*

Vol. 13: *Schriften zur Kunst.*

Vols. 16–17: *Naturwissenschaftliche Schriften.*

———. *Goethes Werke.* (Grossherzogin Sophie edition). Edited by Gustav von Loeper, et al. Weimar: Böhlau, 1887–1919.

———. *The Autobiography.* Translated by John Oxenford. Chicago: University of Chicago Press, 1974.

———. *Faust.* Leipzig: Insel Verlag, n.d.

———. *Lyrische und epische Dichtungen.* 2 vols. Leipzig: Insel Verlag, 1920.

———. *Materialen zur Geschichte der Farbenlehre.* 2 vols. Munich: Deutscher Taschenbuch Verlag, 1963.

*Goethe and the Modern Age: The International Convocation at Aspen, Colorado, 1949.* Chicago, H. Regnery, 1950.

Goldoni, Carlo. *Memoirs.* Translated by John Black. London: Printed for H. Colburn, 1814.

Gooch, George P. "Political Autobiography." in *Studies in Diplomacy and State-craft,* pp. 227–90. London: Longmans, Green, 1942.

Gorki, Maxim. *My Childhood.* Translated by Isidor Schneider. London: Elek Books, 1953.

Gosse, Edmund. *Father and Son: A Study of Two Temperaments.* New York: Norton, 1963.

Gossman, Lionel. "Time and History in Rousseau." *Studies on Voltaire and the Eighteenth Century,* 30 (1964): 311–49.

Gottschalk, Louis, et al. *The Use of Personal Documents in History, Anthropology, and Social Science.* New York: Social Science Research Council, 1945.

Gouhier, Henri Gaston. *Les Méditations métaphysiques de Jean-Jacques Rousseau.* Paris: Vrin, 1970.

———. "Nature et histoire dans la pensée de Rousseau." *Annales de la Société Jean-Jacques Rousseau,* 33 (1953–55): 7–48.

Gran, Gerhard. "La Crise de Vincennes." *Annales de la Société Jean-Jacques Rousseau,* 7 (1911): 1–17.

Gran, Leif. *Peter Abelard: Philosophy and Christianity in the Middle Ages.* Translated by Fred and Charles Crowley. New York: Harcourt Brace, 1970.

Grant, Robert M. *Gnosticism and Early Christianity.* Rev. ed. New York: Harper & Row, 1966.

Gregorius Nazianzus. *Carmina selecta.* Edited by E. Dronke. Göttingen: Vandenhoeck, 1840.

Griffith, Gwilym O. *John Bunyan.* London: Hodder & Stoughton, 1927.

Groethuysen, Bernhard. *J. J. Rousseau.* Paris: Gallimard, 1949.
Grün, Alphonse. *La Vie publique de Michel Montaigne: Etude biographique.* Paris, 1855. Repr., Geneva: Slatkine Reprints, 1970.
Guardini, Romano. *Die Bekehrung des Aurelius Augustinus: Der innere Vorgang in seinen Bekentnissen.* Munich: Kösel, 1959.
———. *The Death of Socrates.* Translated by Basil Wrighton. Cleveland: World Publishing Co., 1962.
Guéhenno, Jean. *Jean-Jacques Rousseau.* Translated by J. & D. Weightman. 2 vols. London: Routledge & Kegan Paul, 1966.
Guerrier, Louis. *Madame Guyon: Sa Vie, sa doctrine et son influence d'après les écrits originaux et des documents inédits.* Paris: Didier, 1881.
Guibert de Nogent. *The Autobiography of Guibert Abbot of Nogent.* Translated by C. C. Swinton Bland. London: Routledge, 1925.
———. *Self and Society in Medieval France: The Memoirs of Abbot Guibert of Nogent (1064?–c. 1125).* Edited by John F. Benton. New York: Harper Torchbooks, 1970.
Guicciardini, Francesco. *Maxims and Reflections of a Renaissance Statesman (Ricordi).* Translated by Mario Domandi. New York: Harper Torchbooks, 1965.
Guillaume, Monk of Saint-Denis. *Vie de Suger.* Collection des Mémoires relatifs à l'histoire de France. Edited by Guizot. Paris: Brière, 1825.
Guigues du Chastel. *Meditations of Guigo, Prior of the Charterhouse.* Translated by John J. Jolin. Milwaukee: Marquette University Press, 1951.
Guillemin, Henri. *"Cette affaire infernale" l'affaire J.-J. Rousseau-Hume-1766.* Paris: Plon, 1942.
———. "Les Affaires de l'Ermitage (1756–57): Examen critique des documents." *Annales de la Société Jean-Jacques Rousseau,* 29 (1941–42): 59–258.
———. *Rousseau à l'Ermitage (1756–57).* Geneva: Milieu du Monde, n.d.
Guilloux, Pierre. "Abelard et le Convent du Paraclet." *Revue d'Histoire ecclésiastique,* 21 (1925): 455–78.
———. "Saint Augustin savait-il le grec?" *Revue d'Histoire ecclésiastique,* 21 (1925): 79–83.
Guitton, Jean. *Le Temps et l'eternité chez Plotin et Saint Augustin.* Paris: Bouvin et cie, 1933.
Gundolf, Friedrich. *Caesar.* Darmstadt: Wissenschaftliche Buchgesellschaft, 1968.
———. *Goethe.* Berlin: Bondi, 1920.
Gusdorf, Georges. *La Découverte de soi.* Paris: Presses Universitaires, 1948.
———. *Mémoire et personne.* Paris: Presses Universitaires, 1951.
Guyon, Jeanne Marie [Bouvier de la Motte]. *La Vie de Madame J. M. B. de la Mothe Guion.* Écrite par elle-même. 3 vols. Cologne: Pierre, 1720.
———. *The Life of Lady Guion written by herself . . . abridged and translated.* 2 vols. Bristol: Farley, 1772.
———. *The Life and Religious Experience of the Celebrated Lady Guyon . . .* New York: Hoyt & Bolmore, 1820.
———. *Life, Religious Opinions, and Experience of Madame de la Mothe Guyon.* Edited by Thomas Upham. London: Sampson Low, 1859.
Haferkamp, Berta. *Bunyan als Künstler: Stilkritische Studien zu seinem Hauptwerk "The Pilgrim's Progress."* Tübingen: Niemeyer, 1963.
Harnack, Adolf von. *Reden und Aufsätze.* 3 vols. Giessen: H. Töpelmann, 1904–16.
Vol. 1: 51–79: "Augustins Confessionen."

Vol. 3: 67–99: "Die Höhepunkte in Augustins Konfessionen."
Hart, Francis R. "Notes for an Anatomy of Modern Autobiography." *New Literary History*, 1 (1969–70): 485–511.
Hatzfeld, Helmuth. "Die spanische Mystik und ihre Ausdrucksmöglichkeiten." *Deutsche Vierteljahrsschrift*, 10 (1932): 597–628.
Hegel, Georg W. F. *Sämmtliche Werke*. 26 vols. (Jubilaeumausgabe) Stuttgart, 1927.
Vol. 2: *Phaenomenologie des Geistes*.
Heinze, Richard. *Die Augusteische Kultur*. Darmstadt: Wissenschaftliche Buchgesellschaft, 1960.
Heinze, Richard. *Vom Geist des Römertums*. Edited by Erich Burck. Darmstadt: Wissenschaftliche Buchgesellschaft, 1960.
Hellweg, Martin. *Der Begriff des Gewissens bei J.-J. Rousseau: Beitrag zu einer Kritik der Demokratie*. Marburger Beiträge zur romanischen Philologie, vol 20. Marburg: Michaelis, 1936.
Hendel, Charles William. *Jean-Jacques Rousseau Moralist*. 2 vols. London: Oxford University Press, 1934.
Herder, Johann Gottfried. *Sämmtliche Werke*. Edited by Bernhard Suphan. 33 vols. Berlin: Weidmann, 1877–1913.
————. *Auch eine Philosophie der Geschichte zur Bildung der Menschheit*. Riga, 1774.
————. *Ideen zur Philosophie der Geschichte der Menschheit*. Edited by Heinrich Kurz. Leipzig: Bibliographisches Institut, n.d.
Hermannus Judaeus. *Opusculum de conversione sua*. Edited by Gerlinde Niemeyer. Monumenta Germaniae historica. Quellen zur Geistesgeschichte des Mittelalters, vol. 4. Weimar: Böhlaus, 1963.
Hoffman, Ernst. "Platonism in Augustine's Philosophy of History." In *Philosophy & History: Essays Presented to Ernst Cassirer*, pp. 173–90. Edited by R. Klibansky, et al. New York: Harper Torchbooks, 1963.
Hoffmeister, Johannes. "Goethes *Urworte-Orphisch*." *Logos: Internationale Zeitschrift für Philosophie der Kultur*, 19 (1930): 173–212.
Holl, Karl. "Augustins innere Entwicklung." In *Gesammelte Aufsätze zur Kirchengeschichte*, 3:54–116. Tübingen: Mohr, 1928.
Holte, Knut Ragnar. *Béatitude et Sagesse: S. Augustin et le problème de la fin de l'homme dans la philosophie ancienne*. Paris: Études augustiniennes; Worchester, Mass.; Augustinian Studies, Assumption College, 1962.
Hönigswald, Richard. "Über J. J. Rousseaus problemgeschichtliche Stellung." *Euphorion*, 28 (1927): 9–21.
Hübinger, Paul Egon, ed. *Zur Frage der Periodengrenze zwischen Altertum und Mittelalter*. Darmstadt: Wissenschaftliche Buchgesellschaft, 1969.
Huizinga, Jacob Herman. *Rousseau: The Self-made Saint*. New York: Viking Press, 1976.
Huizinga, Johan. *Verzamelde Werken*. 9 vols. Harlem: Tjeenk Willink, 1948–53.
"Abaelard." 4:104–22.
"Een praegothieke geest: Johannes van Salisbury." 4:85–103.
*Herfsttij der Middeleeuwen*. 3:3–435.
"Het probleem der Renaissance." 4:231–75.
"Kleine samenspraak over de thema's der Romantiek." 4:381–91.
"Over historische levensidealen." 4:411–32.
"Renaissance en realisme." 4:276–97.
"La Valeur Politique et militaire des idées de chevalerie à la fin du Moyen âge." 3:519–29.
"De Wetenschap der geschiedenis." 7:104–72.

————. *Men and Ideas.* New York: Meridian Books, 1959.

Humboldt, Wilhelm von. *Schriften zur Anthropologie und Geschichte.* Darmstadt: Wissenschaftliche Buchgesellschaft, 1960.

Hume, David. *The Life of David Hume, Esq.* London: W. Strahan, 1777.

Isocrates. *Works. Greek and English.* Translated by George Norlin. 3 vols. Loeb Classical Library. London: Heinemann, 1928–45.

Jacobs, Paul. *Prädestination und Verantwortlichkeit bei Calvin.* Darmstadt: Wissenschaftliche Buchgesellschaft, 1968.

Jaeger, Werner Wilhelm. *Demosthenes: Der Staatsmann und sein Werden.* Berlin: Gruyter, 1963.

————. *Paideia: The Ideals of Greek Culture.* 2d ed. Translated by Gilbert Highet. 3 vols. New York: Oxford University Press, 1945.

Jahn, Kurt. *Goethes Dichtung und Wahrheit: Vorgeschichte, Entstehung, Kritik, Analyse.* Halle: Max Niemeyer, 1908.

Jaime I, king of Aragon. *The Chronicles of James I, King of Aragon, surnamed the Conqueror, (written by himself).* Translated by John Forster. 2 vols. London: Chapman, 1883.

————. *Cronica.* Edited by J. M. Casacuberta. 9 vols. Barcelona: Barcino, 1926–62.

————. *Libre dels feyts.* Biblioteca catalana. Barcelona: 1878.

Jan van Ruysbroeck. *Das Buch von den zwölf Beghinen.* Translated by F. M. Huebner. Leipzig: Insel Verlag, n.d.

————. *Opera Omnia.* Cologne, 1552. Repr., Franborough: Gregg Press, 1967.

Jansen, Albert. "Die Bildnisse Jean-Jacques Rousseau." *Preussische Jahrbücher,* 52 (1883): 444–468.

Jefferson, Thomas. *Autobiography.* New York: Capricorn Books, 1959.

Joachimsen, Paul. "Aus der Entwicklung des italienischen Humanismus." *Historische Zeitschrift,* 121 (1920): 189–223.

John of Salisbury, d. 1180. *Opera Omnia.* Migne, *PL* 199. Paris: Garnier, 1855.

————. *The Letters of John of Salisbury.* (Medieval Texts.). Vol. 1–. London: Nelson, 1955–.

————. *Memoirs of the Papal Court.* Translated by Marjorie Chibnall. Medieval Texts. London: Nelson, 1956.

————. *The Statesman's Book, Being the Fourth, Fifth, & Sixth Books, and Selections from the Seventh and Eighth of the Policraticus.* Translated by John Dickinson. New York: Knopf, 1927.

Jonas, Hans. *The Gnostic Religion.* Boston: Beacon Press, 1958.

Jordan, Elijah. *Forms of Individuality: An Inquiry into the Grounds of Order in Human Relations.* Indianapolis, Ind.: Progress Publishing Co., 1927.

Josephus, Flavius. *Autobiographie.* Texte établi et traduit par André Pelletier. Collection des universités de France. Paris: Les Belles Lettres, 1959.

————. *Josephus.* With an English translation by H. St. J. Thackeray. 9 vols. Loeb Classical Library. London: Heinemann, 1926–65.

————. *Flavius Josephus' Lebensbeschreibung aus dem Griechischen.* Translated and edited by Leo Haefeli. Münster: Aschendorff, 1925.

Joyce, Michael. *Edward Gibbon.* London: Longmans, Greene, 1953.

Justinus Martyr, St. *The Dialogue with Trypho.* Translated by A. Lukyn Williams. Translations of Christian Literature. Series 1: Greek Texts. London: SFPCK, 1930.

Kaegi, Werner. "Voltaire und der Zerfall des christlichen Geschichtbildes." In *Historische Meditationen,* 1:223–48. 2 vols. Zurich: Fretz & Wasmuth, 1942.

Kafka, Franz. *The Diaries 1910–23.* Edited by Max Brod, and translated by Joseph Kresh. 2 vols. New York: Schocken, 1965.

————. *Letter to His Father (Brief an den Vater)*. New York: Schocken, 1953.
Kass, Georg. *Möser und Goethe*. Diss., Göttingen. Berlin: 1909.
Kazin, Alfred. "Autobiography as Narrative." *Michigan Quarterly Review*, 3 (1964): 210–16.
Kemp, Charles, R. *A Pastoral Triumph: The Story of Richard Baxter and His Ministry at Kidderminster*. New York: Macmillan, 1948.
Kindermann, Heinz. *Das Goethebild des 20. Jahrhunderts*. Darmstadt: Wissenschaftliche Buchgesellschaft, 1966.
Kirn, Paul. *Das Bild des Menschen in der Geschichtsschreibung von Polybios bis Ranke*. Göttingen: Vandenhoeck & Ruprecht, 1955.
Kleist, Heinrich von. *Geschichte meiner Seele; das Lebenszeugnis der Briefe*. Edited by Helmut Sembdner. Bremen: Schünemann, 1959.
Klibansky, Raymond. "Peter Abailard and Bernard of Clairvaux: A Letter by Abailard." *Medieval and Renaissance Studies*, 5 (1961): 1–28.
Knauer, G. Nico. "Peregrinatio Animae: Zur Frage der Einheit der Konfessionen." *Hermes*, 85 (1957): 216–48.
Knox, Ronald Arbuthnot. *Enthusiasm*. Oxford: Clarendon Press, 1951.
Korff, Hermann August. *Die Lebensidee Goethes*. Leipzig: Weber, 1925.
————. *Geist der Goethezeit: Versuch einer ideelen Entwicklung der klassisch-romantischen Literaturgeschichte*. 5 vols. Leipzig: Weber, 1925–57.
————. *Humanismus und Romantik: Die Lebensauffassung der Neuzeit und ihre Entwicklung im Zeitalter Goethes*. Leipzig: Weber, 1924.
Kornberg, Jacques. "Wilhelm Dilthey on the Self and History: Some Theoretical Roots of *Geistesgeschichte*." *Central European History*, 5:4 (Dec. 1972): 295–317.
Kristeller, Paul Oskar. *The Classics and Renaissance Thought*. Martin Classical Lectures, vol. 15. Cambridge, Mass.: Harvard University Press, 1955.
————. *Renaissance Thought: The Classic, Scholastic, and Humanist Strains*. A revised and enlarged version of *The Classics and Renaissance Thought*. New York: Harper & Row, 1961.
————. *Renaissance Thought II: Papers on Humanism and the Arts*. New York: Harper & Row, 1965.
Kügelgen, Wilhelm von. *Jugenderinnerungen eines alten Mannes*. Stuttgart: Belser, 1904.
La Bedoyere, Michael de. *The Archbishop and the Lady: The Story of Fénelon and Madame Guyon*. London: Collins, 1956.
Labriolle, Pierre de. *History & Literature of Christianity from Tertullian to Boethius*. Translated by Herbert Wilson. London: Routledge & Kegan Paul, 1968.
La Bruyère, Jean de. *Les Caractères ou les moeurs de ce siècle*. Edited by J. C. Schweighaeuser. Paris: Didot, 1860.
Lammers, Walther, ed. *Geschichtsdenken & Geschichtsbild im Mittelalter*. Darmstadt: Wissenschaftliche Buchgesellschaft, 1965.
Landmann, Michael, et al. *De Homine: der Mensch im Spiegel seines Gedankens*. Orbis Academicus 1:9. Freiburg: K. Alber, 1962.
Langness, Lewis L. *The Life History in Anthropological Science*. New York: Holt, Rinehart & Winston, 1965.
Lanson, Gustave. *Les Essais de Montaigne: Etude et analyse*. Paris: Mellotte, n.d.
————. "L'Unité de la pensée de Jean-Jacques Rousseau." *Annales de la Société Jean-Jacques Rousseau*, 8 (1912): 1–31.
Leclerq, Jean. "Comment fut construit Saint-Denis." *La Clarté-Dieu*, 18 (1945): 1–56.
————. "L'Amitié dans les lettres au Moyen Âge." *Revue du Moyen Âge Latin*, 1 (1945): 391–410.

————. *The Love of Learning and the Desire for God.* Translated by Catherine Misrahi. New York: Mentor Books, 1961.

————. *Pierre le Vénérable.* Paris: de Fontenelle, 1946.

————. "Une 'Lamentation' inédite de Jean de Fécamp." *Revue Bénédictine,* 54 (1942): 41–60.

————., et al. *Un Maître de la vie spirituelle au xi siècle: Jean de Fécamp.* Paris: Vrin, 1946.

Leeuw, Cornelis Arie de. *Aelius Aristides als bron voor de kennis van zijn tijd.* Diss., Utrecht. Amsterdam, n.p. 1939.

Lehmann, Paul. "Autobiographies of the Middle Ages." *Transactions of the Royal Historical Society.* 5th series. 3 (1953): 41–52.

Leibniz, Gottfried Wilhelm. *Philosophische Schriften.* Edited by C. J. Gerhardt. 7 vols. Berlin: Weidmann, 1875–90.

————. *Selections.* Edited by Philip P. Wiener. New York: Scribners, 1951.

————. *Auswahl.* Edited by Friedrich Heer. Frankfurt: Fischer, 1958.

Leisegang, Hans. *Die Gnosis.* Stuttgart: Kröner, 1955.

Le Maitre de Claville, Charles F. *Traité du vrai mérite de l'homme, considéré dans tous les ages et dans toutes les conditions.* 2 vols. 4th ed. Paris: Saugrain, 1742.

Lempp, Otto. *Das Problem der Theodicee in der Philosophie und Literatur des 18. Jahrhunderts bis auf Kant und Schiller.* Leipzig: Dürr, 1910.

Leo, Ulrich. "Petrarca, Ariost und die Unsterblichkeit." *Romanische Forschungen,* 63 (1951): 241–81.

Libanius. *Autobiographische Schriften.* Edited by Peter Wolf. Zurich: Artemis, 1967.

Lichtenstein, Ulrich von. *Frauendienst.* Edited by R. Bechstein. 2 vols. Deutsche Dichtungen des Mittelalters, vols. 6–7. Leipzig: Brockhaus, 1888.

————. *Ulrich von Lichtenstein's Service of Ladies.* Translated in condensed form by J. W. Thomas. University of North Carolina Studies in the German Languages and Literatures, no. 63. Chapel Hill: University of North Carolina Press, 1969.

Liebeschuetz, Hans. *Medieval Humanism in the Life and Writings of John of Salisbury.* Studies of the Warburg Institute, vol. 17. London: Warburg Institute, 1950.

Löwith, Karl. "Vicos Grundsätz: verum et factum convertuntur; seine theologische Prämisse und deren säkulare Konsequenzen." In *Sitzungsberichte der Heidelberger Akademie der Wissenschaften Philosophisch-historische Klasse.* 1968.

Lorenz, Rudolf. "Gnade und Erkenntnis bei Augustinus." *Zeitschrift für Kirchengeschichte,* 75 (1964): 21–78.

Lovejoy, Arthur O. *The Great Chain of Being: A Study of the History of an Idea.* New York: Harper Torchbooks, 1960.

Low, David Morrice. *Edward Gibbon, 1737–1794.* New York: Random House, 1937.

Luscombe, David Edward. *The School of Peter Abelard: The Influence of Abelard's Thought in the Early Scholastic Period.* Cambridge Studies in Medieval Life and Thought, vol. 14. London: Cambridge University Press, 1969.

MacFarlane, Alan. *The Family Life of Ralph Josselin: A Seventeenth Century Clergyman-An Essay in Historical Anthropology.* Cambridge: At the University Press, 1970.

McLaughlin, Mary M. "Abelard as Autobiographer: The Motives and Meaning of his *Story of Calamities." Speculum,* 42 (1967): 463–88.

McNeill, John T. *The History and Character of Calvinism*. New York: Oxford University Press, 1967.

Magalhães-Vilhena, V. de. *Le Problème de Socrate: Le Socrate historique et le Socrate de Platon*. Paris: Presses Universitaires, 1952.

Mahrholz, Werner. *Deutsche Selbstbekenntnisse; ein Beitrag zur Geschichte der Selbstbiographie von der Mystik bis zum Pietismus*. Berlin: Furche, 1919.

Maland, David. *Culture and Society in Seventeenth Century France*. London: Batsford, 1970.

Malcolm X. *The Autobiography of Malcolm X*. New York: Grove Press, 1966.

Mandell, Barrett. "Bunyan and the Autobiographer's Artistic Purpose." *Criticism*, 10 (1968): 225–43.

Mann, Klaus. *André Gide and the Crisis of Modern Thought*. London: Dobson, 1948.

Mann, Thomas. "Goethe als Repräsentant des bürgerlichen Zeitalters." In *Adel des Geistes: Sechzehn Versuche zum Problem der Humanität*, pp. 104–44. Stockholm: Bermann-Fischer, 1948.

Marcus Aurelius [Aurelius Antoninus, Marcus]. *The Meditations of Marcus Aurelius Antoninus*. Translated by John Jackson. Oxford: Clarendon Press, 1906.

————. *The Communings with Himself*. Loeb Classical Library. Cambridge, Mass.: Harvard University Press, 1961.

Martin, Hugh. *Puritanism and Richard Baxter*. London: SCM Press, 1954.

Marrou, Henri-Irénée. *Saint Augustin et la fin de la culture antique*. 4th ed. Paris: de Boccard, 1958.

————. *Histoire de l'éducation dans L'Antiquité*. Paris: Eds. de Seuil, 1948.

Matthews, William. *American Diaries: an annotated bibliography of American diaries written prior to the year 1861*. Berkeley: University of California Press, 1945.

————. *Autobiography, biography, and the novel; papers read at the Clark Library Seminar May 13, 1972*. William Andrews Clark Memorial Library Seminar Papers. Los Angeles: University of California Press, 1973.

————. *British autobiographies; an annotated bibliography of British autobiographies published or written before 1951*. Berkeley: University of California Press, 1955.

————. *British diaries; an annotated bibliography of British diaries written between 1442 and 1942*. Berkeley: University of California Press, 1973.

Maurois, André. *Aspects of Biography*. Translated by Sydney Castle Roberts. New York: D. Appelton & Co., 1929.

Mechtild von Magdeburg. *Die Gesichte der Schwester Mechtild von Magdeburg; aus dem "Fliessenden Licht der Gottheit."* Edited by H. Grimm. Leipzig: Insel Verlag, n.d.

Meer, Frederick van der. *Augustine the Bishop; religion and society at the dawn of the Middle Ages*. Translated by Brian Battershaw, et al. New York: Harper Torchbooks, 1965.

Meinecke, Friedrich. *Die Entstehung des Historismus*. Munich: R. Oldenbourg, 1965.

————. *Historism*. Translated by J. E. Anderson, with a foreword by Sir Isaiah Berlin. London: Routledge and Kegan Paul, 1972.

————. *Die Idee der Staatsräson in der neuren Geschichte*. Munich: Oldenbourg, 1963.

————. *Weltbürgertum und Nationalstaat*. Munich: Oldenbourg, 1962.

*Mensch und Charakter. Handbuch der Philosophie*. Part 3. Munich: Oldenbourg, 1931.

Merlant, Joachim. *De Montaigne à Vauvenargues: Essais sur la vie intérieure et la culture du moi.* Paris, 1914. Repr., Geneva: Slatkine Reprints, 1969.

Mill, John Stuart. *Autobiography.* New York: Signet, 1964.

———. *On Bentham and Coleridge.* New York: Harper Torchbooks, 1962.

Miller, Otto. *Der Individualismus als Schicksal.* Nuremberg: Glock & Lutz, n.d.

Misch, Georg. "Die Autobiographie der französischen Aristokratie des 17. Jahrhunderts." *Deutsche Vierteljahrsschrift,* 1 (1923): 172–213.

———. *Geschichte der Autobiographie.*

   Vol. 1 (in two parts): *Das Altertum.* 3d rev. ed. Bern: Francke, 1949–50.

   Vol. 2: *Das Mittelalter: Die Frühzeit.* Frankfurt: Schulte-Bulmke, 1955.

   Vol. 3: *Das Mittelalter:* Part 1: *Das Hochmittelalter im Anfang.* Frankfurt: Schulte-Bulmke, 1959. Part 2: *Das Hochmittelalter im Anfang.* Frankfurt: Schulte-Bulmke, 1962.

   Vol. 4: Part 1: *Das Hochmittelalter in der Vollendung.* Edited "aus dem Nachlass," by Leo Delfoss. Frankfurt: Schulte-Bulmke, 1967. Part 2: *Von der Renaissance bis zu den autobiographischen Hauptwerken des 18. und 19. Jahrhunderts.* Edited by Bernd Neumann. Frankfurt: Schulte-Bulmke, 1969.

———. *Lebensphilosophie und Phänomenologie.* Darmstadt: Wissenschaftliche Buchgesellschaft, 1967.

———. "Von den Gestaltungen der Persönlichkeit." In *Weltanschauung: Philosophie und Religion in Darstellungen,* pp. 79–126. Edited by Max Frischeisen-Köhler. Berlin: Reichl, 1911.

Möbius, Paul Julius A. *Goethe.* 2 vols. in 1. Leipzig: Barth, 1903.

Möller, Gisela, ed. *Deutsche Selbstbiographien aus drei Jahrhunderten.* Munich: Beck, 1967.

Mönch, Walter. *Deutsche Kultur von der Aufklärung bis zur Gegenwart. Ereignisse-Gestalten-Strömungen.* Munich: Heuber, 1962.

Möser, Justus. *Sämmtliche Werke; historisch-kritische Ausgabe.* Vol. 1–. Oldenburg: Stalling, 1944–.

———. *Osnabrückische Geschichte.* 2 vols. in 1. Berlin: Nicolai, 1780.

Molthagen, Joachim. *Der römische Staat und die Christen im zweiten und dritten Jahrhundert.* Hypomnemata; Untersuchungen zur Antike und ihrem Nachleben, vol 28. Göttingen: Vandenhoeck & Ruprecht, 1970.

Momigliano, Arnaldo. *The Development of Greek Biography; four lectures.* Cambridge: Harvard University Press, 1971.

Mommsen, Momme. *Die Enstehung von Goethes Werken; in Dokumenten.* 2 vols. vol. 2: *Cäcilia bis Dichtung und Wahrheit.* Berlin: Akademie Verlag, 1958.

Monod, Bernard. *Le Moine Guibert et son temps, (1053–1124).* Paris: Hachette, 1905.

Montaigne, Michel de. *Oeuvres complètes. Texte du manuscrit de Bordeaux.* Edited by A. Armaingaud. 12 vols. Paris: Conard, 1924–41.

———. *The Autobiography of Michel de Montaigne.* Edited by Marvin Lowenthal. Boston: Houghton Mifflin, 1935.

———. *The Complete Essays of Montaigne.* Translated by Donald M. Frame. Stanford, Calif.: Stanford University Press, 1958.

———. *The Essays.* Translated by E. J. Trenchmann. 2 vols. in 1. London: Oxford University Press, 1927.

———. *Essais de Montaigne.* Edited by Fortunat Strowski. 5 vols. Bordeaux: Pech, 1906–33.

———. *Oeuvres complètes.* Edited by Albert Thibaudet, et al. Paris: Bibliothèque de la Pleïade, 1962.

Moreau-Rendu, Suzanne. *L'Idée de Bonté naturelle chez J.-J. Rousseau*. Paris: M. Rivière, 1929.

Moritz, Karl Philipp. *Anton Reiser*. Berlin: F. Maurer, 1785–90.

Morley, Henry. *Jerome Cardan: The Life of Girolamo Cardano of Milan, Physician*. 2 vols. London: Chapman, 1854.

Morley, John. *Rousseau*. 2 vols. London: Chapman & Hall, 1873.

Mornet, Daniel. *Le Sentiment de la Nature en France de J. -J. Rousseau à Bernardin de Saint-Pierre*. Paris: Hachette, 1907.

Morris, Colin. *The Discovery of the Individual 1050–1200*. New York: Harper Torchbooks, 1972.

Morris, John N. *Versions of the Self: Studies in English Autobiography from John Bunyan to John Stuart Mill*. New York: Basic Books, 1966.

Mowat, Robert B. *Jean-Jacques Rousseau*. Bristol: Arrowsmith, 1938.

Muckle, Joseph Thomas. "Abelard's Letter of Consolation to a friend (Historia Calamitatum)." *Medieval Studies* , 12 (1950): 163–213.

———. "The Personal Letters between Abelard and Heloise." *Medieval Studies*, 15 (1953): 47–94.

Müller-Freienfels, Richard. "Der Begriff der Individualität als fiktive Konstruktion." *Annalen der Philosophie*, 1 (1919): 70–318.

———. *Philosophie der Individualität*. Leipzig: F. Meiner, 1923.

Munteano, Basil. "La Solitude de J.-J. Rousseau." *Annales de la Société Jean-Jacques Rousseau*, 31 (1946–49): 79–168.

Naves, Raymond. *Voltaire et L'Encyclopédie*. Paris, 1938. Repr., Geneva: Slatkine Reprints, 1970.

Netoliczka, Oskar. *Individualität und Persönlichkeit*. Hermannstadt: Kraft, 1908.

Newman, John Henry Cardinal. *Apologia pro vita sua*. Edited by A. Dwight Culler. Boston: Houghton Mifflin, 1956.

Nisbet, Robert A. *Social Change and History: Aspects of the Western Theory of Development*. New York: Oxford University Press, 1969.

Norden, Eduard. *Die antike Kunstprosa vom 6. Jahrhundert v. Chr. bis in die Zeit der Renaissance*. 2nd ed. 2 vols. Leipzig: B. G. Teubner, 1909.

O'Connell, Robert J. *St. Augustine's Confessions: The Odyssey of Soul*. Cambridge, Mass.: Harvard University Press, 1969.

Olney, James. *Metaphors of Self: The Meaning of Autobiography*. Princeton, N.J.: Princeton University Press, 1972.

O'Meara, John J. "Neoplatonism in the Conversion of Saint Augustine." *Dominican Studies*, 3 (1950): 331–44.

Opperman, Hans, ed. *Römertum: Ausgewählte Aufsätze und Arbeiten aus den Jahren 1921 Bis 1961*. Wege der Forschung, vol. 18. Darmstadt: Wissenschaftliche Buchgesellschaft, 1962.

Ore, Oystein. *Cardano the Gambling Scholar*. With a translation from the Latin of Cardano's <Book on Games of Chance> by Sydney Henry Gould. Princeton, N.J.: Princeton University Press, 1953.

Othlo, monk of St. Emmeram. *Opera Omnia*. Migne, PL 146. Paris: Garnier, 1879.

Otto of Freising. *The Deeds of Frederick Barbarossa (continued by Rahewin)*. Edited by Charles Mierrow. New York: Norton, 1966.

Otto, Rudolf. *Mysticism East and West; a comparative analysis of the nature of mysticism*. Translated by Bertha Bracey and Richenda Payne. New York: Collier Books, 1962.

Otto, Walter F. *Die Gestalt und das Sein*. Darmstadt: Wissenschaftliche Buchgesellschaft, 1955.

Owen, Eric Trevor. *The Story of the Iliad*. Ann Arbor: University of Michigan Press, 1966.

Padover, Saul K. *Confessions and Selfportraits*. Freeport, New York: Books for Libraries Press, 1957.

Panofsky, Erwin. "Abbot Suger of St-Denis." in *Meaning in the Visual Arts: Papers in Art History*, pp. 108–45. Garden City, N.Y.: Anchor Books, 1955.

————. "Dürer's 'Melencolia' I; eine quellen- und typengeschichtliche Untersuchung (with Fritz Saxl). *Studien der Bibliothek Warburg*, vol. 2. Berlin: Teubner, 1923.

————. *Renaissance and Renascences in Western Art*. New York: Harper Torchbooks, 1969.

————., ed. *Abbot Suger on the Abbey Church of St. Denis and Its Art Treasures*. Edited, translated and annotated by E. Panofsky. Princeton, N.J.: Princeton University Press, 1946.

Pascal, Blaise. *Oeuvres complètes*. Edited by Jacques Chevalier. Paris: Bibliothèque de la Pleïade, 1954.

Pascal, Roy. *Design and Truth in Autobiography*. Cambridge, Mass.: Harvard University Press, 1960.

Patrick, St. *Libri Sancti Patrici: The Latin Writings of St. Patrick*. Rev. ed. Edited by Newport J. D. White. London: Society for Promoting Christian Knowledge, 1918.

————. *St. Patrick's Writings*. Translated by Arnold Marsh. Dundalk: Dundalgan Press (W. Tempest), 1961.

Paulinus of Pella. *Benedicti Paulini Petrocorii Poemata et Alia Quaedam Sacrae Antiquitas Fragmenta*. 2 vols in 1. Edited by Christian Daumius. Leipzig: F. Lanckisch, 1686.

Peers, Edgar Allison. *Handbook of the Life and Times of St. Teresa and St. John of the Cross*. London: Burns & Oates, 1954.

————. *The Mystics of Spain*. London: Allen & Unwin, 1951.

————. *Saint Teresa of Jesus and other Essays and Addresses*. London: Faber & Faber, 1953.

————. *Studies of the Spanish Mystics*. 2 vols. London: Sheldon Press, 1927–30.

Petrarca, Francesco. *Edizione nazionale delle Opere*. Vols. 1–14. Florence: Sansoni, 1926–.

————. *Briefe des Francesco Petrarca: Eine Auswahl*. Translated by Hans Nachod. Berlin: Die Runde, 1931.

————. *Dichtungen, Briefe, Schriften*. Edited by Hanns W. Eppelsheimer. Frankfurt: Fischer Bücherei, 1956.

————. *Petrarch at Vaucluse: Letters in Verse and Prose*. Translated by Ernest Hatch Wilkins. Chicago: University of Chicago Press, 1958.

————. *Prose*. Edited by G. Martellotti. Milan: Ricciardi, 1955.

————. *Le Rime di Francesco Petrarca: Francesco Petrarca's italienische Gedichte*. Translated by Karl Förster. 2 vols. Leipzig: Brockhaus, 1818.

Petrus Diaconus of Montecassino, 12th century. *De viris illustribus monasterii Casinensis*. Cum supplemento Placidi Romani et Jo. Baptistae Mari annotationibus. In *Bibliotheca Ecclesiastica*. Edited by Johann Fabricius. Hamburg: C. Liebezeit and T. C. Felginer, 1718.

Peyre, Henri. *Literature and Sincerity*. New Haven, Conn.: Yale University Press, 1963.

Pius II. *Memoirs of a Renaissance Pope; the Commentaries of Pius II: An abridgement*. Translated by Florence A. Gragg. Edited by Leona C. Gabel. New York: Capricorn Books, 1962.

Plato. "The Seventh Letter." In *The Platonic Epistles*, pp. 115–47. Translated by J. Harward. Cambridge: At the University Press, 1932.

———. *Socrates. A Translation of the Apology, Crito, and parts of the Phaedo of Plato*. 6th ed. New York: Scribner's, 1884.

Poole, Reginald L. *Illustrations of the History of Medieval Thought and Learning*. 2d ed. London: SPCK, 1920.

Popkin, Richard H. *The History of Scepticism from Erasmus to Descartes*. Rev. ed. New York: Harper Torchbooks, 1968.

Poulet, Georges. *Studies in Human Time*. Translated by Elliot Coleman. New York: Harper Torchbooks, 1959.

Powicke, Frederick J. *A Life of Reverend Richard Baxter 1615–1691*. Boston: Houghton Mifflin, 1924.

———. *The Reverend Richard Baxter under the Cross (1662–1691)*. London: J. Cape, 1927.

———. "Ailred of Rievaulx and his biographer, Walter Daniel." *John Rylands Library, Manchester Bulletin*, 6 (1921–22): 310–51, 452–521.

———. "Gerald of Wales." *John Rylands Library, Manchester Bulletin*, 12 (1928): 389–410.

Price-Zimmermann, T. C. "Confession and Autobiography in the early Renaissance." In *Renaissance Studies in Honor of Hans Baron*, pp. 121–40. Edited by A. Molho & J. A. Tedeschi. DeKalb: Northern Illinois University Press, 1971.

Pyritz, Hans. *Goethe-Studien*. Cologne: Böhlau, 1962.

Rang, Martin. *Rousseaus Lehre vom Menschen*. Göttingen: Vandenhoeck & Ruprecht, 1959.

Ratzinger, Joseph. "Originalität und Überlieferung in Augustinus Begriff der Confessio." *Revue des études Augustiniennes*, 3 (1957): 375–92.

Ratherius, Bishop of Verona, 890–974. *Opera Omnia*. Migne, *PL* 136. Paris: Garnier, 1844.

———. *Die Briefe des Bischofs Rather von Verona*. Edited by Fritz Weigle. Monumenta Germaniae. Briefe der deutschen Kaiserzeit, vol. 1. (Latin) Weimar: Böhlaus, 1949.

———. *Sermones Ratherii Episcopi Veronensis*. Edited by Benny R. Reece. Worchester, Mass: Holy Cross College, 1969.

Rauschen, Gerhard. *Das griechisch-römische Schulwesen zur Zeit des ausgehenden Heidentums*. Bonn: F. Cohen, 1901.

Ravier, André. *L'Education de l'Homme Nouveau: Essai historique et critique sur le Livre de l'Emile de J.-J. Rousseau*. 2 vols. Issoudun: Ed. Spés, 1941.

Raymond, Marcel. "J.-J. Rousseau: Deux aspects de sa vie intérieure." *Annales de la Société Jean-Jacques Rousseau*, 29 (1941–42): 7–57.

Reichenkron, Günter et al., eds. *Formen der Selbstdarstellung: Analekten zu einer Geschichte des literarischen Selbstporträts*. Festgabe für Fritz Neubert. Berlin: Duncker & Humblot, 1956.

Reinhardt, Karl. *Von Werken und Formen: Vorträge und Aufsätze*. Godesberg: Küpper, 1948.

Renan, Ernest. *Souvenirs d'enfance et de jeunnesse*. Paris: Calmann Lévy, 1883.

de Retz, Cardinal [Jean-François Paul de Gondi]. *Mémoires*. Paris: Bibliothèque de la Pleïade, 1956.

Rinehart, Keith. "The Victorian Approach to Autobiography." *Modern Philology*, 51 (1953): 177–86.

Rixner, Thaddä Anselm et al., eds. *Leben und Lehrmeinungen berühmter Physiker*. Part 2: *Hieronymus Cardano*. Salzbach: Seidel, 1820.

Roethe, Gustav. "Dichtung und Wahrheit." in *Berichte des Freien Deutschen*

*Hochstiftes zu Frankfurt am Main.* N.S. 17 (1901): 1–25.

Röhrs, Hermann. *Jean-Jacques Rousseau: Vision und Wirklichkeit.* Heidelberg: Quelle und Meyer, 1966.

Roldanus, Cornelia W. *Zeventiende Eeuwse Geestesbloei.* Utrecht: Het Spectrum, 1961.

Rossmann, Kurt, ed. *Deutsche Geschichtsphilosophie von Lessing bis Jaspers.* Bremen: C. Schünemann, 1959.

Rousseau, Jean-Jacques. *Oeuvres complètes.* 13 vols. Paris: Hachette, 1909–12.

———. *Oeuvres complètes.* Edited by Bernard Gagnebin and Marcel Raymond et al. 4 vols. Paris: Bibliothèque de la Pléiade, 1959–.

Vol. 1: *Les Confessions et autre textes autobiographiques.* 1959.

Vol. 2: *La Nouvelle Heloïse-Théatre-Poésies-Essais Littéraires.* 1961.

Vol. 3: *Du Contrat Social-Ecrits politiques.* 1964.

———. *Correspondance générale.* Edited by Theophile Dufour. 20 vols. Paris:

———. *Émile ou de l'éducation.* Edited by P. Richard. Paris: Garnier, n.d.

———. *Emile; or Education.* Translated by Barbara Foxley. London: Dent, 1914.

———. *The First and Second Discourses.* Edited by Roger D. Master. New York: St. Martin's Press, 1964.

———. *La Nouvelle Heloïse. Julie or, the new Eloise: Letters of two lovers, inhabitants of a small town at the foot of the Alps.* University Park: Pennsylvania State University Press, 1968.

———. *The Social Contract.* Edited by Charles Frankel. New York: Hafner, 1947.

Ruf, P. and M. Grabmann. "Ein neuaufgefundenes Bruchstück der Apologia Abaelards." *Sitzungsberichte. Akademie der Wissenschaften, München. Philosophisch-Historische Abteilung,* no. 5 (1930): 1–41.

Ruskin, John. *Praeterita.* New York: Merrill and Baker, 1885.

Salomon-Bayet, Claire. *J. -J. Rousseau ou l'impossible unité.* Paris: Seghers, 1968.

Sand, George. *Histoire de ma vie.* Edited by Noëlle Roubaud. Paris: Stock, 1945.

Sartre, Jean-Paul. *The Words.* Translated by Bernard Frechtman. Greenwich: Fawcett, 1968.

Saussure, Hermine de. *Rousseau et les manuscrits des Confessions.* Paris: Boccard, 1958.

Sayre, Robert F. *The Examined Self: Benjamin Franklin, Henry Adams, Henry James.* Princeton, N.J.: Princeton University Press, 1964.

Schadewaldt, Wolfgang. *Goethestudien: Natur und Altertum.* Zurich: Artemis, 1963.

———. *Von Homers Welt und Werk.* Leipzig: Koehler & Anelang, 1944.

Schauwecker, Helga E. *Otloh von St. Emmeram. Ein Beitrag zur Bildungs- und Frömmigkeitsgeschichte des elften Jahrhunderts.* Diss. Würzburg. Munich: n.p., 1965.

Schmalenbach, Hermann. "Individualität und Individualismus." *Kantstudien,* 24 (1919): 365–88.

Schmidt, Martin, et al., eds. *Das Zeitalter des Pietismus.* Klassiker des Protestantismus, vol. 6. Bremen: Schünemann, 1965.

Schmitthenner, Walter, ed. *Augustus.* Darmstadt: Wissenschaftliche Buchgesellschaft, 1969.

Schneider, Carl. *Geistesgeschichte der Christlichen Antike.* abridged ed. Munich: Beck, 1970.

Schulte-Nordholt, Herman Gerrit. *Het Beeld der Renaissance; Een Historiografische Studie.* Bibliotheek voor Theoretische en Cultuurgeschiedenis, vol. 1. Amsterdam: Querido, 1948.

Schultz, Werner. "Das Erlebnis der Individualität bei Wilhelm von Humboldt." *Deutsche Vierteljahrsschrift*, 7 (1929): 654–81.

Schwarz, Richard. *Das Christusbild des deutschen Mystikers Heinrich Seuse.* Deutsches Werden; Greifswalder Forschungen zur deutschen Geistesgeschichte, no. 5. Greifswald: Bamberg, 1934.

Schwietering, Julius. "Der Wandel des Heldenideals in der epischen Dichtung des 12. Jahrhunderts." In *Philologische Schriften*, pp. 304–13. Munich: W. Fink, 1969.

————. "Typologisches in mittelalterlicher Dichtung." In *Vom Werden des Deutsches Geistes*, pp. 40–55. Edited by Paul Merker. Festschrift für Ehrismann. Berlin: Gruyter, 1925.

Seillière, Ernest. *Madame Guyon et Fénelon: Précurseurs de J.-J. Rousseau.* Paris: Alcan, 1918.

Seippel, Paul. "La Personnalité religieuse de J.-J. Rousseau." *Annales de la Société Jean-Jacques Rousseau*, 8 (1912): 205–31.

Seneca, Lucius Annaeus. *Seneca.* With a translation by Thomas Corcoran. Loeb Classical Library. London: Heineman, 1971.

Senn, Richard. *Die Echtheit der Vita Heinrich Seuses.* Sprache und Dichtung, no. 45. Bern: Haupt, 1930.

Seppelt, Franz Xaver ed. *Monumenta Coelestiniana; Quellen zur Geschichte des Papstes Coelestin V.* Paderborn: Schöningh, 1921.

Heinrich Seuse (Suso). *Deutsche Schriften.* Edited by Karl Bihlmeyer. Stuttgart: W. Kohlhammer, 1907.

————. *The Life of Blessed Henry Suso by Himself.* Translated by Thomas F. Knox. London: Methuen, 1913.

————. *The Exemplar.* With a critical introduction and explanatory notes by Nicholas Heller. Translated by Ann Edward. Dubuque, Iowa: Priory Press, 1962.

————. *Das Leben des seligen Heinrich Seuse.* Translated by Georg Hofmann. Düsseldorf: Patmos, 1966.

————. *Das Büchelein der Ewigen Weisheit.* Edited by M. Greiner. Leipzig: Insel Verlag, n.d.

Sharrock, Roger. *John Bunyan.* London: University Library, 1954.

————. "Spiritual Autobiography in the *Pilgrims Progress.*" *Review of English Studies*, 24 (April 1948): 102–19.

Shea, Daniel B. *Spiritual Autobiography in Early America.* Princeton, N.J.: Princeton University Press, 1968.

Shumaker, Wayne. *English Autobiography: Its Emergence, Materials and Forms.* Berkeley: University of California Press, 1954.

Simmel, Georg. *Goethe.* Leipzig: Klinckhardt, 1913.

Simpson, Alan. *Puritanism in Old and New England.* Chicago: University of Chicago Press, 1967.

Sizoo, Alexander. *Toelichting op Augustinus' Belijdenissen.* Delft: Meinema, 1947.

Smalley, Beryl. "Prima Clavis Sapientiae: Augustine and Abelard." *Fritz Saxl Memorial Essays*, pp. 93–101. Edited by D. J. Gordon. London: 1957.

Snell, Bruno. *Die Entdeckung des Geistes: Studien zur Enstehung des europäischen Denkens bei den Griechen.* Hamburg: Claaszen & Goverts, 1946.

————. *The Discovery of Mind: The Greek Origins of European Thought.* Translated by T. G. Rosenmeyer. New York: Harper Torchbooks, 1960.

Southern, Richard William. *The Making of the Middle Ages.* New Haven, Conn.: Yale University Press, 1963.

————. *Medieval Humanism and Other Studies*. Oxford: Blackwell, 1970.

————. *Western Society and the Church in the Middle Ages*. Pelican History of the Church, vol. 2. Penguin Books, 1970.

Spengemann, William et al. "Autobiography and the American Myth." *American Quarterly*, 17 (1965): 501–19.

Spranger, Eduard. *Lebensformen: Geisteswissenschaftliche Psychologie und Ethik der Persönlichkeit*. Halle: Niemeyer, 1927.

Stackelberg, Jürgen von. *Von Rabelais bis Voltaire: Zur Geschichte des französischen Romans*. Munich: Beck, 1970.

Staiger, Emil. *Goethe*. 3 vols. Zurich: Artemis Verlag, 1959.

Starobinski, Jean. *Jean-Jacques Rousseau: La Transparence et l'obstacle, suivi de sept essais sur Rousseau*. Paris: Gallimard, 1971.

Stauffer, Donald Alfred. *The Art of Biography in Eighteenth Century England*. Princeton, N.J.: Princeton University Press, 1941.

————. *English Biography before 1700*. Cambridge: Harvard University Press, 1930.

Stefansky, Georg. "Justus Mösers Geschichtsauffassung im Zusammenhang der deutschen Literatur des 18. Jahrhunderts." *Euphorion: Zeitschrift für Literaturgeschichte*, 28 (1927): 21–34.

Steinen, Wolfram von den. *Der Kosmos des Mittelalters: Von Karl dem Grossen zu Bernhard von Clairvaux*. Bern: Francke, 1959.

Stenzel, Julius. *Kleine Schriften zur griechischen Philosophie*. Darmstadt: Wissenschaftlichen Buchgesellschaft, 1957.

Stiglmayr, Joseph. "Zum Aufbau der Confessions des hl. Augustin." *Scholastik*, 7 (1932): 387–403.

Stockton, David. *Cicero: A Political Biography*. Oxford: Oxford University Press, 1971.

Strassburger, Hermann. *Caesar im Urteil seiner Zeitgenossen*. 2d ed. Darmstadt: Wissenschaftliche Buchgesellschaft, 1968.

Street, Charles L. *Individualism and Individuality in the Philosophy of John Stuart Mill*. Milwaukee, Wisc.: Morehouse, 1926.

Strowski, Fortunat J. *Montaigne, sa vie publique et privée*. Paris: Nouvelle Revue Critique, 1938.

————. *Saint François de Sales; introduction à l'histoire du sentiment religieux en France au dix-septième siècle*. 2d ed. Paris: Plon, 1898.

Sugerius. *Oeuvres complètes de Suger*. Edited by A. Lecoy de la Marche. Paris: J. Renouard, 1867.

Swift, Francis Darwin. *The Life and Times of James the First, the Conqueror, King of Aragon, Valencia, and Majorca*. Oxford: Clarendon Press, 1894.

Tagliacozza, Giorgia, ed. *Giambattista Vico: An International Symposium*. Baltimore, Md.: Johns Hopkins Press, 1967.

Tawney, Richard Henry. *Religion and the Rise of Capitalism*. New York: NAL/Mentor Books, 1954.

Taylor, Alfred Edward. *Socrates*. London: Davies, 1932.

Tellenbach, Gerd. *Church, State, and Christian Society*. Translated by R. F. Bennett. Studies in Medieval History, vol. 3. Oxford: Basil Blackwell, 1966.

Teresa, Saint. *Obras completas*. Edited by Efrén de la Madre de Dios. 2d ed. Biblioteca de autores cristianos, 212. Madrid: 1967.

————. *The Complete Works of Saint Teresa of Jesus*. Translated and edited by E. Allison Peers. 3 vols. London: Sheed & Ward, 1946.

————. *Werken der H. Teresia*. Translated by Titus Brandsma, et al. 2 vols. Bussum: Brand, 1918.

————. *The Life of St. Teresa of Avila including the Relations of Her Spiritual State, Written by Herself.* Translated by David Lewis. London: Burns & Oates, 1962.

TeSelle, Eugene. *Augustine the Theologian.* London: Burns & Oates, 1970.

Thiel, Gerhard. *Bunyans Stellung innerhalb der religiösen Strömungen seiner Zeit.* Sprache und Kultur der Germanisch-Romanischen Völker. Anglistische Reihe, vol. 8. Breslau, 1931.

Thimme, Wilhelm. *Augustins geistige Entwicklung in den ersten Jahren nach seiner Bekehrung, 386–391.* Berlin: Trowitzsch, 1908.

Thomas (Father O.D.C.) et al. *St. Teresa of Avila: Studies in Her Life, Doctrine and Times.* Dublin: Clonmore & Reynolds, 1963.

Thorndike, Lynn. *A History of Magic and Experimental Science.* New York: Columbia University Press, 1941–58. (Vols. 5–8.)

Tolstoy, Leo. *Childhood, Boyhood, Youth.* Translated by Isabel F. Hapgood. New York: T. Y. Crowell, 1886.

Tönnies, Ferdinand. *Gemeinschaft und Gesellschaft; Grundbegriffe der reinen Soziologie.* Darmstadt: Wissenschaftliche Buchgesellschaft, 1963.

Trahard, Pierre. *Les Maitres de la sensibilité française au xviii siècle.* Jean-Jacques Rousseau, vol. 3. Paris: Boivin, 1932.

Tripet, Arnaud. *Pétrarque ou la connaissance de soi.* Travaux d'Humanisme et Renaissance, vol. 91. Geneva: Droz, 1967.

Troeltsch, Ernst. *Aufsätze zur Geistesgeschichte und Religionssoziologie.* Edited by Hans Baron. In *Gesammelte Schriften,* vol. 4. Tübingen: Mohr, 1925.

Trotsky, Leon. *My Life: An Attempt at an Autobiography.* New York: Pathfinder Press, 1970.

Ullmann, Walter. *The Individual and Society in the Middle Ages.* Baltimore, Md.: Johns Hopkins Press, 1966.

Valerius, Saint, Abbot of San Pedro de Montes, 7th cent. *Vita Sancti Fructuosi.* With translation, introduction and commentary by Sister Francis Clare Nock. Washington, D.C.: The Catholic University of America Press, 1946.

Vance, Christie. "Rousseau's Autobiographical Venture: A Process of Negation." *Genre,* 6, no. 1 (March 1973): 98–143.

Van Doren, Carl. *Benjamin Franklin.* New York: Viking, 1964.

Vereker, Charles. *Eighteenth-Century Optimism: A Study of the Interrelations of Moral and Social Theory in English and French Thought between 1689 and 1789.* Liverpool: Liverpool University Press, 1967.

Vico, Giambattista. *Opere.* Edited by G. Ferrari et al. 8 vols in 4. Naples: Stamperia de classici latini, 1858–69.

————. *The Autobiography.* Translated by Max Harold Fisch et al. Ithaca, N.Y.: Cornell University Press, 1963.

————. *The New Science.* Translated from the 3d ed. by Thomas G. Bergin and Max H. Fisch, abridged and revised. Garden City, N.Y.: Anchor Books, 1961.

————. *De nostri temporis studiorum ratione.* Darmstadt: Wissenschaftliche Buchgesellschaft, 1963.

————. *On the Study Methods of Our Time.* Translated by Elio Gianturco. Indianapolis, Ind.: Bobbs-Merrill, 1965.

————. *Opere filosofiche.* Edited by P. Cristofolini. Florence: Sansoni, 1971.

Viëtor, Karl. *Goethe: Dichtung, Wissenschaft, Weltbild.* Bern: Francke, 1949.

Villey, Pierre. *Les Sources et l'évolution des Essais de Montaigne.* 2 vols. 2d rev. ed. Paris: Hachette, 1933.

Vloemans, Antoon. *Cicero.* Kopstukken Uit de Geschiedenis, vol. 16. The Hague: Kruseman, 1964.

Voltaire. *Mélanges*. Edited by Jacques van den Heuvel. Paris: Bibliothèque de la Pleïade, 1961.

————. *Oeuvres historiques*. Edited by René Poemeau. Paris: Bibliothèque de la Pleïade, 1957.

————. *Romans et Contes*. Edited by René Groos. Paris: Bibliothèque de la Pleïade, 1954.

Vossler, Karl. "Benvenuto Cellinis Stil in seiner Vita." In *Festgabe für Gustav Groeber. Beiträge zur romanischen Philologie*, pp. 414–51. Halle: Niemeyer, 1899.

————. *Medieval Culture: An Introduction to Dante and His Times*. Translated by William C. Lawton. 2 vols. New York: Harcourt, Brace, 1929.

Vossler, Otto. *Rousseaus Freiheitslehre*. Göttingen: Vandenhoeck & Ruprecht, 1963.

Waddell, Helen. *The Wandering Scholars*. Boston: Houghton Mifflin, 1929.

Walter Daniel, fl. 1170. *The Life of Ailred of Rievaulx*. Translated by Frederick Maurice Powicke. London: Nelson, 1950.

Ward, Adolphus William. "Goethe and the French Revolution." In *Collected Papers: Historical, Literary, Travel and Miscellaneous*, 4:333–66. 5 vols. Cambridge: At the University Press, 1921.

Ward, John William. "Who was Benjamin Franklin?" *American Scholar*, 33 (1963): 541–53.

Waters, William George. *Jerome Cardan: A Biographical Study*. London: Lawrence & Berllem, 1898.

Watkins, Owen C. *The Puritan Experience*. London: Routledge & Kegan Paul, 1972.

Webb, Beatrice. *My Apprenticeship*. New York: London: Longmans, Green, 1926.

Weber, Ferdinand Wilhelm. *Hermann der Prämonstratenser: oder die Juden und die Kirche des Mittelalters*. Nördlingen: Beck, 1861.

Weber, Max. *The Protestant Ethic and the Spirit of Capitalism*. Translated by Talcott Parsons. New York: Scribner, 1958.

————. *Wirtschaft und Gesellschaft*. Studienausgabe edited by Johannes Winckelmann. 2 vols. Cologne: Kiepenheuer & Witsch, 1964.

Weintraub, Karl J. "Autobiography and Historical Consciousness." *Critical Inquiry* 1, no. 4 (June 1975): 821–848.

Weiser, Christian F. *Shaftesbury und das deutsche Geistesleben*. Leipzig: Teubner, 1916.

Wentzlaff-Eggebert, Friedrich W. "Erscheinungsformen der "unio mystica" in der deutschen Literatur und Dichtung." *Deutsche Vierteljahrsschrift*, 22 (1944): 238–77.

Wethered, Herbert Newton. *The Curious Art of Autobiography from Benvenuto Cellini to Rudyard Kipling*. New York: Philosophical Library, 1956.

Whitman, Cedric H. *Homer and the Heroic Tradition*. Cambridge, Mass.: Harvard University Press, 1958.

Wilamowitz-Moellendorf, Ulrich von. "Die Autobiographie im Altertum." *Internationale Wochenschrift für Wissenschaft, Kunst und Technik* (1907): 1105–14.

————. "Erkenne Dich Selbst." In *Reden und Vorträge*. Berlin: Weidmann, 1926. 2:171–89.

Wilkins, Ernest Hatch. *The Making of the "Canzoniere" and Other Petrarchan Studies*. Rome: Ed di Storia e Letteratura, 1951.

————. *Life of Petrarch*. Chicago: University of Chicago Press, 1961.

————. *Petrarch's Later Years*. Medieval Academy of America. Publication no. 70. Cambridge, Mass.: Medieval Academy of America, 1959.

Wilkinson, Elizabeth M. & Willoughby, L. A. *Goethe: Poet and Thinker*. London: E. Arnold, 1962.

Willey, Basil. *The Eighteenth Century Background: Studies on the Idea of Nature in the Thought of the Period*. Boston: The Beacon Press, 1961.

————. *The Seventeenth Century Background: Studies in the Thought of the Age in Relation to Poetry and Religion*. Garden City, N.Y.: Doubleday, n.d.

Williger, Eduard. "Der Aufbau der Konfessionen Augustins." *Zeitschrift für die Neutestamentliche Wissenschaft*, 28 (1929): 81–106.

Wirszubski, Chaim. *Libertas: As a Political Idea at Rome during the Late Republic and Early Principate*. Cambridge: At the University Press, 1960.

Witcutt, William Purcell. *The Rise and Fall of the Individual*. London: SPCK, 1958.

Wolf, Eugen. *Petrarca: Darstellung seines Lebensgefühls*. Beiträge zur Kulturgeschichte des Mittelalters und der Renaissance, vol. 28. Leipzig: Teubner, 1926.

Workman, Herbert. *The Evolution of the Monastic Ideal: From Earliest Times to the Coming of the Friars*. Boston: Beacon Press, 1962.

Wright, Esmond, ed. *Benjamin Franklin: A Profile*. New York: Hill & Wang, 1970.

Xenophon. *Opera Omnia*. 5 vols. Edited by E. C. Marchant. Oxford: Clarendon Press, 1900–1920.

————. *Xenophon*. With an English translation by C. L. Brownson, O. J. Todd, and E. C. Marchant. Loeb Classical Library. London: Heineman, 1918–.

————. "The Economist." Translated by H. G. Dakyns. In *Works of Xenophon*. London: Macmillan, 1897. 3.1.224–87.

# Index

# THE VALUE OF THE INDIVIDUAL
*Self and Circumstance in Autobiography*
Karl Joachim Weintraub

In this essay, the cultural historian Karl Joachim Weintraub traces the emergence of the concept of individuality as a modern self-image. By analyzing autobiographic writings of many of the men and women who have shaped our culture, Weintraub seeks to show how earlier self-conceptions linked to personality models have gradually given way to that modern self-image, individuality, for which no model exists. Beginning with Augustine's *Confessions*, he comments on a wealth of autobiographies, ending with the *Dichtung und Wahrheit* of Goethe on the very threshold of the modern understanding of individuality.

Autobiographic writings of medieval authors such as Abelard, Guibert of Nogent, Ratherius of Verona, Suger, or Dante reveal lives sufficiently circumscribed by their religious culture that for their mode of self-analysis the notion of individuality was insignificant. Since the Renaissance, such autobiographers as Petrarch, Cellini, Cardano, and Montaigne, engaging in more complex forms of self-analysis, came to value their personal distinctiveness and made use of autobiography for articulating the relation between the person and the surrounding world.